1989

Applying Ethics

Applying Ethics

A TEXT WITH READINGS □ THIRD EDITION

Jeffrey Olen
University of Wisconsin – Stevens Point

Vincent Barry
Bakersfield College

WADSWORTH PUBLISHING COMPANY, BELMONT, CALIFORNIA
A DIVISION OF WADSWORTH, INC.

Philosophy Editor: Kenneth King
Editorial Assistant: Michelle Palacio
Managing Designer: James Chadwick
Text Design: Andrew Ogus
Cover Design: James Chadwick
Print Buyer: Karen Hunt
Production Editor: Harold Humphrey
Cover Illustration: Pablo Picasso, *Family of Saltimbanques*, 1905; oil on canvas, $83\frac{3}{4}''\times 90\frac{3}{8}''$; National
Gallery of Art, Washington, D.C.; Chester Dale Collection

Printed in the United States of America   49

1 2 3 4 5 6 7 8 9 10——93 92 91 90 89

Library of Congress Cataloging-in-Publication Data
Olen, Jeffrey.
    Applying ethics : a text with readings/Jeffrey Olen, Vincent
Barry.—3rd ed.
        p.   cm.
    Rev. ed. of: Applying ethics/Vincent Barry. 2nd ed. © 1985.
    Bibliography: p.
    Includes index.
    ISBN 0-534-10152-6
    1. Social ethics.   2. United States—Moral conditions.   I. Barry,
Vincent E.   II. Barry, Vincent E. Applying ethics.   III. Title.
HM216.B18 1989
170—dc19   88-27738
                                                           CIP

To William Capriotti
—J.O.

To Jim Wilson
—V.B.

CONTENTS

PART II *Issues*

9. World Hunger and Economic Justice   **324**

10. Animal Rights   **378**

PREFACE

The second edition of Vincent Barry's *Applying Ethics* was unique among books of practical ethics. Part I offered chapters on moral theory and informal logic. Part II offered chapters on individual moral problems, each chapter including an essay and case representations by Barry and selections from other sources. In preparing this new edition, I have done my best to preserve that uniqueness.

Part I, while still in the spirit of the second edition, has been totally recast, in the hope of making it even more useful for students and instructors. The first chapter, "Moral Reasons," focuses on the moral principles and considerations relevant to the issues of Part II. Like the corresponding chapter of the earlier edition, it includes the important moral contributions of Aristotle, Kant, Mill, and others. Unlike the earlier chapter, its emphasis is firmly on their roles in moral debate rather than their more theoretical aspects. When the details of particular theories are not directly concerned with the issues of Part II, I have not included them. The second chapter, "Good Reasoning," focuses on critical thinking—in particular, the kinds of thinking most relevant to moral argument. Unlike the corresponding chapter of the second edition, it stresses such matters as supplying missing premises, grasping an argument's structure, and the importance of counterexamples in moral argument, rather than informal fallacies.

Much of Part II, however, remains unchanged. Although I have made some minor changes in the chapters from Barry's edition, the major change is the addition of three new chapters—"Sexual Morality," "Corporate Responsibility," and "Animal Rights."

I am grateful to the reviewers of this edition for their many helpful comments and suggestions: Diedra Flora of St. Petersburg Junior College, Larry McCargar and Steven Sanders of Bridgewater State College, M. J. Abhishaker of Normandale Community College, Ruth Heizer of Georgetown College, James Campbell of Rochester Institute of Technology, and William J. Radke of Seton Hall University.

I am grateful also to Wadsworth philosophy editor Ken King for his assistance and direction, to production editor Hal Humphrey for his suggested improvements, to John Vollrath and Gary Varner for their helpful comments, to Carolee Cote and Corinne Olen for helping me make the change from typewriter to computer, to Jeff Stinebrink for research assistance, and to Vincent Barry, for giving me such a good book to work with.

JEFFREY OLEN
Stevens Point, Wisconsin
June, 1988

Applying Ethics

PART I

Moral Reasoning

1
MORAL REASONS

When we act, we act for reasons. We eat breakfast because we are hungry, or because it gives us the energy we need to get through the morning. We read a book because we want to be entertained, or because we want to learn something. We buy a car because it's reliable, or fun to drive, or affordable.

At any one time, we might—and usually do—have many reasons to do all sorts of things. Most of what we do we do for more than one reason. We buy a car because it's reliable *and* fun to drive *and* affordable, and we read a book because it's entertaining *and* informative.

But not all of our relevant reasons support the same course of action when we choose to do something. Often, we find ourselves faced with conflicting reasons, reasons both to do and not to do something. In addition to our reasons *for* eating breakfast, we might have reasons for *not* eating it. We might be in a hurry, or we might be trying to lose weight.

When our reasons lead us in different directions like that, we must decide which direction to take. Although we can make our decision in a purely arbitrary way—by flipping a coin, perhaps—the rational way to proceed is to weigh the conflicting reasons, to ask ourselves which of the conflicting reasons are the best reasons. If we are lucky, we will answer the question correctly. That is, we will choose the best thing to do, the right course of action. We will do what we ought to do under the circumstances. If we are unlucky, we will choose the wrong course of action. We will do what we ought not do.

Of course, whether we choose correctly is not merely a matter of luck. If it were, rational deliberation would be no more trustworthy than the flip of a coin. Whether we choose correctly is also a matter of how well informed we are, how carefully we reason, how accurately we gauge the pros and cons of the alternatives, how exhaustive our deliberations are. Thus, we can minimize the element of luck when buying a car by test-driving various models, by reading reports in

Car and Driver and *Consumer Reports,* and by giving careful attention to our own needs and preferences. Do we really need a car with this much power? Does appearance matter that much to us? Can we afford all of these options?

We can also minimize the element of luck by making sure that we reason in a reliable way. In the next chapter, we will take a careful look at what makes reasoning reliable. For the rest of this chapter, though, we will concentrate on a particular kind of reasoning—moral reasoning.

Moral Reasoning

To reason morally is not to reason in a certain way. Rather, it is to consider certain kinds of reasons—moral reasons. It is to try to arrive at the best moral reasons for acting, to choose the morally right course of action, to do what we morally ought to do.

There are, after all, many different ways in which an action can be right or wrong. An artist who puts the right finishing touches on a painting does what is aesthetically right. An investor who buys and sells stock at the right times does what is financially right. Someone who gives up smoking cigarettes does what is right for her health. And someone who returns a found wallet does what is morally right. In the first case, we have an action supported by the best aesthetic reasons. In the second, one supported by the best financial reasons. In the third, one supported by the best health-related reasons. In the fourth, one supported by the best moral reasons.

Sometimes, an action will be right in one way but wrong in another. That is, the best reasons of one kind will support it, while the best reasons of another kind will support something else. Reasons of self-interest, for example, might lead us to conclude that we ought to keep a found wallet. Moral reasons, on the other hand, lead us to conclude that we ought to return it. In cases like that, we must decide which kind of reason is best. We must decide what we ought to do, all things considered.

When we make these all-things-considered judgments, we generally do so based on what matters to us most. Some people are willing to risk their health because they enjoy smoking, others are not. Some people are willing to forego a higher paying job for a more pleasant one, others are not. Some people are willing to set aside their self-interest to do what is morally right, others are not.

Although we generally give people a lot of leeway in determining what most matters to them, we do expect them to give moral reasons high priority. And when the moral stakes are very high, we expect people to give moral reasons top priority. We expect them to realize that the morally right course of action is the best course of action, what they ought to do, all things considered.

These are not unreasonable expectations. If we are to live together in society, we must cooperate with one another. And if we are to cooperate with one another, we must trust one another. And we cannot trust people who treat honesty, good faith, and loyalty lightly.

Individual Morality and Social Morality

Honesty, good faith, and loyalty are important considerations of *individual* morality. When each of us, as individuals, must decide what to do, we must, if we are to decide morally, consider whether we are being honest or dishonest, faithful to our commitments to others or unfaithful to them, loyal to those who deserve our loyalty or disloyal to them. The roles that such considerations play in our lives are crucial to our understanding of ourselves as moral people. And the roles that they play in the lives of others are crucial to our moral judgments of both them and their actions.

Because the topics discussed in Part II of this book concern the morality of various kinds of actions, considerations of individual morality will play an important role in those discussions. But so will moral considerations of another kind— *social* morality. In discussing issues like abortion, we will be concerned not only with whether it is moral for an individual woman to have an abortion in various kinds of circumstances. We will also be concerned with how society as a whole should deal with abortion.

The two concerns are related, of course, but, as we shall see, answering the first does not necessarily settle the second. Rape and armed robbery are obviously immoral, and even rational rapists and armed robbers, we can safely suppose, understand why we require laws forbidding such behavior and why we are perfectly justified in locking up people who disobey them. But no rational person believes that every immoral act should be punishable by imprisonment or even made illegal. Who would want to prosecute everyone who cheats in a "friendly" game of tennis?

Also, we might have good reason to want society to regulate various kinds of behavior that do not violate any considerations of individual morality. Many people feel, for instance, that a mature, psychologically sound adult does nothing immoral by enjoying pornography in the privacy of his home, but these same people might also feel that pornography presents serious social dangers and should be curbed or outlawed.

Obviously, what we need are some general principles of social morality to guide us when we ask ourselves how society ought to deal with morally important social issues. And, just as obviously, we need some general principles of individual morality to guide us when we ask ourselves how individuals ought to act in particular situations.

Let's begin with the second.

Principles of Individual Morality

It is easy to think of morality as a system of rules—some telling us not to do certain things, like cheat, lie, break promises, steal, rape, and kill, and others telling us to do certain things, like help others in need, pay our debts, and be loyal to friends and family. But why do we have these rules and not others?

The quick answer is that these are the rules we were taught. And there is no arguing with that answer. Moral rules are the rules accepted by the members of a given society, the rules we agree to follow and expect others to follow, in large part because we were taught to do so. But if we look at morality in just that way, we do both morality and ourselves a disservice. We do morality a disservice by making it look arbitrary. We are in effect saying that we have the moral rules we do because we have the moral rules we do. And we do ourselves a disservice by making ourselves look like mindless followers of arbitrary rules.

But moral rules are not arbitrary. We have the rules we do for good reason. And we are not mindless followers of them. We accept them because we understand that we have them for good reason. And when we feel that reason requires us to change them, we do just that.

Consider one timely example of moral change. Not too long ago, women were expected to live their lives within narrowly defined roles. It was considered their duty to stay home with their children, their obligation to see to various household tasks, and while men might be praised for helping out every now and then, they were not morally required to do so. They were morally required to be the family breadwinner, and women were morally required not to take jobs from other family breadwinners.

All that has changed, of course—or is at least in the process of changing. Many women and an increasing number of men have come to doubt the acceptability of such rules. And what makes them unacceptable is that they are now seen as violating some general moral *principles*—the principle of fairness, most notably. Women do not believe it fair that their lives are so restricted, and many men have come to agree.

What this example shows is that morality is not merely a matter of rules, but also of principles—general standards for evaluating conduct, standards that we apply to all behavior and rules.

Something else shows the same thing. No moral rule is exceptionless. Sometimes we are morally justified in breaking a promise. Sometimes we are morally justified in failing to help someone in need. Consider how easy it is to find yourself in a situation in which you must break a promise to Mary in order to help John or must fail to help John in order to keep your promise to Mary. Unless we allow that the two rules have exceptions and one of them applies here, we are left with a morally immovable object and a morally irresistible force—that is, a morally impossible situation. To resolve the dilemma, we must recognize that one of the rules takes precedence in this particular case and that we are dealing with a legitimate exception to the other. How do we decide which takes precedence? By appealing to some general moral principle.

There is also one more thing that shows the importance of moral principles. The debates of Part II of this book are, in part, about what moral rules we should adopt. Should we adopt a rule that forbids us to give terminally ill patients in great pain a lethal injection if they request it? Should we adopt a rule that permits us to do so? Or should we adopt a rule that requires us to do so? Should we adopt a rule forbidding all abortions, some abortions, or no abortions? If suitable answers are to be found, we must appeal to moral principles.

The Principle of Utility

One of the most well-known general moral principles is closely associated with a number of moral philosophers, most notably the British philosopher John Stuart Mill (1806–1873). It is known as both the *principle of utility* and the *greatest happiness principle*. It tells us to produce the greatest balance of happiness over unhappiness, making sure that we give equal consideration to the happiness and unhappiness of everyone who stands to be affected by our actions.

The principle of utility can be applied in two different ways. The first is to apply it to individual *acts*. How are we to do that? Well, we might ask ourselves every time we act which of the options open to us will maximize happiness, but Mill did not recommend that procedure because it would be much too time consuming. Since we know that lying and stealing and cheating will rarely maximize happiness when everyone is taken equally into account, the sensible thing to do is avoid such behavior without worrying about the principle of utility.

But we sometimes have reason to believe that what usually maximizes happiness might not. Remember the example in which you cannot both keep your promise to Mary and help John. Although keeping promises usually maximizes happiness and helping others usually maximizes happiness, in this case, one will not. That's when Mill tells us to appeal to the principle of utility before we act.

The second way is to apply the principle to *rules*, rather than to acts. Following this method, we appeal to the principle of utility only when we are considering which moral rules we should adopt. We ask ourselves which of the alternatives will maximize happiness if generally followed by the members of our society. Would a moral rule permitting mercy killing maximize happiness, or would one forbidding it? Whichever one would, that's the rule we ought to adopt.

The principle of utility is certainly a reasonable moral principle, whether applied to acts or rules. How our behavior affects others should be of moral concern to us. Moreover, we want our moral rules to make our society a good society, and it is hard to argue against the claim that a happy society is better than an unhappy society. So it is not surprising that utilitarian considerations play an important role in the moral reasoning of many individuals. Nor is it surprising that they play an important role in many of the arguments of Part II.

Still, most people believe that it would be a mistake to make the principle of utility the final arbiter of *all* moral decisions. Suppose Bill borrows ten dollars from Carol on the condition that he pay her back tomorrow. Doesn't that create an obligation to her? And since it does, does Bill have the moral right to neglect that obligation merely because he can maximize happiness by doing something else with the money?

That's one reason for recognizing limits to the principle. Another is that it is a very demanding principle. Very rarely, after all, do most of us take into equal account everybody's happiness before we act. Often we think that our own happiness and the happiness of people who most matter to us should take precedence. That's why we sometimes splurge on presents for our families, even though we might create greater happiness by spending our money on the poor instead. Although we might agree that it would be commendable to do otherwise, it hardly seems *wrong* to splurge on the people we love.

Even when applied to rules, rather than acts, the principle of utility seems to have its limitations. Although we want our moral rules to create happiness and avoid unhappiness, we don't want them to do only that. We also want them to be fair. And we sometimes find that the principle of utility justifies unfair rules. For example, we can easily imagine rules allowing researchers to experiment on selectively chosen human beings. Such rules might very well create the greatest balance of happiness over unhappiness but still be morally unacceptable—because the chosen few would be involuntary subjects, or because they would have to be "sacrificed" during the experiments. Although the medical knowledge gained might benefit the rest of us so enormously that it outweighs the harm to the subjects, it is unfair of us to benefit at their expense that way.

So the principle of utility cannot be, as Mill thought, the one fundamental moral principle that underlies all of morality. But the effect of our actions and moral rules on the happiness and unhappiness of people remains an important moral consideration all the same.

Fairness

Fairness, we just saw, often plays a crucial role in moral reasoning. But as we shall see in Part II, it's not always easy to know what the fairest thing to do is. The problem will be especially acute when we discuss affirmative action, an issue in which different but equally important notions of fairness lead to different resolutions. We can't look at all the conceptions of fairness that come into play in moral reasoning here—some are better considered in Part II and some in connection with principles of social morality—but we can look at some.

THE GOLDEN RULE.   Many people take the golden rule to be the best standard of fairness. Certainly, it is a principle that most of us learned very early in our moral education and one that plays a very large role in our moral lives. But applying it is not as simple a matter as most people think.

For most of us, to do unto others as we would have them do unto us is to do much more than we are inclined to do. Even more important, it is to do much more than we think we ought to do. Most of us would be very pleased if utter strangers walked up to us and gave us wads of hundred-dollar bills, for example. Yet we do not think that we ought to do the same for others.

The reason we rarely think of such things when we think of the golden rule is that we usually apply it in the context of other moral rules and principles. That is, we don't necessarily think that we ought to act toward others as we would *like* them to act toward us so much as we think that we ought to act toward others as they *ought* to act toward us. If we are to act morally, we must follow the same moral rules in our dealings with others that we expect them to follow in their dealings with us.

When we look at the golden rule that way, we recognize that none of us is a special case. The same moral standards apply to all of us. That is indeed an important thing to recognize if we are to reason morally, but it doesn't always tell us what those standards are.

The negative version of the golden rule gives us more help here. The negative version tells us *not* to treat others as we would *not* have them treat us. That is certainly one reason we find a moral rule allowing experimentation on unwilling subjects morally unacceptable. We would not have somebody experiment on us against our will.

But even the negative version requires a context of other rules and principles for its application, because not all of us find the same treatment unacceptable. Consider one common example. Some people prefer to be lied to rather than face unpleasant truths, while others insist on the truth come what may (a fact that physicians are probably most aware of). But that does not mean that the people who don't want to hear the truth should withhold it from those who do.

RESPECT FOR PERSONS. Why shouldn't people who want the truth withheld from them withhold it from others who don't? The answer is simple. In such cases, they should respect the wishes of others. How the other person feels about being lied to matters more than how the would-be liar feels.

More generally, we should always treat other people with respect, and many moral philosophers take respect for persons to be *the* fundamental moral principle. The kind of respect they have in mind should not be confused with the kind of respect exemplified by calling people by their appropriate titles. It is a special kind of respect, often called Kantian respect, after the German philosopher Immanuel Kant (1724–1804). Kantian respect is captured by this moral principle: Never use other people merely as a means to your own ends.

Be sure to notice the word "merely" in the principle. It makes a crucial difference, telling us when it is moral to use another person for our own ends and when it is not. It tells us that it is moral to use a bank teller to cash our checks, a waiter to bring our food, a mechanic to fix our cars, and an accountant to prepare our tax forms. Why are they and other like examples moral? Because the people involved are not *merely* serving our own ends. They are serving their own ends as well. They are, among other things, earning their food and rent money.

For an example of using others merely as a means to our own ends, we can return to an earlier one. To experiment on unwilling subjects is a perfect illustration. To do that is to give no consideration to the subjects' ends. It is to treat them as mere things that exist for our own ends, not as persons who have their own ends in life.

Put another way, respect for persons is intimately connected to the recognition that persons are *autonomous* beings. Our behavior is the product of our choices, and our choices are the product of what we take to be the best reasons for acting. And that is what makes us autonomous. We have our own goals and aspirations, we are capable of evaluating and weighing them against one another, we can reject or change them as we see fit, and we can determine how best to achieve those goals and then act accordingly.

To respect persons, then, is to recognize them as autonomous beings and treat them accordingly. It is to recognize that they have their own reasons for acting and to give those reasons the same respect we feel our own reasons warrant from others. And forcing someone to be a subject in a medical experiment is an obvious case of failing to respect his autonomy. So is any kind of coercion—from extortion and armed robbery to slavery and murder.

Many other cases are less obvious. Lying is one. When John lies to Mary, he is trying to manipulate her. His goal is to get her to act as he wants her to act, not as she would act if she knew the truth. Withholding information is another. If Mary wants to borrow John's car for purposes he doesn't approve of, she violates Kantian respect by not telling him. She is manipulating him. And the same thing holds for making commitments we have no intention of honoring.

Does that mean we should never lie, withhold information, or break a promise? Kant thought we should never lie, but we needn't agree with him. Not only do we find white lies permissible, we also think it right to lie in some cases if there is no other way to prevent someone from doing serious harm. Respect for persons certainly justifies the moral rule "Don't lie," but it needn't lead to the conclusion that lying to save an innocent life isn't a legitimate exception. The important thing about respect for persons is that it cannot justify lying merely for our own convenience or merely to maximize happiness.

If we want to know what does count as a legitimate exception, probably the best thing to do is apply the following test. Imagine that a group of reasonable people is trying to decide what rules they ought to follow, and that the rules they pick will include a list of all the exceptions. If it seems likely that they would freely agree to the proposed exception, then we may consider it legitimate.

Many moral philosophers like that test because it manifests Kantian respect. To apply it is to treat others as they would agree to be treated if it were up to them to participate in the making of our moral rules. And to treat them that way is to recognize them as autonomous beings.

Kantian respect is a very powerful notion. It can explain why various kinds of behavior are wrong and why others are right. Also, it is a very reasonable thing to accept as a general moral principle. But many people believe that it's not powerful enough. Since animals are not autonomous beings, it provides no guidelines for our treatment of them. The same can be said about fetuses. Also, Kantian respect seems to permit a variety of practices that many people consider immoral, like homosexuality among consenting adults, or giving lethal injections to terminally ill patients who ask for them.

Whether these practices are immoral is, of course, a matter of great controversy, which is why we will look at them in Part II. Still, the fact that they are controversial shows that many people adhere to other moral principles. Respect for persons may give us an excellent handle on fairness, but, like the principle of utility, it may not be our only fundamental moral principle.

Proper Human Excellences

The moral principles we have looked at so far focus on an individual's obligations to others. They provide general guidelines for how we ought to act toward one another. But ethical thought has also paid close attention to another aspect of human life—the human good. Philosophers who pursue this line of thought do not focus on obligations, but on character traits and activities that are distinctively human and, when taken together, constitute the good life for human beings.

According to this approach to ethics, there are certain excellences uniquely proper to human life, and the full moral life involves the development of these excellences.

Before considering what these excellences might be, let's look at why this line of thought is so appealing. A good place to start is with the ancient Greek philosopher Aristotle (384–322 B.C.). As Aristotle pointed out, human artifacts have distinctive purposes. The purpose of a pen is to write; of a lamp, to give light; of a knife, to cut. And knowing the purpose of any artifact, we also know how to tell whether it is a good or bad one. A knife with a strong blade is better than one with a weak blade. So is a knife with a handle that gives us a sure, comfortable grip better than one with a handle that does not. Thus, a strong blade and a sure, comfortable grip can be called excellences proper to a knife.

Similar remarks hold for human activities—from performing surgery to playing basketball. Each has its own purpose (or purposes) and there are corresponding excellences appropriate to engaging in each of them. A good basketball player is able to shoot, pass, rebound, and make it difficult for his opponent to shoot, pass, and rebound; various physical and mental skills, plus proper conditioning, will help him do just those things.

Of course, not all of us are basketball players—or surgeons, welders, attorneys, or lifeguards, for that matter. So the distinctive excellences proper to those roles need not concern us. But some excellences are proper to all of these roles, and those that are, such as concentration and pride in our work, should concern us. Even more important, we are sons or daughters, friends, neighbors, coworkers, and citizens, and we are—or are likely to be—lovers, spouses, parents, and grandparents. And the excellences proper to these roles—loyalty, generosity, honesty, kindness, and the like—are proper to us all. They are, that is, proper human excellences, what are often called virtues.

Are there proper human excellences apart from our social roles? Aristotle thought so. He believed that there are natural purposes as well as social purposes. To him, everything in nature has a natural purpose or goal—from the acorn, whose natural purpose is to become an oak tree, to the human being. The human being's natural purpose is *eudaimonia*, a Greek word usually translated as "happiness" but better understood as total well-being. It is what all of us naturally strive for.

Aristotle believed that a good part of *eudaimonia* is fulfilling our social roles, but far from all of it. We are not, after all, just social animals (or, as he put it, political animals). We are also rational animals. Indeed, our ability to reason as we do is, he thought, the trait that best defines us. So an essential part of *eudaimonia* must consist in the proper use of reason. And that means that we must live well-ordered lives, lives not given to extremes. We should not let courage turn to foolhardiness or generosity turn to extravagance. Nor should we let our emotions run away with us. We should display them only when appropriate, and then only to the appropriate degree.

To avoid extremes is the key to what Aristotle called practical wisdom, which is one of the two kinds of wisdom that humans are capable of. The other is the wisdom that comes from contemplating the world in which we live. It is a deep understanding of the world, and like practical wisdom it too is a proper human excellence. We cannot achieve total well-being without it.

Aristotle's concern with contemplation takes us far from the issues of Part II, but his other points do have relevance for us. For one thing, many of the issues we'll be discussing relate directly to various social roles and the excellences proper to them. Is it the proper role of health care professionals actively and intentionally to bring about the death of a terminally ill patient? To treat a baby born three months premature one way and a fetus of six months another?

These issues also touch on the more general human excellences. Thus, we will consider compassion for the dying, generosity toward the poor and starving, mercy for those convicted of capital crimes, understanding toward pregnant women, and concern for fetuses.

Moreover, virtue and the notion of a well-ordered life play a large role in the discussion of sexual morality. The Catholic thinker Thomas Aquinas (1225–1274) is most important here. Taking his cue from Aristotle's view on purpose in nature, he argued that our sexual organs have as their natural purpose procreation, and any sexual activity that is not open to that end is disordered and immoral. Catholic thinking since Aquinas has continued to emphasize that purpose, but it has also emphasized another proper purpose of human sexuality—the expression of fully human love and dignity. According to this line of thought, sex that is not such an expression, including all sex outside of marriage, is disordered and immoral.

The Catholic position is, of course, highly controversial. So, for that matter, is Aristotle's view that there are natural purposes in addition to social ones. But those controversies are matters for Part II. For now, the important point is this: Ethical thinking includes consideration of human virtues as well as of obligations to others. And in asking ourselves what moral rules to adopt, we must ask ourselves what kind of people we should be and how we should live our lives.

The Will of God

To many people, religious belief provides the final word on moral questions. And because the issues we'll be looking at later have been addressed by religious traditions of all kinds, many people rely on their religious belief for guidance. It is not surprising, then, that much of the popular debate that we find in such places as the letter-to-the-editor sections of local newspapers is filled with appeals to the will of God.

Why give God the final word in these matters? Two possibilities come readily to mind. The first is that God is the ultimate source of morality. God made the universe and put human beings in it for some purpose, and whether we act rightly or wrongly depends on how well we pursue that purpose. In other words, there are both moral laws and physical laws, and God is the author of both.

According to the other possibility, God is not so much the source of morality as the best authority on morality. What makes God the best authority depends on how we think of morality. Some people think of morality as a collection of moral facts, much as they think of science as a collection of scientific facts. And

God, being all-knowing, knows both kinds of facts. Others think of morality in a different way. To them, the right thing to do is what an ideal observer would consider the best thing to do—an ideal observer being someone who is fully informed about the case at hand and totally impartial. And God alone is in that position.

Reliance on God does raise some problems, though. Can we really be certain what God wants us to do? Different religious traditions do give conflicting answers to various moral questions, and even within any given religious tradition we can often find conflicting answers. Moreover, we should not forget agnostics and atheists, nor should we forget religious individuals who, for one reason or another, sincerely believe that they must look to their own consciences for the ultimate answers to moral questions.

Such considerations needn't lead to disrespect for religious belief, of course, any more than they need lead to the conclusion that religious people should disregard religious belief when making moral decisions. But they do show the limitations of religious belief for purposes of moral argument.

As we shall see in the next chapter, a good argument goes from statements accepted as true to a conclusion well supported by those statements. If the initial statements are not accepted by our opponents, our arguments will have no force. Also, the better our justification for accepting those initial statements as true, the better the argument. And given the role that faith plays in religious belief, statements about God can have less independent justification than the conclusions they are asked to support.

It is for those reasons, more than antipathy toward religious belief, that moral philosophers addressing a varied audience concentrate on arguments that do not rely on statements about God's will. And it is for the same reasons that this book will do the same.

Principles of Social Morality

So far, we have been concerned with how individuals ought to act. Our focus has been on the moral principles that guide individuals when they must determine what they, and others, ought to do.

But we also act collectively, as well as individually. Most important for our purposes, we act as a municipality, as a state, as a nation. We enact laws, we imprison, fine, and execute people, we enter into treaties and wage war. And collective action, like individual action, can be moral or immoral. And whether it is one or the other, like individual action, depends on how well it is supported by moral principles.

As we shall see, the relevant principles are often the same. Individually and collectively, we should be concerned with human happiness, so the principle of utility is an important principle of social morality. Individually and collectively, we should be concerned with fairness, so respect for persons, too, is an important principle of social morality. And when we act collectively, we care about what kind of society we should be as much as we care about what kind of individuals we should be when we act individually.

But collective action does pose one special difficulty. When Congress acts, the United States acts, but many U.S. citizens will invariably disagree with how Congress acts, including some members of Congress itself. Their disagreement notwithstanding, they are bound by the acts of Congress. They must pay taxes for purposes they find abhorrent, they must submit to regulations they find offensive, and they must give up freedoms they hold dear—that, or face fine or imprisonment. Governments, even democratic governments like our own, are inherently coercive. That is the special difficulty, and it is why we need additional principles of social morality.

Social Justice

If we ask ourselves what kind of society we should be, the natural answer is this: a just society. Candidates on the campaign trail may disagree on all sorts of issues, but none will speak out in favor of injustice. Many will speak out in favor of positions that others of us consider to be unjust, but they will argue in turn that our own positions are the unjust ones. We disagree about what justice requires, but not that we are morally required to be just.

In other words, the issue of social justice—what makes a society a just one—is a very controversial matter. People of good will who share the same principles of individual morality—people who are fair, loyal, honest, faithful, and kind—have great difficulty agreeing on principles of social justice.

That difficulty is due largely to the difficulty noted just before. Government action is coercive action. All of us are in principle against coercion, but we also recognize the occasional need for it. Unfortunately, we don't always recognize it on the same occasions. A look at some important principles of social justice will explain why.

Individual Rights

The Bill of Rights explicitly guarantees us a number of individual freedoms—freedoms of speech, press, religion, and assembly, for example. As part of our Constitution, these guarantees are part of the fundamental law of the land, as are the Bill of Rights' guarantees of a fair trial and its protection against unreasonable search and seizure.

Although these guarantees are set forth in plain enough English, many people of good will disagree about how they should be interpreted. That our guarantee of a free press allows us to criticize government policies is not a matter of controversy. That it allows us to print and sell hardcore pornography is. When such controversies arise, they are settled by the courts, which are the ultimate legal arbiters of how these guarantees are to be understood.

The courts also serve as the ultimate legal arbiters in controversies about implicit constitutional guarantees. The right to privacy, to pick an example that will concern us in Part II, is not explicitly mentioned in the Bill of Rights or anywhere else in the Constitution. Still, the courts have held that it is a constitutionally protected one.

If enough of us disagree with the courts, we can amend the Constitution. But barring such amendments, the decisions of the courts remain the law of the land. They set the legal limits on what kinds of individual behavior the various levels of government can regulate and on the ways it can regulate them. Even if we doubt that a woman has a moral right to abort a fetus in the early months of her pregnancy, we cannot doubt, as matters now stand, that she has the legal right to do so.

But ought she have that legal right? Ought consenting adults have the legal right to engage in private homosexual acts? Ought we grant pornography the same protections as weekly newsmagazines? What legal rights should we grant? And why?

NATURAL RIGHTS.   One historically important answer to these questions is this: We ought to have the legal right to do whatever we have the natural right to do, because no government can justly violate our natural rights. That answer was powerfully advanced by the English philosopher John Locke (1632–1704) and echoed by Thomas Jefferson in the Declaration of Independence. Among its most recent champions is the contemporary American philosopher Robert Nozick.

Natural rights are rights that all of us are born with. They belong to us in virtue of the fact that we are human beings and no one has the right to interfere with our exercise of them. Locke and Nozick list them as life, liberty, and property; Jefferson as life, liberty, and the pursuit of happiness. Because no one can interfere with the exercise of our natural rights, we cannot interfere with anyone else's. And that places the only legitimate limits on our exercise of those rights. Our right to swing our arms, the popular saying has it, stops at someone else's nose. But as long as no one's nose (or property, for that matter) is in the way, we are free to swing.

Even the government, according to natural rights theorists, has no right to interfere. The reason is simple. The government derives its rightful powers from the governed, and the governed cannot transfer to the government any rights they do not have by nature. Since all of us have the right to protect our natural rights, we can transfer the right to protect our lives, liberty, and property to the government. Since none of us has the right to interfere with anyone else's natural rights, we cannot transfer any such right to the government. A just society can have police forces, then, but it cannot tell us what we can and cannot read. It can imprison thieves and rapists, but it cannot imprison its peaceful critics.

These restrictions on government action are more severe than they might at first seem. They leave much behavior—even immoral behavior—free of government interference. The 1964 Civil Rights Act forbidding racial discrimination in privately owned places of public accommodation like theaters and restaurants is, on this view, an unjust law. Since no one has a natural right to enter anyone's property against the owner's wishes, racial exclusion is an exercise of natural property rights that the government cannot interfere with. It goes without saying, then, that this view would not endorse government-mandated affirmative action programs, one of the topics to be considered in Part II. Nor would it endorse government payments to the poor, another topic we will consider. Since no one has the natural right to force others to give to the poor, we cannot transfer that right to the government.

MUTUAL AGREEMENT BEHIND THE VEIL OF IGNORANCE. Many philosophers are suspicious of natural rights. Where do they come from? How do we get them? Locke and Jefferson thought them God-given, but few philosophers today are willing to argue that way. And that leaves the origin of natural rights mysterious at best.

John Rawls, another contemporary American philosopher, takes a different approach to individual rights. Instead of saying that a just society is one that protects but does not interfere with natural rights, he says that the individual rights we ought to have are those that a just society would give us.

What is a just society, according to Rawls? A society in which no one has an unfair advantage over others. And how do we ensure that no one has an unfair advantage over others? By adopting fundamental principles of social justice that pass the following test: They must be principles that we would rationally agree upon behind the veil of ignorance. And what, finally, is it to be behind the veil of ignorance? It is to know how the principles would shape society, but not to know what particular positions each of us would have in that society.

The reason that test would work, Rawls says, is that rational people would not agree to live in any unjust society if they did not know whether they would be the ones who would be unfairly taken advantage of. They would not, for example, be willing to institute slavery if they didn't know whether they'd be slave or master. Anything they would agree to behind the veil of ignorance, therefore, must be just.

What they would agree to are the following two principles:

The equality principle. Every person has a right to the greatest basic freedom compatible with equal freedom for all. That is, there must be equal freedom for all, and if freedom can be increased without violating that requirement, it must be.

The difference principle. All social and economic inequalities must meet two requirements. First, they must be to everyone's advantage, including the people at the bottom. It is, for example, to the advantage of everyone that surgeons make more money than unskilled workers. Everyone, including unskilled workers, benefits by having enough surgeons, and financial rewards help guarantee that enough people will pay the cost in time and money of going through medical school. Second, the inequalities must be attached to positions open to all. If surgeons are to be paid more than unskilled workers, then no one can be excluded from becoming a surgeon because of, say, race or sex.

The first principle gives us many freedoms covered by Locke and Nozick's natural rights, including speech, press, religion, assembly and, more generally, the freedom to do as we please as long as we do not interfere with the rights of others.

The second principle, on the other hand, gives us many individual rights that are not among Locke and Nozick's natural rights. In doing so, it places some important restrictions on Locke and Nozick's natural rights—most important, on property rights. For example, the difference principle gives people at the bottom of the social-economic ladder the right to a minimum level of income. If their income falls below that level, the government has the obligation to supplement it with money collected through taxes. And that, from the viewpoint of natural rights advocates, is an unjust restriction on other people's property rights. The government is taking money that they earned so it can help the poor rather than letting them spend it as they see fit.

Equality

Another central principle of social justice is equality. A society in which all citizens are not treated equally can hardly be considered a just one. On that we all agree, just as we all agree that we ought to be a just society. But we do not all agree on what equal treatment requires of us, any more than we all agree on what justice requires of us.

Consider equal treatment under the law, for example. To many people, equal treatment under the law is merely a procedural matter. As long as each of us is treated according to the same legal procedures, we are granted equal treatment under the law. Thus, what matters in criminal trials, say, is that all defendants be allowed full exercise of their rights, including their rights to counsel, to subpoena witnesses, to cross-examination, and to a jury of their peers. To others, equal treatment under the law means much more. If, for example, juries are more likely to apply the death penalty in cases where the victim is white than in cases where the victim is black, then equal treatment under the law is denied in capital cases, regardless of procedural guarantees.

Similar difficulties muddle the issue of equal opportunity. To some people, equal opportunity means lack of discrimination: As long as employers and universities choose employees and students on the basis of merit, not on the basis of sex or race, equal opportunity is secured. To others, equal opportunity requires affirmative action. Given the history of oppression against blacks, they argue, mere lack of discrimination cannot secure equal opportunity. Others go even further. Can we really believe, they ask, that the son of a millionaire and the daughter of a welfare recipient begin life with equal advantages? How many of you have enjoyed the same opportunities in life as David Rockefeller? Can we really believe that differences in natural endowment make no difference to opportunity? How many of you have enjoyed the same opportunities as Julius Erving or Sophia Loren?

People who argue that way generally conclude that equal treatment requires equality of results. Given that we cannot start out equally, there can be no real equal opportunity. The just thing to do, then, is see that society's wealth is distributed equally. Or they might reach a variation of that conclusion, arguing instead that the just thing to do is see that society's wealth is distributed according to need. Rawls, as we saw, argues in favor of equal distribution, except when it is in everyone's interest that some people have more. The German philosopher Karl Marx (1818–1883) famously advanced another principle: From each according to his abilities, to each according to his needs.

The General Welfare

The doctrine of natural rights greatly influenced the American founding fathers. Its influence appears not only in the Declaration of Independence, but also in the Bill of Rights. The preamble to the Constitution shows another concern of the founding fathers—the general welfare—which brings us to another important principle of social morality: The different levels of government should promote the general welfare, or, as it is often put, the common good, or the public interest.

Thus, we have come to expect our governments to do much in the promotion of the general welfare. We expect public schools and libraries, public funding of highways and medical research, zoning ordinances that guarantee us livable neighborhoods, laws protecting our rivers and air, and much else that is no longer controversial.

Much else that governments do to promote the general welfare is controversial. So is much else that various people propose that our governments do to promote it. Sometimes, the controversy is merely over practical considerations, as when we debate whether one policy or another will better increase worker productivity. Often, though, the controversy is over profoundly moral considerations, as when we debate the issues of Part II of this book.

One particularly profound moral consideration concerns the general welfare itself. Many people of good will differ over what constitutes the general welfare. Another concerns how far the government can rightly go in promoting it. Many people of good will also differ about the proper limits of government action.

PUBLIC DECENCY AND MORALITY.   To most people, the general welfare includes a healthy moral environment. Part of a healthy moral environment is public decency. Some things—like sex between married people—are obviously moral in private but generally considered indecent in public thoroughfares. Other things—like drinking a few Scotches too many—are less obviously moral in private (here reasonable people will differ) and also considered indecent in public thoroughfares. Thus we have laws against indecent exposure and drunk and disorderly conduct, laws that most people agree promote the general welfare.

More controversially, some people feel that the general welfare requires more than that, that a healthy moral environment includes more than public decency. They feel that it includes various restrictions on private behavior, too. Homosexual acts between consenting adults comprise one area of private behavior that is illegal in many jurisdictions. Another involves pornography. In some jurisdictions, certain films cannot be shown in theaters even if minors are kept out and billboards visible to the passing public are not themselves pornographic.

What principles do proponents of these restrictions appeal to? The following three are most important.

The principle of paternalism. John Stuart Mill distinguished what he called self-regarding virtues and vices from other-regarding virtues and vices. Gluttony is an example of a self-regarding vice. Although overeating might cause direct harm to ourselves, it does not cause direct harm to others. A propensity to settle disagreements by beating up those who disagree with us, on the other hand, is an other-regarding vice. It does cause direct harm to others.

The legitimacy of laws forbidding assault and battery is not to be disputed. And the same goes for many similar laws involving other-regarding vices. But when we turn to self-regarding vices, the legitimacy of laws involving them is often disputed. People who steal from us, extort money from us, or rape us violate our most cherished rights, and it is the job of government to protect those rights. Gluttons do not violate our rights. Nor do homosexuals or pornography watchers. If homosexuality and pornography viewing are vices (and reasonable people disagree), they do not on the face of it seem to be other-regarding vices.

Some people justify restrictions on such behavior by appealing to a principle of paternalism: Just as parents are justified in preventing their children from harming themselves, so are governments justified in preventing their citizens from harming themselves. And if homosexuality and pornography cause us moral harm, governments should outlaw them. Otherwise they do not promote the general welfare.

Protecting the public morality. Mill's distinction between self-regarding and other-regarding vices rests on the presence or absence of direct harm to others. Many self-regarding vices, though, can and do cause *indirect* harm to others. A glutton can eat himself into a fatal heart attack, for example, and then his wife and children will suffer.

The courts have made similar claims about the indirect harm that can result from homosexuality and pornography. Sometimes, the harm they refer to is moral harm. If society tolerates behavior it considers immoral, that behavior may spread. And that means that people who engage in that behavior may be causing indirect moral harm to others.

Moreover, the indirect moral harm may come to minors as well as adults. Even if pornography is limited by law to adults only, minors will always find a way to get it. Just as legal drinking ages don't prevent minors from drinking their parents' liquor or getting adults to buy it for them, so do laws prohibiting sales of pornography to minors fail to prevent minors from looking at their parents' pornography or getting adults to buy it for them.

Whether or not the behavior does spread to minors, courts have repeatedly held that governments do have a legitimate interest in protecting the public morality, and that their legitimate interest in doing so does justify prohibiting behavior that many of us would consider self-regarding.

Preventing indirect social costs. The glutton who eats himself into a fatal heart attack may end up harming more than just his wife and children. His death may have social costs as well, especially if his family is forced to go on welfare. Indeed, many self-regarding vices have social costs. Smoking-related illnesses exact enormous costs in lost work hours, medical care, and insurance premiums. So do injuries resulting from failure to use automobile seatbelts.

Much debate over the issues of Part II also involves the social costs of private behavior. Many people have expressed serious concern about the effects of pornography on some people. Does it lead some people to anti-social behavior? Rape? Does it encourage disrespect for women? Violence toward women? Others have expressed concern about the long-term effects of legal tolerance of homosexuality. How will it affect society's family structure? And what changes will that lead to in other areas of society?

Many other people reject the claim that such considerations can justify restrictions on private behavior. Many more reject the principle of paternalism and the principle of protecting the public morality. To them, such principles of collective action lead to unacceptable limits on individual freedom. Some worry that these principles, carried to their extremes, would lead to the outlawing of everything bad for us, including ice cream and other foods high in cholesterol. Others have even stronger objections. Their concern is that such considerations are in principle unacceptable.

People like Nozick would rule them out on the grounds of natural right. If our natural right to liberty is to count for anything, it must include the right to decide for ourselves what is morally harmful to us. Others would rule them out on different grounds. To them, the basic issue is that we live in a free society. In a free society, the general welfare is not to be advanced at the cost of individual freedoms that cause direct harm to nobody else. The government has an obligation to prevent violence toward women, but in a free society, it should fulfill that obligation by educating its citizens and punishing offenders—not by restricting the legitimate freedoms of nonoffenders.

Pluralism and Freedom

In the previous section, we looked at reasons in favor of government action. It's now time to look at reasons against government action. All can be seen as arguments in favor of individual freedom. They can also be seen as arguments in favor of pluralism.

A pluralistic society is a society with many independent centers of power, a society in which no one institution has unlimited power over the others. The more independent and varied the institutions of society are, the more pluralistic the society; the more limits that are placed on the most powerful institution of society, the more pluralistic the society.

In our society, of course, the federal government is the most powerful institution. Among the independent centers of power are the family, the press, religions, business and labor organizations, private (and perhaps even public) universities, and the like. And, to the extent that the government allows these other institutions to pursue their own ends in their own ways, the more pluralistic our own society.

Although pluralism is not highly valued in all societies (the Soviet Union and Iran, for example) it is highly valued in our own. The founding fathers, in placing limits on the powers of the federal government, sought to protect pluralism. And the frequent calls we hear to limit government interference in matters best left to the family, or the medical professions, or any other institutions, are calls to protect or advance pluralism.

INDIVIDUAL FREEDOM.   One reason for valuing pluralism is its close connection to individual freedom. The connection is twofold.

First, to allow institutions to pursue their own ends in their own ways is, more often than not, to allow individuals to pursue their own ends in their own ways. If the government leaves certain areas of concern to the family, it leaves them to individual family members. If it allows research decisions to be made by the scientific community, it allows them to be made by individual scientists. And the less it interferes with media organizations, the less it interferes with individual journalists.

Second, the more independent centers of power there are and the more independent they are permitted to be, the more bulwarks there are against government restrictions on individual freedom. A free press protects the freedoms of all of us, not just of journalists. Independent universities, hospitals, and businesses protect the freedom to choose among varied alternatives of all of us, not just the freedoms of professors, physicians, and managers.

To be sure, independent institutions can also threaten our freedoms. Businesses with monopoly powers, for instance, can greatly restrict our freedom of choice in the marketplace. They can also threaten vital public goods like clean air and water. So we cannot allow them to be unbridled centers of power, any more than we can allow the government to be one. Nor can we give parents unbridled power over their children, or hospitals unbridled power over their patients.

How and where to set these limits fuels many of the controversies of Part II. Is the joint decision to withhold treatment from defective newborns within the proper bounds of parents and physicians? Should private businesses be free to pursue affirmative action, should they be forced to pursue it, or should they be barred from doing so?

How we answer such questions depends on a number of factors, some specific to each issue, others relating to general principles we've been looking at. Fairness, of course, is an important factor. So is the matter of individual rights. But where fairness should lead us and what rights are at stake are not always clear. What is fair to the minority woman might not be fair to the white male. And the question of what rights we ought to extend to a newborn child or fetus is far from settled.

The general welfare is also an important factor. It can, after all, be harmed by government action as well as advanced by government action. So far, we have looked only at ways in which government action can advance it. But pluralists are equally concerned about the ways government action can harm it.

THE SOCIAL UTILITY OF PLURALISM.   For Locke, Jefferson, and Nozick, the individual freedoms that rightfully belong to us are matters of natural right, and they need no further justification than that. For Rawls, the individual freedoms that rightfully belong to us are the ones we would agree to under ideal conditions of fairness. For Mill, the individual freedoms that rightfully belong to us are the ones that will maximize human happiness.

Mill felt very strongly that the only freedom that will not maximize human happiness is the freedom to harm others. He felt that other-regarding vices fall under the legitimate control of governments, but not self-regarding ones. Many of his arguments for this claim center on specific individual freedoms, and it would take us far beyond our purposes here to look at all of them. But two general arguments are very important for us.

The first is one we often hear in political debates: Individuals are in a better position to know what makes them happy than paternalistic governments are. Individuals will make mistakes from time to time, but so will governments. The important point is that individuals will make them less frequently. For one thing, we know ourselves better than our governments know us. For another, each of us is different, and it is extremely unlikely that one judgment about self-regarding behavior made for all individuals in society will promote individual happiness as well as individual judgments made by each of us.

The second deals directly with the link between public morality and the general welfare. According to Mill, the best way to live our lives must always remain an open question. Nobody can now know for certain that certain ways of life are the best ways of life. If we outlaw certain kinds of self-regarding behavior, Mill said, we cut off moral experimentation that might help us discover better ways of life. And even if we can be fairly certain that some ways of life are not good ones, we will not maximize happiness by outlawing them. Bad ways of life may still have some good in them. Also, the rest of us can always learn from bad examples, even if what we learn is only to have greater confidence in the goodness of our own ways of life. A docile citizenry, one that does what it is told rather than what it thinks best, is not a citizenry likely to maximize happiness. Nor, those who agree with Mill might add, are docile hospitals, universities, or media organizations likely to maximize happiness.

Summary and Conclusions

We have looked at a variety of general moral principles in this chapter, some primarily concerned with individual morality, others with social morality. In doing so, we have also looked at the most important considerations we can bring to bear when deciding how we should act, whether individually or collectively. Among them are human happiness, fairness, justice, individual rights, equality, individual freedom, and the general welfare.

What conclusions can we draw from our discussions? Perhaps the most obvious conclusion is that moral questions can be very difficult questions. One moral principle can lead us to one answer, while another equally important moral principle can lead us to another answer. Thus, we may very well be stuck with some very hard choices—between respecting individual freedoms and promoting the general welfare, for example. Also, we may very well find that the same moral principle leads us to different answers. In cases like that, we will find ourselves stuck with hard choices of another kind—between being fair to one group or another, for example, or between protecting one individual's rights or another's.

The existence of such moral dilemmas often leads to a kind of moral skepticism, the view that our answers to moral questions are opinions, not knowledge. Whether that view is correct is a much too complicated matter to deal with here. But even if it is correct, that does not mean that we should give up trying to answer moral questions. They remain very important questions. The answers we eventually decide on will have great impact on the kind of society we are and on the lives of all of us who live in it. We have a responsibility to deal with these questions as best we can, even if we cannot be sure that our answers represent knowledge.

And even if our answers are opinions, not all opinions are equal. At the beginning of a baseball season, nobody can know who will win the World Series, but that doesn't mean that we can't distinguish good picks from bad picks. Few of you can know which career choice will work out best for you, but that doesn't mean that any opinion on the matter is as good as any other. Similarly, perhaps none of us can know whether a woman really has a moral right to an abortion, or whether justice really requires affirmative action, or whether the right to view pornographic material is a right we are really entitled to, but that doesn't mean that we can't distinguish better and worse ways of dealing with those issues.

Basing our judgments on moral principle is one thing we must do if we are to deal with these issues well. But we must also do something else. We must make sure that our debates on these issues are thoughtful, careful, and well reasoned. The combination of good moral principles and faulty reasoning guarantees very little. In this chapter we have looked at the principles. In the next we will look at reasoning.

Selections for Further Reading

Aristotle. *Nicomachean Ethics*, Martin Ostwald, trans. New York: Bobbs-Merrill, 1962.

Fried, Charles. *An Anatomy of Values: Problems of Personal and Social Choice.* Cambridge, Mass.: Harvard University Press, 1970.

Gewirth, Alan. *Reason and Morality.* Chicago: University of Chicago Press, 1978.

Hampshire, Stuart, et al. *Private and Public Morality.* New York: Cambridge University Press, 1978.

Kant, Immanuel. *Foundations of the Metaphysics of Morals*, Lewis White Beck, trans. New York: Bobbs-Merrill, 1959.

Kruschwitz, Robert B. and Robert C. Roberts, eds. *The Virtues: Contemporary Essays on Moral Character.* Belmont, Calif.: Wadsworth, 1987.

Locke, John. *Two Treatises of Government*, Peter Laslett, ed. New York: Cambridge University Press, 1960.

Mill, John Stuart. *On Liberty*, Currin V. Shields, ed. New York: Bobbs-Merrill, 1956.
———. *Utilitarianism.* New York: Bobbs-Merrill, 1957.

Nozick, Robert. *Anarchy, State and Utopia.* New York: Basic Books, 1974.

Rachels, James. *The Elements of Moral Philosophy.* New York: Random House, 1986.

Rawls, John A. *A Theory of Justice.* Cambridge, Mass.: Harvard University Press, 1971.

Ross, W. D. *Foundations of Ethics.* New York: Oxford University Press, 1954.

Sen, Amartya. *On Economic Inequality.* Oxford: Clarendon Press, 1973.

2
GOOD REASONING

Not all opinions are equal, the first chapter concluded, and we looked at a few examples that seemed to show that some opinions are indeed better than others. What we did not do, though, is explain *why* some opinions are better than others.

Of course, given the nature of the examples, explanation might have seemed unnecessary. Let's go back to one of them—the choice of career. If any opinion about the best career for Mary is to be a good one, it must be based on some obvious factors—what she likes to do, what she's good at, availability of jobs, where she would like to live, and so on. Any opinion that ignores these factors is not one that will have much value to her. Similarly, any worthwhile opinion at the beginning of the baseball season regarding the outcome of the World Series must be based on equally obvious factors, like pitching and hitting.

The same thing can be said about any opinion. If it is to be a good one, it must be well grounded. It must be supported by good reasons. And the better the support, the better the opinion, whether it's a scientific opinion or a moral one, an opinion about what's wrong with your car or an opinion about what's wrong with something you did. To be sure, an opinion that is not well grounded may turn out to be correct. Even the most ignorant of ignoramuses are right sometimes. But when they are, it is a matter of pure luck. Their opinions are not to be trusted in the future, because they are not arrived at in a reliable way.

What makes an opinion well grounded? Well, one obvious thing is knowledge. The more relevant details we know about a particular matter, the better grounded our opinions will be. Be sure to notice the word "relevant." It is most important, particularly when we deal with moral problems. In fact, one of the biggest difficulties we will encounter in our dealings with the issues of Part II is trying to decide what the relevant details are.

Another thing is logic. A well-supported opinion is logically arrived at. It comes at the end of a reliable pattern of reasoning. Or, as philosophers often put it, it is the conclusion of a strong *argument*.

Arguments

To philosophers, scientists, attorneys, and others who engage in intellectual debate, an argument is a collection of statements. One of the statements is the *conclusion*. The other statements are called *premises, reasons, evidence, supporting statements,* or *grounds*. Whatever we call them, the important point is this: Their purpose is to show that the conclusion is true, or that it is reasonable to accept the conclusion as true.

Much of Part II will be devoted to arguments for and against various positions. And much of your task in reading Part II will be to do your best to evaluate these arguments. That is, you will have to decide whether the arguments for or against particular positions are the better ones. And to do that, you will have to ask yourself a variety of questions: Are the supporting statements true? If so, do they really lend support to the conclusions, or are they irrelevant to the conclusions? Are the patterns of reasoning followed by these arguments reliable ones? Has anything of importance been left out of these arguments?

In the rest of this chapter, we'll give you some help in answering these questions. But first, we must distinguish two kinds of argument.

Deductive Arguments

Consider the following two sentences:

1.   If Clint Eastwood is a bulldog, then he has four legs.
2.   Clint Eastwood is a bulldog.

Chances are, you know what comes next:

3.   Therefore, Clint Eastwood has four legs.

How did you know that? Not because of anything you know about Clint Eastwood. People may have different opinions about his movies, but all of us agree that he has only two legs. Nor does your knowledge of bulldogs make a difference. Suppose the first sentence had been "If Clint Eastwood is a bulldog, then he has eight legs." Then you would have drawn a different conclusion: "Therefore, Clint Eastwood has eight legs."

What makes the difference is your knowledge of a rule of *deductive logic:*

1.   If A, then B.
2.   A.
3.   Therefore, B.

That rule is called a *truth-preserving* rule. To say that the rule is truth preserving is to say that whenever you follow it, if the first two statements (called the *premises*) are true, the conclusion will also be true. Truth-preserving rules are also called *valid* rules, and any argument that follows only valid rules is called a valid deductive argument.

The notion of a valid deductive argument will prove to be very useful. If we can assure ourselves that all the premises of an argument are true, and if we can also assure ourselves that the argument follows only valid deductive rules, then we can assure ourselves that the conclusion must be true.

There are many valid rules of deductive reasoning, far too many to go into here. Fortunately, we do not need to know all of them to decide whether an argument is valid. Instead, we can use a simple method for detecting invalidity. That method is known as the method of *counter-example*. Consider the following argument, which many people mistakenly think to be valid.

1. If John took a shower, then he got wet.
2. John didn't take a shower.
3. Therefore, John didn't get wet.

That argument follows this rule:

1. If A, then B.
2. A is not true.
3. Therefore, B is not true.

And we can show that *that* rule is not truth preserving by giving a counter-example to the rule. To do that, we find an argument that has true premises, follows the same rule, but has a false conclusion. If we can do that, the rule is certainly not truth preserving. For instance:

1. If Rin Tin Tin had been a collie, then he'd have been a dog.
2. Rin Rin Tin was not a collie.
3. Therefore, Rin Tin Tin was not a dog.

Here's another example of an invalid argument:

1. Some baseball players are left-handed.
2. Some baseball players are pitchers.
3. Therefore, some pitchers are left-handed.

If you don't believe that the argument is invalid, consider this counter-example:

1. Some animals are human.
2. Some animals are fish.
3. Therefore, some fish are human.

And here, finally, is another:

1. All ravens are black.
2. A dove is not a raven.
3. Therefore, a dove is not black.

And here is a counter-example:

1. All ravens are black.

2. A panther is not a raven.

3. Therefore, a panther is not black.

In each of the above cases, we provided a counter-example by constructing an entirely new argument. Sometimes you may find it easier just to ask a few questions about the original argument. Take the argument that concluded that John didn't get wet (because he didn't take a shower). What if he'd taken a bath instead? Or take the argument that concluded that some pitchers are left-handed (because some baseball players are pitchers and some are left-handed). What if all the left-handed players are outfielders? Or take the last one. What if there are black doves?

Fortunately, you will not come upon many invalid arguments in the readings in Part II. Unfortunately, you *will* come across many invalid arguments in other discussions of the same issues—perhaps even in class discussions—so being able to recognize one when you see it is an important skill.

What you are more likely to come across in the readings in Part II are valid but *unsound* arguments. A sound argument is a valid argument with only true premises. If an argument is invalid, or if it has any false premises, then it is unsound. (Our opening example of a valid argument was obviously unsound, since Clint Eastwood is not a bulldog.) So you must be careful to ask whether the premises are true when you evaluate the arguments you encounter.

Inductive Arguments

Most ordinary reasoning is not deductive. The supporting statements, if true, do not guarantee the truth of the conclusion. Rather, they establish that it is more reasonable than not to accept the conclusion. That is, they establish that the conclusion is likely to be true. Arguments of that kind are called *inductive* arguments. The supporting statements of inductive arguments are called *reasons*, *evidence*, or *grounds*, instead of premises, and a good inductive argument is called *warranted*, instead of valid or sound.

When we reason from cause to effect or from effect to cause, we generally reason inductively. If, for example, we hear a loud bang outside, we would most likely conclude that a car had just backfired. Although other explanations are possible—somebody might have shot his neighbor, say—in most neighborhoods a backfiring car is the most probable one. Since our evidence does admit of other possibilities, though, we cannot say that we reasoned deductively. Similarly, when we put a pot of water on the stove and come back later expecting the water to be boiling, we are also reasoning inductively. Various factors may have kept the water from boiling—the gas might have been turned off, for instance—but, more likely than not, the water is boiling.

Most generalizations are also examples of inductive reasoning. We examine a sample taken from a larger population, notice some features shared by a certain percentage of our sample, and then conclude that the same—or nearly the same— pattern occurs in the population at large. Thus, from a sample of green and only green emeralds we conclude that all emeralds are green, and from a sample of

Nielsen families we conclude that more viewers watch NFL football games than NBA basketball games. These generalizations are reliable, but they are not arrived at by deductive reasoning. Because there is always some probability—however small—that the larger population does not match the sample, such reasoning is inductive.

Although inductive reasoning does not have rules in the same way that deductive reasoning does, there are a variety of criteria we use to evaluate inductive arguments. For our purposes, the most important are those that concern *causal* generalizations, since those are the kinds of arguments that will be most prominent in Part II.

Consider this argument:

1. John takes two aspirin tablets every day.

2. John never has a cold.

3. Therefore, aspirin prevents colds.

There is much, of course, that is wrong with that argument. Two flaws are most obvious. First, a sample of one is hardly large enough to support a generalization about all human beings. Second, no care has been taken to rule out other explanations of John's good fortune. Thus, the following are important criteria for evaluating causal generalizations. First, the sample must be large enough to support the generalization. Second, it must also be representative of the larger population that's being generalized about.

Third, to help rule out other explanations, there must be a *control group*— another sample as much like the original sample (called the *experimental group*) as possible except that its members are not exposed to the factor being tested. If we are testing to see whether aspirin prevents colds, for example, we will want to study two groups, one that takes aspirin daily and one that does not. Only after the control group and the experimental group have been compared are we entitled to our causal generalization.

But even then, we must be careful. Statistical links are not the same as causal links. Two factors may be associated without one being the cause of the other. Sneezing and coughing often go together, but one does not cause the other. Rather, both have a common cause—often a flu virus. So even after a statistical link has been established, further experiments may be necessary to establish a causal link.

To be sure, few people are ever in a position to carry out such experiments. For most of us, inductive reasoning is far less formal. We do not have the statistical techniques to evaluate the reliability of our samples, nor do we have the time and money to design and carry out tests on experimental and control groups. That's why we must rely on people who do–scientists—before we can say that a causal generalization has been established. That does not mean, however, that we can't reach reasonable conclusions before science has spoken. We can. Indeed, often we must. But when doing so we must remember two things.

First, we must keep in mind that the more closely our reasoning resembles the scientist's, the better it is. The more numerous and representative the cases we have to generalize from, the better our evidence and the more reasonable our conclusion. And the more justified we are in ruling out other causes, the more reasonable our conclusion.

Second, no matter how reasonable our conclusion may be, we are not entitled to claim that we've established it. Inductive reasoning, unlike deductive reasoning, cannot be neatly divided into the sound and the unsound. Although it *can* be divided into the warranted and the unwarranted, warrant admits of degrees. One sound deductive argument is as conclusive as another. One warranted inductive argument is not as conclusive as another. Our confidence in our conclusions, then, should be no greater than the degree of our warrant. And as long as our inductive reasoning is informal, our degree of warrant requires a corresponding degree of humility.

Moral Arguments

Whether moral arguments are inductive or deductive is a matter of controversy among philosophers. Fortunately, we needn't decide that issue here. For our purposes, what's most important is that it is more useful for us to *treat* them as deductive. To see why, let's look at two arguments that reach opposite conclusions. A common argument for the position that abortion is wrong except to save the life of the mother can be put this way:

1. Taking an innocent life except to save a life is wrong.

2. Abortion is the taking of an innocent life.

3. Therefore, abortion is wrong except to save a life.

4. The only life that can be endangered by a fetus is the mother's.

5. Therefore, abortion is wrong except to save the life of the mother.

Notice that the above argument is a two-step argument. First, it reaches the *intermediate* conclusion of line three. And then, from lines three and four, it reaches the *final* conclusion of line five. That is not at all unusual in moral arguments. The following argument, a common argument in favor of abortion on demand, has even more steps:

1. Women have the right to control their own bodies as long as they don't harm another person.

2. A woman's right to control her body includes the right to have any medical procedure she and her doctor choose.

3. Therefore, a woman has a right to any medical procedure she and her doctor choose as long as it doesn't harm another person.

4. An abortion is a medical procedure.

5. Therefore, a woman has a right to an abortion as long as it doesn't harm another person.

6. An abortion hurts nothing but the fetus, which is not a person.

7. Therefore, women have the right to an abortion.

That argument is a three-step argument. It reaches two intermediate conclusions, at lines three and five, before the final conclusion of line seven.

Both of these arguments are valid, but since they reach opposite conclusions, they cannot both be sound. At least one of them must have at least one false premise. And that is why it is useful for us to treat moral arguments as deductive. If we do so, they become much easier to evaluate. We can lay out opposing arguments in a clear fashion, make sure that we understand the reasoning behind each one, isolate all of the premises, and then examine the premises of each to see whether they are true. The ones with true premises, or with premises more likely to be true, are the ones we should accept.

Evaluating Moral Arguments

Once again, one of your main tasks in dealing with the issues of Part II will be to evaluate arguments in favor of opposing positions. As we just saw, that task breaks down into two sub-tasks. The first is to try to reconstruct each argument as a valid deductive argument. The second is to examine the premises to see if they are true. Let's begin our discussion of these two tasks by looking at an example.

A Sample Evaluation

A common argument in favor of legalized abortion is often put this way: Catholics and fundamentalist Christians have no right to turn their religious beliefs into law. That is a very short argument. If we are to try to turn it into a valid argument, we must ask ourselves what premises are *assumed* by the argument but not explicitly stated by it. That is, we must ask what premises we should *add* in order to make the argument valid.

One way we can make it valid is by adding only one premise. Then the argument would go like this:

1. Catholics and fundamentalist Christians have no right to turn their religious beliefs into law.

2. That abortions should be banned is a religious belief of Catholics and fundamentalist Christians.

3. Therefore, Catholics and fundamentalist Christians have no right to make abortions illegal.

That is a valid argument, to be sure, but it's not very convincing as it stands. After all, why should we pick on Catholics and fundamentalist Christians? Do Presbyterians have the right to turn their religious beliefs into law? Quakers? Jews? Also, the conclusion is a very weak one. It claims that two groups have no right to make abortion illegal, but not that nobody has the right to make abortion illegal.

So let's try another approach:

1. No religious group has the right to turn its religious beliefs into law.

2. Opponents of abortion are trying to turn their religious beliefs into law.

3. Therefore, opponents of abortion have no right to make abortion illegal.

That's a little better. At least it doesn't pick on two religious groups unfairly. Still, the premises are not very plausible. The trouble with the first is that *many* religious beliefs have been turned into law, often rightfully. Religious beliefs against murder, armed robbery, and rape come most readily to mind. The trouble with the second is that many opponents of abortion oppose it for nonreligious reasons. If the argument is to have any force, then, further changes must be made.

For example:

1. If there are no good nonreligious reasons for turning some group's religious beliefs into law, then nobody has the right to turn those beliefs into law.

2. That abortion should be banned is a religious belief of some groups.

3. Therefore, if there are no good nonreligious reasons for making abortion illegal, nobody has the right to make it illegal.

4. There are no good nonreligious reasons for making abortion illegal.

5. Therefore, nobody has the right to make abortion illegal.

Is that much better? Not really. For one thing, line four is not obviously true. Indeed, whether it *is* true is precisely what the debate over abortion is all about. For another thing, what the argument now boils down to is this:

1. If there are no good reasons to make abortion illegal, it should be legal.

2. There are no good reasons to make abortion illegal.

3. Therefore, abortion should be legal.

And that is not much of an argument at all. Granted, it is certainly valid, but until we have an argument in favor of premise two, opponents of abortion have no reason to take it seriously.

Reconstructing Arguments

What we did in the previous section is not nearly as difficult as it might first appear. All it takes is a little common sense plus the knowledge of a few valid rules of deductive logic. And those few rules are also common sense. One, which we already looked at in our Clint Eastwood example, is:

1. If A, then B.

2. A.

3. Therefore, B.

That is a rule that all of you already knew. No doubt you know the others as well. For example:

1. Either John is home or he's at the library.
2. He's not home.
3. Therefore, what?

The answer, obviously, is that he's at the library. And the rule is:

1. A or B.
2. A is not true.
3. Therefore, B.

Here's another:

1. If Mary is home, she's in the den.
2. She's not in the den.
3. Therefore, what?

The answer here is that she's not home. And the rule is:

1. If A, then B.
2. B is not true.
3. Therefore, A is not true.

There are only three others you need to know (and no doubt already know), and they are equally matters of common sense. Examples are:

1. All dogs are mammals.
2. Lassie is a dog.
3. Therefore, Lassie is a mammal.

And:

1. All dogs are mammals.
2. My parrot is not a mammal.
3. Therefore, my parrot is not a dog.

And:

1. No pigs can fly.
2. Robins can fly.
3. Therefore, robins aren't pigs.

And the rules are:

1. All A is B.
2. C is A.
3. Therefore, C is B.

And:

1. All A is B.
2. C is not B.
3. Therefore, C is not A.

And:

1. No A is B.
2. C is B.
3. Therefore, C is not A.

Armed with these common-sense rules, you will be able to turn any logical moral argument into a valid deductive argument. That is, as long as the argument doesn't depend on any invalid rules, you can do what we did in the previous section. For example, we often hear that homosexuality is wrong because it's unnatural. That claim is really an abbreviated argument:

1. Anything unnatural is morally wrong.
2. Homosexuality is unnatural.
3. Therefore, homosexuality is morally wrong.

Of course, few people actually put it that way. The first premise is generally left unsaid, but common sense tells us that something like the first premise is required if the argument is to be valid. Along the same lines, common sense tells us that something must be added when people claim that capital punishment is wrong because it does not deter crime any better than life imprisonment does. When we add what is needed, we get:

1. If one punishment is more severe than another, it is wrong to impose the more severe one if it is not a better deterrent than the less severe one.
2. Capital punishment is more severe than life imprisonment.
3. Therefore, it is wrong to impose capital punishment if it is not a better deterrent than life imprisonment.
4. Capital punishment is not a better deterrent than life imprisonment.
5. Therefore, it is wrong to impose capital punishment.

How do we know which premises to add? There is no precise formula that anybody can give, but we can give some general directions. First, we must choose premises that can be used with valid deductive rules. When we look at the claim that homosexuality is wrong because it's unnatural, for instance, we know that the conclusion is "Homosexuality is wrong" and that one premise is "Homosexuality is unnatural." What we need, then, is a premise like "If anything is unnatural it's wrong," or "All unnatural behavior is wrong."

Second, we must make sure that our added premises are *general* enough to look like real moral principles, not prejudices. That is why we put "anything" and "all unnatural behavior" in the above premises, not "homosexuality" and "all homosexual acts." If we make the premise read "If homosexuality is unnatural, then it's wrong," somebody could justifiably ask us "Why just homosexuality?" That's why we changed "Catholics and ·fundamentalist Christians" to "religious groups" in an earlier example. In moral arguments, we must appeal to moral principles, and the more general a statement is, the more like a genuine moral principle and the less like an expression of prejudice it is.

Third, we must add *enough* premises to make the argument valid. That requirement is not just a matter of logic. If we are to evaluate an argument adequately, we must be able to examine all of its premises. And if we don't have enough premises to make the argument valid, we are lacking at least one assumed premise.

Fourth, we must use a little *charity*, even if we don't agree with the argument's conclusion. We must allow our opponents the best arguments we can if we are to give them a fair hearing. That means that we must do our best to give them *plausible* premises. A few pages back, for example, we looked at the claim that a woman has the right to an abortion because she has the right to control her own body. One of the premises we added was "A woman's right to control her own body includes the right to have any medical procedure she and her doctor choose." Now that may or may not be true, but it is certainly plausible. On the other hand, the following premise is most certainly not: "A woman's right to control her body includes the right to murder her children." Granted, many abortion foes believe that pro-choice advocates are claiming that, but it is most unfair to make it a premise in their arguments.

Fifth, we must do our best to make sure that the premises we add are *faithful* to the beliefs of the person putting forth the argument. Although we cannot always be sure on this point, there are ways to increase our confidence. If we add a premise that is inconsistent with sentences that appear elsewhere in the reading, we have probably failed. Of course, sometimes people *are* inconsistent, but if it is possible to read them in a way that makes them consistent, we should do so. (That, of course, is required of us by the principle of charity.)

Also, arguers often give us hints of their broader commitments. In his reading arguing against abortion, for example, John T. Noonan makes it clear that he agrees with much of traditional Catholic theology, although he attempts to rest his arguments on purely secular grounds. And in her reading arguing against sexist pornography, Ann Garry lets us know that she shares many feminist sympathies. We should not supply anti-Catholic premises to Noonan or anti-feminist premises to Garry.

Sixth, we must be careful not to beg any questions. To *beg a question* is to assume what you are trying to prove, and a *question-begging argument* is one that contains the conclusion as one of its premises. Sometimes, that cannot be helped. If John says that he believes Mary because she's honest, and he knows she's honest because she told him so, and he believed her because she's honest, there is not much we can do to save his argument. On the other hand, we are not forced to beg any questions when reconstructing the pro-choice argument based on a woman's right to control her own body. In that case, we should not add the following:

2. A woman's right to control her body includes the right to do anything moral.

3. Abortions are moral.

4. Therefore, a woman has the right to an abortion.

Although premise three is not precisely the same as the conclusion, it is certainly close enough to qualify as question-begging.

Seventh, we must be careful not to *equivocate*. That is, we must not allow the argument to turn on different meanings of the same word. For example, the word "unnatural" can mean either "perverse" or "out of the ordinary." Many things, like writing poetry or skydiving, are unnatural in the second sense of the word but not the first. Anyone who argues that skydiving is out of the ordinary, and therefore unnatural, and therefore perverse is guilty of equivocating. Of course, sometimes the arguments we are trying to reconstruct *will* turn on equivocations. Some arguments against homosexuality, for example, may turn on an equivocation on "natural" much like the one we just looked at. In those cases, we have no choice but to give up. An argument that turns on an equivocation is not a valid one, and we cannot make it valid without creating an entirely different argument.

Examining Premises

Once we have a valid argument before us, we must next ask whether it is a sound argument. The first premises to look at are the general ones, since they are most likely to be questionable. Although many statements with words like "all" and "every" and "any" and "no" are true, many others are not.

Consider the general statements that appear in our pro- and anti-abortion arguments, for example. Is it really true that a woman's right to control her own body includes the right to have *any* medical procedure she and her doctor choose? What about experimental procedures that have not been approved for the general public? Or procedures that have been outlawed because they are ineffective or dangerous?

Similarly, is it really true that taking an innocent life is *always* wrong except to save another life? (The word "always" did not appear in the premise of our argument, but, as in many general statements, the general word is assumed. With a sentence like "Dogs are mammals," or even "A dog is a mammal," we should understand it as being about all dogs unless we are told otherwise.) Judith Jarvis Thomson, in her defense of abortion that appears in Part II, doesn't think so, and she provides examples to back up her point.

Thomson's examples are meant to be *counter-examples* to the generalization in the anti-abortion argument, just as the examples of unapproved medical procedures were offered as counter-examples to the generalization in the pro-abortion argument. That is, they are meant to be examples in which the generalization breaks down.

If the proposed counter-examples are genuine counter-examples, we may still be able to save the premise in a slightly altered form. Suppose we grant that a woman does not have the right to an unapproved medical procedure. All we have to do is add the phrase "medically approved" to that premise and other premises in which it is now needed to make the argument valid. The additions will not harm the argument, because most abortions are medically approved.

On the other hand, the counter-examples may be decisive. That is, there may be no way to alter the premise without destroying the argument. Whether Thomson's counter-examples are decisive is not for us to decide now, but we can look at another case in which counter-examples are decisive. Take this argument:

1. Lying is wrong.
2. Telling a friend that her ugly baby is cute is lying.
3. Therefore, telling a friend that her ugly baby is cute is wrong.

Most of us agree that white lies are genuine counter-examples to the first premise. Honesty is commendable, but not when it causes our friends great hurt and the lie is an innocuous one. But once we change the first premise to exempt white lies, the argument falls apart.

One way to challenge a general premise, then, is to find a decisive counter-example. Another way is to question the assumptions it rests on. Many people, for example, take issue with premise six of the pro-abortion argument, which says that a fetus is not a person (or no fetus is a person, or all fetuses are not persons). They cannot point to a counter-example that abortion proponents will accept, because the view that fetuses are not persons is based on certain assumptions about what it is to be a person—and those assumptions rule out all fetuses. What abortion opponents must do, then, is challenge the assumptions. That is, they must show that the other side is wrong about what it is to be a person and that a proper understanding would show that all or most or some fetuses are persons.

Very often, the challenged assumptions will be moral assumptions. An argument may conclude that something is right because it is justified by the principle of utility, say. Someone who disagrees with the argument, on the other hand, might feel that respect for persons must take precedence in this instance. Another argument may conclude that justice requires us to do one thing, while someone who disagrees might feel that justice requires us to do something else.

Such disagreements are, of course, very hard to settle. They often boil down to what philosophers call conflicting *moral intuitions*. By moral intuition, we do not mean some mysterious sixth sense for divining moral truths. Rather, we mean only a moral conviction arrived at after careful consideration of the relevant facts—a conviction that strikes us as right, but not provable. But even though they are not provable, moral intuitions can be challenged, discussed, and even changed on reasonable grounds.

The idea is to think of a variety of cases—some ordinary, some a bit fanciful—and see if consideration of these cases has any effect on our intuitions. What these cases add is new relevant information. Many of our moral intuitions, after all, are based on a small sample of possible cases. Some of them may be generalizations we've arrived at a little too quickly. Often, we can benefit by opening them up to some careful scrutiny. So when you come across arguments that rest on moral assumptions that conflict with your intuitions, the best thing to do is examine both the assumptions and your intuitions as carefully as possible.

Other general statements that require careful scrutiny are causal generalizations. Although many causal generalizations are extremely well established—friction causes heat, for example—many others are controversial at best. Among the most controversial are those that some readings in Part II rely on—about the harmful or beneficial effects of pornography, or the deterrent effects of capital punishment, or the effects of various social programs on the poor. Most of us have our own opinions on these matters, but more often than not they are based on what we take to be common sense rather than on well-designed studies.

By well-designed studies, of course, we mean studies with large representative samples and adequate controls. Sometimes such studies exist, but they are inconclusive. Sometimes different studies on the same issue will come to conflicting conclusions. Sometimes they just don't exist. How, then, can we evaluate causal generalizations under such conditions?

The first thing to do is see how they are supported. Often, they are supported by *analogies*. Many opponents of pornography, for example, draw an analogy between pornography and prostitution. Similarly, opponents of mercy killing and abortion sometimes draw analogies between those practices and what went on in Nazi death camps. When faced with such analogies, we must ask in what ways they hold up and in what ways they do not. Are there relevant differences that suggest that the compared practices will have different effects? Are there better analogies than the ones being drawn?

Causal claims might also be supported by an argument called the *slippery slope* argument. The idea here is that what at first looks like one small step is just the beginning of a series of small steps that will be difficult or impossible to stop after we've taken the first one. J. Gay-Williams, in a reading included in Part II, argues that administering lethal injections to pain-wracked terminally ill patients who ask for them is the beginning of such a slippery slope—and that at the bottom we will find ourselves ordering the deaths of undesirables as a matter of social policy.

Whether Gay-Williams is right about that is again something that is not for us to decide here. But as a general rule, we should scrutinize such arguments carefully. Not all slopes are as slippery as they first appear. Perhaps there are very good reasons for taking the first step and very good reasons for *not* taking the second. Perhaps there are principled reasons for digging in our heels somewhere along the way and nothing to stop us from doing so.

Also, causal generalizations might be "supported" by a kind of hand-waving. That is, the argument might boil down to a non-argument, something like "Everybody knows that . . ." To be sure, there are many things that everybody *does* know, and things that everybody knows are the best premises for an argument we can find. But we must be careful, especially when dealing with causal generalizations, and even more especially when dealing with causal generalizations about human behavior, to ask whether *anybody*, let alone everybody, really knows that they're true.

Moreover, the mere fact that we don't know that they're false is insufficient support for them. The proper response to ignorance is to try to learn more. If we must decide what to do before we can learn more, we must do the same kind of calculating that's required whenever we try to make a rational decision under conditions of uncertainty. That is, we must ask ourselves what we stand to gain and lose by acting on a belief we don't know to be true. (For an example of this kind of reasoning, see Ernest Van Den Haag's defense of capital punishment in Part II.)

Finally, causal generalizations might be supported by inductive arguments based on things we *do* know. Since these arguments will not support their conclusions as strongly as well-designed studies can, they must be approached very carefully. At best, they can establish their conclusions as reasonable, perhaps even more reasonable than their competitors, given what we now know. But what we now know, we must remember, is incomplete. That is why well-designed studies are so important. They fill in the many gaps in current knowledge, and once those gaps are filled, we may find that what was once the most reasonable conclusion is false.

Two other kinds of general premises deserve consideration here. These are generalizations about the arguer's supporters and opponents. For example, you may come across the claim that social scientists agree that such and such is true. To make the argument valid, you must add a premise like "Whatever social scientists agree on is true," or the weaker "If social scientists agree on something, we should accept it as true." You might also hear someone argue that you should not accept opponents' arguments because the opponents are untrustworthy for one reason or another. Then you must add a premise like "Arguments by untrustworthy people are unsound."

The first two of these premises appeal to the authority of social scientists. Are they true? Not as they now stand. On the other hand, this variation probably is: "If social scientists agree on a generalization about human behavior that is based on strong research, we should accept it as true." Of course, not being social scientists ourselves, we cannot adequately evaluate their research, but if social scientists at respectable universities claim that their agreement is based on strong research, we are certainly justified in believing them. If their agreement is just a widely shared hunch, however, then their authority is lessened. And if their agreement is on a matter other than human behavior—if it is on the best brand of toothpaste, say—then their authority evaporates.

The third of the three premises, about untrustworthy opponents, is an example of what is called an *ad hominem* argument (from the Latin phrase for "to the man"). Like appeals to authority, they may or may not be acceptable. The premise at hand is not. Granted, untrustworthy people often do present unsound arguments, but as long as they do present arguments, we should evaluate those arguments, not the arguers. (Even paranoids have enemies, as the saying has it.) On the other hand, when someone offers us nothing better than an unsupported claim, rather than an argument, all we can go on is the trustworthiness of the person making the offer.

Trying Alternative Premises

One of the things we saw in the previous sections is that we sometimes have to change an argument's premise. Often, the reason is that the premise is questionable, or downright false. Why change it rather than just reject the argument? The principle of charity gives us one answer. But we are interested in more than just fairness to our opponents. We are also interested in solving moral problems, and that interest should also lead us to consider the strongest arguments possible.

For example, let's return to our argument against capital punishment. The first premise read:

1. If one punishment is more severe than another, it is wrong to impose the more severe one if it is not a better deterrent than the less severe one.

There seem to be many counter-examples to that. Is the threat of a ten-year prison term a greater deterrent than the threat of a nine-year prison term? Is the threat of life imprisonment a greater deterrent than the threat of a thirty-year prison term? Although we can't be absolutely sure about the answers to these questions, the more plausible answer is no. Still, we see nothing wrong in giving some people thirty-year sentences and others life sentences.

More generally, though, we can say this: Deterrence is not the only consideration in determining a just sentence. Another is our concern to protect other people from people convicted of serious crimes. Still another is our feeling that the severity of the punishment should reflect the severity of the crime. Presumably, people who argue against capital punishment on the grounds that it does not deter know that. So we might recast the premise this way:

1. If two punishments equally reflect the severity of the crime and offer equal protection from the convicted criminal, it is wrong to impose the more severe one if it is not a better deterrent.

Notice how this procedure helps us focus on the important issues. By exposing points that the argument takes for granted, it allows us to evaluate them as well as the points it does not take for granted. Now we must add new premises—that life imprisonment protects others from convicted criminals as well as capital punishment protects them, and that life imprisonment reflects the severity of capital crimes as adequately as capital punishment does. And we must then evaluate them.

Moreover, we might want to evaluate the new version of the first premise. Why, we might ask, must punishment *always* reflect the severity of the crime? If we really believe that it must, shouldn't we have even more awful punishments than we now have? If a man brutally rapes and tortures a half dozen women before killing them, does that mean that we should subject him to something equally horrible? Or should we recognize instead that there are moral limits to the severity of punishment regardless of other factors, and maybe those limits mean we should stop short of capital punishment?

In short, trying new premises helps us do more than just evaluate arguments. It helps us think clearly and thoroughly about the problems at hand.

Another example also helps show this. Sometimes we should try new premises because the ones we first added are not the only reasonable possibilities. That reason applies to one of the premises in the pro-abortion argument we looked at:

2.   A woman's right to control her body includes the right to have any medically approved medical procedure she and her doctor choose.

Perhaps people who defend the right to an abortion on the grounds of a woman's right to control her own body mean something else, like:

2.   A woman's right to control her body includes the right not to have her body used for purposes she does not want it used for.

In that case, we get a new intermediate conclusion:

3.   A woman has the right not to have her body used for purposes she does not want it used for as long as she does not harm another person.

Then we add this premise:

4.   A woman carrying an unwanted fetus is having her body used for purposes she does not want it used for.

And then we get this intermediate conclusion:

5.   Therefore, a woman has the right not to carry an unwanted fetus as long as she does not harm another person.

Whether this version or the original version of the argument is sound is, once again, not to be decided here. But looking at both can be important. Judith Jarvis Thomson's article, for example, focuses on the new interpretation of a woman's right to control her own body, not the original one, and it might make an important difference. The reason it might is that Thomson believes a woman has the right not to have her body used in a way she doesn't want it to be used even in some cases where an innocent person *is* harmed, even fatally. Thus, she defends a woman's right to have an abortion without the premise that fetuses are not persons.

Questions of Relevance

Whether a premise is really relevant to the moral issue at hand is, of course, an important matter. Much of the advice for evaluating arguments that we've been looking at has been closely connected to the question of relevance.

Most important has been the advice about supplying and evaluating implicit general premises. If the implicit general premise turns out to be false, that is often because an explicit premise is irrelevant. To pick an obvious example, remember the implicit premise in our sample *ad hominem* argument: Arguments by untrustworthy people are unsound. Any premise that requires a general premise like that is irrelevant. That is why we need not, in general, pay any attention to *ad hominem* arguments. It is also why the arguments we will find in the readings in Part II will not depend on many of the emotion-laden phrases we often find in the letters columns of local newspapers, phrases like "bra burners," "Bible thumpers," "secular humanists," "bleeding hearts," and "ultra-rightists."

Irrelevancies that are intended to distract our attention from the real issues are known as *red herrings*. Because red herrings often involve appeals to our emotions, many textbooks caution their readers to be extremely wary of emotional appeals. That is good advice, if not taken too far—especially in moral arguments. When emotion takes us where reason does not, appeals to emotion are certainly out of order. On the other hand, appeals to emotion are unavoidable in moral debate. Any argument in favor of voluntary euthanasia, for example, must appeal to our sympathy for pain-wracked terminally ill patients. Any argument in favor of capital punishment must appeal to our fear and loathing of brutal murderers. Such appeals will be there even if unintended. Important moral issues are emotional ones, and there is no getting around it.

But if we cannot altogether separate emotion from moral argument, we can still question particular connections in particular cases. Are our emotions being whipped up by flamboyant language? By questionable claims? By sentimental anecdotes that are unrepresentative of most relevant cases? Is our attention being diverted from relevant facts? From important moral considerations like individual rights and obligations? If so, we are being victimized by red herrings.

We must also take care not to be victimized by another kind of irrelevancy— the *straw man*. Sustained arguments for a position usually include criticisms of opposing arguments. If the opposing arguments are faithfully rendered, all is as it should be. But if they are unfaithfully rendered, the arguer is attacking a straw man. And whatever defects the straw man may have, they are irrelevant to what really matters—the opponent's real arguments. So one thing you must always be careful to ask is this: Is *that* what the people on the other side are *really* saying?

Summary and Conclusions

In a play by the seventeenth-century French playwright Molière, the main character is delighted to learn that he has been speaking prose for as long as he has been talking. One thing you might have learned during the course of this chapter is that you have been reasoning logically for as long as you have been thinking. But some people speak better prose than others, and some people reason more logically than others. In each case, what often makes the difference is a bit of reflection on what distinguishes good prose or logical reasoning, followed by a little practice.

This chapter has picked out some of the features that distinguish logical reasoning, and it has applied them to various moral arguments. So should you apply them to the moral arguments of Part II. If you do, you will provide yourself with more than just a little practice. Before we turn to Part II, though, we should make a few final remarks.

First, don't be intimidated by the task of evaluating arguments. You don't have to write out every argument and then rewrite it every time you think of an alternative missing premise. All you have to do is *think* as you read or listen. And that holds not just for the readings in Part II, but for any argument you encounter—in a newspaper, a conversation, another course, or anyplace else. Passive reading or listening is never good reading or listening, especially when the writer or speaker is trying to convince you of something.

Second, the techniques for evaluating arguments we have looked at are intended not only for other people's arguments, but our own too. Whenever we arrive at a conclusion, we do so for reasons, and our reasons may be good or bad, better or worse. It is important, then, that we challenge ourselves as well as others.

Third, this is a book in applied ethics, as its title makes clear. Although every textbook is (or at least should be) an exercise in applied logic (as well as applied prose), our basic concern is to come to grips with some important moral problems. And that means that you should apply the material in *both* chapters of Part I to the material in Part II. We want our moral conclusions to be based on both our most general moral principles and good reasoning.

Since this chapter has said little about those principles so far, it should close by tying them to what it has said. Each of the sample moral arguments we looked at contained at least one moral principle—about a woman's rights, or the taking of innocent life, or the justification of punishment, to mention just three. Some were more general than others, but none was as general as the principle of utility, say, or respect for persons. That does not mean, though, that these most general principles have no important work to do in moral arguments. Why not?

For one thing, the less general principles are based on the most general ones. We accept them because we believe the most general ones require us to accept them. If we think that some kinds of punishment are unjustified, it's because we think them unfair, or inconsistent with respect for persons, or because we think they will not maximize utility. Also, if we think that there are legitimate exceptions to the less general principles, it's because we think that the most general ones require the exceptions. Thus, we justify white lies, for example, because a principle more general than honesty—the principle of utility, say—requires it. So these most general principles did play an important role in our sample arguments, even though we did not make them explicit.

Sometimes, however, they *must* be made explicit. That happens when a less general principle, or a proposed exception to a less general principle, is controversial. When that does happen, we need an argument for the principle or its proposed exception, and that will take us back to the most general principles. We will have to ask whether any of our most general principles support the controversial premise. If they don't, we can reject it. If they do, then we will have to ask whether any of our other most general principles give a conflicting answer. If they don't do that, we can accept the premise. If they do, we will have to ask which of the conflicting principles should take precedence.

That last question is a particularly difficult one to answer, and moral problems that turn on it are particularly difficult to resolve to everyone's satisfaction. Men and women of good will may, in the end, come to different resolutions, because they cannot agree on which principle takes precedence. Not surprisingly, many of the problems of Part II turn on precisely that question, which is why they are still with us. But difficult is not the same as impossible, which is why many similar problems are no longer with us.

If we were writing this book thirty years ago, we might have included a chapter on civil disobedience—we might have looked at arguments for and against the view that people have the moral right to protest laws they consider unjust by peacefully and publicly violating those laws. Also, our chapter on discrimination would have been very different. Instead of looking at arguments for and against *reverse* discrimination, we might very well have been considering whether private employers have the right to discriminate *against* minorities and women. Today, such chapters would be unthinkable. The extraordinarily powerful moral arguments of people like Martin Luther King, Jr. have made them unthinkable. Perhaps in another thirty years we will be able to say the same thing about some of the chapters in the book you are now reading.

Selections for Further Reading

Barry, Vincent E. *Invitation to Critical Thinking.* New York: Holt, Rinehart & Winston, 1984.

Bergman, Merrie, et al. *The Logic Book.* New York: Knopf, 1980.

Damer, Edward T. *Attacking Faulty Reasoning.* Belmont, Calif.: Wadsworth, 1980.

Kahane, Howard. *Logic and Contemporary Rhetoric*, 4th ed. Belmont, Calif.: Wadsworth, 1984.

Quine, W. V. and J. S. Ulliah. *The Web of Belief.* New York: Random House, 1978.

Richards, D. A. *A Theory of Reasons for Actions.* Oxford: Clarendon Press, 1971.

Schwartz, Thomas. *The Art of Logical Reasoning.* New York: Random House, 1980.

Toulmin, Stephen. *An Examination of the Place of Reason in Ethics.* New York: Cambridge University Press, 1950.

PART II

Issues

3
SEXUAL MORALITY

A decade ago, the United States was abuzz with talk of the "new morality" and the "sexual revolution." Almost everywhere, people were discussing singles bars, casual sex, one-night stands, open marriage, unwed motherhood, creative divorce, cohabitation, group sex, teen sex, and sexual preference. Traditional sexual morality was breaking or had already broken down.

To traditionalists, the changes were at best disturbing and at worst alarming. They worried about the future of their children, of the family, and of society. What they saw when they looked around was moral decline. To those caught up in the revolution, on the other hand, the changes were liberating. What they saw when they looked around were new options, new freedoms, new manners of expression, and fulfillment.

Many of you are likely to take the sexual revolution as much for granted as you take the American Revolution. Some of you may even wonder what all the fuss was about. Others may think of the old morality as quaint. You might ask: Were women really supposed to remain virgins until marriage? Did people really think that living together was immoral? Could a talented and beautiful movie star like Ingrid Bergman really be run out of Hollywood for having an affair with a married man? Did parents and universities really insist on separate dorms for male and female students?

Of course, others of you do not take the new morality for granted. Some of you probably agree totally with the traditionalists, despite the pressures you might feel from your peers. Some of you probably accept parts of the new morality but not others. Perhaps you believe in nonmarital sex but feel that the people involved should love each other. Perhaps you find nothing wrong with premarital sex but draw the line at adultery. Perhaps you accept total freedom when it comes to heterosexual sex but believe that homosexuality is immoral.

Such differences show that the victory of the sexual revolution was not total. Moreover, certain trends in today's world suggest that we may be in store for some counterrevolutionary changes. The risk of AIDS seems to be affecting the sexual behavior of both heterosexuals and homosexuals. The large number of teenage pregnancies is also causing doubts about the new morality. And some feminists have begun calling for a "new celibacy."

For these reasons and others, debate about sexual morality continues. The issues involved are many and complex. The best place to start, no doubt, is with the two extreme positions: the traditional and the libertarian.

The Traditional View

The traditional view can be put quite simply: All sex outside marriage is wrong. Although people have held the traditional view for a variety of reasons, its most influential line of defense comes from the Roman Catholic church.

As we saw in Part I, Catholic moral teaching was greatly influenced by Aristotle, the ancient Greek philosopher whose ideas were incorporated into church doctrine by the medieval thinker St. Thomas Aquinas. Four of Aristotle's ideas are particularly important here. First, everything in nature has a purpose. Second, everything in nature has an essential nature—certain features that constitute its defining features. Third, everything in nature has its proper good. Fourth, something's natural purpose, its essential nature, and its proper good are intimately related.

That the Roman Catholic church believes that the natural purpose of sex is reproduction is well known. Equally well known is one consequence that the church draws from that belief—that artificial means of birth control are immoral. Less well known are other, related, beliefs that are also directly related to sexual morality. These beliefs are spelled out in the Vatican's 1976 "Declaration on Certain Questions Concerning Sexual Ethics."

There, the authors stress what they take to be an essential characteristic of human beings—the ability to engage in fully human love, which includes genuine caring, sincerity, respect, commitment, and fidelity. Moreover, the declaration argues, fully human love does not stop at romantic love; it naturally evolves into parental love. That is, true human love is made complete by love for the children produced by that love. These facts about human sexuality are what set it apart from mere animal sexuality. They are also what make it more valuable. Equally important, they are what give human sex and sexual relationships their special dignity.

To engage in sex without love, then, or to engage in sex not open to the possibility of procreation, is to engage in sex that violates our essential nature and dignity. And since to violate our essential nature and dignity is to turn away from the proper human good, to engage in sex without love or sex not open to procreation is to engage in wrongful sex. That does not mean, however, that unmarried sex with love and without contraception is moral in the church's view. Given the changeableness of human desire and commitment, we need added guarantees of sincerity and fidelity. And only marriage can provide those guarantees.

The Libertarian View

According to the libertarian view, sex is an activity like any other—tennis, say, or conversation, or studying—and what determines whether any sexual act is moral or immoral is no different from what determines whether any other act is moral or immoral. As long as the act involves no dishonesty, exploitation, or coercion, and as long as it does not violate any obligations to others, it is not immoral.

Consider premarital sex. Many things can make it immoral. If John tells Mary that he loves her and wants to take her home to meet his parents and she goes to bed with him as a result, John acts immorally if he doesn't mean what he tells her. If Mary has a venereal disease and does not warn John ahead of time, then she acts immorally. If John tries to coerce Mary into performing sexual acts she dislikes, then he acts immorally. But if neither of them is looking for anything more than a one-night stand, and if neither holds back any important information, and if neither resorts to any coercion or breaks any promise, and if neither violates any obligation to a third person, then neither does anything wrong.

Of course, we are assuming here that both John and Mary are adults. Children are incapable of the kind of informed consent required to ensure that they are not being exploited. But there are other things we need not assume. For example, we need not assume that the adults involved are of different sexes. Whatever holds for John and Mary also holds for John and Bill or for Jane and Mary. Nor need we assume that only *two* adults are involved. Group sex that violates none of our conditions is perfectly acceptable to the libertarian. Furthermore, we need not even assume that John and Mary are not close relatives, like brother and sister. Even incest is acceptable to the libertarian, as long as there is no dishonesty, coercion, or exploitation, and as long as reliable means of contraception are used.

Similar remarks hold for adultery. Even though marriage involves the promise of fidelity, husbands and wives are perfectly free to release each other from their vows, just as we are all free to release one another from any other promise. If a married couple agrees that both members would be happier if they could have extramarital affairs, then they are morally free to do so—provided, of course, that they do not keep their marriage a secret from sexual partners who do not wish to have affairs with married people.

Arguments in favor of sexual libertarianism are basically of the "why not?" sort. Why *shouldn't* sex be treated like any other activity? Why should we consider it moral to play tennis with somebody we don't love but immoral to have sex with somebody we don't love? Why should we consider it moral to eat lunch with somebody of the same sex but immoral to have sex with that very same person? Why should we be permitted to go to a movie purely for pleasure but not have sex purely for pleasure? What's so different about sex that it requires such special rules? Why can't sexual morality be determined by the same general moral principles—the principle of utility, respect for persons, the golden rule, and so forth—that determine right and wrong in the rest of our lives?

Treating Sex Differently

We have already looked at one answer to the libertarian's questions, the one offered by the Vatican. Not surprisingly, sexual libertarians reject it. Many of their reasons for rejecting it will become apparent throughout this chapter, but for now, let's just mention one. Libertarians generally feel that it is up to each individual to determine his or her own good. Human dignity lies in our capacity to pursue our own good as we see fit—provided we do not interfere with another person's pursuit of his or her own good—not in adhering to any particular sexual morality. Sex between consenting adults is a private matter, and private matters are matters of individual conscience.

Many other answers to the libertarians' arguments focus on the social context of sex. The sex lives of any particular individuals may be private, but the widespread adoption of any particular sexual morality can have far-reaching social ramifications. Let's look at several of these issues.

Venereal Diseases and AIDS

Gonorrhea, syphilis, and other venereal diseases are familiar hazards of sex. Although some can be extremely serious—even fatal—if left untreated, they *are* treatable. Because they are, fear of contracting them rarely interferes with most people's sex lives. When genital herpes burst on the scene in the seventies, however, fear did begin to play a role in many people's sexual decisions. Although not as dangerous as syphilis, herpes is a chronic condition.

In the eighties, a new and far more dangerous threat appeared—AIDS (acquired immune deficiency syndrome). There is no known cure for AIDS, nor has a vaccine been developed to prevent its spread, and that leaves its victims with the hopeless prospect of a protracted, agonizing death and leaves potential victims with a terrifying question mark.

Although there is much controversy over how AIDS is transmitted, five means of transmission are well established: anal sex, vaginal sex, intravenous needles and syringes, blood transfusions, and pregnancy. (Other feared possibilities, like "deep" kissing and eating utensils, have not been established as means of transmitting the disease.) Because of the controversy over transmission of AIDS, there is a corresponding controversy over its potential victims. Still, statistics show that the groups facing the highest risk are male homosexuals, intravenous drug users, hemophiliacs, the sex partners of members of these three groups, and children of women at risk when pregnant.

AIDS has already taken a terrible toll among the homosexual population. Whether we can expect it to affect the general heterosexual population as severely is, given the other controversies, also a matter of controversy. But whether AIDS can or cannot be spread by casual contact, whether all of us or only those of us in high risk groups need be immediately concerned for our own safety, AIDS does raise serious concerns about sexual morality. Given what we do know, sexual promiscuity—both heterosexual and homosexual—increases the risk of AIDS, not only to ourselves, but to our spouses and future children.

At the minimum, then, people who cannot be certain about their sexual partners should engage in "safe" sex. That is, they should use condoms. Even libertarians can agree on that point. Other people go further. Some argue that the threat of AIDS should cause us to return to traditional sexual morality. Others claim that we need not go that far. Perhaps we should retreat from promiscuity, they say, but monogamous relationships among unmarried people can be just as safe as among married people. Still others claim that the threat of AIDS does not even require monogamy, as long as we do not engage in sex with people in high risk groups.

Threats to the Family

One of the most alarming trends in recent years is the sharp rise in single parent households. Although different people find different things about the trend alarming, one concern is shared by all. Most single parents are women, and single women and their children are often poor. They comprise the vast majority of the residents of major cities' homeless shelters, and they receive more welfare payments than any other group.

That many single parents are teenagers is another concern shared by all. Whether they are forced to drop out of school or manage to continue their educations, teenage motherhood places a great burden on them, their children, and society.

The causes of single parenthood are complex. Any list of contributing factors would have to include a variety of social conditions, including, most notably, poverty. But nothing can be more evident than this: No sex, no children. Another point is equally evident: The fewer the divorces, the fewer the single parents. And it is these two points that critics of sexual libertarianism stress.

Regarding the first, they say that the spread of the sexual revolution from adults to teenagers was inevitable. When unmarried rock stars and other teen heroes openly live together and have children, when the media are filled with representations of casual sex, how can teenagers not be affected? And given their lack of maturity and responsibility, the normal confusions of adolescence, and various pressures that many teens feel, how could we have expected anything less than an explosion of teen pregnancies?

The connection between the sexual revolution and divorce may seem more tenuous, but to some people it is no less real. If sex outside of marriage is freely available and without moral stigma, if sexual adventure and variety are prized at least as much as monogamy, if love and commitment are no longer seen as natural accompaniments to sex, then marital ties inevitably weaken.

What makes sex different, according to this line of argument, then, is the intimate connection between sexual behavior and the health of the family, plus the social costs that the decline of the family entails. If sexual morality concerned only the individuals involved in any particular sexual act, then perhaps we could treat sex like tennis. But it doesn't, so we can't.

Personal Fulfillment

For those of us with no aspirations to be Ivan Lendl or Martina Navratilova, tennis is little more than an enjoyable game, a pleasant way to get fresh air and exercise, or a welcome opportunity for camaraderie. Even if such things are important to us, and even if tennis is our favorite way to get them, the role of tennis in our lives remains relatively limited.

Can we say the same about sex? Hardly. For one thing, there is a strong biological component to our sexual lives. Thus, both biological and behavioral scientists talk of sex *drives* as well as desires. For another, sexual development cannot be separated from psychological development. How we learn to deal with our sexuality is crucial to the kind of person we become, and our sexual identity is a critical feature of our personal identity. For yet another, our sexual relationships are among the most powerful and influential relationships we can have.

Critics of sexual libertarianism often charge that to treat sex like any other activity is to miss everything that is important about sex and its role in our lives. In particular, it is to ignore its importance to personal growth and fulfillment. Any sexual morality must take account of that fact. Such critics don't necessarily call for a return to traditional morality, but they do insist that we view sex as more than merely a pleasant activity. What we should do is ask ourselves questions like these: Does our sex life contribute to our sense of worth and dignity? Is it consistent with our most important goals in life? Does it reflect the kind of person we most want to be? Is it the sex life of a mature, well-adjusted person? Does it help us develop or maintain the character traits that most matter to us? Does it enhance our lives as much as it might? Does it help us build the kind of relationships we most value?

To ask such questions is to steer a middle course between the sexual traditionalist and the sexual libertarian. The questions are, after all, very much in the spirit of the Vatican declaration. The concerns they raise—fundamental values, personal dignity and fulfillment, the quality of our lives and relationships—are the same. But unlike the authors of the declaration, many people who insist that we ask these questions do not assume that our answers must follow any particular line. In that respect, they are more like the libertarians. For example, they allow that many people engaged in loving homosexual relationships can answer yes to all these questions. So can many unmarried heterosexuals with active sex lives.

People who support this way of treating sex, then, are like the traditionalists in that they do not treat sex like any other activity, but like the libertarians in that they make room for a variety of personal decisions about sex.

The Naturalness Argument

Another line of attack against sexual libertarianism also shares certain features with the Vatican declaration. According to this line, sex organs and sexual activity are natural phenomena, and like any other natural phenomenon, they have their own natural manifestations and purposes. In that case, we can distinguish natural from unnatural sex, and natural from unnatural use of our sex organs. And, since what is natural is moral and what is unnatural is immoral, we can distinguish moral from immoral sex.

Although the Vatican declaration applies this reasoning to a variety of sexual behaviors—masturbation and the use of contraception, for instance, as well as homosexuality—many people confine it to homosexuality alone.

What is it that makes homosexuality unnatural? Various answers are given. Homosexual behavior violates the laws of nature, some people say. Or it is an abnormal occurrence in nature. Or it involves an unnatural use of sex organs.

Libertarian Objections

Many libertarians share some of the concerns we have just looked at. They do not, however, conclude that these concerns justify a retreat from full sexual freedom. Sexual libertarians do not advocate moral irresponsibility, they say, but only sexual freedom. And sexual libertarianism can be just as morally responsible as sexual traditionalism.

Consider the AIDS threat. Certainly, libertarians say, we all have an obligation to avoid behavior that might cause us to become carriers of the virus and pass it on to others. And just as certainly, that obligation involves taking necessary precautions like using condoms when we cannot be sure about our sexual partners. But as long as we do take such necessary precautions, we have no obligation to turn to chastity or heterosexual monogamy.

As for teen pregnancy and single parenthood, sexual libertarians argue that the blame for these problems does not rest with them. As long as they behave responsibly, they cannot be held accountable for the irresponsibility of others. Nor should they be morally required to restrict their sex lives. The solution to such social problems lies in education, easy access to birth control counseling, and social programs to alleviate poverty and hopelessness—not in the restriction of sexual freedom.

What about personal fulfillment? Many libertarians might well agree with many of the remarks in that argument, as long as each individual is free to supply his or her own answers to the recommended questions. Others, though, might wonder why sex need be taken so seriously. If Jane is satisfied enough with her life, even though she takes a very casual approach to sex, why should she feel any more pressure to involve herself in any soul-searching about sex than about any other aspect of her life? No doubt sex and sexual relationships are very important to many people, but if other people feel differently, who's to say they shouldn't?

Finally, there is the naturalness argument. Here, libertarians remain totally unimpressed. Does homosexuality really violate the laws of nature? No, because *nothing* can violate the laws of nature. Natural laws are not like criminal laws. They describe how the world actually works. They do not tell us how we ought to behave. Everything that happens, then, must be in accord with natural law. Is homosexuality an abnormal occurrence in nature? Perhaps, but that does not make it immoral. After all, great genius, great basketball talent, and great musical ability are even more abnormal, but we prize them when they occur, not condemn them. Does homosexuality involve the unnatural use of our sex organs?

Again, perhaps, but how does that differ from using our ears for holding earrings, our eyes for giving playful winks, or our thumbs for hitching rides?

Arguments for Sexual Libertarianism

1. *Sex is a private matter.*

POINT: "Whatever goes on between consenting adults in private is nobody's business but their own, and that holds as much for sex as for anything else. Why should anybody even care whether Mary has fifteen lovers or none, whether Jack prefers sex with Bill to sex with Jane, or whether married couples like to 'swing' with other married couples? Just because you personally disapprove of such things doesn't make them wrong. We all have the right to live our lives as we see fit as long as we don't interfere with the rights of others to live their lives as they see fit. Promiscuous people, homosexuals, and swingers don't tell you how to live your life. Don't tell them how to live theirs."

COUNTERPOINT: "Sex isn't nearly as private as you think. All of society is affected by the sexual revolution you're so fond of. Who do you think has to pick up the tab for all the illegitimate children your libertarianism is giving us? The taxpayers. And who has to pick up the tab for AIDS research? The taxpayers. And who has to live with all the abortion mills, the fear of AIDS, and the worry over how all of this free sex will affect our children? All of us."

2. *You can't turn the clock back on the sexual revolution.*

POINT: "Whether you approve of what's happened to sexual morality or not, one thing's certain: You can't turn the clock back. Once people get a taste of freedom—sexual or any other kind—they don't want to give it up. Do you really think that sexually active unmarried people are going to turn to celibacy, or that homosexuals are going to deny their sexual identity and pretend to be something they're not, or that married couples who feel that open marriage works better for them than fidelity are going to settle for fidelity? Let's face it. Human nature just doesn't work that way."

COUNTERPOINT: "Maybe not, but that doesn't make the sexual revolution right. The whole point of morality is to curb some of the excesses of human nature, to try to get people to exercise their freedoms responsibly. Besides, nobody expects to turn everything around overnight. The point is to insist that certain behavior is wrong, to make young people understand the proper place of sex in their lives, and to get them to make responsible choices about sex. It'll take some time, but eventually the changes can come."

3. *Curbing sexual freedom is unfair.*

POINT: "You're neglecting an important point here—fairness. The crux of the issue isn't just that people don't *want* to turn back the clock, but that it's *unfair* to make them turn it back. You're comfortable with your traditional morality, but to other people it can be a straitjacket. For them, it's impossible to live fulfilling lives under those conditions. The worst victims, of course, would be the homosexuals. What are they supposed to do—live a heterosexual lie, or give up sex and love altogether? But they wouldn't be the only victims. Some people are totally unsuited to marriage. Others are totally unsuited to monogamy. They have as much right to fulfilling sex lives as you do."

COUNTERPOINT: "Nobody has the right to seek fulfillment immorally. And there's nothing unfair about making people turn away from immoral behavior. I'm not denying that traditional sexual morality is more demanding for some people than it is for others, but that doesn't make it any different from any other area of moral concern. Pathological liars and kleptomaniacs have a harder time doing right than the rest of us do, but our sympathy for them can't lead us to approve of their lies and thefts. The same holds for homosexuals. We can sympathize, but we can't condone."

4. *Traditional sexual morality is hypocritical.*

POINT: "What you're really calling for is a return to hypocrisy. Let's all pretend to be faithful heterosexual monogamists while we do whatever we feel like doing on the sly. Adultery, premarital sex, promiscuity, and homosexuality aren't new, you know. The only thing that's changed is that people are more honest about them now. And that's a change for the good."

COUNTERPOINT: "Adultery, premarital sex, promiscuity, and homosexuality may not be new, but they're sure a lot more prevalent than they used to be. And you can thank your precious honesty for that. Once people start being proud about things like that, once they start going public about them, it has to start affecting other people's behavior. They start thinking: If it's good enough for Dick and Jane, maybe I should give it a try. In other words, a little bit of hypocrisy is a good thing. You don't want armed robbers telling their kids there's nothing wrong with armed robbery, do you? Well, I don't want unwed mothers telling their kids there's nothing wrong with premarital sex."

Arguments against Sexual Libertarianism

1. *Sexual libertarianism undermines public morality.*

POINT: "Morality is like law. Once you encourage disrespect for a particular law, you encourage disrespect for all laws. And once you encourage disrespect for sexual morality, you encourage disrespect for all of morality. That's why it's no surprise that the sexual revolution brought with it an explosion of pornography and abortion. It's also why I wouldn't be surprised to learn that people don't care as much about loyalty and honesty as they used to. After all, a large part of your revolution is that marriage vows don't have to mean anything."

COUNTERPOINT: "Sexual libertarianism isn't about disrespect for morality. It's about moral change. If you want to talk about disrespect for morality, the real culprit is your traditional sexual morality. That's a morality that people won't adhere to, and a morality like that is bound to breed disrespect. And don't confuse sexual libertarianism with disloyalty and dishonesty. A husband and wife who agree that affairs with other people will make their marriage better aren't being disloyal to each other—and they're certainly not being dishonest."

2. *Sex without love is empty.*

POINT: "One of the biggest problems with your view is that it erases the connection between sex and love. Even you have to admit that sex with someone you love is better than sex with someone you don't love. With someone you love, sex isn't mere empty pleasure. It's communication, it's sharing, it's an expression of affection and care. It *means* something. The sex that you advocate means nothing at all. It's sterile, and it adds nothing of worth to our lives. What you're really doing is reducing human sexuality to animal sexuality. We might as well be rabbits, according to you. But we're not rabbits, and because we're not, loveless sex can't possibly satisfy us or be fulfilling for us."

COUNTERPOINT: "First of all, I'm not advocating any kind of sex. All I'm advocating is people's moral right to engage in the kinds of sex they prefer as long as they don't hurt anyone. Second, who are you to declare that the kind of sex you prefer is the best kind of sex for anyone else? Third, even if you're right— even if loving sex is better than loveless sex—what morally important difference does that make? Some cars are better than others, but there's nothing immoral about driving the inferior ones. Or, to pick an even closer analogy, celebrating good news with someone you love is probably better than celebrating good news with someone you don't love, but nobody's going to say you're doing wrong if you do celebrate good news with someone you don't love."

3. *Sexual libertarianism undermines marriage.*

POINT: "If society adopts your position, we might as well forget about the institution of marriage. Unmarried people will have no good reason to get married, because sex will be freely available. Even having children won't count as a good reason anymore, as it becomes more and more acceptable to be an unmarried parent. And married people will have little reason to stay married. After all, once marital fidelity goes, there goes the most important bond between husband and wife. And even if some kind of bond remains, how can it stand up against the constant temptations that married people will face? Or the jealousies? Or the insecurities?"

COUNTERPOINT: "Aren't you being a little too cynical? People get married for lots of reasons other than sex, and they stay married because of a variety of bonds and intimacies. I'm not going to deny that sexual libertarianism can have some negative effects on marriage, but I *am* going to deny that the effects are all negative. For one thing, people with sexual experience before marriage are less likely to confuse sex with love, and that makes it less likely that they'll choose their spouses unwisely. For another, they're less likely to feel they've missed something before getting married, and that should help protect them from temptation. And for still another, some marriages actually gain from being open to extramarital affairs. If married people feel the need for sexual variety, the possibility of having an open marriage can remove a reason for divorce."

4. *Sexual libertarianism is turning society upside down.*

POINT: "Your views have led to a number of crazy consequences. I'm not just talking about such tragedies as teen mothers, but things like the gay rights movement. First we have homosexuals demanding the right to teach in elementary schools, then we have homosexual couples demanding the right to adopt children, then we have them demanding that homosexual 'spouses' be included in family medical plans and the like. I have no idea where all this is ultimately heading, but it's certainly not in the right direction. We can't let children grow up believing that homosexuality is just another life-style, and we can't have society treating homosexual relationships like real marriages. No society can survive that."

COUNTERPOINT: "Why not? If homosexuality isn't immoral to begin with, what's wrong with giving homosexuals the same rights as heterosexuals? If you're afraid that we'd end up raising an entire generation of homosexual children, you're just being unrealistic. Besides, you're mixing up two different issues. Whether homosexuality is moral is one thing. Whether homosexual relationships should have the same legal status as heterosexual marriages is another."

The Human Venture in Sex, Love and Marriage

Peter A. Bertocci

In this selection from his book The Human Venture in Sex, Love and Marriage, *Peter A. Bertocci defends a traditional view of sexual morality. Bertocci begins by attacking the position that associates sex exclusively with self-satisfaction. In Bertocci's view, sex that has self-satisfaction as its primary goal is not as fulfilling as sex dedicated to other objectives.*

Bertocci takes issue with those who view human life, including sex, as essentially no different from the life of higher animals. In such a view, the sexual behavior of humans is as automatic and mechanical as it is in other animals. Thus, from this strictly biological viewpoint, the only relevant arguments against, say, premarital sex relate to the physical effects of sexual promiscuity, the danger of sexual diseases, and the possibility of pregnancy. But Bertocci feels that this biological perspective neglects the human significance of sex, which must take into consideration the human's total psychological being. When the total human is taken into account, then a whole cluster of other arguments against sex outside marriage arise.

The thrust of Bertocci's argument is that the meaning and value of sex cannot be divorced from the meaning and value of life itself. For Bertocci, love, marriage, and family are among the "supreme values of human existence." Thus, he feels that sex must be viewed and understood within the context of love, marriage, and family.

Bertocci goes on to develop a "love progression," in which love leads to marriage, marriage to family, family to social responsibility. He feels that sex lust, while pleasurable and seemingly satisfactory in itself, is ultimately inadequate because it does not tap into this love progression,

From Peter A. Bertocci, The Human Venture in Sex, Love and Marriage (*Chicago: Association Press/Follett Publishing Company, 1949), pp. 61–71, 95–106, 110–115. Reprinted by permission of Follett Publishing Company, a division of Follett Corporation.*

*which brings completeness, growth in character and personality, and a sense of social
responsibility. Indeed, sex love (or affectional sex) without marriage is inadequate for the same
reasons.*

*In short, love, marriage, family, and social responsibility are the highest values of human
existence, according to Bertocci. If sex is to provide its deepest, most lasting, and most profound
satisfaction, it must symbolically express these other values.*

The Significance of Sexual Intercourse in Married Life

In trying to give Harry and Judith a reasonable answer [to the question of why it may be wrong for two persons who care for each other to have intercourse before marriage] we must assume that the basic motive behind their desire for premarital sexual intercourse is love. Judith and Harry are not in lust with each other, but in love with each other. The main motive is not exploitation, not the pleasure of satisfying sexual desire as such, but the desire to express in a physical way the unity that they feel spiritually. The sexual act would here symbolize the yearning of each person to unite himself more completely with the beloved; it becomes one of the best ways of saying, "I love you."

It is because we believe that this motive is psychologically and ethically sound that we wish to elaborate further what seems to be the profoundest meaning of the sexual act, before trying to show that sexual intercourse before marriage endangers that meaning. We cannot take the argument on its own ground without evaluating the place of sex in the marriage of lovers.

The act of sexual intercourse between a man and a woman gives pleasure at the purely biological level. As the expression of feelings that involve their whole psychophysical being, especially when they are stirred to a high emotional pitch, it is highly satisfying. The psychological satisfaction is deepest when the couple experience orgasm together, when in these brief rhythmic moments of mutual physiological response, both persons reach the climax of their emotional expression at the same time. If human beings were simply physiological organisms, and if this act could be dissociated from other human needs, the physiological and psychological pleasure and satisfaction involved in it would justify it as an end in itself. *But because human beings are more than physiological reactions, because these responses mean more than they themselves as actions in intercourse are, sexual intercourse can seldom, if ever, be an isolated experience of satisfaction.* This physiological transaction can become a source either of much mental discontent, moral guilt, and aesthetic disgust, or of profound mental peace, moral satisfaction, and aesthetic delight, not to mention the possibilities of religious value.

Here, for human beings, is the crux of the sexual problem in life. Sex is a means of communicating a variety of meanings; it objectifies or symbolizes a variety of feelings and ideas that human beings have about themselves and others. It can mean simply, "I'm sexually hungry and I want satisfaction through you." It can mean, "I love you and I want to be identified as far as possible with you." Or it can mean, "We love each other. Life means so much to us that we want children to share its creative joy and values." There are other meanings, of course—as many meanings as the mates find possible in and through each other. These three stages need not exclude each other though the first may endanger the next two. But for two persons who love each other, and therefore find life's meaning heightened and focused in that love, there can hardly be conceived a more expressive symbol of the yearning for unity than a mutual, harmonious orgasm. Two persons find their deepest satisfaction not in mere self-satisfaction, but in making it possible for the loved one to express his feelings in and through his own contribution to a harmonious act.

The testimony of married persons who have found it possible so to discipline their reaction as to find mutuality in orgasm gives clear corroboration at this point. To feel that one's partner encourages and enjoys one's own activity and responses, to feel that one can meet the needs of the person one loves even as one expresses the intensity and meaning of one's own desires, is, indeed, a human experience worth cherishing. We cannot emphasize enough the qualitative enjoyment and meaning of this experience. What two lovers experience, especially in simultaneous orgasm, is not so much physiological simultaneity but the meanings that they, as two human beings dedicated to each other, so want to express. No wonder lovers who have experienced exhaustion in the psychological and physical release of their tension can continue to embrace each other in the afterglow of mental peace, physiological relaxation, and grateful appreciation. How clearly this act can symbolize what the marriage of two loving persons means, the dedication of one's being to the growing happiness of another.

This is an experience that does work creatively in the lives of two persons, for it renews confidence and infuses new meaning. The amazing fact about it is that it can, on the same physiological base, go on being a source of renewal. Youth, middle age, and maturity find different levels of meaning and renewal thereby. This would hardly be so were it not that through sexual intercourse the lovers who are now parents (or the lovers who are now the center of responsibilities and joys in family and civic life, or the lovers who are now older physically but more mature as persons) go on using it to communicate meanings that never find adequate expression in words.

If what I have been saying is true, it is clear that both the harmony of sex experience and the expressive significance of that unity are such sources of strength and enjoyment in married life that they deserve the needed preparation and protection. Violins cannot create music if they are not tuned, or if the violinist cannot control his feelings, thoughts, and muscles to suit his meaning. If there is no "music" in the violinist, even the greatest skill in playing will not produce "music with a soul." To carry this figure further, violinists cannot create music when they are not playing the same score or when they have not been able to synchronize their playing in accordance with their respective parts in the musical whole. Harmony, physiological and spiritual, requires more than good will; it requires careful discriminating thought, sensitive and sincere feeling, and self-discipline that subordinates tensions for the sake of the whole.

It may seem that we are making too much of the unity of intercourse, but if that be an error it is one that needs underscoring since we are purposely insisting upon the quality of the experience. Sexual intercourse has its greatest value when the minds and actions of two persons communicate their meanings. From this viewpoint, it is unfortunate that so many persons, in and out of marriage, are forfeiting such a high quality of experience, frequently without realizing that they are doing so. They are expressing lust, decreasing sexual tension, experiencing different depths of pleasure. But they are usually sacrificing, or jeopardizing, richer values otherwise open to them.

Let us pause here and attempt to avoid misunderstanding.

We are not saying that young men and women, for whom sex has been simply a pleasurable outlet, or who have been unable, for differing reasons, to live controlled sexual lives, are inevitably barred from mutuality in orgasm (or that those who have remained virginal will by that very fact have guaranteed mutuality). But other things being equal, a personal history of relative promiscuity and a loss of self-confidence and adequate self-control are not conducive to achievement of mutuality. While it is important to realize that many other psychological factors will enter into the achievement of mutual orgasm at any one point in married life, we fly in the face of all we know about psychological habits and associations if we allow ourselves to think that a relatively undisciplined past, with all its associations and psychological effects upon the individual, will not become an obstacle—not necessarily insuperable to be sure—to mutuality.

To continue, part of our central thesis is that human beings have been and are, in fact, losing much of the joy possible in sex and love because they are thinking too much of sex expression and not enough about expressing values through sex and in love. We cannot be said to be educating persons with regard to sex until we are as much concerned about the objectives of complete sexual experience as we have been about removing inhibitions. Sex expression is not self-expression. And self-expression is not necessarily the expression of love. We have taken too little cognizance of the probable fact that multitudes of men and women are disappointed with their sexual experience; it becomes, like ordinary eating, a means of regularly satisfying an otherwise discomforting need. The less persons understand about the meaning that sex can have in their lives, the more likely are they to find the most direct means of expression.[1] The very fact that the physical pleasure of releasing tension is theirs blinds them to higher values that would both intensify the physiological pleasure and also lead to more complete fulfillment of their total being.

From this point of view of quality in sex experience, there is very little value in Kinsey's data with regard to the relation of premarital intercourse and sexual effectiveness in marriage. He says:

> It is sometimes asserted that all persons who have premarital intercourse subsequently regret the experience, and that such regrets may constitute a major cloud on their lives. There are a few males whose histories seem to indicate that they have so reacted to their premarital experience, but a high proportion of the thousands of experienced males whom we have questioned on this point indicated that they did not regret having had such an experience, and that the premarital intercourse had not caused any trouble in their subsequent marital adjustments (p. 562).[2]

As Kinsey realizes, even at this level of description one needs accurate data from the wives. But the ambiguous words in his statement are "trouble" and "regret." If "no trouble" means simply that there were no special inhibitions, or feelings of guilt that hindered physiological reaction, or that no serious disunity between the partners was involved, the crux of the problem is not touched. Assuming—what we doubt can be assumed—that "experienced males" would admit that they had been deceived by their desires, what we need to know (and cannot find out probably from men habituated to satisfy desires conveniently) is the effect upon the quality of their marital relation, both sexually and as a whole. Did it make for greater loyalty, for deeper appreciation and respect, both of oneself, one's partner, and the act itself?

When Kinsey continues, "It is notable that most of the males who did regret the experience were individuals who had had very little premarital intercourse, amounting in most cases to not more than one or two experiences" (p. 563), is the conclusion to be drawn that if they had further indulged they would have ceased being disturbed? Or does this also suggest that some persons expected more from themselves and from the sexual experience, and that they realized how little sex as a merely biological or even sociable experience had to contribute to their lives? Obviously, there are no definite conclusions to be drawn from such data.

But Kinsey goes so far in trying to avoid any generalization condemning premarital experience that he makes "the significance of premarital intercourse" depend "upon the situations under which it is had" (p. 561), upon whether the experience is free from fear or "satisfying." This again begs the real question of the kind of fear and the quality of satisfaction. The whole problem is: Can a person outside of married love find the most that sex can bring to human life? Can experiences in which one's fundamental concern is the satisfaction of one's own desire become the psychological basis for an experience in which concern for another's complete well-being is symbolized in the sexual act? Can ego-centered habituation, in idea, in motive, in emotion, in action, be a help in establishing a relation in which another human being, a home, and children call for self-mastery?

A little reflection, then, will make clear the task before any two married persons. It will be evident that much discipline may be required if mutuality is to be realized at the psychophysiological level. Even assuming that past experience with sex has been without serious conflict, so that both persons are emotionally free and are ready to discover the full meaning of sex in their relations to each other, they cannot be sure that the experience of unity will readily be theirs. The sexual responsiveness of the male and female orgasm is by no means the same, and every couple has to work out the modes of mutual response suited to their own particular natures.

At this point of physiological unity one cannot dogmatize about the prerequisites in terms of past sexual experience. As already suggested, one cannot universalize the statement that habits of response derived from premarital experience will interfere necessarily with present adjustment to one's partner. A person's attitude toward his or her past experience, the effect of it upon his emotional life, the attitude of the mate, the total import of the other values in a marriage are always probably more important than the mere fact of abstinence or non-abstinence. But even from the point of view of physiological unity, are not the probabilities on our side when we say that, other things being normal, the chances of harmonizing responses are much greater when two lovers come together who have a history of self-mastery and confidence with regard to sex? Will not "a past of pleasure" be a threat to the more important psychological, moral, aesthetic, and religious overtones—those which transform physical notes into a human symphony.

We need not here go into the different physical and psychological causes that might well lead to an initial disharmony and to a long struggle to achieve the kind of mental freedom and control necessary for increasing sexual harmony. Suffice it to say that one of the greatest misconceptions that young people bring to marriage is that there will be no sex problem in marriage. The fact is that marriage may create as many sex problems as it solves. Too many honeymoons have found two persons who loved each other not a little disturbed, and sometimes shocked, by inability to enjoy the kind of sexual harmony for which their spirits were prepared. To repeat, then, any couple that looks forward to married life needs to face honestly and resolutely the fact that the finest psychophysical expression of their love may have to await the patient discipline and understanding for which their particular response patterns call. Fortunately their meaning to each other, the unity they feel, can be expressed in other ways as they work for greater unity in the sexual satisfaction of their love.

One of the strongest reasons for urging that a person come through adolescence feeling that he is in control of sex (and not sex in control of him) should now be clear. For the less he can control his mind and body, the more difficult his readjustment to his beloved may be at the very time he is most anxious to suceed. The more he is conditioned to a certain form of sexual progression, the more habituated he has become to certain modes of response, the greater the variety of thoughts and associations that come crowding into his mind now that he is trying to meet the needs of his life partner, the harder it is to make the new adjustment that has to be made to his loved one. The person whose past experience with sex has been that of the hungry animal, or that of the egotistic philanderer who has thought of his partner essentially as a means to his enjoyment, will not have an easy time meeting a new situation in which his highest nature wants expression for the sake of his beloved. From the point of view of married life as a whole, the person who has learned to think of human beings as "males" or "females" who can be "used" may indeed find and create more trouble than he can imagine.

It would be tragic to underemphasize the importance of such psychological influences. Let two persons bring wandering thoughts, feelings of insecurity and guilt, desires for self-aggrandizement, or any other expectations foreign to the unique problem of welding two lives together, and the marriage of their spirits will have this much more to overcome.

Are Not Our Sexual Standards Artificial?

We must now turn to another lingering doubt, which is related to what we have been saying about the conflict between the sex desire and the social code. For I am sure that someone will say: In other societies, where no one expects young people to abstain from the satisfaction of their sexual desires, and where the element of fear and social ostracism is reduced to a minimum, there are no bad results, and people seem to be healthier in their attitudes toward sex. May it not be, then, that in developing our social codes and laws we have created problems for young people that did not have to arise at all? Indeed, if a person just does not care about what society thinks, if he has no moral compunctions and, therefore, no resultant sense of guilt about his free sexual life, that person does not seem to suffer any of the disturbances associated with sexual repression.

And my reader might add: Are you sure that all the fuss you are making about sexual control, yes, even as a means to a fuller love relation, is worth the bother? Since sex is so recurrent in human life, would it not be better to remove the bars at this point and let individuals (and society) use the energy now spent in combatting "sexual license" for other desirable personal and social objectives? If we are actually pitting individuals against a drive that in their ripening years is a constant thorn in their sides, are we not really flagellating them unnecessarily? Why not make legal and acceptable what so many people are now doing covertly, and at the expense of an artificially created bad conscience?

Indeed, why not be sensible and scientific, and provide persons from adolescence on with knowledge of contraceptives and prophylactics so that they will be able to enjoy sexual relations with a minimum of fear and with a maximum of birth control? If, as they come into marriage, a couple did not expect premarital abstinence any more than they expect abstinence from other forms of social relations, it would not bother them, and marriage would not be undermined. After all, remember that a great many people even now are breaking the social code, for they reject the moral conception on which it is based. They do not seem to be worse for it. Is it not our problem, then, really to recognize that our present moral and legal codes, developed in earlier stages of socioeconomic-religious development, are no longer applicable and are, in fact, creating more problems today than they solve?

Thus many a thoughtful young person will argue. Remembering our own prolonged collegiate harangues and bull sessions, we can honestly say that this line of argument still strikes a sympathetic chord, especially when we note the great amount of time and energy young and old alike, in and out of family, spend in worrying about maintaining chastity. There are many difficult theoretical questions here, and we can no more than hint at an approach to them.

1. Let us not fool ourselves that we would minimize our social problems by making knowledge of prophylactics and contraceptives more available. Such knowledge and the medical attention necessary should be available as soon as possible, but not because in this way unwanted births might be decreased. There are no methods of contraception that are foolproof (aside from medical operations that keep sperm and ovum from making contact). Errors in adjustment and imperfection in the materials—let alone carelessness or even failure to use them—would certainly occur many times. Unless we were to make provision for an enormous program of legal abortions, a multitude of children would be born when neither father nor mother were mature enough or economically able to take care of their children.

Let us make no mistake about the choices before us. If our psychological and sociological investigations have told us much about the sex urge, they have also emphasized the need that infants and children have for feeling wanted and loved. The constant feeling of insecurity makes deeper inroads on healthy living than the frustration of sex as such. Parents must be psychologically and morally mature to help children meet their problems as they grow up. Our central obligation, therefore, is to preserve the kind of parental care that will enable children to feel at home in their world. To suppose that removal of social restraints regarding sexual control would take us nearer to this goal is to be blind to the many problems with which society would then be beset. Are we willing to have many more children born than can receive adequate care psychologically and morally? We might, indeed, decrease the number of sexual disturbances that are (supposedly) due to sexual inhibition, and increase the many other problems that occur when the life ventures of children and adults are rendered insecure and unstable.

Our choice is not between black and white, and any system will work hardship on many persons. But, surely, any suggestions that would tend to increase the number of inadequately cared-for children, let alone endanger the stability that monogamous marriage provides, cannot compare even with our present imperfect system. A main reason why those who now indulge in premarital sex experience, or even extramarital sex experience, can enjoy the supposed benefits of their "freedom" is that there are enough other human beings left who, despite their imperfections, stand by the system that does give the social stability needed. Let the order of the day emphasize not control but convenience, not long-range planning but "doing what I want when I want it," and it will not take long for physical and social decay to set in. Would this be more "natural" than the kind of system we have? Can those who live by such parasitism honestly encourage others to join them as they "use" and endanger the lives of other persons in order to guarantee their own pleasures?

2. We might remind ourselves, before passing to the next point, that what recommends the idea of birth control is not that there may be a limitation in the number of children, but that birth of children can be controlled in a manner designed to ensure the most adequate care of the number of children a given family can absorb and support. We do not face the facts if we allow ourselves to forget that, the imperfections of contraceptives from the point of safety aside, they are aesthetically obnoxious, to say the least, to a large number of married people who use them only because they do want to limit their families or adequately space their children. The purpose of birth control is to help enrich the experience of sexual love by reducing the probability of pregnancy, and to increase the possibilities of health and education in a given family. The goal of birth control is to help improve the quality of adult life and the opportunities of children for sen-

sitive nurture. To consider the use of contraceptives simply as a way of providing individuals with pleasure minus responsibility is to encourage the dilution of the meaning of sexual intercourse.

3. But these considerations are not so important as those pointed out earlier in discussing the sexual progression and the place of self-control in the complete enjoyment of sex experience itself. To express sex as sex with different "congenial" partners is to establish certain modes and tempos of response, many mental and emotional associations, that cannot be sloughed off at will. If we remember that sex itself is not the cause of love (though it is certainly a factor in love), but that love is a profound cause of sexual intimacy in human experience, we are confronted with another stubborn fact of our psychological nature that forces us to make a choice.

Let us assume that Dick and Jane have, as the supporter of sexual freedom would advocate, moved through their adolescence and early youth indulging their sexual urge discreetly and prudently. Since they have felt no rigorous moral compunctions or morbid sense of guilt, they are not vulnerable to mental disease, and, let us grant, they have enjoyed good, clean, fun on the sexual level. For they have experienced the release of sexual tension when they were really bothered, and they have been fortunate enough to find suitable partners with whom they shared normal, companionable relations and friendships. Let us make their case even stronger by assuming that their attitudes throughout their varied experience were not dominated by an abnormal, aggressive desire for mastery.

With this psychological orientation to men and women and sex, let us suppose that Dick and Jane meet each other and fall in love. They now *fall in love*, but their past experience has been of *falling in lust*. They now no longer anticipate a good-for-a-while relationship, but a lifelong partnership in which they may share as much of life's meaning as possible with each other and make each other the home base for all adventures in value. Two persons like these (whatever their past, I am assuming) want to be one; they want to feel unified in every way. For them the sexual experience, even if they had never had it before, would now be an opportunity demanded by the total impetus of their love and not merely their lust. This love dictates loyalty to

each other, for it represents the fact that the other is valued above all others.

Is it now more serious psychologically and spiritually to disappoint the natural desires of sex than the natural desires of love for loyalty and concentrated devotion? What Dick and Jane want now supremely is love; and, speaking objectively, what they need is love if their lives are to have the quality and inspiration that love contributes to life. Yet the Dick-and-Jane-in-love are confronted by the Dick-and-Jane-in-lust, and the habits of the past—such as finding the attractive physical specimen to share the pleasure of lust, such as desiring sexual experience every so often and in a certain manner or mode—now assert themselves. Here, let us emphasize, *it is not society that is making artificial laws which cause conflict and make them unhappy; it is the psychological laws of their natures as human beings.* Lust and the habit of lust stand in conflict with love and the demands of love. The past of life, enhanced and strengthened by habit, stands in defiance of the development of life as a whole. Dick and Jane want each other completely, dependably, forever. They do not want to feel that the sexual habits of the past may break up something which they now so wholly approve. They dread the thought that their past may threaten the foundations of their happiness together as central units of a family. If Jane and Dick are honest with themselves and with each other, they may well pause and face the fact that, much as they wish to follow the high, broad avenue of growth, because of their past habits they are better fitted to travel the lower, narrower streets of sexual satisfaction.

Let us now assume that, having become engaged, they find it impossible because of established habits to refrain from sexual intercourse. But the sexual intercourse they now want is more than the satisfaction of a strong urge. They want to express their love by the very actions which in the past have expressed lust. They want so much to have this experience say what they cannot say in words. They want everything to be perfect. But now past habits of response, and many past associations with this act, crowd in upon the activity of mind and body, barring the way to the kind of unity and satisfaction their love calls for. It is not society which is barring their way to joy and peace now, but their own past in conflict with the present. Society and its laws did not artificially create this situation. It is the psychological structure of Jane and Dick—the way their natures work out once they have made certain choices. The problem they have—the struggle between self-satisfying lust and other-regarding love—is one their natures would develop in *any* social situation (assuming the value of love). They may, indeed, after a kind of discipline they are not used to, be able to make their way to a harmonious unity of confident love, but the struggle before them is not artificially created by society.

It will not be forgotten, of course, that two other persons, Harry and Judith, despite their controlled psychological past, may have difficulty in achieving the kind of sexual unity that will adequately recreate their bodies and minds. But, we hold out much more hope for their achievement of this unity and for the prolongation and enrichment of this love than we do for Jane and Dick. And happily it cannot be asserted that Jane and Dick may not under the incentive and inspiration of their love find their way with patience, mutual forgiveness, and persistent self-discipline to the kind of unity, mutual confidence, and loyalty to which their love aspires. Nevertheless, the moral attitudes and psychological habits of Dick and Jane may well stand in the way of the present satisfaction of their love. These attitudes and habits may destroy more than one moment of peace and trust, especially when the other tensions of married partnership and home building come into their lives. Once more, then, we come back to a question we have been asking over and over in these pages: When we are honest with the facts of our lives, and when we consider what we desire from life as a whole, is the satisfaction of sex lust along the way worth it? Do we not, in fact, endanger or sacrifice our unique heritage of love for a mess of pottage by thinking that we have solved the sex problem by convenient expression?

In a society where people came together physically and separated whenever they pleased, one might be tempted to think that artificial frustrations would be avoided. But how sure could we be that both persons would find it convenient to separate at the same time? The one who gets caught by love suffers. In the midst of their enjoyment can they keep from being haunted by the knowledge that on their principle of action one or the other

may change his mind when he pleases? These are not problems society's codes create. They are snares into which our human nature falls once we play fast and loose with it.

4. Before closing this section, we must dwell a little longer on another aspect of the suggestion that it is society which makes all the trouble by imposing unnatural standards of conduct on the young. When we talk this way, we seem to assume that our forebears had somehow discovered and forced upon their children a group of moral edicts that had no intimate relation to their needs. Now, it is certainly true that this attitude of the law enforcer has been present in a great deal of societal restriction on human beings. No doubt many laws have been enforced that took little or no account of the needs and desires of the persons who were expected to live by them. They do reflect a slave morality.

Some philosophical and theological theories of law easily lend themselves to manipulation of persons rather than to a regard for the growth of persons. Against them let us assert quite vigorously that human beings are not to be considered the playthings of the gods or, for that matter, of fate, let alone of society or state or church. But it is a great calamity that persons whom study should have at least rendered more cautious make the puerile assertion that the restrictions upon sexual behavior have been imposed only by the philosophical rationalizations of ascetic kill-joys who had little regard for the normal enjoyments of normal persons. It is true that sexual restraint has been advocated in the name of, and as the will of, God. But let it be remembered that God was usually considered not the torturer of little children, but the lover of men. If more of the truth be known, we suspect that the will of God was indeed called in to back up what was shrewdly observed to be a law of the human nature—which, incidentally, God had made that way! This is not the place to review and refute different theories, for the question is an involved one. But it seems fair to say that it is erroneous to maintain that the grounds of sexual control lie not in the nature of human experience and experiment, but in artificial restraints imposed without any realistic justification by society.

That there must be some control of sexual activity is patent in any reflective analysis of the problem of human beings as they come together. Different societies may exercise different controls in order to preserve their form of social organization. Sometimes the controls may be to encourage persons to have more sexual experience, more wives or husbands, and more children. However, we make serious mistakes in the study of values when we compare a mode of behavior in one society with a similar mode of behavior in another without carefully evaluating each mode in the light of the total pattern of values and customs in each society. The fact is that each society must pay in some way or other for the controls that it seeks to enforce on sex, or on property, education, or anything else, for that matter.

The real question, therefore, is: What form of society, what kind of institutions will help human beings in their situations to complete their lives and fulfill their potentialities in the richest possible manner and with the minimum of fruitless frustration? One part of this large question seems clear, namely, that a monogamous home built about confident, controlled love is the best kind of insurance for the growth of human beings and the symphonic satisfaction of human drives.

We can imagine societies in which ideological, economic, and social problems would be such that the kind of love and home we have in mind is beyond present reach and grasp. Theirs, then, would have to be a different form of social code, and that code might work better for them without home-building possibilities than it would for us. But it does not mean that they too would not be better off if they could pay the price for the kind of human love and nurture that joins two lovers and their progeny in a common pursuit of creative living. The problem every person and every society has to face is: Do we want to protect the experience of love even more than the experience of sex? If we agree that the experience of love, given the structure of human beings, is endangered by the expression of sex as an end in itself, then we must organize our institutions and educational efforts to encourage love. And we must discipline sex for the sake of love. . . .

Is Sexual Guilt Not an Artificial Barrier?

If boy or girl were not taught to inhibit their sexual desires, and if as young people they felt no moral guilt or anxiety about it, would it have any bad effect on their lives? The answer is: If, indeed, they had no moral compunctions about free sexual expression, it would not produce mental disturbance, for no real conflict would be set up in their lives. But if these persons ever decided to move into the area of love, they might well expect conflict, and then other disturbances would have to be faced. No one could predict the outcome.

But when we say that some sexual promiscuity will not have a bad effect, I suspect we have in mind mental disorder rooted in the sex-conscience conflict. It is unfortunate that so many of us have got into the habit of thinking that if we do not develop a neurosis we are not being badly affected. But here we really misinterpret what our psychology does in fact teach us. As might be expected, we know the diseased extreme better than we understand what makes for the most effective and enduring health.

Does the fact that a person does not develop a neurosis, owing to the fact that he has no moral compunctions about premarital or extramarital sex-expression, mean that he is better off because he is expressing sex? Study that person's life carefully— his attitudes toward himself, his sense of responsibility for the needs of others—and you may well discover a weakness of moral fiber, of capacity to get the most out of himself despite hardship and sacrifice. What does such a person do in the presence of frustration now? What will he do if he ever undertakes a vocation and marriage, in which there will be great need for willingness to forego present personal pleasures for the sake of later satisfactions? The person who can pleasurably indulge in sexual intercourse owing to his freedom from moral guilt may escape a "complex" or specific mental disorder, but when the total quality of his life is analyzed, when his human sensitiveness and his capacity to forego self-indulgence for the sake of others is evaluated, the deficit in his personality may be more serious than he realizes.

One other fact of experience must be emphasized in relation to this question. I have listened frequently to young men and women, some of them engaged, who because of their thwarted desires for sexual intercourse have wished that they had never been brought up to think it's "bad." And some have concluded that "since we only think it's bad and it really isn't, there really is no good reason why we shouldn't express our desires." Many young people who have gone this way have discovered, to their dismay and undiminished sense of guilt, that their conscience would not keep quiet just because they told it that it was all wrong.

We cannot here discuss the whole problem of conscience, though we must protest the oversimplified and superficially "scientific" accounts of it given by those who reduce it merely to the watchdog voice of society in us. Whatever final theoretical position we take, the fact cannot be forgotten that it does no good to try to laugh off a "conscience," and it frequently does much harm. Laughing the conscience off is hardly the way to get rid of it, any more than laughing away sex or any other strong desire exiles it. It is not impossible to change the content of one's conscience so that it will take account of the present actualities of life as well as of the past. A person whose conscience tells him that every manifestation of sex is bad may be suffering from a distasteful emotional experience in childhood which he then illogically generalized. It will take him time and effort of thought and will to feel differently about that verdict and change his conscience at that point. During the interlude, when his conscience is changing, he will experience the uncertainty that goes with any new development. One does not, however, make a new conscience simply by breaking the old one. The redirection calls for painstaking insight and effort if it is going to represent a real, unified growth of the personality.

Let us apply this fact to the question before us. Too many young people are sure that, in view of the strength of their desire for each other, they can dismiss the conscientious scruples which have been exerting themselves, enter into sex experience, enjoy it thoroughly, and never feel any aftereffects. "After all," they may say, "this conscience about sex is just a fairy tale I picked up in my childhood, like the idea of Santa Claus." But then they find that the experience does not take up the whole mind, that they did not enjoy it quite as much as they thought they would. Later they find that they do keep on feeling guilty about it. Both the possibility of premarital sex experience and the whole idea of sex experience now evoke guilt. Thus, when the sex experience is later to be used as an expression of marital love, it comes into mind with the guilt feeling attached, to destroy what might otherwise be a communication of undivided devotion and love.

This kind of effect was quite clear in the experience of Arthur and Ethel. Arthur had been brought up on the idea that sex should express love and that it should be a bond in married love only. The war came on when he was a sophomore in college and interrupted his life and the normal course of an excellent relation with Ethel. On one of his three-day leaves Ethel met him half-way across the country, so that they could be together longer. They had earlier discussed the possibility of sexual experience, and we suspect that under normal peacetime conditions they would have abstained from sexual intercourse despite their strong love for each other. Now, however, they convinced each other at their hotel that those compunctions they had been feeling about "going all the way" were silly residuals of childhood. They met each other on several other occasions and shared their love with each other.

The last time we saw Ethel she said that soon after Arthur had returned to college, his work (he had been a college leader and an excellent scholar) had gone to pieces, he had broken his engagement and had written her excoriating letters filled with bitterness and the feeling that she had allowed him to make a mess of his life. Anyway, he was no longer any good. We are afraid that Arthur's conscience is still barking, and that the guilt he has been feeling at this point is so heavy upon him that he has allowed it to seep into other areas of his life. And now Ethel, whose conscience "didn't feel too bad" earlier, is miserable, not only about the breaking of the engagement, but also about his attitude toward himself and toward her. This is only one instance of a truth we need to remember, that our conscience, whatever its ultimate nature, has a way of staying with us, and that we are being more than careless when we think we can change it *simply by breaking it.*

In a chapter in which we have been considering lingering doubts, we must not leave the impression of being satisfied with the present status of morality or custom on these problems. It has been our concern to suggest rather the direction in which we need to go in our thinking. What is really disturbing is the fact that so few people are getting from sex the profound, creative experience possible through it. People are cheating themselves of the deeper possibilities sex experience can open to them *if* it symbolically binds together two personalities committed to each other, to their God, their children, and their civil responsibilities. Comparatively speaking, persons are at present experiencing jazz when they might know the stirring themes of symphonies. Our task is not so much to control sex as it is to increase every opportunity for understanding and for growth of personality. Crusades against sex will not do what we really need to do—work with intelligent commitment to the kind of living in which love for others and respect for self are the magnetic poles.

From the cradle to the grave, literally, our task is to develop appreciation for the enriching responsibilities and activities of human experience and, within these, the meaning of sex and love. And we need, as part of this total conception, to change our attitude toward those who have failed to meet their social responsibilities from one of vindictive punishment to one of understanding redirection. Only thus may such persons re-enter as far as possible for them, into their heritage of sex, love, and family. We do not protect society simply by penalizing its weaker members, especially when this frequently means hurting their children more than they need to be hurt. We help society—indeed, we prove that we have the highest and most stable type of society—when we can help those who fall by the way to rediscover their good potentialities and rebuild them.

Notes

1. This statement finds support in Kinsey's statistics with regard to the differences both in freedom of sex expression and mode of sex expression in persons with little school education—and, one assumes, what that means to the development of human understanding.

2. From A. C. Kinsey, W. B. Pomeroy, and C. E. Martin, *Sexual Behavior in the Human Male* (Philadelphia: W. B. Saunders Co., 1948).

Questions for Analysis

1. Bertocci's key assumption is that "love, marriage and the home are among the supreme values of human existence; that the human beings who cannot enjoy the blessings that love, marriage, and the home bestow are relatively poverty-stricken." Do you agree with this assumption or do you find it questionable? Are there other values that you would suggest are coequal with love, marriage, and the home?

2. On what grounds does Bertocci claim that his sexual standards are not artificial barriers? Do you agree? Why or why not?

3. What are Bertocci's views on sexual guilt? Do you agree with them?

4. What does Bertocci mean by "the progression of love"? How does it relate to sexual progression?

5. Given the changes in sexual morality since this essay was written in 1949, do you think Bertocci's arguments are no longer relevant? How do you think he would respond to the charge?

Plain Sex

Alan H. Goldman

In the following selection, Alan Goldman defends the libertarian position. Central to his argument is his rejection of what he calls "means-ends" analyses of sex—analyses that treat sex as

From Alan H. Goldman, "Plain Sex," *Philosophy & Public Affairs* 6, no. 3. Copyright © 1977 Princeton University Press. Reprinted with permission of Princeton University Press.

essentially a means to some further end like love, reproduction, or communication. To him, sexual desire is just the desire for contact with another person's body, and the goal of sex is the pleasure such contact gives. Sex can also be a means of reproduction or of expressing love, he realizes, but those are extraneous purposes to the act of sex itself.

Given that analysis of sex, he concludes that sexual behavior cannot be morally evaluated by any norms other than those by which we evaluate any other kind of behavior—Kant's principle of respect for persons, for instance. We can distinguish perverted from normal sex, but perversion in this case is just a statistical notion, carrying no moral significance.

I

Several recent articles on sex herald its acceptance as a legitimate topic for analytic philosophers (although it has been a topic in philosophy since Plato). One might have thought conceptual analysis unnecessary in this area; despite the notorious struggles of judges and legislators to define pornography suitably, we all might be expected to know what sex is and to be able to identify at least paradigm sexual desires and activities without much difficulty. Philosophy is nevertheless of relevance here if for no other reason than that the concept of sex remains at the center of moral and social consciousness in our, and perhaps any, society. Before we can get a sensible view of the relation of sex to morality, perversion, social regulation, and marriage, we require a sensible analysis of the concept itself; one which neither understates its animal pleasure nor overstates its importance within a theory or system of value. I say "before," but the order is not quite so clear, for questions in this area, as elsewhere in moral philosophy, are both conceptual and normative at the same time. Our concept of sex will partially determine our moral view of it, but as philosophers we should formulate a concept that will accord with its proper moral status. What we require here, as elsewhere, is "reflective equilibrium," a goal not achieved by traditional and recent analyses together with their moral implications. Because sexual activity, like other natural functions such as eating or exercising, has become imbedded in layers of cultural, moral, and superstitious superstructure, it is hard to conceive it in its simplest terms. But partially for this reason, it is only by thinking about plain sex that we can begin to achieve this conceptual equilibrium.

I shall suggest here that sex continues to be misrepresented in recent writings, at least in philosophical writings, and I shall criticize the predominant form of analysis which I term "means-end analysis." Such conceptions attribute a necessary external goal or purpose to sexual activity, whether it be reproduction, the expression of love, simple communication, or interpersonal awareness. They analyze sexual activity as a means to one of these ends, implying that sexual desire is a desire to reproduce, to love or be loved, or to communicate with others. All definitions of this type suggest false views of the relation of sex to perversion and morality by implying that sex which does not fit one of these models or fulfill one of these functions is in some way deviant or incomplete.

The alternative, simpler analysis with which I will begin is that sexual desire is desire for contact with another person's body and for the pleasure which such contact produces; sexual activity is activity which tends to fulfill such desire of the agent. Whereas Aristotle and Butler were correct in holding that pleasure is normally a byproduct rather than a goal of purposeful action, in the case of sex this is not so clear. The desire for another's body is, principally among other things, the desire for the pleasure that physical contact brings. On the other hand, it is not a desire for a particular sensation detachable from its causal context, a sensation which can be derived in other ways. This definition in terms of the general goal of sexual desire appears preferable to an attempt to more explicitly list or define specific sexual activities, for many activities such as kissing, embracing, massaging, or holding hands may or may not be sexual, depending upon the context and more specifically upon the purposes, needs, or desires into which such activities fit. The generality of the definition also represents a refusal (common in recent psychological texts) to overemphasize orgasm as the goal of sexual desire or genital sex as the only norm of sexual activity (this will be hedged slightly in the discussion of perversion below).

Central to the definition is the fact that the goal of sexual desire and activity is the physical contact itself, rather than something else which this contact might express. By contrast, what I term "means-end analyses" posit ends which I take to be extraneous to plain sex, and they view sex as a means to these ends. Their fault lies not in defining sex in terms of its general goal, but in seeing plain sex as merely a means to other separable ends. I term these "means-end analyses" for convenience, although "means-separable-end analyses," while too cumbersome, might be more fully explanatory. The desire for physical contact with another person is a minimal criterion for (normal) sexual desire, but is both necessary and sufficient to qualify normal desire as sexual. Of course, we may want to express other feelings through sexual acts in various contexts, but without the desire for the physical contact in and for itself, or when it is sought for other reasons, activities in which contact is involved are not predominantly sexual. Furthermore, the desire for physical contact in itself, without the wish to express affection or other feelings through it, is sufficient to render sexual the activity of the agent which fulfills it. Various activities with this goal alone, such as kissing and caressing in certain contexts, qualify as sexual even without the presence of genital symptoms of sexual excitement. The latter are not therefore necessary criteria for sexual activity.

This initial analysis may seem to some either over- or underinclusive. It might seem too broad in leading us to interpret physical contact as sexual desire in activities such as football and other contact sports. In these cases, however, the desire is not for contact with another body per se, it is not directed toward a particular person for that purpose, and it is not the goal of the activity—the goal is winning or exercising or knocking someone down or displaying one's prowess. If the desire is purely for contact with another specific person's body, then to interpret it as sexual does not seem an exaggeration. A slightly more difficult case is that of a baby's desire to be cuddled and our natural response in wanting to cuddle it. In the case of the baby, the desire may be simply for the physical contact, for the pleasure of the caresses. If so, we may characterize this desire, especially in keeping with Freudian theory, as sexual or protosexual. It will differ nevertheless from full-fledged sexual desire in being more amorphous, not directed outward toward another specific person's body. It may also

be that what the infant unconsciously desires is not physical contact per se but signs of affection, tenderness, or security, in which case we have further reason for hesitating to characterize its wants as clearly sexual. The intent of our response to the baby is often the showing of affection, not the pure physical contact, so that our definition in terms of action which fulfills sexual desire *on the part of the agent* does not capture such actions, whatever we say of the baby. (If it is intuitive to characterize our response as sexual as well, there is clearly no problem here for my analysis.) The same can be said of signs of affection (or in some cultures polite greeting) among men or women: these certainly need not be homosexual when the intent is only to show friendship, something extrinsic to plain sex although valuable when added to it.

Our definition of sex in terms of the desire for physical contact may appear too narrow in that a person's personality, not merely her or his body, may be sexually attractive to another, and in that looking or conversing in a certain way can be sexual in a given context without bodily contact. Nevertheless, it is not the contents of one's thoughts per se that are sexually appealing, but one's personality as embodied in certain manners of behavior. Furthermore, if a person is sexually attracted by another's personality, he or she will desire not just further conversation, but actual sexual contact. While looking at or conversing with someone can be interpreted as sexual in given contexts it is so when intended as preliminary to, and hence parasitic upon, elemental sexual interest. Voyeurism or viewing a pornographic movie qualifies as a sexual activity, but only as an imaginative substitute for the real thing (otherwise a deviation from the norm as expressed in our definition). The same is true of masturbation as a sexual activity without a partner.

That the initial definition indicates at least an ingredient of sexual desire and activity is too obvious to argue. We all know what sex is, at least in obvious cases, and do not need philosophers to tell us. My preliminary analysis is meant to serve as a contrast to what sex is not, at least, not necessarily. I concentrate upon the physically manifested desire for another's body, and I take as central the immersion in the physical aspect of one's own existence and attention to the physical embodiment of the other. One may derive pleasure in a sex act from expressing certain feelings to one's partner or from awareness of the attitude of one's partner, but sexual desire is essentially desire for physical contact itself: it is a bodily desire for the body of another that dominates our mental life for more or less brief periods. Traditional writings were correct to emphasize the purely physical or animal aspect of sex; they were wrong only in condemning it. This characterization of sex as an intensely pleasurable physical activity and acute physical desire may seem to some to capture only its barest level. But it is worth distinguishing and focusing upon this least common denominator in order to avoid the false views of sexual morality and perversion which emerge from thinking that sex is essentially something else.

II

We may turn then to what sex is not, to the arguments regarding supposed conceptual connections between sex and other activities which it is necessary to conceptually distinguish. The most comprehensible attempt to build an extraneous purpose into the sex act identifies that purpose as reproduction, its primary biological function. While this may be "nature's" purpose, it certainly need not be ours (the analogy with eating, while sometimes overworked, is pertinent here). While this identification may once have had a rational basis which also grounded the identification of the value and morality of sex with that applicable to reproduction and childrearing, the development of contraception rendered the connection weak. Methods of contraception are by now so familiar and so widely used that it is not necessary to dwell upon the changes wrought by these developments in the concept of sex itself and in a rational sexual ethic dependent upon that concept. In the past, the ever present possibility of children rendered the concepts of sex and sexual morality different from those required at present. There may be good reasons, if the presence and care of both mother and father are beneficial to children, for restricting reproduction to marriage. Insofar as society has a legitimate role in protecting children's interests, it may be justified in giving marriage a legal status, although this question is complicated by the fact (among others) that children born to single mothers deserve no penalties. In any case, the point here is simply that these questions are irrelevant at the present time to those regarding the morality of sex and its

potential social regulation. (Further connections with marriage will be discussed below.)

It is obvious that the desire for sex is not necessarily a desire to reproduce, that the psychological manifestation has become, if it were not always, distinct from its biological roots. There are many parallels, as previously mentioned, with other natural functions. The pleasures of eating and exercising are to a large extent independent of their roles in nourishment or health (as the junk-food industry discovered with a vengeance). Despite the obvious parallel with sex, there is still a tendency for many to think that sex acts which can be reproductive are, if not more moral or less immoral, at least more natural. These categories of morality and "naturalness," or normality, are not to be identified with each other, as will be argued below, and neither is applicable to sex by virtue of its connection to reproduction. The tendency to identify reproduction as the conceptually connected end of sex is most prevalent now in the pronouncements of the Catholic church. There the assumed analysis is clearly tied to a restrictive sexual morality according to which acts become immoral and unnatural when they are not oriented towards reproduction, a morality which has independent roots in the Christian sexual ethic as it derives from Paul. However, the means-end analysis fails to generate a consistent sexual ethic: homosexual and oral-genital sex is condemned while kissing or caressing, acts equally unlikely to lead in themselves to fertilization, even when properly characterized as sexual according to our definition, are not.

III

Before discussing further relations of means-end analyses to false or inconsistent sexual ethics and concepts of perversion, I turn to other examples of these analyses. One common position views sex as essentially an expression of love or affection between the partners. It is generally recognized that there are other types of love besides sexual, but sex itself is taken as an expression of one type, sometimes termed "romantic" love.[1] Various factors again ought to weaken this identification. First, there are other types of love besides that which it is appropriate to express sexually, and "romantic" love itself can be expressed in many other ways. I am not denying that sex can take on heightened value and meaning when it becomes a vehicle for the expression of feelings of love or tenderness, but so can many other usually mundane activities such as getting up early to make breakfast on Sunday, cleaning the house, and so on. Second, sex itself can be used to communicate many other emotions besides love, and, as I will argue below, can communicate nothing in particular and still be good sex.

On a deeper level, an internal tension is bound to result from an identification of sex, which I have described as a physical-psychological desire, with love as a long-term, deep emotional relationship between two individuals. As this type of relationship, love is permanent, at least in intent, and more or less exclusive. A normal person cannot deeply love more than a few individuals even in a lifetime. We may be suspicious that those who attempt or claim to love many love them weakly if at all. Yet, fleeting sexual desire can arise in relation to a variety of other individuals one finds sexually attractive. It may even be, as some have claimed, that sexual desire in humans naturally seeks variety, while this is obviously false of love. For this reason, monogamous sex, even if justified, almost always represents a sacrifice or the exercise of self-control on the part of the spouses, while monogamous love generally does not. There is no such thing as casual love in the sense in which I intend the term "love." It may occasionally happen that a spouse falls deeply in love with someone else (especially when sex is conceived in terms of love), but this is relatively rare in comparison to passing sexual desires for others; and while the former often indicates a weakness or fault in the marriage relation, the latter does not.

If love is indeed more exclusive in its objects than is sexual desire, this explains why those who view sex as essentially an expression of love would again tend to hold a repressive or restrictive sexual ethic. As in the case of reproduction, there may be good reasons for reserving the total commitment of deep love to the context of marriage and family—the normal personality may not withstand additional divisions of ultimate commitment and allegiance. There is no question that marriage itself is best sustained by a deep relation of love and affection; and even if love is not naturally monogamous, the benefits of family units to children provide additional reason to avoid serious commitments elsewhere which weaken family ties. It can be argued similarly that monogamous sex strengthens families by restricting and at the same time guaranteeing an outlet for sexual desire in marriage. But there is more force to the argument that recognition of a clear distinction between sex and love in society would help avoid disastrous marriages which result from adolescent confusion of the two when sexual desire is mistaken for permanent love, and would weaken damaging jealousies which arise in marriages in relation to passing sexual desires. The love and affection of a sound marriage certainly differs from the adolescent romantic variety, which is often a mere substitute for sex in the context of a repressive sexual ethic.

In fact, the restrictive sexual ethic tied to the means-end analysis in terms of love again has failed to be consistent. At least, it has not been applied consistently, but forms part of the double standard which has curtailed the freedom of women. It is predictable in light of this history that some women would now advocate using sex as another kind of means, as a political weapon or as a way to increase unjustly denied power and freedom. The inconsistency in the sexual ethic typically attached to the sex-love analysis, according to which it has generally been taken with a grain of salt when applied to men, is simply another example of the impossibility of tailoring a plausible moral theory in this area to a conception of sex which builds in conceptually extraneous factors.

I am not suggesting here that sex ought never to be connected with love or that it is not a more significant and valuable activity when it is. Nor am I denying that individuals need love as much as sex and perhaps emotionally need at least one complete relationship which encompasses both. Just as sex can express love and take on heightened significance when it does, so love is often naturally accompanied by an intermittent desire for sex. But again love is accompanied appropriately by desires for other shared activities as well. What makes the desire for sex seem more intimately connected with love is the intimacy which is seen to be a natural feature of mutual sex acts. Like love, sex is held to lay one bare psychologically as well as physically. Sex is unquestionably intimate, but beyond that the psychological toll often attached may be a function of the restrictive sexual ethic itself, rather than a legitimate apology for it. The intimacy involved in love is psychologically consuming in a generally healthy way, while the psychological tolls of sexual relations, often including embarrassment as a correlate of intimacy, are too often the result of artificial sexual ethics and taboos. The intimacy involved in both love and sex is insufficient in any case in light of previous points to render a means-end analysis in these terms appropriate.

IV

In recent articles, Thomas Nagel and Robert Solomon, who recognize that sex is not merely a means to communicate love, nevertheless retain the form of this analysis while broadening it. For Solomon, sex remains a means of communicating (he explicitly uses the metaphor of body language), although the feelings that can be communicated now include, in addition to love and tenderness, domination, dependence, anger, trust, and so on.[2] Nagel does not refer explicitly to communication, but his analysis is similar in that he views sex as a complex form of interpersonal awareness in which desire itself is consciously communicated on several different levels. In sex, according to his analysis, two people are aroused by each other, aware of the other's arousal, and further aroused by this awareness.[3] Such multileveled conscious awareness of one's own and the other's desire is taken as the norm of a sexual relation, and this model is therefore close to that which views sex as a means of interpersonal communication.

Solomon's analysis is beset by the same difficulties as those pointed out in relation to the narrower sex-love concept. Just as love can be communicated by many activities other than sex, which do not therefore become properly analyzed as essentially vehicles of communication (making breakfast, cleaning the house, and so on), the same is true of the other feelings mentioned by Solomon. Domination can be communicated through economic manipulation, trust by a joint savings account. Driving a car can be simultaneously expressing anger, pride, joy, and so on. We may, in fact, communicate or express feelings in anything we do, but this does not make everything we do into language. Driving a car is not to be defined as an automotive means of communication, although with a little ingenuity we might work out an automotive

vocabulary (tailgating as an expression of aggression or impatience; beating another car away from a stoplight as expressing domination) to match the vocabulary of "body language." That one can communicate various feelings during sex acts does not make these acts merely or primarily a means of communicating.

More importantly, to analyze sex as a means of communication is to overlook the intrinsic nature and value of the act itself. Sex is not a gesture or series of gestures, in fact not necessarily a means to any other end, but a physical activity intensely pleasurable in itself. When a language is used, the symbols normally have no importance in themselves; they function merely as vehicles for what can be communicated by them. Furthermore skill in the use of language is a technical achievement that must be carefully learned; if better sex is more successful communication by means of a more skillful use of body language, then we had all better be well schooled in the vocabulary and grammar. Solomon's analysis, which uses the language metaphor, suggests the appropriateness of a sex-manual approach, the substitution of a bit of technological prowess for the natural pleasure of the unforced surrender to feeling and desire.

It may be that Solomon's position could be improved by using the analogy of music rather than that of language, as an aesthetic form of communication. Music might be thought of as a form of aesthetic communicating, in which the experience of the "phonemes" themselves is generally pleasing. And listening to music is perhaps more of a sexual experience than having someone talk to you. Yet, it seems to me that insofar as music is aesthetic and pleasing in itself, it is not best conceived as primarily a means for communicating specific feelings. Such an analysis does injustice to aesthetic experience in much the same way as the sex-communication analysis debases sexual experience itself.[4]

For Solomon, sex that is not a totally self-conscious communicative art tends toward vulgarity,[5] whereas I would have thought it the other way around. This is another illustration of the tendency of means-end analyses to condemn what appears perfectly natural or normal sex on my account. Both Solomon and Nagel use their definitions, however, not primarily to stipulate moral norms for sex, as we saw in earlier analyses, but to define norms against which to measure perversion. Once again, neither is capable of generating consistency or reflective equilibrium with our firm intuitions as to what counts as subnormal sex, the problem being that both build factors into their norms which are extraneous to an unromanticized view of normal sexual desire and activity. If perversion represents a breakdown in communication, as Solomon maintains, then any unsuccessful or misunderstood advance should count as perverted. Furthermore, sex between husband and wife married for several years, or between any partners already familiar with each other, would be, if not perverted, nevertheless subnormal or trite and dull, in that the communicative content would be minimal in lacking all novelty. In fact the pleasures of sex need not wear off with familiarity, as they would if dependent upon the communicative content of the feelings. Finally, rather than a release or relief from physical desire through a substitute imaginative outlet, masturbation would become a way of practicing or rehearsing one's technique or vocabulary on oneself, or simply a way of talking to oneself, as Solomon himself says.[6]

Nagel fares no better in the implications of his overintellectualized norm. Spontaneous and heated sex between two familiar partners may well lack the complex conscious multileveled interpersonal awareness of which he speaks without being in the least perverted. The egotistical desire that one's partner be aroused by one's own desire does not seem a primary element of the sexual urge, and during sex acts one may like one's partner to be sometimes active and aroused, sometimes more passive. Just as sex can be more significant when love is communicated, so it can sometimes be heightened by an awareness of the other's desire. But at other times this awareness of an avid desire of one's partner can be merely distracting. The conscious awareness to which Nagel refers may actually impede the immersion in the physical of which I spoke above, just as may concentration upon one's "vocabulary" or technique. Sex is a way of relating to another, but primarily a physical rather than intellectual way. For Nagel, the ultimate in degeneration or perversion would have to be what he calls "mutual epidermal stimulation"[7] without mutual awareness of each other's state of mind. But this sounds like normal, if not ideal, sex to me (perhaps only a minimal description of it). His model

certainly seems more appropriate to a sophisticated seduction scene than to the sex act itself,[8] which according to the model would often have to count as a subnormal anticlimax to the intellectual foreplay. While Nagel's account resembles Solomon's means-end analysis of sex, here the sex act itself does not even qualify as a preferred or central means to the end of interpersonal communication.

V

I have now criticized various types of analysis sharing or suggesting a common means-end form. I have suggested that analyses of this form relate to attempts to limit moral or natural sex to that which fulfills some purpose or function extraneous to basic sexual desire. The attempts to brand forms of sex outside the idealized models as immoral or perverted fail to achieve consistency with intuitions that they themselves do not directly question. The reproductive model brands oral-genital sex a deviation, but cannot account for kissing or holding hands; the communication account holds voyeurism to be perverted but cannot accommodate sex acts without much conscious thought or seductive nonphysical foreplay; the sex-love model makes most sexual desire seem degrading or base. The first and last condemn extramarital sex on the sound but irrelevant grounds that reproduction and deep commitment are best confined to family contexts. The romanticization of sex and the confusion of sexual desire with love operate in both directions: sex outside the context of romantic love is repressed; once it is repressed, partners become more difficult to find and sex becomes romanticized further, out of proportion to its real value for the individual.

What all these analyses share in addition to a common form is accordance with and perhaps derivation from the Platonic-Christian moral tradition, according to which the animal or purely physical element of humans is the source of immorality, and plain sex in the sense I defined it is an expression of this element, hence in itself to be condemned. All the analyses examined seem to seek a distance from sexual desire itself in attempting to extend it conceptually beyond the physical. The love and communication analyses seek refinement or intellectualization of the desire; plain physical sex becomes vulgar, and too straightforward sexual encounters without an aura of respectable cerebral communicative content are to be avoided. Solomon explicitly argues that sex cannot be a "mere" appetite, his argument being that if it were, subway exhibitionism and other vulgar forms would be pleasing.[9] This fails to recognize that sexual desire can be focused or selective at the same time as being physical. Lower animals are not attracted by every other member of their species, either. Rancid food forced down one's throat is not pleasing, but that certainly fails to show that hunger is not a physical appetite. Sexual desire lets us know that we are physical beings and, indeed, animals; this is why traditional Platonic morality is so thorough in its condemnation. Means-end analyses continue to reflect this tradition, sometimes unwittingly. They show that in conceptualizing sex it is still difficult, despite years of so-called revolution in this area, to free ourselves from the lingering suspicion that plain sex as physical desire is an expression of our "lower selves," that yielding to our animal natures is sub-human or vulgar.

VI

Having criticized these analyses for the sexual ethics and concepts of perversion they imply, it remains to contrast my account along these lines. To the question of what morality might be implied by my analysis, the answer is that there are no moral implications whatever. Any analysis of sex which imputes a moral character to sex acts in themselves is wrong for that reason. There is no morality intrinsic to sex, although general moral rules apply to the treatment of others in sex acts as they apply to all human relations. We can speak of a sexual ethic as we can speak of a business ethic, without implying that business in itself is either moral or immoral or that special rules are required to judge business practices which are not derived from rules that apply elsewhere as well. Sex is not in itself a moral category, although like business it invariably places us into relations with others in which moral rules apply. It gives us opportunity to do what is otherwise recognized as wrong, to harm others, deceive them or manipulate them against their wills. Just as the fact that an act is sexual in itself never renders it wrong or adds to its wrongness if it is wrong on other grounds (sexual acts towards minors are wrong on other grounds, as will be argued below), so no wrong act is to be

excused because done from a sexual motive. If a "crime of passion" is to be excused, it would have to be on grounds of temporary insanity rather than sexual context (whether insanity does constitute a legitimate excuse for certain actions is too big a topic to argue here). Sexual motives are among others which may become deranged, and the fact that they are sexual has no bearing in itself on the moral character, whether negative or exculpatory, of the actions deriving from them. Whatever might be true of war, it is certainly not the case that all's fair in love or sex.

Our first conclusion regarding morality and sex is therefore that no conduct otherwise immoral should be excused because it is sexual conduct, and nothing in sex is immoral unless condemned by rules which apply elsewhere as well. The last clause requires further clarification. Sexual conduct can be governed by particular rules relating only to sex itself. But these precepts must be implied by general moral rules when these are applied to specific sexual relations or types of conduct. The same is true of rules of fair business, ethical medicine, or courtesy in driving a car. In the latter case, particular acts on the road may be reprehensible, such as tailgating or passing on the right, which seem to bear no resemblance as actions to any outside the context of highway safety. Nevertheless their immorality derives from the fact that they place others in danger, a circumstance which, when avoidable, is to be condemned in any context. This structure of general and specifically applicable rules describes a reasonable sexual ethic as well. To take an extreme case, rape is always a sexual act and it is always immoral. A rule against rape can therefore be considered an obvious part of sexual morality which has no bearing on nonsexual conduct. But the immorality of rape derives from its being an extreme violation of a person's body, of the right not to be humiliated, and of the general moral prohibition against using other persons against their wills, not from the fact that it is a sexual act.

The application elsewhere of general moral rules to sexual conduct is further complicated by the fact that it will be relative to the particular desires and preferences of one's partner (these may be influenced by and hence in some sense include misguided beliefs about sexual morality itself). This means that there will be fewer specific rules in the area of sexual ethics than in other areas of conduct, such as driving cars, where the relativity of preference is irrelevant to the prohibition of objectively dangerous conduct. More reliance will have to be placed upon the general moral rule, which in this area holds simply that the preferences, desires, and interests of one's partner or potential partner ought to be taken into account. This rule is certainly not specifically formulated to govern sexual relations; it is a form of the central principle of morality itself. But when applied to sex, it prohibits certain actions, such as molestation of children, which cannot be categorized as violations of the rule without at the same time being classified as sexual. I believe this last case is the closest we can come to an action which is wrong *because* it is sexual, but even here its wrongness is better characterized as deriving from the detrimental effects such behavior can have on the future emotional and sexual life of the naive victims, and from the fact that such behavior therefore involves manipulation of innocent persons without regard for their interests. Hence, this case also involves violation of a general moral rule which applies elsewhere as well.

Aside from faulty conceptual analyses of sex and the influence of the Platonic moral tradition, there are two more plausible reasons for thinking that there are moral dimensions intrinsic to sex acts per se. The first is that such acts are normally intensely pleasurable. According to a hedonistic, utilitarian moral theory they therefore should be at least prima facie morally right, rather than morally neutral in themselves. To me this seems incorrect and reflects unfavorably on the ethical theory in question. The pleasure intrinsic to sex acts is a good, but not, it seems to me, a good with much positive moral significance. Certainly I can have no duty to pursue such pleasure myself, and while it may be nice to give pleasure of any form to others, there is no ethical requirement to do so, given my right over my own body. The exception relates to the context of sex acts themselves, when one partner derives pleasure from the other and ought to return the favor. This duty to reciprocate takes us out of the domain of hedonistic utilitarianism, however, and into a Kantian moral framework, the central principles of which call for just such reciprocity in human relations. Since independent moral judgments regarding sexual activities constitute one area in which ethical theories are to be tested, these observations indicate here, as I believe others indicate elsewhere, the fertility of the Kantian, as opposed to the utilitarian, principle in reconstructing reasoned moral consciousness.

It may appear from this alternative Kantian viewpoint that sexual acts must be at least prima facie wrong in themselves. This is because they invariably involve at different stages the manipulation of one's partner for one's own pleasure, which might appear to be prohibited on the formulation of Kant's principle which holds that one ought not to treat another as a means to such private ends. A more realistic rendering of this formulation, however, one which recognizes its intended equivalence to the first universalizability principle, admits no such absolute prohibition. Many human relations, most economic transactions for example, involve using other individuals for personal benefit. These relations are immoral only when they are one-sided, when the benefits are not mutual, or when the transactions are not freely and rationally endorsed by all parties. The same holds true of sexual acts. The central principle governing them is the Kantian demand for reciprocity in sexual relations. In order to comply with the principle, one must recognize the subjectivity of one's partner (not merely by being aroused by her or his desire, as Nagel describes). Even in an act which by its nature "objectifies" the other, one recognizes a partner as a subject with demands and desires by yielding to those desires, by allowing oneself to be a sexual object as well, by giving pleasure or ensuring that the pleasures of the acts are mutual. It is this kind of reciprocity which forms the basis for morality in sex, which distinguishes right acts from wrong in this area as in others. (Of course, prior to sex acts one must gauge their effects upon potential partners and take these longer range interests into account.)

VII

I suggested earlier that in addition to generating confusion regarding the rightness or wrongness of sex acts, false conceptual analyses of the means-end form cause confusion about the value of sex to the individual. My account recognizes the satisfaction of desire and the pleasure this brings as the central psychological function of the sex act for the individual. Sex affords us a paradigm of pleasure, but not a cornerstone of value. For most of us it is not only a needed outlet for desire but also the most enjoyable form of recreation we know. Its value is nevertheless easily mistaken by being confused with that of love, when it is taken as essentially an expression of that emotion. Although intense, the pleasures of sex are brief and repetitive rather than cumulative. They give value to the specific acts which generate them, but not the lasting kind of value which enhances one's whole life. The briefness of these pleasures contributes to their intensity (or perhaps their intensity makes them necessarily brief), but it also relegates them to the periphery of most rational plans for the good life.

By contrast, love typically develops over a long term relation; while its pleasures may be less intense and physical, they are of more cumulative value. The importance of love to the individual may well be central in a rational system of value. And it has perhaps an even deeper moral significance relating to the identification with the interests of another person, which broadens one's possible relationships with others as well. Marriage is again important in preserving this relation between adults and children, which seems as important to the adults as it is to the children in broadening concerns which have a tendency to become selfish. Sexual desire, by contrast, is desire for another which is nevertheless essentially self-regarding. Sexual pleasure is certainly a good for the individual, and for many it may be necessary in order for them to function in a reasonably cheerful way. But it bears little relation to those other values just discussed, to which some analyses falsely suggest a conceptual connection.

VIII

While my initial analysis lacks moral implications in itself, as it should, it does suggest by contrast a concept of sexual perversion. Since the concept of perversion is itself a sexual concept, it will always be defined relative to some definition of normal sex; and any conception of the norm will imply a contrary notion of perverse forms. The concept suggested by my account again differs sharply from those implied by the means-end analyses examined above. Perversion does not represent a deviation from the reproductive function (or kissing would be perverted), from a loving relationship (or most sexual desire and many hetero-

sexual acts would be perverted), or from efficiency in communicating (or unsuccessful seduction attempts would be perverted). It is a deviation from a norm, but the norm in question is merely statistical. Of course, not all sexual acts that are statistically unusual are perverted—a three-hour continuous sexual act would be unusual but not necessarily abnormal in the requisite sense. The abnormality in question must relate to the *form of the desire* itself in order to constitute sexual perversion; for example, desire, not for contact with another, but for merely looking, for harming or being harmed, for contact with items of clothing. This concept of sexual abnormality is that suggested by my definition of normal sex in terms of its typical desire. However not all unusual desires qualify either, only those with the typical physical sexual effects upon the individual who satisfies them. These effects, such as erection in males, were not built into the original definition of sex in terms of sexual desire, for they do not always occur in activities that are properly characterized as sexual, say, kissing for the pleasure of it. But they do seem to bear a closer relation to the definition of activities as perverted. (For those who consider only genital sex sexual, we could build such symptoms into a narrower definition, then speaking of sex in a broad sense as well as "proper" sex.)

Solomon and Nagel disagree with this statistical notion of perversion. For them the concept is evaluative rather than statistical. I do not deny that the term "perverted" is often used evaluatively (and purely emotively for that matter), or that it has a negative connotation for the average speaker. I do deny that we can find a norm, other than that of statistically usual desire, against which all and only activities that properly count as sexual perversions can be contrasted. Perverted sex is simply abnormal sex, and if the norm is not to be an idealized or romanticized extraneous end or purpose, it must express the way human sexual desires usually manifest themselves. Of course not all norms in other areas of discourse need be statistical in this way. Physical health is an example of a relatively clear norm which does not seem to depend upon the numbers of healthy people. But the concept in this case achieves its clarity through the connection of physical health with other clearly desirable physical functions and characteristics, for example, living longer. In the case of sex, that which is statistically abnormal is not necessarily incapacitating in other ways, and yet these abnormal desires with sexual effects upon their subject do count as perverted to the degree to which their objects deviate from usual ones. The connotations of the concept of perversion beyond those connected with abnormality or statistical deviation derive more from the attitudes of those likely to call certain acts perverted than from specifiable features of the acts themselves. These connotations add to the concept of abnormality that of *sub*normality, but there is no norm against which the latter can be measured intelligibly in accord with all and only acts intuitively called perverted.

The only proper evaluative norms relating to sex involve degrees of pleasure in the acts and moral norms, but neither of these scales coincides with statistical degrees of abnormality, according to which perversion is to be measured. The three parameters operate independently (this was implied for the first two when it was held above that the pleasure of sex is a good, but not necessarily a moral good). Perverted sex may be more or less enjoyable to particular individuals than normal sex, and more or less moral, depending upon the particular relations involved. Raping a sheep may be more perverted than raping a woman, but certainly not more condemnable morally.[10] It is nevertheless true that the evaluative connotations attaching to the term "perverted" derive partly from the fact that most people consider perverted sex highly immoral. Many such acts are forbidden by long standing taboos, and it is sometimes difficult to distinguish what is forbidden from what is immoral. Others, such as sadistic acts, are genuinely immoral, but again not at all because of their connection with sex or abnormality. The principles which condemn these acts would condemn them equally if they were common and nonsexual. It is not true that we properly could continue to consider acts perverted which were found to be very common practice across societies. Such acts, if harmful, might continue to be condemned properly as immoral, but it was just shown that the immorality of an act does not vary with its degree of perversion. If not harmful, common acts previously considered abnormal might continue to be called perverted for a time by the moralistic minority; but the term when applied to such cases would retain only its emotive negative connotation without consistent logical criteria for application. It would represent merely prejudiced moral judgments.

To adequately explain why there is a tendency to so deeply condemn perverted acts would require a treatise in psychology beyond the scope of this paper. Part of the reason undoubtedly relates to the tradition of repressive sexual ethics and false conceptions of sex; another part to the fact that all abnormality seems to disturb and fascinate us at the same time. The former explains why sexual perversion is more abhorrent to many than other forms of abnormality; the latter indicates why we tend to have an emotive and evaluative reaction to perversion in the first place. It may be, as has been suggested according to a Freudian line,[11] that our uneasiness derives from latent desires we are loathe to admit, but this thesis takes us into psychological issues I am not competent to judge. Whatever the psychological explanation, it suffices to point out here that the conceptual connection between perversion and genuine or consistent moral evaluation is spurious and again suggested by misleading means-end idealizations of the concept of sex.

The position I have taken in this paper against those concepts is not totally new. Something similar to it is found in Freud's view of sex, which of course was genuinely revolutionary, and in the body of writings deriving from Freud to the present time. But in his revolt against romanticized and repressive conceptions, Freud went too far—from a refusal to view sex as merely a means to a view of it as the end of all human behavior, although sometimes an elaborately disguised end. This pansexualism led to the thesis (among others) that repression was indeed an inevitable and necessary part of social regulation of any form, a strange consequence of a position that began by opposing the repressive aspects of the means-end view. Perhaps the time finally has arrived when we can achieve a reasonable middle ground in this area, at least in philosophy if not in society.

Notes

1. Even Bertrand Russell, whose writing in this area was a model of rationality, at least for its period, tends to make this identification and to condemn plain sex in the absence of love: "sex intercourse apart from love has little value, and is to be regarded primarily as experimentation with a view

to love." *Marriage and Morals* (New York: Bantam, 1959), p. 87.

2. Robert Solomon, "Sex and Perversion," *Philosophy and Sex*, ed. R. Baker and F. Elliston (Buffalo: Prometheus, 1975).

3. Thomas Nagel, "Sexual Perversion," *The Journal of Philosophy* 66, no. 1 (16 January 1969).

4. Sex might be considered (at least partially) as communication in a very broad sense in the same way as performing ensemble music, in the sense that there is in both ideally a communion or perfectly shared experience with another. This is, however, one possible ideal view whose central feature is not necessary to sexual acts or desire per se. And in emphasizing the communication of specific feelings by means of body language, the analysis

under consideration narrows the end to one clearly extrinsic to plain and even good sex.

5. Solomon, pp. 284–285.

6. Ibid., p. 283. One is reminded of Woody Allen's rejoinder to praise of his technique: "I practice a lot when I'm alone."

7. Nagel, p. 15.

8. Janice Moulton made the same point in a paper at the Pacific APA meeting, March 1976.

9. Solomon, p. 285.

10. The example is like one from Sara Ruddick, "Better Sex," *Philosophy and Sex*, p. 96.

11. See Michael Slote, "Inapplicable Concepts and Sexual Perversion," *Philosophy and Sex*.

Questions for Analysis

1. What is the significance of this essay's title?

2. According to Goldman, "We all know what sex is, at least in obvious cases, and we do not need philosophers to tell us." Do you agree? Does his analysis of sex agree with what we all know?

3. In rejecting the view that the purpose of sex is reproduction, Goldman compares sex to eating. What's the point of the comparison? Is it a good one?

4. What contrasts does Goldman draw between love and sexual desire?

5. Why does Goldman believe that perversion is not an evaluative norm against which we can judge sexual behavior?

6. Goldman claims that there is no morality intrinsic to sex. What does he mean by that? What are his reasons for claiming it?

7. In considering various means-ends analyses of sex, has Goldman missed any purpose of sex that you think important?

Between Consenting Adults

Onora O'Neill

This selection by Onora O'Neill is an examination of sexual relations from a Kantian perspective. Taken from a longer essay on respect for persons, this passage explores some of the more subtle

From Onora O'Neill, "Between Consenting Adults," Philosophy & Public Affairs *14, no. 3. Copyright © 1985 Princeton University Press. Reprinted with permission of Princeton University Press.*

ways that people can violate Kantian respect in both casual affairs and intimate, loving sexual relationships.

Although O'Neill does not argue for any particular position concerning sexual morality, her examination does raise questions relevant to all of them.

Deception is a pervasive possibility in sexual encounters and relationships. Not only are there well-known deceptions, such as seduction and breach of promise, but varied further possibilities. Many of these reflect the peculiarly implicit nature of sexual communication. Commercial and various distanced sexual encounters standardly use the very means of expression which deeper and longer lasting attachments use. But when the endearments and gestures of intimacy are not used to convey what they standardly convey, miscommunication is peculiarly likely. Endearments standardly express not just momentary enthusiasm but affection; the contact of eyes, lips, skin conveys some openness, acceptance, and trust (often enough much more); embrace conveys a commitment which goes beyond a momentary clinging. These are potent gestures of human emotional life. If insufficient trust and commitment are present to warrant such expression, then those who use these endearments and gestures risk giving false messages about feelings, desires, and even commitments. But perhaps, we may think, at least in sexual relationships which are commercial or very casual or largely formal, it is well understood by all concerned that these expressions have been decontextualized and no longer express the underlying intentions or attitudes or principles that they might express in a more wholehearted relationship. But if such expressions are fully decontextualized, what part are they playing in an entirely casual or commercial or formalized encounter? If the expressions are taken at face value, yet what they would standardly express is lacking, each is likely to deceive the other. Relationship of prostitution, casual sexual encounters, and the sexual aspect of faded marriages are not invariably deceptive. Such sexual relations may be either too crudely mechanical to use or misuse expressions of intimacy, or sufficiently informed by trust and concern for the language of intimacy to be appropriate. But relationships and encounters which standardly combine superficial expression of commitment with its underlying absence are

peculiarly vulnerable to deception. Where too much is unexpressed, or misleadingly expressed, each risks duping the other and using him or her as means.

Avoiding deceit and coercion are only the core of treating others as persons in sexual relationships. In avoiding these we avoid clear and obvious ways of using as (mere) means. But to treat another as a person in an intimate, and especially an intimate sexual, relationship requires far more. These further requirements reflect the intimacy rather than the specifically sexual character of a relationship. However, if sexual relationships cannot easily be merely relationships between consenting adults, further requirements for treating another as a person are likely to arise in any sexual relationship. Intimate bodies cannot easily have separate lives.

Intimacy, sexual or not, alters relationships in two ways that are relevant here. First, those who are intimate acquire deep and detailed (but incomplete) knowledge of one another's life, character, and desires. Secondly, each forms some desires which incorporate or refer to the other's desires, and consequently finds his or her happiness in some ways contingent upon the fulfillment of the other's desires.[1] Intimacy is not a merely cognitive relationship, but one where special possibilities for respecting and sharing (alternatively for disrespecting and frustrating) another's ends and desires develop. It is in intimate relationships that we are most able to treat others as persons—and most able to fail to do so.

Intimacy makes failures of respect and of love more possible. Lack of respect in intimate relationships may, for example, take both manipulative and paternalistic forms. The manipulator trades on the fact that the other is not just a possibly consenting adult, but one whose particular desires are known and may depend in part on the manipulator's desires. One who succumbs to so-called "moral" blackmail could have refused without suffering coercion and was not deceived, but was confronted with the dilemma of sacrificing something central to his or her life—perhaps career or integrity or relationships with others, or perhaps mainly the desire to accommodate the manipulator's desires—unless willing to comply. In intimate relationships it is all too easy to make the other an offer he or she cannot refuse; when we are close to others we can undercut their pursuit of ends without coercion or deceit. Modes of bargaining and negotiating with others which do not make dissent impossible for consenting adults in the abstract, and might be acceptable in public contexts, may yet undercut others' pursuit of their ends in intimate relationships. Here it is peculiarly demanding to leave the other "space" for his or her pursuit of ends. To do so, and so maintain respect for those with whom we are intimate, requires us to take account not only of the particular interlock of desires, dependencies, and vulnerabilities that have arisen in a given relationship, but also that we heed any wider social context whose modes of discourse and received opinions may systematically undermine or belittle the other's ends and capacities to pursue them. Respect for others—the most basic aspect of sharing their ends—requires the greatest tact and insight when we are most aware of ways in which others' capacities to pursue ends autonomously are vulnerable.

Contexts which make manipulation hard to avoid also offer opportunities for paternalistic failures of respect. Unlike the manipulator, the paternalist does not deploy knowledge of the other and the other's ends to reduce his or her "space" for pursuit of those ends. The paternalist rather begins from a failure to acknowledge either *what* the other's ends are, or that they are the *other's* ends. This failure of respect entails failures to share those ends, for to the paternalist they are either invisible or else not the other's ends but rather the ends to be sought for the other. The paternalist tries to express beneficence or love by imposing a conception of others' ends or interests. Lack of respect is then compounded by lack of love. Those who try to remake or control the lives of others with whom they are intimate do not merely fail in respect, however sincerely they may claim to seek the other's good. Paternalism towards those who have their own ends is not a form of love. However, since it is only fundamental principles of actions (whether plans, proposals, policies, or intentions) that must meet these standards, superficial departure from them when acting on morally acceptable fundamental principles may be acceptable, or even required. The jokes and surprises in which friendship may be expressed do not count as deceptions; but if they were incident to action on other maxims might constitute fraud or serious disrespect or unacceptable paternalism.[2]

Even in intimate relationships not all failures of love are consequent upon failures of respect. It is not only in manipulative and paternalistic action, where others' ends are respectively used and overlooked, that we may fail to share the ends of those with whom we are intimate. Failures of love also occur when the other's ends are indeed respected, and he or she is left the "space" in which to pursue them, yet no positive encouragement, assistance, or support for their pursuit is given. Vulnerable, finite beings do not treat one another as ends *merely* by leaving each other an appropriate "space." Here again detailed knowledge of others and their desires, strengths, and weaknesses offers wider possibilities. The support, concern, and generosity we need from particular others if our pursuit of ends is to be not merely unprevented but sufficiently shared to be a genuine possibility are quite specific. If we are to treat others with whom we are intimate with love as well as respect, we must both see and (to some extent) support their ends.

Avoiding using others and treating them as persons both demand a lot in intimate relationships. Only the avoidance of coercion demands no more than usual here, perhaps because coercion tends to destroy intimacy. Deception remains a possibility in any relationship, and more so where much is conveyed elliptically or by gesture. In brief sexual encounters as well as in commercial and formalized sexual relations the discrepancy of expression and underlying attitude offers many footholds for deception; even in sustained intimate relationships underlying attitudes and outlook can become, as it were, decoupled from the expression and gesture which convey them to the other, so that the language of intimacy is used deceptively. Intimate relationships also provide appropriate settings for manipulative and paternalistic failures of respect and consequent and other failures of love. But the other side of these gloomy thoughts is that intimacy also offers the best chances for treating others as the persons they are.

Notes

1. By this I don't mean merely that sexual desire may include desires that refer to the other's sexual desires, but more broadly that at least some desires in intimate relationships are altruistic in the strict sense that they can be specified only by reference to the other's desires. This allows for hostile intimacy where desire may be for frustration rather than the fulfillment of the other's desires.

2. A sensitive element of the pattern of casuistry outlined here is determining which principles are the maxim(s) of a given action, and which ancillary. Here counterfactual considerations must always be introduced. We can reject claims that some principle of action is the maxim of a given act when we have reason to believe that, without fundamental changes either in circumstance or in moral outlook, that principle would not have been acted on. A claim to be acting out of friendship rather than disrespect in throwing a surprise party would be rebutted if the party would be thrown even when friendship would require other implementations (the friend is exhausted or ill or bereaved or shy). A claim that demands on another are not coercive but benevolent could be rebutted only if there are good reasons for thinking the actual refusal wholly neurotic, as well as that disregard of the refusal would benefit the refuser. Imposition of, for example, medical treatment or sexual attentions in the face of refusal could be fundamentally respectful and benevolent only if the coercion would be dropped given some evidence that the refusal is not entirely neurotic.

Questions for Analysis

1. What are the more subtle forms of deception in casual affairs that O'Neill discusses?

2. In what ways can (and do) lovers exploit each other's vulnerabilities?

3. What failures of Kantian respect are more likely in loving relationships than casual ones? What failures are more likely in casual ones?

4. Why does sexual intimacy offer the best chances for treating others as the persons they are? Why is it so hard to do?

5. What questions does O'Neill raise for the traditionalist? The libertarian? For middle positions?

6. Does this essay seem to support any one approach to sexual morality over the others? Why or why not?

Gay Basics: Some Questions, Facts, and Values

Richard D. Mohr   for Robert W. Switzer

In this defense of homosexuality and homosexual rights, Richard D. Mohr addresses a variety of issues surrounding homosexuality. He looks at the nature of the stereotypes that many heterosexuals have of homosexuals, the various kinds of discrimination and harassment that homosexuals often face, the moral objections that have been raised against homosexuality, and the effects that full acceptance of homosexuality would likely have on society.

Three of his points are particularly important for our purposes. One is his objection to the way that all homosexuals become stigmatized by the immoral acts of a few, while heterosexuals are not stigmatized as a group when any of them is found guilty of abusive sex crimes. Another is his criticism of the argument that homosexuality is unnatural. The third is his claim that full acceptance of homosexuality and homosexual rights would have a positive moral effect on our society.

Who Are Gays Anyway?

A recent Gallup poll found that only one in five Americans reports having a gay or lesbian acquaintance.[1] This finding is extraordinary given the number of practicing homosexuals in America. Alfred Kinsey's 1948 study of the sex lives of 5,000 white males shocked the nation: 37 percent had at least one homosexual experience to orgasm in their adult lives; an additional 13 percent had homosexual fantasies to orgasm; 4 percent were exclusively homosexual in their practices; another 5 percent had virtually no heterosexual experience; and nearly one-fifth had at least as many homosexual as heterosexual experiences.[2]

Two out of five men one passes on the street have had orgasmic sex with men. Every second family in the country has a member who is essentially homosexual, and many more people regularly have homosexual experiences. Who are homosexuals? They are your friends, your minister, your teacher, your bank teller, your doctor, your mail carrier, your secretary, your congressional representative, your sibling, parent, and spouse. They are everywhere, virtually all ordinary, virtually all unknown.

Several important consequences follow. First, the country is profoundly ignorant of the actual experience of gay people. Second, social attitudes and practices that are harmful to gays have a much greater overall harmful impact on society than is usually realized. Third, most gay people live in hiding—in the closet—making the "coming out" experience the central fixture of gay consciousness and invisibility the chief characteristic of the gay community.

Ignorance, Stereotype, and Morality

Ignorance about gays, however, has not stopped people from having strong opinions about them. The void which ignorance leaves has been filled with stereotypes. Society holds chiefly two groups of antigay stereotypes; the two are an oddly contradictory lot. One set of stereotypes revolves around alleged mistakes in an individual's gender identity: Lesbians are women that want to be, or at least look and act like, men—bulldykes, diesel dykes; while gay men are those who want to be, or at least look and act like, women—queens, fairies, limp-wrists, nellies. These stereotypes of mismatched genders provide the materials through which gays and lesbians become the butts of ethnic-like jokes. These stereotypes and jokes, though derisive, basically view gays and lesbians as ridiculous.

Another set of stereotypes revolves around gays as a pervasive sinister conspiratorial threat. The core stereotype here is the gay person as child molester and, more generally, as sex-crazed maniac. These stereotypes carry with them fears of the very destruction of family and civilization itself. Now, that which is essentially ridiculous can hardly have such a staggering effect. Something must be afoot in this incoherent amalgam.

Sense can be made of this incoherence if the nature of stereotypes is clarified. Stereotypes are not *simply* false generalizations from a skewed sample of cases examined. Admittedly, false generalizing plays some part in the stereotypes a society holds. If, for instance, one takes as one's sample homosexuals who are in psychiatric hospitals or prisons, as was done in nearly all early investigations, not surprisingly one will probably find homosexuals to be of a crazed and criminal cast. Such false generalizations, though, simply confirm beliefs already held on independent grounds, ones that likely led the investigator to the prison and psychiatric ward to begin with. Evelyn Hooker, who in the late '50s carried out the first rigorous studies to use nonclinical gays, found that psychiatrists, when presented with case files including all the standard diagnostic psychological profiles—but omitting indications of sexual orientation—were unable to distinguish gay files from straight ones, even though they believed gays to be crazy and supposed themselves to be experts in detecting craziness.[3] These studies proved a profound embarrassment to the psychiatric establishment, the financial well-being of which has been substantially enhanced by "curing" allegedly insane gays. The studies led the way to the American Psychiatric Association finally dropping homosexuality from its registry of mental illnesses in 1973.[4] Nevertheless, the stereotype of gays as sick continues apace in the mind of America.

False generalizations *help maintain* stereotypes, they do not *form* them. As the history of Hooker's discoveries shows, stereotypes have a life beyond facts; their origin lies in a culture's ideology—the general system of beliefs by which it lives—and they are sustained across generations by diverse cultural transmissions, hardly any of which, including slang and jokes, even purport to have a scientific basis. Stereotypes, then, are not the products of bad science but are social constructions that perform central functions in maintaining society's conception of itself.

On this understanding, it is easy to see that the antigay stereotypes surrounding gender identification are chiefly means of reinforcing still powerful gender roles in society. If, as this stereotype presumes and condemns, one is free to choose one's social roles independently of gender, many guiding social divisions, both domestic and commercial, might be threatened. The socially gender-linked distinctions between breadwinner and homemaker, boss and secretary, doctor and nurse, protector and protected would blur. The accusations "fag" and "dyke" exist in significant part to keep women in their place and to prevent men from breaking ranks and ceding away theirs.

The stereotypes of gays as child molesters, sex-crazed maniacs, and civilization destroyers function to displace (socially irresolvable) problems from their actual source to a foreign (and so, it is thought, manageable) one. Thus, the stereotype of child molester functions to give the family unit a false sheen of absolute innocence. It keeps the unit from being examined too closely for incest, child abuse, wife battering, and the terrorism of constant threats. The stereotype teaches that the problems of the family are not internal to it, but external.[5]

One can see these cultural forces at work in society's and the media's treatment of current reports of violence, especially domestic violence. When a mother kills her child or a father rapes his daughter—regular Section B fare even in major urbane papers—this is never taken by reporters, column-

ists, or pundits as evidence that there is something wrong with heterosexuality or with traditional families. These issues are not even raised. But when a homosexual child molestation is reported, it is taken as confirming evidence of the way homosexuals are. One never hears of heterosexual murders, but one regularly hears of "homosexual" ones. Compare the social treatment of Richard Speck's sexually motivated mass murder of Chicago nurses with that of John Wayne Gacy's murders of Chicago youths. Gacy was in the culture's mind taken as symbolic of gay men in general. To prevent the possibility that "The Family" was viewed as anything but an innocent victim in this affair, the mainstream press knowingly failed to mention that most of Gacy's adolescent victims were homeless hustlers. That knowledge would be too much for the six o'clock news and for cherished beliefs.

Because "the facts" largely don't matter when it comes to the generation and maintenance of stereotypes, the effects of scientific and academic research and of enlightenment generally will be, at best, slight and gradual in the changing fortunes of lesbians and gay men. If this account of stereotypes holds, society has been profoundly immoral. For its treatment of gays is a grand scale rationalization, a moral sleight-of-hand. The problem is not that society's usual standards of evidence and procedure in coming to judgments of social policy have been misapplied to gays; rather, when it comes to gays, the standards themselves have simply been ruled out of court and disregarded in favor of mechanisms that encourage unexamined fear and hatred.

Are Gays Discriminated Against? Does It Matter?

Partly because lots of people suppose they don't know any gay people and partly through willful ignorance of its own workings, society at large is unaware of the many ways in which gays are subject to discrimination in consequence of widespread fear and hatred. Contributing to this social ignorance of discrimination is the difficulty for gay people, as an invisible minority, even to complain of discrimination. For if one is gay, to register a complaint would suddenly target one as a stigmatized person, and so in the absence of any protections against discrimination, would simply invite additional discrimination. Further, many people, especially those who are persistently downtrodden and so lack a firm sense of self to begin with, tend either to blame themselves for their troubles or to view injustice as a matter of bad luck rather than as indicating something wrong with society. The latter recognition would require doing something to rectify wrong, and most people, especially the already beleaguered, simply aren't up to that. So for a number of reasons discrimination against gays, like rape, goes seriously underreported.

First, gays are subject to violence and harassment based simply on their perceived status rather than because of any actions they have performed. A recent extensive study by the National Gay Task Force found that over 90 percent of gays and lesbians had been victimized in some form on the basis of their sexual orientation.[6] Greater than one in five gay men and nearly one in ten lesbians had been punched, hit, or kicked, a quarter of all gays had had objects thrown at them, a third had been chased, a third had been sexually harassed, and 14 percent had been spit on—all just for being perceived as gay.

The most extreme form of antigay violence is queerbashing—where groups of young men target a person who they suppose is a gay man and beat and kick him unconscious and sometimes to death amid a torrent of taunts and slurs. Such seemingly random but in reality socially encouraged violence has the same social origin and function as lynchings of blacks—to keep the whole stigmatized group in line. As with lynchings of the recent past, the police and courts have routinely averted their eyes, giving their implicit approval to the practice.

Few such cases with gay victims reach the courts. Those that do are marked by inequitable procedures and results. Frequently judges will describe queerbashers as "just all-American boys." Recently a District of Columbia judge handed suspended sentences to queerbashers whose victim had been stalked, beaten, stripped at knifepoint, slashed, kicked, threatened with castration, and pissed on, because the judge thought the bashers were good boys at heart—after all, they went to a religious prep school.[7]

Police and juries will simply discount testimony from gays; they typically construe assaults on and murders of gays as "justified" self-defense— the killer need only claim his act was a panicked response to a sexual overture. Alternatively, when guilt seems patent, juries will accept highly implausible "diminished capacity" defenses, as in the case of Dan White's 1978 assassination of openly gay San Francisco city [supervisor] Harvey Milk— Hostess Twinkies made him do it.[8]

These inequitable procedures and results collectively show that the life and liberty of gays, like those of blacks, simply count for less than the life and liberty of members of the dominant culture.

The equitable rule of law is the heart of an orderly society. The collapse of the rule of law for gays shows that society is willing to perpetrate the worst possible injustices against them. Conceptually there is only a difference in degree between the collapse of the rule of law and systematic extermination of members of a population simply for having some group status independently of any act an individual has performed. In the Nazi concentration camps, gays were forced to wear pink triangles as identifying badges, just as Jews were forced to wear yellow stars. In remembrance of that collapse of the rule of law, the pink triangle has become the chief symbol of the gay rights movement.[9]

Gays are subject to widespread discrimination in employment—the very means by which one puts bread on one's table and one of the chief means by which individuals identify themselves to themselves and achieve personal dignity. Governments are leading offenders here. They do a lot of discriminating themselves, require that others do it ([such as] government contractors), and set precedents favoring discrimination in the private sector. The federal government explicitly discriminates against gays in the armed forces, the CIA, FBI, National Security Agency, and the State Department. The federal government refuses to give security clearances to gays and so forces the country's considerable private-sector military and aerospace contractors to fire known gay employees. State and local governments regularly fire gay teachers, policemen, firemen, social workers, and anyone who has contact with the public. Further, states through licensing laws officially bar gays from a vast array of occupations and professions—everything from doctors, lawyers, accountants, and nurses to hairdressers, morticians, and used car dealers. The American Civil Liberties Union's handbook *The Rights of Gay People* lists 307 such prohibited occupations.[10]

Gays are subject to discrimination in a wide variety of other ways, including private-sector employment, public accommodations, housing, immigration and naturalization, insurance of all types, custody and adoption, and zoning regulations that bar "singles" or "nonrelated" couples. All of these discriminations affect central components of a meaningful life; some even reach to the means by which life itself is sustained. In half the states, where gay sex is illegal, the central role of sex to meaningful life is officially denied to gays.

All these sorts of discriminations also affect the ability of people to have significant intimate relations. It is difficult for people to live together as couples without having their sexual orientation perceived in the public realm and so becoming targets for discrimination. Illegality, discrimination, and the absorption by gays of society's hatred of them all interact to impede or block altogether the ability of gays and lesbians to create and maintain significant personal relations with loved ones. So every facet of life is affected by discrimination. Only the most compelling reasons could justify it.

But Aren't They Immoral?

Many people think society's treatment of gays is justified because they think gays are extremely immoral. To evaluate this claim, different senses of *moral* must be distinguished. Sometimes by *morality* is meant the overall beliefs affecting behavior in a society—its mores, norms, and customs. On this understanding, gays certainly are not moral: Lots of people hate them and social customs are designed to register widespread disapproval of gays. The problem here is that this sense of morality is merely a *descriptive* one. On this understanding *every* society has a morality—even Nazi society, which had racism and mob rule as central features of its "morality" understood in this sense. What is needed in order to use the notion of morality to praise or condemn behavior is a sense of morality that is *prescriptive* or *normative*—a sense of morality whereby, for instance, the descriptive morality of the Nazis is found wanting.

As the Nazi example makes clear, that something is descriptively moral is nowhere near enough to make it normatively moral. [The fact that] a lot of people in a society say something is good, even over eons, does not make it so. Our rejection of the long history of socially approved and state-enforced slavery is another good example of this principle at work. Slavery would be wrong even if nearly everyone liked it. So consistency and fairness require that we abandon the belief that gays are immoral simply because most people dislike or disapprove of gays or gay acts, or even because gay sex acts are illegal.

Furthermore, recent historical and anthropological research has shown that opinion about gays has been by no means universally negative. Historically, it has varied widely even within the larger part of the Christian era and even within the church itself.[11] There are even societies—current ones—where homosexuality is not only tolerated but a universal compulsory part of social maturation.[12] Within the last thirty years, American society has undergone a grand turnabout from deeply ingrained, near total condemnation to near total acceptance on two emotionally charged "moral" or "family" issues: contraception and divorce. Society holds its current descriptive morality of gays not because it has to, but because it chooses to.

If popular opinion and custom are not enough to ground moral condemnation of homosexuality, perhaps religion can. Such argument[s] proceed along two lines. One claims that the condemnation is a direct revelation of God, usually through the Bible; the other claims to be able to detect condemnation in God's plan as manifested in nature.

One of the more remarkable discoveries of recent gay research is that the Bible may not be as univocal in its condemnation of homosexuality as has been usually believed.[13] Christ never mention[ed] homosexuality. Recent interpreters of the Old Testament have pointed out that the story of Lot at Sodom is probably intended to condemn inhospitality rather than homosexuality. Further, some of the Old Testament condemnations of homosexuality seem simply to be ways of tarring those of the Israelites' opponents who happen to accept homosexual practices when the Israelites themselves did not. If so, the condemnation is merely a quirk of history and rhetoric rather than a moral precept.

What does seem clear is that those who regularly cite the Bible to condemn an activity like homosexuality do so by reading it selectively. Do ministers who cite what they take to be condemnations of homosexuality in Leviticus maintain in their lives all the hygienic and dietary laws of Leviticus? If they cite the story of Lot at Sodom to condemn homosexuality, do they also cite the story of Lot in the cave to praise incestuous rape? It seems then not that the Bible is being used to ground condemnations of homosexuality as much as society's dislike of homosexuality is being used to interpret the Bible.[14]

Even if a consistent portrait of condemnation could be gleaned from the Bible, what social significance should it be given? One of the guiding principles of society, enshrined in the [U.S.] Constitution as a check against the government, is that decisions affecting social policy are not made on religious grounds. If the real ground of the alleged immorality invoked by governments to discriminate against gays is religious (as it has explicitly been even in some recent court cases involving teachers and guardians), then one of the major commitments of our nation is violated.

But Aren't They Unnatural?

The most noteworthy feature of the accusation of something being unnatural (where a moral rather than an advertising point is being made) is that the plaint is so infrequently made. One used to hear the charge leveled against abortion, but that has pretty much faded as antiabortionists have come to lay all their chips on the hope that people will come to view abortion as murder. Incest used to be considered unnatural but discourse now usually assimilates it to the moral machinery of rape and violated trust. The charge comes up now in ordinary discourse only against homosexuality. This suggests that the charge is highly idiosyncratic and has little, if any, explanatory force. It fails to put homosexuality in a class with anything else so that one can learn by comparison with clear cases of the class just exactly what it is that is allegedly wrong with it.

Though the accusation of unnaturalness looks whimsical, in actual ordinary discourse when applied to homosexuality, it is usually delivered with venom of forethought. It carries a high emotional charge, usually expressing disgust and evincing queasiness. Probably it is nothing but an emotional charge. For people get equally disgusted and queasy at all sorts of things that are perfectly natural—to be expected in nature apart from artifice—and that

could hardly be fit subjects for moral condemnation. Two typical examples in current American culture are some people's responses to mothers' suckling in public and to women who do not shave body hair. When people have strong emotional reactions, as they do in these cases, without being able to give good reasons for them, we think of them not as operating morally, but rather as being obsessed and maniac. So the feelings of disgust that some people have to gays will hardly ground a charge of immorality. People fling the term *unnatural* against gays in the same breath and with the same force as when they call gays "sick" and "gross." When they do this, they give every appearance of being neurotically fearful and incapable of reasoned discourse.

When *nature* is taken in *technical* rather than ordinary usage, it looks like the notion also will not ground a charge of homosexual immorality. When *unnatural* means "by artifice" or "made by humans," it need only be pointed out that virtually everything that is good about life is unnatural in this sense, that the chief feature that distinguishes people from other animals is their very ability to make over the world to meet their needs and desires, and that their well-being depends upon these departures from nature. On this understanding of human nature and the natural, homosexuality is perfectly unobjectionable.

Another technical sense of *natural* is that something is natural, and so, good, if it fulfills some function in nature. Homosexuality on this view is unnatural because it allegedly violates the function of genitals, which is to produce babies. One problem with this view is that lots of bodily parts have lots of functions and just because some one activity can be fulfilled by only one organ (say, the mouth for eating) this activity does not condemn other functions of the organ to immorality (say, the mouth for talking, licking stamps, blowing bubbles, or having sex). So the possible use of the genitals to produce children does not, without more, condemn the use of the genitals for other purposes, say, achieving ecstasy and intimacy.

The functional view of nature will only provide a morally condemnatory sense to the unnatural if a thing which might have many uses has but one proper function to the exclusion of other possible functions. But whether this is so cannot be established simply by looking at the thing. For what is seen is all its possible functions. The notion of function seemed like it might ground moral authority, but instead it turns out that moral authority is needed to define proper function. Some people try to fill in this moral authority by appeal to the "design" or "order" of an organ, saying, for instance, that the genitals are designed for the purpose of procreation. But these people cheat intellectually if they do not make explicit *who* the designer and orderer is. If it is God, we are back to square one—holding others accountable for religious beliefs.

Further, ordinary moral attitudes about child-rearing will not provide the needed supplement, which, in conjunction with the natural function view of bodily parts, would produce a positive obligation to use the genitals for procreation. Society's attitude toward a childless couple is that of pity not censure—even if the couple could have children. The pity may be an unsympathetic one, that is, not registering a course one would choose *for oneself*, but this does not make it a course one would *require* of others. The couple who discovers it cannot have children is viewed not as having thereby had a debt canceled, but rather as having to forgo some of the richness of life, just as a quadriplegic is not viewed as absolved from some moral obligation to hop, skip, and jump, but is viewed as missing some of the richness of life. Consistency requires then that, at most, gays who do not or cannot have children are to be pitied rather than condemned. What *is* immoral is the willful preventing of people from achieving the richness of life. Immorality in this regard lies with those social customs, regulations, and statues that prevent lesbians and gay men from establishing blood or adoptive families, not with gays themselves.

Sometimes people attempt to establish authority for a moral obligation to use bodily parts in a certain fashion simply by claiming that moral laws are natural laws and vice versa. On this account, inanimate objects and plants are good in that they follow natural laws by necessity, animals by instinct, and persons by a rational will. People are special in that they must first discover the laws that govern them. Now, even if one believes the view—dubious in the post-Newtonian, post-Darwinian world—that natural laws in the usual sense ($e = mc^2$, for instance) have some moral content, it is not at all clear how one is to discover the laws in nature that apply to people.

If, on the one hand, one looks to people themselves for a model—and looks hard enough—one finds amazing variety, including homosexuality as a social ideal (upper-class 5th-century Athenians) and even as socially mandatory (Melanesia today). When one looks to people, one is simply unable to strip away the layers of social custom, history, and taboo in order to see what's really there to any degree more specific than that people are the creatures that make over their world and are capable of abstract thought. That this is so should raise doubts that neutral principles are to be found in human nature that will condemn homosexuality.

On the other hand, if one looks to nature apart from people for models, the possibilities are staggering. There are fish that change gender over their lifetimes: Should we "follow nature" and be operative transsexuals? Orangutans, genetically our next of kin, live completely solitary lives without social organization of any kind: Ought we to "follow nature" and be hermits? There are many species where only two members per generation reproduce: Shall we be bees? The search in nature for people's purpose—far from finding sure models for action—is likely to leave one morally rudderless.

But Aren't Gays Willfully the Way They Are?

It is generally conceded that if sexual orientation is something over which an individual—for whatever reason—has virtually no control, then discrimination against gays is especially deplorable, as it is against racial and ethnic classes, because it holds people accountable without regard for anything they themselves have done. And to hold a person accountable for that over which the person has no control is a central form of prejudice.

Attempts to answer the question whether or not sexual orientation is something that is reasonably thought to be within one's own control usually appeal simply to various claims of the biological or "mental" sciences. But the ensuing debate over genes, hormones, twins, early childhood development, and the like is as unnecessary as it is currently inconclusive.[15] All that is needed to answer the question is to look at the actual experience of gays in current society, and it becomes fairly clear that sexual orientation is not likely a matter of choice. For coming to have a homosexual identity simply does not have the same sort of structure that decision-making has.

On the one hand, the "choice" of the gender of a sexual partner does not seem to express a trivial desire which might be as easily well fulfilled by a simple substitution of the desired object. Picking the gender of a sex partner is decidedly dissimilar, that is, to such activities as picking a flavor of ice cream. If an ice-cream parlor is out of one's flavor, one simply picks another. And if people were persecuted, threatened with jail terms, shattered careers, loss of family and housing and the like for eating, say, rocky road ice cream, no one would ever eat it; everyone would pick another easily available flavor. That gay people abide in being gay even in the face of persecution shows that being gay is not a matter of easy choice.

On the other hand, even if establishing a sexual orientation is not like making a relatively trivial choice, perhaps it is nevertheless relevantly like making the central and serious life choices by which individuals try to establish themselves as being of some type. Again, if one examines gay experience, this seems not to be the case. For one never sees anyone setting out to become a homosexual, in the way one does see people setting out to become doctors, lawyers, and bricklayers. One does not find gays-to-be picking some end—"At some point in the future, I want to become a homosexual"—and then set[ting] about planning and acquiring the ways and means to that end, in the way one does see people deciding that they want to become lawyers, and then sees them plan[ning] what courses to take and what sort of temperaments, habits, and skills to develop in order to become lawyers. Typically gays-to-be simply find themselves having homosexual encounters and yet at least initially resisting quite strongly the identification of being homosexual. Such a person even very likely resists having such encounters but ends up having them anyway. Only with time, luck, and great personal effort, but sometimes never, does the person gradually come to accept her or his orientation, to view it as a given material condition of life, coming as materials do with certain capacities and limitations. The person begins to act in accordance with his or her orientation and its capacities, seeing its actualization as a requisite for an integrated personality and as a central component of personal well-being. As a result, the experience of coming out to oneself has

for gays the basic structure of a discovery, not the structure of a choice. And far from signaling immorality, coming out to others affords one of the few remaining opportunities in ever more bureaucratic, mechanistic, and socialistic societies to manifest courage.

How Would Society at Large Be Changed if Gays Were Socially Accepted?

Suggestions to change social policy with regard to gays are invariably met with claims that to do so would invite the destruction of civilization itself: After all, isn't that what did Rome in? Actually Rome's decay paralleled not the flourishing of homosexuality, but its repression under the later Christianized emperors.[16] Predictions of American civilization's imminent demise have been as premature as they have been frequent. Civilization has shown itself rather resilient here, in large part because of the country's traditional commitments to a respect for privacy, to individual liberties, and especially to people minding their own business. These all give society an open texture and the flexibility to try out things to see what works. And because of this one now need not speculate about what changes reforms in gay social policy might bring to society at large. For many reforms have already been tried.

Half the states have decriminalized homosexual acts. Can you guess which of the following states still have sodomy laws? Wisconsin, Minnesota; New Mexico, Arizona; Vermont, New Hampshire; Nebraska, Kansas. One from each pair does and one does not have sodomy laws. And yet one would be hard pressed to point out any substantial difference between the members of each pair. (If you're interested: It is the second of each pair with them.) Empirical studies have shown that there is no increase in other crimes in states that have decriminalized [homosexual acts].[17] Further, sodomy laws are virtually never enforced. They remain on the books not to "protect society" but to insult gays and, for that reason, need to be removed.

Neither has the passage of legislation barring discrimination against gays ushered in the end of civilization. Some 50 counties and municipalities, including some of the country's largest cities (like Los Angeles and Boston) have passed such statutes and among the states and [counties] Wisconsin and the District of Columbia have model protective codes. Again, no more brimstone has fallen in these places than elsewhere. Staunchly antigay cities, like Miami and Houston, have not been spared the AIDS crisis.

Berkeley, California, has even passed domestic partner legislation giving gay couples the same rights to city benefits as married couples, and yet Berkeley has not become more weird than it already was.

Seemingly hysterical predictions that the American family would collapse if such reforms would pass proved false, just as the same dire predictions that the availability of divorce would lessen the ideal and desirability of marriage proved completely unfounded. Indeed, if current discriminations, which drive gays into hiding and into anonymous relations, were lifted, far from seeing gays raze American families, one would see gays forming them.

Virtually all gays express a desire to have a permanent lover. Many would like to raise or foster children—perhaps [from among the] alarming number of gay kids who have been beaten up and thrown out of their "families" for being gay. But currently society makes gay coupling very difficult. A life of hiding is a pressure-cooker existence not easily shared with another. Members of nongay couples are here asked to imagine what it would take to erase every trace of their own sexual orientation for even just a week.

Even against oppressive odds, gays have shown an amazing tendency to nest. And those gay couples who have survived the odds show that the structure of more usual couplings is not a matter of destiny but of personal responsibility. The so-called basic unit of society turns out not to be a unique immutable atom but can adopt different parts, be adapted to different needs, and even be improved. Gays might even have a thing or two to teach others about divisions of labor, the relation of sensuality and intimacy, and stages of development in such relations.

If discrimination ceased, gay men and lesbians would enter the mainstream of the human community openly and with self-respect. The energies that the typical gay person wastes in the anxiety of leading a day-to-day existence of systematic disguise would be released for use in personal flourishing. From this release would be generated the many spin-off benefits that accrue to a society when its individual members thrive.

Society would be richer for acknowledging another aspect of human richness and diversity. Families with gay members would develop relations based on truth and trust rather than lies and fear. And the heterosexual majority would be better off for knowing that they are no longer trampling their gay friends and neighbors.

Finally and perhaps paradoxically, in extending to gays the rights and benefits it has reserved for its dominant culture, America would confirm its deeply held vision of itself as a morally progressing nation, a nation itself advancing and serving as a beacon for others—especially with regard to human rights. The words with which our national pledge ends—"with liberty and justice for all"—are not a description of the present but a call for the future. Ours is a nation given to a prophetic political rhetoric which acknowledges that morality is not arbitrary and that justice is not merely the expression of the current collective will. It is this vision that led the black civil rights movement to its successes. Those congressmen who opposed that movement and its centerpiece, the 1964 Civil Rights Act, on obscurantist grounds, but who lived long enough and were noble enough came in time to express their heartfelt regret and shame at what they had done. It is to be hoped and someday to be expected that those who now grasp at anything to oppose the extension of that which is best about America to gays will one day feel the same.

Notes

1. "Public Fears—and Sympathies," *Newsweek* (August 12, 1985), p. 23.

2. Alfred C. Kinsey, *Sexual Behavior in the Human Male* (Philadelphia: Saunders, 1948), pp. 650–51. On the somewhat lower incidences of lesbianism, see Alfred C. Kinsey, *Sexual Behavior in the Human Female* (Philadelphia: Saunders, 1953), pp. 472–75.

3. Evelyn Hooker, "The Adjustment of the Male Overt Homosexual," *Journal of Projective Techniques* 21 (1957), pp. 18–31, reprinted in Hendrik M. Ruitenbeek, ed., *The Problem of Homosexuality* (New York: Dutton, 1963), pp. 141–61.

4. See Ronald Bayer, *Homosexuality and American Psychiatry* (New York: Basic Books, 1981).

5. For studies showing that gay men are no more likely—indeed, are less likely—than heterosexuals

to be child molesters and that the largest classes and most persistent sexual abusers of children are the children's fathers, stepfathers, or mother's boyfriends, see Vincent De Francis, *Protecting the Child Victim of Sex Crimes Committed by Adults* (Denver: The American Humane Association, 1969), pp. *vii*, 38, 69–70; A. Nicholas Groth, "Adult Sexual Orientation and Attraction to Underage Persons," *Archives of Sexual Behavior* 7 (1978), pp. 175–81; Mary J. Spencer, "Sexual Abuse of Boys," *Pediatrics* 78:1 (July 1986), pp. 133–38.

6. See National Gay Task Force, *Antigay/Lesbian Victimization* (New York: NGTF, 1984).

7. "2 St. John's Students Given Probation in Assault on Gay," *The Washington Post* (May 15, 1984), p. 1.

8. See Randy Shilts, *The Mayor of Castro Street: The Life and Times of Harvey Milk* (New York: St. Martin's, 1982), pp. 308–25.

9. See Richard Plant, *The Pink Triangle: The Nazi War Against Homosexuals* (New York: Holt, 1986).

10. E. Carrington Boggan, *The Rights of Gay People: The Basic ACLU Guide to a Gay Person's Rights*, 1st ed. (New York: Avon, 1975), pp. 211–35.

11. John Boswell, *Christianity, Social Tolerance, and Homosexuality: Gay People in Western Europe from the Beginning of the Christian Era to the Fourteenth Century* (Chicago: The University of Chicago Press, 1980).

12. See Gilbert Herdt, *Guardians of the Flute: Idioms of Masculinity* (New York: McGraw-Hill, 1981), pp. 232–39, 284–88, and see generally Gilbert Herdt, ed., *Ritualized Homosexuality in Melanesia* (Berkeley: University of California Press, 1984). For another eye-opener, see Walter J. Williams, *The Spirit and the Flesh: Sexual Diversity in American Indian Culture* (Boston: Beacon, 1986).

13. See especially Boswell, *op. cit.*, Chapter 4.

14. For Old Testament condemnations of homosexual acts, see Leviticus 18:22, 21:3. For hygienic and dietary codes, see, for example, Leviticus 15:19–27 (on the uncleanliness of women) and Leviticus 11:1–47 (on not eating rabbits, pigs, bats, finless water creatures, legless creeping creatures, and so on). For Lot at Sodom, see Genesis 19:1–25. For Lot in the cave, see Genesis 19:30–38.

15. The preponderance of the scientific evidence supports the view that homosexuality is either genetically determined or a permanent result of early childhood development. See the Kinsey Institute's study by Alan Bell, Martin Weinberg, and Sue Hammersmith, *Sexual Preference: Its Development in Men and Women* (Bloomington: Indiana University Press, 1981); Frederick Whitam and Robin Mathy, *Male Homosexuality in Four Societies* (New York: Praeger, 1986), Chapter 7.

16. See Boswell, *op. cit.*, Chapter 3.

17. See Gilbert Geis, "Reported Consequences of Decriminalization of Consensual Adult Homosexuality in Seven American States," *Journal of Homosexuality* 1:4 (1976), pp. 419–26; Ken Sinclair and Michael Ross, "Consequences of Decriminalization of Homosexuality: A Study of Two Australian States," *Journal of Homosexuality* 12:1 (1985), pp. 119–27.

Questions for Analysis

1. What does Mohr mean by his claim that homosexual stereotypes are "chiefly means of reinforcing still powerful gender roles in society"? How does he support the claim?

2. Are homosexual stereotypes as independent of the facts about homosexuals as Mohr argues they are?

3. Why does Mohr think that discrimination against homosexuals is morally unjustified?

4. According to Mohr, nature gives us no guide to human purpose or action. Why not? What kinds of examples does he provide in support of the claim?

5. Mohr argues that a homosexual's "coming out" is more like a discovery than a decision. What relevance does that have to the issues of whether homosexual behavior is moral and whether society ought to accept homosexuals?

6. *What benefits does Mohr feel that society would get by granting full acceptance to homosexuals? What fears of such acceptance does he reject as unjustified? Why?*

CASE PRESENTATION
Deception or Joke?

They were two unmarried business travelers who met in a limousine on their way to the airport. Since both had some time before their flights, he offered to buy her a drink in the airport bar. She accepted.

One of the first things they learned over their drinks was that they lived two thousand miles apart.

"Excellent," he said. "Will you marry me?"

"What?"

"Look, it'll be perfect. You'll live in your place, I'll live in mine, and we'll get together a few times a year. A marriage like that is bound to last."

He was kidding, of course, but it seemed to be an innocent enough joke. Unfortunately, she was slow to catch on.

"You think so?" she finally asked.

"Absolutely."

"Yes, maybe you're right." She pulled out her appointment book and turned a few pages. "The weekend after next I'm free. Why don't we spend it together, at my place."

And they did just that. On the appointed day, she picked him up at her city's airport and drove him back to her apartment, where they spent the next two nights.

"What next?" she asked during Sunday dinner. It was the last dinner of his visit. His plane was to leave in three hours.

"Well," he laughed, "we'll certainly keep in touch." He meant what he said. He was already looking forward to their next weekend.

"That's it?" She was not smiling. Her eyes were focused on her wine glass.

"What did you expect?"

She said nothing, nor did she look up.

"You're not thinking about what I said in the airport, are you?"

This time she did look up, with a slight smile. "I'm not?"

"But I was joking."

"I wasn't."

He explained to her all the reasons why it would be preposterous for them to get married, chief among them the fact that they hardly knew each other. She explained to him all the reasons that she'd invited him to spend the weekend with her, chief among them the fact that she'd taken his remarks about marriage seriously.

"Nobody could be serious about that," he told her.

"I was. And I thought you were too. That's what attracted me to you. You seemed adventurous, decisive, self-assured, the kind of man who'd get a crazy whim like that and act on it. You do give that impression, you know, but you're a fraud. You're just like the other men I come across. You've got a million reasons for wanting a woman to fall in love with you, and a million and one reasons not to get married."

"But—"

"But nothing. I didn't expect us to set a date, you know. I'm not a total lunatic, whatever you might think. But I certainly expected something more than 'we'll keep in touch.' "

A long period of awkwardness followed, after which she drove him to the airport. Much to his surprise, she kissed him goodbye. A few days later she called to tell him that she didn't want to see him again.

Questions for Analysis

1. *Was it unreasonable of the woman to expect more of the man than he gave her?*

2. *Did the man have any reason to believe that the woman would take him seriously? Should he have made it clear that he was joking?*

3. *What does the incident suggest about the possibility of unintentional deception in such sexual adventures?*

4. *Does the incident suggest that moral casual sex is rarer than the libertarian position might indicate?*

CASE PRESENTATION
AIDS Education

In a statement issued by the U.S. Public Health Service in October 1986, U.S. Surgeon General C. Everett Koop said:

> Many people—especially our youth—are not receiving information that is vital to their future health and well-being because of our reticence in dealing with the subjects of sex, sexual practices, and homosexuality. This silence must end. We can no longer afford to sidestep frank, open discussion about sexual practices—homosexual and heterosexual. Education about AIDS should start at an early age so that children can grow up knowing the behaviors to avoid to protect themselves from exposure to the AIDS virus.

Considered in terms of public *health* policy, Koop's plea seems unexceptionable. In the face of any medical epidemic, the more knowledgeable the public, the safer the public. But Koop's plea has *moral* implications as well, and those implications have made it very controversial. According to his opponents, Koop is promoting the teaching of "safe sodomy" to children. They agree that children should be taught to avoid behavior that transmits the AIDS virus, but for them—including Secretary of Education William Bennett—that means teaching sexual abstinence.

No one doubts that abstinence is the surest way of avoiding sexual transmission of AIDS. But Koop and his supporters argue that *teaching* abstinence does not always *lead* to abstinence. Therefore, safe sex must be taught as well.

In the spring of 1988, while the debate continued, the Public Health Service mailed the pamphlet *Understanding AIDS* to every home in the country. Although the pamphlet was intended primarily for adults, the term "safe sex" does not appear anywhere in it. Also, under the heading "Safe Behavior," both abstinence and monogamy with an uninfected partner are listed, but no other sexual behavior. Still, there is a section on condom use as a safety measure, including recommendations concerning what kind of condom to use and how to use it, and elsewhere in the pamphlet mention is made of vaginal, oral, and anal sex and their role in the transmission of AIDS. Why not give the same information in the schools?

One reason given by Koop's opponents is the concern that students will interpret their instruction as *advocacy* of sexual promiscuity and homosexuality as long as condoms are used. Another involves the relative ignorance of schoolchildren. Since many do not know what oral and anal sex are, these acts must be explained to them. But schools should not be in the business of teaching children how to perform sodomy (hence the derisive term "safe sodomy").

Koop's supporters, of course, argue that the information can be conveyed without giving the impression of advocacy and that the AIDS threat requires that children receive it. But that brings us to the heart of the matter. To many people, the AIDS threat cannot require us to teach "immoral" behavior to children. They see such behavior as the problem, not the solution.

Questions for Analysis

1. *Is the surgeon general right? Should we overcome our reticence about sex in the face of the AIDS threat?*

2. *Do moral disagreements about sex have a legitimate role in public health matters, or should policy decisions be made purely on the grounds of effectiveness?*

3. *Can information about safe sex be given to children in a morally neutral way? Would moral neutrality come across as moral acceptance?*

4. *At what age do children become old enough to receive the information the surgeon general thinks they should have?*

5. *Would learning about anal and oral sex hurt schoolchildren?*

Selections for Further Reading

Atkinson, Ronald. *Sexual Morality*. New York: Harcourt Brace and World, 1965.

Baker, Robert, and Frederick Elliston, eds. *Philosophy and Sex*. New rev. ed. Buffalo, N.Y.: Prometheus, 1984.

Jaggar, Alison M., and Paula Rothenberg Struhl, eds. *Feminist Frameworks*. New York: McGraw-Hill, 1978.

Morrison, Eleanor S., and Vera Borosage, eds. *Human Sexuality: Contemporary Perspectives*. 2nd ed. Palo Alto: Mayfield, 1977.

Pierce, Christine, and Donald VanDeVeer, eds. *AIDS: Ethics and Public Policy*. Belmont, Calif.: Wadsworth, 1987.

Punzo, Vincent C. *Reflective Naturalism*. New York: Macmillan, 1969.

Russell, Bertrand. *Marriage and Morals*. New York: Liveright, 1970.

Scruton, Roger. *Sexual Desire: A Moral Philosophy of the Erotic*. New York: The Free Press, 1986.

Soble, Alan, ed. *Philosophy of Sex*. Totowa, N.J.: Littlefield, Adams and Co., 1980.

Taylor, Richard. *Having Love Affairs*. Buffalo, N.Y.: Prometheus, 1982.

Vannoy, Russell. *Sex Without Love: A Philosophical Investigation*. Buffalo, N.Y.: Prometheus, 1980.

Whitely, C. H., and W. M. Whitely. *Sex and Morals*. New York: Basic Books, 1967.

4
PORNOGRAPHY

In 1972 the state of Georgia sought an injunction against the showing of two films by the Paris Adult Theatres I and II of Atlanta. The state claimed that the films—*It All Comes Out in the End* and *Magic Mirror*—were obscene under relevant Georgia standards. The trial court demurred, saying an injunction could be granted only if it could be proved that the films were being shown to minors or nonconsenting adults. The state appealed the decision, and the Georgia Supreme Court reversed it. Eventually the U.S. Supreme Court upheld the reversal by a 5–4 majority.[1]

In writing the majority decision, Chief Justice Warren Burger argued that the state is justified in restricting consenting adults' access to obscene material in order to maintain public safety and a decent society, including a proper tone of commerce. In dissenting, Justice William Brennan wrote that state efforts to totally suppress obscene material inevitably would lead to erosion of protected free speech and overburden the nation's judicial machinery.

Were the films in question "obscene"? If they were, should their showing have been prohibited? Or should consenting adults have been allowed to see the films, even if the films were obscene? These are some of the prominent questions the Supreme Court addressed in *Paris I,* and has in many similar cases. And it's a safe bet that such issues will continue to appear on the Court's docket, for pornography is a multibillion-dollar-a-year business whose seemingly uncontrollable growth has individuals, institutions, and government agencies alarmed.

Among those concerned is the U.S. Congress, which has labeled traffic in pornographic materials a matter of national concern. In 1966 Congress established the Commission on Obscenity and Pornography. The commission's responsibility was to make recommendations based on a thorough study of pornographic and obscene materials. In 1970 the commission submitted its report

1. Paris Adult Theatre I *v.* Slaton. *U.S. Supreme Court, 413, U.S. 49, 1973.*

to the President and Congress recommending that legislation prohibiting the sale, exhibition, and distribution of sexual material to consenting adults be repealed.

The commission's report met with widespread executive, legislative, and popular disapproval. In fact, the commission itself was divided: Six of the eighteen members did not support its recommendation. As a result, implementation has been sporadic.

Whether there should be laws restricting the consenting adult's access to pornography or not is a key moral question in the pornography issue. But an even more basic question—and one that often intrudes on the discussions of the morality of restrictive pornography legislation—is whether there is anything morally objectionable about pornographic materials.

In this chapter we shall consider both questions: the morality of pornographic materials and the morality of restrictive pornography laws. Central to both questions is the definition of pornography, so we shall begin our discussion by considering the problem of defining it. We will then air some of the arguments relative to the two main moral concerns that the pornography issue involves.

The Meaning of Pornography and Obscenity

The precise meanings of *pornography* and *obscenity* are important issues in the debate over our two questions. To decide whether pornography is morally objectionable, we must know what pornography is. And to decide whether some pornography should be censored, we must know what obscenity is.

The need to be clear about pornography is obvious. To understand why we must be clear about obscenity, we must understand the legal importance of the concept. The First Amendment to the Constitution guarantees us, among other things, freedom of expression. It requires that Congress pass "no law" abridging our freedom of speech or press. Despite the phrase "no law," the courts have held that certain kinds of expression are not protected by the First Amendment. We are not, for example, guaranteed the right to libel others, nor are we guaranteed the right to yell "Fire!" in a crowded theater. Nor, the courts have held, are we guaranteed the right to engage in the commercial distribution of obscene material. Obscenity, then, is not protected by the First Amendment. So to decide whether some pornographic material should be censored, we must know how to determine whether it is obscene as well as pornographic.

In general, *pornography* refers to erotic material that is *intended* primarily to cause sexual arousal in its audience or in fact *does* have that primary effect. Erotic drawings by Picasso, say, are not considered pornographic because of the artist's artistic intent and because, even though some viewers may be sexually stimulated by them, most viewers react to them in other ways as well. X-rated films like *Deep Throat*, on the other hand, are considered pornographic.

To call something pornographic, then, is to make a variety of judgments about it—about its artistic value, the intentions of its maker, and its effects on its audience. Although these judgments will vary somewhat from society to society and individual to individual, in the contemporary United States we have at least a rough idea of what counts as pornography and what doesn't. We also agree to a large extent on what counts as "soft-core" pornography—the photographs in *Playboy,* for instance, and the simulated sex scenes in some films—and what counts as "hard-core" pornography—films in which the actors actually engage in sex before the cameras.

That agreement falls apart when it comes to obscenity. For pornography to be obscene, it must also be offensive, disgusting, abominable, or the like. But what some people find offensive, others find pleasurable. What some find disgusting, others find attractive. And what some find abominable, others may find even valuable. In fact, such recognized masters of twentieth-century fiction as James Joyce, D. H. Lawrence, and Vladimir Nabokov have run afoul of American obscenity laws.

Since the First Amendment clearly does protect works of serious literary value, such examples have created a problem for the law. Can we define *obscenity* with enough precision to ensure that obscenity laws do not infringe on our constitutional rights? Supreme Court Justice William Brennan, in his dissenting opinion in the Paris theater case, argued that we cannot.

But Brennan's view remains a minority one on the Court, which continues to apply a definition of *obscenity* laid down in the landmark case *Roth* v. *United States* (1957).

In defining obscene material, the Court cited four basic characteristics. (1) The material must be considered in terms of its appeal to "the average person." This contrasted sharply with earlier definitions, which included material that might affect only those susceptible to it. (2) The material must be "patently offensive because it affronts contemporary community standards relating to the description or representation of sexual matters." (3) The work must be taken as a whole, not piecemeal; the dominant theme must be taken into account rather than material taken out of context. Thus the term *obscene* may be applied only to material whose *theme* satisfies the other elements of the definition. (4) The material must appeal only to "prurient interest." It must be totally lacking in any social value or importance. By the Court's account, then, a work is obscene if, considered in terms of its appeal to the average person, it offends community standards because its theme, taken as a whole, appeals to prurient interests and is without social value.

Is such a definition operational? No, say its detractors. They point out, first, that "average person" is a hopelessly vague phrase. Who, after all, is this so-called average person? And even if we could isolate such a creature, we could not freeze that person's attitudes, outlooks, and appetites so that they never changed.

The Court's critics see similar operational problems in the phrase "contemporary community standards." Just what "community" should we have in mind? The village, town, city, county, state, region, country? And even if we could agree on the community, can we really determine what the community's standards are? Perhaps some citizens' group should represent the view of the community. Or maybe each member of the community should be polled: If more individuals think a work obscene than not, then by the community's standards it is. Of course, we would have no way of knowing that the people judged the work pornographic on "legitimate" grounds: on its appeal to the average person, on its appeal to prurience, on its lack of social value.

In addition, critics argue that any judgment about a work's "prurience" is so subjective as to be useless. In the last analysis, they say, all such judgments will be little more than expressions of someone's beliefs.

Finally, there is the matter of "social value." Who can say what has social value? Sometimes what appears to have no social value turns out to be extremely worthwhile. In a dynamic, evolving society such as ours, it is very difficult, if not impossible, to say with assurance what has value and what does not. Might not a reasonable criterion for judging whether material has any redeeming value be whether it "plays," that is, whether it finds any audience? If it does, then it serves some social purpose; it has some social value. Moreover, the fact that what is repugnant to the vast majority of people can still find a niche in society may itself be a social value in reaffirming the full and open nature of our society.

Of course, the Supreme Court's definition is a legal one. What is ruled legally obscene may not be considered obscene by some individuals, and what is ruled legally not obscene may be considered obscene by some individuals. Ultimately, we all make such judgments based on what is offensive to us. Although his words will obviously not do as a legal definition of obscenity, Supreme Court Justice Potter Stewart did speak for many individuals when he said that he could not define *obscenity*, but "I know it when I see it."

Effects of Pornography

Despite the troublesome definitional problems, the Commission on Obscenity and Pornography did conduct a series of studies whose findings bear on the moral arguments we will consider shortly. At the outset, the commission avoided trying to define *pornographic* and *obscene*. Instead, it chose to discuss "erotic materials," which presumably deal with or arouse sexual feelings or desires. Without passing legal or moral judgment on such materials, the commission sought to determine what effects various erotic material had on people in a variety of contexts. Here are six of the commission's most important findings:

1. A significant number of persons masturbated more often after exposure to erotic materials.

2. Erotic dreams, sexual fantasies, and conversations about sexual matter tended to increase after exposure to erotic materials.

3. Where there was an increase in sexual activity, it generally tended to be temporary and didn't differ in kind from the sexual behavior the person was accustomed to engage in before exposure.

4. Some married couples reported more agreeable marital relations and a greater willingness to discuss sexual matters after exposure than before.

5. Both delinquent and nondelinquent youth have wide exposure to erotic materials.

6. There is no statistical correlation between sex crimes and exposure to erotic materials. (Incidentally, sex crimes decreased appreciably in Denmark after Danish law was changed to permit virtually unrestricted access to erotic materials.)

The commission's overall conclusion was that "empirical research designed to clarify the question has found no evidence to date that exposure to explicit sexual materials plays a significant role in the causation of delinquent or criminal behavior among youths or adults. The commission cannot conclude that exposure to erotic materials is a factor in the causation of sex crime or sex delinquency."[2]

It's worth noting that several commission members protested the commission's findings, and wrote a minority report to that effect. Among other things, the minority report claimed that the commission ignored or underrated important studies in its final report, such as the one that found a definite correlation between juvenile exposure to pornography and precocious heterosexual and deviant sexual behavior. Another study found a direct relation between the frequency with which adolescents saw movies depicting sexual intercourse and the extent to which they themselves engaged in premarital intercourse. Still another study found that rapists were the group reporting the highest rates of excitation to masturbation by pornography in both the adult and adolescent years. The significance of this last study, said the minority dissenters, is in its implication that exposure to pornography does not serve adequately as catharsis to prevent a sex crime, as some researchers have maintained. In fact, the dissenters claimed, it may do just the opposite. As evidence they again invoked this third study, which reported that 80 percent of prisoners who had been exposed to erotic materials said they "wished to try the act" they had seen. When asked whether they had acted on their desires, between 30 and 38 percent said they had. This figure is consistent with still another study, which reported that 39 percent of sex offenders said that pornography had something to do with their committing the crimes they were convicted of.[3]

What are we to make of these studies, whose findings often point to opposed conclusions regarding the effects of pornography? A completely satisfactory evaluation calls for analyses of the surveys' methods to ensure that they were genuinely scientific, a task we can't undertake here. Suffice it to say we should recall that a statistical correlation between two phenomena does not of itself establish a causal connection between them, and simply because one event follows another doesn't necessarily mean that the first caused the second. This is not to say, apropos the minority's view, that there is no causal connection between erotic materials and sexual behavior, only that the jury is still out. We don't have sufficient grounds at present to say that exposure to erotic materials has socially undesirable effects on those exposed to them. By the same token, the presently available evidence does not prove that such materials do not have these effects.

2. The Report of the Commission on Obscenity and Pornography (*New York: Bantam Books, 1970*), p. 31.

3. *Ibid., Part IV.*

Moral Issues

Pornography and obscenity raise numerous moral questions, two of which concern us here. The first may be phrased: Are pornographic materials in and of themselves morally objectionable, or are they not? We will call the various arguments connected with this question "Arguments against Pornographic Materials" and "Arguments for Pornographic Materials." The second question, which concerns the legality of pornography, may be stated: Is it right for the state to limit the consenting adult's access to obscene and pornographic material? In responding to this question, we will present "Arguments for Censorship" and "Arguments against Censorship."

It is most important to distinguish these two questions. Whether pornography is moral is a separate and distinct question from whether consenting adults should be allowed access to it. One could argue consistently that pornography is morally objectionable but that the state has no right to limit an adult's access to it. Or one might argue consistently that pornography is not morally objectionable but that the state ought to limit an adult's access to it.

There is another reason to keep the two issues separate. Often arguments for censorship assume that pornography is morally objectionable and, therefore, should be suppressed. Perhaps what is immoral ought to be suppressed, perhaps not. Whatever the view—and there are grounds for reasonable debate—the issue is strictly academic until it is established that pornography is, in fact, immoral. But often this is ignored; pornography is assumed to be immoral, and the argument moves inexorably toward its censorship.

So keep in mind the distinction between the morality of pornographic material and the morality of laws that restrict the adult's access to pornographic material. While obviously related by common subject, these important questions for the individual and society are significantly different, as we will see in the arguments connected with them.

Arguments against Pornographic Materials

1. *Pornography degrades humans.*

POINT: "Nobody can deny that every piece of pornography shares one thing with every other piece of pornography: It degrades humans. It presents in graphic detail a depraved picture of human life; it portrays humans functioning in a way less than human, wallowing in some animal level of lust and depravity, and inviting the spectators to join them. What's wrong with pornography? It affronts human dignity; in its portrayal of humans, it dehumanizes them."

COUNTERPOINT: "Now, don't tell me you've never had a lustful thought. Why, even a U.S. President once admitted to having lusted in his heart. Let's not kid ourselves: Lust is as much a human emotion as fear, anger, or hatred. And, whether we like to admit it or not, some people do act in depraved ways—and, at times, a lot more than in the average 'porno' flick. So, frankly, I don't see what's so 'dehumanizing' about portraying these aspects of the human personality. Sure, I'd probably agree that they aren't as uplifting as showing the human in its finest hour, as in films like *Gandhi, Chariots of Fire,* and *The Right Stuff.* But that's really irrelevant. We're not judging art here, but morality. I might also agree that some people are scandalized, maybe even 'dehumanized,' by pornography. But that speaks more of their reaction to the material than to any feature of the material itself. Some people are amused by 'porn,' others bored by it. So what are we to say—that there's something inherently amusing or boring about pornography? No, simply that some people react to pornography in a bored or amused way."

2. *Pornography separates sexual passion from affection or love.*

POINT: "In our culture, sexual intimacies generally have been associated with the most profound affection that one human being can show toward another. While it's true that sex doesn't always carry that symbolic meaning, our society still recognizes that it should. And individuals in many cases still expect sex to have that affectionate, caring, loving aspect. But you'll never find this side of sex in pornography. Quite the opposite. Every effort is made in pornography to separate sex from affection, caring, and love. 'Impersonal lust' is the order of the day. In the real world, sex without love is objectionable. It's no less objectionable when portrayed that way on the screen or in a book."

COUNTERPOINT: "Sure, sex with affection may be more enjoyable than affectionless sex. It may even be an ideal. But what falls short of the ideal isn't necessarily wrong. Nor is it wrong to portray what is less than the ideal. In fact, some people would say that without such portrayals we'd lose sight of the ideal. But for the sake of argument, let's assume that affectionless sex is wrong. Even so, it doesn't necessarily follow that to portray affectionless sex, even pornographically, is also wrong. Lots of things are wrong—kidnapping, rape, murder. That doesn't mean that it's wrong to portray these subjects in film or literature. Sure, you might say that a presentation that 'glorifies' these things, a presentation that does not categorically condemn them, is wrong. But what constitutes a 'glorifying' presentation? At what point does a film, for example, not only cease to portray affectionate sexual passion and begin to portray it as a depersonalized sexual desire, but also to glorify that presentation? I don't know; I don't think anybody does. I'm not even sure what criteria you'd use to make such a judgment. So how can you call something wrong when you can't even pin down what it is you're judging objectionable?"

3. *Pornography is anti-female.*

POINT: "Anyone who's seen even one pornographic film or read one obscene book realizes that the pornographic view is an anti-female view. Pornographic material generally portrays women as objects, not persons. They are playthings of a male, machinery to be tinkered with and manipulated. Why, pornography is as much a kind of group defamation as is Nazi propaganda, which degrades Jews. Just as we find anti-Semitic material objectionable on the grounds that it degrades a group of human beings and lessens the inherent respect and dignity they deserve, so we should object to pornography. After all, pornography under-cuts respect for women, reinforces cultural prejudices, and encourages acts of violence against women."

COUNTERPOINT: "First of all, there's a big difference in intent between por-nographic and anti-Semitic material. The latter is motivated by hate and aims not only to degrade Jews, but to incite others to join a loathsome genocidal cause. But hate isn't the impulse behind pornography. Money usually is, sometimes notoriety, even sheer pleasure. But not hate, and certainly not hate of women. Look at the material; study it. I think you'll find that if it does 'dehumanize,' it plays no favorites. Males are 'depersonalized' as much as females. And second, you don't have to get very far into anti-Semitic material before you find examples of viciously cruel, overt defamation. You never find that in pornography. And you won't find any singling out of a vulnerable minority group. On the contrary, porn deals with humans across the board: male and female, black and white, Jew and Gentile. And it certainly doesn't invite the sort of violence against women that anti-Semitic propaganda does against Jews. In fact, there's no evidence of a correlation between pornography and violence directed at women."

4. *Pornography breaks down protective barriers.*

POINT: "Our society subjects us to extensive conditioning on matters of sex. And for good reason: Sex is a most powerful appetite, which, if not carefully controlled, can produce a lot of hardship for ourselves and others. No wonder our families, schools, and churches take such pains to help us develop construc-tive attitudes toward sex and deal with sexual feelings and fantasies which, if pursued, would hurt us and society. If this process is effective, then by the time we're adults we have learned to channel our sexual drives properly and have developed certain barriers to help us do that. But pornography breaks down those barriers; it loosens the wildest of sexual feelings and fantasies. The result is behavior that is neither in the interest of the individual nor in the interest of society. So what makes pornography objectionable is that it threatens to undo the control that individuals exercise over their sexuality and leads to self-destruc-tive and antisocial behavior."

COUNTERPOINT: "You make it sound like anybody who enjoys pornography will turn into some sort of sex fiend! That's absurd. In fact, there's some reason to believe that pornography can be healthful for some people and for society. But beyond this, you blithely assume that society's conditional process is above reproach, even that we must ensure that nothing happens to 'undo' it. Did it ever occur to you that society's sexual values and the way they're taught may in part explain the great popularity of pornography?"

Arguments for Pornographic Materials

1. *Pornography can be beneficial.*

POINT: "Not only is pornography not necessarily degrading, it can actually be beneficial. Obviously, those who produce and willingly participate in it feel neither degraded nor exploited. In fact, they often enjoy considerable financial and professional success as a result. They may even feel that they're contributing something worthwhile to society. But beyond this, pornographic material can be a useful source of information about human sexuality. Even more important, it can serve as a sexual release for those in society who, for one reason or another, can't find or have difficulty finding sexual fulfillment in the absence of such materials. Given these benefits, and that there's no solid evidence that pornography harms anyone, there's no reason to object to it."

COUNTERPOINT: "The fact that pornography may benefit the people involved with it says very little about the morality of pornography. Robbery, murder, and skyjacking may also benefit the participants, but that doesn't make those activities moral. Likewise, lots of people would enjoy the spectacle of a duel with pistols at dawn, but that doesn't make dueling right. As for those poor souls who can find sexual release only through pornography, don't you think it would make more sense for society to identify and help those individuals in ways that are more meaningful for both them and society? But even granting your 'benefits,' they don't nearly begin to offset the liabilities of pornography, including its depraved view of human sexuality and dehumanization of men and women."

2. *Sexually explicit material is morally neutral.*

POINT: "The word *pornography* is loaded. As soon as you use it, you're making a pejorative judgment. That's why I'd prefer to talk about 'sexually explicit material.' That phrase describes the material under discussion but doesn't judge it as offensive or disgusting, thereby biasing a moral evaluation of it. Now, it seems to me that the only way someone can find such material in and of itself objectionable is by finding human sexuality or human sexual passion morally objectionable, because this is what 'sexually explicit material' deals with. As far as I'm concerned, there's nothing dirty, sinful, or evil about sex. Like eating, exercising, or watching TV, sex is morally neutral. Certainly it can raise moral concerns, and so can 'explicit sexual material.' For example, if people were forced to view such material or to participate in it, I'd consider that a violation of their civil rights and therefore wrong. But the material itself is neither good nor bad. It's morally inert. Everything depends on how it's used: when, by whom, and with what results. To call sexually explicit material in and of itself morally objectionable doesn't make sense."

COUNTERPOINT: "You conveniently forget, or ignore, that 'explicit sexual material' serves up more than just human sexuality and sexual passion. It packages sex, and that package, more often than not, is colored by dehumanization, human exploitation, sadism, masochism, and other forms of behavior that degrade human sexuality and human beings. Also, sexually explicit material has a viewpoint, and part of the viewpoint usually is an invitation to the spectator to join the fun. Who are we kidding? 'Sexually explicit material,' as you use that term, is inseparable from debasing forms of sexual behavior. So when you say that such material is in itself morally neutral or inert, you're sadly mistaken. Its content *always* raises serious moral questions about the proper concept of human sexuality, the dignity of human beings, and the treatment that individuals accord one another."

Arguments for Censorship

1. *Pornography leads to crime.*

POINT: "Let's be clear about one thing: Pornography leads to crime. Take, for example, the case of the unstable young man who raped a girl after he'd been aroused by lurid scenes in an obscene comic book. Such cases could multiply. Why, the Gebhard study [1965] confirmed reports of police officers that sex offenders often have pornography in their possession or admit to having seen pornographic materials. If you're still not convinced, just use a little common sense. If good literature can have a salutary effect on readers, then why can't obscene and pornographic material have a harmful effect? It can. And that's why the state must regulate pornography—to help reduce the incidence of crime."

COUNTERPOINT: "I agree there's a large body of material dealing with the relation between pornography and sex crimes. But—and it's a big 'but'—no cause-and-effect relationship has ever been found. In fact, in the Gebhard studies the use of pornography by sex offenders was compared to the experiences of a control group of normal, nonoffender males, and to those of a group of prisoners who weren't sex offenders. Guess what? There was *no* difference among the groups in their use, possession of, or exposure to pornography. If there were any correlations to be drawn, they would be between the use of and exposure to pornography and the individual's age, socioeconomic class, and educational level. And as if that weren't enough, consider this: The study found that sex offenders weren't prone to any greater sexual arousal from viewing pornography than were other groups of males."

2. *The community has the right and obligation to enforce its moral standards.*

POINT: "Like it or not, most people today find pornography repugnant. Sure, there are some people who aren't offended by the obscene, and there are those who even enjoy it. But so what? Society is run by majority rule. When the consensus supports a moral standard, the community has every right to enforce that standard. Indeed, it has an obligation to."

COUNTERPOINT: "For a government to impose conventional moral standards on the individual amounts to a tyranny of the majority. In fact, nothing is more repugnant than to impose the moral standards of the community on all its members, even those who disagree with those decisions. It was the recognition of this fact that led the founding fathers to incorporate the Bill of Rights into the

Constitution, and specifically to draft the First Amendment, which provides that 'Congress shall make no law . . . abridging the freedom of speech, or of the press.' 'No law abridging' means *no* law abridging, not even laws we happen to agree with, or anti-obscenity laws. What could be more clear? The supreme law of the land has fixed its own value on freedom of speech and press by putting these freedoms beyond the reach of federal power to abridge."

3.   *The government has the right and duty to suppress views that are incompatible with the security and well-being of the community.*

POINT: "Nobody objects when the government polices individuals who don't maintain standards of health and who threaten society. By the same token, why shouldn't the government be concerned with the moral health of individuals, since this too can affect societal well-being? We all know that pornographic materials have the effect of preoccupying men and women with gratification of their own sensual desires. They also lead to impersonal expressions of sexuality, the destruction of love, and the psychological deprivation of children unfortunate enough to be under the guardianship of adults who indulge in pornography. Since all this can undermine the moral foundations of society, it seems clear to me that government has the right and duty to regulate pornographic and obscene materials."

COUNTERPOINT: "Sure, government has the right, even the obligation to secure and protect its citizens from physical harm if it is difficult or impossible for them to protect themselves. But physical threats are quite different from what you term moral threats, and the physical health of society differs markedly from its moral health. Yes, a government ought to ensure that diseases aren't spread by indifferent or uncaring individuals; it's justified in quarantining, even imposing treatment on certain individuals in order to protect society. But 'pornography' isn't smallpox; it's not a disease which, if unchecked, will rage and consume the population. The litany of 'effects' you say pornography produces just doesn't wash. Of course, viewing or reading erotic materials is sexually arousing for a large number of people. In your view, such sexual stimulation presumably will lead the normal individual to all sorts of unspeakable, unhealthful acts. But there's no reason, not one iota of evidence, for believing that the sexual stimulation of normal individuals leads to anything other than fantasies and normal sexual activity. Now, I find nothing inherently wrong with fantasies, even sexual ones; nor do I find anything objectionable about normal sexual activity."

4.   *People need standards of decency and direction in sexual matters.*

POINT: "Generally speaking, people need direction, standards of decency, particularly regarding sex. The home, church, and school are unable to provide this necessary guidance alone. Law is needed. Law must hold up an authoritative standard for guidance of opinion and judgment. So laws that regulate pornography and obscenity perform a needed educative function. They alert people to the fact that the organized community draws a line between the decent and the indecent. In effect, such laws say: 'This is what we believe is decent, and this is what we believe is indecent; this is what's right, and this is what's wrong; this is what our community will permit, and this is what it will not permit.' The beneficial, long-term effect of such standards on people's moral values and attitudes can't be underestimated. By the same token, there's no calculating the negative long-term impact on values and attitudes in the absence of legal guidelines."

COUNTERPOINT: "Frankly, I resent the paternalistic cut of your argument. There's more than a hint of: 'Now, don't worry, folks, we're doing this for your own good.' Thank you, but no thanks. Certainly government has a right and duty to intervene in matters where there's a clear and present threat of harm. But in the case of pornography, there is none. Thus the government has no right to restrict our access to pornographic material, even for our own good. Individuals should be the judges of what's for their own good, not government. In short, I find the paternalistic principle you propose unacceptable justification for limiting personal liberty."

Arguments against Censorship

1. *No operationally meaningful definition of* obscene *is possible.*

POINT: "It's obvious that individuals bring to a film or a book their own concepts of offensiveness, which may differ from time to time in the same individuals. Also, there's no way of knowing the impact of materials on the public because of all the variables involved. What's more, in trying to define obscenity, one inevitably tries to do so in terms of the 'average person.' The fact is, there is no such animal, and so any definition or description of the obscene that ties it to an 'average person' is simply foolish. Another definitional problem arises in trying to define the 'community' whose standards we're supposed to use. Finally, it's impossible to determine with anything that even approaches objectivity which works have 'redeeming social value,' presumably a criterion for exempting material from censorship. The bottom line is that we don't have any meaningfully operational definition of *obscene* and *pornographic*. If you can't even define these terms, how can you write laws about them? You can't and you shouldn't."

COUNTERPOINT: "The problem with your argument is that it fails to distinguish between the impossibility of formulating a definition and the difficulty of applying one. I grant you that even the Supreme Court's definition of what's obscene may pose operational problems. But this isn't an uncommon problem in law. Law is, in part, based on a set of definitional assumptions. Whether or not a particular phenomenon falls within that definitional assumption always involves some interpretation. Certainly this is true of obscenity and pornography. Sometimes there's very little difficulty in applying the definition; other times considerably more interpretation is involved. If a law is difficult to interpret and apply, then we should refine it. But we shouldn't conclude that an operational difficulty proves that it's impossible to define terms in any meaningfully operational way and, therefore, that a law can't and shouldn't be formulated."

2.   *Governmental abuse will follow such legislation.*

POINT: "Asking government to serve as censor to our films and literature is like asking a fox to guard the hen house. Why, if government is allowed to oversee what people can read and view in sexual matters, there's no telling what government will attempt to regulate next—and it won't wait to be asked, either. Invite government in, and don't be at all surprised if it then proceeds to limit our religious and political freedoms, using, again, deviations from the standards of the nonexistent 'average' person and 'the community' as its justification."

COUNTERPOINT: "Oh, come now. You know as well as I that the passage of anti-smut laws doesn't at all mean the end of our religious and political freedoms. There's no reason whatever to suspect that government will invade any other aspects of people's reading or viewing, as, for example, by censoring politically 'unorthodox' material. Don't you realize that during World War II the government was given wide-ranging liberty-limiting powers? Certainly it had far greater censorship prerogatives than it would under proposed obscenity and pornography legislation. What better opportunity did government have to extend these powers than it had after the war? But it never happened. In the end, each of your fears poses a separate and distinct issue from pornography and obscenity legislation. If the time ever came when political or religious censorship was a serious social consideration, then it would have to be debated on its own merits. In no way would it, or should it, necessarily be tied to anti-smut laws."

3.   *Censorship raises insurmountable operational problems.*

POINT: "Think about the operational problems that censorship raises. The chief one is: Which works won't be censored? Some have said that the 'classics' will and should be exempt from censorship. Okay, but what's a 'classic'? Any traditional definition probably would exclude new works, since a work usually can't be recognized as a classic until some time after its release. Fine, but what does that mean? It means that the censor must determine which works will become classics—an absurdly impossible task. As a result, censors will have little choice but to ban these 'nonclassics' that smack of smut. You probably think this is an idle fear. Is it? Plenty of works of art and literature that today are considered classics once were banned: works by Chaucer, Shakespeare, Swift, and Twain, just to mention a few. And more recently, William Faulkner, Ernest Hemingway, and James Joyce found their works banned. Just imagine what creative artists would suffer, who must compose with the specter of the censor haunting their every move. One of the world's greatest writers, Leo Tolstoy, said it all. 'You would not believe,' wrote the Russian novelist, 'how from the very commencement of my activity that horrible censor question has tormented me. I wanted to write what I felt; but at the same time it occurred to me that what I wrote would not be permitted, and involuntarily I had to abandon the work. I abandoned and went on abandoning and meanwhile the years passed away.' "

COUNTERPOINT: "As an intelligent person who's interested in the arts generally and literature in particular, and as one who's sensitive to the state of the artist in society, I share your concerns. Like you, I don't want an atmosphere that inhibits our artists, nor do I want simpletons censoring works of merit. Furthermore, I don't for a minute deny that some abuses have accompanied anti-obscenity laws. Despite all that, let me ask you this: What law ever has been free from potential abuse at the hands of the overzealous, the narrow-minded, the ill-informed, and, yes, the lame-brained? My point is that the objections you raise really speak to the implementations of anti-obscenity laws and not to the justifiability of the laws themselves. To me what you say is like arguing against capital punishment legislation because capital punishment laws are unfairly applied. If there is inequity in the application of the law, then let's correct that. But let's not abolish the law. The problem isn't with the law, but with how it's implemented."

4. *Government has no right to limit liberty where there is no danger of harm.*

POINT: "When is a government justified in limiting individual liberty? When there's evidence of harm to others. But there's no evidence that pornography presents a clear and present danger to members of society. So the government has no right to pass laws restricting an adult's access to pornography."

COUNTERPOINT: "I disagree that pornography presents no danger to society. Even if we are uncertain that pornography leads to crime, why assume that it doesn't? It seems to me more prudent to assume that it does, until the overwhelming weight of evidence proves otherwise. After all, assuming that pornography is innocuous is far riskier than assuming that it is harmful. Actually, I think there's pretty good reason for assuming that pornography probably is harmful. At the very least it often deals with things like exhibitionism, voyeurism, prostitution, sadism, child molestation, and other forms of sexual perversion, many of which involve harm to people. Besides, much of the stuff portrayed is illegal. So in trafficking in this smut, pornography encourages disrespect for and even disobedience of the law. Surely this is a threat to a peaceful society. But all this aside, I think that, freed of censorship, pornography poses a direct and immediate threat to the style and quality of life we want and value. To say, then, that pornography poses no threat or harm to society is incorrect. On the contrary, pornography threatens the peace, security, and values of our society. The government has a right and duty to prevent such harm through the passage of anti-obscenity laws."

5. *Pornography can be beneficial.*

POINT: "Much that is positive may be said on behalf of pornography. For one thing, it can aid normal sexual development. For another, it can invigorate flagging sexual relations. Why, it's even been used successfully in sex therapy sessions, to treat various sexual dysfunctions. And there's little question that pornographic materials can provide some people release from sexual tensions. It can provide an acceptable sexual substitute for those who might otherwise be sexually frustrated. Finally, it's at least possible that exposure to pornography has prevented people from acting in a harmful way, perhaps from committing sex crimes."

COUNTERPOINT: "Regarding your last claim—that exposure to pornography may actually prevent antisocial acts—I suggest you read the minority report offered by several members of the Commission on Obscenity and Pornography. It mentions a study that finds the group reporting the highest rates of excitation to masturbation by pornography were rapists. Now, surely you can't say that pornography served as an adequate catharsis for these people. If it had, why did they go out and rape someone? In still another study, 39 percent of sex offenders reported that pornography had something to do with their committing the sex offense. As for your claim that pornography serves as a 'release' for some people, perhaps it does. But what kind of release? Escape might be a better term—escape from reality into fantasy and narcissism. Some release! Who knows that the darkly private, short-lived release you speak of doesn't eventuate in greater tension, frustration and, worst of all, despair and self-loathing?

Beyond the (Garbage) Pale, or Democracy, Censorship and the Arts

Walter Berns

About twenty years ago, political scientist Walter Berns wrote an essay that referred to a New York Times *editorial (1 April 1969) entitled "Beyond the (Garbage) Pale." In effect, the editorial called for the censorship of explicit portrayal of sexual intercourse on the stage. Hence the title of Berns's essay, a part of which appears here.*

While Berns's argument for censorship of pornography is not a new one, it is not the most common in contemporary pro-censorship literature. Pruned to its essentials, the argument goes something like this: Pornography can have political consequences, intended or not. The chief political consequence is that it makes us "shameless." Indeed, one of the purposes of pornography seems to be to convince us that shame is unnatural. But, in Berns's view, shame is not only natural but necessary for the proper functioning and stability of society. Without shame, individuals are "unruly and unrulable." Having lost all measure of self-restraint, individuals will have to be ruled by tyrants. Thus tyranny, not democracy, is the proper government for the shameless and self-indulgent. Since pornography induces shamelessness and self-indulgence, it undercuts democracy.

In support of his contention, Berns refers to a number of "thoughtful men" who were familiar with this censorship argument at the time modern democracies were being constituted. He, and presumably they, claims that censorship is not only compatible with a democracy but a necessary part of it.

The case for censorship is at least as old as the case against it, and, contrary to what is usually thought today, has been made under decent and democratic auspices and by intelligent men. To the extent to which it is known today, however, it is thought to be pernicious or, at best, irrelevant to the enlight-ened conditions of the twentieth century. It begins from the premise that the laws cannot remain indifferent to the manner in which men amuse themselves, or to the kinds of amusement offered them. "The object of art," as Lessing put the case, "is pleasure, and pleasure is not indispensable. What kind

From Walter Berns, "Beyond the (Garbage) Pale, or Democracy, Censorship and the Arts," in Censorship and Freedom of Expression, *Harry M. Clor, ed. (Chicago: Rand McNally, 1971). Reprinted by permission of Harry M. Clor.*

and what degree of pleasure shall be permitted may justly depend on the law-giver."[1] Such a view, especially in this uncompromising form, appears excessively Spartan and illiberal to us; yet Lessing was one of the greatest lovers of art who ever lived and wrote.

We turn to the arts—to literature, films, and the theatre, as well as to the graphic arts which were the special concern of Lessing—for the pleasure to be derived from them, and pleasure has the capacity to form our tastes and thereby to affect our lives, and the kind of people we become, and the lives of those with whom and among whom we live. Is it politically uninteresting whether men and women derive pleasure from performing their duties as citizens, parents, and spouses or, on the other hand, from watching their laws and customs and institutions ridiculed on the stage? Whether the passions are excited by, and the affections drawn to, what is noble or what is base? Whether the relations between men and women are depicted in terms of an eroticism wholly divorced from love and calculated to destroy the capacity for love and the institutions, such as the family, that depend on love? Whether a dramatist uses pleasure to attach man to what is beautiful or to what is ugly? We may not be accustomed to thinking of these things in this manner, but it is not strange that so much of the obscenity from which so many of us derive our pleasure today has an avowed political purpose.[2] It would seem that these pornographers know intuitively what liberals—for example, Morris Ernst—have forgotten, namely, that there is indeed a "causal relationship . . . between word or pictures and human behavior." At least they are not waiting for behavioral science to discover this fact.

The purpose is sometimes directly political and sometimes political in the sense that it will have political consequences intended or not. This latter purpose is to make us shameless, and it seems to be succeeding with astonishing speed. Activities that were once confined to the private scene—to the "ob-scene," to make an etymological assumption—are now presented for our delectation and emulation in [sic] center stage. Nothing that is appropriate to one place is inappropriate to any other place. No act, we are to infer, no human possibility, no possible physical combination or connection, is shameful. Even our lawmakers now so declare. "However plebeian my tastes may be," Justice Douglas asked somewhat disingenuously in the *Ginzburg* case, "who am I to say that others' tastes must be so limited and that others' tastes have no 'social importance'?" Nothing prevents a dog from enjoying sexual intercourse in the marketplace, and it is unnatural to deprive man of the same pleasure, either actively or as voyeurs in the theatre. Shame itself is unnatural, a convention devised by hypocrites to inhibit the pleasures of the body. We must get rid of our "hangups."

But what if, contrary to Freud and to what is generally assumed, shame is natural to man in the sense of being an original feature of human existence, and shamelessness unnatural in the sense of having to be acquired? What if the beauty that we are capable of knowing and achieving in our lives with each other derives from the fact that man is naturally a "blushing creature," the only creature capable of blushing? Consider the case of voyeurism, a case that, under the circumstances, comes quickly to mind. Some of us—I have even known students to confess to it—experience discomfort watching others on the stage or screen performing sexual acts, or even the acts preparatory to sexual acts, such as the disrobing of a woman by a man. This discomfort is caused by shame or is akin to shame. True, it could derive from the fear of being discovered enjoying what society still sees as a forbidden game. The voyeur who experiences shame in this sense is judging himself by the conventions of his society and, according to the usual modern account, the greater the distance separating him from his society in space or time, the less he will experience this kind of shame. This shame, which may be denoted as concealing shame, is a function of the fear of discovery by one's own group. The group may have its reasons for forbidding a particular act, and thereby leading those who engage in it to conceal it—to be ashamed of it—but these reasons have nothing to do with the nature of man. Voyeurism, according to this account, is a perversion only because society says it is, and a man guided only by nature would not be ashamed of it.

According to another view, however, not to be ashamed—to be a shameless voyeur—is more likely to require explanation, for voyeurism is by nature a perversion.

Anyone who draws his sexual gratification from looking at another lives continuously at a distance. If it is normal to approach and unite with the partner, then it is precisely characteristic of the voyeur that he remains alone, without a partner, an outsider who acts in a stealthy and furtive manner. To keep his distance when it is essential to draw near is one of the paradoxes of his perversion. The looking of the voyeur is of course also a looking at and, as such, is as different from the looks exchanged by lovers as medical palpation from the gentle caress of the hand.[3]

From this point of view, voyeurism is perversion not merely because it is contrary to convention, but because it is contrary to nature. Convention here follows nature. Whereas sexual attraction brings man and woman together seeking a unity that culminates in the living being they together create, the voyeur maintains a distance; and because he maintains a distance he looks at, he does not communicate; and because he looks at he objectifies, he makes an object of that with which it is natural to join. Objectifying, he is incapable of uniting and therefore of love. The need to conceal voyeurism—the concealing shame—is a corollary of the protective shame, the shame that impels lovers to search for privacy and for an experience protected from the profane and the eyes of the stranger. The stranger is "at odds with the shared unity of the [erotic couple], and his mere presence tends to introduce some objectification into every immediate relationship."[4] Shame, both concealing and protective, protects lovers and therefore love. And a polity without love—without the tenderness and the charming sentiments and the poetry and the beauty and the uniquely human things that depend on it and derive from it—a polity without love would be an unnatural monstrosity.[5]

To speak in a manner that is more obviously political, such a polity may even be impossible, except in a form unacceptable to free men. There is a connection between self-restraint and shame, and therefore a connection between shame and self-government or democracy. There is therefore a danger in promoting shamelessness and the fullest self-expression or indulgence. To live together requires rules and a governing of the passions, and those who are without shame will be unruly and unrulable; having lost the ability to restrain themselves by observing the rules they collectively give themselves, they will have to be ruled by others. Tyranny is the mode of government for the shameless and self-indulgent who have carried liberty beyond any restraint, natural and conventional.

Such was the argument made prior to the twentieth century, when it was generally understood that democracy, more than any other form of government, required self-restraint, which it would inculcate through moral education and impose on itself through laws, including laws governing the manner of public amusements. It was the tyrant who could usually allow the people to indulge themselves. Indulgence of the sort we are now witnessing did not threaten his rule, because his rule did not depend on a citizenry of good character. Anyone can be ruled by a tyrant, and the more debased his subjects the safer his rule. A case can be made for complete freedom of the arts among such people, whose pleasures are derived from activities divorced from their labors and any duties associated with citizenship. Among them a theatre, for example, can serve to divert the search for pleasure from what the tyrant regards as more dangerous or pernicious pursuits.[6]

Such an argument was not unknown among thoughtful men at the time modern democracies were being constituted. It is to be found in Jean-Jacques Rousseau's *Letter to M. d'Alembert on the Theatre*. Its principles were known by Washington and Jefferson, to say nothing of the antifederalists, and later on by Lincoln, all of whom insisted that democracy would not work without citizens of good character; and until recently no justice of the Supreme Court and no man in public life doubted the necessity for the law to make at least a modest effort to promote that good character, if only by protecting the effort of other institutions, such as the church and the family, to promote and maintain it. The case for censorship, at first glance, was made wholly with a view to the political good, and it had as its premise that what was good for the arts and sciences was *not* necessarily good for the polity.

Notes

1. *Laocoön* (New York: Noonday Press), ch. 1, p. 10.

2. *Che!* and *Hair,* for example, are political plays. . . .

3. Erwin W. Straus, *Phenomenological Psychology* (Basic Books, New York, 1966), p. 219. I have no doubt that it is possible to want to observe sexual acts for reasons unrelated to voyeurism. Just as a physician has a clinical interest in the parts of the body,

philosophers will have an interest in the parts of the soul, or in the varieties of human things which are manifestations of the body and the soul. Such a "looking" would not be voyeurism and would be unaccompanied by shame; or the desire to see and to understand would require the "seer" to overcome shame. (Plato, *Republic*, 439e) In any event, the case of the philosopher is politically irrelevant, and aesthetically irrelevant as well.

4. Straus, p. 221.

5. It is easy to prove that shamefulness is not the only principle governing the question of what may properly be presented on the stage; shamefulness would not, for example, govern the case of a scene showing the copulating of a married couple who love each other very much. That is not intrinsically shameful—on the contrary—yet it ought not to be shown. The principle here is, I think, an aesthetic one: Such a scene is dramatically weak because the response of the audience would be characterized by prurience and not by a sympathy with what the scene is intended to portray, a beautiful love. This statement can be tested by joining a college-town movie audience; it is confirmed unintentionally by a defender of nudity on the stage. . . .

6. The modern tyrant does not encourage passivity among his subjects; on the contrary, they are expected by him to be public-spirited: to work for the State, to exceed production schedules, to be citizen soldiers in the huge armies, and to love Big Brother. Indeed, in Nazi Germany and the Soviet Union alike, the private life was and is discouraged, and with it erotic love and the private attachments it fosters. Censorship in a modern tyrannical state is designed to abolish the private life to the extent that this is possible. George Orwell understood this perfectly. This severe censorship that characterizes modern tyranny, and distinguishes it sharply from premodern tyranny, derives from the basis of modern tyrannical rule: Both Nazism and Communism have roots in theory, and more precisely, a kind of utopian theory. The modern tyrant parades as a political philosopher, the heir of Nietzsche or Marx, with a historical mission to perform. He cannot leave his subjects alone.

Questions for Analysis

1. *Do you agree with Berns that what is good for the arts and sciences is not necessarily good for society?*

2. *Do you agree that one of the purposes of pornography is to make us shameless?*

3. *Why does Berns believe that shame is necessary for the protection of lovers and love, and what does that have to do with the justification of censorship?*

4. *To what extent does Berns's argument depend on the principle of utility?*

5. *In what sense could Berns's argument be said to fly in the face of popular conceptions of democracy?*

Pornography and Respect for Women

Ann Garry

Recently some feminists and nonfeminists alike have argued that pornography is anti-female, that it's designed to humiliate women. Professor of philosophy Ann Garry agrees. Arguing in a Kantian way, Garry objects to most pornography because it encourages attitudes and behavior that violate the moral principle of respect for people. Does that mean that pornography is always

This article first appeared in Social Theory and Practice, *Vol. 4 (Summer 1978), pp. 395–421. Reprinted here by permission of the author as it appears in* Philosophy and Women, *edited by Sharon Bishop and Marjorie Weinzweig (Belmont, CA.: Wadsworth, 1979).*

evil? Not necessarily, says Garry. It is possible, she claims, for pornography to be nonsexist and nondegrading and, therefore, morally acceptable.

Pornography, like rape, is a male invention, designed to dehumanize women, to reduce the female to an object of sexual access, not to free sensuality from moralistic or parental inhibition. . . . Pornography is the undiluted essence of anti-female propaganda.
—Susan Brownmiller, *Against Our Will: Men, Women and Rape*[1]

It is often asserted that a distinguishing characteristic of sexually explicit material is the degrading and demeaning portrayal of the role and status of the human female. It has been argued that erotic materials describe the female as a mere sexual object to be exploited and manipulated sexually. . . . A recent survey shows that 41 percent of American males and 46 percent of the females believe that "sexual materials lead people to lose respect for women." . . . Recent experiments suggest that such fears are probably unwarranted.
—Presidential Commission on Obscenity and Pornography[2]

The kind of apparent conflict illustrated in these passages is easy to find in one's own thinking as well. For example, I have been inclined to think that pornography is innocuous and to dismiss "moral" arguments for censoring it because many such arguments rest on an assumption I do not share—that sex is an evil to be controlled. At the same time I believe that it is wrong to exploit or degrade human beings, particularly women and others who are especially susceptible. So if pornography degrades human beings, then even if I would oppose its censorship I surely cannot find it morally innocuous.

In an attempt to resolve this apparent conflict I discuss three questions: Does pornography degrade (or exploit or dehumanize) human beings? If so, does it degrade women in ways or to an extent that it does not degrade men? If so, must pornography degrade women, as Brownmiller thinks, or could genuinely innocuous, nonsexist pornography exist? Although much current pornography does degrade women, I will argue that it is possible to have nondegrading, nonsexist pornography.

However, this possibility rests on our making certain fundamental changes in our conceptions of sex and sex roles. . . .

I

The . . . argument I will consider [here] is that pornography is morally objectionable, not because it leads people to show disrespect for women, but because pornography itself exemplifies and recommends behavior that violates the moral principle to respect persons. The content of pornography is what one objects to. It treats women as mere sex objects "to be exploited and manipulated" and degrades the role and status of women. In order to evaluate this argument, I will first clarify what it would mean for pornography itself to treat someone as a sex object in a degrading manner. I will then deal with three issues central to the discussion of pornography and respect for women: how "losing respect" for a woman is connected with treating her as a sex object; what is wrong with treating someone as a sex object; and why it is worse to treat women rather than men as sex objects. I will argue that the current content of pornography sometimes violates the moral principle to respect persons. Then, in [the concluding part] of this paper, I will suggest that pornography need not violate this principle if certain fundamental changes were to occur in attitudes about sex.

To many people, including Brownmiller and some other feminists, it appears to be an obvious truth that pornography treats people, especially women, as sex objects in a degrading manner. And if we omit "in a degrading manner," the statement seems hard to dispute: How could pornography *not* treat people as sex objects?

First, is it permissible to say that either the content of pornography or pornography itself degrades people or treats people as sex objects? It is not difficult to find examples of degrading content in which women are treated as sex objects. Some pornographic films convey the message that all women really want to be raped, that their resisting struggle is not to be believed. By portraying women in this manner, the content of the movie degrades women. Degrading women is morally objectionable. While seeing the movie need not cause anyone to imitate the behavior shown, we can call the content degrading to women because of the character of the behavior and attitudes it recommends. The same kind of point can be made about films (or books or TV commercials) with other kinds of degrading, thus morally objectionable, content—for example, racist messages.

The next step in the argument is to infer that, because the content or message of pornography is morally objectionable, we can call pornography itself morally objectionable. Support for this step can be found in an analogy. If a person takes every opportunity to recommend that men rape women, we would think not only that his recommendation is immoral but that he is immoral too. In the case of pornography, the objection to making an inference from recommended behavior to the person who recommends is that we ascribe predicates such as "immoral" differently to people than to films or books. A film vehicle for an objectionable message is still an object independent of its message, its director, its producer, those who act in it, and those who respond to it. Hence one cannot make an unsupported inference from "the content of the film is morally objectionable" to "the film is morally objectionable." Because the central points in this paper do not depend on whether pornography itself (in addition to its content) is morally objectionable, I will not try to support this inference. (The question about the relation of content to the work itself is, of course, extremely interesting; but in part because I cannot decide which side of the argument is more persuasive, I will pass.[3]) Certainly one appropriate way to evaluate pornography is in terms of the moral features of its content. If a pornographic film exemplifies and recommends morally objectionable attitudes or behavior, then its content is morally objectionable.

Let us now turn to the first of our three questions about respect and sex objects: What is the connection between losing respect for a woman and treating her as a sex object? Some people who have lived through the era in which women were taught to worry about men "losing respect" for them if they engaged in sex in inappropriate circumstances find it troublesome (or at least amusing) that feminists—supposedly "liberated" women—are outraged at being treated as sex objects, either by pornography or in any other way. The apparent alignment between feminists and traditionally "proper" women need not surprise us when we look at it more closely.

The "respect" that men have traditionally believed they have for women—hence a respect they can lose—is not a general respect for persons as autonomous beings; nor is it respect that is earned because of one's personal merits or achievements. It is respect that is an outgrowth of the "double standard." Women are to be respected because they are more pure, delicate, and fragile than men, have more refined sensibilities, and so on. Because some women clearly do not have these qualities, thus do not deserve respect, women must be divided into two groups—the good ones on the pedestal and the bad ones who have fallen from it. One's mother, grandmother, Sunday School teacher, and usually one's wife are "good" women. The appropriate behavior by which to express respect for good women would be, for example, not swearing or telling dirty jokes in front of them, giving them seats on buses, and other "chivalrous" acts. This kind of "respect" for good women is the sort that adolescent boys in the back seats of cars used to "promise" not to lose. Note that men define, display, and lose this kind of respect. If women lose respect for women, it is not typically a loss of respect for (other) women as a class but a loss of self-respect.

It has now become commonplace to acknowledge that, although a place on the pedestal might have advantages over a place in the "gutter" beneath it, a place on the pedestal is not at all equal to the place occupied by other people (i.e., men). "Respect" for those on the pedestal was not respect for whole, full-fledged people but for a special class of inferior beings.

If a person makes two traditional assumptions—that (at least some) sex is dirty and that women fall into two classes, good and bad—it is easy to see how that person might think that pornography could lead people to lose respect for women or that pornography is itself disrespectful to women. Pornography describes or shows women engaging in activities inappropriate for good women to engage in—or at least inappropriate for them to be seen by strangers engaging in. If one sees these women as symbolic representatives of all women, then all women fall from grace with these women. This fall is possible, I believe, because the traditional "respect" that men have had for women is not genuine, wholehearted respect for full-fledged human beings but half-hearted respect for lesser beings, some of whom they feel the need to glorify and purify.[4] It is easy to fall from a pedestal. Can we imagine 41 percent of men and 46 percent of women answering "yes" to the question "Do movies showing men engaging in violent acts lead people to lose respect for men?"

Two interesting asymmetries appear. The first is that losing respect for men as a class (men with power, typically Anglo men) is more difficult than losing respect for women or ethnic minorities as a class. Anglo men whose behavior warrants disrespect are more likely to be seen as exceptional cases than are women or minorities (whose "transgressions" may be far less serious). Think of the following: women are temptresses; blacks cheat the welfare system; Italians are gangsters; but the men of the Nixon administration are exceptions—Anglo men as a class did not lose respect because of Watergate and related scandals.

The second asymmetry concerns the active and passive roles of the sexes. Men are seen in the active role. If men lose respect for women because of something "evil" done by women (such as appearing in pornography), the fear is that men will then do harm to women—not that women will do harm to men. Whereas if women lose respect for male politicians because of Watergate, the fear is still that male politicians will do harm, not that women will do harm to male politicians. This asymmetry might be a result of one way in which our society thinks of sex as bad—as harm that men do to women (or to the person playing a female role, as in a homosexual rape). Robert Baker calls attention to this point in " 'Pricks' and 'Chicks': A Plea for 'Persons.' "[5] Our slang words for sexual intercourse—'fuck,' 'screw,' or older words such as 'take' or 'have'—not only can mean harm but have traditionally taken a male subject and a female object. The active male screws (harms) the passive female. A "bad" woman only tempts men to hurt her further.

It is easy to understand why one's proper grandmother would not want men to see pornography or lose respect for women. But feminists reject these "proper" assumptions: good and bad classes of women do not exist; and sex is not dirty (though many people believe it is). Why then are feminists

angry at the treatment of women as sex objects, and why are some feminists opposed to pornography?

The answer is that feminists as well as proper grandparents are concerned with respect. However, there are differences. A feminist's distinction between treating a woman as a full-fledged person and treating her as merely a sex object does not correspond to the good-bad woman distinction. In the latter distinction, "good" and "bad" are properties applicable to groups of women. In the feminist view, all women are full-fledged people—some, however, are treated as sex objects and perhaps think of themselves as sex objects. A further difference is that, although "bad" women correspond to those thought to deserve treatment as sex objects, good women have not corresponded to full fledged people; only men have been full-fledged people. Given the feminist's distinction, she has no difficulty whatever in saying that pornography treats women as sex objects, not as full-fledged people. She can morally object to pornography or anything else that treats women as sex objects.

One might wonder whether any objection to treatment as a sex object implies that the person objecting still believes, deep down, that sex is dirty. I don't think so. Several other possibilities emerge. First, even if I believe intellectually and emotionally that sex is healthy, I might object to being treated *only* as a sex object. In the same spirit, I would object to being treated *only* as a maker of chocolate chip cookies or *only* as a tennis partner, because only one of my talents is being valued. Second, perhaps I feel that sex is healthy, but it is apparent to me that you think sex is dirty; so I don't want you to treat me as a sex object. Third, being treated as any kind of object, not just as a sex object, is unappealing. I would rather be a partner (sexual or otherwise) than an object. Fourth, and more plausible than the first three possibilities, is Robert Baker's view mentioned above. Both (1) our traditional double standard of sexual behavior for men and women and (2) the linguistic evidence that we connect the concept of sex with the concept of harm point to what is wrong with treating women as sex objects. As I said earlier, 'fuck' and 'screw,' in their traditional uses, have taken a male subject, a female object, and have had at least two meanings: harm and have sexual intercourse with. (In addition, a prick is a man who harms people ruthlessly; and a motherfucker is so low that he would do something very harmful to his own dear mother.)[6] Because in our culture we connect sex with harm that men do to women, and because we think of the female role in sex as that of harmed object, we can see that to treat a woman as a sex object is automatically to treat her as less than fully human. To say this does not imply that no healthy sexual relationships exist; nor does it say anything about individual men's conscious intentions to degrade women by desiring them sexually (though no doubt some men have these intentions). It is merely to make a point about the concepts embodied in our language.

Psychoanalytic support for the connection between sex and harm comes from Robert J. Stoller. Stoller thinks that sexual excitement is linked with a wish to harm someone (and with at least a whisper of hostility). The key process of sexual excitement can be seen as dehumanization (fetishization) in fantasy of the desired person. He speculates that this is true in some degree of everyone, both men and women, with "normal" or "perverted" activities and fantasies.[7]

Thinking of sex objects as harmed objects enables us to explain some of the first three reasons why one wouldn't want to be treated as a sex object: (1) I may object to being treated only as a tennis partner, but being a tennis partner is not connected in our culture with being a harmed object; and (2) I may not think that sex is dirty and that I would be a harmed object; I may not know what your view is; but what bothers me is that this is the view embodied in our language and culture.

Awareness of the connection between sex and harm helps explain other interesting points. Women are angry about being treated as sex objects in situations or roles in which they do not intend to be regarded in that manner—for example, while serving on a committee or attending a discussion. It is not merely that a sexual role is inappropriate for the circumstances; it is thought to be a less fully human role than the one in which they intended to function.

Finally, the sex-harm connection makes clear why it is worse to treat women as sex objects than to treat men as sex objects, and why some men have had difficulty understanding women's anger about the matter. It is more difficult for heterosex-

ual men than for women to assume the role of "harmed object" in sex; for men have the self-concept of sexual agents, not of passive objects. This is also related to my earlier point concerning the difference in the solidity of respect for men and for women; respect for women is more fragile. Despite exceptions, it is generally harder for people to degrade men, either sexually or nonsexually, than to degrade women. Men and women have grown up with different patterns of self-respect and expectations regarding the extent to which they deserve and will receive respect or degradation. The man who doesn't understand why women do not want to be treated as sex objects (because he'd sure like to be) would not think of himself as being harmed by that treatment; a woman might.[8] Pornography, probably more than any other contemporary institution, succeeds in treating men as sex objects.

Having seen that the connection between sex and harm helps explain both what is wrong with treating someone as a sex object and why it is worse to treat a woman in this way, I want to use the sex-harm connection to try to resolve a dispute about pornography and women. Brownmiller's view, remember, was that pornography is "the undiluted essence of anti-female propaganda" whose purpose is to degrade women. Some people object to Brownmiller's view by saying that, since pornography treats both men and women as sex objects for the purpose of arousing the viewer, it is neither sexist, antifemale, nor designed to degrade women; it just happens that degrading of women arouses some men. How can this dispute be resolved?

Suppose we were to rate the content of all pornography from most morally objectionable to least morally objectionable. Among the most objectionable would be the most degrading—for example, "snuff" films and movies which recommend that men rape women, molest children and puppies, and treat nonmasochists very sadistically.

Next we would find a large amount of material (probably most pornography) not quite so blatantly offensive. With this material it is relevant to use the analysis of sex objects given above. As long as sex is connected with harm done to women, it will be very difficult not to see pornography as degrading to women. We can agree with Brownmiller's opponent that pornography treats men as sex objects, too, but we maintain that this is only pseudoequality: such treatment is still more degrading to women.[9]

In addition, pornography often exemplifies the active/passive, harmer/harmed object roles in a very obvious way. Because pornography today is male-oriented and is supposed to make a profit, the content is designed to appeal to male fantasies. Judging from the content of the most popular legally available pornography, male fantasies still run along the lines of stereotypical sex roles—and, if Stoller is right, include elements of hostility. In much pornography the women's purpose is to cater to male desires, to service the man or men. Her own pleasure is rarely emphasized for its own sake; she is merely allowed a little heavy breathing, perhaps in order to show her dependence on the great male "lover" who produces her pleasure. In addition, women are clearly made into passive objects in still photographs showing only close-ups of their genitals. Even in movies marketed to appeal to heterosexual couples, such as *Behind the Green Door*, the woman is passive and undemanding (and in this case kidnapped and hypnotized as well). Although many kinds of specialty magazines and films are gauged for different sexual tastes, very little contemporary pornography goes against traditional sex roles. There is certainly no significant attempt to replace the harmer/harmed distinction with anything more positive and healthy. In some stag movies, of course, men are treated sadistically by women; but this is an attempt to turn the tables on degradation, not a positive improvement.

What would cases toward the least objectionable end of the spectrum be like? They would be increasingly less degrading and sexist. The genuinely nonobjectionable cases would be nonsexist and nondegrading; but commercial examples do not readily spring to mind.[10] The question is: Does or could any pornography have nonsexist, nondegrading content?

II

I want to start with the easier question: Is it possible for pornography to have nonsexist, morally acceptable content? Then I will consider whether any pornography of this sort currently exists.

Imagine the following situation, which exists only rarely today: Two fairly conventional people who love each other enjoy playing tennis and bridge together, cooking good food together, and having sex together. In all these activities they are free from hang-ups, guilt, and tendencies to dominate or objectify each other. These two people like to watch tennis matches and old romantic movies on TV, like to watch Julia Child cook, like to read the bridge column in the newspaper, and like to watch pornographic movies. Imagine further that this couple is not at all uncommon in society and that nonsexist pornography is as common as this kind of nonsexist sexual relationship. This situation sounds fine and healthy to me. I see no reason to think that an interest in pornography would disappear in these circumstances. People seem to enjoy watching others experience or do (especially do well) what they enjoy experiencing, doing, or wish they could do themselves. We do not morally object to people watching tennis on TV; why would we object to these hypothetical people watching pornography?

Can we go from the situation today to the situation just imagined? In much current pornography, people are treated in morally objectionable ways. In the scene just imagined, however, pornography would be nonsexist, nondegrading, morally acceptable. The key to making the change is to break the connection between sex and harm. If Stoller is right, this task may be impossible without changing the scenarios of our sexual lives—scenarios that we have been writing since early childhood. (Stoller does not indicate whether he thinks it possible for adults to rewrite their scenarios or for social change to bring about the possibility of new scenarios in future generations.) But even if we believe that people can change their sexual scenarios, the sex-harm connection is deeply entrenched and has widespread implications. What is needed is a thorough change in people's deep-seated attitudes and feelings about sex roles in general, as well as about sex and roles in sex (sexual roles). Although I cannot even sketch a general outline of such changes here, changes in pornography should be part of a comprehensive program. Television, children's educational material, and nonpornographic movies and novels may be far better avenues for attempting to change attitudes; but one does not want to take the chance that pornography is working against one.

What can be done about pornography in particular? If one wanted to work within the current institutions, one's attempt to use pornography as a tool for the education of male pornography audiences would have to be fairly subtle at first; nonsexist pornography must become familiar enough to sell and be watched. One should realize too that any positive educational value that nonsexist pornography might have may well be as short-lived as most of the effects of pornography. But given these limitations, what could one do?

Two kinds of films must be considered. First is the short film with no plot or character development, just depicted sexual activity in which nonsexist pornography would treat men and women as equal sex partners.[11] The man would not control the circumstances in which the partners had sex or the choice of positions or acts; the woman's preference would be counted equally. There would be no suggestion of a power play or conquest on the man's part, no suggestion that "she likes it when I hurt her." Sexual intercourse would not be portrayed as primarily for the purpose of male ejaculation—his orgasm is not "the best part" of the movie. In addition, both the man and woman would express their enjoyment; the man need not be cool and detached.

The film with a plot provides even more opportunity for nonsexist education. Today's pornography often portrays the female characters as playthings even when not engaging in sexual activity. Nonsexist pornography could show women and men in roles equally valued by society, and sex equality would amount to more than possession of equally functional genitalia. Characters would customarily treat each other with respect and consideration, with no attempt to treat men or women brutally or thoughtlessly. The local Pussycat Theater showed a film written and directed by a woman (The Passions of Carol), which exhibited a few of the features just mentioned. The main female character in it was the editor of a magazine parody of Viva. The fact that some of the characters treated each other very nicely, warmly, and tenderly did not detract from the pornographic features of the movie. This did not surprise us, for even in traditional male-oriented films, lesbian scenes usually exhibit tenderness and kindness.

Plots for nonsexist films could include women in traditionally male jobs (e.g., long-distance truck-driver) or in positions usually held in respect by pornography audiences. For example, a high-ranking female Army officer, treated with respect by men and women alike, could be shown not only in various sexual encounters with other people but also carrying out her job in a humane manner.[12] Or perhaps the main character could be a female urologist. She could interact with nurses and other medical personnel, diagnose illnesses brilliantly, and treat patients with great sympathy as well as have sex with them. When the Army officer or the urologist engages in sexual activities, she will treat her partners and be treated by them in some of the considerate ways described above.

In the circumstances we imagined at the beginning of [this part of the] paper, our nonsexist films could be appreciated in the proper spirit. Under these conditions the content of our new pornography would clearly be nonsexist and morally acceptable. But would the content of such a film be morally acceptable if shown to a typical pornography audience today? It might seem strange for us to change our moral evaluation of the content on the basis of a different audience, but an audience today is likely to see the "respected" urologist and Army officer as playthings or unusual prostitutes—even if our intention in showing the film is to counteract this view. The effect is that although the content of the film seems morally acceptable and our intention in showing it is morally flawless, women are still degraded.[13] The fact that audience attitude is so important makes one wary of giving wholehearted approval to any pornography seen today.

The fact that good intentions and content are insufficient does not imply that one's efforts toward change would be entirely in vain. Of course, I could not deny that anyone who tries to change an institution from within faces serious difficulties. This is particularly evident when one is trying to change both pornography and a whole set of related attitudes, feelings, and institutions concerning sex and sex roles. But in conjunction with other attempts to change this set of attitudes, it seems preferable to try to change pornography instead of closing one's eyes in the hope that it will go away. For I suspect that pornography is here to stay.[14]

Notes

1. (New York: Simon and Schuster, 1975), p. 394.
2. The Report of the Commission on Obscenity and Pornography (Washington, D.C., 1970), p. 201. This

article first appeared in *Social Theory and Practice*, vol. 4 (Summer 1978), pp. 395–421. It is reprinted here, by permission of the author, as it appears in *Philosophy and Women*, edited by Sharon Bishop and Marjorie Weinzweig (Belmont, Calif.: Wadsworth, 1979).

3. In order to help one determine which position one feels inclined to take, consider the following statement: It is morally objectionable to write, make, sell, act in, use, and enjoy pornography; in addition, the content of pornography is immoral; however, pornography itself is not morally objectionable. If this statement seems extremely problematic, then one might well be satisfied with the claim that pornography is degrading because its content is.

4. Many feminists point this out. One of the most accessible references is Shulamith Firestone, *The Dialectic of Sex: The Case for the Feminist Revolution* (New York: Bantam, 1970), especially pp. 128–32.

5. In Richard Wasserstrom, ed., *Today's Moral Problems* (New York: Macmillan, 1975), pp. 152—71. Also in Robert Baker and Frederick Elliston, eds., *Philosophy and Sex* (Buffalo, N.Y.: Prometheus Books, 1975).

6. Baker, in Wasserstrom, *Today's Moral Problems*, pp. 168–169.

7. "Sexual Excitement," *Archives of General Psychiatry* 33 (1976): 899–909, especially p. 903. The extent to which Stoller sees men and women in different positions with respect to harm and hostility is not clear. He often treats men and women alike, but in *Perversion: The Erotic Form of Hatred* (New York: Pantheon, 1975), pp. 89–91, he calls attention to differences between men and women especially regarding their responses to pornography and lack of understanding by men of women's sexuality. Given that Stoller finds hostility to be an essential element in male-oriented pornography, and given that women have not responded readily to such pornography, one can speculate about the possibilities for women's sexuality: their hostility might follow a different scenario; they might not be as hostile, and so on.

8. Men seem to be developing more sensitivity to being treated as sex objects. Many homosexual men have long understood the problem. As women become more sexually aggressive, some heterosexual men I know are beginning to feel treated as sex objects. A man can feel that he is not being taken seriously if a woman looks lustfully at him while he is holding forth about the French

judicial system or the failure of liberal politics. Some of his most important talents are not being properly valued.

9. I don't agree with Brownmiller that the purpose of pornography is to dehumanize women, rather it is to arouse the audience. The differences between our views can be explained, in part, by the points from which we begin. She is writing about rape; her views about pornography grow out of her views about rape. I begin by thinking of pornography as merely depicted sexual activity, though I am well aware of the male hostility and contempt for women that it often expresses. That pornography degrades women and excites men is an illustration of this contempt.

10. Virginia Wright Wexman uses the film *Group Marriage* (Stephanie Rottman, 1973) as an example of "more enlightened erotica." Wexman also asks the following questions in an attempt to point out sexism in pornographic films:

> Does it [the film] portray rape as pleasurable to women? Does it consistently show females nude but present men fully clothed? Does it present women as childlike creatures whose sexual interests must be guided by knowing experienced men? Does it show sexually aggressive women as castrating viragos? Does it pretend that sex is exclusively the prerogative of women under twenty-five? Does it focus on the physical aspects of lovemaking rather than the emotional ones? Does it portray women as purely sexual beings? ("Sexism of X-rated Films." *Chicago Sun-Times*, 28 March 1976.)

11. If it is a lesbian or male homosexual film, no one would play a caricatured male or female role. The reader has probably noticed that I have limited my discussion to heterosexual pornography, but there are many interesting analogies to be drawn with male homosexual pornography. Very little lesbian pornography exists, though lesbian scenes are commonly found in male-oriented pornography.

12. One should note that behavior of this kind is still considered unacceptable by the military. A female officer resigned from the U.S. Navy recently rather than be court-martialed for having sex with several enlisted men whom she met in a class on interpersonal relations.

13. The content may seem morally acceptable only if one disregards such questions as, "Should a doc-

tor have sex with her patients during office hours?" More important is the propriety of evaluating content wholly apart from the attitudes and reactions of the audience; one might not find it strange to say that one film has morally unacceptable content when shown tonight at the Pussycat Theater but acceptable content when shown tomorrow at a feminist conference.

14. [Two] "final" points must be made:

1. I have not seriously considered censorship as an alternative course of action. . . . Brownmiller . . . [is] not averse to it. But . . . other principles seem too valuable to sacrifice when other options are available. I believe that even if moral objections to pornography exist, one must preclude any simple inference from "pornography is immoral" to "pornography should be censored" because of other important values and principles such as freedom of expression and self-determination. In addition, before justifying censorship on moral grounds one would want to compare pornography to other possibly offensive material: advertising using sex and racial stereotypes, violence in TV and films, and so on.

2. In discussing the audience for nonsexist pornography, I have focused on the male audience. But there is no reason why pornography could not educate and appeal to women as well.

Questions for Analysis

1. What is the "apparent conflict" that Garry refers to in the opening paragraph?

2. Briefly explain why Garry believes that the current content of pornography violates the moral principle of respect for persons.

3. What's the connection between losing respect for a woman and treating her as a sex object?

4. What does Garry mean when she says, ". . . pornography often exemplifies the active/passive, harmer/harmed object roles in a very obvious way"? How is this relevant to her argument?

5. Feminist Susan Brownmiller, whom Garry refers to, argues that tolerance of pornography undercuts respect for women and is a kind of group defamation, much like Nazi propaganda degrades Jews. Therefore, Brownmiller concludes, pornography should be suppressed. Do you think Garry would agree with Brownmiller's conclusion?

6. What does Garry believe is needed for pornography to be nonsexist, nondegrading, and morally acceptable?

7. The traditional Judeo-Christian objection to pornography is that pornography involves the pursuit of pleasure for its own sake, thereby excluding the higher purposes and values to which pleasure is attached. Pornography exemplifies and encourages impersonal sexual activity, which is debasing and a violation of human dignity. Compare and contrast Garry's position with this view.

Dissenting Opinion in *United States* v. *Roth*

Judge Jerome Frank

A man named Roth conducted a business in New York publishing books, photographs, and magazines. He used sexually explicit circulars and advertising material to solicit sales. Charges were brought against him of mailing obscene circulars and advertising and of mailing an obscene book, all in violation of the federal obscenity statute. He was convicted by a jury in the District Court for the Southern District of New York on four counts of a twenty-six-count indictment. In 1956, his conviction was affirmed by the Court of Appeals for the Second Circuit, and subsequently upheld by the U.S. Supreme Court.

What follows is the dissenting opinion in the Court of Appeals ruling, written by Judge Jerome Frank. Frank's comprehensive opinion is often regarded as a classic statement against censorship of obscenity. Although written prior to the Supreme Court's disposition of the First Amendment issue and legal definition of obscenity in United States v. Roth (354 U.S. 476, 1957), Frank's viewpoint remains highly influential. It deals with a wide range of pertinent issues and continues to furnish supporting material for those who claim that censorship of pornography is unconstitutional, unwise, or immoral.

Here Frank's opinion has been edited to less than half its original length. Most footnotes have been deleted, the remainder renumbered.

I agree with my colleagues that since ours is an inferior court, we should not hold invalid a statute which our superior has . . . often said is constitutional (albeit without any full discussion). Yet I think it not improper to set forth, as I do in the Appendix, considerations concerning the obscenity statute's validity with which, up to now, I think the Supreme Court has not dealt in any of its opinions. I do not suggest the inevitability of the conclusion that the statute is unconstitutional. I do suggest that it is hard to avoid that conclusion, if one applies to that legislation the reasoning the Supreme Court has applied to other sorts of legislation. Perhaps I have overlooked conceivable compelling contrary arguments. If so, maybe my Appendix will evoke them.

To preclude misunderstanding of my purpose in stirring doubts about this statute, I think it well to add the following:

(a) As many of the publications mailed by defendant offend my personal taste, I would not cross a street to obtain them for nothing; I happen not to be interested in so-called "pornography," and I think defendant's motives obnoxious. But if the statute were invalid, the merit of those publications would be irrelevant. . . . So, too, as to defendant's motives: "Although the defendant may be the worst of men . . . the rights of the best of men are secure only as the rights of the vilest and most abhorrent are protected."[1]

(b) It is most doubtful (as explained in the Appendix) whether anyone can now demonstrate that children's reading or looking at obscene matter has a probable causal relation to the children's antisocial conduct. If, however, such a probable causal relation could be shown, there could be little, I think, of the validity of a statute (if so worded as to avoid undue ambiguity) which specifically prohibits the distribution by mail of obscene publications for sale to young people. But discussion of such legislation is here irrelevant, since, to repeat, the existing federal statute is not thus restricted.

(c) Congress undoubtedly has wide power to protect public morals. But the First Amendment severely limits that power in the area of free speech and free press. . . .

(e) The First Amendment, of course, does not prevent any private body or group (including any church) from instructing, or seeking to persuade, its adherents or others not to read or distribute obscene (or other) publications. That constitutional provision—safeguarding a principle indispensable in a true democracy—leaves unhampered all non-governmental means of molding public opinion about not reading literature which some think undesirable; and, in that respect, experience teaches that democratically exercised censorship by public opinion has far more potency, and is far less easily evaded, than censorship by government. The incessant struggle to influence public opinion is of the very essence of the democratic process. A basic purpose of the First Amendment is to keep that struggle alive, by not permitting the dominant public opinion of the present to become embodied in legislation which will prevent the formation of a different dominant public opinion in the future.

(f) At first glance it may seem almost frivolous to raise any question about the constitutionality of the obscenity statute at a time when many seemingly graver First Amendment problems confront the courts. But (for reasons stated in more detail in the Appendix) governmental censorship of writings, merely because they may stimulate, in the reader, sexual thoughts the legislature deems undesirable, has more serious implications than appear at first glance: We have been warned by eminent thinkers of the easy path from any apparently mild governmental control of what adult citizens may read to governmental control of adults' political and religious reading. John Milton, Thomas Jefferson, James Madison, John Stuart Mill and Alexis de Tocqueville have pointed out that any paternalistic guardianship by government of the thoughts of grown-up citizens enervates their spirit, keeps them immature, all too ready to adopt towards government officers the attitude that, in general, "Papa knows best." If the government possesses the power to censor publications which arouse sexual thoughts, regardless of whether those thoughts tend probably to transform themselves into anti-social behavior, why may not the government censor political and religious publications regardless of any causal relation to probably dangerous deeds? And even if we confine attention to official censorship of publications tending to stimulate sexual thoughts, it should be asked why, at any moment, that censorship cannot be extended to advertise-

ments and true reports or photographs, in our daily press, which, fully as much, may stimulate such thoughts?

(g) Assuming *arguendo*, that a statute aims at an altogether desirable end, nevertheless its desirability does not render it constitutional. . . .

Appendix

In 1799, eight years after the adoption of the First Amendment, Madison, in an address to the General Assembly of Virginia,[2] said that the "truth of opinion" ought not to be subject to "imprisonment, to be inflicted by those of a different opinion"; he there also asserted that it would subvert the First Amendment to make a "distinction between the freedom and the licentiousness of the press." Previously, in 1792, he wrote that "a man has property in his opinions and free communication of them," and that a government which "violates the property which individuals have in their opinion . . . is not a pattern for the United States."[3] Jefferson's proposed Constitution for Virginia (1776) provided: "Printing presses shall be free, except so far as by commission of private injury cause may be given of private action."[4] In his Second Inaugural Address (1805), he said:

> No inference is here intended that the laws provided by the State against false and defamatory publications should not be enforced. . . . The press, confined to truth, needs no other restraint . . . ; and no other definite line can be drawn between the inestimable liberty of the press and demoralizing licentiousness. If there still be improprieties which this rule would not restrain, its supplement must be sought in the censorship of public opinion.

. . . Jefferson, in 1798, quoting the First Amendment, said it guarded "in the same sentence, and under the same words, the freedom of religion, of speech, and of the press; insomuch, that whatever violates either throws down the sanctuary which covers the others."[5] In 1814, he wrote in a letter,

> I am really mortified to be told that in the United States of America, a fact like this (the sale of a book) can become a subject of inquiry, and of criminal inquiry too, as an

offense against religion; that (such) a question can be carried before the civil magistrate. Is this then our freedom of religion? And are we to have a censor whose imprimatur shall say what books may be sold and what we may buy? . . . Whose foot is to be the measure to which ours are all to be cut or stretched?[6]

Those utterances highlight this fact: Freedom to speak publicly and to publish has, as its inevitable and important correlative, the private rights to hear, to read, and to think and to feel about what one hears and reads. The First Amendment protects those private rights of hearers and readers. . . .

The question therefore arises whether the courts, in enforcing the First Amendment, should interpret it in accord with the views prevalent among those who sponsored and adopted it or in accord with subsequently developed views which would sanction legislation more restrictive of free speech and free press.

So the following becomes pertinent: Some of those who in the twentieth century endorse legislation suppressing "obscene" literature have an attitude toward freedom of expression which does not match that of the framers of the First Amendment (adopted at the end of the eighteenth century) but does stem from an attitude toward writings dealing with sex which arose decades later, in the mid-nineteenth century, and is therefore labeled—doubtless too sweepingly—"Victorian." It was a dogma of "Victorian morality" that sexual misbehavior would be encouraged if one were to "acknowledge its existence or at any rate to present it vividly enough to form a lifelike image of it in the reader's mind"; this morality rested on a "faith that you could best conquer evil by shutting your eyes to its existence,"[7] and on a kind of word magic.[8] The demands at that time for "decency" in published words did not comport with the actual sexual conduct of many of those who made those demands: "The Victorians, as a general rule, managed to conceal the 'coarser' side of their lives so thoroughly under a mask of respectability that we often fail to realize how 'coarse' it really was. . . ." Could we have recourse to the vast unwritten literature of bawdry, we should be able to form a more veracious notion of life as it (then) really was. The respectables of those days often, "with unblushing license," held "high revels" in "night houses."[9] Thanks to them, Mrs. Warren's profes-

sion flourished, but it was considered sinful to talk about it in books.[10] Such a prudish and purely verbal moral code, at odds (more or less hypocritically) with the actual conduct of its adherents, was (as we have seen) not the moral code of those who framed the First Amendment. One would suppose, then, that the courts should interpret and enforce that Amendment according to the views of those framers, not according to the later "Victorian" code. . . .

The Statute, as Judicially Interpreted, Authorizes Punishment for Inducing Mere Thoughts, and Feelings, or Desires

For a time, American courts adopted the test of obscenity contrived in 1868 by L. J. Cockburn, in *Queen* v. *Hicklin*, L.R. 3 Q.B. 360: "I think the test of obscenity is this, whether the tendency of the matter charged as obscenity is to deprave and corrupt those whose minds are open to such immoral influences, and into whose hands a publication of this sort might fall." He added that the book there in question "would suggest . . . thoughts of a most impure and libidinous character."

The test in most federal courts has changed: They do not now speak of the thoughts of "those whose minds are open to . . . immoral influences" but, instead, of the thoughts of average adult normal men and women, determining what these thoughts are, not by proof at the trial, but by the standard of "the average conscience of the time," the current "social sense of what is right."

Yet the courts still define obscenity in terms of the assumed average normal adult reader's sexual thoughts or desires or impulses, without reference to any relation between those "subjective" reactions and his subsequent conduct. The judicial opinions use such key phrases as this: "suggesting lewd thoughts and exciting sensual desires," "arouse the salacity of the reader," "allowing or implanting . . . obscene, lewd, or lascivious thoughts or desires," "arouse sexual desires." The judge's charge in the instant case reads accordingly: "It must tend to stir sexual impulses and lead to sexually impure thoughts." Thus the statute, as the courts construe it, appears to provide criminal punishment for inducing no more than thoughts, feelings, desires.

No Adequate Knowledge Is Available Concerning the Effects on the Conduct of Normal Adults of Reading or Seeing the "Obscene"

Suppose we assume, *arguendo*, that sexual thoughts or feelings, stirred by the "obscene," probably will often issue into overt conduct. Still it does not at all follow that that conduct will be antisocial. For no sane person can believe it socially harmful if sexual desires lead to normal, and not antisocial, sexual behavior since, without such behavior, the human race would soon disappear.

Doubtless, Congress could validly provide punishment for mailing any publications if there were some moderately substantial reliable data showing that reading or seeing those publications probably conduces to seriously harmful sexual conduct on the part of normal adult human beings. But we have no such data.

Suppose it argued that whatever excites sexual longings might *possibly* produce sexual misconduct. That cannot suffice: Notoriously, perfumes sometimes act as aphrodisiacs, yet no one will suggest that therefore Congress may constitutionally legislate punishment for mailing perfumes. It may be that among the stimuli to irregular sexual conduct, by normal men and women, may be almost anything—the odor of carnations or cheese, the sight of a cane or a candle or a shoe, the touch of silk or a gunnysack. For all anyone now knows, stimuli of that sort may be far more provocative of such misconduct than reading obscene books or seeing obscene pictures. Said John Milton, "Evil manners are as perfectly learnt, without books, a thousand other ways that cannot be stopped."

Effect of "Obscenity" on Adult Conduct

To date there exist, I think, no thoroughgoing studies by competent persons which justify the conclusion that normal adults' reading or seeing of the "obscene" probably induces antisocial conduct. Such competent studies as have been made do conclude that so complex and numerous are the causes of sexual vice that it is impossible to assert with any assurance that "obscenity" represents a ponderable causal factor in sexually deviant adult behavior. "Although the whole subject of obscenity censorship hinges upon the unproved assumption that 'obscene' literature is a significant factor in causing sexual deviation from the community standard, no report can be found of a single effort at genuine research to test this assumption by singling out as a factor for study the effect of sex literature upon sexual behavior."[11] What little competent research has been done points definitely in a direction precisely opposite to that assumption.

Alpert reports[12] that, when, in the 1920s, 409 women college graduates were asked to state in writing what things stimulated them sexually, they answered thus: 218 said men; 95 said books; 40 said drama; 29 said dancing; 18 said pictures; 9 said music. Of those who replied "that the source of their sex information came from books, not one specified a 'dirty' book as the source. Instead, the books listed were: The Bible, the dictionary, the encyclopedia, novels from Dickens to Henry James, circulars about venereal diseases, medical books, and Motley's *Rise of the Dutch Republic*." Macaulay, replying to advocates of the suppression of obscene books, said: "We find it difficult to believe that in a world so full of temptations as this, any gentleman whose life would have been virtuous if he had not read Aristophanes or Juvenal, will be vicious by reading them." Echoing Macaulay, Jimmy Walker, former mayor of New York City, remarked that he had never heard of a woman seduced by a book. New Mexico has never had an obscenity statute; there is no evidence that, in that state, sexual misconduct is proportionately greater than elsewhere.

Effect on Conduct of Young People

. . . Judge Clark[13] speaks of "the strongly held views of those with competence in the premises as to the very direct connection" of obscenity "with the development of juvenile delinquency." . . . One of the cited writings is a report, by Dr. [Marie] Jahoda and associates, entitled "The Impact of Literature: A Psychological Discussion of Some Assumptions in the Censorship Debate" (1954). I have read this report (which is a careful survey of all available studies and psychological theories). I think it expresses an attitude quite contrary to that indicated by Judge Clark. In order to avoid any possible bias in my interpretation of that report, I thought it well to ask Dr. Jahoda to write her own summary of it, which, with her permission, I shall quote.

Dr. Jahoda's summary reads as follows:

Persons who argue for increased censorship of printed matter often operate on the assumption that reading about sexual matters or about violence and brutality leads to anti-social actions, particularly to juvenile delinquency. An examination of the pertinent psychological literature has led to the following conclusions:

1. There exists no research evidence either to prove or to disprove this assumption definitely.

2. In the absence of scientific proof two lines of psychological approach to the examination of the assumption are possible: (a) a review of what is known on the causes of juvenile delinquency; and (b) a review of what is known about the effect of literature on the mind of the reader.

3. In the vast research literature on the causes of juvenile delinquency there is no evidence to justify the assumption that reading about sexual matters or about violence leads to delinquent acts. Experts on juvenile delinquency agree that it has no single cause. Most of them regard early childhood events, which precede the reading age, as a necessary condition for later delinquency. At a later age, the nature of personal relations is assumed to have much greater power in determining a delinquent career than the vicarious experiences provided by reading matter. Juvenile delinquents as a group read less, and less easily, than nondelinquents. Individual instances are reported in which so-called "good" books allegedly influenced a delinquent in the manner in which "bad" books are assumed to influence him.

Where childhood experiences and subsequent events have combined to make delinquency psychologically likely, reading could have one of two effects: It could serve a trigger function releasing the criminal act or it could provide for a substitute outlet of aggression in fantasy, dispensing with the need for criminal action. There is no empirical evidence in either direction.

4. With regard to the impact of literature on the mind of the reader, it must be pointed out that there is a vast overlap in content between all media of mass communication.

The daily press, television, radio, movies, books and comics all present their share of so-called "bad" material, some with great realism as reports of actual events, some in clearly fictionalized form. It is virtually impossible to isolate the impact of one of these media on a population exposed to all of them. Some evidence suggests that the particular communications which arrest the attention of an individual are in good part a matter of choice. As a rule, people do not expose themselves to everything that is offered, but only to what agrees with their inclinations.

Children, who have often not yet crystallized their preferences and have more unspecific curiosity than many adults, are therefore perhaps more open to accidental influences from literature. This may present a danger to youngsters who are insecure or maladjusted who find in reading (of "bad" books as well as of "good" books) an escape from reality which they do not dare face. Needs which are not met in the real world are gratified in a fantasy world. It is likely, though not fully demonstrated, that excessive reading of comic books will intensify in children those qualities which drove them to the comic book world to begin with: an inability to face the world, apathy, a belief that the individual is hopelessly impotent and driven by uncontrollable forces and, hence, an acceptance of violence and brutality in the real world.

It should be noted that insofar as causal sequence is implied, insecurity and maladjustment in a child must precede this exposure to the written word in order to lead to these potential effects. Unfortunately, perhaps, the reading of Shakespeare's tragedies or of Andersen's and Grimm's fairy tales might do much the same.

Maybe someday we will have enough reliable data to show that obscene books and pictures do tend to influence children's sexual conduct adversely. Then a federal statute could be enacted which would avoid constitutional defects by authorizing punishment for using the mails or interstate shipments in the sale of such books and pictures to children.

It is, however, not at all clear that children would be ignorant, in any considerable measure, of obscenity, if no obscene publications ever came into their hands. Youngsters get a vast deal of education in sexual smut from companions of their own age. A verbatim report of conversations among young teen-age boys (from average respectable homes) will disclose their amazing proficiency in obscene language, learned from other boys. Replying to the argument of the need for censorship to protect the young, Milton said: "Who shall regulate all the . . . conversation of our youth . . . appoint what shall be discussed . . . ?" Most judges who reject that view are long past their youth and have probably forgotten the conversational ways of that period of life: "I remember when I was a little boy," said Dr. Dooley, "but I don't remember how I was a little boy."

The Obscenity Statute and the Reputable Press

Let it be assumed, for the sake of the argument, that contemplation of published matter dealing with sex has a significant impact on children's conduct. On that assumption, we cannot overlook the fact that our most reputable newspapers and periodicals carry advertisements and photographs displaying women in what decidedly are sexually alluring postures, and at times emphasizing the importance of "sex appeal." That women are there shown scantily clad increases "the mystery and allure of the bodies that are hidden," writes an eminent psychiatrist. "A leg covered by a silk stocking is much more attractive than a naked one; a bosom pushed into shape by a brassiere is more alluring than the pendant realities."[14] Either, then, the statute must be sternly applied to prevent the mailing of many reputable newspapers and periodicals containing such ads and photographs, or else we must acknowledge that they have created a cultural atmosphere for children in which, at a maximum, only the most trifling additional effect can be imputed to children's perusal of the kind of matter mailed by the defendant. . . .

Da Capo: Available Data Seem Wholly Insufficient to Show That the Obscenity Statutes Come Within Any Exception to the First Amendment

I repeat that because that statute is not restricted to obscene publications mailed for sale to minors,

its validity should be tested in terms of the evil effects of adult reading of obscenity on adult conduct. With the present lack of evidence that publications probably have such effects, how can the government discharge its burden of demonstrating sufficiently that the statute is within the narrow exceptions to the scope of the First Amendment? One would think that the mere possibility of a causal relation to misconduct ought surely not be enough. . . .

If the Obscenity Statute Is Valid, Why May Congress Not Validly Provide Punishment for Mailing Books Which Will Provoke Thoughts It Considers Undesirable About Religion or Politics?

If the statute is valid, then, considering the foregoing, it would seem that its validity must rest on this ground: Congress, by statute, may constitutionally provide punishment for the mailing of books evoking mere thoughts or feelings about sex, if Congress considers them socially dangerous, even in the absence of any satisfactory evidence that those thoughts or feelings will tend to bring about socially harmful deeds. If that be correct, it is hard to understand why, similarly, Congress may not constitutionally provide punishment for such distribution of books evoking mere thoughts or feelings about religion or politics which Congress considers socially dangerous, even in the absence of any satisfactory evidence that those thoughts or feelings will tend to bring about socially dangerous deeds.

The Judicial Exception of the "Classics"

As I have said, I have no doubt the jury could reasonably find, beyond a reasonable doubt, that many of the publications mailed by defendant were obscene within the current judicial definition of the term as explained by the trial judge in his charge to the jury. But so, too, are a multitude of recognized works of art found in public libraries. Compare, for instance, the books which are exhibits in this case with Montaigne's *Essay on Some Lines of Virgil* or with Chaucer. Or consider the many nude pictures which the defendant transmitted through the mails, and then turn to the reproductions in the articles on paintings and sculptures in the *Encyclopaedia Britannica* (14th edition). Some of the latter are no less "obscene" than those which led to the defendant's conviction. Yet these Encyclopedia volumes are readily accessible to everyone, young or old, and, without let or hindrance, are frequently mailed to all parts of the country. Catalogues of famous art museums, almost equally accessible and also often mailed, contain reproductions of paintings and sculpture, by great masters, no less "obscene."

To the argument that such books (and such reproductions of famous paintings and works of sculpture) fall within the statutory ban, the courts have answered that they are "classics"—books of "literary distinction" or works which have "an accepted place in the arts," including, so this court has held, Ovid's *Art of Love* and Boccaccio's *Decameron*. There is a "curious dilemma" involved in this answer that the statute condemns "only books which are dull and without merit," that in no event will the statute be applied to the "classics," that is, books "of literary distinction."[15] The courts have not explained how they escape that dilemma, but instead seem to have gone to sleep (although rather uncomfortably) on its horns.

. . . No one can rationally justify the judge-made exception. The contention would scarcely pass as rational that the "classics will be read or seen solely by an intellectual or artistic elite"; for, even ignoring the snobbish, undemocratic nature of this contention, there is no evidence that the elite has a moral fortitude (an immunity from moral corruption) superior to that of the "masses." And if the exception, to make it rational, were taken as meaning that a contemporary book is exempt if it equates in "literary distinction" with the "classics," the result would be amazing: Judges would have to serve as literary critics; jurisprudence would merge with aesthetics; authors and publishers would consult the legal digests for legal-artistic precedents; we would some day have a Legal Restatement of the Canons of Literary Taste. . . .

How Censorship Under the Statute Actually Operates

Prosecutors, as censors, actually exercise prior restraint. Fear of punishment serves as a powerful restraint on publication, and fear of punishment often means, practically, fear of prosecution. For most men dread indictment and prosecution; the publicity alone terrifies, and to defend a criminal action is expensive. If the definition of obscenity had a limited and fairly well-known scope, that fear might deter restricted sorts of publications only. But on account of the extremely vague judicial definition of the obscene, a person threatened with prosecution if he mails (or otherwise sends in interstate commerce) almost any book which deals in an unconventional, unorthodox manner with sex may well apprehend that, should the threat be carried out, he will be punished. As a result, each prosecutor becomes a literary censor (dictator) with immense unbridled power, a virtually uncontrolled discretion. A statute would be invalid which gave the Postmaster General the power, without reference to any standard, to close the mails to any publication he happened to dislike. Yet a federal prosecutor, under the federal obscenity statute, approximates that position: Within wide limits, he can (on the advice of the Postmaster General or on no one's advice) exercise such a censorship by threat without a trial, without any judicial supervision, capriciously and arbitrarily. Having no special qualifications for that task, nevertheless, he can, in large measure, determine at his will what those within his district may not read on sexual subjects. In that way, the statute brings about an actual prior restraint of free speech and free press which strikingly flouts the First Amendment. . . .

The Dangerously Infectious Nature of Governmental Censorship of Books

Governmental control of ideas or personal preferences is alien to a democracy. And the yearning to use governmental censorship of any kind is infectious. It may spread insidiously. Commencing with suppression of books as obscene, it is not unlikely to develop into official lust for the power of thought-control in the areas of religion, politics, and elsewhere. Milton observed that "licensing of books . . . necessarily pulls along with it so many other kinds of licensing." Mill noted that the "bounds of what may be called moral police" may easily extend "until it encroaches on the most unquestionably legitimate liberty of the individual." We should beware of a recrudescence of the undemocratic doctrine uttered in the seventeenth century by Berkeley, Governor of Virginia: "Thank God there are no free schools or preaching, for learning has brought disobedience into the world, and printing has divulged them. God keep us from both."

The People as Self-Guardians: Censorship by Public Opinion, Not by Government

Plato, who detested democracy, proposed to banish all poets; and his rulers were to serve as guardians of the people, telling lies for the people's good, vigorously suppressing writings these guardians thought dangerous. Governmental guardianship is repugnant to the basic tenet of our democracy: According to our ideals, our adult citizens are self-guardians, to act as their own fathers, and thus become self-dependent. When our governmental officials act towards our citizens on the thesis that "Papa knows best what's good for you," they enervate the spirit of the citizens: To treat grown men like infants is to make them infantile, dependent, immature.

So have sagacious men often insisted. Milton, in his *Areopagitica*, denounced such paternalism: "We censure them for a giddy, vicious and unguided people, in such sick and weak (a) state of faith and discretion as to be able to take down nothing but through the pipe of a licensor." "We both consider the people as our children," wrote Jefferson to Dupont de Nemours, "but you love them as infants whom you are afraid to trust without nurses, and I as adults whom I freely leave to self-government." Tocqueville sagely remarked: "No form or combination of social policy has yet been devised to make an energetic people of a community of pusillanimous and enfeebled citizens." "Man," warned Goethe, "is easily accustomed to slavery and learns quickly to be obedient when his freedom is taken from him." Said Carl Becker, "Self-government, and the spirit of freedom that sustains it, can be maintained only if the people have sufficient intelligence and honesty to maintain them with a minimum of legal compulsion. This heavy responsibility is the price of freedom."[16] The "great art," according to Milton, "lies to discern in what the law is to bid restraint and punishment, and in what things persuasion only is to work." So, we come back, once more, to Jefferson's advice: The only completely democratic way to control publications which arouse mere thoughts or feelings is through nongovernmental censorship by public opinion.

The Seeming Paradox of the First Amendment

Here we encounter an apparent paradox: The First Amendment, judicially enforced, curbs public opinion when translated into a statute which restricts freedom of expression (except that which will probably induce undesirable conduct). The paradox is unreal: The Amendment ensures that public opinion—the "common conscience of the time"—shall not commit suicide through legislation which chokes off today the free expression of minority views which may become the majority public opinion of tomorrow.

Private Persons or Groups May Validly Try to Influence Public Opinion

The First Amendment obviously has nothing to do with the way persons or groups, not a part of government, influence public opinion as to what constitutes "decency" or "obscenity." The Catholic Church, for example, has a constitutional right to persuade or instruct its adherents not to read designated books or kinds of books.

The Fine Arts Are Within the First Amendment's Protection

"The framers of the First Amendment," writes Chafee, "must have had literature and art in mind, because our first national statement on the subject of freedom of the press, the 1774 address of the Continental Congress to the inhabitants of Quebec, declared, 'The importance of this (freedom of the press) consists, beside the advancement of truth, science, morality and *arts* in general, in its diffusion of liberal sentiments on the administration of government.' "[17] One hundred and sixty-five years later, President Franklin Roosevelt said, "The arts cannot thrive except where men are free to be themselves and to be in charge of the discipline of their own energies and ardors. The conditions for democracy and for art are one and the same. What we call liberty in politics results in freedom of the arts."[18] The converse is also true.

In our industrial era when, perforce, economic pursuits must be, increasingly, governmentally regulated, it is especially important that the realm of art—the noneconomic realm—should remain free, unregimented, the domain of free enterprise, of unhampered competition at its maximum. An individual's taste is his own private concern. *De gustibus non [est] disputandum* represents a valued democratic maxim.

Milton wrote: "For though a licenser should happen to be judicious more than the ordinary, yet his very office . . . enjoins him to let pass nothing but what is vulgarly received already." He asked, "What a fine conformity would it starch us all into? We may fall . . . into a gross conformity stupidly. . . ." In 1859 Mill, in his essay *On Liberty*, maintained that conformity in taste is not a virtue, but a vice. "The danger," he wrote, "is not the excess but the deficiency of personal impulses and preferences. By dint of not following their own nature (men) have no nature to follow. . . . Individual spontaneity is entitled to free exercise   That so few men dare to be eccentric marks the chief danger of the time." Pressed by the demand for conformity, a people degenerate into "the deep slumber of a decided opinion," yield a "dull and torpid consent" to the accustomed. "Mental despotism" ensues. For "whatever crushes individuality is despotism by whatever name it be called. . . . It is not by wearing down into uniformity all that is individual in themselves, but by cultivating it, and calling it forth, within the limits imposed by the rights and interests of others, that human beings become a noble and beautiful object of contemplation; and as the works partake the character of those who do them, by the same process human life also becomes rich, diversified, and animating. . . . In proportion to the development of his individuality, each person becomes more valuable to himself, and is therefore capable of being more valuble to others. There is a greater fullness of life about his own existence, and when there is more life in the units there is more in the mass which is composed of them."

To vest a few fallible men—prosecutors, judges, jurors—with vast powers of literary or artistic censorship, to convert them into what Mill called a "moral police," is to make them despotic arbiters of literary products. If one day they ban mediocre books as obscene, another day they may do likewise to a work of genius. Originality, not too plentiful, should be cherished, not stifled. An author's imagination may be cramped if he must write with one eye on prosecutors or juries; authors must cope with publishers who, fearful about the judgments of governmental censors, may refuse to accept the manuscripts of contemporary Shelleys or Mark Twains or Whitmans.

Some few men stubbornly fight for the right to write or publish or distribute books which the great majority at the time consider loathsome. If we jail those few, the community may appear to have suffered nothing. The appearance is deceptive. For the conviction and punishment of these few will terrify writers who are more sensitive, less eager for a fight. What, as a result, they do not write might have been major literary contributions. "Suppression," Spinoza said, "is paring down the state till it is too small to harbor men of talent."

Notes

1. Judge Cuthbert Pound dissenting in *People v. Gitlow*, 234 N.Y. 132, 158, 136 N.E. 317, 327.

2. Padover, *The Complete Madison* (1953), pp. 295–296.

3. Padover, *The Complete Madison* (1953), pp. 267, 268–269.

4. Padover, *The Complete Jefferson* (1943), p. 109.

5. Padover, *The Complete Jefferson* (1943), p. 130.

6. Padover, *The Complete Jefferson* (1943), p. 889.

7. Wingfield-Stratford, *Those Earnest Victorians* (1930), p. 151.

8. See Kaplan, "Obscenity as an Esthetic Category," 20 *Law and Contemporary Problems* (1955), pp. 544, 550: "In many cultures, obscenity has an important part in magical rituals. In our own, its magical character is betrayed in the puritan's supposition that words alone can work evil, and that evil will be averted if only the words are not uttered."

9. Wingfield-Stratford, *Victorians*, pp. 296–297.

10. Paradoxically, this attitude apparently tends to "create" obscenity, for the foundation of obscenity seems to be secrecy and shame: "The secret becomes shameful because of its secrecy." Kaplan, "Obscenity as an Esthetic Category," 20 *Law and Contemporary Problems* (1955), pp. 544, 556.

11. Lockhart and McClure, "Obscenity and the Courts," 20 *Law and Contemporary Problems* (1955), pp. 587, 595.

12. Alpert, "Judicial Censorship and the Press," 52 *Harvard Law Review* (1938), pp. 40, 72.

13. The majority opinion upholding Roth's conviction was delivered by Chief Judge Clark, U.S. Court of Appeals, Second Circuit. [The Editor]

14. Myerson, *Speaking of Man* (1950), p. 92.

15. *Ruth v. Goldman*, 2 Cir., 172 F.2d 788.

16. Becker, *Freedom and Responsibility in the American Way of Life* (1945), p. 42.

17. Chafee, *Government and Mass Communication* (1947), p. 53.

18. Message at dedicating exercises of the New York Museum of Modern Art, May 8, 1939.

Questions for Analysis

1. What evidence does Frank offer for the claim "Freedom to speak publicly and to publish has, as its inevitable and important correlative, the private right to hear, to read, and to think about what one hears and reads"? Do you agree?

2. Do you agree that pro-censorship views can be traced to Victorian influences?

3. On what grounds does Frank dispute the claim that there is a connection between pornography and conduct?

4. Would it be accurate to say that Frank would oppose even pornography aimed at minors?

5. Do you think, as Frank claims, that a prohibition against the dissemination of sexual materials would logically justify a prohibition against other things considered "socially dangerous"?

6. Frank contends that government control of ideas or personal preferences is alien to a democracy. Contrast this view with Walter Berns's view in "Beyond the (Garbage) Pale, or Democracy, Censorship and the Arts."

7. Distinguish the utilitarian from the nonutilitarian considerations that make up Frank's argument.

The Moral Theory of Free Speech and Obscenity Law

David A. J. Richards

In Chapter 1 you were introduced to the social-justice theory of John Rawls. In Rawls's view, basic political rights are not, as utilitarians believe, justified by appeal to consequences, nor may they be overridden in order to further social welfare. Rawls has argued for a comprehensive theory of justice that holds that principles of justice can be discovered by consideration of which principles for regulating their basic social structures a group of people would choose if they were coming together to form a society. Rawls imposes the condition that the people are not to know what positions in society they will occupy. Such a procedure, he claims, would represent a fair choice of principles. He argues further that given the constraints of the principles of justice that would be selected, such people would further choose the protections of basic political rights, including that of free speech.

The following essay is a good illustration of how Rawls's thought, which applies primarily to economic transactions, is useful in other situations. David A. J. Richards outlines a theory of the First Amendment based on a Rawlsian conception of justice. After carefully examining the nature *of pornography, Richards argues that the Supreme Court's reasoning in* Paris Adult Theatre *cannot be accepted. Specifically, Richards argues that regulating obscene communications subverts the central moral purpose of the First Amendment, which, in his view, is to secure the greatest equal liberty of communication compatible with a like liberty for all. This, of course, is an application of Rawls's first principle of justice, the equality principle.*

. . . We begin with a discussion of the moral theory underlying the First Amendment. Then, we turn to the examination of the notion of the obscene. The contours of the notion are not self-evident. In order to understand the law of obscenity, some precision must be given to this notion itself. Finally, the analysis will focus on the issue of the constitutionality of obscenity law. . . .

In interpreting and enforcing the First Amendment, courts must determine the proper standards under which their responsibility is to be discharged. On the basis of our formulation of applicable principles of justice, the constitutional notions of free speech and free press should be understood in terms of certain relevant requirements of the first principle of justice, namely, the greatest equal liberty of communication compatible with a like liberty for all. Thus, all legal prohibitions and regulations which constrain liberty of communication in a manner incompatible with this idea should be constitutionally forbidden and invalid. But how are we to understand the concrete application of the equal liberty idea?[1]

One important point is that in applying the equal liberty principle, the basic liberties must be assessed as an interrelated system. The weights of each kind of liberty may depend on the specification of other kinds of liberty. The liberties of expression constitute both a right to communicate and a right to be the object of communication. Obviously, these liberties must be adjusted to one another in such a way as to best realize the underlying values of autonomous self-determination. The morally preferable adjustment is a liberty to communicate to any audience that is itself at liberty to choose to be or not to be an audience. Given this interpretation, the liberty to communicate and other liberties are to be assessed as a whole in the light of the principle requiring the greatest equal liberty compatible with a like liberty for all.

The crucial analytic question is whether institutions and practices governing human expression, assessed as a system,[2] violate or cohere with

the idea of a system of greatest equal liberty compatible with a like liberty for all. For example, it is clear that procedural rules of order, time, and place, which regulate a reasonable pattern of communications, cohere with this idea, for they enlarge the equal liberty of communication compatible with a like liberty for all.[3] Without such rules of order, time, and place, the liberty of communication of one will be used to violate the liberty of communication of another so that the system of liberties is not the greatest *equal* liberty compatible with a like liberty for all.

Similarly, the punishment of communications that are an indispensable part of actions designed to and capable of overthrowing the constitutional order—for example, communicating military secrets to the enemy—does not violate this equal liberty of communications, for such communications would help to overthrow the system of equal liberties. The proof that such communications do advance the overthrow of the constitutional order must, however, appeal to general principles of empirical induction and inference. No special principles of inference, not admissible in deciding on the principles of justice, are admissible in the interpretation of those principles. Thus, special a priori views regarding the relation of certain communications to the decline and fall of the constitutional order, not justified on generally acceptable empirical grounds, are not morally tolerable as reasons for limiting such communications.

Attempts by the state to prohibit certain contents of communication per se are fundamentally incompatible with the moral and constitutional principle of equal liberty. Notwithstanding the outrage felt by the majority toward certain contents of communication, the equal liberty principle absolutely forbids the prohibition of such communications on the ground of such outrage alone. Otherwise, the liberty of expression, instead of the vigorous and potent defense of individual autonomy that it is, would be a pitifully meager permission allowing people to communicate only in ways to which no one has any serious objection. The interest of the few in free expression is not to be sacrificed on such grounds to the interest of the many. Conventional attitudes are not to be the procrustean measure of the exercise of human expressive and judgmental competence.

On this view, the constitutionally protected liberty of free expression is the legal embodiment of a moral principle which ensures to each person the maximum equal liberty of communication compatible with a like liberty for all. Importantly, if the First Amendment freedoms rest on a fundamental moral principle, they have no necessary justificatory relation to the liberty of equal voting rights. No doubt, both rights advance values of self-direction and autonomy, but a maximum equal liberty of self-expression is neither a necessary nor a sufficient condition of democratic voting rights or the competent exercise of those rights. Voting rights may exist and be competently exercised in a regime where expression is not in general free, but is limited to a small class of talented technicians who circulate relevant data on policy issues to the electorate. Similarly, free expression may exist in a political aristocracy or in a democracy where voting rights are not competently exercised because of illiteracy or political apathy.

The independent status of the value of free expression shows that its value is not intrinsically political but rests on deeper moral premises regarding the general exercise of autonomous expressive and judgmental capacity and the good that this affords in human life. It follows that the attempt to limit the constitutional protection of free expression to the political[4] must be rejected on moral and constitutional grounds.[5]

The foregoing account makes clear that strong moral ideas are implicit in the First Amendment and that moral analysis may clarify the proper constitutional interpretation and application of those ideas. It is significant in this connection that the account here proposed clarifies many concrete features of First Amendment adjudications,[6] for example, the propriety of reasonable regulations of time, place, and procedure,[7] the insistence that majority dislike of protected expression has no constitutional weight,[8] the basis of the clear and present danger test,[9] and the refusal to limit the First Amendment to the political.[10] It is equally clear that this account provides a framework from which the case law may be crucially assessed both as regards proper extensions of First Amendment rights, such as rights of access to the media,[11] and the criticism of anomalies in existing case law which depart from its deepest moral strains.

The Concept of the Obscene

A satisfying philosophical explication of the notion of the obscene would clarify the notion itself, its connections to related notions (such as the pornographic, the indecent, and the immoral), its uses in speech, and its relations to fundamental attitudes which explain how the notion comes to have moving appeal to conduct. Initially, we must describe some general marks of the obscene. Then, a constructive account of the notion will be proposed, and, finally, an attempt will be made to connect the account to related notions, especially the pornographic.

The Marks of the Obscene

The etymology of *obscene* is obscure. The *Oxford English Dictionary* notes that the etymology is "doubtful,"[12] while *Webster's* suggests a derivation from the Latin *ob*, meaning *to, before, against*, and the Latin *caenum*, meaning *filth*.[13] Other commentators suggest alternative derivations from the Latin *obscurus*, meaning *concealed*,[14] or a derivation as a corruption of the Latin *scena* meaning *what takes place off stage*.[15] In the latter sense, blinding Gloucester on stage in *King Lear* would have been an obscenity for a Greek playwright like Sophocles (thus, Oedipus is blinded offstage), but it was not for an Elizabethan playwright like Shakespeare, who was imbued with the bloodthirstiness of Senecan tragedy.

The standard dictionary definition of *obscene* turns on notions of what is disgusting, filthy, or offensive to decency.[16] While contemporary legal discussions emphasize the applicability of *obscene* to depictions, it is clearly significantly applied to acts themselves. Shakespeare, for example, speaks of an obscene deed,[17] and Sartre discusses obscene movements of the body.[18] In the law it is notable that the earliest English obscenity conviction was for obscene acts.[19] Judicial decisions[20] and legal and general[21] commentary emphasize the connections of the obscene to the notion of shame. It is clear that in European thought the notion of the obscene has long been connected to the scatological[22] and the sexually lascivious,[23] a connection emphasized in Anglo-American legal history.[24] This history also makes clear the significant relation of the obscene to the notion of the morally corrupting. Many of these connections were summarized in the language of the Comstock Act, which, in forbidding the mailing of obscene material in interstate commerce in the United States, speaks of "obscene, lewd, or lascivious . . . publication(s)" and included in its prohibitions contraceptives and abortifacients or anything else "for any indecent or immoral use."[25]

The most significant class of speech acts involving the notion of the obscene is that class of epithets, known as *obscenities*, which relate to excretory or sexual functions.[26] Such expressions are, at least in reasonably well-educated circles, conventionalized ways of expressing attitudes of disgust and contempt which depend for their sometimes shocking and bracing effect on the impropriety of their use.[27] In circles, like the army, where the verbal obscenities are constantly employed, their function seems quite different;[28] there they are used as a kind of manly, transgression-braving vocabulary whose use is a criterion of intimate membership in the group. Related to this is the use of obscenities among intimate friends and even as a language of love.

The verbal obscenities demonstrate the relation of the obscene not only to shock and offense, but to the anxiety-producing loss of control. On hearing or using such expressions in reasonably well-educated circles, one has the sense of a loss of control, a sudden frustration, or an explosion of pique, which may surprise the speaker as much as the listener.

In the light of these functions and marks of the verbal obscenities, one can better understand the functions of literature which employs obscene contents—for example, some works of Swift[29] and Pope.[30] By employing contents known to be offensive to the conventional proprieties, such literature can express complex communicative intentions of bitter satire and burlesque in ways related to the capacity of the verbal obscenities to express disgust and contempt.[31] Similarly, one can understand the use of the obscene in literary humor as well as in the smutty joke and obscene witticism.[32] Obviously, such effects of the obscene are in some important way tied to attitudes, the existence of which accounts for these effects.

An Explication of the Obscene

The concept of the obscene is identical with the concept of those actions, representations, works, or states which display an exercise of bodily or personal function which in certain circumstances constitutes an abuse of that function, as dictated by standards in which one has invested self-esteem, so that the supposed abuse of function is regarded as a demeaning object of self-contempt and self-disgust.[33]

On this view, the obscene is a subcategory of the objects of shame. Shame is, I believe, properly understood in terms of a fall from one's self-concept in the exercise of capacities which one desires to exercise competently. The objects of shame, thus, are explained by reference to the notions of personal competence and self-respect which are their bases. One feels ashamed because, for example, one has been cowardly, failing to exercise courageous self-control over fear when danger threatened. A characteristic mark of such failure is self-contempt or self-disgust.

The obscene identifies a special class of the possible objects of shame which are explained by reference to certain defined notions of competence in bodily or personal function. Thus, just as one explains to a child that it is an abuse and misuse of the function of a knife or fork to put either in the ear, so too one explains the proper exercise of bodily function. The use of the body is thought to have precise and sharply defined functions and ends. This idea, found widely among primitive peoples and the most ancient cultures,[34] including, significantly, ancient Judaism,[35] rigidly defines certain clear proprieties of bodily function as pure or clean. Failure to so exercise bodily function is unclean, polluting, an abomination, in short, obscene.[36]

The obscene, thus, is a conceptual residuum of very ancient ways of thinking about human conduct. Human beings are thought of as clusters of strengths or virtues and corresponding weaknesses or vices, where virtues and vices are not conceived in narrow moral terms.[37] Obscenity within this view is a kind of vice, a wasting and abuse of the natural employment of bodily or personal function. Hence, a culture's definition of the obscene will indicate those areas of bodily or personal function in which the culture centrally invests its self-esteem and in which deviance provokes the deepest anxieties. For example, incompetence with respect to excretory function typically defines the frailest members of society, infants and the senile. Where frailty and declining powers are a source of anxiety, excretory impropriety is likely to be regarded as obscene. Moreover, where the sexual function is regarded as akin to the excretory function, as it easily may be,[38] sexual behavior will come to share this condemnation.

This explication is intended to apply cross-culturally.[39] To the extent people in different cultures take different attitudes to certain bodily or personal functions, those cultures will take different views of those things that are obscene, though the cultures share the concept of the obscene as an abuse of bodily or personal function. A striking example is provided by the Tahitians, who do not take the Western view of the competent exercise of sexual function, but do take a rather stringent view of eating; thus for Tahitians, displays of coitus are not obscene, but displays of eating are.[40] For us, aside from contexts of satirical humor,[41] eating conventional food would be obscene only in extreme circumstances of gluttonous self-indulgence[42] or in circumstances where eating is associated with aphrodisiacal allure.[43]

Similarly, this explication is true over time as well. For example, English society in the eighteenth century was apparently very tolerant of obscene literature, despite the fact that obscene libel had become a common-law offense.[44] But in the nineteenth century, changing moral standards gave rise to groups like the Society for the Suppression of Vice and prosecutions for obscene libel increased rapidly.[45] Concern over the explosion of pornographic literature[46] finally received expression in English statutes.[47] In the same way, contemporary attitudes evince a shift in the application of the obscene; a growing modern usage applies the notion, for example, to violence and death and displays of violence and death (based on the idea, I believe, that these represent demeaning abuses of competences of the person),[48] but no longer applies the notion to sex or sexual displays.[49]

Significantly, this explication accounts for the application of *obscene* to acts as well as to depictions of acts. Both acts and depictions are obscene if they display certain exercises of bodily function; whether by the act itself or by depiction, our anxiety is aroused when we become aware of phenomena which threaten our self-esteem. It does not follow, of course, that obscene depictions are only of obscene acts. Normal heterosexual intercourse between a married couple is not typically viewed as obscene; but a public depiction of such intercourse would, by some people, be viewed as obscene. Nonetheless, there is little question that the obscenity of an act is a sufficient condition for the obscenity of a depiction of that act. Most cases of obscene depictions fall into this category. At one time obscenity convictions were granted for the mere sympathetic discussion of homosexuality or advocacy of birth control or abortion, apart from any pornographic representation of any kind.[50] The idea seems to have been that since homosexuality, birth control, and abortion were obscene, any favorable discussion of them was obscene. Even today, it is clear that courts are quickest to make or affirm judgments of obscenity with respect to depictions of sexual acts such as cunnilingus, fellatio, sodomy, sadomasochism, and bestiality that are regarded as obscene in themselves.[51] The view that these acts are obscene is the basis for judging their depiction to be obscene.

The connection between the obscenity of acts and depictions of acts distinguishes the obscene from the indecent. The distinctive mark of the indecent is the public exhibition of that which, while unobjectionable in private, is offensive and embarrassing when done in public.[52] The obscene, by contrast, may be and often is condemned whether or not it involves a public display.

Finally, this linkage between the act and its depiction accounts for the use of obscenities to express contempt and disgust. Since the obscene identifies a disgusting abuse of bodily function, it is wholly natural that it should be used to express disgust. It follows that if one does not find certain communicative contents obscene, one may tendentiously advocate the abandonment of speech acts using those contents to express disgust.[53]

The Obscene and the Pornographic

Pornography etymologically derives from the Greek *pornographos*, meaning *writing of harlots*, literally, writing concerning or descriptive of prostitutes in their profession.[54] Thus, the depictions of various forms of sexual intercourse on the walls of a certain building in Pompeii, intended as aphrodisiacs for the orgiastic bacchanales housed there, were literally *pornographos*.[55] Pornography in this sense is identified by its sexually explicit content, its depiction of varied forms of sexual intercourse, turgid genitalia, and so on.[56]

Pornography is neither conceptually nor factually identical with the obscene. Conceptually, the notion of sexually explicit, aphrodisiacal depictions is not the same idea as that of the abuse of a bodily or personal function. Many cultures, though sharing the fundamental concept of the obscene, do not regard pornography as obscene.[57] Individuals within our culture may find coprophagy (eating feces) obscene,[58] but do not find pornography obscene,[59] because they fail to take a certain attitude toward "proper" sexual function although they do have ideas about "proper" excretory function. For such people, viewing sex or depictions of sex as obscene is an unfortunate blending of the sexual and the excremental.[60]

If there is no necessary connection between the pornographic and the obscene, how did the connection between them arise?

One account of the sexual morality behind this connection is that of Catholic canon law which

> holds, as a basic and cardinal fact, that complete sexual activity and pleasure is licit and moral only in a naturally completed act in valid marriage. All acts which, of their psychological and physical nature, are designed to be preparatory to the complete act, take their licitness and their morality from the complete act. If, therefore, they are entirely divorced from the complete act, they are distorted, warped, meaningless, and hence immoral.[61]

This view of course derives from St. Augustine's classic conception that the only proper "genital commotion"[62] is one with the voluntary aim of reproduction of the species.[63] It follows from this view that only certain rigidly defined kinds of "natural" intercourse in conventional marriage are moral; "unnatural" forms of such intercourse are forbidden; extramarital and of course homosexual intercourse are forbidden. Further, all material that will induce to "genital commotion" not within mar-

riage is forbidden. Pornography is obscene not only in itself, because it displays intercourse not within marriage, but also because it tempts to intercourse outside marriage or to masturbation, which are independently obscene acts because they are forms of sexual conduct that violate minimum standards of proper bodily function and thus cause disgust.

While this specific Catholic view is not the universal basis for the connection of the obscene and the pornographic, this general kind of view seems always present. Sexual function of certain rigidly defined kinds is alone the correct and competent exercise of sexual function. All other forms are marked by failure, weakness, and disgust. Masturbation in particular is a moral wrong.

Clearly this general notion, premised on supposed medical as well as theological facts, was behind the extraordinary explosion in obscenity legislation in England and the United States in the 1850s, 1860s, and 1870s. This legislation rested squarely on the remarkable Victorian medical view relating masturbation and sexual excess in general to insanity.[64] Pornography, being in part masturbation fantasy, was condemned on medical as well as theological grounds, so that Anthony Comstock, the father of the Comstock Act, could point with the support of medical authority to the fact that pornography's "most deadly effects are felt by the victims in the habit of secret vices."[65]

Significantly, Victorian medical literature and pornography[66] make transparent that sexual function was construed on the model of excretory function.[67] The proper exercise of sexual function was rigidly defined in terms of one mode, marital reproductive sexuality. Within that mode, the proper function was one of regularity and moderation. Thus, doctors condemned sexual excess within marriage[68] and deprecated infertile sexual activity within marriage as "conjugal onanism."[69] This rigid and narrow conception of sexual function was obviously profoundly opposed to pornography which would expose, in the words of one prominent Victorian court, "the minds of those hitherto pure . . . to the danger of contamination and pollution from the impurity it contains."[70]

Similar views regarding the evils of masturbation are echoed in contemporary writers who condemn pornography. Thus, D. H. Lawrence emphasized the corrosive effects of autoeroticism on the capacity for the central spiritual experience, for Lawrence, of sexual mutuality between partners.[71]

Whatever the form of theological, medical, or psychological belief underlying the association of the obscene and the pornographic, some such belief always prevails, so that there is a significant correlation between judgments of obscenity and the judgments that a certain work is both sexually arousing and quite unpleasant.[72]

The Constitutionality of Obscenity Law

It should now be possible to apply the foregoing explication of the obscene and the moral analysis of the First Amendment to the issue raised in *Miller* v. *California* and *Paris Adult Theatre I* v. *Slaton*—the constitutionally permissible concept of the obscene.

Miller reaffirmed the holding of *Roth* v. *United States* that obscene expression is not protected by the First Amendment. In addition, the Court, speaking through the Chief Justice, formulated a constitutional test for obscenity. The test is threefold:

> (a) whether "the average person, applying contemporary community standards" would find that the work, taken as a whole, appeals to the prurient interest . . . ; (b) whether the work depicts or describes, in a patently offensive way, sexual conduct specifically defined by the applicable state law; and (c) whether the work, taken as a whole, lacks serious literary, artistic, political, or scientific value.[73]

This test imposes on states that wish to ban obscenity an obligation to formulate specific standards. Moreover, *Miller* limits the obscene to "representations or descriptions of ultimate sexual acts, normal or perverted, actual or simulated" or "of masturbation, excretory functions and lewd exhibition of the genitals."[74] In effect, only hard-core scatology and pornography may be banned.[75]

On the other hand, the *Miller* test permits censorship wherever the allegedly obscene work is without "serious" value.[76] Thus, a lighter burden is imposed on the prosecution than was imposed under the prior "utterly without redeeming social value" test.[77] Moreover, reliance on local standards,[78] within the bounds of the court's test, permits a variety of constitutionally permissible restrictions. Hence, a person's First Amendment rights may be restricted in one jurisdiction without appeal to a national standard.[79]

The *Miller* case involved a conviction for mailing unsolicited sexually explicit material, which is, of course, a problem of nonconsensual intrusion of offensive material. In *Paris Adult Theatre I* v. *Slaton*, however, a majority of the Court, again speaking through Chief Justice Burger, applied the *Miller* criteria for obscenity to an adult's fully informed and consensual access to obscene materials. The Court thus narrowly limited the holding of *Stanley* v. *Georgia*[80] to its facts. There the Court invalidated a state statute prohibiting the possession and private use in one's home of obscene (pornographic) materials on the grounds of infringing the constitutional right of privacy. In *Paris Adult Theatre*, and other cases decided concurrently, the Court made clear that the constitutional right of privacy as regards the use of obscene materials applies only to one's home, not to any theater, nor even to the transport of such materials in one's traveling bags for private use.[81]

Miller and *Paris Adult Theatre*, then, find obscenity, even for consenting adults, to be outside the protection of the First Amendment, but the analysis here presented suggests that the Court's decisions are wrong. An understanding of the moral function of the First Amendment compels a conclusion contrary to the Court's; there should be a presumption that obscenity, like other forms of expression, falls within the protection of the First Amendment.

To summarize, obscene communications, it has been proposed, implicate the idea of the abuse of basic bodily functions, the proper exercise of which is an object of basic self-esteem and the improper use of which is an object of shame and disgust. A sufficient, though not a necessary, condition of the obscenity of a communication is that the act depicted be obscene.

On this view, the precise application of the notion of the obscure crucially depends on beliefs and attitudes involving precise and rigid definitions of the proper exercise of bodily functions. Thus, different cultures, with different beliefs and attitudes, may regard dissimilar acts or objects as obscene. Similarly, within a culture, individuals may apply the label *obscene* to different phenomena. In the United States, for example, many people regard pornography as obscene because it reflects, for them, an improper exercise of sexual function. But others, not sharing their beliefs and attitudes, do not regard

pornography as obscene,[82] though they may think
that other things, like depictions of coprophagy or
gratuitous violence, are obscene.

An obscenity law, then, must be understood
as a political expression of broader popular attitudes toward the putative proper and improper use
of the body. It is no accident that such laws have
been used to forbid the transport of abortifacient
and contraceptive information[83] and dissemination
of sex manuals[84] and to prosecute advocacy of contraception and population control.[85] The moral attitudes behind such laws, directed against a supposed "abuse" of the body, were founded on a
compound of religious, psychological, and medical
beliefs basic to which was a deep fear of masturbation.[86] Masturbation, it was believed, led directly
to physical debility and even death,[87] as well as
crime and civil disorder.[88]

In judicial interpretation of the notion of the
obscene, courts implicitly decide on and enforce
popular attitudes about bodily function. Whatever
may be the constitutional legitimacy of regulating
obscene acts, it is impossible to see how regulating
obscene communications can avoid raising the
deepest First Amendment problems. Because judicial application of obscenity laws necessarily enforces
a particular attitude, albeit presumably majoritar-
ian, about the contents of communication, it seems
to be obnoxious in principle to the central moral
purpose of the First Amendment—to secure the
greatest equal liberty of communication compatible
with a like liberty for all.

Notes

1. For an interesting consideration of this general
problem, see J. Feinberg, "Limits to the Free
Expression of Opinion," J. Feinberg and H. Gross,
Philosophy of Law, pp. 135–151.

2. I take the notion of a system of free expression
from T. Emerson, *The System of Freedom of Expression* (1970).

3. See A. Meiklejohn, *Political Freedom* 21–28 (1960).

4. See A. Meiklejohn, *supra* note 3. Meiklejohn
attempted to defend his view by interpreting the
political quite broadly. A. Meiklejohn, "The First
Amendment Is an Absolute," 1961 *Sup. Ct. Rev.*
245, 255–257, 262–263.

5. See Z. Chafee, Book Review, 62 *Harv. L. Rev.* 891,
896–898 (1949).

6. As an explication, this account seems to have more
explanatory power than other comparable general
theories of the First Amendment. Unlike Meiklejohn's theory, it accounts for the fact that free
expression is not limited to politics. See Meiklejohn, *supra* note 3. It also accounts for the clear
and present danger test, unlike the work of
Thomas Emerson. See T. Emerson, *supra* note 2; T.
Emerson, *Toward a General Theory of the First Amendment* (1966).

7. See, e.g., Cox v. Louisiana, 379 U.S. 536, 554–55
(1965); Poulos v. New Hampshire, 345 U.S. 395,
405 (1953); Kovacs v. Cooper, 336 U.S. 77 (1949).

8. See, e.g., A Book Named "John Cleland's Memoirs
of a Woman of Pleasure" v. Attorney General, 383
U.S. 413, 427 (1966) (Douglas, J., concurring);
Kingsley International Pictures Corp. v. Regents,
360 U.S. 684, 688–89 (1959); Roth v. United States,
354 U.S. 476, 484 (1957); Terminiello v. Chicago,
337 U.S. 1, 3–5 (1949).

9. See, e.g., Brandenburg v. Ohio, 395 U.S. 444
(1969); Dennis v. United States, 341 U.S. 494
(1951).

10. See, e.g., Roth v. United States, 354 U.S. 476, 484
(1957) (all ideas with the slightest redeeming social
value have First Amendment protection); Joseph
Burstyn, Inc. v. Wilson, 343 U.S. 495 (1952).

11. See J. Barron, "Access to the Press–a New First
Amendment Right," 80 *Harv. L. Rev.* 1641 (1967).

12. See 7 *Oxford English Dictionary* 0.26 (1961).

13. See *Webster's Third New International Dictionary* 1557
(1965).

14. A. Kaplan, "Obscenity as an Esthetic Category," 20
Law & Contemp. Prob. 544, 550 (1955).

15. H. Ellis, *On Life and Sex* 175 (1962); G. Gorer, *The
Danger of Equality* 218 (1966); W. Allen, "The Writer
and the Frontiers of Tolerance," in *"To Deprave and
Corrupt . . ."* 141, 147 (J. Chandos ed. 1962).

16. See notes 12 and 13 *supra.*

17. "O, forfend it, God, that, in a Christian climate,
souls refin'd should show so heinous, black,
obscene a deed!" W. Shakespeare, *Richard II,* act 4,
sc. 1. The deed in question is a subject's judging
his king.

18. J. P. Sartre, *Being and Nothingness* 401–402 (H.
Barnes trans. 1956): cf. the notion of "the jest
obscene," as used in Nitocris's condemnation of
her son in Handel, *Belshazzar,* act I, sc. 4 (1744).

19. *Sir Charles Sedley's Case,* 83 Eng. Rep. 1146 (K.B.
1663). Sir Charles Sedley was here convicted "for
shewing himself naked in a balcony, and throwing

down bottles (pist in) vi & armis among the people in Covent Garden, contra pacem and to the scandal of the Government," *Id.* at 1146–1147. Sedley's conduct was condemned for its intrinsic obscenity as well as on the four additional grounds of indecent exposure, blasphemy, throwing missiles containing urine, and inciting to the small riot that ensued. See L. M. Alpert, "Judicial Censorship of Obscene Literature," 52 *Harv. L. Rev.* 40, 41–43 (1938). One commentary on these events states that Sedley also excreted in public. See A. Craig, *The Banned Books of England* 23–24 (1962); D. Thomas, *A Long Time Burning* 81 (1969).

20. Thus, the prurient interest test for obscenity, established in Roth v. United States, 354 U.S. 476, 487 (1957), and reaffirmed in Miller v. California, 413 U.S. 15, 24 (1973), and Paris Adult Theatre I v. Slaton, 413 U.S. 49 (1973), is defined in terms of "a shameful or morbid interest in nudity, sex, or excretion."

21. See *Model Penal Code* §207.10, Comment at 1, 10, 29–31 (Tent. Draft No. 6 1957), and commentary thereon in L. B. Schwartz, "Morals Offenses and the Model Penal Code," 63 *Col. L. Rev.* 669 (1963), reprinted in Feinberg and Gross, *Philosophy of Law* 152–161. See also Kaplan, *supra* note 14, at 556.

22. For example, Alexander Pope in his remarkable denunciations of Curl in *The Dunciad* uses "obscene" in excretory contexts. See A. Pope, *The Dunciad* 299, 300 (J. Sutherland ed. 1963) (first published 1728, 1743).

23. For example, in Cavalli's characteristically lascivious opera *La Calisto* (ca. 1650), Calisto's amorous approach to the goddess Diana is rejected with "Taci, lascia, taci/ Qual, qual delirio osceno/ l'ingeno ti confonde?" meaning, "Silence, lascivious girl!/ What, what obscene delirium/ has come over your reason?" Cavalli, *La Calisto*, act I, sc. 1.

24. For a useful general account, see Alpert, *supra* note 19. For accounts of English legal development, see D. Thomas, *supra* 19; N. St. John-Stevas, *Obscenity and the Law* (1956). For the best general account of earlier American developments, see W. B. Lockhart and R. C. McClure, "Literature, the Law of Obscenity, and the Constitution," 38 *Minn. L. Rev.* 295 (1954).

25. Comstock Act §2, ch. 258, §2, 17 Stat. 598, 599 (1873), as amended, 18 U.S.C. 1461 (1970).

26. See E. Sagarin, *The Anatomy of Dirty Words* (1962); Read, "An Obscenity Symbol," 9 *Am. Speech* 264 (1934).

27. For the force of such expressions in psychoanalysis, see S. Ferenczi, *Sex in Psychoanalysis* 132–153 (E. Jones trans. 1950); cf. Stone, "On the Principal Obscene Word of the English Language," 33 *Int'l J. Psycho-Anal.* 30 (1954).

28. See *Songs and Slang of the British Soldier* 1914–1918, at 15 (3d ed. Brophy & Partridge eds. 1931).

29. See, e.g., J. Swift, *A Tale of a Tub*, in *Gulliver's Travels and Other Writings* 245, 327–329, 334–336 (L. Landa ed. 1960); J. Swift, *A Voyage to Lilliput*, in *id.* 3, 34–35.

30. See A. Pope, *supra* note 22, at 299–300, 303–304, 306, 308–314.

31. Cf. D. Thomas, *supra* note 19, at 273–274, 010–014 (1969); S. Sontag, *Styles of Radical Will* 35–73 (1969).

32. Cf. S. Freud, *Wit and Its Relation to the Unconscious*, in *The Basic Writings of Sigmund Freud* 631, 692–697 (A. Brill trans. & ed. 1938).

33. I am indebted, for this idea of the relevance of the demeaning to the obscene, to criticisms of John Kleining.

34. See M. Douglas, *Purity and Danger* (1966).

35. See *id.* 41–57.

36. See, e.g., *Leviticus* 11–15, 17–18.

37. See Aristotle *Nicomachean Ethics* 116–251 (M. Ostwald trans. 1962).

38. See notes 66 and 67 *infra* and accompanying text.

39. Cf. Honigman, "A Cultural Theory of Obscenity," in *Sexual Behavior and Personality Characteristics* 31 (M. DeMartino ed. 1963).

40. See W. LaBarre, "Obscenity: An Anthropological Appraisal," 20 *Law and Contemp. Prob.* 533, 541–542 (1955). Geoffrey Gorer cites the Trobriand Islanders as a people who finds public eating of solid food an obscenity; G. Gorer, *supra* note 15. For a discussion of the Indian idea that eating may be polluting, see M. Douglas, *supra* note 34, at 33–34.

41. The suggestion of the reversal of the roles of eating and excretion (namely, that eating would be obscene and excretion a social occasion) is the subject of one scene of hilarious social satire in L. Bunuel's movie *Le Fantôme de la Liberté* (1974).

42. E.g., the movie *La Grande Bouffe* (1974).

43. E.g., the famous eating scene in the movie *Tom Jones* (1963).

44. Rex v. Curl, 93 Eng. Rep. 849 (K.B. 1727).

45. See N. St. John-Stevas, *supra* note 24, at 29–65.

46. For a literary analysis of some notable examples of Victorian pornography, see S. Marcus, *The Other Victorians* (1966).

47. E.g., the Customs Consolidating Act of 1853. 16 & 17 Vict., c. 107 (repealed by Customs Consolidat-

ing Act of 1876, 39 & 40 Vict., c. 36 paragraphs 42, 288); and Lord Campbell's Act of 1857, 20 & 21 Vict., c. 83 (repealed by Obscene Publications Act of 1959, 7 & 8 Eliz. 2, c. 66, paragraph 3(8)).

48. In 1948, the Supreme Court expressly declined to find that depictions of violence could be obscene, Winters v. New York, 333 U.S. 507 (1948), but this holding seems quite questionable today in view of growing modern usage. My views on the obscenity of violence and death gratefully acknowledge helpful criticisms of Joel Feinberg.

49. See note 59 *infra* and associated text.

50. See H. M. Hyde, *A History of Pornography* 3–8 (1964); N. St. John-Stevas, *supra* note 24, at 70–74, 98–103. See also notes 83, 84, and 85 *infra*.

51. Compare, e.g., Paris Adult Theatre I v. Slaton, 413 U.S. 49, 52 (Burger, C. J., emphasized the occurrence of "scenes of simulated fellatio, cunnilingus, and group sex intercourse") and Mishkin v. New York, 383 U.S. 502, 508 (1965) (depictions of flagellation, fetishism, and lesbianism held obscene), with Sunshine Book Co. v. Summerfield, 355 U.S. 372 (1958) (per curiam), rev'd 249 F.2d 114 (D.C. Cir. 1957), aff'd 128 F. Supp. 564 (D.D.C. 1955) (nudity per se not obscene). Cf. R. Kuh, *Foolish Figleaves?* 306–307 (1967) (suggesting that pictured bestiality and homosexuality are more obscene than comparable pictured heterosexuality).

52. See J. Feinberg, " 'Harmless Immoralities' and Offensive Nuisances," in *Issues in Law and Morality* 83, 87 (N. Care and T. Trelogan eds. 1973).

53. This proposal has been made with respect to sexual contents. See E. Sagarin, *supra* note 26, at 9–12, 160–174. Lenny Bruce, according to the show *The World of Lenny Bruce*, sc. 1 (1974), predicted the day when, pursuant to his view of the nonobscenity of sex, the erstwhile sexual obscenities would be used as forms of congratulation and good wishes.

54. See, e.g., *Webster's Third New International Dictionary* 1767 (1966).

55. See H. M. Hyde, *supra* note 50 at 1, 10.

56. See, e.g., M. Peckham *Art and Pornography* 46–47 (1969); A. Kinsey, *Sexual Behavior in the Human Female* 671–672 (1953); E. Kronhausen and P. Kronhausen, *Pornography and the Law* 262, 265 (1959).

57. See H. M. Hyde, *supra* note 50, at 30–58; D. Loth, *The Erotic in Literature* 41–68 (1961); M. Peckham, *supra* note 56, at 257–301: La Barre *supra* note 40, at 533–35.

58. The example of coprophagy occurs in M. de Sade, *120 Days of Sodom*, in 2 *The Complete Marquis De Sade* 215, 222 (P. Gillette trans. 1966). De Sade sug-

gests other examples, such as eating vomit, which someone might find obscene, even if he would not find pornography obscene. *Id.* 215.

59. See R. Haney, *Comstockery in America* 58–59, 67–69, 75 (1960); D. Loth, *supra* note 57, at 208–233; L. Marcuse, *Obscene: The History of an Indignation* 307–327 (K. Gershon trans. 1965); M. Peckham, *supra* note 56, t 19–20; B. Russell, *Marriage and Morals* 93–117 (1929).

60. See H. Ellis, *supra* note 15, at 21–37; E. Kronhausen and P. Kronhausen, *supra* note 56, at 167; B. Russell, *supra* note 59, at 106–107.

61. H. Gardiner, "Moral Principles toward a Definition of the Obscene," 20 *Law & Contemp. Prob.* 560, 564 (1955).

62. This quaint phrase appears in Gardiner, *id.* 567.

63. See Augustine, *The City of God* 470–472 (M. Dods trans. 1950). St. Thomas is in accord with Augustine's view. Of the emission of semen apart from generation in marriage, he wrote, "after the sin of homicide whereby a human nature already in existence is destroyed, this type of sin appears to take next place, for by it the generation of human nature is precluded." T. Aquinas, *On the Truth of the Catholic Faith: Summa Contra Gentiles* 146 (V. Bourke trans. 1946).

64. See A. Comfort, *The Anxiety Makers* (1970); J. Haller and R. Haller, *The Physician and Sexuality in Victorian America* 199–234 (1974); S. Marcus, *supra* note 46; E. H. Hare, "Masturbational Insanity: The History of an Idea," 108 *J. Mental Science* 1, 6–9 (1962).

65. A. Comstock, *Traps for the Young* 136 (R. Bremner ed. 1967). See also *id.* 132–133, 139, 145, 169, 179, 205; A. Comstock, *Frauds Exposed* 388–389, 416, 437–438, 440–441 (1880; reprinted 1969).

66. See S. Marcus, *supra* note 46, at 24–25, 233, 243.

67. See H. Ellis, *supra* note 19, at 21–25. On the fundamental mistake involved in confusing sexual and excretory function, see W. Masters and V. Johnson, *Human Sexual Inadequacy* 10 (1970), who state: "Seemingly, many cultures and certainly many religions have risen and fallen on their interpretation and misinterpretation of one basic physiological fact. Sexual functioning is a natural physiological process, yet it has a unique facility that no other natural physiological process, such as respiratory, bladder, or bowel function, can imitate. *Sexual responsivity can be delayed indefinitely or functionally denied for a lifetime.* No other basic physiological process can claim such malleability of physical expression."

68. A. Comfort, *supra* note 64, at 57.

69. *Id.* 155, 161.

70. The Queen v. Hicklin, L. R. 3 Q.B. 359, 372 (1868).

71. See D. H. Lawrence, *Sex, Literature, and Censorship* 64–81 (1953). For similar sentiments, see M. Mead, "Sex and Censorship in Contemporary Society," in *New World Writing,* 7, 19–21 (1953).

72. See *United States Comm'n on Obscenity and Pornography, Report of the Comm'n on Obscenity and Pornography* 210–212 (GPO ed. 1979) [hereinafter *Report*] cf. J. W. Higgins & M. B. Katzman, "Determinants in the Judgment of Obscenity," 125 *Am. J. Psychiat.* 1733 (1969).

73. 413 U.S. at 24 (quoting Roth, 354 U.S. at 489).

74. *Id.* 25. In Jenkins v. Georgia, 418 U.S. 153 (1974), the Court made clear the force of these requirements; the movie *Carnal Knowledge* could not constitutionally be found obscene, for the depictions therein are not sexually explicit within the meaning of the *Miller* tests.

75. 413 U.S. at 27–28.

76. 413 U.S. at 24–25.

77. A Book Named "John Cleland's Memoirs of a Woman of Pleasure" v. Massachusetts, 383 U.S. 413, 419 (1966).

78. 413 U.S. at 30–34.

79. The Court thus rejected the previously urged view that the standards to be applied were national, not local. E.g., Jacobellis v. Ohio, 378 U.S. 184, 192–193 (1974) (Brennan, J.).

80. 394 U.S. 557 (1969).

81. United States v. Orito, 413 U.S. 139 (1973); United States v. 12 200-Ft. Reels of Film, 413 U.S. 123 (1973).

82. See notes 57 to 60 *supra.*

83. See note 25 *supra*; 18 U.S.C. paragraph 1461 (1964), as amended, 18 U.S.C. paragraph 1461 (1970) (mail); 18 U.S.C. paragraph 1462(c), as amended, 18 U.S.C. paragraph 1462(c) (1970) (interstate commerce).

84. See, e.g., United States v. Chesman, 19 F. 497 (E.D. Mo. 1881).

85. See, e.g., United States v. Bennett, 24 F. Cas, 1093, No. 14, 571 (C.C.S.D.N.Y. 1879); Regina v. Bradlaugh, 2 Q.B.D. 569 (1977), *rev'd on other grounds,* 3 A.B.D. 607 (1878).

86. See text accompanying notes 61 to 70, *supra.*

87. Comstock, for example, noted the case of a thirteen-year-old girl, in whose bureau he "found a quantity of the most debasing and foul-worded matter. The last heard from this child was she was in a dying condition, the result of habits induced by this foul reading." A. Comstock, *Traps for the Young* 139 (R. Bremner ed. 1967).

88. Comstock cited a number of instances where, in his view, access to obscene material led to robbery, burglary, and murder. A. Comstock, *Frauds Exposed* 437–39 (1880, reprinted 1969). See also A. Comstock, *supra* note 87, at 132–33, 169, 179).

Questions for Analysis

1. *Why does Richards think "Attempts by the state to prohibit certain contents of communication per se are fundamentally incompatible with the moral and constitutional principle of equal liberty"?*

2. *What reasons does Richards give for asserting that "strong moral ideas are implicit in the First Amendment"?*

3. *What, in Richards's view, are the "marks of the obscene"?*

4. *According to Richards, what does the precise application of the notion of the obscene depend on?*

5. *What do the courts implicitly decide on and enforce in their interpretations of the notion of the obscene?*

6. *Richards concludes that the regulation of obscene communications is "obnoxious in principle to the central moral purpose of the First Amendment—to securing the greatest equal liberty of communication compatible with a like liberty for all." Precisely how does such regulation sully this central moral purpose?*

CASE PRESENTATION
Ginzburg *v.* United States *(1966)*

Ralph Ginzburg, publisher of *Eros* and other erotic magazines, was convicted under an obscenity statute for publishing or circulating obscene materials. In appealing the conviction to the U.S. Supreme Court, Ginzburg's lawyers felt they had a good chance of having the conviction overturned, for the Court had consistently overturned similar convictions (and, incidentally, has since). But their optimism went unfulfilled: In 1966 the Court upheld the conviction, and Ginzburg went to prison.

The Court held that Ginzburg had been properly convicted because the materials he sold were obscene under the *Roth* definition and because he had engaged in "pandering": He had not only published and distributed erotic materials, but had "purveyed textual or graphic matter openly advertised to appeal to the erotic interest" of his customers.

For example, Ginzburg admittedly sought out a town with a sexually suggestive name from which to mail his publications. Intercourse, Pennsylvania, was his first choice, but its post office couldn't handle the volume of mail. So he chose Middlesex, New Jersey. In advertising *Eros,* Ginzburg portrayed the magazine as a child of its times, the result of recent court decisions safeguarding freedom of expression, *the* magazine of sexual candor. And in direct-mail advertising for *Eros* and other Ginzburg publications, the publisher guaranteed customers a full refund should the magazines fail to reach them because of U.S. Post Office censorship interference.

In a dissenting opinion, Justice Hugo Black contended that the criteria employed by the Court in upholding the conviction of Ginzburg were "so vague and meaningless that they practically leave the fate of a person charged with violating censorship statutes to the unbridled discretion, whim and caprice of the judge or jury which tries him."[4] Black then elaborated on these criteria:

> (a) The first element considered necessary for determining obscenity is that the dominant theme of the material taken as a whole must appeal to the prurient interest in sex. It seems quite apparent to me that human beings, serving either as judges or jurors, could not be expected to give any sort of decision on this element which would even remotely promise any kind of uniformity in the enforcement of this law. What conclusion an individual, be he judge or juror, would reach about whether the material appeals to "prurient interest in sex" would depend largely in the long run not upon testimony of witnesses such as can be given in ordinary criminal cases where conduct is under scrutiny, but would depend to a large extent upon the judge's or juror's personality, habits, inclinations, attitudes and other individual characteristics. In one community or in one courthouse a matter would be condemned as

4. *Ginzburg* v. *United States*, 383 U.S. 463 (1966).

obscene under this so-called criterion but in another community, maybe only a few miles away, or in another courthouse in the same community, the material could be given a clean bill of health. In the final analysis the submission of such an issue as this to a judge or jury amounts to practically nothing more than a request for the judge or juror to assert his own personal beliefs about whether the matter should be allowed to be legally distributed. Upon this subjective determination the law becomes certain for the first and last time.

(b) The second element for determining obscenity . . . is [supposedly] that the material must be "patently offensive because it affronts contemporary community standards relating to the description or representation of sexual matters. . . ." Nothing . . . that has been said . . . leaves me with any kind of certainty as to whether the "community standards" referred to are world-wide, nation-wide, section-wide, state-wide, country-wide, precinct-wide, or township-wide. But even if some definite areas were mentioned, who is capable of assessing "community standards" on such a subject? Could one expect the same application of standards by jurors in Mississippi as in New York City, in Vermont as in California? So here again the guilt or innocence of a defendant charged with obscenity must depend in the final analysis upon the personal judgment and attitude of particular individuals and the place where the trial is held. . . .

(c) A third element which [is supposedly] required to establish obscenity is that the material must be "utterly without redeeming social value." This element seems to me to be as uncertain, if not even more uncertain, than is the unknown substance of the Milky Way. If we are to have a free society as contemplated by the Bill of Rights, then I can find little defense for leaving the liberty of American individuals subject to the judgment of a judge or jury as to whether material that provokes thought or stimulates desire is "utterly without redeeming social value. . . ." Whether a particular treatment of a particular subject is with or without social value in this evolving, dynamic society of ours is a question upon which no uniform agreement could possibly be reached among politicians, statesmen, professors, philosophers, scientists, religious groups or any other type of group. A case-by-case assessment of social values by individual judges and jurors is, I think, a dangerous technique for government to utilize in determining whether a man stays in or out of the penitentiary.

My conclusion is that . . . no person, not even the most learned judge, much less a layman, is capable of knowing in advance of an ultimate decision in his particular case by this Court whether certain material comes within the area of "obscenity" as that term is confused by the Court today.[5]

Questions for Analysis

1. *Would you agree with the majority in* Ginzburg *that Ginzburg had engaged in "pandering"?*

2. *In your view, what, if anything, is morally objectionable about pandering?*

3. *Black claimed that a determination of obscenity on the basis of prurient interest in sex must of necessity be subjective. Do you agree?*

5. *Ginzburg* v. *United States.*

4. *Do you agree with Black's rejection of community standards as a basis for determining obscenity?*

5. *Is it impossible, as Black claimed, to determine what is "utterly without socially redeeming social value"? Can you cite an illustration of what you would regard a depiction utterly without socially redeeming social value?*

6. *The law aside, what moral judgment, if any, are you prepared to make of publishers like Ginzburg, Hugh Hefner (Playboy), and Larry Flynt (Hustler) who publish erotic materials for sale? Do you consider their publishing activities moral, immoral, or nonmoral? Explain. If immoral, do you also think that they should be prohibited from publishing these magazines?*

7. *Comment on the morality of buying and reading magazines like those mentioned in the preceding question. Do you think those who do are acting immorally, or is their behavior nonmoral? Explain.*

8. *Under what circumstances do you think individuals or institutions should (that is, are morally obliged to) limit access to erotic materials? For example, should your college bookstore refuse to carry for sale magazines like the aforementioned? Do you think it would be morally obligated to offer them if a majority of its customers wanted it to? If the bookstore did carry these publications, would how it displayed them raise a moral issue (for example, on a stand with other publications such as* Time *and* Newsweek, *as opposed to keeping them behind the counter and indicating that they are available)?*

CASE PRESENTATION
From Chaplin to Disney: A Censorship Retrospective

Some defenders of the right to publish, display, distribute, and sell allegedly pornographic materials invoke the Bill of Rights. The First Amendment, they remind us, guarantees the right of free expression, both in speech and in the press. For their part, anti-pornographers claim that this right does not extend to allegedly pornographic materials. *Really obscene* books, films, and magazines, they say, should be censored. But what's *really obscene?* free-expressionists want to know. Let the censors ban so-called really obscene materials, they warn, and they will soon be passing judgment on serious works of art and political and social thought that they deem antisocial, subversive, or offensive.

Just how far *do* censors go? And what do they base their opinions on? Does the slippery-slope argument of the free-expressionists have any validity? The following instances of film censorship may throw some light on these questions:[6]

Walt Disney's nature film *The Vanishing Prairie:* Officials in some cities deleted a sequence showing the birth of a buffalo.

6. *Burton M. Leiser,* Liberty, Justice, and Morals: Contemporary Value Conflicts *(New York: Macmillan, 1973), p. 163.*

The "March of Time" documentary *Inside Nazi Germany* and Charlie Chaplin's satire on Hitler, *The Great Dictator:* Before World War II the Chicago censor denied licenses to these and some other films critical of life in Nazi Germany, apparently out of deference to Chicago's large German population.

Anatomy of a Murder: In 1959, the Chicago censor refused to license the film because the words *rape* and *contraceptive* were objectionable.

The Southerner and *Curley:* Memphis censors banned the first because it dealt with poverty among tenant farmers, a theme which presumably would reflect badly on the South. It banned the second because the film contained scenes of black and white children in school together.

Lost Boundaries: In 1950, Atlanta censors banned this film about a black physician and his family who "passed" for white. Reason for ban: the film's anticipated adverse effect on the "peace, morals and good order of Atlanta."

The Russian film *Professor Mamlock:* Ohio censors banned this film, which dealt with Nazi persecution of Jews, because the film probably would "stir up hatred and ill will and gain nothing." Police in Providence, Rhode Island, wouldn't permit the film to be shown there because it was "communist propaganda."

Carmen: Various state censors rejected this film for sundry reasons, among which that the girls who worked in the cigar factory smoked in public and that a kiss lasted too long.

New York censors forbade discussion in films of pregnancy, venereal disease, eugenics, birth control, abortion, illegitimacy, prostitution, miscegenation, and divorce.

Questions for Analysis

1. Which, if any, of the preceding acts of censorship do you think were morally justified? Explain.

2. Do you think the fact that censors have on occasion gone to extremes offers a compelling argument against censorship of allegedly obscene materials? If not, what other considerations would you introduce?

3. Do you think a community is morally justified in imposing its moral standards on all its members with regard to what films and publications its citizens have access to?

4. Can censorship laws be written in a way that prevents excessive restrictions?

Selections for Further Reading

Boyer, Paul S. *Purity in Print.* New York: Scribner's, 1968.

Clor, Harry M. *Obscenity and Public Morality: Censorship in a Liberal Society.* Chicago: University of Chicago Press, 1969.

Comstock, Anthony. *Traps for the Young*. Cambridge, Mass.: Harvard University Press, 1967.

Copp, David and Susan Wendel, eds. *Pornography and Censorship*. Buffalo, N.Y.: Prometheus, 1983.

Emerson, Thomas I. *The System of Freedom of Expression*. New York: Random House, 1970.

————. *Toward a General Theory of the First Amendment*. New York: Random House, 1966.

Gerber, Albert. *Sex, Pornography, and the Law*. 2nd rev. ed. New York: Ballantine, 1964.

Gilmore, Donald H. *Sex, Censorship and Pornography*. San Diego: Greenleaf Classics, 1969.

Holbrook, David, ed. *The Case Against Pornography*. New York: The Library Press, 1973.

Hoyt, Olga G., and Edwin P. Hoyt. *Censorship in America*. New York: Seabury Press, 1962.

Lederer, Laura, ed. *Take Back the Night: Women on Pornography*. New York: Morrow, 1980.

Marcuse, Ludwig. *Obscene: The History of an Indignation*. New York: Fernhill House, 1965.

Rembar, Charles. *The End of Obscenity*. New York: Simon and Schuster, 1970.

St. John-Stevas, Norman. *Obscenity and The Law*. London: Secker and Warburg, 1956.

Sharp, Donald B., ed. *Commentaries on Obscenity*. Metuchen, N.J.: Scarecrow Press, 1970.

5

ABORTION

Jane Roe was an unmarried pregnant woman who wished to have an abortion, an intentional termination of a pregnancy by inducing the loss of the fetus. But Ms. Roe lived in Texas, where statutes forbade abortion except to save the life of the mother. So she went to court to prove that the statutes were unconstitutional.

The three-judge district court ruled that Jane Roe had reason to sue, that the Texas criminal abortion statutes were void on their face, and, most important, that the right to choose whether to have children was protected by the Ninth through the Fourteenth Amendments. Since the district court denied a number of other aspects of the suit, the case went to the United States Supreme Court. On 22 January 1973, in the now famous *Roe* v. *Wade* decision, the Supreme Court affirmed the district court's judgment.[1]

Expressing the views of seven members of the Court, Justice Blackmun pointed out that the right to privacy applies to a woman's decision on whether to terminate her pregnancy, but that her right to terminate is not absolute. Her right may be limited by the state's legitimate interests in safeguarding the woman's health, in maintaining proper medical standards, and in protecting human life. Blackmun went on to point out that fetuses are not included within the definition of *person* as used in the Fourteenth Amendment. Most important, he indicated that prior to the end of the first trimester of pregnancy, the state may not interfere with or regulate an attending physician's decision, reached in consultation with the patient, that the patient's pregnancy should be terminated. After the first trimester and until the fetus is viable, the state may regulate the abortion procedure only for the health of the mother. After the fetus becomes viable, the state may prohibit all abortions except those necessary to preserve the health or life of the mother.

1. *See* U.S. Supreme Court Reports, *October Term 1972, lawyers' edition* (Rochester, N.Y.: Lawyers' Cooperative Publishing, 1974), p. 147.

In dissenting, Justices White and Rehnquist said that nothing in the language or history of the U.S. Constitution supported the Court's judgment, that the Court had simply manufactured a new constitutional right for pregnant women. The abortion issue, they said, should have been left with the people and the political processes they had devised to govern their affairs.

So for the time being at least, the abortion question has been resolved legally. But the issue is hardly settled. A number of anti-abortion movements have surfaced, which indicates not only that some people think abortion should be illegal, but that many believe it is wrong. Abortion, whether legal or not, still remains a most personal moral concern for those who must confront it. Obviously its legality provides options that may not have been present before, but these can make the moral dilemma that much thornier; in the past one could always rationalize away the possibility of an abortion on the basis of its illegality.

Some say an abortion is right if (1) it is therapeutic—that is, when it is necessary to preserve the physical or mental health of the woman; (2) it prevents the birth of a severely handicapped child; or (3) it ends a pregnancy resulting from some criminal act of sexual intercourse. Others say that even therapeutic abortions are immoral. Still others argue that any restrictive abortion legislation is wrong and must be liberalized to allow a woman to have an abortion on demand—that is, at the request of her and her physician, regardless or even in the absence of reasons. In order to evaluate such claims, it is helpful to know some biological background and to consider what sort of entities the unborn are and whether they have rights.

Biological Background

Since most of the controversy surrounding the abortion issue concerns precisely when a human individual or "person" is considered to exist, it is important to have some background about the development of the human fetus and familiarity with the terms that designate the various developmental stages. Conception or fertilization occurs when a female germ cell, or *ovum*, is penetrated by a male germ cell, or *spermatozoon*. The result is a single cell, containing a full genetic code of forty-six chromosomes, called the *zygote*. The zygote then journeys down the fallopian tube, which carries ova from the ovary to the uterus. This passage generally takes two or three days. During the journey the zygote begins a process of cellular division that increases its size. Occasionally, the zygote ends its journey in the fallopian tube, where it continues to develop. Because the tube is so narrow, such a pregnancy generally must be terminated by surgery.

When the multicell zygote reaches the uterus, it floats free in the intrauterine fluid and develops into what is termed a *blastocyst*, a ball of cells surrounding a fluid-filled cavity. By the end of the second week, the blastocyst implants itself in the uterine wall. From the end of the second week until the end of the eighth week, the unborn entity is termed an *embryo*. In the interim (four to five weeks), organ systems begin to develop, and the embryo takes on distinctly human external features.

The eighth week is important in the biological development and in a discussion of abortion, because it is then that brain activity generally becomes detectable. From this point until birth, the embryo is termed a *fetus*, although in common parlance *fetus* is used to designate the unborn entity at whatever stage.

Two other terms that designate events in fetal development are worth noting because they sometimes arise in abortion discussions. One is *quickening*, which refers to when the mother begins to feel the movements of the fetus. This occurs somewhere between the thirteenth and twentieth weeks. The second term is *viability*, the point at which the fetus is capable of surviving outside the womb. The fetus ordinarily reaches viability around the twenty-fourth week. Generally, then, events during pregnancy unfold as follows:

Developmental Timetable

zygote: first through third day
blastocyst: second day through second week
embryo: third week through eighth week
fetus: ninth week until birth
quickening: thirteenth week through twentieth week
viability: around twenty-fourth week

Should the unborn entity be terminated at any point in this timetable, an abortion is said to occur. Thus, *abortion simply refers to the termination of a pregnancy.*

Abortions can happen for a number of reasons. Sometimes the abortion occurs "spontaneously," because of internal biochemical factors or because of an injury to the woman. Such spontaneous abortions are ordinarily termed *miscarriages.* These generally involve no moral issues.

Abortions also can result directly from human intervention, which can occur in a variety of ways. Sometimes it happens very early, as when a woman takes a drug such as the "morning-after pill" in order to prevent the blastocyst from implanting in the uterine wall. Subsequent intervention during the first trimester (through the twelfth week) usually takes one of two forms: (1) uterine or vacuum aspiration; (2) dilation and curettage.

In *uterine or vacuum aspiration* the narrow opening of the uterus, the *cervix*, is dilated. A small tube is then inserted into the uterus, and its contents are vacuumed or emptied by suction. In *dilation and curettage* (D&C), the cervix is also widened, and the contents of the uterus are scraped out by means of a spoon-shaped surgical instrument called a curette. These two procedures can sometimes be done through the sixteenth week, but after that the fetus is generally too large to make the procedures practical.

The most common abortion technique after the sixteenth week is called *saline injection.* In this procedure the amniotic fluid (the fluid in the amnion, which is a membrane sac surrounding the fetus) is drawn out through a hollow needle and replaced by a solution of salt and water. This leads to a miscarriage.

Another but far rarer method after the sixteenth week is the *hysterotomy.* This is a surgical procedure whereby the fetus is removed from the uterus through an incision. This procedure is generally called a cesarean section and is rarely performed for an abortion.

We can list the various abortion possibilities as follows:

1. Internally induced:

   a. Spontaneous abortion: anytime

2. Externally induced:

   a. Drug such as "morning-after pill": immediately following intercourse

   b. Uterine or vacuum aspiration: through week 12

   c. Dilation and curettage: through week 12

   d. Saline injection: after week 16

   e. Hysterotomy (extremely rare): after week 16

The Moral Problem

The key moral problem of abortion is: Under what conditions, if any, is abortion morally justifiable? In answer to this question, three positions are broadly identifiable.

(1) The so-called conservative view holds that abortion is never morally justifiable, or, at most, justifiable only when the abortion is necessary to save the mother's life. This view is commonly associated with Roman Catholics, although they are certainly not the only persons who espouse it. (2) The so-called liberal view holds that abortion is always morally justifiable, regardless of the reasons or the time in fetal development. (3) The so-called intermediate or moderate views consider abortion morally acceptable up to a certain point in fetal development and/or claim that some reasons, not all, provide a sufficient justification for abortion.

While there is no consensus on the moral acceptability of abortion, there is agreement that any answer to the question depends on one's view of what sort of entities fetuses are and whether such entities have rights. These two important problems generally are referred to as the ontological and moral status of the fetus.

The Ontological Status of the Fetus

In philosophy the term *ontology* refers to the theory and nature of being and existence. When we speak of the ontological status of the fetus, we mean the kind of entity the fetus is. Determining the ontological status of fetuses bears directly on the issue of fetal rights and, subsequently, on permissible treatment of the fetus.

Actually, the problem of ontological status embraces a number of questions, such as: (1) whether the fetus is an individual organism; (2) whether the fetus is biologically a human being; (3) whether the fetus is psychologically a human being; (4) whether the fetus is a person.[2] Presumably, to affirm question (2) is to attribute more significant status to the fetus than to affirm question (1); and to affirm question (3) is to assign even greater status. To affirm question (4), that the fetus is a person, probably is to assign the most significant status to the fetus, although this, as well as the other presumptions, depends on the precise meaning of the concepts involved.

Complicating the question of the fetus's ontological status is the meaning of the expression *human life*. The concept of "human life" can be used in at least two different ways. On the one hand, it can refer to *biological* human life, that is, to a set of biological characteristics that distinguish the human species from other nonhuman species. In this sense, "human life" may be coextensive with "individual organism," as in question (1). On the other hand, "human life" may refer to *psychological* human life, that is, to life that is characterized by the properties that are distinctly human. Among these properties might be the abilities to use symbols, to think, and to imagine. Abortion discussions can easily founder when these distinctions are not made. For example, many who would agree that abortion involves the taking of human life in the biological sense would deny that it involves taking human life in the psychological sense. Moreover, they might see nothing immoral about taking life exclusively in the biological sense, although they would consider taking life in the psychological sense morally unacceptable. Thus they find nothing morally objectionable about abortion. Of course, at the root of this judgment is an assumption about the meaning of *human life*.

Intertwined with one's concept of human life is one's concept of "personhood." The concept of personhood may or may not differ from either the biological or the psychological sense of "human life." Some would argue that to be a person is simply to have the biological and/or psychological properties that make an organism human. However, others would propose additional conditions for personhood, such as consciousness, self-consciousness, rationality, even the capacities for communication and moral judgment. In this view, an entity must satisfy some or all of these criteria, even additional ones, to be a person. Still other theorists would extend the concept of personhood to include properties bestowed by human evaluation, in addition to the factual properties possessed by a person. Thus they might argue that a person must be the bearer of legal rights and social responsibilities, and must be capable of being assigned moral responsibility, of being praised or blamed.

Clearly the conditions that one believes are necessary for "person" status directly affect the ontological status of the fetus. For example, if the condition is only of an elementary biological nature, then the fetus can more easily qualify as a person than if the conditions include a list of factual properties. Further, if "personhood" must be analyzable in terms of properties bestowed by human evaluation, it becomes infinitely more difficult for the fetus to qualify as a person.

In the final analysis, the ontological status of fetuses remains an open issue. But some viewpoint ultimately underpins any position on the morality of abor-

---

2. *Tom L. Beauchamp and Le Roy Walters,* Contemporary Issues in Bioethics *(Belmont, Calif.: Dickenson, 1978), p. 188.*

tion. Whether conservative, liberal, or moderate, one must be prepared eventually to defend one's view of the ontological status of fetuses.

When Ontological Status Is Attained

Further complicating the problem of the ontological status is the question of when in fetal development the fetus gains full ontological status. Whether one claims the fetus is an individual organism, a biological human being, a psychological human being, or a full-fledged person, one must specify at what point in its biological development the fetus attains this status. It is one thing to say what status the fetus has; it is another to say *when* it has attained such status. A judgment about *when* the fetus has the status bears as directly on abortion views as does a judgment of the status itself.

We can identify a number of positions on when status is attained. An extreme conservative position would argue that the fetus has full ontological status from conception; at the time of conception the fetus must be regarded as an individual person. In direct contrast to this view is the extreme liberal position, which holds that the fetus never achieves ontological status.

Viewing these as polar positions, we can identify a cluster of moderate views that fall between them. In every instance, the moderate view tries to pinpoint full ontological status somewhere between conception and birth. For example, some would draw the line when brain activity is first present; others draw it at quickening; still others would draw the line at viability.

The Moral Status of the Fetus

The issue of moral status of the fetus is generally, but not always, discussed in terms of the fetus's rights. What rights, if any, does it have? Any position on abortion must at some point address this question, and all seriously argued positions do, at least by implication.

Various views on the moral status of the fetus are currently circulating. Each view can be associated with one or another of the views on the fetus's ontological status. For example, claiming that the fetus has full ontological status at conception, the extreme conservative view also holds that it has full moral status at the same stage. From the moment of conception on, the unborn entity enjoys the same rights we attribute to any adult human. In this view, abortion would be a case of denying the unborn the right to life. Therefore, abortion could never be undertaken without reasons sufficient to override the unborn's claim to life. In other words, only conditions that would justify the killing of an adult human—for example, self-defense—would morally justify an abortion.

Liberals similarly derive their view of moral status from their theory of ontological status. The extreme liberal view would deny the fetus any moral status. In this view, abortion is not considered comparable to killing an adult person. Indeed, abortion may be viewed as removing a mass of organic material, not unlike an appendectomy. Its removal raises no serious moral problems. A somewhat less liberal view, while granting the fetus ontological status as being biologically human, claims it is not human in any significant moral sense and thus has no significant rights.

Likewise, moderates would assign moral status to the fetus at the point that the entity attained full ontological status. If brain activity is taken as the point of ontological status, for example, then abortions conducted before that time would not raise serious moral questions; those conducted subsequent to that development would. Currently, viability seems to be an especially popular point at which to assign ontological status. And so, many moderate theorists today insist that abortion raises significant moral questions only *after* the fetus has attained viability. This view is reflected in some of the opinions delivered in the *Roe* v. *Wade* case.

It is important to note that granting the fetus moral status does not at all deny moral status to the woman. Indeed, the question of whose rights should take precedence when a conflict develops raises thorny questions, especially for conservatives and moderates. For example, while granting the fetus full moral status, some conservatives nonetheless approve of therapeutic abortions—abortions performed to save the woman's life or to correct some life-threatening condition. These are often viewed as cases of self-defense or justifiable homicide. Since self-defense and justifiable homicide commonly are considered acceptable grounds for killing an adult person, they are also taken as moral justification for killing a fetus. But other conservatives disapprove of even therapeutic abortions.

Similarly, while moderates grant the fetus moral status at some point in development, they too must arbitrate cases of conflicting rights. They must determine just what conditions are sufficient for allowing the woman's right to override the fetus's right to life. Here the whole gamut of conditions involving the pregnancy must be evaluated, including rape, incest, fetal deformity, and of course physical or psychological harm to the woman.

Moral Implications

Determining the moral status of the fetus, then, is directly related to determining when the fetus is actually a human. There is no question that even at the zygote stage, and from then on, the fetus is at least potentially human (until it becomes actually so). At whatever point it becomes actually human, we face a set of serious moral issues regarding abortion, among which are:

1. Does the fetus have a right to be carried to full term?

2. Under what circumstances, if ever, can we take an innocent human life?

3. Is any other right more important than the right to life—for example, the woman's right to privacy?

4. If the woman's life is in danger because of the pregnancy, how do we decide whose right prevails?

If, as is the case at present, we can't determine with reasonable certainty at what point the fetus becomes fully human, we're confronted with another set of problems:

1. Can we morally disregard the possibility that the fetus may be actually human (or may not)? If we do, does that imply, at best, an indifference to an important moral value? And is not such an attitude of not caring about a moral value itself morally questionable at least?

2. Can we ever act morally on a doubt—for example, a doubt about our obligation, the morally relevant facts, the morally correct means? How are we to resolve our doubt?

Pro-Life Arguments (against Abortion)

1. *Abortion is murder.*

POINT: "You don't have to be a lawyer to know what murder means: the intentional ending of an innocent human life. Who can imagine an uglier and more outrageous act? Well, I can think of at least one: abortion. At least when you kill adults, they usually have a chance to defend themselves. But what chance does a fetus have? None. Try as you will, you can't escape the inevitable fact that abortion is murder."

COUNTERPOINT: "You make it sound like fetuses can go out and buy ice cream cones whenever they want, as well as think, imagine, wonder, hope, dream, and create. Why, a fetus isn't any more a 'human being' than cake batter is a cake. Certainly murder is a terrible thing—the murder of a full-fledged walking, talking human being, not a glob of protoplasm."

2. *Abortion sets a dangerous precedent.*

POINT: "Everybody would agree that any action leading to a casual attitude toward life is wrong. But that's just what abortion is. And that includes therapeutic abortion. As for abortions committed in the case of severely deformed fetuses, they're no more than the first step to 'putting away' the severely handicapped, the dysfunctional, the senile, and the incurably ill in our society. No, abortion leads to a shabby attitude toward life; it opens a Pandora's box of unspeakable affronts to human dignity and worth. Remember: The Holocaust under Hitler began with the legalization of abortion. Every abortion that's demanded or performed takes us one step closer to a systematic recognition of abortion, and everything that implies."

COUNTERPOINT: "Why do you assume that the practice of abortion inevitably will lead to disrespect for life and usher in an age of nightmarish inhumanity? In fact, anthropological studies indicate that societies condoning abortion have better records on 'civil rights' and 'protections' than those that don't. You and I both know that issues dealing with the severely handicapped or incurably ill are separate and distinct questions from abortion and must be examined on their own merits. As for your Hitler reference, that has nothing to do with the question of whether abortion's right or wrong. It's outrageously irrelevant. Besides, legal abortion didn't produce the Holocaust; Hitler's madness and those who cooperated with it did. Even if your point had any merit, it really argues against *allowing* abortions, and not their morality."

3. *Abortion involves psychological risks for the woman.*

POINT: "Let's face it: A woman and the child she's bearing are about as close as any two humans can ever get. And I don't mean just biologically, but emotionally and psychologically, too. Ask any mother—she'll tell you. For a woman to intentionally harm her unborn violates the deepest levels of her unconscious needs, impulses, and desires. And she's bound to pay a big price for this psychologically. Plenty of women already have—ask the psychologists. There's no question about it: The woman who has an abortion not only kills her unborn, she also seriously damages herself."

COUNTERPOINT: "If there was an annual award for sweeping generalizations, you'd certainly get it. You talk of 'women' as if they were all the same. Sure, lots of women, maybe even most, want to carry their unborn to term. But *lots* and *most* don't mean *all*. Who knows what lurks in the so-called unconscious mind? Maybe a woman who outwardly wants to bear children secretly doesn't. Ask the psychologists, you say. All right, ask them. And while you're at it, ask about child abuse, post- and neonatal trauma, and nervous breakdowns. What makes you think every woman is suited to be a mother? Some women discover only after giving birth that they genuinely *don't* want the child. They assumed they did largely because of environmental conditioning which, as you well illustrated, has had the effect of heaping guilt on the poor woman who might honestly admit she does not want to carry, bear, and rear children. It's time we put aside these stereotypes about women for good. And while we're at it, let's not confuse what women actually want to do with what we believe they *should* want to do."

4. *Alternatives to abortion are available.*

POINT: "All this talk about unwanted pregnancies and bringing undesired and unloved children into the world just won't cut it. Whom are we kidding? There are countless individuals and couples who are dying to have kids but can't. If a woman doesn't want to carry a child to term, that's no reason to abort it. Just put it up for adoption at birth. As for the tragically deformed infant no one may want to adopt, there are plenty of institutions and agencies set up for those pitiful souls."

COUNTERPOINT: "Sure, there are plenty of people willing and able to adopt. But even if the child will be adopted, the woman still has to carry it for nine months. And she may be either unwilling or unable to do that. What's more, giving up your child for adoption is no emotional picnic, you know. And often it's no easier on the child. Plenty of adoptees anguish over unresolved feelings of parental rejection. As for the deformed, why make society foot the bill for someone else's responsibility? I for one don't want my hard-earned tax dollars spent caring for someone else's problems that easily could have been prevented in the first place."

5. *The woman must be responsible for her sexual activity.*

POINT: "No woman *has* to get pregnant. You don't have to be the 'happy hooker' to know that there are plenty of readily available contraceptives. When a woman doesn't practice some form of birth control, she takes responsibility for what happens. For a woman to sacrifice an innocent human life just because she's been careless, ignorant, or indiscreet is the height of sexual and moral irresponsibility."

COUNTERPOINT: "Come now, everybody knows that there's no surefire birth control method, except abstinence. Any woman who has sex stands the same chance of getting pregnant as a driver of having an accident. Why, even if a driver drives recklessly and has a serious accident, we allow her the opportunity to repair the damage to herself and others, don't we? In fact, we help her do it! To make a woman bear a child out of some warped sense of 'personal responsibility' is like turning our back on a torn and bloody motorist because 'she got what she deserved.' Such an attitude reflects more vindictiveness and punishment than commitment to the principle of personal responsibility. No matter why a woman gets pregnant, she still has the right to dispose of her pregnancy as she sees fit. Sure, she may have been irresponsible, but that's a separate issue from what she then chooses to do about the result of her indiscretion."

Pro-Choice Arguments (for Abortion)

1. *Pregnancies are dangerous for the woman.*

POINT: "There are very few adults, if any, who haven't had a direct or indirect experience that shows how dangerous pregnancies can be to the life and health of women. Let those without such knowledge look at the record. They'll see that in some cases the woman's life is actually on the line. In other cases, the woman must endure heroic suffering and hardship during the term. In still other cases, the woman must endure lifelong health problems that are the direct result of the pregnancy. Given these possible risks, women should have the say about whether they want to run them or not."

COUNTERPOINT: "Your argument would be very persuasive if this were the nineteenth century. Where have you been for the last thirty years? Don't you realize that modern medicine has, in effect, wiped out the dangers connected with pregnancy? Sure, there remain some cases where the woman's life is in jeopardy. But even in those cases, why assume that her life must be saved at all costs? There's another human life at stake, you know. As for your long-term ill effects of pregnancy, what did you have in mind—varicose veins, hemorrhoids, and an aching back? When such 'horrors' become justification for abortion, we're really in trouble. What will be acceptable justification next—a ski trip to Aspen which, unluckily for the fetus, pops up in the seventh month?"

2. *Many unborn are unwanted or deformed.*

POINT: "Everybody knows that society has serious population, pollution, and poverty problems—not to mention crime, disease, and world hunger. These problems already are taxing our financial capacity to deal with them. One way we can begin to deal with them is to make sure every child that's brought into the world is wanted and healthy. Ignoring this, we just worsen the world's problems. Fortunately, we've got lots of ways to ensure that unwanted and unhealthy children are never born. Contraceptives are one way. But for one reason or another, some people don't play it safe, and it's usually those who can least afford to maintain children physically and emotionally. Such people need an alternative form of birth control: abortion. Abortion's especially necessary in the case of monstrously deformed fetuses. If a woman is willing and able to bear and care for the deformed or unintended child, fine. But if she isn't willing or can't, it's unfair to make the rest of us pay the price for the problem she's created and the responsibility she's shirked.

COUNTERPOINT: "You make it sound like the unloved and the deformed are responsible for every social and global problem we have; if we can just keep these 'undesirables' from being born, all our headaches will vanish. Sure, we have considerable problems, but lots of things account for them, including human mismanagement of resources, inadequate or misguided technology, nearsighted and unimaginative leadership, as well as the age-old conditions of human greed, prejudice, and downright stupidity. The idea that abortions can help improve these conditions is exactly the kind of mindless proposal that contributes to our problems. It's unfair, you say, to make society pay the price for maintaining the unwanted or deformed child. What's so unfair about it? I always thought that part of a society's function was to provide for those least able to fend for themselves. What would you suggest we do with our mental health services and facilities? Discontinue them, I guess. How about simply exterminating the mentally defective? That would really save us a bundle. And how about just executing criminals instead of incarcerating them? You shouldn't find that objectionable. After all, what could be more 'unfair' by your standard than making society pay the price for maintaining those who have flouted society's conventions?"

3. *Some pregnancies result from rape or incest.*

POINT: "There's no more heinous a crime committed against a woman than rape or incest. To oblige a woman morally to bear the child of such an outrage goes beyond adding insult to injury. It's brutally barbaric. Nothing short of the woman's free choice would morally justify going through with a rape or incest pregnancy."

COUNTERPOINT: "Agreed, rape and incest are ugly. But pregnancies resulting from them are rare. You're so concerned with not punishing the woman who has already been sexually abused. Well, by the same token, why punish the unborn by making them give up their lives? If making a woman carry to term a fetus that's resulted from rape or incest is a case of making the innocent suffer, then how much more innocent suffering is terminating the life of the fetus? Besides, nobody is asking the woman to raise a child she doesn't want or can't maintain. There are plenty of individuals and institutions who'll do that if she's unwilling or unable."

4. *Women have rights over their own bodies.*

POINT: "Women bear the full and exclusive burden of carrying a fetus to term. They must endure the physical and emotional risks, the discomfort, the disruptions of career and routine living. Given this burden, they have the right to decide whether or not they want to go through with a pregnancy. But beyond this, the unborn is a part of the woman's body, and she should have absolute say over whether or not it's going to remain in her body and be allowed to be born. To deny her that right is about as crude and basic a violation of free choice as anything imaginable."

COUNTERPOINT: "Of course women have certain rights over their own bodies. But having basic rights doesn't mean that those rights are absolute and take precedence over all others' rights. My right to free speech doesn't justify my yelling 'Fire!' in a crowded theater when, in fact, there is no fire. Nor does the woman's right over her own body mean she's justified in taking the life of the unborn. As soon as a woman gets pregnant, a relationship exists between her and the unborn. And like any other relationship, this one must involve a careful defining, assigning, and setting the priorities of rights and responsibilities. This is especially important in pregnancies because the unborn are in no position to argue for or defend their own rights. Let the woman who's so concerned about her own body make sure she doesn't get pregnant in the first place. But once she gets pregnant, her right takes a back seat to the unborn's right to life, certainly so long as the unborn's life doesn't threaten the woman's life."

Legal Considerations

We began this chapter by referring to a landmark abortion ruling. It is important to recognize that the question of whether a woman ought to have a legal right to an abortion is related to, but different from, the question of whether an abortion is ever morally justifiable.

Naturally, the morality of abortion can and does bear on the morality of restrictive abortion legislation. Thus people who believe that abortion is in and of itself morally objectionable often object to nonrestrictive legislation. And those who believe that abortion is unobjectionable often support nonrestrictive legislation. But it is also perfectly consistent to object to abortion while opposing restrictive abortion legislation because, say, such laws would abridge the individual's right to free choice. And it is perfectly consistent, and common, to argue that individual acts of abortion may be moral, even obligatory, while opposing a loosening of abortion laws because, for example, such a systematic policy may lead to abuses. In short, one can be opposed to abortion but also opposed to restrictive abortion legislation, or in favor of individual acts of abortion but against nonrestrictive legislation.

Any of the pro-life arguments can be marshaled in support of restrictive legislation, and any of the pro-choice arguments can be marshaled on behalf of nonrestrictive legislation. So one could argue that since abortion is murder, the state has a moral obligation to protect its citizens by preventing their murder; or, since abortion involves risks for women, the state has an obligation to protect its citizens from such risks. A person could also argue that the state has an obligation to relieve society's burden of caring for the unwanted or deformed unborn by making abortions possible for women; or that the state has an obligation to minimize the profound hardship a rape or incest pregnancy causes a woman by allowing her to have an abortion.

Especially relevant to the legislation question are the probable consequences of restrictive legislation, some of which can best be anticipated by considering some statistics prior to the Roe decision. By some estimates, in the early 1960s a million women obtained abortions, most of which were illegal.[3] Whatever the exact figure, before 1973 most abortions were obtained clandestinely. Poor women seemed to have been particularly vulnerable to the health-threatening conditions that often accompanied clandestine abortions, particularly those that were self-induced or performed by unqualified persons. In 1960 alone, 50 percent of the deaths in New York City associated with pregnancy and births resulted from illegal abortions.[4] It's a safe guess, then, that if abortion is returned to its pre-1973 legal status there will likely be an increase in clandestine abortions, with the poor bearing the brunt of the riskiest procedures.

In addition, physicians who believe in the morality of nontherapeutic abortions in the first trimester will presumably be forced to choose between obeying the law and following their conscience. Furthermore, restrictive legislation may create a fee system that borders on price-gouging. These concerns should at least be part of an analysis of the morality of proposed abortion legislation.

All the same, a knot of moral problems has developed since the passage of nonrestrictive legislation. For one thing, women today are often subjected to humiliating encounters with medical personnel. For example, sometimes they are asked to sign fetal "death certificates." In some cases machines are set next to them that record fetal heartbeats; abortions are performed in the same wards where other women are giving birth. Still other times women are given bags with a picture of a fetus that they are expected to return to the hospital after aborting at home.[5] At minimum, such procedures are callous and raise doubt about how well some health professionals and institutions are meeting their obligations to provide adequate care for the pregnant woman and to respect her autonomy.

3. N. Lee, The Search for an Abortionist *(Chicago: University of Chicago Press, 1969), pp. 5–6.*

4. A. F. Guttmacher, "Abortion—Yesterday, Today, Tomorrow," *in* The Case for Legalized Abortion, *ed. A. F. Guttmacher (Berkeley, Calif.: Diablo Press, 1967), pp. 8–9.*

5. *Ellen Frankfort,* Vaginal Politics *(New York: Quadrangle Books, 1972), pp. xxiii–xxv.*

In addition, legalization of abortion has not necessarily meant an end to profiteering, inadequate facilities, or poorly trained personnel.[6] Nor does abortion reform appear to have significantly altered the plight of the poor. On the contrary, some evidence indicates that first- and second-trimester abortions are sometimes not available to institutional patients, whereas in the very same institution abortions are being performed on private patients.[7] More important, according to recent federal legislation, Medicaid payments are permitted only for medical care following termination of a pregnancy by miscarriage or by an abortion to save the life of the mother; Medicaid payments are prohibited for all abortions except those performed to save the life of the mother.[8]

Undoubtedly, then, any proposed abortion legislation will be fraught with serious moral questions about autonomy, suffering, adequate care, and social justice. Discussions of the morality of the legislation must address these issues.

6. S. Burth Rauzek, The Women's Health Movement: Feminist Alternatives to Medical Control (New York: Praeger, 1979), pp. 26–27.

7. Diane Scully, Men Who Control Women's Health: The Miseducation of Obstetrician-Gynecologists (Boston: Houghton-Mifflin, 1980), pp. 229–30.

8. The Child Health Assurance Program (CHAP) was passed by the House of Representatives on December 11, 1979, HR 4962. For a synopsis of the bill, see Health Policy: The Legislative Agenda (Washington, D.C.: Congressional Quarterly, Inc., 1980), p. 90.

An Almost Absolute Value in History

John T. Noonan

Like many authors on the subject of abortion, law professor John T. Noonan locates the central issue in the ontological status of the fetus. In his essay Noonan assigns the fetus full ontological status at the moment of conception.

Noonan not only puts this view in the context of traditional Christian theology, he also tests its strength compared with the other distinctions of ontological status that are commonly made: viability, experience, quickening, attitude of parents, and social visibility. Noonan shows why he thinks each of these distinctions is unsound.

In addition to the unique problems that each of these distinctions has, Noonan believes that they share one overriding problem: They are distinctions that appear to be arbitrary. Noonan feels that if distinctions leading to moral judgments are not to appear arbitrary, they should relate to some real difference in probabilities. He argues that his position passes this test, because it recognizes the fact that 80 percent of the zygotes formed will develop into new beings. For Noonan this probability is a most compelling reason for granting the conceptus (fetus) full ontological status.

In short, conception is the decisive moment of humanization, for it is then that the fetus receives the genetic code of the parents. These arguments lead Noonan to condemn abortion, except in cases of self-defense.

From John T. Noonan, "An Almost Absolute Value in History," in Morality of Abortion: Legal and Historical Perspectives, ed. John T. Noonan (Harvard University Press, 1970). Reprinted by permission of the author.

The most fundamental question involved in the long history of thought on abortion is: How do you determine the humanity of a being? To phrase the question that way is to put in comprehensive humanistic terms what the theologians either dealt with as an explicitly theological question under the heading of "ensoulment" or dealt with implicitly in their treatment of abortion. The Christian position as it originated did not depend on a narrow theological or philosophical concept. It had no relation to theories of infant baptism. It appealed to no special theory of instantaneous ensoulment. It took the world's view on ensoulment as that view changed from Aristotle to Zacchia. There was, indeed, theological influence affecting the theory of ensoulment finally adopted, and, of course, ensoulment itself was a theological concept, so that the position was always explained in theological terms. But the theological notion of ensoulment could easily be translated into humanistic language by substituting "human" for "rational soul"; the problem of knowing when a man is a man is common to theology and humanism.

If one steps outside the specific categories used by the theologians, the answer they gave can be analyzed as a refusal to discriminate among human beings on the basis of their varying potentialities. Once conceived, the being was recognized as man because he had man's potential. The criterion for humanity, thus, was simple and all-embracing: If you are conceived by human parents, you are human.

The strength of this position may be tested by a review of some of the other distinctions offered in the contemporary controversy over legalizing abortion. Perhaps the most popular distinction is in terms of viability. Before an age of so many months, the fetus is not viable, that is, it cannot be removed from the mother's womb and live apart from her. To that extent, the life of the fetus is absolutely dependent on the life of the mother. This dependence is made the basis of denying recognition to its humanity.

There are difficulties with this distinction. One is that the perfection of artificial incubation may make the fetus viable at any time: It may be removed and artificially sustained. Experiments with animals already show that such a procedure is possible. This hypothetical extreme case relates to an actual difficulty: there is considerable elasticity to the idea of viability. Mere length of life is not an exact measure. The viability of the fetus depends on the extent of its anatomical and functional development. The weight and length of the fetus are better guides to the state of its development than age, but weight and length vary. Moreover, different racial groups have different ages at which their fetuses are viable. Some evidence, for example, suggests that Negro fetuses mature more quickly than white fetuses. If viability is the norm, the standard would vary with race and with many individual circumstances.

The most important objection to this approach is that dependence is not ended by viability. The fetus is still absolutely dependent on someone's care in order to continue existence; indeed a child of one or three or even five years of age is absolutely dependent on another's care for existence; uncared for, the older fetus or the younger child will die as surely as the early fetus detached from the mother. The unsubstantial lessening in dependence at viability does not seem to signify any special acquisition of humanity.

A second distinction has been attempted in terms of experience. A being who has had experience, has lived and suffered, who possesses memories, is more human than one who has not. Humanity depends on formation by experience. The fetus is thus "unformed" in the most basic human sense.

This distinction is not serviceable for the embryo which is already experiencing and reacting. The embryo is responsive to touch after eight weeks and at least at that point is experiencing. At an earlier stage the zygote is certainly alive and responding to its environment. The distinction may also be challenged by the rare case where aphasia has erased adult memory: Has it erased humanity? More fundamentally, this distinction leaves even the older fetus or the younger child to be treated as an unformed inhuman thing. Finally, it is not clear why experience as such confers humanity. It could be argued that certain central experiences such as loving or learning are necessary to make a man human. But then human beings who have failed to love or to learn might be excluded from the class called man.

A third distinction is made by appeal to the

sentiments of adults. If a fetus dies, the grief of the parents is not the grief they would have for a living child. The fetus is an unnamed "it" till birth, and is not perceived as personality until at least the fourth month of existence, when movements in the womb manifest a vigorous presence demanding joyful recognition by the parents.

Yet feeling is notoriously an unsure guide to the humanity of others. Many groups of humans have had difficulty in feeling that persons of another tongue, color, religion, sex, are as human as they. Apart from reactions to alien groups, we mourn the loss of a ten-year-old boy more than the loss of his one-day-old brother or his 90-year-old grandfather. The difference felt and the grief expressed vary with the potentialities extinguished, or the experience wiped out; they do not seem to point to any substantial difference in the humanity of baby, boy, or grandfather.

Distinctions are also made in terms of sensation by the parents. The embryo is felt within the womb only after about the fourth month. The embryo is seen only at birth. What can be neither seen nor felt is different from what is tangible. If the fetus cannot be seen or touched at all, it cannot be perceived as man.

Yet experience shows that sight is even more untrustworthy than feeling in determining humanity. By sight, color became an appropriate index for saying who was a man, and the evil of racial discrimination was given foundation. Nor can touch provide the test; a being confined by sickness, "out of touch" with others, does not thereby seem to lose his humanity. To the extent that touch still has appeal as a criterion, it appears to be a survival of the old English idea of "quickening"— a possible mistranslation of the Latin *animatus* used in the canon law. To that extent, touch as a criterion seems to be dependent on the Aristotelian notion of ensoulment, and to fall when this notion is discarded.

Finally, a distinction is sought in social visibility. The fetus is not socially perceived as human. It cannot communicate with others. Thus, both subjectively and objectively, it is not a member of society. As moral rules are rules for the behavior of members of society to each other, they cannot be made for behavior toward what is not yet a member. Excluded from the society of men, the fetus is excluded from the humanity of men.

By force of the argument from the consequences, this distinction is to be rejected. It is more subtle than that founded on an appeal to physical sensation, but it is equally dangerous in its implications. If humanity depends on social recognition, individuals or whole groups may be dehumanized by being denied any status in their society. Such a fate is fictionally portrayed in *1984* and has actually been the lot of many men in many societies. In the Roman empire, for example, condemnation to slavery meant the practical denial of most human rights; in the Chinese Communist world, landlords have been classified as enemies of the people and so treated as nonpersons by the state. Humanity does not depend on social recognition, though often the failure of society to recognize the prisoner, the alien, the heterodox as human has led to the destruction of human beings. Anyone conceived by a man and a woman is human. Recognition of this condition by society follows a real event in the objective order, however imperfect and halting the recognition. Any attempt to limit humanity to exclude some group runs the risk of furnishing authority and precedent for excluding other groups in the name of the consciousness or perception of the controlling group in the society.

A philosopher may reject the appeal to the humanity of the fetus because he views "humanity" as a secular view of the soul and because he doubts the existence of anything real and objective which can be identified as humanity. One answer to such a philosopher is to ask how he reasons about moral questions without supposing that there is a sense in which he and the others of whom he speaks are human. Whatever group is taken as the society which determines who may be killed is thereby taken as human. A second answer is to ask if he does not believe that there is a right and wrong way of deciding moral questions. If there is such a difference, experience may be appealed to: To decide who is human on the basis of the sentiment of a given society has led to consequences which rational men would characterize as monstrous.

The rejection of the attempted distinctions based on viability and visibility, experience and feeling, may be buttressed by the following considerations: Moral judgments often rest on distinctions, but if the distinctions are not to appear arbitrary fiat, they should relate to some real difference in probabilities. There is a kind of continuity in all life, but the earlier stages of the elements of human life possess tiny probabilities of development. Consider, for example, the spermatozoa in any normal ejaculate: There are about 200,000,000 in any single ejaculate, of which one has a chance of developing into a zygote. Consider the oocytes which may become ova: There are 100,000 to 1,000,000 oocytes in a female infant, of which a maximum of 390 are ovulated. But once spermatozoon and ovum meet and the conceptus is formed, such studies as have been made show that roughly in only 20 percent of the cases will spontaneous abortion occur. In other words, the chances are about 4 out of 5 that this new being will develop. At this stage in the life of the being there is a sharp shift in probabilities, an immense jump in potentialities. To make a distinction between the rights of spermatozoa and the rights of the fertilized ovum is to respond to an enormous shift in possibilities. For about twenty days after conception, the egg may split to form twins or combine with another egg to form a chimera, but the probability of either event happening is very small.

It may be asked, What does a change in biological probabilities have to do with establishing humanity? The argument from probabilities is not aimed at establishing humanity but at establishing an objective discontinuity which may be taken into account in moral discourse. As life itself is a matter of probabilities, as most moral reasoning is an estimate of probabilities, so it seems in accord with the structure of reality and the nature of moral thought to found a moral judgment on the change in probabilities at conception. The appeal to probabilities is the most commonsensical of arguments; to a greater or smaller degree all of us base our actions on probabilities, and in morals, as in law, prudence and negligence are often measured by the account one has taken of the probabilities. If the chance is 200,000,000 to 1 that the movement in the bushes into which you shoot is a man's, I doubt if many persons would hold you careless in shooting; but if the chances are 4 out of 5 that the movement is a human being's, few would acquit you of blame. Would the argument be different if only one out of ten children conceived came to term? Of course this argument would be different. This argument is an appeal to probabilities that actually exist, not to any and all states of affairs which may be imagined.

The probabilities as they do exist do not show the humanity of the embryo in the sense of a demonstration in logic any more than the probabilities of the movement in the bush being a man demonstrate beyond all doubt that the being is a man. The appeal is a "buttressing" consideration, showing the plausibility of the standard adopted. The argument focuses on the decisional factor in any moral judgment and assumes that part of the business of a moralist is drawing lines. One evidence of the nonarbitrary character of the line drawn is the difference of probabilities on either side of it. If a spermatozoon is destroyed, one destroys a being which had a chance of far less than 1 in 200 million of developing into a reasonable being, possessed of the genetic code, a heart and other organs, and capable of pain. If a fetus is destroyed, one destroys a being already possessed of the genetic code, organs, and sensitivity to pain, and one which had an 80 percent chance of developing further into a baby, outside the womb, who, in time, would reason.

The positive argument for conception as the decisive moment of humanization is that at conception the new being receives the genetic code. It is this genetic information which determines his characteristics, which is the biological carrier of the possibility of human wisdom, which makes him a self-evolving being. A being with a human genetic code is man.

This review of current controversy over the humanity of the fetus emphasizes what a fundamental question the theologians resolved in asserting the inviolability of the fetus. To regard the fetus as possessed of equal rights with other humans was not, however, to decide every case where abortion might be employed. It did decide the case where the argument was that the fetus should be aborted for its own good. To say a being was human was to say it had a destiny to decide for itself which could not be taken from it by another man's decision. But human beings with equal rights often come in conflict with each other, and some decision must be made as to whose claims are to prevail. Cases of conflict involving the fetus are different only in two respects: the total inability of the fetus to speak for itself and the fact that the right of the fetus regularly at stake is the right to life itself.

The approach taken by the theologians to these conflicts was articulated in terms of "direct" and "indirect." Again, to look at what they were doing from outside their categories, they may be said to have been drawing lines or "balancing values." "Direct" and "indirect" are spatial metaphors: "line-drawing" is another. "To weigh" or "to balance" values is a metaphor of a more complicated mathematical sort hinting at the process which goes on in moral judgments. All the metaphors suggest that, in the moral judgments made, comparisons were necessary, that no value completely controlled. The principle of double effect was no doctrine fallen from heaven, but a method of analysis appropriate where two relative values were being compared. In Catholic moral theology, as it developed, life even of the innocent was not taken as an absolute. Judgments on acts affecting life issued from a process of weighing. In the weighing, the fetus was always given a value greater than zero, always a value separate and independent from its parents. This valuation was crucial and fundamental in all Christian thought on the subject and marked it off from any approach which considered that only the parents' interests needed to be considered.

Even with the fetus weighed as human, one interest could be weighed as equal or superior: that of the mother in her own life. The casuists between 1450 and 1895 were willing to weigh this interest as superior. Since 1895, that interest was given decisive weight only in the two special cases of the cancerous uterus and the ectopic pregnancy. In both of these cases the fetus itself had little chance of survival even if the abortion were not performed. As the balance was once struck in favor of the mother whenever her life was endangered, it could be so struck again. The balance reached between 1895 and 1930 attempted prudentially and pastorally to forestall a multitude of exceptions for interests less than life.

The perception of the humanity of the fetus and the weighing of fetal rights against other human rights constituted the work of the moral analysts. But what spirit animated their abstract judgments? For the Christian community it was the injunction of Scripture to love your neighbor as yourself. The fetus as human was a neighbor; his life had parity with one's own. The commandment gave life to what otherwise would have been only rational calculation.

The commandment could be put in humanistic as well as theological terms: Do not injure your fellow man without reason. In these terms, once the humanity of the fetus is perceived, abortion is never right except in self-defense. When life must be taken to save life, reason alone cannot say that a mother must prefer a child's life to her own. With this exception, now of great rarity, abortion violates the rational humanist tenet of the equality of human lives.

For Christians the commandment to love had received a special imprint in that the exemplar proposed of love was the love of the Lord for his disciples. In the light given by this example, self-sacrifice carried to the point of death seemed in the extreme situations not without meaning. In the less extreme cases, preference for one's own interests to the life of another seemed to express cruelty or selfishness irreconcilable with the demands of love.

Questions for Analysis

1. *Do you agree that considering the unborn a person from the moment of conception poses fewer problems than any of the alternative views?*

2. *What problems does Noonan see in distinctions based on: (a) viability, (b) experience, (c) feelings of adults, (d) social visibility?*

3. *Explain how Noonan used "biological probabilities" to buttress his view of the unborn as a person from the moment of conception. Is his argument persuasive?*

4. *On what grounds does Noonan object to abortion?*

5. *Is it accurate to say that Noonan finds abortion always impermissible?*

In Defense of Abortion and Infanticide

Michael Tooley

In the following essay, professor of philosophy Michael Tooley focuses on the basic moral objection traditionally raised to abortion and infanticide, namely, that the unborn and newborn have a right to life. In testing this assumption, Tooley attempts to isolate the properties a thing must possess in order to have a right to life.

In Tooley's view, only if an entity is capable of having an interest in its own continued existence can it have a right to life, and only if an entity possesses at some time the concept of a continuing self is it capable of having an interest in its own continued existence. Since fetuses and infants cannot satisfy these conditions, Tooley concludes that they have no right to life—their potential for satisfying these conditions notwithstanding. Therefore, barring other objections besides the traditional one, Tooley considers both abortion and infanticide morally acceptable. In contrast, he thinks that since adult members of nonhuman species may satisfy these conditions, our treatment of them may be morally suspect.

It's important to realize that Tooley is not arguing for indiscriminate abortion and infanticide, but trying to make a case for the moral permissibility of acts of abortion and infanticide that might be considered immoral because they violate a right-to-life claim. It doesn't necessarily follow that every act of abortion and infanticide would therefore be morally permissible.

This essay deals with the question of the morality of abortion and infanticide. The fundamental ethical objection traditionally advanced against these practices rests on the contention that human fetuses and infants have a right to life. It is this claim which will be the focus of attention here. The basic issue to be discussed, then, is what properties a thing must possess in order to have a right to life. My approach will be to set out and defend a basic moral principle specifying a condition an organism must satisfy if it is to have a right to life. It will be seen that this condition is not satisfied by human fetuses and infants, and thus that they do not have a right to life. So unless there are other objections to abortion and infanticide which are sound, one is forced to conclude that these practices are morally acceptable ones.[1] In contrast, it may turn out that our treatment of adult members of some other species is morally indefensible. For it is quite possible that some nonhuman animals do possess properties that endow them with a right to life.

I. Abortion and Infanticide

What reason is there for raising the question of the morality of infanticide? One reason is that it seems very difficult to formulate a completely satisfactory pro-abortion position without coming to grips with the infanticide issue. For the problem that the liberal on abortion encounters here is that of specifying a cutoff point which is not arbitrary: at what stage in the development of a human being does it cease to be morally permissible to destroy it, and why?

It is important to be clear about the difficulty here. The problem is not, as some have thought, that since there is a continuous line of development from a zygote to a newborn baby, one cannot hold that it is seriously wrong to destroy a newborn baby without also holding that it is seriously wrong to destroy a zygote, or any intermediate stage in the development of a human being. The problem is rather that if one says that it is wrong to destroy a newborn baby but not a zygote or some intermediate stage, one should be prepared to point to a

This article first appeared in The Problem of Abortion, *edited by Joel Feinberg (Belmont, Calif.: Wadsworth, 1984). Reprinted here by permission of the author.*

morally relevant difference between a newborn baby and the earlier stage in the development of a human being.

Precisely the same difficulty can, of course, be raised for a person who holds that infanticide is morally permissible, since one can ask what morally relevant difference there is between an adult human being and a newborn baby. What makes it morally permissible to destroy a baby, but wrong to kill an adult? So the challenge remains. But I shall argue that in the latter case there is an extremely plausible answer.

Reflecting on the morality of infanticide forces one to face up to this challenge. In the case of abortion a number of events—quickening or viability, for instance—might be taken as cutoff points, and it is easy to overlook the fact that none of these events involves any morally significant change in the developing human. In contrast, if one is going to defend infanticide, one has to get very clear about what it is that gives something a right to life.

One of the interesting ways in which the abortion issue differs from most other moral issues is that the plausible positions on abortion appear to be extreme ones. For if a human fetus has a right to life, one is inclined to say that, in general, one would be justified in killing it only to save the life of the mother, and perhaps not even in that case.[2] Such is the extreme anti-abortion position. On the other hand, if the fetus does not have a right to life, why should it be seriously wrong to destroy it? Why would one need to point to special circumstances—such as the presence of genetic disease, or a threat to the woman's health—in order to justify such action? The upshot is that there does not appear to be any room for a moderate position on abortion such as one finds, for example, in the Model Penal Code recommendations.[3]

Aside from the light it may shed on the abortion question, the issue of infanticide is both interesting and important in its own right. The theoretical interest has been mentioned above: it forces one to face up to the question of what it is that gives something a right to life. The practical importance need not be labored. Most people would prefer to raise children who do not suffer from gross deformities or from severe physical, emotional, or intellectual handicaps. If it could be shown that there is no moral objection to infanticide, the happiness of society could be significantly and justifiably increased.

The suggestion that infanticide may be morally permissible is not an idea that many people are able to consider dispassionately. Even philosophers tend to react in a way which seems primarily visceral—offering no arguments, and dismissing infanticide out of hand.

Some philosophers have argued, however, that such a reaction is not inappropriate, on the ground that, first, moral principles must, in the final analysis, be justified by reference to our moral feelings, or intuitions, and secondly, infanticide is one practice that is judged wrong by virtually everyone's moral intuition. I believe, however, that this line of thought is unsound, and I have argued elsewhere that even if [one] grants, at least for the sake of argument, that moral intuitions are the final court of appeal regarding the acceptability of moral principles, the question of the morality of infanticide is not one that can be settled by an appeal to our intuitions concerning it.[4] If infanticide is to be rejected, an argument is needed, and I believe that the considerations advanced in this essay show that it is unlikely that such an argument is forthcoming.

II. What Sort of Being Can Possess a Right to Life?

The issues of the morality of abortion and of infanticide seem to turn primarily upon the answers to the following four questions:

(1) What properties, other than potentialities, give something a right to life?

(2) Do the corresponding potentialities also endow something with a right to life?

(3) If not, do they at least make it seriously wrong to destroy it?

(4) At what point in its development does a member of the biologically defined species *Homo sapiens* first possess those nonpotential properties that give something a right to life? The argument to be developed in the present section bears upon the answers to the first two questions.

How can one determine what properties endow a being with a right to life? An approach that I believe is very promising starts out from the observation that there appear to be two radically different sorts of reasons why an entity may lack a certain right. Compare, for example, the following two claims:

(1)   A child does not have a right to smoke.

(2)   A newspaper does not have a right not to be torn up.

The first claim raises a substantive moral issue. People might well disagree about it, and support their conflicting views by appealing to different moral theories. The second dispute, in contrast, seems an unlikely candidate for moral dispute. It is natural to say that newspapers just are not the sort of thing that can have any rights at all, including a right not to be torn up. So there is no need to appeal to a substantive moral theory to resolve the question whether a newspaper has a right not to be torn up.

One way of characterizing this difference, albeit one that will not especially commend itself to philosophers of a Quincan[5] bent, is to say that the second claim, unlike the first, is true in virtue of a certain *conceptual* connection, and that is why no moral theory is needed in order to see that it is true. The explanation, then, of why it is that a newspaper does not have a right not to be torn up, is that there is some property P such that, first, newspapers lack property P, and secondly, it is a conceptual truth that only things with property P can be possessors of rights.

What might property P be? A plausible answer, I believe, is set out and defended by Joel Feinberg in his paper, "The Rights of Animals and Unborn Generations."[6] It takes the form of what Feinberg refers to as the *interest principle:* ". . . the sorts of beings who *can* have rights are precisely those who have (or can have) interests."[7] And then, since "interests must be compounded somehow out of conations,"[8] it follows that things devoid of desires, such as newspapers, can have neither interests nor rights. Here, then, is one account of the difference in status between judgments such as (1) and (2) above.

Let us now consider the right to life. The interest principle tells us that an entity cannot have any rights at all, and *a fortiori*, cannot have a right to life, unless it is capable of having interests. This in itself may be a conclusion of considerable importance. Consider, for example, a fertilized human egg cell. Someday it will come to have desires and interests. As a zygote, however, it does not have

desires, nor even the *capacity* for having desires. What about interests? This depends upon the account one offers of the relationship between desires and interests. It seems to me that a zygote cannot properly be spoken of as a subject of interests. My reason is roughly this. What is in a thing's interest is a function of its present and future desires, both those it will actually have and those it could have. In the case of an entity that is not presently capable of any desires, its interest must be based entirely upon the satisfaction of future desires. Then, since the satisfaction of future desires presupposes the continued existence of the entity in question, anything which has an interest which is based upon the satisfaction of future desires must also have an interest in its own continued existence. Therefore, something which is not presently capable of having any desires at all—like a zygote—cannot have any interests at all unless it has an interest in its own continued existence. I shall argue shortly, however, that a zygote cannot have such an interest. From this it will follow that it cannot have any interests at all, and this conclusion, together with the interest principle, entails that not all members of the species *Homo sapiens* have a right to life.

The interest principle involves, then, a thesis concerning a necessary condition which something must satisfy if it is to have a right to life, and it is a thesis which has important moral implications. It implies, for example, that abortions, if performed sufficiently early, do not involve any violation of a right to life. But on the other hand, the interest principle provides no help with the question of the moral status of human organisms once they have developed to the point where they do have desires, and thus are capable of having interests. The interest principle states that they *can* have rights. It does not state whether they *do* have rights—including, in particular, a right not to be destroyed.

It is possible, however, that the interest principle does not exhaust the conceptual connections between rights and interests. It formulates only a very general connection: a thing cannot have any rights at all unless it is capable of having at least some interest. May there not be more specific connections, between particular rights and particular sorts of interests? The following line of thought lends plausibility to this suggestion. Consider animals such as cats. Some philosophers are inclined to hold that animals such as cats do not have any rights at all. But let us assume, for the purpose of the present discussion, that cats do have some rights, such as a right not to be tortured, and consider the following claim:

(3)   A cat does not have a right to a university education.

How is this statement to be regarded? In particular, is it comparable in status to the claim that children do not have a right to smoke, or, instead, to the claim that newspapers do not have a right not to be torn up? To the latter, surely. Just as a newspaper is not the sort of thing that can have any rights at all, including a right not to be destroyed, so one is inclined to say that a cat, though it may have some rights, such as a right not to be tortured, is not the sort of thing that can possibly have a right to a university education.

This intuitive judgment about the status of claims such as (3) is reinforced, moreover, if one turns to the question of the grounds of the interest principle. Consider, for example, the account offered by Feinberg, which he summarizes as follows:

> Now we can extract from our discussion of animal rights a crucial principle for tentative use in the resolution of the other riddles about the applicability of the concept of a right, namely, that the sorts of beings who *can* have rights are precisely those who have (or can have) interests. I have come to this tentative conclusion for two reasons: (1) because a right holder must be capable of being represented and it is impossible to represent a being that has no interests, and (2) because a right holder must be capable of being a beneficiary in his own person, and a being without interests is a being that is incapable of being harmed or benefited, having no good or 'sake' of its own. Thus a being without interests has no 'behalf' to act in, and no 'sake' to act for.[9]

If this justification of the interest principle is sound, it can also be employed to support principles connecting particular rights with specific sorts of interests. Just as one cannot represent a being that has no interests at all, so one cannot, in demanding a university education for a cat, be representing the cat unless one is thereby representing some interest that the cat has, and that would be served by its receiving a university education. Similarly, one cannot be acting for the sake of a cat in arguing that it should receive a university education unless the

cat has some interest that will thereby be furthered. The conclusion, therefore, is that if Feinberg's defense of the interest principle is sound, other more specific principles must also be correct. These more specific principles can be summed up, albeit somewhat vaguely, by the following *particular-interests principle*:

> It is a conceptual truth that an entity cannot have a particular right, R, unless it is at least capable of having some interest, I, which is furthered by its having right R.

Given this particular-interests principle, certain familiar facts, whose importance has not often been appreciated, become comprehensible. Compare an act of killing a normal adult human being with an act of torturing one for five minutes. Though both acts are seriously wrong, they are not equally so. Here, as in most cases, to violate an individual's right to life is more seriously wrong than to violate his right not to have pain inflicted upon him. Consider, however, the corresponding actions in the case of a newborn kitten. Most people feel that it is seriously wrong to torture a kitten for five minutes, but not to kill it painlessly. How is this difference in the moral ordering of the two types of acts, between the human case and the kitten case, to be explained? One answer is that while normal adult human beings have both a right to life and a right not to be tortured, a kitten has only the latter. But why should this be so? The particular-interests principle suggests a possible explanation. Though kittens have some interests, including, in particular, an interest in not being tortured, which derives from their capacity to feel pain, they do not have an interest in their own continued existence, and hence do not have a right not to be destroyed. This answer contains, of course, a large promissory element. One needs a defense of the view that kittens have no interest in continued existence. But the point here is simply that there is an important question about the rationale underlying the moral ordering of certain sorts of acts, and that the particular-interests principle points to a possible answer.

This fact lends further plausibility, I believe, to the particular-interests principle. What one would ultimately like to do, of course, is to set out an analysis of the concept of a right, show that the analysis is indeed satisfactory, and then show that the particular-interests principle is entailed by the analysis. Unfortunately, it will not be possible to pursue such an approach here, since formulating an acceptable analysis of the concept of a right is a far from trivial matter. What I should like to do, however, is to touch briefly upon the problem of providing such an analysis, and then to indicate the account that seems to me most satisfactory—an account which does entail the particular-interests principle.

It would be widely agreed, I believe, both that rights impose obligations, and that the obligations they impose upon others are *conditional* upon certain factors. The difficulty arises when one attempts to specify what the obligations are conditional upon. There seem to be two main views in this area. According to the one, rights impose obligations that are conditional upon the interests of the possessor of the right. To say that Sandra has a right to something is thus to say, roughly, that if it is in Sandra's interest to have that thing, then others are under an obligation not to deprive her of it. According to the second view, rights impose obligations that are conditional upon the right's not having been waived. To say that Sandra has a right to something is to say, roughly, that if Sandra has not given others permission to take the thing, then they are under an obligation not to deprive her of it.

Both views encounter serious difficulties. On the one hand, in the case of minors, and nonhuman animals, it would seem that the obligations that rights impose must be taken as conditional upon the interests of those individuals, rather than upon whether they have given one permission to do certain things. On the other, in the case of individuals who are capable of making informed and rational decisions, if that person has not given one permission to take something that belongs to him, it would seem that one is, in general, still under an obligation not to deprive him of it, even if having that thing is no longer in his interest.

As a result, it seems that a more complex account is needed of the factors upon which the obligations imposed by rights are conditional. The account which I now prefer, and which I have defended elsewhere,[10] is this:

> A has a right to X

means the same as

> A is such that it can be in A's interest to have X, and *either* (1) A is not capable of making an informed and rational choice whether

to grant others permission to deprive him of X, in which case, if it is in A's interest not to be deprived of X, then, by that fact alone, others are under a prima facie obligation not to deprive A of X, *or* (2) A is capable of making an informed and rational choice whether to grant others permission to deprive him of X, in which case others are under a prima facie obligation not to deprive A of X if and only if A has not granted them permission to do so.

And if this account, or something rather similar, is correct, then so is the particular-interests principle.

What I now want to do is to apply the particular-interests principle to the case of the right to life. First, however, one needs to notice that the expression "right to life" is not entirely happy, since it suggests that the right in question concerns the continued existence of a biological organism. That this is incorrect can be brought out by considering possible ways of violating an individual's right to life. Suppose, for example, that future technological developments make it possible to change completely the neural networks in a brain, and that the brain of some normal adult human being is thus completely reprogrammed, so that the organism in question winds up with memories (or rather, apparent memories), beliefs, attitudes, and personality traits totally different from those associated with it before it was subjected to reprogramming. (The pope is programmed, say, on the model of Bertrand Russell.) In such a case, however beneficial the change might be, one would surely want to say that *someone* had been destroyed, that an adult human being's right to life had been violated, even though no biological organism had been killed. This shows that the expression "right to life" is misleading, since what one is concerned about is not just the continued existence of a biological organism.

How, then, might the right in question be more accurately described? A natural suggestion is that the expression "right to life" refers to the right of a subject of experiences and other mental states to continue to exist. It might be contended, however, that this interpretation begs the question against certain possible views. For someone might hold—and surely some people in fact do—that while continuing subjects of experiences and other mental states certainly have a right to life, so do some other organisms that are only potentially such continuing subjects, such as human fetuses. A right to life, on this view, is *either* the right of a subject of experiences to continue to exist, *or* the right of something that is only potentially a continuing subject of experiences to become such an entity.

This view is, I believe, to be rejected, for at least two reasons. In the first place, this view appears to be clearly incompatible with the interest principle, as well as with the particular-interests principle. Secondly, this position entails that the destruction of potential persons is, in general, prima facie seriously wrong, and I shall argue, in the next section, that the latter view is incorrect.

Let us consider, then, the right of a subject of experiences and other mental states to continue to exist. The particular-interests principle implies that something cannot possibly have such a right unless its continued existence can be in its interest. We need to ask, then, what must be the case if the continued existence of something is to be in its interest.

It will help to focus our thinking, I believe, if we consider a crucial case, stressed by Derek Parfit. Imagine a human baby that has developed to the point of being sentient, and of having simple desires, but that is not yet capable of having any desire for continued existence. Suppose, further, that the baby will enjoy a happy life, and will be glad that it was not destroyed. Can we or can we not say that it is in the baby's interest not to be destroyed?

To approach this case, let us consider a closely related one, namely, that of a human embryo that has not developed sufficiently far to have any desires, or even any states of consciousness at all, but that will develop into an individual who will enjoy a happy life, and who will be glad that his mother did not have an abortion. Can we or can we not say that it is the embryo's interest not to be destroyed?

Why might someone be tempted to say that it is in the embryo's interest not to be destroyed? One line of thought which, I believe, tempts some people is this. Let Mary be an individual who enjoys a happy life. Then, though some philosophers have expressed serious doubts about this, it might very well be said that it was certainly in Mary's interest that a certain embryo was not destroyed several years earlier. And this claim, together with the tendency to use expressions such as "Mary before she was born" to refer to the embryo in question, may

lead one to think that it was in the embryo's interest not to be destroyed. But this way of thinking involves conceptual confusion. A subject of interests, in the relevant sense of "interest," must necessarily be a subject of conscious states, including experiences and desires. This means that in identifying Mary with the embryo, and attributing to it her interest in its earlier nondestruction, one is treating the embryo as if it were itself a subject of consciousness. But by hypothesis, the embryo being considered has not developed to the point where there is any subject of consciousness associated with it. It cannot, therefore, have any interests at all, and *a furtiori*, it cannot have any interest in its own continued existence.

Let us now return to the first case—that of a human baby that is sentient, and which has simple desires, but which is not yet capable of having more complex desires, such as a desire for its own continued existence. Given that it will develop into an individual who will lead a happy life, and who will be glad that the baby was not destroyed, does one want to say that the baby's not being destroyed is in the baby's own interest?

Again, the following line of thought may seem initially tempting. If Mary is the resulting individual, then it was in Mary's interest that the baby not have been destroyed. But the baby *is* Mary when she was young. So it must have been in the baby's interest that it not have been destroyed.

Indeed, this argument is considerably more tempting in the present case than in the former, since here there is something that is a subject of consciousness, and which it is natural to identify with Mary. I suggest, however, that when one reflects upon the case, it becomes clear that such an identification is justified only if certain further things are the case. Thus, on the one hand, suppose that Mary is able to remember quite clearly some of the experiences that the baby enjoyed. Given that sort of causal and psychological connection, it would seem perfectly reasonble to hold that Mary and the baby are one and the same subject of consciousness, and thus, that if it is in Mary's interest that the baby not have been destroyed, then this must also have been in the baby's interest. On the other hand, suppose that not only does Mary, at a much later time, not remember any of the baby's experiences, but the experiences in question are not psychologically linked, either via memory or in any other way, to mental states enjoyed by the human organism in question at *any* later time. Here it seems to me clearly incorrect to say that Mary and the baby are one and the same subject of consciousness, and therefore it cannot be correct to transfer, from Mary to the baby, Mary's interest in the baby's not having been destroyed.

Let us now return to the question of what must be the case if the continued existence of something is to be in [its] own interest. The picture that emerges from the two cases just discussed is this. In the first place, nothing at all can be in an entity's interest unless it has desires at some time or other. But more than this is required if the continued existence of the entity is to be in its own interest. One possibility, which will generally be sufficient, is that the individual have, at the time in question, a desire for its own continued existence. Yet it also seems clear that an individual's continued existence can be in its own interest even when such a desire is not present. What is needed, apparently, is that the continued existence of the individual will make possible the satisfaction of some desires existing at other times. But not just any desires existing at other times will do. Indeed, as is illustrated both by the case of the baby just discussed, and by the deprogramming/reprogramming example, it is not even sufficient that they be desires associated with the same physical organism. It is crucial that they be desires that belong to one and the same subject of consciousness.

The critical question, then, concerns the conditions under which desires existing at different times can be correctly attributed to a single, continuing subject of consciousness. This question raises a number of difficult issues which cannot be considered here. Part of the rationale underlying the view I wish to advance will be clear, however, if one considers the role played by memory in the psychological unity of an individual over time. When I remember a past experience, what I know is not merely that there was a certain experience which someone or other had, but that there was an experience that belonged to the *same* individual as the present memory beliefs, and it seems clear that this feature of one's memories is, in general, a crucial part of what it is that makes one a continuing subject of experiences, rather than merely a series of

psychologically isolated, momentary subjects of consciousness. This suggests something like the following principle:

> Desires existing at different times can belong to a single, continuing subject of consciousness only if that subject of consciousness possesses, at some time, the concept of a continuing self or mental substance.[11]

Given this principle, together with the particular-rights principle, one can set out the following argument in support of a claim concerning a necessary condition which an entity must satisfy if it is to have a right to life:

(1) The concept of a right is such that an individual cannot have a right at time *t* to continued existence unless the individual is such that it can be in its interest at time *t* that it continue to exist.

(2) The continued existence of a given subject of consciousness cannot be in that individual's interest at time *t* unless *either* that individual has a desire, at time *t*, to continue to exist as a subject of consciousness, *or* that individual can have desires at other times.

(3) An individual cannot have a desire to continue to exist as a subject of consciousness unless it possesses the concept of a continuing self or mental substance.

(4) An individual existing at one time cannot have desires at other times unless there is at least one time at which it possesses the concept of a continuing self or mental substance.

Therefore:

(5) An individual cannot have a right to continued existence unless there is at least one time at which it possesses the concept of a continuing self or mental substance.

This conclusion is obviously significant. But precisely what implications does it have with respect to the morality of abortion and infanticide? The answer will depend upon what relationship there is between, on the one hand, the behavioral and neurophysiological development of a human being, and, on the other, the development of that individual's mind. Some people believe that there is no relationship at all. They believe that a human mind, with all its mature capacities, is present in a human from conception onward, and so is there before the brain has even begun to develop, and before the individual has begun to exhibit behavior expressive of higher mental functioning. Most philosophers, however, reject this view. They believe, on the one hand, that there is, in general, a rather close relation between an individual's behavioral capacities and its mental functioning, and, on the other, that there is a very intimate relationship between the mind and the brain. As regards the latter, some philosophers hold that the mind is in fact identical with the brain. Others maintain that the mind is distinct from the brain, but causally dependent upon it. In either case, the result is a view according to which the development of the mind and the brain are necessarily closely tied to one another.

If one does adopt the view that there is a close relation between the behavioral and neurophysiological development of a human being and the development of its mind, then the above conclusion has a very important, and possibly decisive implication with respect to the morality of abortion and infanticide. For when human development, both behavioral and neurophysiological, is closely examined, it is seen to be most unlikely that human fetuses, or even newborn babies, possess any concept of a continuing self.[12] And in the light of the above conclusion, this means that such individuals do not possess a right to life.

But is it reasonable to hold that there is a close relation between human behavioral and neurophysiological development and the development of the human mind? Approached from a scientific perspective, I believe that there is excellent reason for doing so. Consider, for example, what is known about how, at later stages, human mental capacities proceed in step with brain development, or what is known about how damage to different parts of the brain can affect, in different ways, an individual's intellectual capacities.

Why, then, do some people reject the view that there is a close relationship between the development of the human mind and the behavioral and neurophysiological development of human beings? There are, I think, two main reasons. First, some philosophers believe that the scientific evidence is irrelevant, because they believe that it is possible to establish, by means of a purely metaphysical

argument, that a human mind, with its mature capacities, is present in a human from conception onward. I have argued elsewhere that the argument in question is unsound.[13]

Secondly, and more commonly, some people appeal to the idea that it is a divinely revealed truth that human beings have minds from conception onward. There are a number of points to be made about such an appeal. In the first place, the belief that a mind, or soul, is infused into a human body at conception by God is not an essential belief within many of the world religions. Secondly, even within religious traditions, such as Roman Catholicism, where that belief is a very common one, it is by no means universally accepted. Thus, for example, the well known Catholic philosopher Joseph Donceel has argued very strongly for the claim that the correct position on the question of ensoulment is that the soul enters the body only when the human brain has undergone a sufficient process of development.[14] Thirdly, there is the question of whether it is reasonable to accept the religious outlook which is being appealed to in support of the contention that humans have minds which are capable of higher intellectual activities from conception onward. This question raises very large issues in philosophy of religion which cannot be pursued here. But it should at least be said that many contemporary philosophers who have reflected upon religious beliefs have come to the view that there is not sufficient reason even for believing in the existence of God, let alone for accepting the much more detailed religious claims which are part of a religion such as Christianity. Finally, suppose that one nonetheless decides to accept the contention that it is a divinely revealed truth that humans have, from conception onward, minds that are capable of higher mental activities, and that one appeals to this purported revelation in order to support the claim that all humans have a right to life. One needs to notice that if one then goes on to argue, not merely that abortion is morally wrong, but that there should be a law against it, one will encounter a very serious objection. For it is surely true that it is inappropriate, at least in a pluralistic society, to appeal to specific religious beliefs of a nonmoral sort—such as the belief that God infuses souls into human bodies at conception—in support of legislation that will be binding upon everyone, including those who either accept different religious beliefs, or none at all.

III. Summary and Conclusions

In this paper I have advanced three main philosophical contentions:

(1) An entity cannot have a right to life unless it is capable of having an interest in its own continued existence.

(2) An entity is not capable of having an interest in its own continued existence unless it possesses, at some time, the concept of a continuing self, or subject of experiences and other mental states.

(3) The fact that an entity will, if not destroyed, come to have properties that would give it a right to life does not in itself make it seriously wrong to destroy it. [15]

If these philosophical contentions are correct, the crucial question is a factual one: At what point does a developing human being acquire the concept of a continuing self, and at what point is it capable of having an interest in its own continued existence? I have not examined this issue in detail here, but I have suggested that careful scientific studies of human development, both behavioral and neurophysiological, strongly support the view that even newborn humans do not have the capacities in question. If this is right, then it would seem that infanticide during a time interval shortly after birth must be viewed as morally acceptable.

But where is the line to be drawn? What is the precise cutoff point? If one maintained, as some philosophers do, that an individual can possess a concept only if it is capable of expressing that concept linguistically, then it would be a relatively simple matter to determine whether a given organism possessed the concept of a continuing subject of experiences and other mental states. It is far from clear, however, that this claim about the necessary connection between the possession of concepts and the having of linguistic capabilities is correct. I would argue, for example, that one wants to ascribe mental states of a conceptual sort—such as beliefs and desires—to animals that are incapable of learning a language, and that an individual cannot have beliefs and desires unless it possesses the concepts involved in those beliefs and desires. And if that view is right—if an organism can acquire concepts without thereby acquiring a way of expressing those concepts linguistically—then the question of whether an individual possesses the concept of a continuing self may be one that requires quite subtle experimental techniques to answer.

If this view of the matter is roughly correct, there are two worries that one is left with at the level of practical moral decisions, one of which may turn out to be deeply disturbing. The lesser worry is the question just raised: Where is the line to be drawn in the case of infanticide? This is not really a troubling question since there is no serious need to know the exact point at which a human infant acquires a right to life. For in the vast majority of cases in which infanticide is desirable due to serious defects from which the baby suffers, its desirability will be apparent at birth or within a very short time thereafter. Since it seems clear that an infant at this point in its development is not capable of possessing the concept of a continuing subject of experiences and other mental states, and so is incapable of having an interest in its own continued existence, infanticide will be morally permissible in the vast majority of cases in which it is, for one reason or another, desirable. The practical moral problem can thus be satisfactorily handled by choosing some short period of time, such as a week after birth, as the interval during which infanticide will be permitted.

The troubling issue which arises out of the above reflections concerns whether adult animals belonging to species other than *Homo sapiens* may not also possess a right to life. For once one allows that an individual can possess concepts, and have beliefs and desires, without being able to express those concepts, or those beliefs and desires, linguistically, then it becomes very much an open question whether animals belonging to other species do not possess properties that give them a right to life. Indeed, I am strongly inclined to think that adult members of at least some nonhuman species do have a right to life. My reason is that, first I believe that some nonhuman animals are capable of envisaging a future for themselves, and of having desires about future states of themselves. Secondly, that anything which exercises these capacities has an interest in its own continued existence. And thirdly, that having an interest in one's own continued existence is not merely a necessary, but also a sufficient, condition for having a right to life.

The suggestion that at least some nonhuman animals have a right to life is not unfamiliar, but it is one that most of us are accustomed to dismissing very casually. The line of thought advanced here suggests that this attitude may very well turn out to be tragically mistaken. Once one reflects upon the question of the *basic* moral principles involved in the ascription of a right to life to organisms, one may find oneself driven to the conclusion that our everyday treatment of members of other species is morally indefensible, and that we are in fact murdering innocent persons.

Notes

1. My forthcoming book, *Abortion and Infanticide*, contains a detailed examination of other important objections.

2. Judith Jarvis Thomson, in her article "A Defense of Abortion," *Philosophy & Public Affairs*, vol. 1, no. 1, 1971, pp. 47–66, argues very forcefully for the view that this conclusion is incorrect. For a critical discussion of her argument, see Chapter 3 of *Abortion and Infanticide*.

3. Section 230.3 of the American Law Institute's *Model Penal Code* (Philadelphia, 1962).

4. *Abortion and Infanticide*, Chapter 10.

5. Editor's note: Followers of the Harvard philosopher Willard van Orman Quine.

6. In *Philosophy and Environmental Crisis*, edited by William T. Blackstone (Athens, Georgia, 1974), pp. 43–68.

7. Ibid., p. 51.

8. Ibid., pp. 49–50.

9. Ibid., p. 51.

10. *Abortion and Infanticide*, section 5.2.

11. For a fuller discussion, and defense of this principle, see *Abortion and Infanticide*, section 5.3.

12. For a detailed survey of the scientific evidence concerning human development, see *Abortion and Infanticide*, section 11.5.

13. *Abortion and Infanticide*, section 11.42.

14. For a brief discussion, see Joseph F. Donceel, "A Liberal Catholic's View," in *Abortion in a Changing World*, Volume I, edited by R. E. Hall, New York, 1970 [*supra*, pp. 15–20]. A more detailed philosophical discussion can be found in Donceel's "Immediate Animation and Delayed Hominization," *Theological Studies*, Volume 31, 1970, pp. 76–105.

15. Editor's note: Readers wishing to sample Tooley's arguments for this contention, which have been deleted here, are referred to Tooley's original article in *Philosophy & Public Affairs*, vol. 2, no. 1 (Fall 1972), or his forthcoming book.

Questions for Analysis

1. How can infanticide shed light on the abortion question?

2. Why does Tooley consider infanticide an interesting and important question by itself?

3. How is the "interest principle" used in distinguishing between entities that have rights and those that don't?

4. What does Tooley mean by "particular-interests principle"?

5. Tooley states, "The particular-interests principle implies that something cannot possibly have such a right [to life] unless its continued existence can be in its interest." What, in his view, must be the case if the continued existence of something is to be in its own interest?

6. What response does Tooley make to the question "At what point does a developing human being acquire the concept of a continuing self, and at what point is it capable of having an interest in its own continued existence?"

7. Why does Tooley believe that adult members of at least some nonhuman species have a right to life?

Abortion: Law, Choice, and Morality

Daniel Callahan

Philosopher Daniel Callahan's viewpoint regarding the status of the fetus is positioned somewhere between the two extremes of Noonan and Tooley. In Callahan's view, as developed in his book Abortion: Law, Choice and Morality, *the unborn is neither just a mass of protoplasm nor a full-fledged person. As a result, Callahan believes it is equally improper to deny the fetus any moral status or to assign it full moral status.*

Essentially, Callahan believes that an abortion choice is a private choice: Individuals ought to be allowed to make their own decisions. But he quickly points out that a legal freedom to choose does not dissolve the serious moral questions that an abortion choice always raises.

The thrust of Callahan's essay, therefore, addresses the question of how a woman ought to go about making an abortion choice, if her action is to be considered moral. He isolates a number of factors to consider in any serious and responsible evaluation of an abortion choice: the biological evidence, the philosophical assumptions implied in the term human, *a philosophical theory of biological analysis, the social consequences of the different analyses of and the meaning of the word* human, *and consistency of meaning and use. He especially warns against making a personal choice easy either through intellectual ignorance or by appeal to personal convenience.*

In the last analysis, Callahan suggests that the woman who faces an abortion choice keep foremost in mind the sanctity of life and the fact that abortion always involves a violation of that sanctity. In that way she will remain sensitive to the moral gravity of an abortion decision and weigh her reasons for wanting an abortion accordingly.

The strength of pluralistic societies lies in the personal freedom they afford individuals. One is free to choose among religious, philosophical, ideological, and political creeds; or one can create one's own highly personal, idiosyncratic moral code and view of the universe. Increasingly, the individual is free to ignore the morals, manners and mores of society. The only limitations are upon those actions which seem to present clear and present dangers to the common good, and even there the range of prohibited actions is diminishing as more and more choices are left to personal and private decisions. I have contended that, apart from some regulatory laws, abortion decisions should be left, finally, up to the women themselves. Whatever one may think of the morality of abortion, it cannot be established that it poses a clear and present danger to the common good. Thus society does not have the right decisively to interpose itself between a woman and the abortion she wants. It can only intervene where it can be shown that some of its own interests are at stake *qua* society. Regulatory laws of a minimal kind therefore seem in order, since in a variety of ways already mentioned society will be affected by the number, kind, and quality of legal abortions. In short, with a few important stipulations, what I have been urging is tantamount to saying that abortion decisions should be private decisions. It is to accept, in principle, the contention of those who believe that, in a free, pluralistic society, the woman should be allowed to make her own moral choice on abortion and be allowed to implement that choice.

But pluralistic societies also lay a few traps for the unwary. It is not a large psychological step from saying that individuals should be left free to make up their own minds on some crucial moral issues (of which abortion is one) to an adoption of the view that one personal decision is as good as another, that any decision is a good one as long as it is honest or sincere, that a free decision equals a correct decision. However short the psychological step, the logical gap is very large. An absence of cant, hypocrisy and coercion may prepare the way for good personal decisions. But that is only to clean the room, and something must then be put in it. The hazard is that, once cleaned, it will be filled with capriciousness, sentimentality, a thinly disguised conformity to the reigning moral taste, or strongly felt but inadequately analyzed moral opinions. This is a particular danger in affluent pluralistic societies, heavily dominated by popular tastes, communication media and the absence of shared values. Philosophically, the view that all values are equally good and all private moral choices on a par is all but dead; but it still has a strong life at the popular level, where there is a tendency to act as if, once personal freedom is legally and socially achieved, moral questions cease to exist.

A considerable quantity of literature exists in the field of ethics concerned with such problems as subjective and objective values, the meaning and use of ethical principles and moral rules, the role of intentionality. That literature need not be reviewed here. But it is directly to the point to observe that a particular failing of the abortion-on-request literature is that it persistently scants the moral problem of how a woman, if granted the desired legal freedom to make her own decision about abortion, should go about making that decision. Up to a point, this deficiency is understandable. The immediate tactical problem has been to get the laws changed or repealed; that has been the burden of the public struggle, which has concentrated on statutes and legislators rather than on the moral contents and problems of personal decision-making. It is reasonable and legitimate to say that a woman should be left free to make the decision in the light of her own personal values; that is, I believe, the best legal solution. But it leaves totally untouched the question of how, once freedom is achieved, she ought to go about the personal business of forming a coherent, rational, sensitive moral perspective and opinion on abortion. After freedom, what then? Society may have no right to demand that a woman give it good reasons why she should have an abortion before permitting it. But this does not entail that the woman should not, as a morally responsible person, have good reasons to justify her desires or acts in her own eyes.

This is only to say that a solution of the legal problem is not the same as a solution to the moral problem. That the moral struggle is transferred from the public to the private sphere should not be taken to mean that the moral problem has been solved; only its public aspect, under a permissive law or a repeal of all laws, has been dealt with. The personal problem will remain.

Some women will be part of a religious group or ethical tradition which they freely choose and which can offer them something, possibly very much, in the way of helpful moral insight consistent with that tradition. The obvious course in that instance is for them to turn to their tradition to see what it has to offer them on the particular problem of abortion. But what of those who have no tradition to repair to or those who find their tradition wanting on this problem? One way or another, they will have to find some way of developing a set of ethical principles and moral rules to help them act responsibly, to justify their own conduct in their own eyes. To press the problem to a finer point, what ought they to think about as they try to work out their own views on abortion?

Only a few suggestions will be made here, taking the form of arguing for an ethic of personal responsibility which tries, in the process of decision-making, to make itself aware of a number of things. The biological evidence should be considered, just as the problem of methodology must be considered; the philosophical assumptions implicit in different uses of the word "human" need to be considered; a philosophical theory of biological analysis is required; the social consequences of different kinds of analyses and different meanings of the word "human" should be thought through; consistency of meaning and use should be sought to avoid *ad hoc* and arbitrary solutions.

It is my own conviction that the "developmental school" offers the most helpful and illuminating approach to the problem of the beginning of human life, avoiding, on the one hand, a too narrow genetic criterion of human life and, on the other, a too broad and socially dangerous social definition of the "human." Yet the kinds of problems which appear in any attempt to decide upon the beginning of life suggest that no one position can be either proved or disproved from biological evidence alone. It becomes a question of trying to do justice to the evidence while, at the same time, realizing that how the evidence is approached and used will be a function of one's way of looking at reality, one's moral policy, the values and rights one believes need balancing, and the type of questions one thinks need to be asked. At the very least, however, the genetic evidence for the uniqueness of zygotes and embryos (a uniqueness of a different kind than that of the uniqueness of sperm and ova), their potentiality for development into a human person, their early development of human characteristics, their genetic and organic distinctness from the organism of the mother, appear to rule out a treatment even of zygotes, much less the more developed stages of the conceptus, as mere pieces of "tissue," of no human significance or value. The "tissue" theory of the significance of the conceptus can only be made plausible by a systematic disregard of the biological evidence. Moreover, though one may conclude that a conceptus is only potential human life, in the process of continually actualizing its potential through growth and development, a respect for the sanctity of life, with its bias in favor even of undeveloped life, is enough to make the taking of such life a moral problem. There is a choice to be made and it is a moral choice. In the near future, it is likely that some kind of simple, safe abortifacient drug will be developed, which either prevents implantation or destroys the conceptus before it can develop. It will be tempting then to think that the moral dilemma has vanished, but I do not believe it will have.

It is possible to imagine a huge number of situations where a woman could, in good and sensitive conscience, choose abortion as a moral solution to her personal or social difficulties. But, at the very least, the bounds of morality are overstepped when either through a systematic intellectual negligence or a willful choosing of that moral solution most personally convenient, personal choice is deliberately made easy and problem-free. Yet it seems to me that a pressure in that direction is a growing part of the ethos of technological societies; it is easily possible to find people to reassure us that we need have no scruples about the way we act, whether the issue is war, the suppression of rebellion and revolution, discrimination against minorities or the use of technological advances. Pluralism makes possible the achieving of freer, more subtle moral thinking; but it is a possibility constantly endangered by cultural pressures which would simplify or dissolve moral doubts and anguish.

The question of abortion "indications" returns at the level of personal choice. I have contended that the advent of permissive laws should not mean a cessation of efforts to explore the problem of "indications." When a woman asks herself, as she ought, whether her reasons for wanting an abortion are sound reasons—which presumes abortion is a serious enough moral issue to warrant the need to provide oneself with good reasons for choosing it—she will be asking herself about justifiable indications. Thus, transposed from the legal to the personal level, the kinds of concerns adumbrated in the earlier chapters on indications remain fully pertinent. It was argued in those chapters that, with the possible exception of exceedingly rare instances of a direct threat to the physical life of the mother, one cannot speak of general categories of abortion indications as *necessitating* an abortion. In a number of circumstances, abortion may be a wise and justifiable solution to a distressed pregnancy. But when the language of necessity is used, the implication is that no other conceivable alternative is available. It may be granted, willingly enough, that some set of practical circumstances in some (possibly very many) concrete cases may indicate that abortion is the only feasible option open. But these cases cannot readily be determined in advance, and, for that reason, it is necessary to say that no formal indication as such (e.g., a psychiatric indication) entails a necessary, predetermined choice in favor of abortion.

The word "indication" remains the best word, suggesting that a number of given circumstances will bring the possibility or desirability of abortion to the fore. But to escalate the concept of an indication into that of a required procedure is to go too far. Abortion is *one* way to solve the problem of an unwanted or hazardous pregnancy (physically, psychologically, economically or socially), but it is rarely the only way, at least in affluent societies (I would be considerably less certain about making the same statement about poor societies). Even in the most extreme cases—rape, incest, psychosis, for instance—alternatives will usually be available and different choices open. It is not necessarily the end of every woman's chance for a happy, meaningful life to bear an illegitimate child. It is not necessarily the automatic destruction of a family to have a seriously defective child born into it. It is not necessarily the ruination of every family living in overcrowded housing to have still another child. It is not inevitable that every immature woman would become even more so if she bore a child or another child. It is not inevitable that a gravely handicapped child can hope for nothing from life. It is not inevitable that every unwanted child is doomed to misery. It is not written in the essence of things, as a fixed law of human nature, that a woman cannot come to accept, love and be a good mother to a child who was initially unwanted. Nor is it a fixed law that she could not come to cherish a grossly deformed child. Naturally, these are only generalizations. The point is only that human beings are as a rule flexible, capable of doing more than they sometimes think they can, able to surmount serious dangers and challenges, able to grow and mature, able to transform inauspicious beginnings into satisfactory conclusions. Everything in life, even in procreative and family life, is not fixed in advance; the future is never wholly unalterable.

Yet the problem of personal question-asking must be pushed a step farther. The way the questions are answered will be very much determined by a woman's way of looking at herself and at life. A woman who has decided, as a personal moral policy, that nothing should be allowed to stand in the way of her own happiness, goals and self-interest will have no trouble solving the moral problem. For her, an unwanted pregnancy will, by definition, be a pregnancy to be terminated. But only by a Pickwickian use of words could this form of reasoning be called moral. It would preclude any need to consult the opinion of others, any need to examine the validity of one's own viewpoint, any need to, for instance, ask when human life begins, any need to interrogate oneself in any way, intellectually or morally; will and desire would be king.

Assuming, however, that most women would seek a broader ethical horizon than that of their exclusively personal self-interest, what might they think about when faced with an abortion decision? A respect for the sanctity of human life should, I believe, incline them toward a general and strong bias against abortion. Abortion is an act of killing, the violent, direct destruction of potential human life, already in the process of development. That fact should not be disguised, or glossed over by euphemism and circumlocution. It is not the destruction of a human person—for at no stage of its development does the conceptus fulfill the definition of a person, which implies a developed capacity for reasoning, willing, desiring and relating to others—but it is the destruction of an important and valuable form of human life. Its value and its potentiality are not dependent upon the attitude of the woman toward it; it grows by its own biological dynamism and has a genetic and morphological potential distinct from that of the woman. It has its own distinctive and individual future. If contraception and abortion are both seen as forms of birth limitation, they are distinctly different acts; the former precludes the possibility of a conceptus being formed, while the latter stops a conceptus already in existence from developing. The bias implied by the principle of the sanctity of human life is toward the protection of all forms of human life, especially, in ordinary circumstances, the protection of the right to life. That right should be accorded even to doubtful life; its existence should not be wholly dependent upon the personal self-interest of the woman.

Yet she has her own rights as well, and her own set of responsibilities to those around her; that is why she may have to choose abortion. In extreme situations of overpopulation, she may also have a responsibility for the survival of the species or of a people. In many circumstances, then, a decision in favor of abortion—one which overrides the right to life of that potential human being she carries within—can be a responsible moral decision, worthy neither of the condemnation of others nor of self-condemnation. But the bias of the principle of the sanctity of life is against a routine, unthinking employment of abortion; it bends over backwards not to take life and gives the benefit of the doubt to life. It does not seek to diminish the range of responsibility toward life—potential or actual—but to extend it. It does not seek the narrowest definition of life, but the widest and the richest. It is mindful of individual possibility, on the one hand, and of a destructive human tendency, on the other, to exclude from the category of "the human" or deny rights to those beings whose existence is or could prove burdensome to others.

The language used to describe abortion will have an important bearing on the sensitivities and imagination of those women who must make abortion decisions. Abortion can be talked about in the language of medical technology and technique—as, say, "a therapeutic procedure involving the emptying of the uterine contents." That language is neutral, clinical, unemotional. Or abortion can be talked about in the emotive language of relieving woman from suffering, or meeting the need for freedom among women, or saving a nation from a devastating overpopulation. Both kinds of language have their place, for abortion has more than one result and meaning and abortion can legitimately be talked about in more than one way. What is objectionable is a conscious manipulation of language to incite an irrational emotional response, to allay doubts or to mislead the imagination. Particularly misleading is one commonly employed mixture of rhetorical modes by advocates of abortion on request. That is the use of a detached, clinical language to describe the actual operation itself combined with an emotive rhetoric to evoke the personal and social goods which an abortion can bring about. Thus, when every effort is made to suggest that emotion and feeling are perfectly appropriate to describe the social and personal goals of abortion, but that a clinical language only is appropriate when the actual technique and medical objective of an abortion are described, then the moral imagination is being misled.

Any human act can be described in impersonal, technological language, just as any act can be described in emotive language. What is wanted is an equity in the language. It is fair enough and to the point to say that in many circumstances abortion will save a woman's health or her family. It only becomes misleading when the act itself, as distinguished from its therapeutic goal, is talked about in an entirely different way. For abortion is not just an "emptying of the uterine contents." It is also an act of killing; there will be no abortion unless the conceptus is killed (or its further existence made impossible, which amounts to the same thing). If it is appropriate to evoke the imagination and elicit sympathy for those women in a distressed pregnancy who could be helped by abortion, it is no less appropriate to evoke the imagination about what actually occurs in an abortion "procedure."

Imagination should also come into play at another point. It is often argued by proponents of abortion that there is no need for a woman ever to take any chances in a distressed pregnancy, particularly in the instance of an otherwise healthy woman who, if she has an abortion on one occasion, could simply get pregnant again on another, more auspicious occasion. This might be termed the "replacement theory" of abortion indications: since fetus "x" can be replaced by fetus "y," then there is no reason why a woman should have any scruples about such a replacement. This way of conceiving the choices effectively dissolves them; it becomes important only to know whether a woman can get pregnant again when she wants to. But this strategy can be employed only at the price of convincing oneself that there is no difference whatever among embryos or fetuses, that they all have exactly the same potentiality. But even the sketchiest knowledge of the genetic uniqueness of each conceptus (save in the instance of monozygotic twins), and thus the different genetic potentialities of each, should raise doubts on that point. Yet, having said that, I would not want to deny that the possibility of a further pregnancy could have an important bearing on the moral reasoning of a woman whose present pregnancy was threatening. If, out of a sense of responsibility toward her present children or her present life situation, a woman decided that an abortion was the wisest, most moral course, then the possibility that she could become pregnant later, when these responsibilities would be less pressing, would be a pertinent consideration.

The goal of these remarks is to keep alive in the consciences of women who have an abortion choice a moral tension; and it is to hope that they will be willing to bear the pain and the uncertainty of having to make a moral choice. It is the automatic, unthinking and unimaginative personal solution of abortion questions which women themselves should be extremely wary of, either for or against an abortion. A woman can, with little trouble, find both people and books to reassure her that there is no problem about abortion at all; or people and books to convince her that she would be a moral monster if she chose abortion. A woman can choose in advance the views she will listen to and thus have her predispositions confirmed. Yet a willingness to keep alive a moral tension, and to be wary of precipitous solutions, presupposes two things. First, that the woman herself wants to do what is right, realizing that what is right may not always be that which is most convenient, most easy or most immediately apt to solve a pressing problem. It is simply not the case that what one wants to do, or would like to do, or is predisposed to do is necessarily the right thing to do. A willingness seriously to entertain that moral perception—which, of course, does not in itself imply a decision for or against abortion—is one sign of moral seriousness.

Second, moral seriousness presupposes one is concerned with the protection and furthering of life. This means that, out of respect for human life, one bends over backwards not to eliminate human life, not to desensitize oneself to the meaning and value of potential life, not to seek definitions of the "human" which serve one's self-interest only. A desire to respect human life in all of its forms means, therefore, that one voluntarily imposes upon oneself a pressure against the taking of life; that one demands of oneself serious reasons for doing so, even in the case of a very early embryo; that one use not only the mind but also the imagination when a decision is being made; that one seeks not to evade the moral issues but to face them; that one

searches out the alternatives and conscientiously entertains them before turning to abortion. A bias in favor of the sanctity of human life in all of its forms would include a bias against abortion on the part of women; it would be the last rather than the first choice when unwanted pregnancies occurred. It would be an act to be avoided if at all possible.

A bias of this kind, voluntarily imposed by a woman upon herself, would not trap her; for it is also part of a respect for the dignity of life to leave the way open for an abortion when other reasonable choices are not available. For she also has duties toward herself, her family and her society. There can be good reasons for taking the life even of a very late fetus; once that also is seen and seen as a counterpoise in particular cases to the general bias against the taking of potential life, the way is open to choose abortion. The bias of the moral policy implies the need for moral rules which seek to preserve life. But, as a policy which leaves room for choice—rather than entailing a fixed set of rules—it is open to flexible interpretation when the circumstances point to the wisdom of taking exception to the normal ordering of the rules in particular cases. Yet, in that case, one is not genuinely taking exception to the rules. More accurately, one would be deciding that, for the preservation or furtherance of other values or rights—species-rights, person-rights—a choice in favor of abortion would be serving the sanctity of life. That there would be, in that case, conflict between rights, with one set of rights set aside (reluctantly) to serve another set, goes without saying. A subversion of the principle occurs when it is made out that there is no conflict and thus nothing to decide.

Questions for Analysis

1. What does Callahan mean by a "pluralistic society"?

2. When are regulatory laws justifiable? Is this a utilitarian justification?

3. Callahan says ". . . a solution of the legal problem is not the same as a solution to the moral problem." What does this mean? How does it apply to an abortion choice?

4. What is the "tissue theory" and why does Callahan reject it?

5. *Callahan claims a woman's abortion decision will very much be determined by her way of looking at herself and at life. What does he mean, and do you agree?*

6. *In Callahan's view, are there any formal indications that entail a necessary choice in favor of an abortion? How does this view relate to his cautions about abortion decisions?*

7. *What does Callahan mean by keeping alive a "moral tension" in the conscience of a woman who faces an abortion choice?*

8. *Would it be accurate to say that Callahan considers some acts of abortion morally justifiable? If so, under what conditions would such abortions be justifiable?*

A Defense of Abortion

Judith Jarvis Thomson

Philosopher Judith Jarvis Thomson wrote this essay in 1971. It has since become a classic in the literature of abortion.

What makes her treatment of the pro-choice position unique is that it begins by conceding, for the sake of argument, that the fetus is a person from the moment of conception. This concession is significant because, as Thomson points out, most opposition to abortion builds on the assumption that the fetus has person status and rights from the moment of conception.

Thomson focuses her essay on an important question: Granted that the fetus is a person from the moment of conception, does it necessarily follow that abortion is always wrong? She thinks not. Relying primarily on a series of analogies, she attacks the argument that the immorality of abortion is entailed by the premise that asserts the person status of the fetus.

Toward the end of her essay, Thomson admits that anti-abortionists might object that the immorality of abortion follows not so much from the fact that the fetus is a person as from the special relationship between the fetus and the mother. Thus, anti-abortionists claim that the fetus is a person for whom the woman has a unique kind of responsibility because she is the mother.

In responding to this claim, Thomson argues that we have no responsibility for another person unless we have assumed it. If parents do not take any birth control measures, if they do not elect an abortion, if they choose to take the child home with them from the hospital, then certainly they have a responsibility to and for the child. For they then have assumed responsibility, implicitly and explicitly, in all their actions. But if a couple has taken measures to prevent conception, this implies quite the opposite of any "special responsibility" for the unintended and unwanted fetus. Thus, in Thomson's view, the woman has no special responsibility to the fetus simply because of a biological relationship.

Ironically, as Thomson points out, many pro-choice advocates object to her argument for a couple of reasons. First, while Thomson argues that abortion is not impermissible, she does not think that it is always permissible. There may be times, for example, when carrying the child to term requires only minimal inconvenience; in such cases the woman would be required by

From Judith Jarvis Thomson, "A Defense of Abortion," Philosophy & Public Affairs, 1, no. 1 (Fall 1971). Copyright © 1971 by Princeton University Press. Reprinted by permission of Princeton University Press. Ms. Thomson acknowledges her indebtedness to James Thomson for discussion, criticism, and many helpful suggestions.

"Minimally Decent Samaritanism" to have the child. Those supporting abortion on demand object to such a limitation of choice.

Second, while Thomson, like act utilitarians, would sanction some acts of abortion, she is not arguing for the right to kill the unborn child. That is, removing a nonviable fetus from the mother's body and thereby guaranteeing its death is not the same as removing a viable fetus from the mother's body and then killing it. In Thomson's view, the former may be permissible; the latter never is. Again, some pro-choice advocates object to this limitation of choice.

Most opposition to abortion relies on the premise that the fetus is a human being, a person, from the moment of conception. The premise is argued for, but, as I think, not well. Take, for example, the most common argument. We are asked to notice that the development of a human being from conception through birth into childhood is continuous; then it is said that to draw a line, to choose a point in this development and say "before this point the thing is not a person, after this point it is a person" is to make an arbitrary choice, a choice for which in the nature of things no good reason can be given. It is concluded that the fetus is, or anyway that we had better say it is, a person from the moment of conception. But this conclusion does not follow. Similar things might be said about the development of an acorn into an oak tree, and it does not follow that acorns are oak trees, or that we had better say they are. Arguments of this form are sometimes called "slippery slope arguments"—the phrase is perhaps self-explanatory—and it is dismaying that opponents of abortion rely on them so heavily and uncritically.

I am inclined to agree, however, that the prospects for "drawing a line" in the development of the fetus look dim. I am inclined to think also that we shall probably have to agree that the fetus has already become a human person well before birth. Indeed, it comes as a surprise when one first learns how early in its life it begins to acquire human characteristics. By the tenth week, for example, it already has a face, arms and legs, fingers and toes; it has internal organs, and brain activity is detectable.[1] On the other hand, I think that the premise is false, that the fetus is not a person from the moment of conception. A newly fertilized ovum, a newly implanted clump of cells, is no more a person than an acorn is an oak tree. But I shall not discuss any of this. For it seems to me to be of great interest to ask what happens if, for the sake of argument, we allow the premise. How, precisely, are we sup-

posed to get from there to the conclusion that abortion is morally impermissible? Opponents of abortion commonly spend most of their time establishing that the fetus is a person, and hardly any time explaining the step from there to the impermissibility of abortion. Perhaps they think the step too simple and obvious to require much comment. Or perhaps instead they are simply being economical in argument. Many of those who defend abortion rely on the premise that the fetus is not a person, but only a bit of tissue that will become a person at birth; and why pay out more arguments than you have to? Whatever the explanation, I suggest that the step they take is neither easy nor obvious, that it calls for closer examination than it is commonly given, and that when we do give it this closer examination we shall feel inclined to reject it.

I propose, then, that we grant that the fetus is a person from the moment of conception. How does the argument go from here? Something like this, I take it. Every person has a right to life. So the fetus has a right to life. No doubt the mother has a right to decide what shall happen in and to her body; everyone would grant that. But surely a person's right to life is stronger and more stringent than the mother's right to decide what happens in and to her body, and so outweighs it. So the fetus may not be killed; an abortion may not be performed.

It sounds plausible. But now let me ask you to imagine this. You wake up in the morning and find yourself back to back in bed with an unconscious violinist. A famous unconscious violinist. He has been found to have a fatal kidney ailment, and the Society of Music Lovers has canvassed all the available medical records and found that you alone have the right blood type to help. They have therefore kidnapped you, and last night the violinist's circulatory system was plugged into yours, so that your kidneys can be used to extract poisons from his blood as well as your own. The director of the hospital now tells you, "Look, we're sorry the Society of Music Lovers did this to you—we would never have permitted it if we had known. But still, they did it, and the violinist now is plugged into you. To unplug you would be to kill him. But never mind, it's only for nine months. By then he will have recovered from his ailment, and can safely be unplugged from you." Is it morally incumbent on you to accede to this situation? No doubt it would be very nice of you if you did, a great kindness. But do you *have* to accede to it? What if it were not nine months, but nine years? Or longer still? What if the director of the hospital says, "Tough luck, I agree, but you've now got to stay in bed, with the violinist plugged into you, for the rest of your life. Because remember this. All persons have a right to life, and violinists are persons. Granted you have a right to decide what happens in and to your body, but a person's right to life outweighs your right to decide what happens in and to your body. So you cannot ever be unplugged from him." I imagine you would regard this as outrageous, which suggests that something really is wrong with that plausible-sounding argument I mentioned a moment ago.

In this case, of course, you were kidnapped; you didn't volunteer for the operation that plugged the violinist into your kidneys. Can those who oppose abortion on the ground I mentioned make an exception for a pregnancy due to rape? Certainly. They can say that persons have a right to life only if they didn't come into existence because of rape; or they can say that all persons have a right to life, but that some have less of a right to life than others, in particular, that those who came into existence because of rape have less. But these statements have a rather unpleasant sound. Surely the question of whether you have a right to life at all, or how much of it you have, shouldn't turn on the question of whether or not you are the product of a rape. And in fact the people who oppose abortion on the ground I mentioned do not make this distinction, and hence do not make an exception in the case of rape.

Nor do they make an exception for a case in which the mother has to spend the nine months of her pregnancy in bed. They would agree that would be a great pity, and hard on the mother; but all the same, all persons have a right to life, the fetus is a person, and so on. I suspect, in fact, that they would not make an exception for a case in which, mirac-

ulously enough, the pregnancy went on for nine years, or even the rest of the mother's life.

Some won't even make an exception for a case in which continuation of the pregnancy is likely to shorten the mother's life; they regard abortion as impermissible even to save the mother's life. Such cases are nowadays very rare, and many opponents of abortion do not accept this extreme view. All the same, it is a good place to begin: A number of points of interest come out in respect to it.

1. Let us call the view that abortion is impermissible even to save the mother's life "the extreme view." I want to suggest first that it does not issue from the argument I mentioned earlier without the addition of some fairly powerful premises. Suppose a woman has become pregnant, and now learns that she has a cardiac condition such that she will die if she carries the baby to term. What may be done for her? The fetus, being a person, has a right to life, but as the mother is a person too, so has she a right to life. Presumably they have an equal right to life. How is it supposed to come out that an abortion may not be performed? If mother and child have an equal right to life, shouldn't we perhaps flip a coin? Or should we add to the mother's right to life her right to decide what happens in and to her body, which everybody seems to be ready to grant—the sum of her rights now outweighing the fetus' right to life?

The most familiar argument here is the following. We are told that performing the abortion would be directly killing[2] the child, whereas doing nothing would not be killing the mother, but only letting her die. Moreover, in killing the child, one would be killing an innocent person, for the child has committed no crime, and is not aiming at his mother's death. And then there are a variety of ways in which this might be continued. (1) But as directly killing an innocent person is always and absolutely impermissible, an abortion may not be performed. Or, (2) as directly killing an innocent person is murder, and murder is always and absolutely impermissible, an abortion may not be performed.[3] Or, (3) as one's duty to refrain from directly killing an innocent person is more stringent than one's duty to keep a person from dying, an abortion may not be performed. Or, (4) if one's only options are directly killing an innocent person or letting a person die, one must prefer letting the person die, and thus an abortion may not be performed.[4]

Some people seem to have thought that these are not further premises which must be added if the conclusion is to be reached, but that they follow from the very fact that an innocent person has a right to life.[5] But this seems to me to be a mistake, and perhaps the simplest way to show this is to bring out that while we must certainly grant that innocent persons have a right to life, the theses in (1) through (4) are all false. Take (2), for example. If directly killing an innocent person is murder, and thus is impermissible, then the mother's directly killing the innocent person inside her is murder, and thus is impermissible. But it cannot seriously be thought to be murder if the mother performs an abortion on herself to save her life. It cannot seriously be said that she *must* refrain, that she *must* sit passively by and wait for her death. Let us look again at the case of you and the violinist. There you are, in bed with the violinist, and the director of the hospital says to you, "It's all most distressing, and I deeply sympathize, but you see this is putting an additional strain on your kidneys, and you'll be dead within the month. But you *have* to stay where you are all the same. Because unplugging you would be directly killing an innocent violinist, and that's murder, and that's impermissible." If anything in the world is true, it is that you do not commit murder, you do not do what is impermissible, if you reach around to your back and unplug yourself from that violinist to save your life.

The main focus of attention in writings on abortion has been on what a third party may or may not do in answer to a request from a woman for an abortion. This is in a way understandable. Things being as they are, there isn't much a woman can safely do to abort herself. So the question asked is what a third party may do, and what the mother may do, if it is mentioned at all, is deduced, almost as an afterthought, from what it is concluded that third parties may do. But it seems to me that to treat the matter in this way is to refuse to grant to the mother that very status of person which is so firmly insisted on for the fetus. For we cannot simply read off what a person may do from what a third party may do. Suppose you find yourself trapped in a tiny house with a growing child. I mean a very tiny house, and a rapidly growing child—you are already up against the wall of the house and in a few minutes you'll be crushed to death. The child on the other hand won't be crushed

to death; if nothing is done to stop him from growing he'll be hurt, but in the end he'll simply burst open the house and walk out a free man. Now I could well understand it if a bystander were to say, "There's nothing we can do for you. We cannot choose between your life and his, we cannot be the ones to decide who is to live, we cannot intervene." But it cannot be concluded that you too can do nothing, that you cannot attack it to save your life. However innocent the child may be, you do not have to wait passively while it crushes you to death. Perhaps a pregnant woman is vaguely felt to have the status of house, to which we don't allow the right of self-defense. But if the woman houses the child, it should be remembered that she is a person who houses it.

I should perhaps stop to say explicitly that I am not claiming that people have a right to do anything whatever to save their lives. I think, rather, that there are drastic limits to the right of self-defense. If someone threatens you with death unless you torture someone else to death, I think you have not the right, even to save your life, to do so. But the case under consideration here is very different. In our case there are only two people involved, one whose life is threatened, and one who threatens it. Both are innocent: The one who is threatened is not threatened because of any fault, the one who threatens does not threaten because of any fault. For this reason we may feel that we bystanders cannot intervene. But the person threatened can.

In sum, a woman surely can defend her life against the threat to it posed by the unborn child, even if doing so involves its death. And this shows not merely that the theses in (1) through (4) are false; it shows also that the extreme view of abortion is false, and so we need not canvass any other possible ways of arriving at it from the argument I mentioned at the outset.

2. The extreme view could of course be weakened to say that while abortion is permissible to save the mother's life, it may not be performed by a third party, but only by the mother herself. But this cannot be right either. For what we have to keep in mind is that the mother and the unborn child are not like two tenants in a small house which has, by an unfortunate mistake, been rented to both: The mother *owns* the house. The fact that she does adds to the offensiveness of deducing that the mother can do nothing from the supposition that

third parties can do nothing. But it does more than this: It casts a bright light on the supposition that third parties can do nothing. Certainly it lets us see that a third party who says "I cannot choose between you" is fooling himself if he thinks this is impartiality. If Jones has found and fastened on a certain coat, which he needs to keep him from freezing, but which Smith also needs to keep him from freezing, then it is not impartiality that says "I cannot choose between you" when Smith owns the coat. Women have said again and again "This body is *my* body!" and they have reason to feel angry, reason to feel that it has been like shouting into the wind. Smith, after all, is hardly likely to bless us if we say to him, "Of course it's your coat, anybody would grant that it is. But no one may choose between you and Jones who is to have it."

We should really ask what it is that says "no one may choose" in the face of the fact that the body that houses the child is the mother's body. It may be simply a failure to appreciate this fact. But it may be something more interesting, namely the sense that one has a right to refuse to lay hands on people, even where it would be just and fair to do so, even where justice seems to require that somebody do so. Thus justice might call for somebody to get Smith's coat back from Jones, and yet you have a right to refuse to be the one to lay hands on Jones, a right to refuse to do physical violence to him. This, I think, must be granted. But then what should be said is not "no one may choose," but only "*I* cannot choose," and indeed not even this, but "*I* will not *act*," leaving it open that somebody else can or should, and in particular that anyone in a position of authority, with the job of securing people's rights, both can and should. So this is no difficulty. I have not been arguing that any given third party must accede to the mother's request that he perform an abortion to save her life, but only that he may.

I suppose that in some views of human life the mother's body is only on loan to her, the loan not being one which gives her any prior claim to it. One who held this view might well think it impartiality to say "I cannot choose." But I shall simply ignore this possibility. My own view is that if a human being has any just, prior claim to anything at all, he has a just, prior claim to his own body. And perhaps this needn't be argued for here anyway, since, as I mentioned, the arguments against abortion we are looking at do grant that the woman has a right to decide what happens in and to her body.

But although they do grant it, I have tried to show that they do not take seriously what is done in granting it. I suggest the same thing will reappear even more clearly when we turn away from cases in which the mother's life is at stake, and attend, as I propose we now do, to the vastly more common cases in which a woman wants an abortion for some less weighty reason than preserving her own life.

3. Where the mother's life is not at stake, the argument I mentioned at the outset seems to have a much stronger pull. "Everyone has a right to life, so the unborn person has a right to life." And isn't the child's right to life weightier than anything other than the mother's own right to life, which she might put forward as ground for an abortion?

This argument treats the right to life as if it were unproblematic. It is not, and this seems to me to be precisely the source of the mistake.

For we should now, at long last, ask what it comes to, to have a right to life. In some views having a right to life includes having a right to be given at least the bare minimum one needs for continued life. But suppose that what in fact *is* the bare minimum a man needs for continued life is something he has no right at all to be given? If I am sick unto death, and the only thing that will save my life is the touch of Henry Fonda's cool hand on my fevered brow, then all the same, I have no right to be given the touch of Henry Fonda's cool hand on my fevered brow. It would be frightfully nice of him to fly in from the West Coast to provide it. It would be less nice, though no doubt well meant, if my friends flew out to the West Coast and carried Henry Fonda back with them. But I have no right at all against anybody that he should do this for me. Or again, to return to the story I told earlier, the fact that for continued life that violinist needs the continued use of your kidneys does not establish that he has a right to be given the continued use of your kidneys. He certainly has no right against you that *you* should give him continued use of your kidneys. For nobody has any right to use your kidneys unless you give him such a right; and nobody has the right against you that you shall give him this right—if you do allow him to go on using your kidneys, this is a kindness on your part, and not something he can claim from you as his due. Nor has he any right against anybody else that *they* should give him continued use of your kidneys. Certainly he had no right against the Society of Music Lovers that they should plug him into you in the first place. And if you now start to unplug yourself, having learned that you will otherwise have to spend nine years in bed with him, there is nobody in the world who must try to prevent you, in order to see to it that he is given something he has a right to be given.

Some people are rather stricter about the right to life. In their view, it does not include the right to be given anything, but amounts to, and only to, the right not to be killed by anybody. But here a related difficulty arises. If everybody is to refrain from killing that violinist, then everybody must refrain from doing a great many different sorts of things. Everybody must refrain from slitting his throat, everybody must refrain from shooting him— and everybody must refrain from unplugging you from him. But does he have a right against everybody that they shall refrain from unplugging you from him? To refrain from doing this is to allow him to continue to use your kidneys. It could be argued that he has a right against us that *we* should allow him to continue to use your kidneys. That is, while he had no right against us that we should give him the use of your kidneys, it might be argued that he anyway has a right against us that we shall not now intervene and deprive him of the use of your kidneys. I shall come back to third-party interventions later. But certainly the violinist has no right against you that *you* shall allow him to continue to use your kidneys. As I said, if you do allow him to use them, it is a kindness on your part, and not something you owe him.

The difficulty I point to here is not peculiar to the right of life. It reappears in connection with all the other natural rights; and it is something which an adequate account of rights must deal with. For present purposes it is enough just to draw attention to it. But I would stress that I am not arguing that people do not have a right to life—quite to the contrary, it seems to me that the primary control we must place on the acceptability of an account of rights is that it should turn out in that account to be a truth that all persons have a right to life. I am arguing only that having a right to life does not guarantee having either a right to be given the use of or a right to be allowed continued use of another

person's body—even if one needs it for life itself. So the right to life will not serve the opponents of abortion in the very simple and clear way in which they seem to have thought it would.

4. There is another way to bring out the difficulty. In the most ordinary sort of case, to deprive someone of what he has a right to is to treat him unjustly. Suppose a boy and his small brother are jointly given a box of chocolates for Christmas. If the older boy takes the box and refuses to give his brother any of the chocolates, he is unjust to him, for the brother has been given a right to half of them. But suppose that, having learned that otherwise it means nine years in bed with that violinist, you unplug yourself from him. You surely are not being unjust to him, for you gave him no right to use your kidneys, and no one else can have given him any such right. But we have to notice that in unplugging yourself, you are killing him; and violinists, like everybody else, have a right to life, and thus in the view we were considering just now, the right not to be killed. So here you do what he supposedly has a right you shall not do, but you do not act unjustly to him in doing it.

The emendation which may be made at this point is this: The right to life consists not in the right not to be killed, but rather in the right not to be killed unjustly. This runs a risk of circularity, but never mind: It would enable us to square the fact that the violinist has a right to life with the fact that you do not act unjustly toward him in unplugging yourself, thereby killing him. For if you do not kill him unjustly, you do not violate his right to life, and so it is no wonder you do him no injustice.

But if this emendation is accepted, the gap in the argument against abortion stares us plainly in the face: It is by no means enough to show that the fetus is a person, and to remind us that all persons have a right to life—we need to be shown also that killing the fetus violates its right to life, i.e., that abortion is unjust killing. And is it?

I suppose we may take it as a datum that in the case of pregnancy due to rape the mother has not given the unborn person a right to the use of her body for food and shelter. Indeed, in what pregnancy should it be supposed that the mother has given the unborn person such a right? It is not as if there were unborn persons drifting about the world, to whom a woman who wants a child says "I invite you in."

But it might be argued that there are other ways one can have acquired a right to the use of another person's body than by having been invited to use it by that person. Suppose a woman voluntarily indulges in intercourse, knowing of the chance it will issue in pregnancy, and then she does become pregnant; is she not in part responsible for the presence, in fact the very existence, of the unborn person inside? No doubt she did not invite it in. But doesn't her partial responsibility for its being there itself give it a right to the use of her body?[6] If so, then her aborting it would be more like the boy's taking away the chocolates, and less like your unplugging yourself from the violinist—doing so would be depriving it of what it does have a right to, and thus would be doing it an injustice.

And then, too, it might be asked whether or not she can kill it even to save her own life: If she voluntarily called it into existence, how can she now kill it, even in self-defense?

The first thing to be said about this is that it is something new. Opponents of abortion have been so concerned to make out the independence of the fetus, in order to establish that it has a right to life, just as its mother does, that they have tended to overlook the possible support they might gain from making out that the fetus is *dependent* on the mother, in order to establish that she has a special kind of responsibility for it, a responsibility that gives it rights against her which are not possessed by any independent person—such as an ailing violinist who is a stranger to her.

On the other hand, this argument would give the unborn person a right to its mother's body only if her pregnancy resulted from a voluntary act, undertaken in full knowledge of the chance a pregnancy might result from it. It would leave out entirely the unborn person whose existence is due to rape. Pending the availability of some further argument, then, we would be left with the conclusion that unborn persons whose existence is due to rape have no right to the use of their mothers' bodies, and thus that aborting them is not depriving them of anything they have a right to and hence is not unjust killing.

And we should also notice that it is not at all plain that this argument really does go even as far as it purports to. For there are cases and cases, and the details make a difference. If the room is stuffy, and I therefore open a window to air it, and a burglar climbs in, it would be absurd to say, "Ah, now he can stay, she's given him a right to the use of her house—for she is partially responsible for his presence there, having voluntarily done what enabled him to get in, in full knowledge that there are such things as burglars, and that burglars burgle." It would be still more absurd to say this if I had had bars installed outside my windows, precisely to prevent burglars from getting in, and a burglar got in only because of a defect in the bars. It remains equally absurd if we imagine it is not a burglar who climbs in, but an innocent person who blunders or falls in. Again, suppose it were like this: Peopleseeds drift about in the air like pollen, and if you open your windows, one may drift in and take root in your carpets or upholstery. You don't want children, so you fix up your windows with fine mesh screens, the very best you can buy. As can happen, however, and on very, very rare occasions does happen, one of the screens is defective; and a seed drifts in and takes root. Does the personplant who now develops have a right to the use of your house? Surely not—despite the fact that you voluntarily opened your windows, you knowingly kept carpets and upholstered furniture, and you knew that screens were sometimes defective. Someone may argue that you are responsible for its rooting, that it does have a right to your house, because after all you *could* have lived out your life with bare floors and furniture, or with sealed windows and doors. But this won't do—for by the same token anyone can avoid a pregnancy due to rape by having a hysterectomy, or anyway by never leaving home without a (reliable!) army.

It seems to me that the argument we are looking at can establish at most that there are *some* cases in which the unborn person has a right to the use of its mother's body, and therefore *some* cases in which abortion is unjust killing. There is room for much discussion and argument as to precisely which, if any. But I think we should sidestep this issue and leave it open, for at any rate the argument certainly does not establish that all abortion is unjust killing.

5. There is room for yet another argument here, however. We surely must grant that there may be cases in which it would be morally indecent to detach a person from your body at the cost of his life. Suppose you learn that what the violinist needs is not nine years of your life, but only one hour: All

you need do to save his life is spend one hour in that bed with him. Suppose also that letting him use your kidneys for that one hour would not affect your health in the slightest. Admittedly you were kidnapped. Admittedly you did not give anyone permission to plug him into you. Nevertheless it seems to me plain you *ought* to allow him to use your kidneys for that hour—it would be indecent to refuse.

Again, suppose pregnancy lasted only an hour, and constituted no threat to life or death [sic]. And suppose that a woman becomes pregnant as a result of rape. Admittedly she did not voluntarily do anything to bring about the existence of a child. Admittedly she did nothing at all which would give the unborn person a right to the use of her body. All the same it might well be said, as in the newly emended violinist story, that she *ought* to allow it to remain for that hour—that it would be indecent in her to refuse.

Now some people are inclined to use the term "right" in such a way that it follows from the fact that you ought to allow a person to use your body for the hour he needs, that he has a right to use your body for the hour he needs, even though he has not been given that right by any person or act. They may say that it follows also that if you refuse, you act unjustly toward him. This use of the term is perhaps so common that it cannot be called wrong; nevertheless it seems to me to be an unfortunate loosening of what we would do better to keep a tight rein on. Suppose that box of chocolates I mentioned earlier had not been given to both boys jointly, but was given only to the older boy. There he sits, stolidly eating his way through the box, his small brother watching enviously. Here we are likely to say "You ought not to be so mean. You ought to give your brother some of those chocolates." My own view is that it just does not follow from the truth of this that the brother has any right to any of the chocolates. If the boy refuses to give his brother any, he is greedy, stingy, callous—but not unjust. I suppose that the people I have in mind will say it does follow that the brother has a right to some of the chocolates, and thus that the boy does act unjustly if he refuses to give his brother any. But the effect of saying this is to obscure what we should keep distinct, namely the difference between the boy's refusal in this case and the boy's refusal in the earlier case, in which the box was

given to both boys jointly, and in which the small brother thus had what was from any point of view clear title to half.

A further objection to so using the term "right" that from the fact that A ought to do a thing for B, it follows that B has a right against A that A do it for him, is that it is going to make the question of whether or not a man has a right to a thing turn on how easy it is to provide him with it; and this seems not merely unfortunate, but morally unacceptable. Take the case of Henry Fonda again. I said earlier that I had no right to the touch of his cool hand on my fevered brow, even though I needed it to save my life. I said it would be frightfully nice of him to fly in from the West Coast to provide me with it, but that I had no right against him that he should do so. But suppose he isn't on the West Coast. Suppose he has only to walk across the room, place a hand briefly on my brow—and lo, my life is saved. Then surely he ought to do it, it would be indecent to refuse. Is it to be said, "Ah, well, it follows that in this case she has a right to the touch of his hand on her brow, and so it would be an unjustice in him to refuse"? So that I have a right to it when it is easy for him to provide it, though no right when it's hard? It's rather a shocking idea that anyone's rights should fade away and disappear as it gets harder and harder to accord them to him.

So my own view is that even though you ought to let the violinist use your kidneys for the one hour he needs, we should not conclude that he has a right to do so—we should say that if you refuse, you are, like the boy who owns all the chocolates and will give none away, self-centered and callous, indecent in fact, but not unjust. And similarly, that even supposing a case in which a woman pregnant due to rape ought to allow the unborn person to use her body for the hour he needs, we should not conclude that he has a right to do so; we should conclude that she is self-centered, callous, indecent, but not unjust, if she refuses. The complaints are no less grave; they are just different. However, there is no need to insist on this point. If anyone does wish to deduce "he has a right" from "you ought," then all the same he must surely grant that there are cases in which it is not morally required of you that you allow that violinist to use your kidneys, and in which he does not have a right to use them, and in which you do not do him an injustice if you refuse. And so also for mother and unborn child. Except in such cases as the unborn person has a right to demand it—and we were leaving open the possibility that there may be such cases—nobody is morally *required* to make large sacrifices, of health, of all other interests and concerns, of all other duties and commitments, for nine years, or even for nine months, in order to keep another person alive.

6. We have in fact to distinguish between the two kinds of Samaritan: the Good Samaritan and what we might call the Minimally Decent Samaritan. The story of the Good Samaritan, you will remember, goes like this:

> A certain man went down from Jerusalem to Jericho, and fell among thieves, which stripped him of his raiment, and wounded him, and departed, leaving him half dead.
>
> And by chance there came down a certain priest that way; and when he saw him, he passed by on the other side.
>
> And likewise a Levite, when he was at the place, came and looked on him, and passed by on the other side.
>
> But a certain Samaritan, as he journeyed, came where he was; and when he saw him he had compassion on him.
>
> And went to him, and bound up his wounds, pouring in oil and wine, and set him on his own beast, and brought him to an inn, and took care of him.
>
> And on the morrow, when he departed, he took out two pence, and gave them to the host, and said unto him, "Take care of him; and whatsoever thou spendest more, when I come again, I will repay thee."
>
> (Luke 10:30–35)

The Good Samaritan went out of his way, at some cost to himself, to help one in need of it. We are not told what the options were, that is, whether or not the priest and the Levite could have helped by doing less than the Good Samaritan did, but assuming they could have, then the fact they did nothing at all shows they were not even Minimally Decent Samaritans, not because they were not Samaritans, but because they were not even minimally decent.

These things are a matter of degree, of course, but there is a difference, and it comes out perhaps most clearly in the story of Kitty Genovese, who, as you will remember, was murdered while thirty-eight people watched or listened, and did nothing at all to help her. A Good Samaritan would have rushed out to give direct assistance against the murderer. Or perhaps we had better allow that it would have been a Splendid Samaritan who did this, on the ground that it would have involved a risk of death for himself. But the thirty-eight not only did not do this, they did not even trouble to pick up a phone to call the police. Minimally Decent Samaritanism would call for doing at least that, and their not having done it was monstrous.

After telling the story of the Good Samaritan, Jesus said, "Go, and do thou likewise." Perhaps he meant that we are morally required to act as the Good Samaritan did. Perhaps he was urging people to do more than is morally required of them. At all events it seems plain that it was not morally required of any of the thirty-eight that he rush out to give direct assistance at the risk of his own life, and that it is not morally required of anyone that he give long stretches of his life—nine years or nine months—to sustaining the life of a person who has no special right (we were leaving open the possibility of this) to demand it.

Indeed, with one rather striking class of exceptions, no one in any country in the world is *legally* required to do anywhere near as much as this for anyone else. The class of exceptions is obvious. My main concern here is not the state of the law in respect to abortion, but it is worth drawing attention to the fact that in no state in this country is any man compelled by law to be even a Minimally Decent Samaritan to any person; there is no law under which charges could be brought against the thirty-eight who stood by while Kitty Genovese died. By contrast, in most states in this country women are compelled by law to be not merely Minimally Decent Samaritans, but Good Samaritans to unborn persons inside them. This doesn't by itself settle anything one way or the other, because it may well be argued that there should be laws in this country—as there are in many European countries—compelling at least Minimally Decent Samaritanism.[7] But it does show that there is a gross injustice in the existing state of the law. And it shows also that the groups currently working against liberalization of abortion laws, in fact working toward having it declared unconstitutional for a state to permit abortion, had better start working for the adoption of Good Samaritan laws generally, or earn the charge that they are acting in bad faith.

I should think, myself, that Minimally Decent Samaritan laws would be one thing, Good Samaritan laws quite another, and in fact highly improper. But we are not here concerned with the law. What we should ask is not whether anybody should be compelled by law to be a Good Samaritan, but whether we must accede to a situation in which somebody is being compelled—by nature, perhaps—to be a Good Samaritan. We have, in other words, to look now at third-party interventions. I have been arguing that no person is morally required to make large sacrifices to sustain the life of another who has no right to demand them, and this even where the sacrifices do not include life itself; we are not morally required to be Good Samaritans or anyway Very Good Samaritans to one another. But what if a man cannot extricate himself from such a situation? What if he appeals to us to extricate him? It seems to me plain that there are cases in which we can, cases in which a Good Samaritan would extricate him. There you are, you were kidnapped, and nine years in bed with that violinist lie ahead of you. You have your own life to lead. You are sorry, but you simply cannot see giving up so much of your life to the sustaining of his. You cannot extricate yourself, and ask us to do so. I should have thought that—in light of his having no right to the use of your body—it was obvious that we do not have to accede to your being forced to give up so much. We can do what you ask. There is no injustice to the violinist in our doing so.

7. Following the lead of the opponents of abortion, I have throughout been speaking of the fetus merely as a person, and what I have been asking is whether or not the argument we began with, which proceeds only from the fetus' being a person, really does establish its conclusion. I have argued that it does not.

But of course there are arguments and arguments, and it may be said that I have simply fastened on the wrong one. It may be said that what is important is not merely the fact that the fetus is a person, but that it is a person for whom the woman has a special kind of responsibility issuing from the fact that she is its mother. And it might be argued that all my analogies are therefore irrelevant—for you do not have that special kind of responsibility for that violinist, Henry Fonda does not have that special kind of responsibility for me. And our attention might be drawn to the fact that men and

women both *are* compelled by law to provide support for their children.

I have in effect dealt (briefly) with this argument in section 4 above; but a (still briefer) recapitulation now may be in order. Surely we do not have any such "special responsibility" for a person unless we have assumed it, explicitly or implicitly. If a set of parents do not try to prevent pregnancy, do not obtain an abortion, but rather take it home with them, then they have assumed responsibility for it, they have given it rights, and they cannot *now* withdraw support from it at the cost of its life because they now find it difficult to go on providing for it. But if they have taken all reasonable precautions against having a child, they do not simply by virtue of their biological relationship to the child who comes into existence have a special responsibility for it. They may wish to assume responsibility for it, or they may not wish to. And I am suggesting that if assuming responsibility for it would require large sacrifices, then they may refuse. A Good Samaritan would not refuse—or anyway, a Splendid Samaritan, if the sacrifices that had to be made were enormous. But then so would a Good Samaritan assume responsibility for that violinist; so would Henry Fonda, if he is a Good Samaritan, fly in from the West Coast and assume responsibility for me.

8. My argument will be found unsatisfactory on two counts by many of those who want to regard abortion as morally permissible. First, while I do argue that abortion is not impermissible, I do not argue that it is always permissible. There may well be cases in which carrying the child to term requires only Minimally Decent Samaritanism of the mother, and this is a standard we must not fall below. I am inclined to think it a merit of my account precisely that it does *not* give a general yes or a general no. It allows for and supports our sense that, for example, a sick and desperately frightened fourteen-year-old schoolgirl, pregnant due to rape, may of *course* choose abortion, and that any law which rules this out is an insane law. And it also allows for and supports our sense that in other cases resort to abortion is even positively indecent. It would be indecent in the woman to request an abortion, and indecent in a doctor to perform it, if she is in her seventh month, and wants the abortion just to avoid the nuisance of postponing a trip abroad. The very fact that the arguments I have been drawing atten-

tion to treat all cases of abortion, or even all cases of abortion in which the mother's life is not at stake, as morally on a par ought to have made them suspect at the outset.

Secondly, while I am arguing for the permissibility of abortion in some cases, I am not arguing for the right to secure the death of the unborn child. It is easy to confuse these two things in that up to a certain point in the life of the fetus it is not able to survive outside the mother's body; hence removing it from her body guarantees its death. But they are importantly different. I have argued that you are not morally required to spend nine months in bed, sustaining the life of that violinist; but to say this is by no means to say that if, when you unplug yourself, there is a miracle and he survives, you then have a right to turn around and slit his throat. You may detach yourself even if this costs him his life; you have no right to be guaranteed his death, by some other means, if unplugging yourself does not kill him. There are some people who will feel dissatisfied by this feature of my argument. A woman may be utterly devastated by the thought of a child, a bit of herself, put out for adoption and never seen or heard of again. She may therefore want not merely that the child be detached from her, but more, that it die. Some opponents of abortion are inclined to regard this as beneath contempt—thereby showing insensitivity to what is surely a powerful source of despair. All the same, I agree that the desire for the child's death is not one which anybody may gratify, should it turn out to be possible to detach the child alive.

At this place, however, it should be remembered that we have only been pretending throughout that the fetus is a human being from the moment of conception. A very early abortion is surely not the killing of a person, and so is not dealt with by anything I have said here.

Notes

1. Daniel Callahan, *Abortion: Law, Choice and Morality* (New York, 1970), p. 373. This book gives a fascinating survey of the available information on abortion. The Jewish tradition in David M. Feldman, *Birth Control in Jewish Law* (New York, 1963), part 5; the Catholic tradition in John T. Noonan, Jr., "An Almost Absolute Value in History," in *The Morality of Abortion*, ed. John T. Noonan, Jr. (Cambridge, Mass., 1970).

2. The term "direct" in the arguments I refer to is a technical one. Roughly, what is meant by "direct killing" is either killing as an end in itself, or killing as a means to some end, for example, the end of saving someone else's life. See note 5 on this page, for an example of its use.

3. Cf. *Encyclical Letter of Pope Pius XI on Christian Marriage*, St. Paul Editions (Boston, n.d.), p. 32: "However much we may pity the mother whose health and even life is gravely imperiled in the performance of the duty allotted to her by nature, nevertheless what could ever be a sufficient reason for excusing in any way the direct murder of the innocent? This is precisely what we are dealing with here." Noonan (*The Morality of Abortion*, p. 43) reads this as follows: "What cause can ever avail to excuse in any way the direct killing of the innocent? For it is a question of that."

4. The thesis in (4) is in an interesting way weaker than those in (1), (2), and (3): They rule out abortion even in cases in which both mother *and* child will die if the abortion is not performed. By contrast, one who held the view expressed in (4) could consistently say that one needn't prefer letting two persons die to killing one.

5. Cf. the following passage from Pius XII, *Address to the Italian Catholic Society of Midwives:* "The baby in the maternal breast has the right to life immediately from God.—Hence there is no man, no human authority, no science, no medical, eugenic, social, economic or moral 'indication' which can establish or grant a valid juridical ground for a direct deliberate disposition of an innocent human life, that is a disposition which looks to its destruction either as an end or as a means to another end perhaps in itself not illicit.—The baby, still not born, is a man in the same degree and for the same reason as the mother" (quoted in Noonan, *The Morality of Abortion*, p. 45).

6. The need for a discussion of this argument was brought home to me by members of the Society for Ethical and Legal Philosophy, to whom this paper was originally presented.

7. For a discussion of the difficulties involved, and a survey of the European experience with such laws, see *The Good Samaritan and the Law*, ed. James M. Ratcliffe (New York, 1966).

Questions for Analysis

1. *Does the belief that abortion is always impermissible necessarily result from the argument that the unborn is a person from the moment of conception? If not, what additional premises are necessary?*

2. *Why does Thomson conclude that "a woman surely can defend her life against the threat to it posed by the unborn child, even if doing so involves its death"?*

3. *How does Thomson answer the claim that the fetus's right to life weighs more (in the moral sense) than anything other than the mother's own right to life?*

4. *Does Thomson feel that there may be cases in which it would be wrong for a woman to have an abortion? Explain.*

5. *Distinguish between a "Good Samaritan" and a "Minimally Decent Samaritan."*

CASE PRESENTATION
Mrs. Sherri Finkbine and the Thalidomide Tragedy

In 1962 Mrs. Sherri Finkbine, the mother of four normal children, found herself pregnant. The pregnancy was going well, except that Mrs. Finkbine was experiencing trouble sleeping. Instead of consulting her physician, she simply took some of the tranquilizers her husband had brought back from a trip to Europe, where the sedative was a widely used over-the-counter-drug.

A short time later, Mrs. Finkbine read an article concerning the great increase in the number of deformed children being born in Europe. Some of the children's limbs failed to develop, or developed only in malformed ways; some of the children were born blind and deaf, or had seriously defective internal organs. What alarmed Mrs. Finkbine was that the birth defects had been traced to the use in pregnancy of a supposedly harmless and widely used tranquilizer, whose active ingredient was thalidomide.

A visit to her physician confirmed Mrs. Finkbine's worst fears: The tranquilizer she had taken did indeed contain thalidomide. Convinced that his patient stood little chance of delivering an undeformed baby, the physician recommended termination of the pregnancy. He explained to Mrs. Finkbine that getting approval for an abortion under such conditions should prove simple. All she had to do was explain them to the three-member medical board of Phoenix. Mrs. Finkbine followed her physician's counsel, which proved correct: The board granted approval for the abortion.

Concerned about other women who might have unwittingly taken thalidomide, Mrs. Finkbine then called a local newspaper and told her story to the editor. While agreeing not to identify her, the editor ran the story bordered in black on the front page under the headline "Baby-Deforming Drug May Cost Woman Her Child Here."

The wire services picked up the story straightaway, and it wasn't long before enterprising reporters discovered and published Mrs. Finkbine's identity. In no time, Mrs. Finkbine became the object of intense anti-abortion sentiment. *L'Osservatore Romano,* the official Vatican newspaper, condemned Mrs. Finkbine and her husband as murderers. Although she received some letters of support, many were abusive. "'I hope someone takes the other four children and strangles them,' one person wrote, "because it's all the same thing." Another wrote from the perspective of the fetus: "Mommy, please dear Mommy, let me live. Please please, I want to live. Let me love you, let me see the light of day, let me smell a rose, let me sing a song, let me look into your face, let me say Mommy."

In the heat of the controversy, the medical board members decided that, if challenged, their approval could not survive a court test, for Arizona statute legally sanctioned abortion only when it was required to save the mother's life. Rather than attempt to defend its judgment if asked to, it withdrew its approval.

Thwarted in her attempt to get a legal abortion in some other state, Mrs. Finkbine went to Sweden. After a rigorous investigation by a medical board there, she was given an abortion in a Swedish hospital.

Questions for Analysis

1. *Do you think Mrs. Finkbine acted rightly or wrongly in having an abortion?*

2. *What bearing, if any, do you think probable or certain deformities have on the person status of the unborn?*

3. *How would you assess this argument: "If you're willing to permit abortions for the reason operating in the Finkbine case, then it follows that you should permit the termination of the existence of similarly defective infants and adults."*

4. *Do you believe that a government has a right and perhaps even a duty to prohibit abortions in cases like Mrs. Finkbine's? Or do you believe it doesn't? Explain with reference to concepts of justice and freedom.*

5. *Which of the moral principles discussed in Chapter 1 do you think are especially relevant to cases like this one?*

CASE PRESENTATION
"CONCEIVED IN VIOLENCE, BORN IN HATE"[9]

Shortly after returning home, a twenty-seven-year-old mother was gagged, tied up, and raped by a 220-pound guard from a nearby Air Force base who had forced his way into her home. The woman received medical treatment at a hospital and from her own physician. Nevertheless, the episode had left her pregnant.

9.   *Reported in Burton M. Leiser,* Liberty, Justice, and Morals: Contemporary Value Conflicts *(New York: Macmillan, 1973), p. 96.*

Not wanting the child, the woman sought an abortion. Although the state's abortion law was, at the time (1955), one of the least restrictive, no hospital in her state would permit her to have an abortion.

Unable to afford to travel abroad for a legal abortion, the woman and her husband were left with two choices: a clandestine illegal abortion or having the baby. Deeply religious and law abiding, the couple chose to carry the baby to term.

During her pregnancy, the woman admitted to hating the fetus she was carrying and to eagerly awaiting the time she would be rid of it. "Thus the child, conceived in violence and born in hatred, came into the world."[10]

10.   *Leiser,* Liberty, Justice, and Morals: Contemporary Value Conflicts, *p. 96.*

Questions for Analysis

1. *Do you think abortion should or should not be legal in cases like the preceding?*

2. *The traditional Roman Catholic position on abortion rests on the assumption that the unborn is a person from conception. Since the fetus is an innocent person, even when a pregnancy is due to rape or incest the fetus may not be held accountable and made to suffer through its death. According to Roman Catholicism, then, a* direct *abortion is never morally justifiable. (Although the fetus may never be deliberately killed, it may be allowed to die as a consequence of an action that is intended to save the life of the mother, such as the removal of a malignant uterus.) By this account, an abortion in the preceding case would be immoral. Evaluate this position.*

3. *Christian moralist Joseph Fletcher has written: "No unwanted and unintended baby should ever be born."[11] Do you think such a rule would produce the greatest social benefit?*

4. *Do you think Rawls's first principle of social justice has any relevance to the abortion issue?*

11.   *Joseph Fletcher,* Situation Ethics: The New Morality *(Philadelphia: Westminster Press, 1966), p. 39.*

Selections for Further Reading

Braggin, Mary V.; Frederick Elliston; and Jane English, eds. *Feminism and Philosophy,* Section 7. Totowa, N.J.: Littlefield, Adams, 1977.

Brody, B. *Abortion and the Sanctity of Human Life.* Cambridge, Mass.: Harvard University Press, 1975.

Callahan, Daniel. *Abortion: Law, Choice, and Morality.* New York: Macmillan, 1970.

Cohen, Marshall; Thomas Nagen; and Thomas Scanlon, eds. *The Rights and Wrongs of Abortion.* Princeton, N.J.: Princeton University Press, 1974.

Denes, Magda. *In Necessity and Sorrow: Life and Death in an Abortion Hospital.* New York: Penguin Books, 1977.

Feinberg, Joel. *The Problem of Abortion*, 2nd ed. Belmont, Calif.: Wadsworth, 1974.

Finnish, J., et al. *The Rights and Wrongs of Abortion*. Princeton, N.J.: Princeton University Press, 1974.

Nicholson, Susan. *Abortion and the Roman Catholic Church*. Knoxville, Tenn.: Religious Ethics, 1978.

Noonan, John T. *The Morality of Abortion: Legal and Historical Perspectives*. Cambridge, Mass.: Harvard University Press, 1970.

Perkins, Robert L., ed. *Abortion: Pro and Con*. Cambridge: Mass.: Schenkman, 1974.

Summer, L. W. *Abortion and Moral Theory*. Princeton, N.J.: Princeton University Press, 1981.

Tooley, Michael. *Abortion and Infanticide*. New York: Oxford University Press, 1983.

6
EUTHANASIA

The case of Karen Ann Quinlan has probably done more than any other in recent decades to rivet public attention on the legal and moral aspects of euthanasia, which generally refers to the act of painlessly putting to death a person suffering from a terminal or incurable disease or condition. On the night of April 15, 1975, for reasons still unclear, Karen Ann Quinlan ceased breathing for at least two 15-minute periods. Failing to respond to mouth-to-mouth resuscitation by friends, she was taken by ambulance to Newton Memorial Hospital in New Jersey. She had a temperature of 100 degrees, her pupils were unreactive, and she did not respond even to deep pain. Physicians who examined her characterized Karen as being in a "chronic, persistent, vegetative state," and later it was judged that no form of treatment could restore her to cognitive life. Her father, Joseph Quinlan, asked to be appointed her legal guardian with the expressed purpose of discontinuing the use of the respirator by which Karen was being sustained. Eventually the Supreme Court of New Jersey granted the request. The respirator was turned off. However, Karen Ann Quinlan remained alive but comatose until June 11, 1985, when she died at the age of thirty-one. Although widely publicized, the Quinlan case is by no means the only one that has raised questions concerning euthanasia.

In fact, improvements in biomedical technology have made euthanasia an issue that more and more individuals and institutions must confront and that society must address. Respirators, artificial kidneys, intravenous feeding, new drugs—all have made it possible to sustain an individual's life artificially, that is, long after the individual has lost the capacity to sustain life independently. In cases like Quinlan's, individuals have fallen into a state of irreversible coma, what some health professionals term a vegetative state. In other instances, such as after severe accidents or with congenital brain disease, the individual's consciousness has been so dulled and the personality has so deteriorated that he or she lacks the capacity for development and growth. In still other cases, such as with terminal cancer, individuals vacillate between agonizing pain and a drug-induced stupor, with no possibility of ever again enjoying life. Not too long ago, "nature would have taken its course"; such patients would have died. Today we have the technological capacity to keep them alive artificially. Should we? Or, at least in some instances, are we justified in not doing this, even obliged not to?

As with abortion and pornography, euthanasia raises two basic moral issues that must be distinguished. The first deals with the morality of euthanasia itself; the second concerns the morality of euthanasia legislation. We will consider both issues in this chapter.

Before discussing the arguments related to these issues, we must clarify a number of concepts central to euthanasia. Among them are the meanings of *personhood* and *death*, the difference between "ordinary" and "extraordinary" treatment, the distinctions between "killing" and "allowing to die," the various meanings of *euthanasia*, and the difference between "voluntary" and "nonvoluntary" euthanasia.

Personhood

The question of personhood bears as much on euthanasia as on abortion debates. What conditions should be used as the criteria of personhood? Can an entity be considered a person merely because it possesses certain biological properties? Or should other factors be introduced, such as consciousness, self-consciousness, rationality, and the capacities for communication and moral judgment? If personhood is just an elementary biological matter, then patients like Karen Ann Quinlan can qualify as persons more easily than if personhood depends on a complex list of psychosocial factors.

In part, the significance of the personhood issue lies in the assignment of basic patient rights; once the criteria for personhood are established, those qualifying presumably enjoy the same general rights as any other patient. Conversely, for those who do not qualify and have no reasonable chance of ever qualifying, the rights issue is far less problematic. This doesn't mean that a death decision necessarily follows when an entity is determined to be a nonperson. But it does mean that whatever may be inherently objectionable about allowing or causing a *person* to die dissolves, because the entity is no longer a person. So the concept of personhood bears directly on a death decision.

Death

Related to personhood is the conceptual issue of death. To get some idea of the complexities enshrouding the concept of death, consider this episode, which is based on an actual case.[1]

A terrible auto accident has occurred. One of the cars was occupied by a husband and wife. Authorities on the scene pronounce the man dead and rush the unconscious woman to a hospital, where she spends the next seventeen days in a coma due to severe brain damage. On the morning of the eighteenth day,

1. Smith *v.* Smith, *229 Arkansas 579, 3175.W, 2d, 275, 1958.*

she dies. Some time afterward, a relative contesting the couple's estate claims that the two people died simultaneously. Did they?

Not too long ago, legal and medical experts would have said yes. But when this case went to the Supreme Court of Arkansas in 1958, the court ruled that since the woman was breathing after the accident, she was alive, even though unconscious. The court relied on the time-honored definition of death as "the cessation of life; the ceasing to exist; defined by physicians as a total stoppage of the circulation of blood and a cessation of the animal and vital functions consequent thereon, such as respiration, pulsation, etc."[2] By this definition, death occurs if and only if there is a total cessation of respiration and blood flow.

Using heart-lung functioning as a criterion for death served well enough until recent developments in biomedical technology made it questionable. One of these developments is the increasing and widespread use of devices that can sustain respiration and heartbeat indefinitely, even when there is no brain activity. If the traditional heart-lung criterion is applied in cases like the preceding, then these individuals are technically still alive. Yet to many—including relatives of the comatose and those who must treat them—such people are, for all intents and purposes, dead.

Another development that has cast doubt on the traditional definition of death is the need for still-viable organs in transplant surgery. In general, a transplant is most successful if the organs are removed immediately after death. Thus there is intense pressure on transplant teams to harvest organs as soon as possible. The moral implications of this pressure are serious, as we'll see shortly.

But these developments are only part of what makes the whole issue of defining death so nettlesome. Also relevant are three distinct categories of concerns that can be identified in any discussion of death: the philosophical, the physiological, and the methodical.

Philosophical Concerns

The philosophical level refers to one's basic concept of death, which inevitably springs from some view of what it means to be human. For example, if we believe it is the capacity to think and reason that makes one a human, we will likely associate the loss of personhood with the loss of rationality. If we consider consciousness as the defining characteristic, we will be more inclined to consider a person to have lost that status when a number of characteristics such as the capacities to remember, enjoy, worry, and will are gone. Although the absence of rational or experimental capacities would not necessarily define death, it would dispose us toward such a definition, since we are already disposed to accept the absence of personhood in the absence of those criteria. So there is interplay between our concepts of personhood and death.

Physiological Concerns

These relate to the functioning of specific body systems or organs. The traditional physiological standard for recognizing death has been irreversible loss

2. Black's Law Dictionary, *rev. 4th ed. (St. Paul Minn.: West Publishing), 1968, p. 488.*

of circulatory and respiratory functions. More recent physiological standards defined by the Harvard Ad Hoc Committee (1968) have focused on the central nervous system—the brain and spinal cord. Specifically, these standards are the irreversible loss of reflex activity mediated through the brain or spinal cord, electrical activity in the cerebral neocortex, and/or cerebral blood flow. Whether traditional or recent, these physiological standards can be used individually or in combination. The significance of the physiological category in death decisions is that a patient who might be declared alive by one set of criteria might be ruled dead by another. If a patient is considered dead, obviously euthanasia becomes academic; if the person is considered alive, euthanasia is a real concern.

Methodical Concerns

This category refers to specific means for determining physiological standards. The method used to determine traditional heart-lung standards has been taking the pulse or reading an electrocardiogram, or both. For the central nervous system, electroencephalographs can be used to measure electrical activity in the neocortex, and radioactive tracers can be injected into the circulatory system for detecting cerebral blood flow.

Moral Implications

What makes defining death so important in discussions of euthanasia and the general study of bioethics is the interplay between definitional and moral considerations. To illustrate, suppose an attacker has clubbed a woman into a comatose condition. She is rushed to a hospital, is determined to have suffered profound and irreversible brain damage, and is put on an artificial respirator. Efforts to identify her fail. As the team tending her debates whether to remove her from the respirator, one member, using one of the brain-death criteria, claims she is already dead. Therefore, withdrawing the respirator poses no special problems. Another member demurs. Using the heart-lung criterion, she insists that the woman is still alive and that the team has an obligation to sustain her life. What ought the team do?

One answer is, Let the law decide. But some states lack an adequate definition of death. Complicating matters, some states allow either of the two alternative definitions. And even where the law is decisive, moral problems remain about the rightness of the standard itself. Beyond this, even when the law sanctions a brain-death criterion, as it now does in most states, it does not *compel* health professionals or anyone else to implement it. So although brain-death law may legally protect health professionals, it does not obligate them to act. Health professionals, presumably in consultation with others, must still wrestle with moral decisions in cases of irreversible coma.

Then there is the phenomenon of organ transplants, which promises to become of even greater concern as technology and techniques improve. A number of interests are identifiable in such cases. First there are the interests of recipients, whose welfare depends on the availability of organs. Then there are the interests of health teams, who are obliged to provide adequate health care, which may include appropriate quality organs. There are also the interests of the donors, who may fear that their organs will be pirated prior to death or that their own health-care providers will perform less than adequately in trying to sustain their lives. Moreover, there are the obligations of health teams to guard donors against physical violations as well as the psychological threat of violations, and to guard themselves against developing a cannibalistic image. And finally, society at large must be watchful that the rights of its citizens to protection are not flouted, while at the same time ensuring that its ill citizens are not denied needed medical care and treatment, which may involve transplants.

Ordinary vs. Extraordinary Treatment

A third issue that arises in euthanasia discussions involves the concept of ordinary as opposed to extraordinary treatment, terms used to differentiate two broad categories of medical intervention. Although the terms are often applied facilely, they elude hard-and-fast definition.

Moralist Paul Ramsey, for one, has applied *ordinary* to all medicines, treatments, and surgical procedures that offer a reasonable hope of benefit to the patient but do not involve excessive pain, expense, or other inconveniences. In contrast, he has identified *extraordinary* as measures that are unusual, extremely difficult, dangerous, inordinately expensive, or that offer no reasonable hope of benefit to the patient.[3]

Such descriptions are useful and probably find widespread acceptance. But they do raise questions. An obvious one concerns the concepts used to define *ordinary* and *extraordinary*. What can be considered "reasonable hope of benefit to the patient"? What measures qualify as "unusual"? Ramsey mentions cost, but some would claim that cost has no place in a moral calculation. And then there is always the question of whether these criteria should be used individually or in combination; if in combination, what is the proper mix? Furthermore, patient idiosyncrasies inevitably influence a determination of ordinary and extraordinary in a particular case. For example, the use of antibiotics for a pneumonia patient undoubtedly qualifies as ordinary treatment. But does it remain ordinary treatment when the patient with pneumonia happens to have terminal cancer with metastasis to the brain and liver? The institutional setting can also affect evaluations of what constitutes ordinary and extraordinary: What is extraordinary treatment in a small community hospital could well be ordinary in a large teaching hospital.[4]

The significance of trying to pin down these two concepts is that euthanasia arguments often rely on them to distinguish the permissible from the impermissible act of euthanasia. Some moralists argue that health professionals should provide ordinary treatment for the moribund but not extraordinary, which may

3. *Paul Ramsey,* The Patient as Person *(New Haven, Conn.: Yale University Press, 1970), pp. 122–23.*

4. *See A. J. Davis and M. A. Aroskar,* Ethical Dilemmas and Nursing Practice *(New York: Appleton-Century-Crofts, 1978), p. 117.*

be withheld or never started. Others insist that health professionals initiate extraordinary measures. Indeed, the medical profession itself makes similar operational distinctions in making death decisions.

Killing vs. Allowing to Die

A fourth conceptual issue that we should try to clarify is what some consider to be the difference between killing a person and allowing a person to die. Presumably, "killing" a person refers to a definite action taken to end someone's life, as in the case of the physician who, out of mercy, injects a terminally ill patient with air or a lethal dose of a medication. Killing is an act of commission. In contrast, "allowing to die" presumably is an act of omission, whereby the steps needed to preserve someone's life simply are not taken. For example, a doctor, again out of mercy, fails to give an injection of antibiotics to a terminally ill patient who has contracted pneumonia. As a result of this omission, the patient dies.

Those making this distinction, such as the American Medical Association (AMA), say that the distinction is reasonable because in ordinary language and everyday life we distinguish between causing someone harm and permitting the harm to happen to them. If, in cases of euthanasia, the distinction is not made between killing and allowing to die, we lose the important distinction between causing someone harm and permitting that harm to happen.

Proponents also claim that the distinction acknowledges cases in which additional curative treatment would serve no purpose, and in fact would interfere with a person's natural death. It recognizes that medical science will not initiate or sustain extraordinary means to preserve the life of a dying patient when such means would obviously serve no useful purpose for the patient or the patient's family.

Finally, some argue that the distinction is important in determining causation of death, and ultimate responsibility. In instances where the patient dies following nontreatment, the proximate cause of the death is the patient's disease, not the treatment or the person who did not provide it. If we fail to differentiate between killing and allowing to die, we blur this distinction. If allowing to die is subsumed under the category of euthanasia, then the nontreatment is the cause of the death, not the disease.

Not everyone, however, agrees that the distinction is a logical one. Some argue that withholding extraordinary treatment or suspending heroic measures in terminal cases is tantamount to the intentional termination of the life of one human being by another; that is, it is an act of killing. Thus they claim that no logical distinction can be made between killing and allowing to die.

Whether or not the distinction between the two can be sustained logically is only one question raised by the killing-vs.-letting-die debate. Another is the moral relevance of such a distinction. Even if the distinction is logical, does it have any bearing on the rightness or wrongness of acts commonly termed *euthanasia*?

On the one hand, for those making the distinction, allowing a patient to die under carefully circumscribed conditions could be moral. On the other hand, they seemingly would regard the killing of a patient, even out of mercy, an immoral act. But those opposing the killing–letting die distinction would not necessarily accept the close connection between killing a dying patient and an immoral act. For them, while killing may be wrong, in some cases it may be the right thing to do. What determines the morality of killing a patient, what is of moral relevance and importance, is not the manner of causing the death but the circumstances in which the death is caused.

In summary, those distinguishing killing from allowing to die claim that the distinction is logically and morally relevant. Generally, they would condemn any act of killing a patient, while recognizing that some acts of allowing a patient to die may be moral (as, for example, in cases where life is being preserved heroically and death is imminent). In contrast are those who hold that the killing–letting die distinction is not logical, that allowing to die is in effect killing. They claim that killing a patient may be morally justifiable depending on the *circumstances* and not the *manner* in which the death is caused. The debate that surrounds the killing-vs.-allowing-to-die question is basic to the very meaning of *euthanasia*, a fifth conceptual issue that needs clarification.

Meaning of *Euthanasia:* Narrow vs. Broad Interpretations

Construing euthanasia (from the Greek, meaning "good or happy death") narrowly, some philosophers have taken it to be the equivalent of killing. Since allowing someone to die does not involve killing, allowing to die would not actually be an act of euthanasia at all. By this account, then, there are acts of allowing to die, which may be moral, and acts of euthanasia, which are always wrong.

Other philosophers interpret the meaning of *euthanasia* more broadly. For them euthanasia includes not only acts of killing but also acts of allowing to die. In other words, euthanasia can take an active or passive form. *Active* (sometimes termed *positive*) *euthanasia refers to the act of painlessly putting to death persons suffering from incurable conditions or diseases.* Injecting a lethal dosage of medication into a terminally ill patient would constitute active euthanasia. *Passive euthanasia,* in contrast, *refers to any act of allowing a patient to die.* Not providing a terminally ill patient the needed antibiotics to survive pneumonia would be an example of passive euthanasia.

It is tempting to view the debate between the narrow and the broad interpretations of *euthanasia* largely in terms of semantics. While the meaning of *euthanasia* certainly is a factor in the disagreement, the issue involves more than mere word definition.

One side, the narrow interpretation, considers killing a patient always morally wrong. Since euthanasia, by this definition, is killing a patient, euthanasia is always morally wrong. But allowing a patient to die does not involve killing a patient. Therefore, allowing a patient to die does not fall under the moral prohibition that euthanasia does; allowing a patient to die may be morally right.

The other side, the broad interpretation, considers acts of allowing patients to die acts of euthanasia, albeit passive euthanasia. They argue that if euthanasia is wrong, then so is allowing patients to die (since it is a form of euthanasia). But if allowing patients to die is not wrong, then euthanasia is not always wrong. Generally, those favoring the broad interpretation, in fact, claim that allowing patients to die is not always wrong; that euthanasia, therefore, may be morally justifiable. With the possible moral justifiability of euthanasia established, it is conceivable that acts of active euthanasia, as well as passive, may be moral. What determines their morality are the conditions under which the death is caused, and not the manner in which it is caused. It's within these broad interpretations that the most problematic cases of death decisions fall—including the Quinlan case.

Voluntary vs. Nonvoluntary Euthanasia

In addition to the preceding, there is another conceptual issue that arises in discussions of euthanasia. It concerns the difference between voluntary and nonvoluntary decisions about death.

Voluntary decisions about death refer to cases in which a competent adult patient requests or gives informed consent to a particular course of medical treatment or nontreatment. Generally speaking, informed consent exists when patients can understand what they are agreeing to and voluntarily choose it. Voluntary decisions also include cases in which persons take their own lives either directly or by refusing treatment, and cases where patients deputize others to act in their behalf. For example, a woman who is terminally ill instructs her husband and family not to permit antibiotic treatment should she contract pneumonia, or not to use artificial support systems should she lapse into a coma and be unable to speak for herself. Similarly, a man requests that he be given a lethal injection after an industrial explosion has left him with third-degree burns over most of his body and no real hope of recovery. For a decision about death to be voluntary, the individual must give explicit consent.

A nonvoluntary decision about death refers to cases in which the decision is not made by the person who is to die. Such cases would include situations where, because of age, mental impairment, or unconsciousness, patients are not competent to give informed consent to life-or-death decisions and where others make the decisions for them. For example, suppose that as a result of an automobile accident, a man suffers massive and irreparable brain damage, falls into unconsciousness, and can be maintained only by artificial means. Should he regain consciousness, he would likely be little more than a vegetable. Given this prognosis, the man's family, in consultation with his physicians, decide to suspend artificial life-sustaining means and allow him to die.

In actual situations, the difference between voluntary and nonvoluntary decisions about death is not always clear. For example, take the case of a man who has heard his mother say that she would never want to be kept alive with "machines and pumps and tubes." Now that she is, in fact, being kept alive that way, and is unable to express a life-or-death decision, the man is not sure that his mother actually would choose to be allowed to die. Similarly, a doctor might not be certain that the tormented cries of a stomach-cancer patient to be "put out of my misery" is an expression of informed consent or of profound pain and momentary despair.

The voluntary-nonvoluntary distinction is relevant to both the narrow and the broad interpretations of the meaning of *euthanasia*. Each interpretation seemingly distinguishes four kinds of death decisions, in which the voluntary-nonvoluntary distinction plays a part. Thus, the narrow interpretation recognizes cases of:

1. Voluntary euthanasia
2. Nonvoluntary euthanasia
3. Voluntary allowing to die
4. Nonvoluntary allowing to die

By this account, the first two generally are considered immoral; instances of the second two may be moral under carefully circumscribed conditions.

Recognizing no logical or morally relevant distinction between euthanasia and allowing to die, the broad interpretation allows four forms of euthanasia:

1. Voluntary active euthanasia
2. Nonvoluntary active euthanasia
3. Voluntary passive euthanasia
4. Nonvoluntary passive euthanasia

By this account, any of these types of euthanasia may be morally justifiable under carefully circumscribed conditions.

The narrow and the broad interpretations differ sharply in their moral judgment of *deliberate* acts taken to end or shorten a patient's life—that is, acts that the narrow interpretation terms voluntary or nonvoluntary euthanasia, and that the broad interpretation terms voluntary or nonvoluntary *active* euthanasia. Generally, the narrow interpretation considers such acts always morally repugnant; the broad interpretation views them as being morally justifiable under carefully circumscribed conditions.

With these complicated conceptual issues behind us, we can now turn to the arguments for and against death decisions. The most conservative death decisions involve cases of voluntary allowing to die, which we will take as circumstantially a rough equivalent to voluntary passive euthanasia. Having raised the relevant pro and con arguments, we will then see how they can be and are applied to other forms of death decisions.

Arguments for Voluntary
Allowing to Die

1. *Individuals have the right to decide about their own lives and deaths.*

POINT: "What more basic right is there than to decide whether or not you're going to live? There is none. A person under a death sentence who's being kept alive through so-called heroic measures certainly has a fundamental right to say, 'Enough's enough. The treatment's worse than the disease. Leave me alone. Let me die!' Ironically, those who would deny the terminally ill this right do so out of a sense of high morality. Don't they realize that in denying the gravely ill and the suffering the right to release themselves from pain, they commit the arch-villainy?"

COUNTERPOINT: "The way you talk you'd swear people have absolute rights over their bodies and lives: You know as well as I that just isn't true. No individual has absolute freedom. Even 'A Patient's Bill of Rights,' which was drawn up by the American Hospital Association, recognizes this. While acknowledging that patients have the right to refuse treatment, the document also recognizes that they have this right and freedom only to the extent permitted by law. Maybe people should be allowed to die if they want to. But if so, it's not because they have an absolute right to dispose of themselves if they so choose."

2. *The period of suffering can be shortened.*

POINT: "Have you ever been in a terminal-cancer ward? It's grim, but enlightening. Anyone who has knows how much people can suffer before they die. And not just physically. The emotional, even spiritual, agony is often worse. Today our medical hardware is so sophisticated that the period of suffering can be extended beyond the limit of human endurance. What's the point of allowing someone a few more months or days or hours of so-called life when recovery is impossible? There's no point. In fact, it's downright inhumane. When someone under such conditions asks to be allowed to die, it's far more humane to honor that request than deny it."

COUNTERPOINT: "Only a fool would discount the agony that many terminally ill patients endure. And there's no question that by letting them die on request we shorten their period of suffering. But we also shorten their lives. Can you seriously argue that the saving of pain is a greater good than the saving of life? Or that the presence of pain is a greater evil than the loss of life? I don't think so. Of course nobody likes to see a creature suffer, especially when the creature has requested a halt to the suffering. But we have to keep our priorities straight. In the last analysis, life is a greater value than freedom from pain; death is a worse evil than suffering."

3. *People have a right to die with dignity.*

POINT: "Nobody wants to end up plugged into machines and wired to tubes. Who wants to spend his last days lying in a hospital bed wasting away to something that's hardly recognizable as a human being, let alone his former self?

Nobody. And rightly so. Why, the very prospect insults the whole concept of what it means to be a human. People are entitled to dignity, in life *and* in death. Just as we respect people's right to live with dignity, so we must respect their right to die with dignity. In the case of the terminally ill, that means people have the right to refuse life-sustaining treatment when it's obvious to them that the treatment is only eroding their dignity, destroying their self-concept and self-respect, and reducing them to some subhuman level of biological life."

COUNTERPOINT: "Listening to you, someone would swear that the super-human efforts often made to keep someone alive are not worthy of human beings. What could be more dignified, more respectful of human life, than to maintain life against all odds, against all hope? Why, in situations like those, humans live their finest hours. And that includes many patients. All of life is a struggle, and a gamble. Nobody ever knows what the outcome will be. But on we go—dogged in our determination to see things through to a meaningful resolution. Indeed, humans are noblest when they persist in the face of the inevitable. Look at our literature. Reflect on our heroes. They are not those who have capitulated, but those who have endured. No, there's nothing undignified about being hollowed out by a catastrophic disease, about writhing in pain, about wishing it would end. The indignity lies in capitulation."

Arguments against Voluntary Allowing to Die

1. *We should not play God.*

POINT: "Our culture traditionally has recognized that only God gives life, and only God should take life away. When humans take it upon themselves to shorten their lives or have others do that by withdrawing life-sustaining apparatus, they play God. They usurp the divine function; they interfere with the divine plan."

COUNTERPOINT: "Well, I'm impressed! It's not every day that I meet some-body who knows the mind of God. But you obviously do. How you can be so sure about the 'divine plan,' however, quite escapes me. Did it ever occur to you that the intervention of modern medicine to keep people alive who otherwise would have long since died might itself be interfering with God's will? If there is a God and a divine plan, it seems pretty clear that God didn't intend that his creatures should live forever. Judging from history, God meant for all humans to die. Don't you think modern medicine has interfered with this plan? What could be more like 'playing God' than keeping people alive artificially? Let's face it: Nobody knows what God's plan is for allowing people to die."

2. *We cannot be sure consent is voluntary.*

POINT: "Many of those opposed to nonvoluntary death decisions are quick to approve of voluntary ones. What they overlook is that we can't ever be sure consent is voluntary. In fact, the circumstances that surround most terminal cases make voluntary consent impossible. Take the case of terminal patients who have built up a tolerance to drugs and, as a result, are tortured by pain. Just when are we supposed to get their consent? If we get it when they're drugged, then they're not clearheaded enough for the consent to be voluntary. If we withdraw the drugs, then they'll probably be so crazed with pain that their free consent still will be in question. Since consent in such cases can't be voluntary, it can only be presumed. And to allow a death decision on the basis of presumed consent is wrong."

COUNTERPOINT: "Agreed, in the situations you set up, rational free choice is in question. But you've overlooked cases where people facing a death due to a dreadful disease make a death request *before* they're suffering pain. Maybe you'll reply that the consent of people in such situations is uninformed and anticipatory, and that patients can't bind themselves to be killed in the future. Okay, but what about cases where patients not under pain indicate a desire for ultimate euthanasia and reaffirm that request when under pain? Surely, by any realistic criteria, this would constitute voluntary consent."

3. *Diagnoses may be mistaken.*

POINT: "Doctors aren't infallible, that's for sure. The American Medical Association readily admits that far too many medical procedures and operations aren't even necessary. This doesn't mean doctors are malicious, only that they're human. They make mistakes in their diagnoses. Any instance of electing death runs the tragic risk of terminating a life unnecessarily, and for that reason it's wrong."

COUNTERPOINT: "Sure, doctors make mistakes, but not as often as you imply. In fact, in terminal cases mistaken diagnoses are as rare as the kiwi bird. But that fact probably won't satisfy you, because you claim that any risk makes a death decision wrong. Well, by the same token, every diagnosis, from the simplest to most complex, carries a chance of error and with it the possibility of needless treatment. Sometimes the treatment involves operations, and operations always involve some jeopardy for the patient. So what are we to say—that it's wrong for people to opt for procedures that expert medical opinion says they need, because there's always a chance of mistaken diagnosis? Of course not. The fact of the matter is that the correctness of a diagnosis is a separate issue from the individual's right to request and receive treatment. This applies with equal force to death decisions."

4. *There is always a chance of a cure or of some new relief from pain.*

POINT: "People easily forget how final death is. That may sound silly, but it's pertinent to death decisions. After all, people can never be recalled from the grave to benefit from a cure to the diseases that ravage them, or from a new drug to relieve the pain they suffered. Instances of such 'wonder' drugs, even of spontaneous remissions of disease, are common enough to make a death decision precipitate, and therefore wrong."

COUNTERPOINT: "First of all, it's highly unlikely that some kind of cure will benefit those who are already ravaged by a disease. Ask doctors. They'll tell you that a cure is most likely in the early stages of a disease, and most unlikely in its final stages. But the issue of death decisions pertains precisely to people in the final, tortured stages of a disease. So even if a cure is discovered, its likelihood of helping these patients is virtually nonexistent. Another thing: You fail to distinguish between cases where a cure is imminent, cases where it's remote, and those where it falls somewhere in between. To treat all terminal diseases as if they had an equal probability of being cured is unrealistic. Generally speaking, there's a time lapse between a medical discovery and the general availability of a drug. I might agree that it would be 'precipitate' and even wrong to elect death in that interim between discovery and general availability of the drug. But I don't see why it would be precipitate and wrong for a person to elect death when suffering from a terminal disease for which no cure or relief has ever been discovered, or who doesn't want to gamble but to die."

5. *Allowing death decisions will lead to abuses.*

POINT: "Of course it's easy to think of death decisions as isolated instances of individuals electing to die. Looked at this way, those who make such decisions appear to be above moral reproach. But when individuals choose to die and are subsequently allowed to, their actions open the door for all sorts of abuses. The chief abuse is *nonvoluntary* death decisions. A terminal patient who elects to die at the very least brings individuals and society closer to accepting nonvoluntary killing, such as in cases of defective infants, old and senile people, and the hopelessly insane. Indeed, such 'private' decisions will likely set off a chain reaction that will lead to horrible abuses."

COUNTERPOINT: "The treatments of defective infants, old and senile people, and the hopelessly insane are issues separate and distinct from permitting death decisions. There is no causal connection between them and allowing death decisions, such that allowing death decisions will inevitably lead to the abuses you fear. But even if there were a connection, that wouldn't of itself demonstrate that voluntary death decisions are immoral, only that they shouldn't be legalized."

Arguments for and against Other Forms of Death Decisions

The foregoing are the arguments typically marshaled for and against voluntary allowing to die or voluntary passive euthanasia. They, or variations of them, are commonly enlisted in discussions of other forms of death decisions as well.

For example, those arguing for voluntary active euthanasia often stress the inherent freedom of individuals to do as they choose, so long as their actions do not hurt anyone else. They also contend that it is cruel and inhuman to make people suffer when they have requested to have their lives ended. In contrast, those opposing voluntary active euthanasia appeal to the sanctity of human life, arguing that the intentional termination of an innocent human life is always immoral. They also express concern about mistaken diagnoses, the possibility of cure and relief, and especially about the potentially dangerous consequences resulting from such a lessening of respect for human life.

Similarly, those supporting nonvoluntary active or passive euthanasia generally appeal to principles of humanness and human dignity. Those opposing it marshal all the arguments that we have catalogued against a voluntary death decision, while stressing how morally objectionable it is to allow people to die or to kill people without voluntary consent.

Of course, various positions are possible, and likely, within this broad outline. For example, some who support voluntary decisions might well oppose the nonvoluntary. And many who support nonvoluntary allowing to die or nonvoluntary passive euthanasia might object to nonvoluntary active euthanasia. In other words, for some moralists the key factor in determining the morality of a death decision is whether or not it is voluntary. For many, a death decision is moral if and only if it is voluntary. Others concern themselves primarily with the distinction between active and passive, not voluntary and nonvoluntary. In their view, the focus should be not on who makes the death decision, but on whether there is a morally significant difference between active and passive euthanasia, such that even if passive euthanasia is acceptable, the active form is not.

Defective Newborns

Much of the preceding discussion applies to the issue of babies born with serious birth defects, such as Tay-Sachs, a fatal degenerative disease; Down's syndrome, which manifests itself in mental retardation and various physical abnormalities; and duodenal atresia, in which the upper part of the small intestine, the duodenum, is closed off, thus preventing the passage and digestion of food. (Although duodenal atresia usually can be treated effectively through surgery, it often is accompanied by other serious birth defects.) Today physicians can tell much about the health of the fetus through a procedure called amniocentesis, whereby amniotic fluid is withdrawn from the pregnant woman for diagnostic purposes.

It's important to note that in the case of defective newborns, allowing to die includes withholding ordinary and not just extraordinary treatment. For example, ordinary nourishment may be withheld, resulting in the infant's death. Is this moral? In answering this question, it's necessary to come to grips with the central moral issue involving seriously defective infants, which involves determining the conditions, if any, under which it is morally permissible to allow defective newborns to die.

It is possible to identify three broad positions on the moral acceptability of allowing severely defective newborns to die. Underpinning each are controversial value assumptions.

The first and most permissive position is that allowing seriously defective infants to die is morally permissible when there is no significant potential for a meaningful human existence. It also sanctions such an act when the emotional or financial hardship of caring for the infant would place a grave burden on the family. Adherents of this view often argue their case on the grounds that the seriously defective newborn does not have person status, which, as we've seen in Chapter 5, is a controversial assumption.

The second position is that it is permissible only if there is no significant potential for a meaningful human existence. Clearly implied here is a quality-of-life judgment, which, of course, elicits debate.

The third position asserts that it is *never* morally permissible to allow a defective newborn to die. Stated more cautiously, it is never moral to withhold from a defective newborn any treatment that would be provided a normal one. The clear implication here is that the defective infant has full personhood and must be treated accordingly. Just as clearly, this view rejects any quality-of-life or cost factors in determining the acceptability of allowing a defective infant to die. Like the other positions, this one is fraught with debatable value judgments, and in cases of duodenal atresia it ignores that normal infants would not require corrective surgery in order to digest food.

It is quite apparent, then, that whether cases involve defective newborns or adults who are terminally ill, the central moral question concerns the acceptability of a death decision and subsequent action. But there are additional moral problems relating to death decisions in the institutional setting that are worth considering.

Death Decisions in the Institutional Setting

A basic problem related to death decisions in an institutional setting concerns the criteria for the decision. There are several aspects to this issue. One aspect deals with who makes the decision.

Who Should Decide?

Should it be the physician, the patient, the family, a member of the clergy, a board, or some combination? When patients can give informed consent—that is, can understand what they are agreeing to and voluntarily choose it—their rights to autonomy and adequate care would require their participation in the death decision. Cases in which patients are denied their own *request* that life-sustaining treatment be discontinued or that they be permitted to kill themselves raise serious moral questions. For to deny their requests contradicts the standard presumption that it is moral to let adults make for themselves decisions that affect themselves, and that not to do so is to use them as means, not ends, violating the Kantian principle of respect for individuals.

But cases in which patients are not competent to make a death decision are just as troublesome. Some moralists believe death decisions should never be made for patients who cannot themselves ask to die. Thus it would be wrong for health professionals or anyone else to permit or cause the deaths of incompetent older patients being kept alive artificially or of defective newborns. Others disagree, arguing that in such cases the decision rightfully shifts to those most knowledgeable about the patient: parents, guardians, spouses, physicians, or others.

Given the complexities involved in any death decision, it's understandable that many health professionals, especially nurses, prefer a board decision.[5] It's true that in cases of incompetent patients a collective decision (as opposed to a decision made exclusively by the physician, for example) seems most likely to ensure that the legitimate interests of all parties will be considered and that undue personal bias will not color the decision. But there's still the category of competent patients who request death and are denied, say, by a board. To repeat: How does a denial square with the presumption that it's moral, even obligatory, to permit adults who can to make for themselves decisions that affect themselves? To respond by saying, "Yes, such adults should be permitted to make a death decision, but I (the health professional, relative, board, etc.) am under no obligation to help them implement it" misses the point that "not helping" here is equivalent to "not permitting." There may be good reasons for not permitting the death decision in these cases, but one can't have it both ways: One cannot *not* permit and at the same time reasonably claim that one is honoring the individual's right to autonomy.

What Should the Criteria Be?

Under what conditions, if ever, should death decisions be made? The answer to this question inevitably will reflect perspectives on personhood, death, and ordinary vs. extraordinary treatment, as well as general views on allowing to die, euthanasia, and emphasis to be placed on informed consent. The question of who should formulate the criteria is related to this issue.

What Policies Should There Be for Implementation?

Vague physician orders are a problem in this area. Nurses can get caught between their legal obligation to follow physicians' orders, which may imply termination of treatment, and their professional obligation to provide life-preserving services. Such a dilemma can torture personnel in institutions for the elderly, whose nurses may be the patient's and family's own daily resources. Problems for nurses grow even murkier when the patient's family desires a course of action that conflicts with what some rarely present physician has ordered. Certainly physicians are under special obligations to clarify their orders, and by the same token, nurses are obliged to keep physicians informed of family wishes and of changes in the patient's condition that may warrant changes in standing orders. Furthermore, it's worth emphasizing the physician's obligation to draw on the nurse's perceptions of the terminally ill patient. Nurses, because of the daily contact with patients, often know more about the patient's condition than physicians do. This observation is especially relevant to institutions with guidelines for orders not to resuscitate. Although physicians are responsible for recording the decision, they risk considerable harm to patients if they don't consult on

5. N. K. Brown, J. T. Donovan, R. J. Bulger, and E. H. Laws, "How Do Nurses Feel about Euthanasia and Abortion?" American Journal of Nursing, July 1971, pp. 1415–16.

a *continuing* basis with their nurses who may be best informed about the patient's condition.

Although professional staff deal with dying, death, and death decisions more directly than administrative staff do, the bureaucratic line of authority does get involved in these issues, thereby raising additional questions. For one thing, administrators have an obligation to ensure a free flow of communication among health professionals involved in implementing a death decision. For another, administrative and professional staff must make sure their organizational clashes don't jeopardize the care of the dying. Physicians, nurses, and other health professionals tend to identify with the interests of patients. In contrast, administrators tend to view patients as managerial problems, relating specifically to the allocation of scarce hospital resources. When a patient happens to be terminally ill, these incompatible perspectives can cause problems for everyone, especially the patient. Health professionals generally seek to provide treatment tailored to the individual's needs and requests, but they can still be indifferent to the matter of when and under what conditions patients should choose death—especially since the cornerstone of their medical training and of their professional obligation is the preservation of life. Administrators, given their preoccupation with institutional efficiency and equality of services for all patients, can ignore individual needs.[6]

So although determining the moral acceptability of a death decision stands as the central moral issue, there are other questions health professionals and others must face. These pertain to decision criteria and to policies for implementing death decisions in an institutional setting. So complex are these problems that some argue an alternative setting is required, one that effectively minimizes the need for death decisions. Of all the alternative care systems for the dying, the hospice approach has received the most attention in recent years.

The Hospice Approach

Hospices are special settings devoted exclusively to care of the terminally ill. The hospice approach to care of the dying differs from conventional care in several important ways.[7] (1) It stresses comfort and care, including control of pain and symptoms and assistance at all levels to patients and their families. (2) Its nucleus is the hospice "team," which includes physicians, nurses, clergy, social workers, psychologists and psychiatrists, and various therapists and volunteers, as well as patients and family. (3) Hospice practitioners take a preventive rather than reactive approach to control of pain and symptoms. Accordingly, every attempt is made to preclude the patient's having pain, which means that in some cases drugs are administered not only when patients are already in pain but also *before*. (4) Hospices may have both inpatient and outpatient or home-care service.

---

6. A. J. Davis and M. A. Aroskar, Ethical Dilemmas and Nursing Practice (New York: Appleton-Century-Crofts, 1978), p. 127.

7. See Jacques Thiroux, Ethics: Theory and Practice, 2nd ed. (Encino, Calif.: Glencoe, 1980), pp. 187–189.

(5) The hospice approach attempts to help patients' families adjust to death before, during, and—most important—after its occurrence.

Hospice supporters argue that their approach is calculated to relieve the very sources of requests and demands for mercy deaths: suffering and profound feelings of meaninglessness. Of course, there remains that category of patients who do not want even hospice treatment and who would rather die. And there are those for whom hospice treatment doesn't apply: for example, paraplegics, quadriplegics, paralytics, and others suffering from debilitating diseases. For them a mercy death might pose a viable alternative to their conditions. A case in point is Elizabeth Bouvia, the 26-year-old Riverside, California, woman who has cerebral palsy and who has waged an unsuccessful legal battle to compel a nursing home to help her end her life.

Legal Considerations

Even if we decide that some form of euthanasia is morally acceptable, another question arises: Should individuals have a legal right to euthanasia? Ought people be permitted under law to have their lives terminated?

Currently it is illegal to deliberately cause the death of another person. It is generally recognized, however, that people have a right to refuse life-sustaining treatment. In recent years numerous attempts have been made to legislate the individual's right to refuse life-sustaining treatment. By and large these efforts have been rebuffed. Some object to the proposed legislation because of inherent difficulties in trying to define phrases such as "death with dignity," "natural death," "extraordinary means," "heroic measures," and "informed consent." Others observe that such legislation is not needed, since there is already a widely recognized right to reject life-sustaining treatment. Still others express concern that legalizing such a right will lead to abuses.

In the absence of specific legislation, various documents and directives have been developed to allow people to inform others about the nature and extent of the treatment they wish to have should they become seriously ill. Such documents usually are termed *living wills*. While living wills do specify the person's wishes, and relieve others of having to make momentous life or death decisions, generally they are not legally binding. Thus there is no guarantee that the person's wishes will be implemented.

In 1977 the State of California, as part of the "Natural Death Act," created a version of a living will called "Directive to Physicians" (see Figure 1). What makes this document unique is that it guarantees those who execute it the same legal power guaranteed by an estate will. Of course, as with estate wills, the "Directive to Physicians" can be contested. But the document takes a giant step toward granting legal status to living wills.

It is important to remember that the morality of legalizing death decisions is a separate issue from the morality of euthanasia itself. While many of the arguments for and against the legalization of death decisions capitalize on the general arguments previously outlined, it is entirely possible that one could approve of individual death decisions but at the same time object to any systematic social policy permitting them. The objection could be based on a fear that such a policy would lead to abuses by physicians, families, and others, or that it would lead to more permissive legislation allowing, say, nonvoluntary or active euthanasia.

DIRECTIVE TO PHYSICIANS

Directive made this _____ day of _____(month, year).

I _____ , being of sound mind, willfully and voluntarily make known my desire that my life shall not be artificially prolonged under the circumstances set forth below, do hereby declare:

1. If at any time I should have an incurable injury, disease, or illness certified to be a terminal condition by two physicians, and where the application of life-sustaining procedures would serve only to artificially prolong the moment of my death and where my physician determines that my death is imminent whether or not life-sustaining procedures are utilized, I direct that such procedures be withheld or withdrawn, and that I be permitted to die naturally.

2. In the absence of my ability to give directions regarding the use of such life-sustaining procedures, it is my intention that this directive shall be honored by my family and physician(s) as the final expression of my legal right to refuse medical or surgical treatment and accept the consequences from such refusal.

3. If I have been diagnosed as pregnant and that diagnosis is known to my physician, this directive shall have no force or effect during the course of my pregnancy.

4. I have been diagnosed and notified at least 14 days ago as having a terminal condition by _____ , M.D., whose address is _____ , and whose telephone number is _____ . I understand that if I have not filled in the physician's name and address, it shall be presumed that I did not have a terminal condition when I made out this directive.

5. This directive shall have no force or effect five years from the date filled in above.

6. I understand the full import of this directive and I am emotionally and mentally competent to make this directive.

Signed _____

City, County and State of Residence _____

The declarant has been personally known to me and I believe him or her to be of sound mind.

Witness _____

Witness _____

Figure 1

The Wrongfulness of Euthanasia

J. Gay-Williams

In this essay, professor of philosophy J. Gay-Williams defines euthanasia *as intentionally taking the life of a person suffering from some illness or injury from which recovery cannot reasonably be expected. While rejecting* voluntary euthanasia *as a* name *for actions that are usually designated by the phrase, Gay-Williams seems to approve of the actions themselves. He argues that euthanasia as intentional killing goes against natural law because it violates the natural inclination to preserve life. Furthermore, in Gay-Willlums's view, both self-interest and possible practical effects of euthanasia provide reasons for rejecting it.*

My impression is that euthanasia—the idea, if not the practice—is slowly gaining acceptance within our society. Cynics might attribute this to an increasing tendency to devalue human life, but I do not believe this is the major factor. The acceptance is much more likely to be the result of unthinking sympathy and benevolence. Well-publicized, tragic stories like that of Karen Quinlan elicit from us deep feelings of compassion. We think to ourselves, "She and her family would be better off if she were dead." It is an easy step from this very human response to the view that if someone (and others) would be better off dead, then it must be all right to kill that person.[1] Although I respect the compassion that leads to this conclusion, I believe the conclusion is wrong. I want to show that euthanasia is wrong. It is inherently wrong, but it is also wrong judged from the standpoints of self-interest and of practical effects.

Before presenting my arguments to support this claim, it would be well to define "euthanasia." An essential aspect of euthanasia is that it involves taking a human life, either one's own or that of another. Also, the person whose life is taken must be someone who is believed to be suffering from some disease or injury from which recovery cannot reasonably be expected. Finally, the action must be deliberate and intentional. Thus, euthanasia is intentionally taking the life of a presumably hopeless person. Whether the life is one's own or that of another, the taking of it is still euthanasia.

It is important to be clear about the deliberate and intentional aspect of the killing. If a hopeless person is given an injection of the wrong drug by mistake and this causes his death, this is wrongful killing but not euthanasia. The killing cannot be the result of accident. Furthermore, if the person is given an injection of a drug that is believed to be necessary to treat his disease or better his condition and the person dies as a result, then this is neither wrongful killing nor euthanasia. The intention was to make the patient well, not kill him. Similarly, when a patient's condition is such that it is not reasonable to hope that any medical procedures or treatments will save his life, a failure to implement the procedures or treatments is not euthanasia. If the person dies, this will be as a result of his injuries or disease and not because of his failure to receive treatment.

The failure to continue treatment after it has been realized that the patient has little chance of benefitting from it has been characterized by some as "passive euthanasia." This phrase is misleading and mistaken.[2] In such cases, the person involved is not killed (the first essential aspect of euthanasia), nor is the death of the person intended by the withholding of additional treatment (the third essential aspect of euthanasia). The aim may be to spare the person additional and unjustifiable pain, to save him from the indignities of hopeless manipulations, and to avoid increasing the financial and emotional burden on his family. When I buy a pencil it is so that I can use it to write, not to contribute to an increase in the gross national product. This

J. Gay-Williams, "The Wrongfulness of Euthanasia," from Ronald Munson, Intervention and Reflection: Basic Issues in Medical Ethics. *Copyright © 1979 by Wadsworth Publishing Company, Inc., 141–143. Reprinted by permission of the author and publisher.*

may be the unintended consequence of my action, but it is not the aim of my action. So it is with failing to continue the treatment of a dying person. I intend his death no more than I intend to reduce the GNP by not using medical supplies. His is an unintended dying, and so-called "passive euthanasia" is not euthanasia at all.

we are conscious through reason of our nature and our ends. Euthanasia involves acting as if this dual nature—inclination towards survival and awareness of this as an end—did not exist. Thus, euthanasia denies our basic human character and requires that we regard ourselves or others as something less than fully human.

1. The Argument from Nature

Every human being has a natural inclination to continue living. Our reflexes and responses fit us to fight attackers, flee wild animals, and dodge out of the way of trucks. In our daily lives we exercise the caution and care necessary to protect ourselves. Our bodies are similarly structured for survival right down to the molecular level. When we are cut, our capillaries seal shut, our blood clots, and fibrogen is produced to start the process of healing the wound. When we are invaded by bacteria, antibodies are produced to fight against the alien organisms, and their remains are swept out of the body by special cells designed for clean-up work.

Euthanasia does violence to this natural goal of survival. It is literally acting against nature because all the processes of nature are bent towards the end of bodily survival. Euthanasia defeats these subtle mechanisms in a way that, in a particular case, disease and injury might not.

It is possible, but not necessary, to make an appeal to revealed religion in this connection.[3] Man as trustee of his body acts against God, its rightful possessor, when he takes his own life. He also violates the commandment to hold life sacred and never to take it without just and compelling cause. But since this appeal will persuade only those who are prepared to accept that religion has access to revealed truths, I shall not employ this line of argument.

It is enough, I believe, to recognize that the organization of the human body and our patterns of behavioral responses make the continuation of life a natural goal. By reason alone, then, we can recognize that euthanasia sets us against our own nature.[4] Furthermore, in doing so, euthanasia does violence to our dignity. Our dignity comes from seeking our ends. When one of our goals is survival, and actions are taken that eliminate that goal, then our natural dignity suffers. Unlike animals,

2. The Argument from Self-Interest

The above arguments are, I believe, sufficient to show that euthanasia is inherently wrong. But there are reasons for considering it wrong when judged by standards other than reason. Because death is final and irreversible, euthanasia contains within it the possibility that we will work against our own interest if we practice it or allow it to be practiced on us.

Contemporary medicine has high standards of excellence and a proven record of accomplishment, but it does not possess perfect and complete knowledge. A mistaken diagnosis is possible, and so is a mistaken prognosis. Consequently, we may believe that we are dying of a disease when, as a matter of fact, we may not be. We may think that we have no hope of recovery when, as a matter of fact, our chances are quite good. In such circumstances, if euthanasia were permitted, we would die needlessly. Death is final and the chance of error too great to approve the practice of euthanasia.

Also, there is always the possibility that an experimental procedure or a hitherto untried technique will pull us through. We should at least keep this option open, but euthanasia closes it off. Furthermore, spontaneous remission does occur in many cases. For no apparent reason, a patient simply recovers when those all around him, including his physicians, expected him to die. Euthanasia would just guarantee their expectations and leave no room for the "miraculous" recoveries that frequently occur.

Finally, knowing that we can take our life at any time (or ask another to take it) might well incline us to give up too easily. The will to live is strong in all of us, but it can be weakened by pain and suffering and feelings of hopelessness. If during a bad time we allow ourselves to be killed, we never have a chance to reconsider. Recovery from a serious illness requires that we fight for it, and anything that weakens our determination by suggesting that there is an easy way out is ultimately against our own interest. Also, we may be inclined towards euthanasia because of our concern for others. If we see our sickness and suffering as an emotional and financial burden on our family, we may feel that to leave our life is to make their lives easier.[5] The very presence of the possibility of euthanasia may keep us from surviving when we might.

3. The Argument from Practical Effects

Doctors and nurses are, for the most part, totally committed to saving lives. A life lost is, for them, almost a personal failure, an insult to their skills and knowledge. Euthanasia as a practice might well alter this. It could have a corrupting influence so that in any case that is severe doctors and nurses might not try hard enough to save the patient. They might decide that the patient would simply be "better off dead" and take the steps necessary to make that come about. This attitude could then carry over to their dealings with patients less seriously ill. The result would be an overall decline in the quality of medical care.

Finally, euthanasia as a policy is a slippery slope. A person apparently hopelessly ill may be allowed to take his own life. Then he may be permitted to deputize others to do it for him should he no longer be able to act. The judgment of others then becomes the ruling factor. Already at this point euthanasia is not personal and voluntary, for others are acting "on behalf of" the patient as they see fit. This may well incline them to act on behalf of other patients who have not authorized them to exercise their judgment. It is only a short step, then, from voluntary euthanasia (self-inflicted or authorized), to directed euthanasia administered to a patient who has given no authorization, to involuntary euthanasia conducted as part of a social policy.[6] Recently many psychiatrists and sociologists have argued that we define as "mental illness" those forms of behavior that we disapprove of.[7] This gives us license then to lock up those who display the behavior. The category of the "hopelessly ill" provides the possibility of even worse abuse. Embedded in a social policy, it would give society or its representatives the authority to eliminate all those who might be considered too "ill" to function normally any

longer. The dangers of euthanasia are too great to all to run the risk of approving it in any form. The first slippery step may well lead to a serious and harmful fall.

I hope that I have succeeded in showing why the benevolence that inclines us to give approval of euthanasia is misplaced. Euthanasia is inherently wrong because it violates the nature and dignity of human beings. But even those who are not convinced by this must be persuaded that the potential personal and social dangers inherent in euthanasia are sufficient to forbid our approving it either as a personal practice or as a public policy.

Suffering is surely a terrible thing, and we have a clear duty to comfort those in need and to ease their suffering when we can. But suffering is also a natural part of life with values for the individual and for others that we should not overlook. We may legitimately seek for others and for ourselves an easeful death, as Arthur Dyck has pointed out.[8] Euthanasia, however, is not just an easeful death. It is a wrongful death. Euthanasia is not just dying. It is killing.

Notes

1. For a sophisticated defense of this position see Philippa Foot, "Euthanasia," *Philosophy and Public Affairs*, vol. 6 (1977), pp. 85–112. Foot does not endorse the radical conclusion that euthanasia, voluntary and involuntary, is always right.

2. James Rachels rejects the distinction between active and passive euthanasia as morally irrelevant in his "Active and Passive Euthanasia," *New England Journal of Medicine*, vol. 292, pp. 78–80. But see the criticism by Foot, pp. 100–103.

3. For a defense of this view see J. V. Sullivan, "The Immorality of Euthanasia," in *Beneficent Euthanasia*, ed. Marvin Kohl (Buffalo, New York: Prometheus Books, 1975), pp. 34–44.

4. This point is made by Ray V. McIntyre in "Voluntary Euthanasia: The Ultimate Perversion," *Medical Counterpoint*, vol. 2, 26–29.

5. See McIntyre, p. 28.

6. See Sullivan, "Immorality of Euthanasia," pp. 34–44, for a fuller argument in support of this view.

7. See, for example, Thomas S. Szasz, *The Myth of Mental Illness*, rev. ed. (New York: Harper & Row, 1974).

8. Arthur Dyck, "Beneficent Euthanasia and Benemortasia," in Kohl, op. cit., pp. 117–129.

Questions for Analysis

1. *Why doesn't Gay-Williams consider "passive euthanasia" an act of euthanasia? Do you agree with his distinction?*

2. *Would it be accurate to say that Gay-Williams applies both religious and nonreligious interpretations to argue against euthanasia? Explain.*

3. *State his arguments from self-interest.*

4. *State his arguments from practical effects. Which moral principle or type of ethical theory does this reflect?*

5. *What critical inquiries, if any, would you make about the author's arguments against euthanasia?*

6. *Can Gay-Williams's arguments be equally applied against passive euthanasia?*

Active and Passive Euthanasia

James Rachels

The traditional view that there is an important moral difference between active and passive euthanasia is one that was endorsed by J. Gay-Williams in the preceding essay. Active euthanasia involves killing and passive euthanasia letting die, and this fact has led many physicians and philosophers to reject active euthanasia as morally wrong, even while approving of passive euthanasia.

In this essay, professor of philosophy James Rachels challenges both the use and moral significance of this distinction for several reasons. First, active euthanasia is in many cases more humane than passive. Second, the conventional doctrine leads to decisions concerning life and death on irrelevant grounds. Third, the doctrine rests on a distinction between killing and letting die that itself has no moral significance. Fourth, the most common arguments in favor of the doctrine are invalid. Therefore, in Rachels's view, the American Medical Association's policy statement endorsing the active-passive distinction is unwise.

The distinction between active and passive euthanasia is thought to be crucial for medical ethics. The idea is that it is permissible, at least in some cases, to withhold treatment and allow a patient to die, but it is never permissible to take any direct action designed to kill the patient. This doctrine seems to be accepted by most doctors, and it is endorsed in a statement adopted by the House of Delegates of the American Medical Association on December 4, 1973:

> The intentional termination of the life of one human being by another—mercy kill-

ing—is contrary to that for which the medical profession stands and is contrary to the policy of the American Medical Association.

> The cessation of the employment of extraordinary means to prolong the life of the body when there is irrefutable evidence that biological death is imminent is the decision of the patient and/or his immediate family. The advice and judgment of the physician should be freely available to the patient and/or his immediate family.

However, a strong case can be made against this doctrine. In what follows I will set out some of the

From James Rachels, "Active and Passive Euthanasia," New England Journal of Medicine, 292 (January 9, 1975), 78–80. Reprinted by permission of the publisher.

relevant arguments, and urge doctors to reconsider their views on this matter.

To begin with a familiar type of situation, a patient who is dying of incurable cancer of the throat is in terrible pain, which can no longer be satisfactorily alleviated. He is certain to die within a few days, even if present treatment is continued, but he does not want to go on living for those days since the pain is unbearable. So he asks the doctor for an end to it, and his family joins in the request.

Suppose the doctor agrees to withhold treatment, as the conventional doctrine says he may. The justification for his doing so is that the patient is in terrible agony, and since he is going to die anyway, it would be wrong to prolong his suffering needlessly. But now notice this. If one simply withholds treatment, it may take the patient longer to die, and so he may suffer more than he would if more direct action were taken and a lethal injection given. This fact provides strong reason for thinking that, once the initial decision not to prolong his agony has been made, active euthanasia is actually preferable to passive euthanasia, rather than the reverse. To say otherwise is to endorse the option that leads to more suffering rather than less, and is contrary to the humanitarian impulse that prompts the decision not to prolong his life in the first place.

Part of my point is that the process of being "allowed to die" can be relatively slow and painful, whereas being given a lethal injection is relatively quick and painless. Let me give a different sort of example. In the United States about one in 600 babies is born with Down's syndrome. Most of these babies are otherwise healthy—that is, with only the usual pediatric care, they will proceed to an otherwise normal infancy. Some, however, are born with congenital defects such as intestinal obstructions that require operations if they are to live. Sometimes, the patients and the doctor will decide not to operate, and let the infant die. Anthony Shaw describes what happens then:

> . . . When surgery is denied [the doctor] must try to keep the infant from suffering while natural forces sap the baby's life away. As a surgeon whose natural inclination is to use the scalpel to fight off death, standing by and watching a salvageable baby die is the most emotionally enhausting experience I know. It is easy at a conference, in a theoretical discussion, to decide that such infants should be allowed to die. It is altogether dif-

ferent to stand by in the nursery and watch as dehydration and infection wither a tiny being over hours and days. This is a terrible ordeal for me and the hospital staff—much more so than for the parents who never set foot in the nursery.[1]

I can understand why some people are opposed to all euthanasia, and insist that such infants must be allowed to live. I think I can also understand why other people favor destroying these babies quickly and painlessly. But why should anyone favor letting "dehydration and infection wither a tiny being over hours and days"? The doctrine that says that a baby may be allowed to dehydrate and wither, but may not be given an injection that would end its life without suffering, seems so patently cruel as to require no further refutation. The strong language is not intended to offend, but only to put the point in the clearest possible way.

My second argument is that the conventional doctrine leads to decisions concerning life and death made on irrelevant grounds.

Consider again the case of the infants with Down's syndrome who need operations for congenital defects unrelated to the syndrome to live. Sometimes, there is no operation, and the baby dies, but when there is no such defect, the baby lives on. Now, an operation such as that to remove an intestinal obstruction is not prohibitively difficult. The reason why such operations are not performed in these cases is, clearly, that the child has Down's syndrome and the parents and the doctor judge that because of that fact it is better for the child to die.

But notice that this situation is absurd, no matter what view one takes of the lives and potentials of such babies. If the life of such an infant is worth preserving, what does it matter if it needs a simple operation? Or, if one thinks it better that such a baby should not live on, what difference does it make that it happens to have an unobstructed intestinal tract? In either case, the matter of life and death is being decided on irrelevant grounds. It is the Down's syndrome, and not the intestines, that is the issue. The matter should be decided, if at all, on that basis, and not be allowed to depend on the essentially irrelevant question of whether the intestinal tract is blocked.

What makes this situation possible, of course, is the idea that when there is an intestinal blockage, one can "let the baby die," but when there is no such defect there is nothing that can be done, for one must not "kill" it. The fact that this idea leads to such results as deciding life or death on irrelevant grounds is another good reason why the doctrine should be rejected.

One reason why so many people think that there is an important moral difference between active and passive euthanasia is that they think killing someone is morally worse than letting someone die. But is it? Is killing, in itself, worse than letting die? To investigate this issue, two cases may be considered that are exactly alike except that one involves killing whereas the other involves letting someone die. Then, it can be asked whether this difference makes any difference to the moral assessments. It is important that the cases be exactly alike, except for this one difference, since otherwise one cannot be confident that it is this difference and not some other that accounts for any variation in the assessments of the two cases. So, let us consider this pair of cases:

In the first, Smith stands to gain a large inheritance if anything should happen to his six-year-old cousin. One evening while the child is taking his bath, Smith sneaks into the bathroom and drowns the child, and then arranges things so that it will look like an accident.

In the second, Jones also stands to gain if anything should happen to his six-year-old cousin. Like Smith, Jones sneaks in planning to drown the child in his bath. However, just as he enters the bathroom Jones sees the child slip and hit his head, and fall face down in the water. Jones is delighted; he stands by, ready to push the child's head back under if it is necessary, but it is not necessary. With only a little thrashing about, the child drowns all by himself, "accidentally," as Jones watches and does nothing.

Now Smith killed the child, whereas Jones "merely" let the child die. That is the only difference between them. Did either man behave better, from a moral point of view? If the difference between killing and letting die were in itself a morally important matter, one should say that Jones's behavior was less reprehensible than Smith's. But does one really want to say that? I think not. In the first place, both men acted from the same motive, personal gain, and both had exactly the same end in view when they acted. It may be inferred from

Smith's conduct that he is a bad man, although that judgment may be withdrawn or modified if certain further facts are learned about him—for example, that he is mentally deranged. But would not the very same thing be inferred about Jones from his conduct? And would not the same further considerations also be relevant to any modification of this judgment? Moreover, suppose Jones pleaded, in his own defense, "After all, I didn't do anything except just stand there and watch the child drown. I didn't kill him; I only let him die." Again, if letting die were in itself less bad than killing, this defense should have at least some weight. But it does not. Such a "defense" can only be regarded as a grotesque perversion of moral reasoning. Morally speaking, it is no defense at all.

Now, it may be pointed out, quite properly, that the cases of euthanasia with which doctors are concerned are not like this at all. They do not involve personal gain or the destruction of normal healthy children. Doctors are concerned only with cases in which the patient's life is of no further use to him, or in which the patient's life has become or will soon become a terrible burden. However, the point is the same in these cases: The bare difference between killing and letting die does not, in itself, make a moral difference. If a doctor lets a patient die, for humane reasons, he is in the same moral position as if he had given the patient a lethal injection for humane reasons. If his decision was wrong—if, for example, the patient's illness was in fact curable—the decision would be equally regrettable no matter which method was used to carry it out. And if the doctor's decision was the right one, the method used is not in itself important.

The AMA policy statement isolates the crucial issue very well: The crucial issue is "the intentional termination of the life of one human being by another." But after identifying this issue, and forbidding "mercy killing," the statement goes on to deny that the cessation of treatment is the intentional termination of a life. This is where the mistake comes in, for what is the cessation of treatment, in these circumstances, if it is not "the intentional termination of the life of one human being by another"? Of course it is exactly that, and if it were not, there would be no point to it.

Many people will find this judgment hard to accept. One reason, I think, is that it is very easy to conflate the question of whether killing is, in itself, worse than letting die, with the very different question of whether most actual cases of killing are more reprehensible than most actual cases of letting die. Most actual cases of killing are clearly terrible (think, for example, of all the murders reported in the newspapers), and one hears of such cases everyday. On the other hand, one hardly ever hears of a case of letting die, except for the actions of doctors who are motivated by humanitarian reasons. So one learns to think of killing in a much worse light than of letting die. But this does not mean that there is something about killing that makes it in itself worse than letting die, for it is not the bare difference between killing and letting die that makes the difference in these cases. Rather, the other factors—the murderer's motive of personal gain, for example, contrasted with the doctor's humanitarian motivation—account for different reactions to the different cases.

I have argued that killing is not in itself any worse than letting die; if my contention is right, it follows that active euthanasia is not any worse than passive euthanasia. What arguments can be given on the other side? The most common, I believe, is the following:

"The important difference between active and passive euthanasia is that in passive euthanasia, the doctor does not do anything to bring about the patient's death. The doctor does nothing, and the patient dies of whatever ills already afflict him. In active euthanasia, however, the doctor does something to bring about the patient's death: He kills him. The doctor who gives the patient with cancer a lethal injection has himself caused his patient's death; whereas if he merely ceases treatment, the cancer is the cause of death."

A number of points need to be made here. The first is that it is not exactly correct to say that in passive euthanasia the doctor does nothing, for he does do one thing that is very important: He lets the patient die. "Letting someone die" is certainly different, in some respects, from other types of action—mainly in that it is a kind of action that one may perform by way of not performing certain other actions. For example, one may let a patient die by way of not giving medication, just as one may insult someone by way of not shaking his hand. But for any purpose of moral assessment, it is a type of action nonetheless. The decision to let a patient die is subject to moral appraisal in the same way that

a decision to kill him would be subject to moral appraisal: It may be assessed as wise or unwise, compassionate or sadistic, right or wrong. If a doctor deliberately let a patient die who was suffering from a routinely curable illness, the doctor would certainly be to blame for what he had done, just as he would be to blame if he had needlessly killed the patient. Charges against him would then be appropriate. If so, it would be no defense at all for him to insist that he didn't "do anything." He would have done something very serious indeed, for he let his patient die.

Fixing the cause of death may be very important from a legal point of view, for it may determine whether criminal charges are brought against the doctor. But I do not think that this notion can be used to show a moral difference between active and passive euthanasia. The reason why it is considered bad to be the cause of someone's death is that death is regarded as a great evil—and so it is. However, if it has been decided that euthanasia—even passive euthanasia—is desirable in a given case, it has also been decided that in this instance death is no greater an evil than the patient's continued existence. And if this is true, the usual reason for not wanting to be the cause of someone's death simply does not apply.

Finally, doctors may think that all of this is only of academic interest—the sort of thing that philosophers may worry about but that has no practical bearing on their own work. After all, doctors must be concerned about the legal consequences of what they do, and active euthanasia is clearly forbidden by the law. But even so, doctors should also be concerned with the fact that the law is forcing upon them a moral doctrine that may well be indefensible, and has a considerable effect on their practices. Of course, most doctors are not now in the position of being coerced in this matter, for they do not regard themselves as merely going along with what the law requires. Rather, in statements such as the AMA policy statement that I have quoted, they are endorsing this doctrine as a central point of medical ethics. In that statement, active euthanasia is condemned not merely as illegal but as "contrary to that for which the medical profession stands," whereas passive euthanasia is approved. However, the preceding considerations suggest that there is really no moral difference between the two, considered in themselves (there may be important moral differences in some cases in their *consequences*, but, as I pointed out, these differences may make active euthanasia, and not passive euthanasia, the morally preferable option). So, whereas doctors may have to discriminate between active and passive euthanasia to satisfy the law, they should not do any more than that. In particular, they should not give the distinction any added authority and weight by writing it into official statements of medical ethics.

Note

1. A. Shaw, "Doctor, Do We Have a Choice?" *The New York Times Magazine,* January 30, 1972, p. 54.

Questions for Analysis

1. Early in his essay, Rachels sets up a familiar situation involving a throat-cancer patient. What is the point of the example? Do you think that suspending pain-relieving drugs is what people generally understand by "withholding treatment"?

2. Explain, through Rachels's own example of the infant with Down's syndrome, why he thinks the distinction between active and passive euthanasia leads to life-or-death decisions made on irrelevant grounds.

3. Do you agree with Rachels that the cessation of treatment is tantamount to the intentional termination of life?

4. Rachels claims that killing is not necessarily any worse than allowing a person to die. What are the implications of this claim for the morality of active euthanasia?

5. Rachels believes it is inaccurate and misleading to say that a doctor who allows a patient to die does "nothing" to cause the death. Do you agree?

Euthanasia

Philippa Foot

Griffin Professor of Philosophy Philippa Foot, as part of her general concerns in her essay, develops a distinction between active and passive euthanasia by using the notion of a "right to life." She disagrees with Rachels, who criticizes the distinction between active and passive as morally irrelevant and inhumane in application. In contrast, Foot offers cases to show the value of making and using the distinction.

The basic issue Foot considers, however, is whether one is ever morally justified in killing people for their own good. Replying, Foot examines the idea of "ordinary human life" and explores the question of when someone's life might be regarded as not worth living any longer. She doesn't believe that it's legitimate for us to decide that for someone else. In her view, everyone has a right to life in the sense she specifies; it is what a person wants that counts. Thus even if someone would be better off dead, if that person wants to live, we aren't justified in killing him or her. In short, Foot cannot support nonvoluntary active euthanasia. Furthermore, if a person both wants to live and has a right to medical treatment, then involuntary passive euthanasia isn't justified either.

But what of cases involving those whose wishes we don't know—for example, patients in a comatose state? Foot argues that taking the lives of such people would infringe their rights. So she rejects nonvoluntary active euthanasia in these cases. But she does concede that there are cases in which the comatose, were they able, would not want to be kept alive artificially. This leads her to conclude that nonvoluntary passive euthanasia may be sometime morally permissible.

Although Foot does endorse both forms of voluntary euthanasia (active and passive) as morally legitimate, she doesn't believe that we have a duty to kill people who have decided their lives are no longer worth living. For Foot, the explicit consent by such people merely guarantees that we would not be infringing their right to life by following their wishes.

The widely used *Shorter Oxford English Dictionary* gives three meanings for the word "euthanasia": the first, "a quiet and easy death"; the second, "the means of procuring this"; and the third, "the action of inducing a quiet and easy death." It is a curious fact that no one of the three gives an adequate definition of the word as it is usually understood. For "euthanasia" means much more than a quiet and easy death, or the means of procuring it, or the action of inducing it. The definition specifies only the manner of the death, and if this were all that was implied, a murderer, careful to drug his victim, could claim that his act was an act of euthanasia. We find this ridiculous because we take it for granted that in euthanasia it is death itself, not just the manner of death, that must be kind to the one who dies.

To see how important it is that "euthanasia" should not be used as the dictionary definition allows it to be used, merely to signify that a death was quiet and easy, one has only to remember that Hitler's "euthanasia" program traded on this ambiguity. Under this program, planned before the War but brought into full operation by a decree of 1 September 1939, some 275,000 people were gassed in centers which were to be a model for those in which Jews were later exterminated. Anyone in a state institution could be sent to the gas chambers if it was considered that he could not be "rehabilitated" for useful work. As Dr. Leo Alexander reports, relying on the testimony of a neuropathologist who received 500 brains from one of the killing centers,

> In Germany the exterminations included the mentally defective, psychotics (particularly schizophrenics), epileptics and patients suffering from infirmities of old age and from various organic neurological disorders such as infantile paralysis, Parkinsonism, multiple sclerosis and brain tumors. . . . In truth, all those unable to work and considered nonrehabilitable were killed.[1]

These people were killed because they were "useless" and "a burden on society"; only the manner of their deaths could be thought of as relatively easy and quiet.

Let us insist, then, that when we talk about euthanasia we are talking about a death understood as a good or happy event for the one who dies. This stipulation follows etymology, but is itself not exactly in line with current usage, which would be captured by the condition that the death should *not* be an evil rather than that it *should* be a good. That this is how people talk is shown by the fact that the case of Karen Ann Quinlan and others in a state of permanent coma is often discussed under the heading of "euthanasia." Perhaps it is not too late to object to the use of the word "euthanasia" in this sense. Apart from the break with the Greek origins of the word, there are other unfortunate aspects of this extension of the term. For if we say that the death must be supposed to be a good to the subject, we can also specify that it shall be for his sake that an act of euthanasia is performed. If we say merely that death shall not be an evil to him, we cannot stipulate that benefiting him shall be the motive where euthanasia is in question. Given the importance of the question, For whose sake are we acting? It is good to have a definition of euthanasia which brings under this heading only cases of opting for death for the sake of the one who dies. Perhaps what is most important is to say either that euthanasia is to be for the good of the subject or at least that death is to be no evil to him, thus refusing to talk Hitler's language. However, in this paper it is the first condition that will be understood, with the additional proviso that by an act of euthanasia we mean one of inducing or otherwise opting for death for the sake of the one who is to die.

A few lesser points need to be cleared up. In the first place it must be said that the word "act" is not to be taken to exclude omission; we shall speak of an act of euthanasia when someone is deliberately allowed to die, for his own good, and not only when positive measures are taken to see that he does. The very general idea we want is that of a choice of action or inaction directed at another man's death and causally effective in the sense that, in conjunction with actual circumstances, it is a sufficient condition of death. Of complications such as overdetermination, it will not be necessary to speak.

A second, and definitely minor, point about the definition of an act of euthanasia concerns the question of fact versus belief. It has already been implied that one who performs an act of euthanasia thinks that death will be merciful for the subject since we have said that it is on account of this thought that the act is done. But is it enough that he acts with this thought, or must things actually be as he thinks them to be? If one man kills another, or allows him to die, thinking that he is in the last stages of a terrible disease, though in fact he could have been cured, is this an act of euthanasia or not? Nothing much seems to hang on our decision about this. The same condition has got to enter into the definition whether as an element in reality or only as an element in the agent's belief. And however we define an act of euthanasia, culpability or justifiability will be the same: if a man acts through ignorance, his ignorance may be culpable or it may not.[2]

These are relatively easy problems to solve, but one that is dauntingly difficult has been passed over in this discussion of the definition, and must now be faced. It is easy to say, as if this raised no problems, that an act of euthanasia is by definition one aiming at the *good* of the one whose death is in question, and that it is *for his sake* that his death is desired. But how is this to be explained? Presumably we are thinking of some evil already with him or to come on him if he continues to live, and death is thought of as a release from this evil. But this cannot be enough. Most people's lives contain evils such as grief or pain, but we do not therefore think that death would be a blessing to them. On the contrary, life is generally supposed to be a good even for someone who is unusually unhappy or frustrated. How is it that one can ever wish for death for the sake of the one who is to die? This difficult question is central to the discussion of euthanasia, and we shall literally not know what we are talking about if we ask whether acts of euthanasia defined as we have defined them are ever morally permissible without first understanding better the reason for saying that life is a good, and the possibility that it is not always so.

If a man should save my life he would be my benefactor. In normal circumstances this is plainly true; but does one always benefit another in saving his life? It seems certain that he does not. Suppose, for instance, that a man were being tortured to death and was given a drug that lengthened his sufferings; this would not be a benefit but the reverse. Or suppose that in a ghetto in Nazi Germany a doctor saved the life of someone threatened by disease, but that the man once cured was transported to an extermination camp; the doctor might wish for the sake of the patient that he had died of the disease. Nor would a longer stretch of life always be a benefit to the person who was given it. Comparing Hitler's camps with those of Stalin, Dmitri Panin observes that in the latter the method of extermination was made worse by agonies that could stretch out over months.

> Death from a bullet would have been bliss compared with what many millions had to endure while dying of hunger. The kind of death to which they were condemned has nothing to equal it in treachery and sadism.[3]

These examples show that to save or prolong a man's life is not always to do him a service: it may be better for him if he dies earlier rather than later. It must therefore be agreed that while life is normally a benefit to the one who has it, this is not always so.

The judgment is often fairly easy to make—that life is or is not a good to someone—but the basis for it is very hard to find. When life is said to be a benefit or a good, on what grounds is the assertion made?

The difficulty is underestimated if it is supposed that the problem arises from the fact that one who is dead has nothing, so that the good someone gets from being alive cannot be compared with the amount he would otherwise have had. For why should this particular comparison be necessary? Surely it would be enough if one could say whether or not someone whose life was prolonged had more good than evil in the extra stretch of time. Such estimates are not always possible, but frequently they are; we say, for example, "He was very happy in those last years," or, "He had little but unhappiness then." If the balance of good and evil determined whether life was a good to someone, we would expect to find a correlation in the judgments. In fact, of course, we find nothing of the kind. First, a man who has no doubt that existence is a good to him may have no idea about the balance of happiness and unhappiness in his life, or of any other positive and negative factors that may be suggested. So the supposed criteria are not always operating where the judgment is made. And secondly, the application of the criteria gives an answer that is often wrong. Many people have more evil than good in their lives; we do not, however, conclude that we would do these people no service by rescuing them from death.

To get around this last difficulty Thomas Nagel has suggested that experience itself is a good which must be brought in to balance accounts.

> . . . life is worth living even when the bad elements of experience are plentiful, and the good ones too meager to outweigh the bad ones on their own. The additional positive weight is supplied by experience itself, rather than by any of its contents.[4]

This seems implausible because if experience itself is a good it must be so even when what we experience is wholly bad, as in being tortured to death. How should one decide how much to count for this experiencing; and why count anything at all?

Others have tried to solve the problem by arguing that it is a man's desire for life that makes us call life a good: if he wants to live, then anyone who prolongs his life does him a benefit. Yet someone may cling to life where we would say confidently that it would be better for him if he died, and he may admit it too. Speaking of those same conditions in which, as he said, a bullet would have been merciful, Panin writes,

> I should like to pass on my observations concerning the absence of suicides under the extremely severe conditions of our concentration camps. The more that life became desperate, the more a prisoner seemed determined to hold on to it.[5]

One might try to explain this by saying that hope was the ground of this wish to survive for further days and months in the camp. But there is nothing unintelligible in the idea that a man might cling to life though he knew those facts about his future which would make any charitable man wish that he might die.

The problem remains, and it is hard to know where to look for a solution. Is there a conceptual connection between *life* and *good*? Because life is not always a good we are apt to reject this idea, and to think that it must be a contingent fact that life is usually a good, as it is a contingent matter that legacies are usually a benefit, if they are. Yet it seems not to be a contingent matter that to save someone's life is ordinarily to benefit him. The problem is to find where the conceptual connection lies.

It may be good tactics to forget for a time that it is euthanasia we are discussing and to see how *life* and *good* are connected in the case of living beings other than men. Even plants have things done to them that are harmful or beneficial, and what does them good must be related in some way to their living and dying. Let us therefore consider plants and animals, and then come back to human beings. At least we shall get away from the temptation to think that the connection between life and benefit must everywhere be a matter of happiness and unhappiness or of pleasure and pain; the idea being absurd in the case of animals and impossible even to formulate for plants.

In case anyone thinks that the concept of the beneficial applies only in a secondary or analogical way to plants, he should be reminded that we speak quite straightforwardly in saying, for instance, that a certain amount of sunlight is beneficial to most plants. What is in question here is the habitat in which plants of particular species flourish, but we can also talk, in a slightly different way, of what does them good, where there is some suggestion of improvement or remedy. What has the beneficial to do with sustaining life? It is tempting to answer, "everything," thinking that a healthy condition just is the one apt to secure survival. In fact, however, what is beneficial to a plant may have to do with reproduction rather than the survival of the individual member of the species. Nevertheless there is a plain connection between the beneficial and the life-sustaining even for the individual plant; if something makes it better able to survive in conditions normal for that species, it is ipso facto good for it. We need go no further, and could go no further, in explaining why a certain environment or treatment is good for a plant than to show how it helps this plant to survive.[6]

This connection between the life-sustaining and the beneficial is reasonably unproblematic, and there is nothing fanciful or zoomorphic in speaking of benefiting or doing good to plants. A connection with its survival can make something beneficial to a plant. But this is not, of course, to say that we count life as a good to a plant. We may save its life by giving it what is beneficial; we do not benefit it by saving its life.

A more ramified concept of benefit is used in speaking of animal life. New things can be said, such as that an animal is better or worse off for something that happened, or that it was a good or bad thing for it that it did happen. And new things count as benefit. In the first place, there is comfort, which often is, but need not be, related to health. When loosening a collar which is too tight for a dog we can say, "That will be better for it." So we see that the words "better for it" have two different meanings which we mark when necessary by a difference of emphasis, saying "better *for* it" when health is involved. And secondly, an animal can be benefited by having its life saved. "Could you do anything for it?" can be answered by, "Yes, I managed to save its life." Sometimes we may understand this, just as we would for a plant, to mean that we had checked some disease. But we can also do something for an animal by scaring away its predator. If we do this, it is a good thing for the animal that we did, unless of course it immediately meets a more unpleasant end by some other means. Similarly, on the bad side, an animal may be worse off for our intervention, and this is not because it pines or suffers but simply because it gets killed.

The problem that vexes us when we think about euthanasia comes on the scene at this point. For if we can do something for an animal—can benefit it—by relieving its suffering but also by saving its life, where does the greater benefit come when only death will end pain? It seemed that life was a good in its own right; yet pain seemed to be an evil with equal status and could therefore make life not a

good after all. Is it only life without pain that is a good when animals are concerned? This does not seem a crazy suggestion when we are thinking of animals, since unlike human beings they do not have suffering as part of their normal life. But it is perhaps the idea of ordinary life that matters here. We would not say that we had done anything for an animal if we had merely kept it alive, either in an unconscious state or in a condition where, though conscious, it was unable to operate in an ordinary way; and the fact is that animals in severe and continuous pain simply do not operate normally. So we do not, on the whole, have the option of doing the animal good by saving its life though the life would be a life of pain. No doubt there are borderline cases, but that is no problem. We are not trying to make new judgments possible, but rather to find the principle of the ones we do make.

When we reach human life, the problems seem even more troublesome. For now we must take quite new things into account, such as the subject's own view of his life. It is arguable that this places extra constraints on the solution: might it not be counted as a necessary condition of life's being a good to a man that he should see it as such? Is there not some difficulty about the idea that a benefit might be done to him by saving or prolonging his life even though he himself wished for death? Of course he might have a quite mistaken view of his own prospects, but let us ignore this and think only of cases where it is life as he knows it that is in question. Can we think that the prolonging of this life would be a benefit to him even though he would rather have it end than continue? It seems that this cannot be ruled out. That there is no simple incompatibility between life as a good and the wish for death is shown by the possibility that a man should wish himself dead, not for his own sake, but for the sake of someone else. And if we try to amend the thesis to say that life cannot be a good to one who wishes *for his own sake* that he should die, we find the crucial concept slipping through our fingers. As Bishop Butler pointed out long ago, not all ends are either benevolent or self-interested. Does a man wish for death for his own sake in the relevant sense if, for instance, he wishes to revenge himself on another by his death? Or what if he is proud and refuses to stomach dependence or incapacity even though there are many good things left in life for him? The truth seems to be that the wish for death is sometimes compatible with life's being a good and sometimes not, which is possible because the description "wishing for death" is one covering diverse states of mind from that of the determined suicide, pathologically depressed, to that of one who is surprised to find that the thought of a fatal accident is viewed with relief. On the one hand, a man may see his life as a burden but go about his business in a more or less ordinary way; on the other hand, the wish for death may take the form of a rejection of everything that is in life, as it does in severe depression. It seems reasonable to say that life is not a good to one permanently in the latter state, and we must return to this topic later on.

When are we to say that life is a good or a benefit to a man? The dilemma that faces us is this. If we say that life as such is a good, we find ourselves refuted by the examples given at the beginning of this discussion. We therefore incline to think that it is as bringing good things that life is a good, where it is a good. But if life is a good only because it is the condition of good things, why is it not equally an evil when it brings bad things? And how can it be a good even when it brings more evil than good?

It should be noted that the problem has here been formulated in terms of the balance of good and evil, not that of happiness and unhappiness, and that it is not to be solved by the denial (which may be reasonable enough) that unhappiness is the only evil or happiness the only good. In this paper no view has been expressed about the nature of goods other than life itself. The point is that on any view of the goods and evils that life can contain, it seems that a life with more evil than good could still itself be a good.

It may be useful to review the judgments with which our theory must square. Do we think that life can be a good to one who suffers a lot of pain? Clearly we do. What about severely handicapped people; can life be a good to them? Clearly it can be, for even if someone is almost completely paralyzed, perhaps living in an iron lung, perhaps able to move things only by means of a tube held between his lips, we do not rule him out of order if he says that some benefactor saved his life. Nor is it different with mental handicap. There are many fairly severely handicapped people—such as those with Down's Syndrome (Mongolism)—for whom a simple affectionate life is possible. What about senility?

Does this break the normal connection between life and good? Here we must surely distinguish between forms of senility. Some forms leave a life which we count someone as better off having than not having, so that a doctor who prolonged it would benefit the person concerned. With some kinds of senility this is, however, no longer true. There are some in geriatric wards who are barely conscious, though they can move a little and swallow food put into their mouths. To prolong such a state, whether in the old or in the very severely mentally handicapped, is not to do them a service or confer a benefit. But of course it need not be the reverse: only if there is suffering would one wish for the sake of the patient that he should die.

It seems, therefore, that merely being alive even without suffering is not a good, and that we must make a distinction similar to that which we made when animals were our topic. But how is the line to be drawn in the case of men? What is to count as ordinary human life in the relevant sense? If it were only the very senile or very ill who were to be said not to have this life, it might seem right to describe it in terms of *operation*. But it will be hard to find the sense in which the men described by Panin were not operating, given that they dragged themselves out to the forest to work. What is it about the life that the prisoners were living that makes us put it on the other side of the dividing line from that of some severely ill or suffering patients, and from most of the physically or mentally handicapped? It is not that they were in captivity, for life in captivity can certainly be a good. Nor is it merely the unusual nature of their life. In some ways the prisoners were living more as other men do than the patient in an iron lung.

The suggested solution to the problem is, then, that there is a certain conceptual connection between *life* and *good* in the case of human beings as in that of animals and even plants. Here, as there, however, it is not the mere state of being alive that can determine, or itself count as, a good, but rather life coming up to some standard of normality. It was argued that it is as part of ordinary life that the elements of good that a man may have are relevant to the question of whether saving his life counts as benefiting him. Ordinary human lives, even very hard lives, contain a minimum of basic goods, but when these are absent the idea of life is no longer linked to that of good. And since it is in this way that the elements of good contained in a man's life are relevant to the question of whether he is benefited if his life is preserved, there is no reason why it should be the balance of good and evil that counts.

It should be added that evils are relevant in one way when, as in the examples discussed above, they destroy the possibility of ordinary goods, but in a different way when they invade a life from which the goods are already absent for a different reason. So, for instance, the connection between *life* and *good* may be broken because consciousness has sunk to a very low level, as in extreme senility or severe brain damage. In itself this kind of life seems to be neither good nor evil, but if suffering sets in, one would hope for a speedy end.

The idea we need seems to be that of life which is ordinary human life in the following respect— that it contains a minimum of basic human goods. What is ordinary in human life—even in very hard lives—is that a man is not driven to work far beyond his capacity; that he has the support of a family or community; that he can more or less satisfy his hunger; that he has hopes for the future; that he can lie down to rest at night. Such things were denied to the men in the Vyatlag camps described by Panin; not even rest at night was allowed them when they were tormented by bed-bugs, by noise and stench, and by routines such as body-searches and bath-parades—arranged for the night time so that work norms would not be reduced. Disease too can so take over a man's life that the normal human goods disappear. When a patient is so overwhelmed by pain or nausea that he cannot eat with pleasure, if he can eat at all, and is out of the reach of even the most loving voice, he no longer has ordinary human life in the sense in which the words are used here. And we may now pick up a thread from an earlier part of the discussion by remarking that crippling depression can destroy the enjoyment of ordinary goods as effectively as external circumstances can remove them.

This, admittedly inadequate, discussion of the sense in which life is normally a good, and of the reasons why it may not be so in some particular case, completes the account of what euthanasia is here taken to be. An act of euthanasia, whether literally act or rather omission, is attributed to an agent who opts for the death of another because in his case life seems to be an evil rather than a good.

The question now to be asked is whether acts of euthanasia are ever justifiable. But there are two topics here rather than one. For it is one thing to say that some acts of euthanasia considered only in themselves and their results are morally unobjectionable, and another to say that it would be all right to legalize them. Perhaps the practice of euthanasia would allow too many abuses, and perhaps there would be too many mistakes. Moreover, the practice might have very important and highly undesirable side effects, because it is unlikely that we could change our principles about the treatment of the old and the ill without changing fundamental emotional attitudes and social relations. The topics must, therefore, be treated separately. In the next part of the discussion, nothing will be said about the social consequences and possible abuses of the practice of euthanasia, but only about acts of euthanasia considered in themselves.

What we want to know is whether acts of euthanasia, defined as we have defined them, are ever morally permissible. To be more accurate, we want to know whether it is ever sufficient justification of the choice of death for another that death can be counted a benefit rather than harm, and that this is why the choice is made.

It will be impossible to get a clear view of the area to which this topic belongs without first marking the distinct grounds on which objection may lie when one man opts for the death of another. There are two different virtues whose requirements are, in general, contrary to such actions. An unjustified act of killing, or allowing to die, is contrary to justice or to charity, or to both virtues, and the moral failings are distinct. Justice has to do with what men *owe* each other in the way of noninterference and positive service. When used in this wide sense, which has its history in the doctrine of the cardinal virtues, justice is not especially connected with, for instance, law courts but with the whole area of rights, and duties corresponding to rights. Thus murder is one form of injustice, dishonesty another, and wrongful failure to keep contracts a third; chicanery in a law court or defrauding someone of his inheritance are simply other cases of injustice. Justice as such is not directly linked to the good of another, and may require that something be rendered to him even where it will do him harm, as Hume pointed out when he remarked that a debt must be paid even to a profligate debauchee who "would rather receive harm than benefit from large possessions."[7] Charity, on the other hand, is the virtue which attaches us to the good of others. An act of charity is in question only where something is not demanded by justice, but a lack of charity and of justice can be shown where a man is denied something which he both needs and has a right to; both charity and justice demand that widows and orphans are not defrauded, and the man who cheats them is neither charitable nor just.

It is easy to see that the two grounds of objection to inducing death are distinct. A murder is an act of injustice. A culpable failure to come to the aid of someone whose life is threatened is normally contrary, not to justice, but to charity. But where one man is under contract, explicit or implicit, to come to the aid of another, injustice too will be shown. Thus injustice may be involved either in an act or an omission, and the same is true of a lack of charity; charity may demand that someone be aided, but also that an unkind word not be spoken.

The distinction between charity and justice will turn out to be of the first importance when voluntary and nonvoluntary euthanasia are distinguished later on. This is because of the connection between justice and rights, and something should now be said about this. I believe it is true to say that wherever a man acts unjustly he has infringed a right, since justice has to do with whatever a man is owed, and whatever he is owed is his as a matter of right. Something should therefore be said about the different kinds of rights. The distinction commonly made is between having a right in the sense of having a liberty, and having a "claim-right" or "right of recipience."[8] The best way to understand such a distinction seems to be as follows. To say that a man has a right in the sense of a liberty is to say that no one can demand that he do not do the thing which he has a right to do. The fact that he has a right to do it consists in the fact that a certain kind of objection does not lie against his doing it. Thus a man has a right in this sense to walk down a public street or park his car in a public parking space. It does not follow that no one else may prevent him from doing so. If for some reason I want a certain man not to park in a certain place I may lawfully park there myself or get my friends to do so, thus preventing him from doing what he has a right (in the sense of a liberty) to do. It is different,

however, with a claim-right. This is the kind of right which I have in addition to a liberty when, for example, I have a private parking space; now others have duties in the way of noninterference, as in this case, or of service, as in the case where my claim-right is to goods or services promised to me. Sometimes one of these rights gives other people the duty of securing to me that to which I have a right, but at other times their duty is merely to refrain from interference. If a fall of snow blocks my private parking space, there is normally no obligation for anyone else to clear it away. Claim rights generate duties; sometimes these duties are duties of noninterference; sometimes they are duties of service. If your right gives me the duty not to interfere with you, I have "no right" to do it; similarly, if your right gives me the duty to provide something for you, I have "no right" to refuse to do it. What I lack is the right which is a liberty; I am not "at liberty" to interfere with you or to refuse the service.

Where in this picture does the right to life belong? No doubt people have the right to live in the sense of a liberty, but what is important is the cluster of claim-rights brought together under the title of the right to life. The chief of these is, of course, the right to be free from interferences that threaten life. If other people aim their guns at us or try to pour poison into our drink we can, to put it mildly, demand that they desist. And then there are the services we can claim from doctors, health officers, bodyguards, and firemen; the rights that depend on contract or public arrangement. Perhaps there is no particular point in saying that the duties these people owe us belong to the right to life; we might as well say that all the services owed to anyone by tailors, dressmakers, and couturiers belong to a right called the right to be elegant. But contracts such as those understood in the patient-doctor relationship come in an important way when we are discussing the rights and wrongs of euthanasia, and are therefore mentioned here.

Do people have the right to what they need in order to survive, apart from the right conferred by special contracts into which other people have entered for the supplying of these necessities? Do people in the underdeveloped countries in which starvation is rife have the right to the food they so evidently lack? Joel Feinberg, discussing this question, suggests that they should be said to have "a claim," distinguishing this from a "valid claim," which gives a claim-right.

> The manifesto writers on the other side who seem to identify needs, or at least basic needs, with what they call "human rights," are more properly described, I think, as urging upon the world community the moral principle that *all* basic human needs ought to be recognized as *claims* (in the customary *prima facie* sense) worthy of sympathy and serious consideration right now, even though, in many cases, they cannot yet plausibly be treated as *valid* claims, that is, as grounds of any other people's duties. This way of talking avoids the anomaly of ascribing to all human beings now, even those in pre-industrial societies such "economic and social rights" as "periodic holidays with pay."[9]

This seems reasonable, though we notice that there are some actual rights to service which are not based on anything like a contract, as for instance the right that children have to support from their parents and parents to support from their children in old age, though both sets of rights are to some extent dependent on existing social arrangements.

Let us now ask how the right to life affects the morality of acts of euthanasia. Are such acts sometimes or always ruled out by the right to life? This is certainly a possibility; for although an act of euthanasia is, by our definition, a matter of opting for death for the good of the one who is to die, there is, as we noted earlier, no direct connection between that to which a man has a right and that which is for his good. It is true that men have the right only to the kind of thing that is, in general, a good: we do not think that people have the right to garbage or polluted air. Nevertheless, a man may have the right to something which he himself would be better off without; where rights exist, it is a man's will that counts, not his or anyone else's estimate of benefit or harm. So the duties complementary to the right to life—the general duty of noninterference and the duty of service incurred by certain persons—are not affected by the quality of a man's life or by his prospects. Even if it is true that he would be, as we say, "better off dead," so long as he wants to live this does not justify us in killing him and may not justify us in deliberately allowing him to die. All of us have the duty of noninterference, and some of us may have the duty to sustain

his life. Suppose, for example, that a retreating army has to leave behind wounded or exhausted soldiers in the wastes of an arid or snowbound land where the only prospect is death by starvation or at the hands of an enemy notoriously cruel. It has often been the practice to accord a merciful bullet to men in such desperate straits. But suppose that one of them demands that he should be left alive? It seems clear that his comrades have no right to kill him, though it is a quite different question as to whether they should give him a life-prolonging drug. The right to life can sometimes give a duty of positive service, but does not do so here. What it does give is the right to be left alone.

Interestingly enough, we have arrived by way of a consideration of the right to life at the distinction normally labeled "active" versus "passive" euthanasia, and often thought to be irrelevant to the moral issue.[10] Once it is seen that the right to life is a distinct ground of objection to certain acts of euthanasia, and that this right creates a duty of noninterference more widespread than the duties of care, there can be no doubt about the relevance of the distinction between passive and active euthanasia. Where everyone may have the duty to leave someone alone, it may be that no one has the duty to maintain his life, or that only some people do.

Where then do the boundaries of the "active" and "passive" lie? In some ways the words are themselves misleading, because they suggest the difference between act and omission which is not quite what we want. Certainly the act of shooting someone is the kind of thing we were talking about under the heading of "interference," and omitting to give him a drug a case of refusing care. But the act of turning off a respirator should surely be thought of as no different from the decision not to start it; if doctors had decided that a patient should be allowed to die, either course of action might follow, and both should be counted as passive rather than active euthanasia if euthanasia were in question. The point seems to be that interference in a course of treatment is not the same as other interference in a man's life, and particularly if the same body of people are responsible for the treatment and for its discontinuance. In such a case we could speak of the disconnecting of the apparatus as killing the man, or of the hospital as allowing him to die. By and large, it is the act of killing that is ruled out under the heading of noninterference, but not in every case.

Doctors commonly recognize this distinction, and the grounds on which some philosophers have denied it seem untenable. James Rachels, for instance, believes that if the difference between active and passive is relevant anywhere, it should be relevant everywhere, and he has pointed to an example in which it seems to make no difference which is done. If someone saw a child drowning in a bath it would seem just as bad to let it drown as to push its head under water.[11] If "it makes no difference" means that one act would be as iniquitous as the other, this is true. It is not that killing is *worse* than allowing to die, but that the two are contrary to distinct virtues, which gives the possibility that in some circumstances one is impermissible and the other permissible. In the circumstances invented by Rachels, both are wicked: it is contrary to justice to push the child's head under the water—something one has no right to do. To leave it to drown is not contrary to justice, but it is a particularly glaring example of lack of charity. Here it makes no practical difference because the requirements of justice and charity coincide; but in the case of the retreating army they did not: charity would have required that the wounded soldier be killed had not justice required that he be left alive.[12] In such a case it makes all the difference whether a man opts for the death of another in a positive action, or whether he allows him to die. An analogy with the right to property will make the point clear. If a man owns something, he has the right to it even when its possession does him harm, and we have no right to take it from him. But if one day it should blow away, maybe nothing requires us to get it back for him; we could not deprive him of it, but we may allow it to go. This is not to deny that it will often be an unfriendly act or one based on an arrogant judgment when we refuse to do what he wants. Nevertheless, we would be within our rights, and it might be that no moral objection of any kind would lie against our refusal.

It is important to emphasize that a man's rights may stand between us and the action we would dearly like to take for his sake. They may, of course, also prevent action which we would like to take for the sake of others, as when it might be tempting to kill one man to save several. But it is interesting that the limits of allowable interference, however

uncertain, seem stricter in the first case than the second. Perhaps there are no cases in which it would be all right to kill a man against his will *for his own sake* unless they could equally well be described as cases of allowing him to die, as in the example of turning off the respirator. However, there are circumstances, even if these are very rare, in which one man's life would justifiably be sacrificed to save others, and "killing" would be the only description of what was being done. For instance, a vehicle which had gone out of control might be steered from a path on which it would kill more than one man to a path on which it would kill one.[13] But it would not be permissible to steer a vehicle towards someone in order to kill him, against his will, for his own good. An analogy with property rights illustrates the point. One may not destroy a man's property against his will on the grounds that he would be better off without it; there are, however, circumstances in which it could be destroyed for the sake of others. If his house is liable to fall and kill him, that is his affair; it might, however, without injustice be destroyed to stop the spread of a fire.

We see then that the distinction between active and passive, important as it is elsewhere, has a special importance in the area of euthanasia. It should also be clear why James Rachels' other argument, that it is often "more humane" to kill than to allow to die, does not show that the distinction between active and passive euthanasia is morally irrelevant. It might be "more humane" in this sense to deprive a man of the property that brings evils on him, or to refuse to pay what is owed to Hume's profligate debauchee; but if we say this we must admit that an act which is "more humane" than its alternative may be morally objectionable because it infringes rights.

So far we have said very little about the right to service as opposed to the right to noninterference, though it was agreed that both might be brought under the heading of "the right to life." What about the duty to preserve life that may belong to special classes of persons such as bodyguards, firemen, or doctors? Unlike the general public, they are not within their rights if they merely refrain from interfering and do not try to sustain life. The subject's claim-rights are twofold as far as they are concerned, and passive as well as active euthanasia may be ruled out here if it is against his will. This is not to say that he has the right to any and every service needed to save or prolong his life; the rights of other people set limits to what may be demanded, both because they have the right not to be interfered with and because they may have a competing right to services. Furthermore, one must inquire just what the contract or implicit agreement amounts to in each case. Firemen and bodyguards presumably have a duty which is simply to preserve life, within the limits of justice to others and of reasonableness to themselves. With doctors it may, however, be different, since their duty relates not only to preserving life but also to the relief of suffering. It is not clear what a doctor's duties are to his patient if life can be prolonged only at the cost of suffering or suffering relieved only by measures that shorten life. George Fletcher has argued that what the doctor is under contract to do depends on what is generally done, because this is what a patient will reasonably expect.[14] This seems right. If procedures are part of normal medical practice, then it seems that the patient can demand them however much it may be against his interest to do so. Once again, it is not a matter of what is "most humane."

That the patient's right to life may set limits to permissible acts of euthanasia seems undeniable. If he does not want to die, no one has the right to practice active euthanasia on him, and passive euthanasia may also be ruled out where he has a right to the services of doctors or others.

Perhaps few will deny what has so far been said about the impermissibility of acts of euthanasia simply because we have so far spoken about the case of one who positively wants to live, and about his rights, whereas those who advocate euthanasia are usually thinking either about those who wish to die or about those whose wishes cannot be ascertained either because they cannot properly be said to have wishes or because, for one reason or another, we are unable to form a reliable estimate of what they are. The question that must now be asked is whether the latter type of case, where euthanasia though not involuntary would again be nonvoluntary, is different from the one discussed so far. Would we have the right to kill someone for his own good so long as we had no idea that he positively wished to live? And what about the life-prolonging duties of doctors in the same circumstances? This is a very difficult problem. On the one hand, it seems ridiculous to suppose that a man's right to life is something which generates duties only where he has signaled that he wants to live; as a borrower does indeed have a duty to return something lent on indefinite loan only if the lender indicates that he wants it back. On the other hand, it might be argued that there is something illogical about the idea that a right has been infringed if someone incapable of saying whether he wants it or not is deprived of something that is doing him harm rather than good. Yet on the analogy of property we would say that a right has been infringed. Only if someone had earlier told us that in such circumstances he would not want to keep the thing could we think that his right had been waived. Perhaps if we could make confident judgments about what anyone in such circumstances would wish, or what he would have wished beforehand had he considered the matter, we could agree to consider the right to life as "dormant," needing to be asserted if the normal duties were to remain. But as things are, we cannot make any such assumption; we simply do not know what most people would want, or would have wanted, us to do unless they tell us. This is certainly the case so far as active measures to end life are concerned. Possibly it is different, or will become different, in the matter of being kept alive, so general is the feeling against using sophisticated procedures on moribund patients, and so much is this dreaded by people who are old or terminally ill. Once again the distinction between active and passive euthanasia has come on the scene, but this time because most people's attitudes to the two are so different. It is just possible that we might presume, in the absence of specific evidence, that someone would not wish, beyond a certain point, to be kept alive; it is certainly not possible to assume that he would wish to be killed.

In the last paragraph we have begun to broach the topic of voluntary euthanasia, and this we must now discuss. What is to be said about the case in which there is no doubt about someone's wish to die: either he has told us beforehand that he would wish it in circumstances such as he is now in, and has shown no sign of a change of mind, or else he tells us now, being in possession of his faculties and of a steady mind. We should surely say that the objections previously urged against acts of euthanasia, which it must be remembered were all on the ground of rights, had disappeared. It does not seem that one would infringe someone's right to life in killing him with his permission and in fact at his request. Why should someone not be able to waive his right to life, or rather, as would be more likely to happen, to cancel some of the duties of noninterference that this right entails? (He is more likely to say that he should be killed by this man at this time in this manner, than to say that anyone may kill him at any time and in any way.) Similarly, someone may give permission for the destruction of his property, and request it. The important thing is that he gives a critical permission, and it seems that this is enough to cancel the duty normally associated with the right. If someone gives you permission to destroy his property, it can no longer be said that you have no right to do so, and I do not see why it should not be the case with taking a man's life. An objection might be made on the ground that only God has the right to take life, but in this paper religious as opposed to moral arguments are being left aside. Religion apart, there seems to be no case to be made out for an infringement of rights if a man who wishes to die is allowed to die or even killed. But of course it does not follow that there is no moral objection to it. Even with property, which is after all a relatively small matter, one might be wrong to destroy what one had the right to destroy. For, apart from its value to other people, it might be valuable to the man who wanted it destroyed, and charity might require us to hold our hand where justice did not.

Let us review the conclusion of this part of the argument, which has been about euthanasia and the right to life. It has been argued that from this side come stringent restrictions on the acts of euthanasia that could be morally permissible. Active nonvoluntary euthanasia is ruled out by that part of the right to life which creates the duty of noninterference, though passive nonvoluntary euthanasia is not ruled out, except where the right to life-preserving action has been created by some special condition such as a contract between a man and his doctor, and it is not always certain just what such a contract involves. Voluntary euthanasia is another matter: as the preceding paragraph suggested, no right is infringed if a man is allowed to die or even killed at his own request.

Turning now to the other objection that normally holds against inducing the death of another, that it is against charity, or benevolence, we must tell a very different story. Charity is the virtue that gives attachment to the good of others, and because life is normally a good, charity normally demands that it should be saved or prolonged. But as we so defined an act of euthanasia that it seeks a man's death for his own sake—for his good—charity will normally speak in favor of it. This is not, of course, to say that charity can require an act of euthanasia which justice forbids, but if an act of euthanasia is not contrary to justice—that is, it does not infringe rights—charity will rather be in its favor than against.

Once more the distinction between nonvoluntary and voluntary euthanasia must be considered. Could it ever be compatible with charity to seek a man's death although he wanted to live, or at least had not let us know that he wanted to die? It has been argued that in such circumstances active euthanasia would infringe his right to life, but passive euthanasia would not do so, unless he had some special right to life-preserving service from the one who allowed him to die. What would charity dictate? Obviously when a man wants to live there is a presumption that he will be benefited if his life is prolonged, and if it is so the question of euthanasia does not arise. But it is, on the other hand, possible that he wants to live where it would be better for him to die: perhaps he does not realize the desperate situation he is in, or perhaps he is afraid of dying. So, in spite of a very proper resistance to refusing to go along with a man's own wishes in the matter of life and death, someone might justifiably refuse to prolong the life even of someone who asked him to prolong it, as in the case of refusing to give the wounded soldier a drug that would keep him alive to meet a terrible end. And it is even more obvious that charity does not always dictate that life should be prolonged where a man's own wishes, hypothetical or actual, are not known.

So much for the relation of charity to nonvoluntary passive euthanasia, which was not, like nonvoluntary active euthanasia, ruled out by the right to life. Let us now ask what charity has to say about voluntary euthanasia, both active and passive. It was suggested in the discussion of justice that if of sound mind and steady desire, a man might give others the *right* to allow him to die or even to kill him, where otherwise this would be ruled out. But it was pointed out that this would not settle the question of whether the act was morally permissible, and it is this that we must now consider. Could not charity speak against what justice allowed? Indeed it might do so. For while the fact that a man wants to die suggests that his life is wretched, and while his rejection of life may itself tend to take the good out of the things he might have enjoyed, nevertheless his wish to die might here be opposed for his own sake just as it might be if suicide were in question. Perhaps there is hope that his mental condition will improve. Perhaps he is mistaken in thinking his disease incurable. Perhaps he wants to die for the sake of someone else on whom he feels he is a burden, and we are not ready to accept this sacrifice whether for ourselves or others. In such cases, and there will surely be many of them, it could not be for his own sake that we will him or allow him to die, and therefore euthanasia as defined in this paper would not be in question. But this is not to deny that there could be acts of voluntary euthanasia both passive and active against which neither justice nor charity would speak.

We have now considered the morality of euthanasia both voluntary and nonvoluntary, and active and passive. The conclusion has been that nonvoluntary active euthanasia (roughly, killing a man against his will or without his consent) is never justified; that is to say, that a man's being killed for his own good never justifies the act unless he himself has consented to it. A man's rights are infringed by such an action, and it is therefore contrary to justice. However, all the other combinations, nonvoluntary passive euthanasia, voluntary active euthanasia, and voluntary passive euthanasia, are sometimes compatible with both justice and charity. But the strong condition carried in the definition of euthanasia adopted in this paper must not be forgotten; an act of euthanasia as here understood is one whose purpose is to benefit the one who dies.

In the light of this discussion let us look at our present practices. Are they good or are they bad? And what changes might be made, thinking now not only of the morality of particular acts of euthanasia but also of the indirect effects of instituting different practices, of the abuses to which they might be subject and of the changes that might come about if euthanasia became a recognized part of the social scene.

The first thing to notice is that it is wrong to ask whether we should introduce the practice of euthanasia as if it were not something we already had. In fact we do have it. For instance, it is common, where the medical prognosis is very bad, for doctors to recommend against measures to prolong life, and particularly where a process of degeneration producing one medical emergency after another has already set in. If these doctors are not certainly within their legal rights, this is something that is apt to come as a surprise to them as to the general public. It is also obvious that euthanasia is often practiced where old people are concerned. If someone very old and soon to die is attacked by a disease that makes his life wretched, doctors do not always come in with life-prolonging drugs. Perhaps poor patients are more fortunate in this respect than rich patients, being more often left to die in peace; but it is in any case a well recognized piece of medical practice, which is a form of euthanasia.

No doubt the case of infants with mental or physical defects will be suggested as another example of the practice of euthanasia as we already have it, since such infants are sometimes deliberately allowed to die. That they are deliberately allowed to die is certain; children with severe spina bifida malformations are not always operated on even where it is thought that without the operation they will die; and even in the case of children with Down's Syndrome who have intestinal obstructions, the relatively simple operation that would make it possible to feed them is sometimes not performed.[15] Whether this is euthanasia in our sense or only as the Nazis understood it is another matter. We must ask the crucial question, "Is it for the sake of the child himself that the doctors and parents choose his death?" In some cases the answer may really be yes, and, what is more important, it may really be true that the kind of life which is a good is not possible or likely for this child, and that there is little but suffering and frustration in store for him.[16] But this must presuppose that the medical prognosis is wretchedly bad, as it may be for some spina bifida children. With children who are born with Down's Syndrome it is, however, quite different. Most of these are able to live on for quite a time in a reasonably contented way, remaining like children all their lives but capable of affectionate relationships and able to play games and perform simple tasks. The fact is, of course, that the doctors who recommend against lifesaving procedures for handicapped infants are usually thinking not of them but rather of their parents and of other children in the family or of the "burden on society" if the children survive. So it is not for their sake but to avoid trouble to others that they are allowed to die. When brought out into the open this seems unacceptable: at least we do not easily accept the principle that adults who need special care should be counted too burdensome to be kept alive. It must in any case be insisted that if children with Down's Syndrome are deliberately allowed to die this is not a matter of euthanasia except in Hitler's sense. And for our children, since we scruple to gas them, not even the manner of their death is "quiet and easy"; when not treated for an intestinal obstruction a baby simply starves to death. Perhaps some will take this as an argument for allowing active euthanasia, in which case they will be in the company of an S.S. man stationed in the Warthgenau who sent Eichmann a memorandum telling him that "Jews in the coming winter could no longer be fed" and submitting for his consideration a proposal as to whether "it would not be the most humane solution to kill those Jews who were incapable of work through some quicker means."[17] If we say we are *unable* to look after children with handicaps, we are no more telling the truth than was the S.S. man who said that the Jews could not be fed.

Nevertheless, if it is ever right to allow deformed children to die because life will be a misery to them, or not to take measures to prolong for a little the life of a newborn baby whose life cannot extend beyond a few months of intense medical intervention, there is a genuine problem about active as opposed to passive euthanasia. There are well-known cases in which the medical staff has looked on wretchedly while an infant died slowly from starvation and dehydration because they did not feel able to give a lethal injection. According to the principles discussed in the earlier part of this paper they would indeed have had no right to give it, since an infant cannot ask that it should be done. The only possible solution—supposing that voluntary active euthanasia were to be legalized—would be to appoint guardians to act on the infant's behalf. In a different climate of opinion this might not be dangerous, but at present, when people so readily assume that the life of a handicapped baby is of no value, one would be loath to support it.

Finally, on the subject of handicapped children, another word should be said about those with severe mental defects. For them too it might sometimes be right to say that one would wish for death

for their sake. But not even severe mental handicap automatically brings a child within the scope even of a possible act of euthanasia. If the level of consciousness is low enough it could not be said that life is a good to them, any more than in the case of those suffering from extreme senility. Nevertheless, if they do not suffer it will not be an act of euthanasia by which someone opts for their death. Perhaps charity does not demand that strenuous measures are taken to keep people in this state alive, but euthanasia does not come into the matter, any more than it does when someone is, like Karen Ann Quinlan, in a state of permanent coma. Much could be said about this last case. It might even be suggested that in the case of unconsciousness this "life" is not the life to which "the right to life" refers. But that is not our topic here.

What we must consider, even if only briefly, is the possibility that euthanasia, genuine euthanasia, and not contrary to the requirements of justice or charity, should be legalized over a wider area. Here we are up against the really serious problem of abuse. Many people want, and want very badly, to be rid of their elderly relatives and even of their ailing husbands or wives. Would any safeguards ever be able to stop them describing as euthanasia what was really for their own benefit? And would it be possible to prevent the occurrence of acts which were genuinely acts of euthanasia but morally impermissible because infringing the rights of a patient who wished to live?

Perhaps the furthest we should go is to encourage patients to make their own contracts with a doctor by making it known whether they wish him to prolong their life in case of painful terminal illness or of incapacity. A document such as the Living Will seems eminently sensible, and should surely be allowed to give a doctor following the previously expressed wishes of the patient immunity from legal proceedings by relatives.[18] Legalizing active euthanasia is, however, another matter. Apart from the special repugnance doctors feel towards the idea of a lethal injection, it may be of the very greatest importance to keep a psychological barrier up against killing. Moreover, it is active euthanasia which is the most liable to abuse. Hitler would not have been able to kill 275,000 people in his "euthanasia" program if he had had to wait for them to need life-saving treatment. But there are other objections to active euthanasia, even voluntary active euthanasia. In the first place, it would be hard to devise procedures that would protect people from being persuaded into giving their consent. And secondly, the possibility of active voluntary euthanasia might change the social scene in ways that would be very bad. As things are, people do, by and large, expect to be looked after if they are old or ill. This is one of the good things that we have, but we might lose it, and be much worse off without it. It might come to be expected that someone likely to need a lot of looking after should call for the doctor and demand his own death. Something comparable could be good in an extremely poverty-stricken community where the children genuinely suffered from lack of food; but in rich societies such as ours it would surely be a spiritual disaster. Such possibilities should make us very wary of supporting large measures of euthanasia, even where moral principle applied to the individual act does not rule it out.

Notes

I would like to thank Derek Parfit and the editors of *Philosophy & Public Affairs* for their very helpful comments.

1. Leo Alexander, "Medical Science under Dictatorship," *New England Journal of Medicine*, 14 July 1949, p. 40.

2. For a discussion of culpable and nonculpable ignorance see Thomas Aquinas, *Summa Theologica*, First Part of the Second Part, Question 6, article 8, and Question 19, articles 5 and 6.

3. Dmitri Panin, *The Notebooks of Sologdin* (London, 1976), pp. 66–67.

4. Thomas Nagel, "Death," in James Rachels, ed., *Moral Problems* (New York, 1971), p. 362.

5. Panin, *Sologdin*, p. 85.

6. Yet some detail needs to be filled in to explain why we should not say that a scarecrow is beneficial to the plants it protects. Perhaps what is beneficial must either be a feature of the plant itself, such as protective prickles, or else must work on the plant directly, such as a line of trees which give it shade.

7. David Hume, *Treatise*, Book III, Part II, Section 1.

8. See, for example, D. D. Raphael, "Human Rights Old and New," in D. D. Raphael, ed., *Political Theory and the Rights of Man* (London, 1967), and Joel Feinberg, "The Nature and Value of Rights," *The Journal of Value Inquiry* 4, no. 4 (Winter 1970): 243–257. Reprinted in Samuel Gorovitz, ed., *Moral Problems in Medicine* (Englewood Cliffs, New Jersey, 1976).

9. Feinberg, "Human Rights," *Moral Problems in Medicine*, p. 465.

10. See, for example, James Rachels, "Active and Passive Euthanasia," *New England Journal of Medicine* 292, no. 2 (9 Jan. 1975): 78–80.

11. Ibid.

12. It is not, however, that justice and charity conflict. A man does not lack charity because he refrains from an act of injustice which would have been for someone's good.

13. For a discussion of such questions, see my article "The Problem of Abortion and the Doctrine of Double Effect," *Oxford Review*, no. 5 (1967); reprinted in Rachels, *Moral Problems*, and Gorovitz, *Moral Problems in Medicine*.

14. George Fletcher, "Legal Aspects of the Decision not to Prolong Life," *Journal of the American Medical Association* 203, no. 1 (1 Jan. 1968): 119–122. Reprinted in Gorovitz.

15. I have been told this by a pediatrician in a well-known medical center in the United States. It is confirmed by Anthony M. Shaw and Iris A. Shaw, "Dilemma of Informed Consent in Children," *The New England Journal of Medicine* 289, no. 17 (25 Oct. 1973): 885–890. Reprinted in Gorovitz.

16. It must be remembered, however, that many of the social miseries of spina bifida children could be avoided. Professor R. B. Zachary is surely right to insist on this. See, for example, "Ethical and Social Aspects of Spina Bifida," *The Lancet*, 3 Aug. 1968, pp. 274–276. Reprinted in Gorovitz.

17. Quoted by Hannah Arendt, *Eichmann in Jerusalem* (London 1963), p. 90.

18. Details of this document are to be found in J. A. Behnke and Sissela Bok, eds., *The Dilemmas of Euthanasia* (New York, 1975), and in A. B. Downing, ed., *Euthanasia and the Right to Life: The Case for Voluntary Euthanasia* (London, 1969).

Questions for Analysis

1. *What does Foot mean by "right to life," and how does she use this notion to distinguish between active and passive euthanasia?*

2. *Under what conditions might a person's life be regarded as no longer worth living?*

3. *Why does Foot believe it is not legitimate for us to decide when someone else's life is no longer worth living?*

4. *Which forms of euthanasia does Foot regard as legitimate, and which illegitimate? Cite her reasons.*

5. *Why does Foot believe we don't have a duty to kill a person who has decided his or her life is no longer worth living?*

A Moral Principle about Killing

Richard Brandt

The preceding writers, either explicitly or implicitly, dealt with the moral principle "It is morally wrong to kill innocent human beings." In this essay, philosopher Richard Brandt observes that this principle is really more useful in determining blame than for guiding us in making decisions. Brandt thinks a more appropriate principle can be based on the presumed obligation not to kill any human being except in justifiable self-defense—unless we have an even stronger moral obligation to do something that cannot be done without killing. In Brandt's view, that other overriding obligation is not to cause injury to another.

Brandt is distinguishing, then, between killing and causing injury, so that not every act of killing is an act of injury. After citing examples of what he believes are noninjurious killings and specifying conditions under which an act is noninjurious, Brandt argues that a person in irreversible coma is "beyond injury." If such a person has left instructions that his or her life should be ended, then, in Brandt's view, we are under a prima facie obligation to do so. In the absence of explicit instructions, we may attempt to determine what the person's wishes likely would be and carry them out. Of course, if a person has left instructions to be maintained under any circumstances, then we have an obligation to respect that preference.

Throughout the essay, Brandt uses the term prima facie *duty or obligation, which he has borrowed from the English philosopher William David Ross. Prima facie means "at first sight" or "on the surface." Accordingly, a* prima facie *duty is one that dictates what I should do when other relevant factors aren't considered. For example, I have a* prima facie *duty not to lie in every case in which lying is possible. Likewise, I have a* prima facie *duty to prevent the needless suffering of others. In other words, all things being equal, this is what I ought to try to do.*

In this essay, Brandt is taking issue with the commonplace view that killing a person is something that is prima facie *wrong in itself. In his view, killing is wrong only if and because it is an injury to someone, or if and because it runs counter to the person's known preference. In short, Brandt believes that a principle about the* prima facie *wrongness of killing derives from principles about when we are* prima facie *obligated not to injure and when we are* prima facie *obligated to respect a person's wishes.*

One of the Ten Commandments states: "Thou shalt not kill." The commandment does not supply an object for the verb, but the traditional Catholic view has been that the proper object of the verb is "innocent human beings" (except in cases of extreme necessity), where "innocent" is taken to exclude persons convicted of a capital crime or engaged in an unjust assault aimed at killing, such as members of the armed forces of a country prosecuting an unjust war. Thus construed, the prohibition is taken

This article first appeared in the book Beneficent Euthanasia, *edited by Marvin Kohl, published by Prometheus Books, Buffalo, N.Y., 1975, and is reprinted by permission of the publisher.*

to extend to suicide and abortion. (There is a qualification: that we are not to count cases in which the death is not wanted for itself or intended as a *means* to a goal that is wanted for itself, provided that in either case the aim of the act is the avoidance of some evil greater than the death of the person.) Can this view that all killing of innocent human beings is morally wrong be defended, and if not, what alternative principle can be?

This question is one the ground rules for answering which are far from a matter of agreement. I should myself be content if a principle were identified that could be shown to be one that would be included in any moral system that rational and benevolent persons would support for a society in which they expected to live. Apparently others would not be so content; so in what follows I shall simply aim to make some observations that I hope will identify a principle with which the consciences of intelligent people will be comfortable. I believe the rough principle I will suggest is also one that would belong to the moral system rational and benevolent people would want for their society.

Let us begin by reflecting on what it is to kill. The first thing to notice is that *kill* is a biological term. For example, a weed may be killed by being sprayed with a chemical. The verb *kill* involves essentially the broad notion of death—the change from the state of being biologically alive to the state of being dead. It is beyond my powers to give any general characterization of this transition, and it may be impossible to give one. If there is one, it is one that human beings, flies, and ferns all share; and to kill is in some sense to bring that transition about. The next thing to notice is that at least human beings do not live forever, and hence killing a human being at a given time must be construed as *advancing the date* of its death, or as *shortening its life*. Thus it may be brought about that the termination of the life of a person occurs at the time t instead of at the time $t + k$. Killing is thus shortening the span of organic life of something.

There is a third thing to notice about *kill*. It is a term of causal agency and has roots in the legal tradition. As such, it involves complications. For instance, suppose I push a boulder down a mountainside, aiming it at a person X and it indeed strikes X, and he is dead after impact and not before (and not from a coincidental heart attack); in that case we would say that I killed X. On the other hand,

suppose I tell Y that X is in bed with Y's wife, and Y hurries to the scene, discovers them, and shoots X to death; in that case, although the unfolding of events from my action may be as much a matter of causal law as the path of the boulder, we should *not* say that I killed X. Fortunately, for the purpose of principles of the morally right, we can sidestep such complications. For suppose I am choosing whether to do A or B (where one or the other of these "acts" may be construed as essentially *inaction*—for example, *not* doing what I know is the one thing that will *prevent* someone's death); then it is enough if I know, or have reason to think it highly probable, that were I to do A, a state of the world including the death of some person or persons would ensue, whereas were I to do B, a state of the world of some specified different sort would ensue. If a moral principle will tell me in this case whether I am to do A or B, that is all I need. It could be that a moral principle would tell me that I am absolutely never to perform any action A, such that were I to do it the death of some innocent human being would ensue, provided there is some alternative action I might perform, such that were I to do it no such death would ensue.

It is helpful, I think, to reformulate the traditional Catholic view in a way that preserves the spirit and intent of that view (although some philosophers would disagree with this assessment) and at the same time avoids some conceptions that are both vague and more appropriate to a principle about when a person is morally blameworthy for doing something than to a principle about what a person ought morally to do. The terminology I use goes back, in philosophical literature, to a phrase introduced by W. D. Ross, but the conception is quite familiar. The alternative proposal is that there is a *strong prima facie obligation* not to kill any human being except in justifiable self-defense; in the sense (of prima facie) that it is morally *wrong* to kill any human being except in justifiable self-defense *unless* there is an even stronger prima facie moral obligation to do something that cannot be done without killing. (The term *innocent* can now be omitted, since if a person is not innocent, there may be a stronger moral obligation that can only be discharged by killing him; and this change is to the good since it is not obvious that we have no prima facie obligation to avoid killing people even if they are not innocent.) This formulation has the result that sometimes, to decide what is morally right, we have to compare the stringencies of conflicting moral obligations—and that is an elusive business; but the other formulation either conceals the same problem by putting it in another place, or else leads to objectionable implications. (Consider one implication of the traditional formulation for a party of spelunkers in a cave by the oceanside. It is found that a rising tide is bringing water into the cave and all will be drowned unless they escape at once. Unfortunately, the first man to try to squeeze through the exit is fat and gets wedged inextricably in the opening, with his head inside the cave. Somebody in the party has a stick of dynamite. Either they blast the fat man out, killing him, or all of them, including him, will drown. The traditional formulation leads to the conclusion that all must drown.)

Let us then consider the principle: "There is a strong prima facie moral obligation not to kill any human being except in justifiable self-defense." I do not believe we want to accept this principle without further qualification; indeed, its status seems not to be that of a basic principle at all, but derivative from some more-basic principles. W. D. Ross listed what he thought were the main basic prima facie moral obligations; it is noteworthy that he listed a prima facie duty not to *cause injury*, but he did not include an obligation not to kill. Presumably this was no oversight. He might have thought that killing a human being is always an injury, so that the additional listing of an obligation not to kill would be redundant; but he might also have thought that killing is sometimes *not* an injury and that it is prima facie obligatory not to kill only when, and because, so doing would injure a sentient being.

What might be a noninjurious killing? If I come upon a cat that has been mangled but not quite killed by several dogs and is writhing in pain, and I pull myself together and put it out of its misery, I have killed the cat but surely not *injured* it. I do not injure something by relieving its pain. If someone is being tortured and roasted to death and I know he wishes nothing more than a merciful termination of life, I have not injured him if I shoot him; I have done him a favor. In general, it seems I have not injured a person if I treat him in a way in which he would want me to treat him if he were fully rational, or in a way to which he would be indifferent if he were fully rational. (I do not think that terminating the life of a human fetus in the third month is an injury; I admit this view requires discussion.[1])

Consider another type of killing that is not an injury. Consider the case of a human being who has become unconscious and will not, it is known, regain consciousness. He is in a hospital and is being kept alive only through expensive supportive measures. Is there a strong prima facie moral obligation not to withdraw these measures and not to take positive steps to terminate his life? It seems obvious that if he is on the only kidney machine and its use could *save* the life of another person, who could lead a normal life after temporary use, it would be wrong not to take him off. Is there an obligation to continue, or not to terminate, if there is no countering obligation? I would think not, with an exception to be mentioned; and this coincides with the fact that he is *beyond* injury. There is also not an obligation *not* to preserve his life, say, in order to have his organs available for use when they are needed.

There seems, however, to be another morally relevant consideration in such a case—knowledge of the patient's own wishes when he was conscious and in possession of his faculties. Suppose he had feared such an eventuality and prepared a sworn statement requesting his doctor to terminate his life at once in such circumstances. Now, if it is morally obligatory to some degree to carry out a person's wishes for disposal of his body and possessions after his death, it would seem to be equally morally obligatory to respect his wishes in case he becomes a "vegetable." In the event of the existence of such a document, I would think that if he can no longer be injured we are free to withdraw life-sustaining measures and also to take positive steps to terminate life—and are even morally bound, prima facie, to do so. (If, however, the patient had prepared a document directing that his body be preserved alive as long as possible in such circumstances, then there would be a prima facie obligation *not* to cease life-sustaining measures and not to terminate. It would seem obvious, however, that such an obligation would fall far short of giving the patient the right to continued use of a kidney machine when its use by another could save that person's life.) Some persons would not hesitate to discontinue life-sustaining procedures in such a situation, but would balk at more positive measures. But the hesitation to use more positive procedures, which veterinarians employ frequently with animals, is surely nothing but squeamishness; if a person is in the state described, there can be no injury to him in positive termination more than or less than that in allowing him to wither by withdrawing life-supportive procedures.

If I am right in my analysis of this case, we must phrase our basic principle about killing in such a way as to take into account (1) whether the killing would be an injury and (2) the person's own wishes and directives. And perhaps, more important, any moral principle about killing must be viewed simply as an implicate of more basic principles about these matters.

Let us look for corroboration of this proposal to how we feel about another type of case, one in which termination would be of positive benefit to the agent. Let us suppose that a patient has a terminal illness and is in severe pain, subject only to brief remissions, with no prospect of any event that could make his life good, either in the short or long term. It might seem that here, with the patient in severe pain, at least life-supportive measures should be discontinued, or positive termination adopted. But I do not think we would accept this inference, for in this situation the patient, let us suppose, has his preferences and is able to express them. The patient may have strong religious convictions and prefer to go on living despite the pain; if so, surely there is a prima facie moral obligation not positively to terminate his life. Even if, as seemingly in this case, the situation is one in which it would be *rational* for the agent, from the point of view of his own welfare, to direct the termination of his life,[2] it seems that if he (irrationally) does the opposite, there is a prima facie moral obligation not to terminate and some prima facie obligation to sustain it. Evidently a person's own expressed wishes have moral force. (I believe, however, that we think a person's expressed wishes have *less* moral force when we think the wishes are irrational.)

What is the effect, in this case, if the patient himself expresses a preference for termination and would, if he were given the means, terminate his own existence? Is there a prima facie obligation to sustain his life—and pain—against his will? Surely not. Or is there an obligation *not* to take positive measures to terminate his life immediately, thereby saving the patient much discomfort? Again, surely not. What possible reason could be offered to justify the claim that the answer is affirmative, beyond theological ones about God's will and our being bound to stay alive at His pleasure? The only argument I can think of is that there is some consideration of public policy, to the effect that a recognition of such moral permission might lead to abuses or to some other detriment to society in the long run. Such an argument does seem weak.

It might be questioned whether a patient's request should be honored, if made at a time when he is in pain, on the grounds that it is not rational. (The physician may be in a position to see, however, that the patient is quite right about his prospects and that his personal welfare would be maximized by termination.) It might also be questioned whether a patient's formal declaration, written earlier, requesting termination if he were ever in his present circumstances should be honored, on the grounds that at the earlier time he did not know what it would be like to be in his present situation. It would seem odd, however, if *no* circumstances are identifiable in which a patient's request for termination is deemed to have moral force, when his request *not* to terminate is thought morally weighty in the same circumstances even when this request is clearly irrational. I think we may ignore such arguments and hold that, in a situation in which it is rational for a person to choose termination of his life, his expressed wish is morally definitive and removes both the obligation to sustain life and the obligation not to terminate.

Indeed, there is a question whether or not in these circumstances a physician has not a moral obligation at least to withdraw life-supporting measures, and perhaps positively to terminate life. At least there seems to be a general moral obligation to render assistance when a person is in need, when it can be given at small cost to oneself, and when it is requested. The obligation is the stronger when one happens to be the only person in a position to receive such a request or to know about the situation. Furthermore, the physician has acquired a special obligation if there has been a long-standing personal relationship with the patient—just as a friend or relative has special obligations. But since we are discussing not the possible obligation to terminate but the obligation *not* to terminate, I shall not pursue this issue.

The patient's own expression of preference or consent, then, seems to be weighty. But suppose he is unable to express his preference; suppose that his terminal disease not only causes him great pain but has attacked his brain in such a way that he is incapable of thought and of rational speech. May the physician, then, after consultation, take matters into his own hands? We often think we know what is best for another, but we think one person should not make decisions for another. Just as we must respect the decision of a person who has decided after careful reflection that he wants to commit suicide, so we must not take the liberty of deciding to bring another's life to a close contrary to his wishes. So what may be done? Must a person suffer simply because he cannot express consent? There is evidence that can be gathered about what conclusions a person would draw if he were in a state to draw and express them. The patient's friends will have some recollection of things he has said in the past, of his values and general ethical views. Just as we can have good reason to think, for example, that he would vote Democratic if voting for president in a certain year, so we can have good reason to think he would take a certain stand about the termination of his own life in various circumstances. We can know of some persons who because of their religious views would want to keep on living until natural processes bring their lives to a close. About others we can know that they decidedly would not take this view. We can also know what would be the *rational* choice for them to make, and our knowledge of this can be *evidence* about what they would request if they were able. There are, of course, practical complications in the mechanics of a review board of some kind making a determination of this sort, but they are hardly insurmountable.

I wish to consider one other type of case, that of a person who, say, has had a stroke and is leading, and for some time can continue to lead, a life that is comfortable but one on a very low level, *and* who has antecedently requested that his life be terminated if he comes, incurably, into such a situation. May he then be terminated? In this case, unlike the others, there are probably ongoing pleasant experiences, perhaps on the level of some animals, that seem to be a good thing. One can hardly say that *injury* is being done such a person by keeping him alive; and one might say that some slight injury

is being done him by terminating his existence. There is a real problem here. Can the (slight) goodness of these experiences stand against the weight of an earlier firm declaration requesting that life be terminated in a situation of hopeless senility? There is no *injury* in keeping the person alive despite his request, but there seems something *indecent* about keeping a mind alive after a severe stroke, when we know quite well that, could he have anticipated it, his own action would have been to terminate his life. I think that the person's own request should be honored; it should be if a person's expressed preferences have as much moral weight as I think they should have.

What general conclusions are warranted by the preceding discussion? I shall emphasize two. First, there is a prima facie obligation *not* to terminate a person's existence when this would injure him (except in cases of self-defense or of senility of a person whose known wish is to be terminated in such a condition) *or* if he wishes not to be terminated. Second, there is *not* a prima facie obligation not to terminate when there would be *no* injury, or when there would be a positive benefit (release from pain) in so doing, provided the patient has not declared himself otherwise or there is evidence that his wishes are to that effect. Obviously there are two things that are decisive for the morality of terminating a person's life: whether so doing would be an *injury* and whether it conforms to what is known of his *preferences*.

I remarked at the outset that I would be content with some moral principles if it could be made out that rational persons would want those principles incorporated in the consciences of a group among whom they were to live. It is obvious why rational persons would want these principles. They would want injury avoided both because they would not wish others to injure them and because, if they are benevolent, they would not wish others injured. Moreover, they would want weight given to a person's own known preferences. Rational people do want the decision about the termination of their lives, where that is possible; for they would be uncomfortable if they thought it possible that others would be free to terminate their lives without consent. The threat of serious illness is bad enough without that prospect. On the other hand, this discomfort would be removed if they knew that termination would not be undertaken on their behalf without their explicit consent, except after a careful inquiry had been made, both into whether termination would constitute an injury and whether they would request termination under the circumstances if they were in a position to do so.

If I am right in all this, then it appears that killing a person is not something that is just prima facie wrong *in itself;* it is wrong roughly only if and because it is an *injury* of someone, or if and because it is contrary to the *known preferences* of someone. It would seem that a principle about the prima facie wrongness of killing is *derivative* from principles about when we are prima facie obligated not to injure and when we are prima facie obligated to respect a person's wishes, at least about what happens to his own body. I do not, however, have any suggestions for a general statement of principles of this latter sort.

Notes

1. See my "The Morality of Abortion" in *The Monist,* 56 (1972), pp. 503–26; and, in revised form, in *Abortion: Pro and Con,* ed. R. L. Perkins (General Learning Press, 1975).

2. See my "The Morality and Rationality of Suicide," in James Rachels, ed., *Moral Problems* (Harper & Row, 1975); and, in revised form, in E. S. Shneidman, ed., *Suicidology: Current Developments* (Grune & Stratton, 1976).

Questions for Analysis

1. *Under what conditions, according to Brandt, can one person be said to injure another?*

2. *Give an example of killing that causes injury, and of killing that doesn't.*

3. *How do we determine what a comatose person's wishes are, if the person has left no directions about terminating his or her life?*

4. *According to Brandt, under what conditions are we* prima facie *obliged not to terminate a person's existence? Under what conditions is there no such* prima facie *obligation?*

5. *Explain the significance (with respect to mercy deaths) of Brandt's deriving a principle about the* prima facie *wrongness of killing from principles about when we are* prima facie *obligated not to injure and when we are* prima facie *obligated to respect a person's wishes.*

6. *Would you say that Brandt's analysis is consistent or inconsistent with a Kantian view of the morality of euthanasia? (In order to answer this question, you of course should first try to apply Kant's ethics to the problem of euthanasia. Under what conditions, if ever, do you think Kant would approve of a mercy death?)*

CASE PRESENTATION
Earle N. Spring

Seventy-eight-year-old Earle N. Spring was suffering from end-stage kidney disease, which required him to undergo hemodialysis three days a week, five hours a day. He was also suffering from chronic organic brain syndrome, or senility, which left him completely confined and disoriented, and thus mentally incompetent. Physicians considered both the kidney disease and the senility permanent and irreversible, and saw no prospect of a medical breakthrough that would provide a cure for either disease. Without the dialysis treatment, Spring would die; with it, he might survive for months or years.

In 1979, Spring's wife and son, who had been appointed temporary guardian of his father, petitioned a probate court for legal authorization to discontinue Spring's life-sustaining medical treatment. The court appointed a guardian for Spring to look into the matter. Although the guardian opposed the cessation of treatment, the judge authorized it. In response, the guardian appealed the judgment to the Massachusetts Appeals Court, which upheld the judgment of the lower court. Undaunted, the court-appointed guardian made other legal moves. But before any final legal resolution, Earle Spring died in April 1980.

Questions for Analysis

1. *The Massachusetts Appeals Court based its decision on the presumption that if Spring were competent, he would wish to discontinue dialysis treatments (the court felt there was enough circumstantial evidence to warrant this presumption). What moral principle does this ruling implicitly recognize?*

2. *The appeals court based its presumption about Spring's wishes on many factors, but especially on the fact that Spring's family and attending physician were at one regarding the suspension of treatment. Do you think the views of those who best know an incompetent, incurably ill patient such as Spring should be given paramount consideration in determining a course of treatment or nontreatment?*

3. *Suppose the appeals court had overturned the lower court's decision, thereby upholding the court-appointed guardian's request that treatment be continued. Do you think Spring's family would have been morally justified in "taking matters into their own hands," that is, discontinuing Spring's hemodialysis treatment? Or do you think even if they had thought that such an action would have been respecting Spring's autonomous will, their overriding obligation would have been to obey the court's judgment?*

4. *Do you think the court should decide when the use of life-sustaining treatment should be discontinued? Or do you think other parties should—for example, the patient, if competent; the patient's family or physician; or a hospital ethics committee, when the patient is incompetent or even competent?*

CASE PRESENTATION
Baby Jane Doe

In October 1983, Baby Jane Doe, as the infant was called by the court to protect her anonymity, was born with a protruding spinal cord (spina bifida) and a host of other congenital defects. Surgery could be performed to prolong her life, but the prognosis was grim. According to best medical opinion, the child would be severely mentally retarded, bedridden, and suffer considerable pain during her life which, in all likelihood, wouldn't reach beyond twenty-five years. Faced with so tragic a prospect and after agonized consultations with medical experts and religious counselors, Mr. and Mrs. A (as the parents were designated in court documents) decided not to authorize permission for the surgery.

A right-to-life activist lawyer sought to force the surgery, but two New York appeals courts and a state children's agency declined to override the parents. The U.S. Justice Department then sued to obtain the records from the University Hospital in Stony Brook, New York, to determine whether it had violated a federal law that forbids discrimination against the handicapped.[8] Appearing on the *Face the Nation* television program of November 6, 1983, U.S. Surgeon General Dr. C. Everett Koop expressed the view that the government has a moral obligation to intercede on behalf of such infants in order to protect their basic right to life. He implied further that denying Baby Jane Doe the needed corrective surgery was tantamount to saying that as a society we value certain kinds of life more than others. This, in his view, was a most dangerous practice to establish.

Two weeks later, Federal District Judge Leonard Wexler threw out the Justice Department's unprecedented suit. Wexler found no discrimination, only a great deal of caring. The hospital had always been willing to do the surgery, the judge said, and had failed to do so, not because the baby was handicapped, but because her parents had refused to consent to such procedures. Wexler concluded that the parents' decision was a reasonable one based on genuine concern for the best interests of the child.

The day after the ruling, the Justice Department announced an appeal. On February 23, a federal appeals court upheld the lower court ruling, saying that the law forbidding discrimination against the handicapped did not apply to cases involving the treatment of newborn infants. Meanwhile, on January 9, 1984, federal regulations were issued preventing federally funded hospitals from withholding treatment in such cases.

Questions for Analysis

1. *Do you think this is a case of discrimination against the handicapped?*

2. *In a similar case ten years earlier, the Supreme Court of Maine ordered, against parental wishes, that an operation be performed on a grotesquely deformed infant in order to save its life. In defending his ruling, Judge David G. Roberts said: "At the moment of live birth, there does exist a human being entitled to the fullest protection of the law. The most basic right enjoyed by every human being is the right to life itself."[9] Do you agree with Judge Roberts?*

3. *Some would argue that the view shared by the U.S. Justice Department and Judge Roberts is cruel and inhumane—that they, in effect, sentence infants like*

8. *Early in the Reagan Administration a twenty-four-hour "hotline" had been set up to receive calls from anyone who, among other things, thought that the civil rights of infants like Baby Jane Doe were being violated.*

9. *Richard A. McCormick, "To Save or Let Die: The Dilemma of Modern Medicine,"* Journal of the American Medical Association, July 1974, p. 172.

Baby Jane and their families to lives of profound pain, suffering, humiliation, frustration, and unhappiness. They might further charge that these officials are callously insensitive to the feelings and capabilities of the parents. What is your view of such criticisms?

4. Which ethical principles do you think are of utmost concern in cases like Baby Jane Doe?

5. Some people claim that it is morally permissible to allow a seriously and irreversibly defective newborn like Baby Jane to die if and only if there is no significant potential for a meaningful human existence. There comes a point, they say, when an individual life precludes satisfying any human potential, such as establishing meaningful human relationships. Implicit in this argument is that the quality of life not only is morally significant in cases like these but may rank as a higher moral value than mere survival. Do you agree? Or would you say that the sanctity of life, regardless of a particular life's quality or lack of potential for development, is the supreme moral value?

6. If society through its government and judicial system intercedes to preserve the lives of infants like Baby Jane Doe, do you think it then bears the chief responsibility for maintenance costs?

Selections for Further Reading

Behnke, John A., and Sissela Bok. *The Dilemmas of Euthanasia.* New York: Doubleday, Anchor, 1975.

Caughill, R. E., ed. *The Dying Patient: A Supportive Approach.* Boston: Little, Brown, 1976.

Cooper, I. S. *Hard to Leave When the Music's Playing.* New York: Norton, 1977.

Grisez, Germain, and Joseph Boyle. *Life and Death with Liberty and Justice.* Notre Dame, Ind.: University of Notre Dame Press, 1979.

Kluge, Eike-Henner. *The Practice of Death.* New Haven: Yale University Press, 1975.

Kohl, Marvin, ed. *Beneficent Euthanasia.* Buffalo, N.Y.: Prometheus Press, 1975.

Kübler-Ross, Elisabeth. *On Death and Dying.* New York: Macmillan, 1969.

———. *Questions and Answers on Death and Dying.* New York: Macmillan, 1974.

Maguire, Daniel C. *Death by Choice.* Garden City, N.Y.: Doubleday, 1974.

Russell, O. Ruth. *Freedom to Die: Moral and Legal Aspects of Euthanasia.* New York: Human Sciences Press, 1975; Dell, 1976.

Steinbock, Bonnie, ed. *Killing and Letting Die.* Englewood Cliffs, N.J.: Prentice-Hall, 1980.

Weir, Robert F. *Selective Nontreatment of Handicapped Newborns: Moral Dilemmas in Neonatal Medicine.* New York: Oxford University Press, 1984.

7
CAPITAL PUNISHMENT

Late on the night of October 4, 1983, in Huntsville, Texas, convicted killer J. D. Autry was taken from his death-row cell in the penitentiary and strapped to a wheeled cot. Intravenous tubes were connected to both arms, ready to administer a dose of poison.

Outside, a crowd shouted "Kill him, kill him, kill him!" whenever television lights were turned on.

In Washington, Supreme Court Justice Byron White waited for a last-minute application for a stay of execution. The application, written on three sheets of a yellow pad, made a new argument related to another case due to be heard by the Court. Shortly after midnight White granted the stay. The intravenous tubes were disconnected, the straps unbuckled. Autry was returned to his cell. Only in March of 1984 was the execution carried out.

The U.S. Supreme Court decision that paved the way for Autry's execution was *Gregg* v. *Georgia* (1976). In an earlier decision, *Furman* v. *Georgia* (1972), the court had ruled that capital punishment as then administered was cruel and unusual punishment, and therefore unconstitutional. The issue in that case was *standardless discretion*—the freedom of a jury (or, in some cases, a judge) to use its own discretion in determining a sentence without explicit legal standards to guide its decision. In their attempts to get around the decision, some states passed laws making the death penalty mandatory for certain crimes, while others enacted legal standards to guide the discretion of the sentencing jury or judge. In *Woodson* v. *North Carolina* (1976), the Supreme Court ruled laws of the first type unconstitutional. In *Gregg* v. *Georgia*, it upheld laws of the second type for the crime of murder.

Since that decision, capital punishment has withstood one other major legal challenge—*McClesky* v. *Kemp* (1987). In that case, the Supreme Court ruled against Warren McClesky, a black man who had been sentenced to death for killing a white policeman. McClesky argued that the imposition of the death penalty was unconstitutionally affected by racial bias, and in support of his claim he offered studies showing that convicted killers of white victims were more likely to receive the death penalty than were convicted killers of black victims. Although the court did not dispute the studies, it rejected his argument. With almost 1,900 convicted killers waiting on death row, the constitutionality of the death penalty was upheld by a five to four majority.

The death penalty is a form of punishment. Consequently, one's view of the morality of the death penalty usually is influenced by one's view of punishment generally. So the specific moral question under discussion in this chapter is: Is capital punishment ever a justifiable form of punishment?

The Nature and Definition of Punishment

Generally, philosophers discuss punishment in terms of five elements. For something to be punishment it must (1) involve pain, (2) be administered for an offense against a law or rule, (3) be administered to someone who has been judged guilty of an offense, (4) be imposed by someone other than the offender, and (5) be imposed by rightful authority. Whether a punishment is commensurate with an offense, whether it is fair and equitable—these are very important moral and legal questions. But they must be distinguished from the question of what punishment is.

1. *Punishment must involve pain, harm, or some other consequence normally considered unpleasant.* For example, if a convicted robber was sentenced to "five-to-twenty" in a Beverly Hills country club, this would not be considered punishment, since ordinarily it would not involve pain or other unpleasant consequences (unless the robber had to pick up the tab). If he were sentenced to have his hands cut off, this could constitute punishment, though draconian by many people's standards.

2. *The punishment must be administered for an offense against a law or rule.* While punishment involves pain, obviously not all pain involves punishment. If a robber breaks into your house and steals your stereo, he is not "punishing" you, even though his action satisfies element (1). Although it caused you pain, his action is not taken to punish an offense against a law or rule. However, should the robber subsequently be sent to prison for the crime, then *that* action would be administered for breaking a law and thus satisfy element (2).

3. *The punishment must be administered to someone who has been judged guilty of an offense.* Suppose the robber is apprehended and imprisoned, although never judged guilty of the robbery. This would not be considered punishment. However, if he is imprisoned after his conviction for stealing your stereo, then he is being punished.

4. *The punishment must be imposed by someone other than the offender.* It is true that people sometimes speak of "punishing themselves" for a transgression. This, however, is not punishment in the strict sense, but a self-imposed act of

atonement. Suffering from a twinge of conscience as he listens to the latest Willie Nelson album on your stereo, the robber decides to "punish" himself by listening to Robert Goulet, whom he detests, for two hours each day for a year. Properly speaking, this would not be punishment, although it might qualify as masochism.

5. *The punishment must be imposed by rightful authority.* In a strictly legal sense, "rightful authority" would be that constituted by a legal system against whom the offense is committed. In the case of the robber, "rightful authority" likely would be a court judge and jury. In a less legal sense, the authority might be a parent, a teacher, or some official who has a right to harm a person in a particular way for having done something or failed to do something.

These five elements, then, generally constitute the nature of punishment. Combining them produces a useful definition of punishment. Thus a punishment is harm inflicted by a rightful authority on a person who has been judged to have violated a law or rule.[1]

The Moral Acceptability of Punishment

Is punishment ever morally acceptable? This may seem a foolish question to ask, since it is hard to imagine society functioning without an established legal system of punishment. In fact, philosophers generally agree that punishment is morally acceptable. They, like most others, view punishment as a part of rule and law necessary to minimize the occurrence of forbidden acts. In short, law without punishment is toothless.

Still, there are people who do not share this view. They argue that society should be restructured so that a legal system of punishment is unnecessary. Just how this can or should be done remains problematic. The method most often proposed involves some form of therapeutic treatment or behavior modification for antisocial behavior, rather than a traditional form of punishment. Among the most morally controversial procedures for modifying undesirable social behavior are those associated with some startling advances in biomedicine. Such cases rarely can be resolved by a simple appeal to the individual's right to obtain appropriate treatment on request, and are even less likely to be resolved by an appeal to society's right to order such treatment.

Consider one case provided by a leading research scientist in the field, Dr. J. R. Delgado. A number of years ago, Delgado recalls, an attractive twenty-four-year-old woman of average intelligence and education and a long record of arrests for disorderly conduct approached him and his associates. The patient explained that she had been repeatedly involved in bar brawls in which she would entice men to fight over her. Having spent a number of years in jail and mental institutions, the woman expressed a strong desire but inability to change her behavior. Because past psychological therapy had proved ineffective, both she and her mother urgently requested that some sort of brain surgery be performed to control her antisocial and destructive behavior. As Delgado said: "They asked

1. See Burton M. Leiser, Liberty, Justice, and Morals *(New York: Macmillan, 1973), pp. 195–97.*

specifically that electrodes be implanted to orient a possible electrocoagulation of a limited cerebral area; and if that wasn't possible, they wanted a lobotomy."[2]

At that time, medical knowledge could not determine whether such procedures could help resolve the woman's problem, so the physicians rejected surgical intervention. When Delgado and his colleagues explained their decision to the woman and her mother, the two reacted with disappointment and anxiety: "What is the future? Only jail or the hospital?"[3]

What is the future, indeed? The day could very well come when such therapeutic treatment renders traditional kinds of punishment obsolete, perhaps barbaric. But even then, pressing moral questions will remain concerning society's right to alter an individual's personality against his or her will. For now, most agree that punishment is a morally acceptable practice. What they do not agree on, however, is the aim of punishment.

Aims of Punishment

The aims of punishment can be divided into two categories: (1) in terms of giving people what they deserve, or (2) in terms of its desirable consequences. The first category includes retributive theories of punishment; the second includes preventive, deterrent, and reformative theories.

Retribution

The term *retribution* refers to punishment given in return for some wrong done. This view of punishment holds that we should punish people simply because they deserve it. Traditionally, retributive theorists have considered punishment a principle of justice, whereby offenders are made to suffer in kind for the harm they have caused others. Arguments in favor of capital punishment commonly make this point.

But another version of retribution associates punishment not with revenge, but with respect for persons, both noncriminals and criminals. Proponents of this theory argue that the robber, for example, like everyone else in society, ought to live under the same limitations of freedom. When the robber steals your stereo, he is taking unfair advantage of you, disrupting the balance of equal limitations. When the state subsequently punishes him, the punishment is viewed as an attempt to restore this disrupted balance, to reaffirm society's commitment to fair treatment for all. This version of retribution focuses on the noncriminal generally and the victim in particular, claiming that respect for the parties who abide by society's limitations requires punishment of those who flout those limitations.

The other side of the respect-retribution theory concerns respect for the offender. Proponents of retribution sometimes argue that failure to punish is tantamount to treating offenders with disrespect because it denies them autonomy and responsibility for their actions. Showing respect entails giving people

2. J. R. Delgado, Physical Control of the Mind: Toward a Psycho-Civilized Society *(New York: Harper & Row, 1969)*, p. 85.

3. *Ibid.*

what they deserve, whether that be reward or punishment. To deny praise to a deserving person is disrespectful. By the same token, to deny punishment to a deserving person is equally disrespectful. Both views of respect-retribution can be used in defense of capital punishment.

Prevention

The prevention view of punishment holds that we should punish to ensure that offenders do not repeat their offense and so further injure society. Thus robbers should be punished, perhaps imprisoned, so that they will not steal anything else. Prevention is one of the most common justifications for capital punishment.

Deterrence

The deterrence view holds that we should punish in order to discourage others from committing similar offenses. Like the prevention theory, it aims to minimize the crime rate. Thus when other potential thieves see that the robber has been punished for the crime, they will be less likely to steal. Deterrence is perhaps the most common argument made on behalf of capital punishment, and thus is the one that those against capital punishment often focus on. For the moment, we will simply observe that if a punishment is to function effectively as a deterrent, it must be severe enough to be undesirable and, just as important, it must be known and certain. Thus, potential offenders must be aware of the kind and severity of the punishment that awaits them, and they must be convinced that they will receive it if they commit the offense.

Reform

The reform theory holds that one should punish in order to induce people to conform to standards of behavior they have tended to ignore or violate. The idea here is that people will emerge from punishment better than they were before, insofar as they will be less likely to breach conventional standards of behavior.

Although rehabilitation often accompanies reform, the aims of each are different. Rehabilitation aims not to punish but to offer the offenders opportunities to find a useful place in society on release from prison. Modern penal institutions attempt to accomplish this by providing various recreational, educational, and vocational services for prisoners.

It's important to keep in mind that the aforementioned aims of punishment are not mutually exclusive. It's possible for more than one purpose of punishment to be morally legitimate. In fact, perhaps all four, in varying degrees, might be called for.

Retentionist and *Abolitionist* Defined

Having briefly examined some aspects of punishment, including its nature and definition, its moral acceptability, and its aims, let us now turn to the particular form of punishment that is the topic of this chapter: capital punishment.

The central moral question that concerns us is: Is capital punishment ever a justifiable form of punishment?

Those who support retaining or reinstituting capital punishment can be termed *retentionists*. Retentionists are not agreed that all the arguments supporting capital punishment are acceptable or on the conditions under which capital punishment should be imposed. But they do agree that capital punishment is at least sometimes morally justifiable. Those who oppose capital punishment are commonly termed *abolitionists*. Like retentionists, abolitionists disagree among themselves about which arguments against capital punishment are acceptable. But all abolitionists share the belief that capital punishment is never morally justifiable.

One common argument enlisted by both retentionists and abolitionists concerns capital punishment as a deterrent. As we'll see, retentionists sometimes claim that capital punishment deters potential murderers, and therefore should be kept. For their part, some abolitionists claim that capital punishment does not serve as a deterrent, and offer this—usually with other reasons—for abolishing the death penalty. Because the deterrent argument figures so prominently in capital punishment debates, we should inspect it before beginning this chapter's dialogues.

Capital Punishment as Deterrent

Does capital punishment succeed in deterring potential murderers? At first glance, the answer seems to be a resounding yes. After all, virtually everyone seems deterred from lawbreaking by relatively mild intimidation—for example, being towed away for illegal parking or losing one's driver's license for recklessness. How much more, common sense suggests, must potential murderers be intimidated by the threat of their own death at the executioner's hand. In this instance, however, common sense misleads by failing to recognize that murderers differ from the rest of us in important respects.

First, there's the large category of murderers who kill in a fit of rage or passion. A barroom brawl escalates and one man kills another; in a gang fight a member of one group kills a member of another, perhaps to save face or avenge a harm; in a family quarrel a person kills a relative when things get out of hand. The list goes on and on. Such murders, of which there are many, are committed not with forethought of the consequences, but in a moment of white-hot anger. Hence not even the death penalty is likely to deter these murderers. (In fact, in instances of gang killings it might have the opposite effect: In risking their own lives at the hands of the state, killers might feel they're proving their mettle or giving ultimate evidence of gang loyalty.)

Then there's the category of so-called professional criminals, those who deliberately calculate when, where, and how to commit crimes. It's not at all clear that this type of criminal is deterred by the death penalty. In fact, if professional criminals perceive the likely punishment for nonhomicidal crimes (e.g., robbery, burglary, rape, and so forth) as overly severe, they might be encouraged to kill their victims and witnesses rather than risk getting caught: Killing these people greatly increases the criminals' chances of getting away with their crimes, and so they may not in the least be deterred by the threat of the death penalty.

Besides these kinds of potential murderers are those who seemingly have a death wish. The annals of psychiatry are replete with cases of people so emotionally disturbed that they kill in order to win the death penalty to end their tortured existence. In effect, their murderous acts are expressions of suicidal impulses. Since they lack the nerve to kill themselves, they want someone else to do it for them—in this case, the state.

But what about cases of so-called normal, nonsuicidal persons who carefully weigh the risks before killing? Are these potential murderers deterred by the death penalty? Even here, the deterrent effect of capital punishment is by no means obvious or certain. What's required is a determination of how many, if any, calculating potential murderers (a small class to begin with) who are not deterred by the threat of life imprisonment would be deterred by the threat of death. Even if such a determination is possible, it's not obvious or certain that there would be any such people at all, or much more than a small number annually.

A further complication in assessing the death penalty as deterrent relates not to factual questions such as the preceding, but to the moral and legal costs of deterrence. Some claim there's a basic incompatibility between the deterrent efficacy of the death penalty and due process, which refers to a constitutionally guaranteed, specific, systematic procedure of appeal. The death penalty can be deterrent, the argument goes, only if due process is sacrificed. Conversely, due process can govern the inflicting of capital punishment but at the cost of deterrence. When human life is at issue—as of course it is in capital punishment cases—the courts have been understandably scrupulous in reviewing cases for error and ensuring that basic rights have been respected. The consequences of this process of rigorous judicial review are quite apparent: increasing delays of execution, an ever-increasing percentage of those convicted who are never executed, and large numbers of convictions overturned. When fully exercised, the right of appeal can lead to costly, protracted litigation, in which a criminal's fate may hinge as much on the quality of legal representation as on any other factor. Given the delay between murder and the death penalty, and the uncertainty that a death sentence will ever be carried out, one wonders about the death penalty's deterrent effect. On the other hand, to ensure swiftness and certainty mocks one of the most cherished ideals of our system of justice: due process.

Currently, the consensus among social scientists is that no statistical studies on the deterrent effect of capital punishment yield a conclusive answer. We simply don't know whether the threat of death deters people from killing. Given this picture, some argue that since there is a moral presumption against the taking of life, the burden of proving capital punishment is a deterrent should fall on those who advocate the taking of life in the form of capital punishment. But by the same token, one could contend that abolitionists should bear the burden of proof: Since we don't know for sure whether the death penalty is a deterrent, we should give the benefit of doubt to the lives of potential victims of murderers rather than to the murderers. This tack is especially forceful when applied to measures intended to reserve the death penalty for the intentional killings of law-enforcement agents and others who need special protection, which they might get from the threat of the death penalty.

Abolitionist Arguments
(against Capital Punishment)

1. *Every life has dignity and worth, even that of a convicted murderer.*

POINT: "I'm sure you'll agree that every individual has inherent dignity and worth. While the taking of human life is sometimes morally permissible—for example, in self-defense—it's always a very serious matter and should not be permitted in the absence of weighty overriding reasons. The death penalty is cruel and inhuman. Since retentionists haven't marshaled substantial reasons in its defense, it must be judged morally unacceptable and should be prohibited.

"I expect you'll consider my absolute prohibition against capital punishment improbable since what I'm saying is that even when the end in question is the net saving of human lives, capital punishment is still absolutely impermissible morally. But I suggest that you look at your own presumably 'absolutist' view of torturing to death as a possible punishment. Suppose, for example, we had good reason to believe that by reinstituting death by torture for murder, we could save 100 percent of victims' lives a year. I think that you and almost everyone would reject such a penalty. No matter its positive social effect, you'd probably agree torture simply is not an eligible instrument of social policy in a civilized nation. Well, I feel the same way about the gallows or the electric chair, or any other form of capital punishment. In short, executing people, no matter how heinous their offenses, is an insult to the highest principle of morality and civilization: the sanctity of life."

COUNTERPOINT: "I share your reverence for life. I also agree that there are times when the taking of a human life is morally permissible. Where we part company is on whether the infliction of the death penalty can be one of the morally permissible occasions for taking life. If retentionists had not made a compelling case for the death penalty, I'd agree with you that the death penalty is cruel and inhuman. But, as I'll try to show later, I think we have.

"But let me just ask you to think about the notion of 'cruel and inhuman.' On what grounds do you say with such conviction that inflicting the death penalty is cruel and inhuman, but presumably that life imprisonment is not, or at least is less so? It's conceivable, isn't it, that a young killer facing a life sentence for murder with no chance of parole and all the indignities associated with prison life might consider this sentence more cruel than just being put to death? What are we to say of this? That the person is simply misinformed or demented? It seems to me that respecting the dignity and worth of a human being begins with respect for the person's autonomous will as a rational being. To call the death penalty cruel and inhuman, in effect, denies the party most affected by the punishment any voice in deciding which of two sentences—life imprisonment without possibility of parole, or death—is worse from his or her viewpoint. Of course, you'd probably say that a convicted murderer should not be given the choice, that society should determine what passes for cruel or inhuman punishment. But how is denying the convicted murderer a say consistent with honoring the dignity and worth of human beings? To me, *that* seems like a most cruel and inhuman way of treating people. In short, I think you're operating from a rather fuzzy concept of 'cruel and inhuman,' which you're treating as so clearly defined as to make capital punishment morally impermissible."

2. *Capital punishment does not deter crime.*

POINT: "A comparative analysis of states that have capital punishment and those that don't indicates that the murder rate in capital-punishment states frequently is no lower than in those states that don't have capital punishment. In some cases, it's higher. It's obvious, therefore, that capital punishment simply doesn't deter crime. And since capital punishment does not function as an effective deterrent to crime, it should be abolished."

COUNTERPOINT: "A statistical correlation does not establish a causal connection. Many things influence the commission of crimes, including economic, political, sociological, and psychological factors. A high crime rate in a non-capital-punishment state may be accounted for in a variety of ways, none of which bears on the absence of capital punishment. Conversely, a low crime rate in a non-capital-punishment state doesn't in itself disprove the deterrent value of capital punishment."

3. *Capital punishment is implemented with a class bias.*

POINT: "Statistics indicate that the poor, the underprivileged, and members of minority groups are executed proportionately in far greater numbers than the rich, the influential, and white people. Thus, capital punishment actually serves to oppress the most disadvantaged in our society. This is patently unfair and must be stopped."

COUNTERPOINT: "Your point is irrelevant because it addresses the inequity of the penalty's *distribution*, not whether it's a justifiable form of punishment. If the rich, white, or influential escape capital punishment for crimes that other people are executed for, then the problem lies with our judicial system, not with the punishment. Of course it's unfair that comparable crimes don't get the same penalties, no matter who the offender is. But let's remedy the system that allows this injustice, and not throw out the penalty."

4. *The innocent may die.*

POINT: "It's no secret that innocent people are often convicted of crimes. This is always tragic. Such a deplorable occurrence is reversible with every kind of punishment except capital punishment. We can't call the innocent back from their graves to make our apologies and offer reparation. Even if only one innocent person is executed, that's inexcusable. The very existence of capital punishment allows for such a heinous possibility, and therefore it should be abolished."

COUNTERPOINT: "Actually, very few innocent people are ever executed. True, the execution of even one innocent person is tragic and diminishes all of us and our system of justice. But no institution is perfect, certainly not the judicial system. Laws and the institutions that enforce them are made by humans, and the human factor always spells potential error. This doesn't mean we shouldn't minimize the possibility that someone will be executed for something he or she didn't do. Of course we should, and the death penalty ought never be given casually. But at the same time, we must recognize the fallibility of people and their institutions, and consequently view the rare execution of an innocent person in that sobering light."

5. *Retribution is uncivilized.*

POINT: "Putting someone to death can't bring back the victim or in any meaningful way repay the victim's loved ones. So what's the function of capital punishment? Clearly, it is to satisfy the primitive and apparently irrepressible urge for revenge. Such a motive isn't worthy of a society that considers itself civilized."

COUNTERPOINT: "Your argument focuses on only one aspect of retributive justice. Even if the desire for revenge is an unwholesome basis for punishment, one can still make a case for respect-retribution. Furthermore, your argument assumes that capital punishment can be only retributive. But punishment can have aims other than that—for example, deterrence."

6. *Capital punishment precludes reform.*

POINT: "When people are put to death, the chance that they can be restored to a useful place in society dies with them. How tragic that society should compound one heinous deed by committing another. The fact is, society bears as much responsibility for crime as criminals do. After all, societal influences help shape individuals into the criminals they subsequently become."

COUNTERPOINT: "Why assume that the sole or at least primary function of punishment is reform? And I categorically reject that societal influence can be so strong that people lose their sense of right and wrong, or have their will so constrained they cannot help committing heinous crimes. Such a degree of societal influence over individuals has never been established. In fact, many individuals who function as admirable citizens have been exposed to more sinister environmental influences than those who commit murder. Finally, your argument confuses social responsibility with personal responsibility. Where personal responsibility is involved, one can rightly assign blame. But to speak of 'social responsibility' is to blame everyone and no one. Pushed far enough, the concept of social responsibility ends up holding no one personally responsible for anything."

7. *Capital punishment injures the judicial system.*

POINT: "Capital punishment actually has the effect of making judges and juries soft on crime. It makes a mockery of the judicial system. Where capital punishment has been a mandatory sentence, judges and juries have been known to strain the evidence to acquit rather than sentence to death. And to make matters worse, cases of capital punishment inevitably involve years of costly appeals. This not only delays justice but subjects the people who are directly and indirectly involved to cruel and inhuman punishment."

COUNTERPOINT: "If judges and juries would rather acquit a guilty party than sentence the person to death, then the trouble lies not with capital punishment but with judges and juries. The same applies to the duration of capital-offense cases: The trouble isn't with capital punishment but with the judicial system. Yes, make the system more responsive, efficient, and accountable. But don't throw out capital punishment. That would be like throwing the baby out with the bathwater."

Retentionist Arguments (for Capital Punishment)

1. *Capital punishment is the only prevention against certain crimes.*

POINT: "Certain major crimes cannot be deterred in any way other than by capital punishment. Take, for example, the case of political revolutionaries or terrorists. These people won't be deterred from violent acts by threats of life imprisonment, because in their view they'll eventually gain freedom, even acclaim when their cause succeeds. Then there are those who are prone to violence, unreformable individuals whose very existence constitutes a potential threat to society. The only way society can protect itself from the possibility that such people will strike again is to execute them."

COUNTERPOINT: "Your argument assumes that those bent on murder or revolution will be deterred by capital punishment. But there's no evidence for this. In fact, it's more sensible to believe that the fanatical mind is indifferent to any potential punishment, no matter how severe. As for the unreformable, since society has never unflinchingly committed itself to a concept of punishment as rehabilitation, we have no way of knowing who, if anyone, is unreformable. This aside, protecting ourselves through executing people seems to be treating the symptoms, not the disease. The root causes of crime are social: poverty, prejudice, sickness, despair. Thinking that we're protecting ourselves through capital punishment is an illusion. The real way to protect ourselves is to root out the conditions that breed crime."

2. *Capital punishment balances the scales of justice.*

POINT: "When someone wantonly takes another's life, that person upsets the balance of equal limitations under which everyone in society ought to live. This disruption must be balanced. The only way to do this is to impose a punishment equal to the offense that upset the balance. Let the punishment fit the crime. Thus those who murder forfeit their own claim to life. The state has the right and the duty to execute them."

COUNTERPOINT: "Why do you take for granted the retributive view of punishment? Surely that theory is at least questionable. Just what is this 'balance of equal limitations' you talk about? The fact is that for no other crime except a capital offense is there a one-to-one correspondence between the crime and the punishment. Thieves aren't punished by having something stolen from them; blackmailers aren't punished by being blackmailed; muggers aren't punished by being mugged. Why should murderers necessarily be punished by being executed? It's true that, generally, punishment is given according to the crime committed. The robber is punished differently from the drunken driver, and the murderer should be punished differently from the robber. But 'difference' doesn't necessarily entail capital punishment for the murderer."

3. *Capital punishment deters crime.*

POINT: "When potential murderers realize they may have to pay for their crimes with their lives, they'll think twice before killing. There's no telling how many potential murderers have been deterred from murdering because of capital punishment. It's just common sense that people will think more seriously about committing a murder if they know they can lose their own lives as a result."

COUNTERPOINT: "The statistics on this point are inconclusive. We just don't know for sure that capital punishment does or doesn't deter crime. Until we know for sure, your assumption is unsupported."

4. *Capital punishment is an economical way to punish offenders.*

POINT: "There's no conclusive evidence that murderers can be reformed. That means society is faced with having to foot the bill for their incarceration. But is this fair? Why should innocent people be made to pay for the care of those who have wantonly violated society's conventions when there's no evidence that such care will reform them?"

COUNTERPOINT: "That is a crass disregard for the value of human life. How can you seriously measure the worth of a life, even a criminal's, in dollars and cents? Surely such considerations are beneath the dignity of a society that considers itself civilized. Destroying a human life, even a murderer's, because it's the most economical thing to do is an outrage."

Gregg v. *Georgia* (1976)[4]

Troy Gregg was charged with committing armed robbery and murder. In accordance with Georgia procedure in capital cases, the trial had two stages: a guilt stage and a penalty stage.

In the guilt stage, the jury found Gregg guilty of two counts of armed robbery and two counts of murder. At the penalty stage, which took place before the same jury, the trial judge instructed the jury that it could recommend either a death sentence or a life prison sentence on each count. The jury returned verdicts of death on each count.

On appeal, the Supreme Court of Georgia affirmed the convictions and the imposition of the death sentence for murder, but it vacated the death sentence imposed for armed robbery on grounds that the death penalty had rarely been imposed in Georgia for that offense.

4. *Gregg v. Georgia*, U.S. Supreme Court, 238 U.S. (1976).

Eventually, the U.S. Supreme Court heard the case of Gregg v. Georgia. *The issue before the Court was whether capital punishment violated the Eighth Amendment's prohibition of cruel and unusual punishment. The majority of the Court held that it did not because: (1) capital punishment accords with contemporary standards of decency, (2) capital punishment may serve some deterrent or retributive purpose that is not degrading to human dignity, and (3) in the case of the Georgia law under review, capital punishment is no longer arbitrarily applied. (In* Furman v. Georgia, *1972, the court had ruled that the death penalty was unconstitutional as then administered, but did not comprehensively rule that it was unconstitutional by its very nature.)*

Dissenting, Justice Thurgood Marshall objected to the majority's decision on the grounds that: (1) capital punishment is not necessary for deterrence, (2) a retributive purpose for capital punishment is not consistent with human dignity, and (3) contemporary standards for decency with respect to capital punishment are not based on informed opinion. The following are excerpts from the majority and the dissenting views.

Majority Opinion (Written by Justice Potter Stewart)

We address initially the basic contention that the punishment of death for the crime of murder is, under all circumstances, "cruel and unusual" in violation of the Eighth and Fourteenth Amendments of the Constitution.

The Court on a number of occasions has both assumed and asserted the constitutionality of capital punishments. In several cases that assumption provided a necessary foundation for the decision, as the Court was asked to decide whether a particular method of carrying out a capital sentence would be allowed to stand under the Eighth Amendment. But until Furman v. Georgia, 408 U.S. 238 (1972), the Court never confronted squarely the fundamental claim that the punishment of death always, regardless of the enormity of the offense or the procedure followed in imposing the sentence, is cruel and unusual punishment in violation of the Constitution.

Although the issue was presented and addressed in Furman, it was not resolved by the Court. Four Justices would have held that capital punishment is not constitutional per se; two Justices would have reached the opposite conclusion; and three Justices, while agreeing that the statutes then before the Court were invalid as applied, left open the question whether such punishment may ever be imposed. We now hold that the punishment of death does not invariably violate the Constitution.

It is clear from the foregoing precedents that the Eighth Amendment has not been regarded as a static concept. As Chief Justice Warren said, in an oftquoted phrase, "[the] amendment must draw its meaning from the evolving standards of decency that mark the progress of a maturing society." Thus, an assessment of contemporary values concerning the infliction of a challenged sanction is relevant to the application of the Eighth Amendment. As we develop below more fully, this assessment does not call for a subjective judgment. It requires, rather, that we look to objective indicia that reflect the public attitude toward a given sanction.

But our cases also make clear that public perceptions of standards of decency with respect to criminal sanctions are not conclusive. A penalty also must accord with "the dignity of man," which is the "basic concept underlying the Eighth Amendment." This means, at least, that the punishment not be "excessive." When a form of punishment in the abstract (in this case, whether capital punishment may ever be imposed as a sanction for murder) rather than in the particular (the propriety of death as a penalty to be applied to a specific defendant for a specific crime) is under consideration, the inquiry into "excessiveness" has two aspects. First, the punishment must not involve the unnecessary and wanton infliction of pain. Second, the punishment must not be grossly out of proportion to the severity of the crime.

Of course, the requirements of the Eighth Amendment must be applied with an awareness of the limited role to be played by the courts. This does not mean that judges have no role to play, for the Eighth Amendment is a restraint upon the exercise of legislative power.

But, while we have an obligation to insure that constitutional bounds are not overreached, we may not act as judges as we might as legislators.

Therefore, in assessing a punishment by a democratically elected legislature against the constitutional measure, we presume its validity. We may not require the legislature to select the least severe penalty possible so long as the penalty selected is not cruelly inhumane or disproportionate to the crime involved. And a heavy burden rests on those who would attack the judgment of the representatives of the people.

This is true in part because the constitutional test is intertwined with an assessment of contemporary standards and legislative judgment weighs heavily in ascertaining such standards.

The deference we owe to the decisions of the state legislatures under our Federal system is enhanced where the specification of punishment is concerned, for "these are peculiarly questions of legislative policy." A decision that a given punishment is impermissible under the Eighth Amendment cannot be reversed short of a constitutional amendment. The ability of the people to express their preference through the normal democratic process, as well as through ballot referenda, is shut off. Revisions cannot be made in the light of further experience. We now consider specifically whether the sentence of death for the crime of murder is a per se violation of the Eighth and Fourteenth Amendments to the Constitution.

We note first that history and precedent strongly support a negative answer to this question.

The imposition of the death penalty for the crime of murder has a long history of acceptance both in the United States and in England. The common-law rule imposed a mandatory death sentence on all convicted murderers. And the penalty continued to be used into the 20th century by most American states, although the breadth of the common-law rule was diminished, initially by narrowing the class of murders to be punished by death and subsequently by widespread adoption of laws expressly granting judges the discretion to recommend mercy.

It is apparent from the text of the Constitution itself that the existence of capital punishment was accepted by the framers. At the time the Eighth Amendment was ratified, capital punishment was a common sanction in every state. Indeed, the first Congress of the United States enacted legislation providing death as the penalty for specified crimes.

For nearly two centuries, this Court, repeatedly and often expressly, has recognized that capital punishment is not invalid per se.

Four years ago, the petitioners in Furman and its companion cases predicated their argument primarily upon the asserted proposition that standards of decency had evolved to the point where capital punishment no longer could be tolerated. The petitioners in those cases said, in effect, that the evolutionary process had come to an end, and that standards of decency required that the Eighth amendment be construed finally as prohibiting capital punishment for any crime regardless of its depravity and impact on society.

The petitioners in the capital cases before the Court today renew the "standards of decency" argument, but developments during the four years since Furman have undercut substantially the assumptions upon which their argument rested. Despite the continuing debate, dating back to the 19th century, over the morality and utility of capital punishment, it is now evident that a large proportion of American society continues to regard it as an appropriate and necessary sanction.

The most marked indication of society's endorsement of the death penalty for murder is the legislative response to Furman. The legislatures of at least 35 states have enacted new statutes that provide for the death penalty for at least some crimes that result in the death of another person. And the Congress of the United States, in 1974, enacted a statute providing the death penalty for aircraft piracy that results in death.

As we have seen, however, the Eighth Amendment demands more than that a challenged punishment be acceptable to contemporary society. The Court also must ask whether it comports with the basic concept of human dignity at the core of the amendment. Although we cannot "invalidate a category of penalties because we deem less severe penalties adequate to serve the ends of penology," the sanction imposed cannot be so totally without penological justification that it results in the gratuitous infliction of suffering.

The death penalty is said to serve two principal social purposes: retribution and deterrence of capital crimes by prospective offenders.

In part, capital punishment is an expression of society's moral outrage at particularly offensive conduct. This function may be unappealing to many, but it is essential in an ordered society that asks its citizens to rely on legal processes rather than self-help to vindicate their wrongs.

Statistical attempts to evaluate the worth of the death penalty as a deterrent to crimes by potential offenders have occasioned a great deal of debate. The results simply have been inconclusive.

Although some of the studies suggest that the death penalty may not function as a significantly greater deterrent than lesser penalties, there is no convincing empirical evidence either supporting or refuting this view. We may nevertheless assume safely that there are murderers, such as those who act in passion, for whom the threat of death has little or no deterrent effect. But for many others, the death penalty undoubtedly is a significant deterrent. There are carefully contemplated murders, such as murder for hire, where the possible penalty of death may well enter into the cold calculus that precedes the decision to act. And there are some categories of murder, such as murder by a life prisoner, where other sanctions may not be adequate.

In sum, we cannot say that the judgment of the Georgia Legislature that capital punishment may be necessary in some cases is clearly wrong. Considerations of federalism, as well as respect for the ability of a legislature to evaluate, in terms of its particular state, the moral consensus concerning the death penalty and its social utility as a sanction, require us to conclude, in the absence of more convincing evidence, that the infliction of death as a punishment for murder is not without justification and thus is not unconstitutionally severe.

Finally, we must consider whether the punishment of death is disproportionate in relation to the crime for which it is imposed. There is no question that death as a punishment is unique in its severity and irrevocability. When a defendant's life is at stake, the Court has been particularly sensitive to insure that every safeguard is observed.

But we are concerned here only with the imposition of capital punishment for the crime of murder, and when a life has been taken deliberately by the offender, we cannot say that the punishment is invariably disproportionate to the crime. It is an extreme sanction, suitable to the most extreme of crimes.

We hold that the death penalty is not a form of punishment that may never be imposed, regardless of the circumstances of the offense, regardless of the character of the offender, and regardless of the procedure followed in reaching the decision to impose it.

We now consider whether Georgia may impose the death penalty on the petitioner in this case.

The basic concern of Furman centered on those defendants who were being condemned to death capriciously and arbitrarily. Under the procedures before the Court in that case, sentencing authorities were not directed to give attention to the nature or circumstances of the crime committed or to the character or record of the defendant. Left unguided, juries imposed the death sentence in a way that could only be called freakish. The new Georgia sentencing procedures, by contrast, focus the jury's attention on the particularized characteristics of the individual defendant. While the jury is permitted to consider any aggravating or mitigating circumstances, it must find and identify at least one statutory aggravating factor before it may impose a penalty of death. In this way the jury's discretion is channeled. No longer can a jury wantonly and freakishly impose the death sentence; it is always circumscribed by the legislative guidelines. In addition, the review function of the Supreme Court of Georgia affords additional assurance that the concerns that prompted our decision in Furman are not present to any significant degree in the Georgia procedure applied here.

For the reasons expressed in this opinion, we hold that the statutory system under which Gregg was sentenced to death does not violate the Constitution. Accordingly, the judgment of the Georgia Supreme Court is affirmed.

It is so ordered.

Mr. Justice Brennan, Dissenting

This Court inescapably has the duty, as the ultimate arbiter of the meaning of our Constitution, to say whether, when individuals condemned to death stand before our bar, "moral concepts" require us to hold that the law has progressed to the point where we should declare that the punishment of death, like punishments on the rack, the screw and the wheel, is no longer morally tolerable in our civilized society. My opinion in Furman v. Georgia concluded that our civilization and the law had progressed to this point and therefore the punishment of death, for whatever crime and under all circumstances, is "cruel and unusual" in violation of the Eighth and Fourteenth Amendments of the Constitution. I shall not again canvass the reasons that led to that conclusion. I emphasize only that foremost among the "moral concepts" recognized in our cases and inherent in the clause is the primary moral principle that the state, even as it punishes, must treat its citizens in a manner consistent with their intrinsic worth as human beings—a punishment must not be so severe as to be degrading to human dignity. A judicial determination whether the punishment of death comports with human dignity is therefore not only permitted but compelled by the clause.

Death is not only an unusually severe punishment, unusual in its pain, in its finality, and in its enormity, but it serves no penal purpose more effectively than a less severe punishment; therefore the principle inherent in the clause that prohibits pointless infliction of excessive punishment when less severe punishment can adequately achieve the same purposes invalidates the punishment.

Mr. Justice Marshall, Dissenting

My sole purposes here are to consider the suggestion that my conclusion in Furman has been undercut by developments since then, and briefly to evaluate the basis for my brethren's holding that the extinction of life is a permissible form of punishment under the cruel and unusual punishments clause.

In Furman I concluded that the death penalty is constitutionally invalid for two reasons. First, the death penalty is excessive. And second, the American people, fully informed as to the purposes of the death penalty and its liabilities, would in my view reject it as morally unacceptable.

Since the decision in Furman, the legislatures of 35 states have enacted new statutes, authorizing the imposition of the death sentence for certain crimes, and Congress has enacted a law providing the death penalty for air piracy resulting in death. I would be less than candid if I did not acknowledge that these developments have a significant bearing on a realistic assessment of the moral acceptability of the death penalty to the American people. But if the constitutionality of the death penalty turns, as I have urged, on the opinion of an informed citizenry, then even the enactment of new death statutes cannot be viewed as conclusive. In Furman, I observed that the American people are largely unaware of the information critical to a judgment on the morality of the death penalty, and concluded that if they were better informed they would consider it shocking, unjust, and unacceptable.

Even assuming, however, that the post-Furman enactment of statutes authorizing the death penalty renders the prediction of the views of an informed citizenry an uncertain basis for a constitutional decision, the enactment of those statutes has no bearing whatsoever on the conclusion that the death penalty is unconstitutional because it is excessive. An excessive penalty is invalid under the cruel and unusual punishments clause "even though popular sentiment may favor" it. The inquiry here, then, is simply whether the death penalty is necessary to accomplish the legitimate legislative purposes in punishment, or whether a less severe penalty—life imprisonment—would do as well.

The two purposes that sustain the death penalty as nonexcessive in the Court's view are general deterrence and retribution.

The Solicitor General in his amicus brief in these cases relies heavily on a study by Isaac Ehrlich, reported a year after Furman, to support the contention that the death penalty does deter murder.

The Ehrlich study, in short, is of little, if any, assistance in assessing the deterrent impact of the death penalty. The evidence I reviewed in Furman remains convincing, in my view, that "capital punishment is not necessary as a deterrent to crime in our society." The justification for the death penalty must be found elsewhere.

The other principal purpose said to be served by the death penalty is retribution. The notion that retribution can serve as a moral justification for the sanction of death finds credence in the opinion of my brothers Stewart, Powell, and Stevens, and that of my brother White in Roberts vs. Louisiana. It is this notion that I find to be the most disturbing aspect of today's unfortunate decision.

The foregoing contentions—that society's expression of moral outrage through the imposition of the death penalty pre-empts the citizenry from taking the law into its own hands and reinforces moral values—are not retributive in the purest sense. They are essentially utilitarian in that they portray the death penalty as valuable because of its beneficial results. These justifications for the death penalty are inadequate because the penalty is, quite clearly I think, not necessary to the accomplishment of those results.

There remains for consideration, however, what might be termed the purely retributive justification for the death penalty—that the death penalty is appropriate, not because of its beneficial effect on society, but because the taking of the murderer's life is itself morally good. Some of the language of the plurality's opinion appears positively to embrace this notion of retribution for its own sake as a justification for capital punishment.

The mere fact that the community demands the murderer's life in return for the evil he has done cannot sustain the death penalty, for as the plurality reminds us, "the Eighth Amendment demands more than that a challenged punishment be acceptable to contemporary society." To be sustained under the Eighth Amendment, the death penalty must "[comport] with the basic concept of human dignity at the core of the amendment"; the objective in imposing it must be "[consistent] with our respect for the dignity of other men." Under these standards, the taking of life "because the wrongdoer deserves it" surely must fall, for such a punishment has as its very basis the total denial of the wrongdoer's dignity and worth.

The death penalty, unnecessary to promote the goal of deterrence or to further any legitimate notion of retribution, is an excessive penalty forbidden by the Eighth and Fourteenth Amendments. I respectfully dissent from the Court's judgment upholding the sentences of death imposed upon the petitioners in these cases.

Questions for Analysis

1. *Writing the majority view, Justices Stewart, Powell, and Stevens explained: "The instinct for retribution is part of the nature of man, and channeling that instinct in the administration of criminal justice serves an important purpose in promoting the stability of a society governed by law. When people begin to believe that organized society is unwilling or unable to impose upon criminal offenders the punishment they 'deserve,' then there are sown the seeds of anarchy—of self help, vigilante justice, and lynch law." Do you think that is essentially a retributivist or utilitarian argument? In dissenting, Justice Marshall called the majority statement "wholly inadequate to justify the death penalty." With whom would you agree—the majority or Marshall?*

2. *Here's another quotation from the majority view: "[The] decision that capital punishment may be the appropriate sanction in extreme cases is an expression of the community's belief that certain crimes are themselves so grievous an affront to humanity that the only adequate response may be the penalty of death. . . . The truth is that some crimes are so outrageous that society insists on adequate punishment, because the wrong-doer deserves it, irrespective of whether it is a deterrent or not." Do you think this notion of retribution for its own sake is consistent with the basic concept of human dignity and worth which is at the base of the Eighth Amendment?*

The Death Sentence

Sidney Hook

In this essay, professor of philosophy Sidney Hook suggests that much of the debate about capital punishment suffers from vindictiveness and sentimentality. For example, abolitionists often argue that capital punishment is no more than an act of revenge, that it is the ultimate inhumanity. Hook is no more sympathetic, however, to the thrust of retentionist arguments. He points out that capital punishment has never been established as a deterrent to crime. Furthermore, he rejects as question-begging the retentionist argument that capital punishment is justified because it fulfills a community need, or that it is the only appropriate punishment for certain unspeakable offenses.

So where does Hook stand on the issue? Despite his feelings that no valid case for capital punishment has thus far been made, Hook is not categorically opposed to it. Indeed, he cites two conditions under which he believes capital punishment is justified. The first is in cases where criminals facing a life-imprisonment sentence request it. The second involves cases of convicted murderers who murder again. Hook regards the abolitionist objections to these exceptions as expressions of sentimentalism, even cruelty.

Is there anything new that can be said for or against capital punishment? Anyone familiar with the subject knows that unless extraneous issues are introduced, a large measure of agreement about it can be, and has been, won. For example, during the last 150 years the death penalty for criminal offenses has been abolished, or remains unenforced, in many countries; just as important, the number of crimes punishable by death has been sharply reduced in all countries. But while the progress has been encouraging, it still seems to me that greater clarity on the issues involved is desirable. Much of the continuing polemic still suffers from one or the other of the twin evils of vindictiveness and sentimentality.

Sentimentality, together with a great deal of confusion about determinism, is found in Clarence Darrow's speeches and writings on the subject. Darrow was an attractive and likeable human being but a very confused thinker. He argued against capital punishment on the ground that the murderer was always a victim of heredity and environment—and therefore it was unjust to execute him. ("Back of every murder and back of every human

act are sufficient causes that move the human machine beyond their control.") The crucifiers and the crucified, the lynch mob and its prey are equally moved by causes beyond their control and the relevant differences between them are therewith ignored. Although Darrow passionately asserted that no one knows what justice is and that no one can measure it, he nonetheless was passionately convinced that capital punishment was unjust.

It should be clear that if Darrow's argument were valid, it would be an argument not only against capital punishment but against all punishment. Very few of us would be prepared to accept this. But the argument is absurd. Even if we are all victims of our heredity and environment, it is still possible to alter the environment by meting out capital punishment to deter crimes of murder. If no one can help doing what he does, if no one is responsible for his actions, then surely this holds just as much for those who advocate and administer capital punishment as for the criminal. The denunciation of capital punishment as unjust, therefore, would be senseless. The question of universal determinism is irrelevant. If capital punishment actually were a

From Sidney Hook, "The Death Sentence," The New Leader, *vol. 44 (April 3, 1961). Copyright © The American Labor Conference on International Affairs, Inc. Reprinted, with three paragraphs added, by permission of the publisher. Cf. the original version which appeared in* The New York Law Forum *(August 1961), pp. 278–83, as an address before the New York State District Attorneys' Association.*

deterrent to murder, and there existed no other more effective deterrent, and none as effective but more humane, a case could be made for it.

Nor am I impressed with the argument against capital punishment on the ground of its inhumanity. Of course it is inhumane. So is murder. If it could be shown that the inhumanity of murder can be decreased in no other way than by the inhumanity of capital punishment acting as a deterrent, this would be a valid argument for such punishment.

I have stressed the hypothetical character of these arguments because it makes apparent how crucially the wisdom of our policy depends upon the alleged facts. Does capital punishment serve as the most effective deterrent we have against murder? Most people who favor its retention believe that it does. But any sober examination of the facts will show that this has never been established. It seems plausible, but not everything which is plausible or intuitively credible is true.

The experience of countries and states which have abolished capital punishment shows that there has been no perceptible increase of murders after abolition—although it would be illegitimate to infer from this that the fear of capital punishment never deterred anybody. The fact that "the state with the very lowest murder rate is Maine, which abolished capital punishment in 1870" may be explained by the hypothesis that fishermen, like fish, tend to be cold-blooded, or by some less fanciful hypothesis. The relevant question is: What objective evidence exists which would justify the conclusion that if Maine had not abolished capital punishment, its death rate would have been higher? The answer is: No evidence exists.

The opinion of many jurists and law enforcement officers from Cesare Beccaria (the eighteenth-century Italian criminologist) to the present is that swift and certain punishment of some degree of severity is a more effective deterrent of murder than the punishment of maximum severity when it is slow and uncertain. Although this opinion requires substantiation, too, it carries the weight which we normally extend to pronouncements by individuals who report on their life experience. And in the absence of convincing evidence that capital punishment is a more effective and/or humane form of punishment for murder than any other punishment, there remains no other reasonable ground for retaining it.

This is contested by those who speak of the necessity for capital punishment as an expression of the "community need of justice," or as the fulfillment of "an instinctive urge to punish injustice." Such views lie at the basis of some forms of the retributive theory. It has been alleged that the retributive theory is nothing more than a desire for revenge, but it is a great and arrogant error to assume that all who hold it are vindictive. The theory has been defended by secular saints like G. E. Moore and Immanuel Kant, whose dispassionate interest in justice cannot reasonably be challenged. Even if one accepted the retributive theory or believed in the desirability of meeting the community need of justice, it doesn't in the least follow that this justifies capital punishment. Other forms of punishment may be retributive, too.

I suppose that what one means by community need or feeling and the necessity of regarding it is that not only must justice be done, it must be seen to be done. A requirement of good law is that it must be consonant with the feeling of the community, something which is sometimes called "the living law." Otherwise it is unenforceable and brings the whole system of law into disrepute. Meeting community feeling is a necessary condition for good law, but not a sufficient condition for good law. This is what Justice Holmes meant when he wrote in *The Common Law* that "The first requirement of a sound body of law is that it should correspond with the actual feelings and demands of the community, whether right or wrong." But I think he would admit that sound law is sounder still if in addition to being enforceable it is also just. Our moral obligation as citizens is to build a community feeling and demand which is right rather than wrong.

Those who wish to retain capital punishment on the ground that it fulfills a community need or feeling must believe either that community feeling *per se* is always justified, or that to disregard it in any particular situation is inexpedient because of the consequences, *viz.*, increase in murder. In either case they beg the question—in the first case, the question of justice, and in the second, the question of deterrence.

One thing is incontestable. From the standpoint of those who base the argument for retention of capital punishment on the necessity of satisfying community needs there could be no justification whatsoever for any *mandatory* death sentence. For a mandatory death sentence attempts to determine in advance what the community need and feeling will be, and closes the door to fresh inquiry about the justice as well as the deterrent consequences of any proposed punishment.

Community need and feeling are notoriously fickle. When a verdict of guilty necessarily entails a death sentence, the jury may not feel the sentence warranted and may bring in a verdict of not guilty even when some punishment seems to be legally and morally justified. Even when the death sentence is not mandatory, there is an argument, not decisive but still significant, against any death sentence. This is its incorrigibility. Our judgment of a convicted man's guilt may change. If he has been executed in the meantime, we can only do him "posthumous justice." But can justice ever really be posthumous to the victim? Rarely has evidence, even when it is beyond reasonable doubt, the same finality about its probative force as the awful finality of death. The weight of this argument against capital punishment is all the stronger if community need and feeling are taken as the prime criteria of what is just or fitting.

What about heinous political offenses? Usually when arguments fail to sustain the demand for capital punishment in ordinary murder cases, the names of Adolf Hitler, Adolf Eichmann, Joseph Stalin and Ilse Koch are introduced and flaunted before the audience to inflame their feelings. Certain distinctions are in order here. Justice, of course, requires severe punishment. But why is it assumed that capital punishment is, in these cases, the severest and most just of sentences? How can any equation be drawn between the punishment of one man and the sufferings of his numerous victims? After all, we cannot kill Eichmann six million times or Stalin twelve million times (a conservative estimate of the number of people who died by their order).

If we wish to keep alive the memory of political infamy, if we wish to use it as a political lesson to prevent its recurrence, it may be educationally far more effective to keep men like Eichmann in existence. Few people think of the dead. By the same token, it may be necessary to execute a politically monstrous figure to prevent him from becoming the object of allegiance of a restoration movement. Eichmann does not have to be executed. He is more useful alive if we wish to keep before mankind the enormity of his offense. But if Hitler had been taken alive, his death would have been required as a matter of political necessity, to prevent him from becoming a living symbol or rallying cry of Nazi diehards and irreconcilables.

There is an enormous amount of historical evidence which shows that certain political tyrants, after they lose power, become the focus of restoration movements that are a chronic source of bloodshed and civil strife. No matter how infamous a tyrant's actions, there is usually some group which has profited by it, resents being deprived of its privileges, and schemes for a return to power. In difficult situations, the dethroned tyrant also becomes a symbol of legitimacy around which discontented elements rally who might otherwise have waited for the normal processes of government to relieve their lot. A *mystique* develops around the tyrant, appeals are made to the "good old days," when his bread and circuses were used to distract attention from the myriads of his tortured victims, plots seethe around him until they boil over into violence and bloodshed again. I did not approve of the way Mussolini was killed. Even he deserved due process. But I have no doubt whatsoever that had he been sentenced merely to life imprisonment, the Fascist movement in Italy today would be a much more formidable movement, and that sooner or later, many lives would have been lost in consequence of the actions of Fascist legitimists.

Where matters of ordinary crime are concerned these political considerations are irrelevant. I conclude, therefore, that no valid case has so far been made for the retention of capital punishment, that the argument from deterrence is inconclusive and inconsistent (in the sense that we do not do other things to reinforce its deterrent effect if we believe it has such an effect), and that the argument from community feeling is invalid.

However, since I am not a fanatic or absolutist, I do not wish to go on record as being categorically opposed to the death sentence in all circumstances. I should like to recognize two exceptions. A defendant convicted of murder and sentenced to life should be permitted to choose the death sentence instead. Not so long ago a defendant sentenced to life imprisonment made this request and was rebuked by the judge for his impertinence. I can see no valid grounds for denying such a request out of hand. It may sometimes be denied, particularly if a way can be found to make the defendant labor for the benefit of the dependents of his victim, as is done in some European countries. Unless such considerations are present, I do not see on what reasonable ground the request can be denied, particularly by those who believe in capital punishment. Once they argue that life imprisonment is either a more effective deterrent or more justly punitive, they have abandoned their position.

In passing, I should state that I am in favor of permitting *any* criminal defendant, sentenced to life imprisonment, the right to choose death. I can understand why certain jurists, who believe that the defendant wants thereby to cheat the state out of its mode of punishment, should be indignant at the idea. They are usually the ones who believe that even the attempt at suicide should be deemed a crime—in effect saying to the unfortunate person that if he doesn't succeed in his act of suicide, the state will punish him for it. But I am baffled to understand why the absolute abolitionist, dripping with treacly humanitarianism, should oppose this proposal. I have heard some people actually oppose capital punishment in certain cases on the ground that: "Death is too good for the vile wretch! Let him live and suffer to the end of his days." But the absolute abolitionist should be the last person in the world to oppose the wish of the lifer, who regards this form of punishment as torture worse than death, to leave our world.

My second class of exceptions consists of those who having been sentenced once to prison for premeditated murder, murder again. In these particular cases we have evidence that imprisonment is not a sufficient deterrent for the individual in question. If the evidence shows that the prisoner is so psychologically constituted that, without being insane, the fact that he can kill again with impunity may lead to further murderous behavior, the court should have the discretionary power to pass the death sentence if the criminal is found guilty of a second murder.

In saying that the death sentence should be *discretionary* in cases where a man has killed more than once, I am *not* saying that a murderer who murders again is more deserving of death than the murderer who murders once. Bluebeard was not twelve times more deserving of death when he was finally caught. I am saying simply this: that in a sub-class of murderers, i.e., those who murder several times, there may be a special group of sane murderers who, knowing that they will not be executed, will not hesitate to kill again and again. For *them* the argument from deterrence is obviously valid. Those who say that there must be no exceptions to the abolition of capital punishment cannot rule out the existence of such cases on *a priori* grounds. If they admit that there is a reasonable probability that such murderers will murder again or attempt to murder again, a probability which usually grows with the number of repeated murders, and still insist they would *never* approve of capital punishment, I would conclude that they are indifferent to the lives of the human beings doomed, on their position, to be victims. What fancies itself as a humanitarian attitude is sometimes an expression of sentimentalism. The reverse coin of sentimentalism is often cruelty.

Our charity for all human beings must not deprive us of our common sense. Nor should our charity be less for the future or potential victims of the murderer than for the murderer himself. There are crimes in this world which are, like acts of nature, beyond the power of men to anticipate or control. But not all or most crimes are of this character. So long as human beings are responsible and educable, they will respond to praise and blame and punishment. It is hard to imagine it, but even Hitler and Stalin were once infants. Once you *can* imagine them as infants, however, it is hard to believe that they were already monsters in their cradles. Every confirmed criminal was once an amateur. The existence of confirmed criminals testifies to the defects of our education—where they can be reformed—and of our penology—where they cannot. That is why we are under the moral obligation to be intelligent about crime and punishment. Intelligence should teach us that the best educational and penological system is the one which prevents crimes rather than punishes them; the next best is one which punishes crime in such a way as to prevent it from happening again.

Questions for Analysis

1. Why does Hook say that if Darrow's argument were valid, it would be an argument not against capital punishment but against all punishment?

2. Why is Hook not impressed by the claim that capital punishment is inhumane? Do you agree with him?

3. Why does Hook feel that those who justify capital punishment by appeal to community feeling beg the question? Do you accept his argument?

4. How does Hook respond to the retentionist claim that capital punishment is justified for politically heinous offenses?

5. Do you agree that a "lifer's" request for capital punishment ought to be honored? Is Hook's justification for his position utilitarian or nonutilitarian? Explain.

6. Why does Hook believe capital punishment is justified when a convicted murderer murders again? Is his defense utilitarian? Explain.

7. Do you agree with Hook that what are called "humanitarian" objections to his two exceptions are really expressions of sentimentalism, even cruelty?

On Deterrence and the Death Penalty

Ernest Van Den Haag

Professor of social philosophy Ernest Van Den Haag begins his essay by conceding that capital punishment cannot be defended on grounds of rehabilitation or protection of society from unrehabilitated offenders. But he does believe that the ultimate punishment can be justified on grounds of deterrence.

To make his point, Van Den Haag at some length provides a psychological basis for deterrence. He associates deterrence with human responses to danger. Law functions to change social dangers into individual ones: Legal threats are designed to deter individuals from actions that threaten society. Most of us, Van Den Haag argues, transfer these external penalty dangers into internal ones; that is, we each develop a conscience that threatens us if we do wrong. But this conscience is and needs to be reinforced by external authority, which imposes penalties for antisocial behavior.

Van Den Haag then critically examines the reason punishment has fallen into disrepute as a deterrent to crime: the claim that slums, ghettos, and personality disorders are the real causes of crime. He dismisses these as spurious explanations, and insists that only punishment can deter crime. In Van Den Haag's view, whether individuals will commit crimes depends exclusively on whether they perceive the penalty risks as worth it.

While he concedes that the death penalty cannot be proved to deter crime, Van Den Haag observes that this in no way means capital punishment lacks a deterrent value. Indeed, it is this very uncertainty about its deterrence that impels Van Den Haag to argue for its retention. In the last analysis, he believes that retaining capital punishment leads to a net gain for society, notwithstanding the occasional abuse of it. In arguing for capital punishment, then, Van Den Haag takes a utilitarian viewpoint.

Reprinted by special permission of the Journal of Criminal Law, Criminology, and Police Science, © *1969 by Northwestern University School of Law, Vol. 60, No. 2.*

I

If rehabilitation and the protection of society from unrehabilitated offenders were the only purposes of legal punishment, the death penalty could be abolished: It cannot attain the first end, and is not needed for the second. No case for the death penalty can be made unless "doing justice" or "deterring others" is among our penal aims.[1] Each of these purposes can justify capital punishment by itself; opponents, therefore, must show that neither actually does, while proponents can rest their case on either.

Although the argument from justice is intellectually more interesting, and, in my view, decisive enough, utilitarian arguments have more appeal: The claim that capital punishment is useless because it does not deter others is most persuasive. I shall, therefore, focus on this claim. Lest the argument be thought to be unduly narrow, I shall show, nonetheless, that some claims of injustice rest on premises which the claimants reject when arguments for capital punishment are derived therefrom; while other claims of injustice have no independent standing: Their weight depends on the weight given to deterrence.

II

Capital punishment is regarded as unjust because it may lead to the execution of innocents, or because the guilty poor (or disadvantaged) are more likely to be executed than the guilty rich.

Regardless of merit, these claims are relevant only if "doing justice" is one purpose of punishment. Unless one regards it as good, or, at least, better, that the guilty be punished rather than the innocent, and that the equally guilty be punished equally,[2] unless, that is, one wants penalties to be just, one cannot object to them because they are not. However, if one does include justice among the purposes of punishment, it becomes possible to justify any one punishment—even death—on grounds of justice. Yet, those who object to the death penalty because of its alleged injustice usually deny not only the merits, or the sufficiency, of specific arguments based on justice, but the propriety of justice as an argument: They exclude "doing justice" as a purpose of legal punishment. If justice is not a purpose of penalties, injustice cannot be an objection to the death penalty, or to any other; if it is, justice cannot be ruled out as an argument for any penalty.

Consider the claim of injustice on its merits now. A convicted man may be found to have been innocent; if he was executed, the penalty cannot be reversed. Except for fines, penalties never can be reversed. Time spent in prison cannot be returned. However, a prison sentence may be remitted once the prisoner serving it is found innocent; and he can be compensated for the time served (although compensation ordinarily cannot repair the harm). Thus, though (nearly) all penalties are irreversible, the death penalty, unlike others, is irrevocable as well.

Despite all precautions, errors will occur in judicial proceedings: The innocent may be found guilty,[3] or the guilty rich may more easily escape conviction, or receive lesser penalties than the guilty poor. However, these injustices do not reside in the penalties inflicted but in their maldistribution. It is not the penalty—whether death or prison—which is unjust when inflicted on the innocent, but its imposition on the innocent. Inequity between poor and rich also involves distribution, not the penalty distributed.[4] Thus injustice is not an objection to the death penalty but to the distributive process—the trial. Trials are more likely to be fair when life is at stake—the death penalty is probably less often unjustly inflicted than others. It requires special consideration not because it is more, or more often, unjust than other penalties, but because it is always irrevocable.

Can any amount of deterrence justify the possibility of irrevocable injustice? Surely injustice is unjustifiable in each actual individual case; it must be objected to whenever it occurs. But we are concerned here with the process that may produce injustice, and with the penalty that would make it irrevocable—not with the actual individual cases produced, but with the general rules which may produce them. To consider objections to a general rule (the provision of any penalties by law) we must compare the likely net result of alternative rules and select the rule (or penalty) likely to produce the least injustice. For however one defines justice, to support it cannot mean less than to favor the least injustice. If the death of innocents because of judicial error is unjust, so is the death of innocents by murder. If some murders could be avoided by a penalty conceivably more deterrent than others—

such as the death penalty—then the question becomes: Which penalty will minimize the number of innocents killed (by crime and by punishment)? It follows that the irrevocable injustice sometimes inflicted by the death penalty would not significantly militate against it, if capital punishment deters enough murders to reduce the total number of innocents killed so that fewer are lost than would be lost without it.

In general, the possibility of injustice argues against penalization of any kind only if the expected usefulness of penalization is less important than the probable harm (particularly to innocents) and the probable inequities. The possibility of injustice argues against the death penalty only inasmuch as the added usefulness (deterrence) expected from irrevocability is thought less important than the added harm. (Were my argument specifically concerned with justice, I could compare the injustice inflicted by the courts with the injustice—outside the courts—avoided by the judicial process. *I.e.,* "important" here may be used to include everything to which importance is attached.)

We must briefly examine now the general use and effectiveness of deterrence to decide whether the death penalty could add enough deterrence to be warranted.

III

Does any punishment "deter others" at all? Doubts have been thrown on this effect because it is thought to depend on the incorrect rationalistic psychology of some of its 18th- and 19th-century proponents. Actually deterrence does not depend on rational calculation, on rationality or even on capacity for it; nor do arguments for it depend on rationalistic psychology. Deterrence depends on the likelihood and on the regularity—not on the rationality—of human responses to danger; and further on the possibility of reinforcing internal controls by vicarious external experiences.

Responsiveness to danger is generally found in human behavior; the danger can, but need not, come from the law or from society; nor need it be explicitly verbalized. Unless intent on suicide, people do not jump from high mountain cliffs, however tempted to fly through the air; and they take precautions against falling. The mere risk of injury often restrains us from doing what is otherwise

attractive; we refrain even when we have no direct experience, and usually without explicit computation of probabilities, let alone conscious weighing of expected pleasure against possible pain. One abstains from dangerous acts because of vague, inchoate, habitual and, above all, preconscious fears. Risks and rewards are more often felt than calculated; one abstains without accounting to oneself, because "it isn't done," or because one literally does not conceive of the action one refrains from. Animals as well refrain from painful or injurious experiences presumably without calculation; and the threat of punishment can be used to regulate their conduct.

Unlike natural dangers, legal threats are constructed deliberately by legislators to restrain actions which may impair the social order. Thus legislation transforms social into individual dangers. Most people further transform external into internal danger: They acquire a sense of moral obligation, a conscience, which threatens them, should they do what is wrong. Arising originally from the external authority of rulers and rules, conscience is internalized and becomes independent of external forces. However, conscience is constantly reinforced in those whom it controls by the coercive imposition of external authority on recalcitrants and on those who have not acquired it. Most people refrain from offenses because they feel an obligation to behave lawfully. But this obligation would scarcely be felt if those who do not feel or follow it were not to suffer punishment.

Although the legislators may calculate their threats and the responses to be produced, the effectiveness of the threats neither requires nor depends on calculations by those responding. The predictor (or producer) of effects must calculate; those whose responses are predicted (or produced) need not. Hence, although legislation (and legislators) should be rational, subjects, to be deterred as intended, need not be: They need only be responsive.

Punishments deter those who have not violated the law for the same reasons—and in the same degrees (apart from internalization: moral obligation) as do natural dangers. Often natural dangers—all dangers not deliberately created by legislation (*e.g.*, injury of the criminal inflicted by the crime victim) are insufficient. Thus, the fear of injury (natural danger) does not suffice to control city traffic; it must be reinforced by the legal punishment meted out to those who violate the rules. These punishments keep most people observing the regulations. However, where (in the absence of natural danger) the threatened punishment is so light that the advantage of violating rules tends to exceed the disadvantage of being punished (divided by the risk), the rule is violated (*i.e.*, parking fines are too light). In this case the feeling of obligation tends to vanish as well. Elsewhere punishment deters.

To be sure, not everybody responds to threatened punishment. Non-responsive persons may be (a) self-destructive or (b) incapable of responding to threats, or even of grasping them. Increases in the size, or certainty, of penalties would not affect these two groups. A third group (c) might respond to more certain or more severe penalties.[5] If the punishment threatened for burglary, robbery, or rape were a $5 fine in North Carolina, and 5 years in prison in South Carolina, I have no doubt that the North Carolina treasury would become quite opulent until vigilante justice would provide the deterrence not provided by law. Whether to increase penalties (or improve enforcement) depends on the importance of the rule to society, the size and likely reaction of the group that did not respond before, and the acceptance of the added punishment and enforcement required to deter it. Observation would have to locate the points—likely to differ in different times and places—at which diminishing, zero, and negative returns set in. There is no reason to believe that all present and future offenders belong to the *a priori* non-responsive groups, or that all penalties have reached the point of diminishing, let alone zero returns.

IV

Even though its effectiveness seems obvious, punishment as a deterrent has fallen into disrepute. Some ideas which help explain this progressive heedlessness were uttered by Lester Pearson, then Prime Minister of Canada, when, in opposing the death penalty, he proposed that instead "the state seek to eradicate the causes of crime—slums, ghettos and personality disorders."[6]

"Slums, ghettos, and personality disorders" have not been shown, singly or collectively, to be "the causes" of crime.

(1) The crime rate in the slums is indeed higher than elsewhere; but so is the death rate in hospitals. Slums are no more "causes" of crime than hospitals are of death; they are locations of crime, as hospitals are of death. Slums and hospitals attract people selectively; neither is the "cause" of the condition (disease in hospitals, poverty in slums) that leads to the selective attraction.

As for poverty which draws people into slums, and, sometimes, into crime, any relative disadvantage may lead to ambition, frustration, resentment and, if insufficiently restrained, to crime. Not all relative disadvantages can be eliminated; indeed very few can be, and their elimination increases the resentment generated by the remaining ones; not even relative poverty can be removed altogether. (Absolute poverty—whatever that may be—hardly affects crime.) However, though contributory, relative disadvantages are not a necessary or sufficient cause of crime: Most poor people do not commit crimes, and some rich people do. Hence, "eradication of poverty" would, at most, remove one (doubtful) cause of crime.

In the United States, the decline of poverty has not been associated with a reduction of crime. Poverty measured in dollars of constant purchasing power, according to present government standards and statistics, was the condition of ½ of all our families in 1920; of ⅕ in 1962; and of less than ⅙ in 1966. In 1967, 5.3 million families out of 49.8 million were poor—⅑ of all families in the United States. If crime has been reduced in a similar manner, it is a well-kept secret.

Those who regard poverty as a cause of crime often draw a wrong inference from a true proposition: The rich will not commit certain crimes—Rockefeller never riots; nor does he steal. (He mugs, but only on T. V.) Yet while wealth may be the cause of not committing (certain) crimes, it does not follow that poverty (absence of wealth) is the cause of committing them. Water extinguishes or prevents fire; but its absence is not the cause of fire. Thus, if poverty could be abolished, if everybody had all "necessities" (I don't pretend to know what this would mean), crime would remain, for, in the words of Aristotle, "the greatest crimes are committed not for the sake of basic necessities but for the sake of superfluities." Superfluities cannot be provided by the government; they would be what the government does not provide.

(2) Negro ghettos have a high, Chinese ghettos have a low crime rate. Ethnic separation, voluntary or forced, obviously has little to do with crime; I can think of no reason why it should.[7]

(3) I cannot see how the state could "eradicate" personality disorders even if all causes and cures were known and available. (They are not.) Further, the known incidence of personality disorders within the prison population does not exceed the known incidence outside—though our knowledge of both is tenuous. Nor are personality disorders necessary or sufficient causes for criminal offenses, unless these be identified by means of (moral, not clinical) definition with personality disorders. In this case, Mr. Pearson would have proposed to "eradicate" crime by eradicating crime—certainly a sound, but not a helpful idea.

Mr. Pearson's views are part as well of the mental furniture of the former U.S. Attorney General Ramsey Clark, who told a congressional committee that ". . . only the elimination of the causes of crime can make a significant and lasting difference in the incidence of crime." Uncharitably interpreted, Mr. Clark revealed that only the elimination of causes eliminates effects—a sleazy cliché and wrong to boot. Given the benefit of the doubt, Mr. Clark probably meant that the causes of crime are social; and that therefore crime can be reduced "only" by non-penal (social) measures.

This view suggests a fireman who declines fire-fighting apparatus by pointing out that "in the long run only the elimination of the causes" of fire "can make a significant and lasting difference in the incidence" of fire, and that fire-fighting equipment does not eliminate "the causes"—except that such a fireman would probably not rise to fire chief. Actually, whether fires are checked depends on equipment and on the efforts of the firemen using it no less than on the presence of "the causes": inflammable materials. So with crimes. Laws, courts and police actions are no less important in restraining them than "the causes" are in impelling them. If firemen (or attorneys general) pass the buck and refuse to use the means available, we may all be burned while waiting for "the long run" and "the elimination of the causes."

Whether any activity—be it lawful or unlawful—takes place depends on whether the desire for it, or for whatever is to be secured by it, is stronger than the desire to avoid the costs involved. Accord-

ingly people work, attend college, commit crimes, go to the movies—or refrain from any of these activities. Attendance at a theatre may be high because the show is entertaining and because the price of admission is low. Obviously the attendance depends on both—on the combination of expected gratification and cost. The wish, motive or impulse for doing anything—the experienced, or expected, gratification—is the cause of doing it; the wish to avoid the cost is the cause of not doing it. One is no more and no less "cause" than the other. (Common speech supports this use of "cause" no less than logic: "Why did you go to Jamaica?" "*Because* it is such a beautiful place." "Why didn't you go to Jamaica?" "*Because* it is too expensive."—"Why do you buy this?" "*Because* it is so cheap." "Why don't you buy that?" "*Because* it is too expensive.") Penalties (costs) are causes of lawfulness, or (if too low or uncertain) of unlawfulness, of crime. People do commit crimes because, given their conditions, the desire for the satisfaction sought prevails. They refrain if the desire to avoid the cost prevails. Given the desire, low cost (penalty) causes the action, and high cost restraint. Given the cost, desire becomes the causal variable. Neither is intrinsically more causal than the other. The crime rate increases if the cost is reduced or the desire raised. It can be decreased by raising the cost or by reducing the desire.

The cost of crime is more easily and swiftly changed than the conditions producing the inclination to it. Further, the costs are very largely within the power of the government to change, whereas the conditions producing propensity to crime are often only indirectly affected by government action, and some are altogether beyond the control of the government. Our unilateral emphasis on these conditions and our undue neglect of costs may contribute to an unnecessarily high crime rate.

V

The foregoing suggests the question posed by the death penalty: Is the deterrence added (return) sufficiently above zero to warrant irrevocability (or other, less clear, disadvantages)? The question is not only whether the penalty deters, but whether it deters more than alternatives and whether the difference exceeds the cost of irrevocability. (I shall assume that the alternative is actual life imprisonment so as to exclude the complication produced by the release of the unrehabilitated.)

In some fairly infrequent but important circumstances the death penalty is the only possible deterrent. Thus, in case of acute *coups d'état*, or of acute substantial attempts to overthrow the government, prospective rebels would altogether discount the threat of any prison sentence. They would not be deterred because they believe the swift victory of the revolution will invalidate a prison sentence and turn it into an advantage. Execution would be the only deterrent because, unlike prison sentences, it cannot be revoked by victorious rebels. The same reasoning applies to deterring spies or traitors in wartime. Finally, men who, by virtue of past acts, are already serving, or are threatened, by a life sentence could be deterred from further offenses only by the threat of the death penalty.[8]

What about criminals who do not fall into any of these (often ignored) classes? Prof. Thorsten Sellin has made a careful study of the available statistics: He concluded that they do not yield evidence for the deterring effect of the death penalty.[9] Somewhat surprisingly, Prof. Sellin seems to think that this lack of evidence for deterrence is evidence for the lack of deterrence. It is not. It means that deterrence has not been demonstrated statistically—not that non-deterrence has been.

It is entirely possible, indeed likely (as Prof. Sellin appears willing to concede), that the statistics used, though the best available, are nonetheless too slender a reed to rest conclusions on. They indicate that the homicide rate does not vary greatly between similar areas with or without the death penalty, and in the same area before and after abolition. However, the similar areas are not similar enough; the periods are not long enough; many social differences and changes, other than the abolition of the death penalty, may account for the variation (or lack of it) in homicide rates with and without, before and after abolition; some of these social differences and changes are likely to have affected homicide rates. I am unaware of any statistical analysis which adjusts for such changes and differences. And logically, it is quite consistent with the postulated deterrent effect of capital punishment that there be less homicide after abolition: With retention there might have been still less.

Homicide rates do not depend exclusively on penalties any more than do other crime rates. A number of conditions which influence the propensity to crime, demographic, economic or generally social changes or differences—even such matters as changes of the divorce laws or of the cotton price—may influence the homicide rate. Therefore variation or constancy cannot be attributed to variations or constancy of the penalties, unless we know that no other factor influencing the homicide rate has changed. Usually we don't. To believe the death penalty deterrent does not require one to believe that the death penalty, or any other, is the only or the decisive causal variable; this would be as absurd as the converse mistake that "social causes" are the only or always the decisive factor. To favor capital punishment, the efficacy of neither variable need be denied. It is enough to affirm that the severity of the penalty may influence some potential criminals, and that the added severity of the death penalty adds to deterrence, or may do so. It is quite possible that such a deterrent effect may be offset (or intensified) by non-penal factors which affect propensity; its presence or absence therefore may be hard, and perhaps impossible to demonstrate.

Contrary to what Prof. Sellin *et al.* seem to presume, I doubt that offenders are aware of the absence or presence of the death penalty state by state or period by period. Such unawareness argues against the assumption of a calculating murderer. However, unawareness does not argue against the death penalty if by deterrence we mean a preconscious, general response to a severe, but not necessarily specifically and explicitly apprehended, or calculated threat. A constant homicide rate, despite abolition, may occur because of unawareness and not because of lack of deterrence: People remain deterred for a lengthy interval by the severity of the penalty in the past, or by the severity of penalties used in similar circumstances nearby.

I do not argue for a version of deterrence which would require me to believe that an individual shuns murder while in North Dakota, because of the death penalty, and merrily goes to it in South Dakota since it has been abolished there; or that he will start the murderous career from which he had hitherto refrained, after abolition. I hold that the generalized threat of the death penalty may be a deterrent, and the more so, the more generally applied. Deterrence will not cease in the particular areas of abolition or at the particular times of abolition.

Rather, general deterrence will be somewhat weakened, through local (partial) abolition. Even such weakening will be hard to detect owing to changes in many offsetting, or reinforcing, factors.

For all of these reasons, I doubt that the presence or absence of a deterrent effect of the death penalty is likely to be demonstrable by statistical means. The statistics presented by Prof. Sellin *et al.* show only that there is no statistical proof for the deterrent effect of the death penalty. But they do not show that there is no deterrent effect. Not to demonstrate presence of the effect is not the same as to demonstrate its absence; certainly not when there are plausible explanations for the non-demonstrability of the effect.

It is on our uncertainty that the case for deterrence must rest.[10]

VI

If we do not know whether the death penalty will deter others, we are confronted with two uncertainties. If we impose the death penalty, and achieve no deterrent effect thereby, the life of a convicted murderer has been expended in vain (from a deterrent viewpoint). There is a net loss. If we impose the death sentence and thereby deter some future murderers, we spared the lives of some future victims (the prospective murderers gain too; they are spared punishment because they were deterred). In this case, the death penalty has led to a net gain, unless the life of a convicted murderer is valued more highly than that of the unknown victim, or victims (and the non-imprisonment of the deterred non-murderer).

The calculation can be turned around, of course. The absence of the death penalty may harm no one and therefore produce a gain—the life of the convicted murderer. Or it may kill future victims of murderers who could have been deterred, and thus produce a loss—their life.

To be sure, we must risk something certain—the death (or life) of the convicted man, for something uncertain—the death (or life) of the victims of murderers who may be deterred. This is in the nature of uncertainty—when we invest, or gamble, we risk the money we have for an uncertain gain. Many human actions, most commitments—including marriage and crime—share this characteristic with the deterrent purpose of any penal-

ization, and with its rehabilitative purpose (and even with the protective).

More proof is demanded for the deterrent effect of the death penalty than is demanded for the deterrent effect of other penalties. This is not justified by the absence of other utilitarian purposes such as protection and rehabilitation; they involve no less uncertainty than deterrence.[11]

Irrevocability may support a demand for some reason to expect more deterrence than revocable penalties might produce, but not a demand for more proof of deterrence, as has been pointed out above. The reason for expecting more deterrence lies in the greater severity, the terrifying effect inherent in finality. Since it seems more important to spare victims than to spare murderers, the burden of proving that the greater severity inherent in irrevocability adds nothing to deterrence lies on those who oppose capital punishment. Proponents of the death penalty need show only that there is no more uncertainty about it than about greater severity in general.

The demand that the death penalty be proved more deterrent than alternatives can not be satisfied any more than the demand that six years in prison be proved to be more deterrent than three. But the uncertainty which confronts us favors the death penalty as long as by imposing it we might save future victims of murder. This effect is as plausible as the general idea that penalties have deter-effects which increase with their severity. Though we have no proof of the positive deterrence of the penalty, we also have no proof of zero or negative effectiveness. I believe we have no right to risk additional future victims of murder for the sake of sparing convicted murderers; on the contrary, our moral obligation is to risk the possible ineffectiveness of executions. However rationalized, the opposite view appears to be motivated by the simple fact that executions are more subjected to social control than murder. However, this applies to all penalties and does not argue for the abolition of any.

Notes

1. Social solidarity of "community feeling" (here to be ignored) might be dealt with as a form of deterrence.
2. Certainly a major meaning of *suum cuique tribue.*

3. I am not concerned here with the converse injustice, *which I regard as no less grave.*

4. Such inequity, though likely, has not been demonstrated. Note that, since there are more poor than rich, there are likely to be more guilty poor; and, if poverty contributes to crime, the proportion of the poor who are criminals also should be higher than of the rich.

5. I neglect those motivated by civil disobedience or, generally, moral or political passion. Deterring them depends less on penalties than on the moral support they receive, though penalties play a role. I also neglect those who may belong to all three groups listed, some successively, some even simultaneously, such as drug addicts. Finally, I must altogether omit the far-from-negligible role that problems of apprehension and conviction play in deterrence—beyond saying that, by reducing the government's ability to apprehend and convict, courts are able to reduce the risks of offenders.

6. I quote from the *New York Times* (November 24, 1967, p. 22). The actual psychological and other factors which bear on the disrepute—as distinguished from the rationalizations—cannot be examined here.

7. Mixed areas, incidentally, have higher crime rates than segregated ones (see, e.g., R. Ross and E. van den Haag, *The Fabric of Society* (New York: Harcourt, Brace & Co., 1957), pp. 102–4. Because slums are bad (morally) and crime is, many people seem to reason that "slums spawn crime"—which confuses some sort of moral with a causal relation.

8. Cautious revolutionaries, uncertain of final victory, might be impressed by prison sentences—but not in the acute stage, when faith in victory is high. And one can increase even the severity of a life sentence in prison. Finally, harsh punishment of rebels can intensify rebellious impulses. These points, though they qualify it, hardly impair the force of the argument.

9. Sellin considered mainly homicide statistics. His work may be found in his *Capital Punishment* (New York: Harper & Row, 1967); or, most conveniently, in H. A. Bedau, *The Death Penalty in America* (Garden City, N.Y.: Doubleday & Co., 1964), which also offers other material, mainly against the death penalty.

10. In view of the strong emotions aroused (itself an indication of effectiveness to me: Might not murderers be as upset over the death penalty as those who wish to spare them?) and because I believe penalties must reflect community feeling to be effective, I oppose mandatory death sentences and favor optional, and perhaps binding, recommendations by juries after their finding of guilt. The opposite course risks the non-conviction of guilty defendants by juries who do not want to see them executed.

11. Rehabilitation or protection are of minor importance in our actual penal system (though not in our theory). We confine many people who do not need rehabilitation and against whom we do not need protection (e.g., the exasperated husband who killed his wife); we release many unrehabilitated offenders against whom protection is needed. Certainly rehabilitation and protection are not, and deterrence is, the main actual function of legal punishment if we disregard non-utilitarian ones.

Questions for Analysis

1. *Van Den Haag claims that injustice is an objection not to the death penalty but to the distributive process. What does he mean? Is his distinction between penalty and distribution germane?*

2. *What does deterrence depend on, in Van Den Haag's view?*

3. *How does punishment differ from natural dangers?*

4. *What kinds of people do not respond to threatened punishment? Would you be persuaded by the anti-capital-punishment argument that insists the death penalty simply does not deter certain people?*

5. *What determines whether penalties ought to be increased? Explain how this is a utilitarian argument.*

6. *Does Van Den Haag convince you that slums and ghettos are "no more 'causes' of crimes than hospitals are of death"?*

7. *In Van Den Haag's view, what is the sole determinant of whether people will or will not commit crimes? Do you agree?*

8. *Why does Van Den Haag not believe that the presence or absence of a deterrent effect of the death penalty is likely to be proved statistically? Does this weaken, strengthen, or have no effect on his own retentionist position?*

9. *Explain why Van Den Haag believes there is more to be gained by retaining the death penalty than by abolishing it.*

The Death Penalty as a Deterrent: Argument and Evidence

Hugo Adam Bedau

The following article was written by a leading abolitionist, philosophy professor Hugo Adam Bedau. Bedau applies the scalpel of logical analysis to the contentions made by Van Den Haag in the preceding essay.

Bedau isolates five main points made by Van Den Haag, and then critically analyzes each of them. First, Bedau objects to Van Den Haag's claim that the utilitarian abolitionist considers capital punishment useless because it does not deter crime. Bedau says that Van Den Haag's point founders on the concept of "deterrence," which is "too ill-formulated to be of any serious use." Second, Bedau rejects Van Den Haag's claim that the death penalty is the only way to deter certain classes of criminals.

Third, Bedau spends considerable time critically analyzing Van Den Haag's contention that no statistical case can be made for capital punishment as a nondeterrent. Bedau points out that the issue of abolishing the death penalty is not whether the death penalty is a deterrent but whether it is a superior deterrent to life imprisonment. There is no evidence, in Bedau's view, that points to the superiority of the death penalty as a deterrent. Indeed, he suggests, there is evidence that capital punishment is not a superior deterrent to life imprisonment.

Fourth, therefore, Bedau rejects the claim that the death penalty should be favored to life imprisonment because it may add to deterrence. And fifth, he likewise rejects the contention that abolitionists must prove that capital punishment does not add to deterrence.

Apart from further advancing the debate on capital punishment, Bedau's essay well illustrates the rigorous analysis that philosophers apply to moral questions and positions on them.

Professor Van Den Haag's recent article, "On Deterrence and the Death Penalty,"[1] raises a number of points of that mixed (i.e., empirical-and-conceptual-and-normative) character which typifies most actual reasoning in social and political controversy but which (except when its purely formal aspects are in question) tends to be ignored by philosophers. I pass by any number of tempting points in his critique in order to focus in detail only on those which affect his account of what he says is

From Hugo Adam Bedau, "The Death Penalty as a Deterrent: Argument and Evidence," Ethics 80 (1970), 205–217. Copyright
©1970 by The University of Chicago Press. Reprinted by permission of the publisher and the author.

the major topic, namely, the argument for retaining or abolishing the death penalty as that issue turns on the question of *deterrence*.

On this topic, Van Den Haag's main contentions seem to be these five: (I) Abolitionists of a utilitarian persuasion "claim that capital punishment is useless because it does not deter others" (p. 280, col. 1). (II) There are some classes of criminals and some circumstances in which "the death penalty is the only possible deterrent" (p. 284, col. 2). (III) As things currently stand, "deterrence [namely of criminal homicide by the death penalty] has not been demonstrated statistically"; but it is mistaken to think that "non-deterrence" has been demonstrated statistically (p. 285, col. 1). (IV) The death penalty is to be favored over imprisonment, because "the added severity of the death penalty adds to deterrence, or may do so" (p. 285, col. 2; cf. p. 286, col. 1). (V) "Since it seems more important to spare victims than to spare murderers, the burden of proving that the greater severity inherent in irrevocability adds nothing to deterrence lies on those who oppose capital punishment" (p. 287, col. 1).

Succinctly, I shall argue as follows: (I) is not reasonably attributable to abolitionists, and in any case it is false; (II) is misleading and, in the interesting cases, is empirically insignificant; (III), which is the heart of the dispute, is correct in what it affirms but wrong and utterly misleading in what it denies; (IV) is unempirical and one-sided as well; and (V) is a muddle and a dodge.

The reasons for pursuing in some detail what at first might appear to be mere polemical controversy is not that Professor Van Den Haag's essay is so persuasive or likely to be of unusual influence. The reason is that the issues he raises, even though they are familiar, have not been nearly adequately discussed, despite a dozen state, congressional, and foreign government investigations into capital punishment in recent years. In Massachusetts, for example, several persons under sentence of death have been granted stays of execution pending the final report of a special legislative commission to investigate the death penalty. The exclusive mandate of this commission is to study the question of deterrence.[2] Its provisional conclusions, published late in 1968, though not in the vein of Van Den Haag's views, are liable to the kind of criticism he makes. This suggests that his reasoning may be representative of many who have tried to understand the arguments and research studies brought forward by those who would abolish the death penalty, and therefore that his errors are worth exposure and correction once and for all.

I

The claim Van Den Haag professes to find "most persuasive," namely, "capital punishment is useless because it does not deter others," is strange, and it is strange that he finds it so persuasive. Anyone who would make this claim must assume that only deterrent efficacy is relevant to assessing the utility of a punishment. In a footnote, Van Den Haag implicitly concedes that deterrence may not be the only utilitarian consideration, when he asserts that whatever our penal "theory" may tell us, "deterrence is . . . the *main actual* function of legal punishment if we disregard non-utilitarian ones" (italics added). But he does not pursue this qualification. Now we may concede that if by "function" we mean intended or professed function, deterrence is the main function of punishment. But what is deterrence? Not what Van Den Haag says it is, namely, "a preconscious, general response to a severe but not necessarily specifically and explicitly apprehended or calculated threat" (pp. 285–86). How can we count as evidence of deterrence, as we may under this rubric of "general response," the desire of persons to avoid capture and punishment for the crimes they commit? Some criminologists have thought this is precisely what severe punishments tend to accomplish; if so, then they accomplish this effect only if they have failed as a deterrent. Van Den Haag's conception of deterrence is too ill-formulated to be of any serious use, since it does not discriminate between fundamentally different types of "general response" to the threat of punishment.

Let us say (definition 1) that a given punishment (P) is a *deterrent* for a given person (A) with respect to a given crime (C) at a given time (t) if and only if A does not commit C at t because he believes he runs some risk of P if he commits C, and A prefers, *ceteris paribus*, not to suffer P for committing C. This definition does not presuppose that P really is the punishment for C (a person could be deterred through a mistaken belief); it does not presuppose that A runs a high risk of incurring P (the degree of risk could be zero); or that A consciously thinks of P prior to t (it is left open as to the sort of theory needed to account for the operation of A's beliefs and preferences on his conduct). Nor does it presuppose that anyone ever suffers P (P could be a "perfect" deterrent), or that only P could have deterred A from C (some sanction less severe than P might have worked as well); and, finally, it does not presuppose that because P deters A at t from C, therefore P would deter A at any other time or anyone else at t. The definition insures that we cannot argue from the absence of instances of C to the conclusion that P has succeeded as a deterrent: The definition contains conditions (and, moreover, contains them intentionally) which prevent this. But the definition does allow us to argue from occurrences of C to the conclusion that P has failed on each such occasion as a deterrent.

Definition 1 suggests a general functional analogue appropriate to express scientific measurements of *differential deterrent efficacy* of a given punishment for a given crime with respect to a given population (definition 2). Let us say that a given Punishment, P, deters a given population, H, from a crime, C, to the degree, D, that the members of H do not commit C because they believe that they run some risk of P if they commit C and, *ceteris paribus,* they prefer not to suffer P for committing C. If $D = 0$, then P has completely failed as a deterrent, whereas if $D = 1$, P has proved to be a perfect deterrent. Given this definition and the appropriate empirical results for various values of P, C, and H, it should be possible to establish on inductive grounds the relative effectiveness of a given punishment as a deterrent.

Definition 2 in turn leads to the following corollary for assertions of relative superior deterrent efficacy of one punishment over another. A given Punishment, P_1, is a superior deterrent to another punishment, P_2, with respect to some crime, C, and some population, H, if and only if: If the members of H, believing that they are liable to P_1 upon committing C, commit C to the degree D_1; whereas if the members of H believe that they are liable to P_2 upon committing C, they commit C to the degree D_2, and $D_1 > D_2$. This formulation plainly allows that P_1 may be a more effective deterrent than P_2 for C_1 and yet less effective as a deterrent than P_2 for a different crime C_2 (with H constant), and so forth, for other possibilities. When speaking about deterrence in the sections which follow, I shall presuppose these definitions and this corollary. For the present, it is sufficient to notice that they have, at least, the virtue of eliminating the vagueness in Van Den Haag's definition complained of earlier.

Even if we analyze the notion of deterrence to accommodate the above improvements, we are left with the central objection to Van Den Haag's claim. Neither classic nor contemporary utilitarians have argued for or against the death penalty *solely* on the ground of deterrence, nor would their ethical theory entitle them to do so. One measure of the non-deterrent utility of the death penalty derives from its elimination (through death of a known criminal) of future possible crimes from that source; another arises from the elimination of the criminal's probable adverse influence upon others to emulate his ways; another lies in the generally lower budgetary outlays of tax moneys needed to finance a system of capital punishment as opposed to long-term imprisonment. There are still further consequences apart from deterrence which the scrupulous utilitarian must weigh, along with the three I have mentioned. Therefore, it is incorrect, because insufficient, to think that if it could be demonstrated that the death penalty is not a deterrent then we would be entitled to infer, on utilitarian assumptions, that "the death penalty is useless" and therefore ought to be abolished. The problem for the utilitarian is to make commensurable such diverse social utilities as those measured by deterrent efficacy, administrative costs, etc., and then to determine which penal policy in fact maximizes utility. Finally, inspection of sample arguments actually used by abolitionists[3] will show that Van Den Haag has attacked a straw man: There are few if any contemporary abolitionists (and Van Den Haag names none) who argue solely from professional utilitarian assumptions, and it is doubtful whether there are any nonutilitarians who would abolish the death penalty solely on grounds of its deterrent inefficacy.

II

Governments faced by incipient rebellion or threatened by a coup d'état may well conclude, as Van Den Haag insists they should, that rebels (as well as traitors and spies) can be deterred, if at all, by the threat of death, since "swift victory" of the revolution "will invalidate [the deterrent efficacy] of a prison sentence" (pp. 284–85).[4] This does not yet tell us how important it is that such deterrence be provided, any more than the fact that a threat of expulsion is the severest deterrent available to university authorities tells them whether they ought to insist on expelling campus rebels. Also, such severe penalties might have the opposite effect of inducing martyrdom, of provoking attempts to overthrow the government to secure a kind of political sainthood. This possibility Van Den Haag recognizes, but claims in a footnote that it "hardly impair[s] the force of the argument" (p. 288). Well, from a logical point of view it impairs it considerably; from an empirical point of view, since we are wholly without any reliable facts or hypotheses on politics in such extreme situations, the entire controversy remains quite speculative.

The one important class of criminals deterrable, if at all, by the death penalty consists, according to Van Den Haag, of those already under "life" sentence or guilty of a crime punishable by "life." In a trivial sense, he is correct; a person already suffering a given punishment, P, for a given crime, C_1, could not be expected to be deterred by anticipating the reinfliction of P were he to commit C_2. For if the anticipation of P did not deter him from committing C_1, how could the anticipation of P deter him from committing C_2, given that he is already experiencing P? This generalization seems to apply whenever P = "life" imprisonment. Actually, the truth is a bit more complex, because in practice (as Van Den Haag concedes, again in a footnote) so-called "life" imprisonment always has its aggravations (e.g., solitary confinement) and its mitigations (parole eligibility). These make it logically possible to deter a person already convicted of criminal homicide and serving "life" imprisonment from committing another such crime. I admit that the aggravations available are not in practice likely to provide much added deterrent effect; but exactly how likely or unlikely this effect is remains a matter for empirical investigation, not idle guesswork. Van Den Haag's seeming truism, therefore, relies for its plausibility on the false assumption that "life" imprisonment is a uniform punishment not open to further deterrence-relevant aggravations and mitigations.

Empirically, the objection to his point is that persons already serving a "life" sentence do not in general constitute a source of genuine alarm to custodial personnel. Being already incarcerated and integrated into the reward structure of prison life, they do not seem to need the deterrent controls allegedly necessary for other prisoners and the general public.[5] There are exceptions to this generalization, but there is no known way of identifying them in advance, their number has proved to be not large, and it would be irrational, therefore, to design a penal policy (as several states have)[6] which invokes the death penalty in the professed hope of deterring such convicted offenders from further criminal homicide. Van Den Haag cites no evidence that such policies accomplish their alleged purpose, and I know of none. As for the real question which Van Den Haag's argument raises— is there any class of actual or potential criminals for which the death penalty exerts a marginally superior deterrent effect over every less severe alternative?—we have no evidence at all, one way or the other. Until this proposition, or some corollary, is actually tested and confirmed, there is no reason to indulge Van Den Haag in his speculations.

III

It is not clear why Van Den Haag is so anxious to discuss whether there is evidence that the death penalty is a deterrent, or whether—as he thinks— there is no evidence that it is not a deterrent. For the issue over abolishing the death penalty, as all serious students of the subject have known for decades, is not whether (1) *the death penalty is a deterrent*, but whether (2) *the death penalty is a superior deterrent to "life" imprisonment*, and consequently the evidential dispute is also not over (1) but only over (2). As I have argued elsewhere,[7] abolitionists have reason to contest (1) only if they are against *all* punitive alternatives to the death penalty; since few abolitionists (and none cited by Van Den Haag) take this extreme view, it may be ignored here. We should notice in passing, however, that if it were demonstrated that (1) were false, there would be no need for abolitionists to go on to marshal evidence against (2), since the truth of (1) is a presupposition of the truth of (2). Now it is true that some abolitionists may be faulted for writing as if the falsity of (1) followed from the falsity of (2), but this is not a complaint Van Den Haag makes nor is it an error vital to the abolitionist argument against the death penalty. Similar considerations inveigh against certain pro-death-penalty arguments. Proponents must do more than establish (1), they must also provide evidence in favor of (2); and they cannot infer from evidence which establishes (1) that (2) is true or even probable (unless, of course, that evidence would establish [2] independently). These considerations show us how important it is to distinguish (1) and (2) and the questions of evidence which each raises. Van Den Haag never directly discusses (2), except when he observes in passing that "the question is not only whether the death penalty deters but whether it deters more than alternatives" (p. 284, col. 2). But since he explicitly argues only over the evidential status of (1), it is unclear whether he wishes to ignore (2) or whether he thinks that his arguments regarding (1) also have consequences for the evidential status of (2). Perhaps Van Den Haag thinks that if there is no evidence disconfirming (1), then there can be no evidence disconfirming (2); or perhaps he thinks that none of the evidence disconfirming (2) also disconfirms (1). (If he thinks either, he is wrong.) Or perhaps he is careless, conceding on the one hand that (2) is important to the issue of abolition of the death penalty, only to slide back into a discussion exclusively about (1).

He writes as if his chief contentions were these two: We must not confuse (a) the assertion that there is no evidence that not-(1) (i.e., evidence that [1] is false); and abolitionists have asserted (b) whereas all they are entitled to assert is (a).[8] I wish to proceed on the assumption that since (1) is not chiefly at issue, neither is (a) nor (b) (though I grant, as anyone must, that the distinction between [a] and [b] is legitimate and important). What is chiefly at issue, even though Van Den Haag's discussion obscures the point, is whether abolitionists must content themselves with asserting that there is no evidence against (2), or whether they may go further and assert that there is evidence that not-(2) (i.e., evidence that [2] is false). I shall argue that abolitionists may make the stronger (latter) assertion.

In order to see the issue fairly, it is necessary to see how (2) has so far been submitted to empirical tests. First of all, the issue has been confined to the death penalty for criminal homicide; consequently, it is not (2) but a subsidiary proposition which critics of the death penalty have tested, namely, (2a) *the death penalty is a superior deterrent to "life" imprisonment for the crime of criminal homicide.* The falsification of (2a) does not entail the falsity of (2); the death penalty could still be a superior deterrent to "life" imprisonment for the crime of burglary, etc. However, the disconfirmation of (2a) is obviously a partial disconfirmation of (2). Second, (2a) has not been tested directly but only indirectly. No one has devised a way to count or estimate directly the number of persons in a given population who have been deterred from criminal homicide by the fear of the penalty. The difficulties in doing so are plain enough. For instance, it would be possible to infer from the countable numbers who have not been deterred (because they did commit a given crime) that everyone else in the population was deterred, but only on the assumption that the only reason why a person did not commit a given crime is because he was deterred. Unfortunately for this argument (though happily enough otherwise) this assumption is almost certainly false. Other ways in which one might devise to test (2a) directly have proved equally unfeasible. Yet it would be absurd to insist that there can be no *evidence* for or against (2a) unless it is *direct* evidence for or against it. Because Van Den Haag nowhere indicated what he thinks would count as evidence, direct or indirect, for or against (1), much less (2), his insistence upon the distinction between (a) and (b) and his rebuke to abolitionists is in danger of implicitly relying upon just this absurdity.

How, then, has the indirect argument over (2a) proceeded? During the past generation, at least six different hypotheses have been formulated, as corollaries of (2a), as follows:[9]

i. death-penalty jurisdictions should have a lower annual rate of criminal homicide than abolition jurisdictions;

ii. jurisdictions which abolished the death penalty should show an increased annual rate of criminal homicide after abolition;

iii. jurisdictions which reintroduced the death penalty should show a decreased annual rate of criminal homicide after reintroduction;

iv. given two contiguous jurisdictions differing chiefly in that one has the death penalty and the other does not, the latter should show a higher annual rate of criminal homicide;

v. police officers on duty should suffer a higher annual rate of criminal assault and homicide in abolition jurisdictions than in death-penalty jurisdictions;

vi. prisoners and prison personnel should suffer a higher annual rate of criminal assault and homicide from life-term prisoners in abolition jurisdictions than in death-penalty jurisdictions.

It could be objected to these six hypotheses that they are, as a set, insufficient to settle the question posed by (2a) no matter what the evidence for them may be (i.e., that falsity of [i]–[vi] does not entail the falsity of [2]). Or it could be argued that each of (i)–(vi) has been inadequately tested or insufficiently (dis)confirmed so as to establish any (dis)confirmation of (2a), even though it is conceded that if these hypotheses were highly (dis)confirmed they would (dis)confirm (2a). Van Den Haag's line of attack is not entirely clear as between these two alternatives. It looks as if he ought to take the former line of criticism in its most extreme version. How else could he argue his chief point, that the research used by abolitionists has so far failed to produce *any* evidence against (1)— we may take him to mean (2) or (2a). Only if (i)–(vi) were *irrelevant* to (2a) could it be fairly concluded from the evidential disconfirmation of (i)–(vi) that there is still no disconfirmation of (2a). And this is Van Den Haag's central contention. The other ways to construe Van Den Haag's reasoning are simply too preposterous to be considered: He cannot think that the evidence is indifferent to or *confirms* (i)–(vi); nor can he think that there has been no *attempt* at all to disconfirm (2a); nor can he think that the evidence which disconfirms (i)–(vi) is not therewith also evidence which confirms the negations of (i)–(vi). If any of these three was true, it would be a good reason for saying that there is "no evidence" against (2a); but each is patently false. If one inspects (i)–(vi) and (2a), it is difficult to see how one could argue that (dis)confirmation of the former does not constitute (dis)confirmation of the latter, even if it might be argued that verification of the former does not constitute verification of the latter. I think, therefore, that there is nothing to be gained by pursuing further this first line of attack.

Elsewhere, it looks as though Van Den Haag takes the other alternative of criticism, albeit rather crudely, as when he argues (against [iv], I suppose, since he nowhere formulated [i]–[vi]) that "the similar areas are not similar enough" (p. 285, col. 1). As to why, for example, the rates of criminal homicide in Michigan and in Illinois from 1920 to 1960

are not relevant because the states aren't "similar enough," he does not try to explain. But his criticism does strictly concede that if the jurisdictions *were* "similar enough," then it would be logically possible to argue from the evidence against (iv) to the disconfirmation of (2a). And this seems to be in keeping with the nature of the case; it is this second line of attack which needs closer examination.

Van Den Haag's own position and objections apart, what is likely to strike the neutral observer who studies the ways in which (i)–(vi) have been tested and declared disconfirmed is that their disconfirmation, and, a fortiori, the disconfirmation of (2a), is imperfect for two related reasons. First, all the tests rely upon *unproved empirical assumptions;* second, it is not known whether there is any *statistical significance* to the results of the tests. It is important to make these concessions, and abolitionists and other disbelievers in the deterrent efficacy of the death penalty have not always done so.

It is not possible here to review all the evidence and to reach a judgment on the empirical status of (i)–(vi). But it is possible and desirable to illustrate how the two qualifications cited above must be understood, and then to assess their effect on the empirical status of (2a). The absence of statistical significance may be illustrated by reference to hypothesis (v). According to the published studies, the annual rate of assaults upon on-duty policemen in abolition jurisdictions is lower than in death-penalty jurisdictions (i.e., a rate of 1.2 attacks per 100,000 population in the former as opposed to 1.3 per 100,000 in the latter). But is this difference statistically significant or not? The studies do not answer this question because the data were not submitted to tests of statistical significance. Nor is there any way, to my knowledge, that these data could be subjected to any such tests. This is, of course, no reason to suppose that the evidence is really not evidence after all, or that though it is evidence against (i) it is not evidence against (2a). Statistical significance is, after all, only a measure of the strength of evidence, not a *sine qua non* of evidential status.

The qualification concerning unproved assumptions is more important, and is worth examining somewhat more fully (though, again, only illustratively). Consider hypothesis (i). Are we entitled to infer that (i) is disconfirmed because in fact a study of the annual homicide rates (as measured by vital statistics showing cause of death) unquestionably indicates that the rate in all abolition states is consistently lower than in all death-penalty states? To make this inference we must assume that (A_1) homicides as measured by vital statistics are in a generally constant ratio to criminal homicides, (A_2) the years for which the evidence has been gathered are representative and not atypical, (A_3) however much fluctuations in the homicide rate owe to other factors, there is a nonnegligible proportion which is a function of the penalty, and (A_4) the deterrent effect of a penalty is not significantly weakened by its infrequent imposition. (There are, of course, other assumptions, but these are central and sufficiently representative here.) Assumption A_1 is effectively unmeasurable because the concept of a criminal homicide is the concept of a homicide which *deserves* to be criminally prosecuted.[10] Nevertheless, A_1 has been accepted by criminologists for over a generation. A_2 is confirmable, on the other hand, and bit by bit, a year at a time, seems to be being confirmed. Assumption A_3 is rather more interesting. To the degree to which it is admitted or insisted that other factors than the severity of the penalty affect the volume of homicide, to that degree A_3 becomes increasingly dubious; but at the same time testing (2a) by (i) becomes increasingly unimportant. The urgency of testing (2a) rests upon the assumption that it is the deterrent efficacy of penalties which is the chief factor in the volume of crimes, and it is absurd to hold that assumption and at the same time doubt A_3. On the other hand, A_4 is almost certainly false (and has been believed so by Bentham and other social theorists for nearly two hundred years). The falsity of A_4, however, is not of fatal harm to the disconfirmation of (i) because it is not known how frequently or infrequently a severe penalty such as death or life imprisonment needs to be imposed in order to maximize its deterrent efficacy. Such information as we do have on this point leads one to doubt that for the general population the frequency with which the death sentence is imposed makes any significant difference to the volume of criminal homicide.[11]

I suggest that these four assumptions and the way in which they bear upon interpretation and evaluation of the evidence against (i), and therefore the disconfirmation of (2a), are typical of what one finds as one examines the work of criminologists

as it relates to the rest of these corollaries of (2a). Is it reasonable, in the light of these considerations, to infer that we have no evidence against (i)–(vi), or that although we do have evidence against (i)–(vi), we have none against (2a)? I do not think so. Short of unidentified and probably unobtainable "crucial experiments," we shall never be able to marshal evidence for (2a) or for (i)–(vi) except by means of certain additional assumptions such as A_1–A_4. To reason otherwise is to rely on nothing more than the fact that it is logically possible to grant the evidence against (i)–(vi) and yet deny that (2a) is false; or it is to insist that the assumptions which the inference relies upon are not plausible assumptions at all (or though plausible are themselves false or disconfirmed) and that no other assumptions can be brought forward which will both be immune to objections and still preserve the linkage between the evidence and the corollaries and (2a). The danger now is that one will repudiate assumptions such as A_1–A_4 in order to guarantee the failure of efforts to disconfirm (2a) via disconfirmation of (i)–(vi); or else that one will place the standards of evidence too high before one accepts the disconfirmation. In either case one has begun to engage in the familiar but discreditable practice of "protecting the hypothesis" by making it, in effect, immune to any kind of disconfirmation.

On my view things stand in this way. An empirical proposition not directly testable, (2), has a significant corollary, (2a), which in turn suggests a number of corollaries, (i)–(vi), each of which is testable with varying degrees of indirectness. Each of (i)–(vi) has been tested. To accept the results as evidence disconfirming (i)–(vi) and as therefore disconfirming (2a), it is necessary to make certain assumptions, of which A_1–A_4 are typical. These assumptions in turn are not all testable, much less directly tested; some of them, in their most plausible formulation, may even be false (but not in that formulation necessary to the inference, however). Since this structure of indirect testing, corollary hypotheses, unproved assumptions, is typical of the circumstances which face us when we wish to consider the evidence for or against any complex empirical hypothesis such as (2), I conclude that while (2) has by no means been disproved (whatever that might mean), it is equally clear that (2) has been disconfirmed, rather than confirmed or left untouched by the inductive arguments we have surveyed.

I have attempted to review and appraise the chief "statistical" arguments (as Van Den Haag calls them) marshaled during the past fifteen years or so in this country by those critical of the death penalty. But in order to assess these arguments more adequately, it is helpful to keep in mind two other considerations. First, most of the criminologists skeptical of (1) are led to this attitude not by the route we have examined—the argument against (2)—but by a general theory of the causation of crimes of personal violence. Given their confidence in that theory, and the evidence for it, they tend not to credit seriously the idea that the death penalty deters (very much), much less the idea that it is a superior deterrent to a severe alternative such as "life" imprisonment (which may not deter very much, either). The interested reader should consult in particular Professor Marvin Wolfgang's monograph, *Patterns of Criminal Homicide* (1958). Second, very little of the empirical research purporting to establish the presence or absence of deterrent efficacy of a given punishment is entirely reliable because almost no effort has been made to isolate the relevant variables. Surely, it is platitudinously true that *some* persons in *some* situations considering *some* crimes can be deterred from committing them by *some* penalties. To go beyond this, however, and supplant these variables with a series of well-confirmed functional hypotheses about the deterrent effect of current legal sanctions is not possible today.

Even if one cannot argue, as Van Den Haag does, that there is no evidence against the claim that the death penalty is a better deterrent than life imprisonment, this does not yet tell us how good this evidence is, how reliable it is, how extensive, and how probative. Van Den Haag could, after all, give up his extreme initial position and retreat to the concession that although there is evidence against the superior deterrent efficacy of the death penalty, still, the evidence is not very good, indeed, not good enough to make reasonable the policy of abolishing the death penalty. Again, it is not possible to undertake to settle this question short of a close examination of each of the empirical studies which confirm (i)–(vi). The reply, so far as there is one, short of further empirical studies (which undoubtedly are desirable—I should not want to obscure that), is twofold: The evidence, such as it

is, for (i)–(vi) is uniformly confirmatory in all cases; and the argument of Section IV which follows.

IV

Van Den Haag's "argument" rests considerable weight on the claims that "the added severity of the death penalty adds to deterrence, or may do so"; and that "the generalized threat of the death penalty may be a deterrent, and the more so, the more generally applied." These claims are open to criticism on at least three grounds.

First, as the modal auxiliaries signal, Van Den Haag has not really committed himself to any affirmative empirical claim, but only to a truism. It is always logically possible, no matter what the evidence, that a given penalty which is *ex hypothesi* more severe than an alternative, may be a better deterrent under some conditions not often realized, and be proven so by evidence not ever detectable. For this reason, there is no possible way to prove that Van Den Haag's claims are false, no possible preponderance of evidence against his conclusions which must, logically, force him to give them up. One would have hoped those who believe in the deterrent superiority of the death penalty could, at this late date, offer their critics something more persuasive than logical possibilities. As it is, Van Den Haag's appeal to possible evidence comes perilously close to an argument from ignorance: The possible evidence we might gather is used to offset the actual evidence we have gathered.

Second, Van Den Haag rightly regards his conclusion above as merely an instance of the general principle that, *ceteris paribus,* "the Greater the Severity the Greater the Deterrence," a "plausible" idea, as he says (p. 287). Yet the advantage on behalf of the death penalty produced by this principle is a function entirely of the evidence for the principle itself. But we are offered no evidence at all to make this plausible principle into a confirmed hypothesis of contemporary criminological theory of special relevance to crimes of personal violence. Until we see evidence concerning specific crimes, specific penalties, specific criminal populations, which show that in general the Greater the Severity the Greater the Deterrence, we run the risk of stupefying ourselves by the merely plausible. Besides, without any evidence for this principle we will find ourselves at a complete standoff with the abolitionist (who, of course, can play the same game), because he has his own equally plausible first principle: The Greater the Severity of Punishment the Greater the Brutality Provoked throughout Society. When at last, exhausted and frustrated by mere plausibilities, we once again turn to study the evidence, we will find that the current literature on deterrence in criminology does not encourage us to believe in Van Den Haag's principle.[12]

Third, Van Den Haag has not given any reason why, in the quest for deterrent efficacy, one should fasten (as he does) on the severity of the punishments in question, rather than (as Bentham long ago counseled) on the relevant factors, notably the ease and speed and reliability with which the punishment can be inflicted. Van Den Haag cannot hope to convince anyone who has studied the matter that the death penalty and "life" imprisonment differ only in their severity, and that in all other respects affecting deterrent efficacy they are equivalent; and if he believes this himself it would be interesting to have seen his evidence for it. The only thing to be said in favor of fastening exclusively upon the question of severity in the appraisal of punishments for their relative deterrent efficacy is that augmenting the severity of a punishment in and of itself usually imposes little if any added direct cost to operate the penal system; it even may be cheaper. This is bound to please the harried taxpayer, and at the same time gratify the demand on government to "do something" about crime. Beyond that, emphasizing the severity of punishments as the main (or indeed the sole) variable relevant to deterrent efficacy is unbelievably superficial.

V

Van Den Haag's final point concerning where the burden of proof lies is based, he admits, on playing off a certainty (the death of the persons executed) against a risk (that innocent persons, otherwise the would-be victims of those deterrable only by the death penalty, would be killed).[13] This is not as analogous as he seems to think it is to the general nature of gambling, investment, and other risk-taking enterprises. In none of them do we deliberately cause anything to be killed, as we do, for instance, when we weed out carrot seedlings

to enable those remaining to grow larger (a eugenic analogy, by the way, which might be more useful to Van Den Haag's purpose). In none, that is, do we venture a sacrifice in the hope of a future net gain; we only *risk* a present loss in that hope. Moreover, in gambling ventures we recoup what we risked if we win, whereas in executions we must lose something (the lives of persons executed) no matter if we lose or win (the lives of innocents protected). Van Den Haag's attempt to locate the burden of proof by appeal to principles of gambling is a failure.

Far more significantly, Van Den Haag frames the issue in such a way that the abolitionist has no chance of discharging the burden of proof once he accepts it. For what evidence could be marshaled to prove what Van Den Haag wants proved, namely, that "the greater severity inherent in irrevocability [of the death penalty] . . . adds nothing to deterrence"? The evidence alluded to at the end of Section IV does tend to show that this generalization (the negation of Van Den Haag's own principle) is indeed true, but it does not prove it. I conclude, therefore, that either Van Den Haag is wrong in his argument which shows the locus of burden of proof to lie on the abolitionist, or one must accept less than proof in order to discharge this burden (in which case, the very argument Van Den Haag advances shows that the burden of proof now lies on those who would retain the death penalty).

"Burden of proof" in areas outside judicial precincts where evidentiary questions are at stake tends to be a rhetorical phrase and nothing more. Anyone interested in the truth of a matter will not defer gathering evidence pending a determination of where the burden of proof lies. For those who do think there is a question of burden of proof, as Van Den Haag does, they should consider this: Advocacy of the death penalty is advocacy of a rule of penal law which empowers the state to deliberately take human life and in general to threaten the public with the taking of life. *Ceteris paribus*, one would think anyone favoring such a rule would be ready to offer considerable evidence for its necessity and efficacy. Surely, some showing of necessity, some evidentiary proof, is to be expected to satisfy the skeptical. Exactly when and in what circumstances have the apologists for capital punishment offered evidence to support their contentions? Where is that evidence recorded for us to inspect, comparable to the evidence cited in Section III against the superior deterrent efficacy of the death penalty? Van Den Haag conspicuously cited no such evidence and so it is with all other proponents of the death penalty. The insistence that the burden of proof lies on abolitionists, therefore, is nothing but the rhetorical demand of every defender of the status quo who insists upon evidence from those who would effect change, while reserving throughout the right to dictate criteria and standards of proof and refusing to offer evidence for his own view.[14]

I should have thought that the death penalty was a sufficiently momentous matter and of sufficient controversy that the admittedly imperfect evidence assembled over the past generation by those friendly to abolition would have been countered by evidence tending to support the opposite, retentionist, position. It remains a somewhat sad curiosity that nothing of the sort has happened; no one has ever published research tending to show, however inconclusively, that the death penalty after all is a deterrent, and a superior deterrent to "life" imprisonment. Among scholars at least, if not among legislators and other politicians, the perennial appeal to burden of proof really ought to give way to offering of proof by those interested enough to argue the issue.

TUFTS UNIVERSITY

Notes

1. *Ethics* 78 (July 1968):280–88. Van Den Haag later published a "revised version" under the same title in *Journal of Criminal Law, Criminology and Police Science* 60 (1969):141–47. I am grateful to Professor Van Den Haag for providing me with a reprint of each version. I should add that his revisions in the later version were minimal, especially in his Section V which is mainly what I shall criticize. All page references in the text are to the version published in *Ethics*.

2. See Massachusetts Laws, chap. 150, Resolves of 1967; "Interim Report of the Special Commission Established to Make an Investigation and Study Relative to the Effectiveness of Capital Punishment as a Deterrent to Crime," mimeographed (Boston: Clerk, Great and General Court, State House, 1968).

3. See the several essays reprinted in Bedau, ed., *The Death Penalty in America*, rev. ed. (New York, 1967),

chap. 4 and the articles cited therein at pp. 166–70.

4. The same argument has been advanced earlier by Sidney Hook (see the *New York Law Forum* [1961], pp. 278–83, and the revised version of this argument published in Bedau, pp. 150–51).

5. See, e.g., Thorsten Sellin, "Prison Homicides," in *Capital Punishment*, ed. Sellin (New York, 1967), pp. 154–60.

6. Rhode Island (1852), North Dakota (1915), New York (1965), Vermont (1965), and New Mexico (1969), have all qualified their abolition of the death penalty in this way; for further details, see Bedau, p. 12.

7. Bedau, pp. 260–61.

8. Van Den Haag accuses Professor Thorsten Sellin, a criminologist "who has made a careful study of the available statistics," of seeming to "think that this lack of evidence for deterrence is evidence for the lack of deterrence" (p. 285, col. 1), that is, of thinking that (a) is (b)! In none of Sellin's writings which I have studied (see, for a partial listing, note 9, below) do I see any evidence that Sellin "thinks" the one "is" the other. What will be found is a certain vacillation in his various published writings, which span the years from 1953 to 1967, between the two ways of putting his conclusions. His most recent statement is unqualifiedly in the (b) form (see his *Capital Punishment*, p. 138). Since Van Den Haag also cited my *Death Penalty in America* (though not in this connection), I might add that there I did distinguish between (a) and (b) but did not insist, as I do now, that the argument entitles abolitionists to assert (b) (see Bedau, pp. 264–65). It is perhaps worth noting here some other writers, all criminologists, who have recently stated the same or a stronger conclusion. "Capital punishment does not act as an effective deterrent to murder" (William J. Chambliss, "Types of Deviance and the Effectiveness of Legal Sanctions," *Wisconsin Law Review* [1967], p. 706); "The capital punishment controversy has produced the most reliable information on the general deterrent effect of a criminal sanction. It now seems established and accepted that . . . the death penalty makes no difference to the homicide rate" (Norval Morris and Frank Zimring, "Deterrence and Corrections," *Annals* 381 [January 1969]:143); "the evidence indicates that it [namely, the death penalty for murder] has no discernible effects in the United States" (Walter C. Reckless, "The Use of the Death Penalty," *Crime and Delinquency* 15 [January 1969]:52); "Capital punishment is ineffective in deterring murder" (Eugene Doleschal, "The Deterrent Effect

of Legal Punishment," *Information Review on Crime and Delinquency* 1 [June 1969]:7).

9. The relevant research, regarding each of the six hypotheses in the text, is as follows: (i) Karl Schuessler, "The Deterrent Influence of the Death Penalty," *Annals* 284 (November 1952):57; Walter C. Reckless, "The Use of the Death Penalty—a Factual Statement," *Crime and Delinquency* 15 (1969):52, table 9. (ii) Thorsten Sellin, *The Death Penalty* (Philadelphia: American Law Institute, 1959), pp. 19–24, reprinted in Bedau, pp. 274–84; updated in Sellin, *Capital Punishment*, 135–38. (iii) Sellin, *The Death Penalty*, pp. 34–38, reprinted in Bedau, pp. 339–43. (iv) See works cited in (iii), above. (v) Canada, *Minutes and Proceedings of Evidence*, Joint Committee of the Senate and House of Commons on Capital Punishment and Corporal Punishment and Lotteries (1955), appendix F, pt. 1, pp. 718–28; "The Death Penalty and Police Safety," reprinted in Bedau, pp. 284–301, and in Sellin, *Capital Punishment*, pp. 138–54, with postscript (1967); Canada, "The State Police and the Death Penalty," pp. 729–35, reprinted in Bedau, pp. 301–15. (vi) *Massachusetts, Report and Recommendations of the Special Commission . . . [on] the Death Penalty . . .* (1958), pp. 21–22, reprinted in Bedau, p. 400; Thorsten Sellin, "Prison Homicides," in Sellin, *Capital Punishment*, pp. 154–60.

10. See, for discussion surrounding this point, Bedau, pp. 56–74.

11. See Robert H. Dann, *The Deterrent Effect of Capital Punishment* (Philadelphia, 1935); Leonard H. Savitz, "A Study in Capital Punishment," *Journal of Criminal Law, Criminology and Police Science* 49 (1958):338–41, reprinted in Bedau, pp. 315–32; William F. Graves, "A Doctor Looks at Capital Punishment," *Medical Arts and Sciences* 10 (1956):137–41, reprinted in Bedau, pp. 322–32, with addenda (1964).

12. See, for a general review, Eugene Doleschal, "The Deterrent Effect of Legal Punishment: A Review of the Literature," *Information Review on Crime and Delinquency* 1 (June 1969):1–17, and the many research studies cited therein, especially the survey by Norval Morris and Frank Zimring, "Deterrence and Corrections," *Annals* 381 (January 1969):137–46; also Gordon Hawkins, "Punishment and Deterrence," *Wisconsin Law Review* (1969), pp. 550–65.

13. The same objection has been raised earlier by Joel Feinberg (see his review of Bedau in *Ethics* 76 [October 1965]:63).

14. For a general discussion which is not inconsistent with the position I have taken, and which illuminates the logicorhetorical character of the appeal to burden of proof in philosophical argument, see Robert Brown, "The Burden of Proof," *American Philosophical Quarterly* 7 (1970):74–82.

Questions for Analysis

1. Explain why Bedau believes that Van Den Haag's definition of deterrence is "too ill-formulated to be of any serious use." Do you agree?

2. On what grounds does Bedau dismiss Van Den Haag's contention that the death penalty is the only possible deterrent for some classes of criminals?

3. Why does Bedau feel it is so important to distinguish (1) the death penalty as a deterrent from (2) the death penalty as a superior deterrent to life imprisonment? Does the falsity of (1) necessarily follow from the falsity of (2)? Does the establishment of (1) thereby establish (2)?

4. What hypotheses have been formulated to test the proposition that the death penalty is a superior deterrent to life imprisonment for the crime of criminal homicide? What have been the results? What are Van Den Haag's objections to these tests, and how does Bedau respond to the objections? Do you feel that Bedau has adequately met the objections?

5. Regarding the same hypotheses, Bedau concedes that their disconfirmation is imperfect for two related reasons. What are those reasons? Does Bedau go on to turn these concessions to his own advantage? If so, how?

6. *Why does Bedau reject Van Den Haag's argument that the severity of the death penalty may add to deterrence?*

7. *How does Bedau respond to Van Den Haag's claim that abolitionists must prove that capital punishment adds nothing to deterrence?*

CASE PRESENTATION
J. D. Autry: Death in Texas

High on booze, pot, and pills, James David (J. D.) Autry and his companion John Alton Sandifer had been bumping around Port Arthur, Texas, in a borrowed pickup one warm Sunday night in April 1980, when they stopped at a convenience store for more beer. What then happened is unclear. But a jury concluded, and a succession of appellate courts affirmed, that there had been a drunken attempt at a robbery and that Autry had shot the cashier between the eyes when she resisted. Then, fleeing the store, Autry had run into two men, both of whom he shot. One was killed, and the other was crippled for life in mind and body. Autry's net profit for the bloodshed was a $2.70 six-pack.

Before the year was out, Autry was convicted of capital murder and delivered in chains to death row—protesting his innocence all the way.

A half hour before his scheduled death by lethal injection in October 1983, Autry was plucked off the gurney. Supreme Court Justice Byron White had granted a last-minute reprieve, a chance to re-examine and reargue the question of whether a killer should die. The reprieve meant that not only Autry but all death-row inmates in Texas and California, who account for about one-quarter of the nation's condemned population, might not even be considered for execution until the spring of 1984.

In the following months the Supreme Court heard arguments in a case from California that posed the question of a condemned prisoner's being entitled to a judicial review of his or her sentence to determine whether it is "proportional"; that is, whether like crimes typically warrant the death penalty. In the 1976 decisions that restored the death penalty, the Court noted with approval that both the Georgia and Florida courts made proportionality reviews to make sure the penalty wouldn't be imposed arbitrarily. Since then, the Court has struck down as "disproportional" death sentences for rapists and defendants who neither killed nor attempted to kill the victim. At the same time, it has upheld state statutes like that in Texas which make no mention of comparative sentence review. The Court decided that the absence of a proportionality review is not grounds to stay an execution. Shortly thereafter, on the morning of March 14, 1984, J. D. Autry was executed by lethal injection.

Questions for Analysis

1. *Do you think states should have proportionality reviews to ensure that the death penalty is not imposed arbitrarily? Do you think justice requires this?*

2. *Critics say proportionality-review systems don't work. They point out that the state courts have failed to set standards for real comparisons, collect complete information on the sentences of all killers, and provide other judges with guidance. Discuss the implications of these charges with regard to the equitable administration of the death penalty.*

3. *Do you think proportionality is relevant to whether the death penalty is ever morally permissible? Explain.*

4. *Some say the Autry case is just another example of delay that results in a denial of justice. Both retentionists and abolitionists view such delays as support for their positions. For example, retentionists argue that the obvious difficulties in carrying out the death penalty undermine confidence in the legal system. For their part, abolitionists claim that the very tortuousness of the appeals process demonstrates there is no way to make capital punishment work. On various occasions the Supreme Court has expressed its own concern with the delays. Justice William Rehnquist charged in 1981 that his colleagues were making a mockery of the criminal-justice system by countenancing extended appeals. In 1983 Justice Lewis F. Powell, Jr., told a group of federal judges that unless the judiciary can find a more efficient way to handle death cases, capital punishment should be abolished. And in granting Autry his last-minute stay, Justice White called for a change in the law to limit repetitive appeals. Despite the high court's impatience, it is obliged to keep reviewing death-penalty cases. Do you think that delays do, in fact, result in a denial of justice? Explain. Do they make stronger the retentionist or the abolitionist position?*

CASE PRESENTATION
Paul Crump: Death Despite Rehabilitation?[5]

When Warden Jack Johnson met Paul Crump in 1955, Crump was, according to Johnson, "choked up with hatred." "He was animalistic and belligerent," the warden said. "Self-preservation was the only law he knew." A jury had agreed, for it had sentenced Crump to death for a vicious murder.

Before Johnson's arrival at the "scandal-ridden, riot-scarred" Illinois prison, the institution had been an "abomination." Overcrowded and understaffed, it

---

5. *See Ronald Bailey, "Facing Death: A New Life Perhaps Too Late," Life, July 27, 1962, pp. 28–29, or Tom L. Beauchamp, William T. Blackstone, Joel Feinberg, Philosophy and the Human Condition, Englewood Cliffs, N.J.: Prentice-Hall, 1980, pp. 324–327.*

was an ugly throwback to a bygone era. Guards not only wore guns but armed themselves with brass knuckles, blackjacks, and miniature baseball bats. On death row, prisoners were locked up in four-by-eight-foot cells. Handcuffed and dragging leg irons, they exercised for two hours a day in the cellblock corridor. Slumbred Crump described coming to jail as being "transplanted from one jail to another." "If I hadn't been an animal," he said, "I wouldn't have survived."

Johnson immediately instituted a series of reforms. He de-emphasized punishment, disarmed the guards, ended the death-row lockup, and tried, as he put it, "a few simple words of love." Taking personal charge of death row, Johnson made daily visits there. He installed two telephones outside the tier and invited inmates to call him whenever they felt like talking. Johnson then started bringing in the men in groups of three or four for discussions with the new prison sociologists and psychologists. Eventually, Johnson created a new climate, one in which Paul Crump had a chance to change and grow.

Responding to the warden's reforms, Crump started work on his autobiographical novel, *Burn, Killer, Burn*. Limited by his ninth-grade education, Crump enlisted the aid of the assistant warden, who gave him an informal course in analytic reading. With his newly acquired skills and his awakened intellect, Crump read poetry, fiction, philosophy—virtually everything he could obtain. "I read and read and read," he said, "and some old distortions were swept away. I had thought that anything good that happened to me was all gravy, just accident. I started seeing that things don't happen by accident but because of the good will of people and their belief in the basic goodness of man."

When Johnson obtained a typewriter for him, Crump proceeded to crank out short stories, articles, and poems, which were published in small magazines. He started a second novel and began corresponding with interested and sympathetic people around the world.

Crump also began to take an interest in the problems of his fellow prisoners. Johnson made Crump "barn boss," or head of the convalescent tier for the new jail hospital. As barn boss, Crump, in the words of one guard, was "mother, father, priest, and social worker" for some fifty prisoners. An array of men came to Crump's tier: epileptics, diabetics, heart patients, old men suffering from DTs, drug addicts in withdrawal. Johnson also sent him problem prisoners and inmates needing special protection: teenagers, former policemen, potential suicides. Ministering to his charges at all hours of the day and night, Crump soon grew legendary. On various occasions, he bathed senile men unable to bathe themselves; he set aside a corner of the cellblock so that an orthodox Jew could worship in privacy; he broke up fights and prevented guards from getting hurt. Learning that the cousin of one of the guards was born with a heart defect and desperately needed blood, Crump collected the signatures of fifty men who promised to donate blood.

The rehabilitation of Paul Crump occurred over a period of seven years. If Crump underwent a dramatic change, so did Warden Jack Johnson. When he came to the prison, Johnson was ambivalent about capital punishment. But Crump turned Johnson into a vigorous opponent of capital punishment. "Paul Crump is completely rehabilitated," Johnson said, just prior to the State of Illinois's final decision on whether Crump would be executed. "Should society demand Paul's life at this point, it would be capital vengeance, not punishment. If it were humanly possible, I would put Paul back on the street tomorrow. I have no fear of any antisocial behavior on his part. I would stake my life on it. And I would trust him with my life."

On August 1, 1962, Illinois Governor Otto Kerner commuted Crump's death sentence to 199 years imprisonment without possibility of parole.

Questions for Analysis

1. *Do you think the governor's decision was proper?*

2. *How strong an argument do you think the Paul Crump case makes for the abolition of capital punishment?*

3. *Do you think it would have been morally justifiable to execute Crump despite his apparent rehabilitation? Explain.*

4. *What moral principle or principles do you think underlay Johnson's rehabilitation efforts?*

5. *Assuming Crump had been rehabilitated, do you think the governor should have been more lenient—perhaps commuting Crump's death sentence to, say, twenty additional years in prison? Explain by appeal to concepts of punishment.*

Selections for Further Reading

Adenaes, Johannes. *Punishment and Deterrence.* Ann Arbor: University of Michigan Press, 1974.

Bedau, Hugo Adam. *The Death Penalty in America.* New York: Oxford University Press, 1982.

Bedau, Hugo Adam, and C. M. Pierce, eds. *Capital Punishment in the United States.* New York: AMS Press, 1976.

Berns, Walter. *For Capital Punishment.* New York: Basic Books, 1979.

Black, Charles Jr. *Capital Punishment: The Inevitability of Caprice and Mistake.* New York: W. W. Norton, 1974.

Camus, Albert. *Reflections on the Guillotine: An Essay on Capital Punishment,* Richard Howard, trans. Michigan City, Ind.: Fridtjog-Karla Press, 1959.

Ezorsky, Gertrude, ed. *Philosophical Perspectives on Punishment.* Albany, N.Y.: State University of New York Press, 1972.

Feinberg, Joel, and Hyman Gross. *Philosophy of Law.* Belmont, Calif.: Wadsworth, 1980.

Goldinger, Milton, ed. *Punishment and Human Rights.* Cambridge, Mass.: Schenkman, 1974.

McCafferty, Jeffrie G. *Retribution, Justice, and Therapy.* Boston: D. Reidel, 1979.

Van Den Haag, Ernest. *Punishing Criminals.* New York: Basic Books, 1975.

_____ and John P. Conrad. *The Death Penalty: A Debate.* New York: Plenum, 1983.

8
JOB DISCRIMINATION

On December 10, 1970, the Equal Employment Opportunity Commission (EEOC) petitioned the Federal Communication Commission not to back a request by American Telephone and Telegraph (AT&T) for a rate increase on the grounds that AT&T was engaging in pervasive, systemwide, and blatantly unlawful discrimination against women, blacks, Spanish-surnamed Americans, and other minorities. After nearly two years of negotiation with the EEOC, AT&T finally reached an agreement with the government on December 28, 1972, whereby it agreed, among other things, not to discriminate in the future, and to set up goals and timetables for hiring women and minorities into all nonmanagement job classifications where they were underrepresented. For its part, the EEOC agreed to drop all outstanding equal-employment actions against AT&T.

Three years later, on December 8, 1975, AT&T was sued by Dan McAleer, an AT&T service representative. McAleer claimed he had lost out on a promotion to a less qualified female employee as a result of AT&T's implementation of its agreement with the EEOC. McAleer had worked for AT&T for five years and had scored thirty-four out of thirty-five on the company's performance rating. Sharon Hullery, the woman who beat out McAleer for the promotion, had worked at AT&T for less than five years and had scored thirty points.

On June 9, 1976, the U.S. District Court in Washington, D.C., ruled that AT&T owed McAleer monetary compensation, but not the promotion. AT&T owed McAleer the money, said the court, because he was an innocent victim of an agreement intended to remedy the company's wrongdoing. But the court didn't think AT&T owed McAleer the promotion because that, in the court's view, might help perpetuate and prolong the effects of the discrimination that the AT&T–EEOC agreement was designed to eliminate.

On January 18, 1979, the agreement between AT&T and the EEOC expired. AT&T had reached 99.7 percent of the female-hiring goals it had set up in 1973.

In recent years, laws have been passed and programs formulated to ensure fair and equal treatment of all people in employment practices. Nevertheless, unequal practices still exist. To help remedy these, the federal government in the early 1970s instituted an affirmative-action program.

Before affirmative action, many institutions already followed nondiscriminatory as well as merit-hiring employment practices to equalize employment opportunities. In proposing affirmative action, the government recognized the worth of such endeavors, but said that it did not think they were enough. Affirmative action, therefore, refers to positive measures beyond neutral nondiscriminatory and merit-hiring employment practices. It is an aggressive program intended to identify and remedy unfair discrimination practiced against many people who are qualified for jobs.

Among the most controversial aspects of affirmative action are its preferential and quota-hiring systems. *Preferential hiring* is an employment practice designed to give special consideration to people from groups that traditionally have been victimized by racism, sexism, or other forms of discrimination. *Quota hiring* is the policy of hiring and employing people in direct proportion to their numbers in society or in the community. According to affirmative-action guidelines, preferential and quota hiring go hand in glove; thus, for simplicity, we will refer to both by the phrase *preferential treatment*. Courts are increasingly requiring companies and unions to provide apprentice and reapprentice training to hire, promote, and train minorities and women in specified numerical ratios, in specified job categories, until specified remedial goals are reached. But critics charge that at least in some instances, implementing affirmative-action guidelines has led to *reverse discrimination—that is, the unfair treatment of a majority member (usually a white male).* Presumably this was the basis for McAleer's complaint. Was he treated unfairly? Was AT&T's action moral? Would it have been fairer had the employees' names been thrown into a hat from which one was drawn? Obviously such preferential programs raise questions of social justice.

Undoubtedly some will wonder: Why not focus directly on the morality of sexism? By *sexism* we mean the unfair treatment of a person exclusively on the basis of sex. Perhaps we should focus on it, but consider that in all our discussions so far we have made reasonable cases for at least two sides of an issue. True, perhaps one side was more flawed than another, but in all cases reasonable people could disagree. But the fact is that few seriously argue anymore that sexism, as defined, is moral. So if we focused on sexism we would be inviting a most lopsided discussion. This would be unfortunate in the light of so many aspects of sexism that genuinely deserve moral debate. One of these aspects involves such proposed remedies as preferential treatment.

Another reason for not considering sexism exclusively is that this chapter, as well as the next, naturally raises questions of social justice. Many discussions of social justice founder because they remain abstract, content to theorize while scrupulously avoiding practice. For example, it is easy and safe to argue that a government must remedy racial injustice. It is far more controversial to argue that a government must implement forced busing to do so. The same applies to sexism. Most would agree that the government has an obligation to correct the social injustice of sexism, but how?

It is one thing to recognize, deplore, and want to correct any injustice. It is entirely another thing to remedy the injustice fairly. Sadly, too many discussions of social justice ignore means entirely, often offering the defense that the means vary from situation to situation. Undoubtedly. But the debate flying around so many social justice questions today concerns proposed means. We should learn to examine every situation's means and also the common but agonizing predicament of applauding the intention and even the probable consequences of an action, but deploring the action itself. For many people, preferential treatment is just such a problem.

Job Discrimination: Its Nature and Forms

To discriminate in employment is to make an adverse decision against employees based on their membership in a certain class.[1] Included in the preceding definition of discrimination in employment are three basic elements: (1) The decision is against employees solely because of their membership in a certain group. (2) The decision is based on the assumption that the group is in some way inferior to some other group, and thus deserving of unequal treatment. (3) The decision in some way harms those it's aimed at. Since, traditionally, most of the discrimination in the American workplace has been aimed at women and minorities such as blacks and Hispanics, the following discussion will focus on these groups.

On-the-job discrimination can be intentional or unintentional, practiced by a single individual or individuals in a company or by the institution itself. "Intentional" here means knowingly or consciously; "unintentional" means unthinkingly or not consciously. "Institution" refers to the business, company, corporation, profession, or even the system within which the discrimination operates. These distinctions provide a basis for identifying four forms of discrimination: (1) intentional individual, (2) unintentional individual, (3) intentional institutional, and (4) unintentional institutional.

1. *Intentional individual* discrimination is an isolated act of discrimination *knowingly* performed by some individual out of personal prejudice. Example: A male personnel director routinely passes over females for supervisory jobs because he believes and knowingly acts on the belief that "lady bosses mean trouble."

2. *Unintentional individual* discrimination is an isolated act of discrimination performed by some individual who *unthinkingly* or *unconsciously* adopts traditional practices and stereotypes. Example: If the male in the preceding case

1. *Manuel G. Velasquez,* Business Ethics: Concepts and Cases *(Englewood Cliffs, N.J.: Prentice-Hall, 1982), p. 266.*

acted without being aware of the bias underlying his decisions, his action would fall into this category.

3. *Intentional institutional* discrimination is an act of discrimination that is part of the reactive behavior of a company or profession which knowingly discriminates out of the personal prejudices of its members. Example: The male personnel director passes over women for supervisory jobs because "the boys in the company don't like to take orders from females."

4. *Unintentional institutional* discrimination is an act of discrimination that is part of the routine behavior of a company or profession that has unknowingly incorporated sexually or racially prejudicial practices into its operating procedures. Example: An engineering firm routinely avoids hiring women because of the stereotypical assumption that women don't make good engineers or that its clients won't do business with women.

In recent years, discussions of discrimination have focused on institutional forms of discrimination, with special emphasis on the unintentional institutional. In fact, it's been this kind of discrimination that some believe only affirmative-action programs can root out. Others consider programs like this inherently unjust or counterproductive. They say that workplace discrimination can be corrected through strict enforcement of anti-discrimination law without resorting to preferential-treatment programs. The force of these positions depends, in part, on whether the body of anti-discriminatory legislation that has developed over the past twenty years has, in fact, tended to reduce discrimination in the workplace. If it has, then it would lend weight to the anti-affirmative-action positions. If it hasn't, then the pro-affirmative-action position would be strengthened. So before inspecting the two positions, let's briefly examine the relative positions of whites and minorities and of males and females in the American workplace to see if they say anything about ongoing discrimination.

Evidence of Discrimination

Determining the presence of discrimination isn't easy, because many factors could possibly account for the relative positions of various groups in the work world. But generally speaking, there are reasonable grounds for thinking that an institution is practicing discrimination (intentional or unintentional) when (1) statistics indicate that members of a group are being treated unequally in comparison with other groups, and (2) endemic attitudes, and formal and informal practices and policies, seem to account for the skewed statistics.

Statistical Evidence

Overwhelming statistical evidence points to the fact that a disproportionate number of women and minority members hold the less desirable jobs and get paid less than their white male counterparts. For example, at all occupational levels, women make less money than men—even for the same work—despite legislation forbidding discrimination on the basis of sex. According to Census Bureau statistics from 1988, the median weekly income of male workers in 1986 was $419, while the median weekly income of female workers for the same year was only $290—69 percent of the male figure.[2] Although that percentage is better than it was in 1955, years before the advent of federal anti-discrimination laws and affirmative action programs, it represents a gain of only 5 percentage points.[3] Also, the disparity between men and women cuts across all occupational categories, from executive and managerial (the highest paid) to farming, forestry, and fishing (the lowest paid). Moreover, even though much of the gap between men and women reflects differences among older workers, the median income of women between the ages of sixteen and twenty-four years was less than 90 percent of the median income of their male counterparts. Comparative figures for the incomes of whites and minorities turn up similar disparities.[4]

Another body of statistics points to unequal distribution of positions. As of 1986, the most desirable occupations (in management and administration, professions and technical jobs, and nonretail sales) were dominated by whites, while the least desirable occupations (such low-paying service jobs as maids and janitors, for example) were held by a disproportionate number of blacks and Hispanics. Although differences of educational level can account for some of these disparities, the 1988 figures for 1985 (the most recent year for which the figures are available) show that whites out-earned blacks and Hispanics of the same educational level at every educational level.[5] These and other statistical studies indicate that women and minorities are not treated as equals of white men.

Attitudinal Evidence

Although some would disagree, the statistics alone don't establish discrimination, for one could always argue that other things account for these disparities. But there are indications of widespread attitudes and formal and informal institutional practices and policies which, taken collectively, point to discrimination as the cause of these statistical disparities.

For example, in a questionnaire submitted to 5,000 of its subscribers in 1974, the *Harvard Business Review* found a double standard with regard to managerial expectations of men and women. In sum, managers expect male employees to put job before family when conflicting obligations arise, but they expect females to sacrifice their career to family responsibilities. Also, when personal conduct threatens an employee's job, managers go to greater lengths to retain a valuable male employee than an equally qualified female. The survey also turned up anti-

2. *U.S. Bureau of the Census*, Statistical Abstract of the U.S. 1988, *108th ed. (Washington, D.C.: U.S. Government Printing Office, 1988), p. 394.*

3. *U.S. Department of Labor,* The Earnings Gap between Men and Women *(Washington, D.C.: U.S. Government Printing Office, 1979), p. 6.*

4. Statistical Abstract of the U.S. 1988, *pp. 394–95.*

5. *Ibid., pp. 376, 429.*

female bias: In employee selection and promotion and in career-development decisions, managers clearly favor males.[6]

Another study has found that men prefer male supervisors and feel uncomfortable with female supervisors.[7] And over the years, various reports indicate that myths, stereotypes, and false preconceptions victimize women and minorities.

Then there's the commonplace practice in many trades and industries of filling positions by word-of-mouth recruitment policies. In jobs dominated by white males, the word of a job vacancy tends to reach other white males. Furthermore, on several occasions the EEOC has found that interviewers for non-white-collar positions have biased attitudes that lead them to treat the applications of minorities and women systematically differently from those of white males. The EEOC considers these practices so flagrant and typical that it deems strict word-of-mouth recruitment policies prima facie evidence of discrimination. And according to some, the practice is as common in professional white-collar hiring.[8]

Taken together, the statistics, personal and institutional attitudes, assumptions, and practices provide powerful evidence of intractable discrimination against women and minorities in the American workplace. Recognizing the existence of such discrimination and believing that, for a variety of reasons, it's wrong, we have as a nation passed laws expressly forbidding discrimination in recruitment, screening, promotion, compensation, and firing practices. In short, specific laws have been enacted to ensure equal opportunity in employment. The aim of these policies is to prevent further discrimination, and they probably have prevented egregious instances of discrimination. But the evidence indicates that they have not had the effect of providing equal opportunity to women and minorities as groups. Furthermore, anti-discrimination laws do not address the present-day effects of past discrimination. They ignore, for example, the fact that because of past discrimination women and minorities in general lack the skills of white males and are disproportionately underrepresented in the more prestigious and better-paying jobs. In order to remedy the effects of past discrimination and seeing no other way to counteract apparently visceral racism and sexism, many people today call for specific affirmative-action programs.

Affirmative Action: Preferential Treatment

As amended by the Equal Employment Opportunity Act of 1972, the Civil Rights Act of 1964 requires businesses that have substantial dealings with the

6. *Benson Rosen and Thomas H. Jerdee, "Sex Stereotyping in the Executive Suite,"* Harvard Business Review, *May–June 1974, pp. 45–58.*

7. *Bernard M. Bass, Judith Krusell, Ralph A. Alexander, "Male Managers' Attitudes Toward Working Women,"* American Behavioral Scientist, *November 1977, p. 223.*

8. *See Gertrude Ezorsky, "The Fight Over University Women,"* New York Review of Books, *May 16, 1974, pp. 32–39.*

federal government to undertake affirmative-action programs. *Affirmative-action programs are plans designed to correct imbalances in employment that exist directly as a result of past discrimination.* Even though these acts do not technically require companies to undertake affirmative-action programs, in recent years courts have responded to acts of job discrimination by ordering the offending firms to implement such programs to combat the effects of past discrimination. In effect, then, all business institutions must adopt affirmative-action programs either in theory or in fact. They must be able to prove that they have not been practicing institutional sexism or racism, and if they cannot prove this, they must undertake programs to ensure against racism or sexism.

What do affirmative-action programs involve? The EEOC lists general guidelines as steps to affirmative action. Under these steps, firms must issue a written equal-employment policy and an affirmative-action commitment. They must appoint a top official with responsibility and authority to direct and implement their program and to publicize their policy and affirmative-action commitment. In addition, firms must survey current female and minority employment by department and job classification. Where underrepresentation of these groups is evident, firms must develop goals and timetables to improve in each area of underrepresentation. They then must develop specific programs to achieve these goals, establish an internal audit system to monitor them, and evaluate progress in each aspect of the program. Finally, companies must develop supportive in-house and community programs to combat discrimination.

In implementing such programs, some companies have adopted a policy of preferential treatment for women and minorities. *Preferential treatment refers to the practice of giving individuals favored consideration in hiring or promotions for other than job-related reasons* (such as the person is female or black). Those espousing preferential treatment argue that such a policy is the only way to remedy traditional sexism and racism, or at least that it is the most expeditious and fairest way to do it. In some instances preferential treatment for women and minorities takes the form of a quota system, that is, *an employment policy of representing women and minorities in the firm in direct proportion to their numbers in society or in the community at large.* Thus a firm operating in a community which has a 20 percent black population might try to ensure that 20 percent of its work force be black.[9]

To unravel some of the complex moral issues affirmative-action programs can raise, let's look at a specific instance of quota hiring. Suppose an equally qualified man and woman are applying for a job. The employer, conscious of affirmative-action guidelines and realizing that the company has historically discriminated against women in its employment policies, adopts a quota-hiring system. Since males are already disproportionately well represented and females underrepresented, the quota system gives the female applicant a decided advantage. As a result, the employer hires the female. Is this action moral? Are affirmative-action programs that operate in the preferential way moral?

9.   *Some institutions simply reserve a number of places for women and minority members. The University of California at Davis, for example, had such a policy in its medical school when it denied Alan Bakke admission. Bakke appealed to the Supreme Court, which—in a 5–4 decision—found in his favor. He was presumably more qualified than some minority students who had been admitted.*

Many people argue that affirmative-action programs are inherently discriminatory and therefore unjust. In this context, *discriminatory* should be understood to refer to policies that favor individuals on non-job-related grounds (for example, on the basis of sex, color, or ethnic heritage). It has been argued that quota hiring is unjust because it involves giving preferential treatment to women and minorities over equally qualified white males, a practice that is clearly discriminatory, albeit in reverse.

Those in favor of affirmative action, however, generally attempt to rebut this objection by appealing to principles of *compensatory justice. Since women and minorities clearly continue to be victimized directly and indirectly by traditional discrimination in the workplace, they are entitled to some compensation.* This is the basis for preferential treatment. The soundness of this contention seems to rely on at least two factors: (1) that affirmative-action programs involving preferential treatment will in fact provide adequate compensation, and (2) that they will provide compensation more fairly than any other alternative.[10] Since the justice and the morality of affirmative-action programs depend to a large degree on these assumptions, we should examine them.

The question that comes to mind in regard to the first assumption is: adequate compensation for whom? The answer seems obvious: for women and minorities. But does this mean *individual* women and minority-group members, or women and minorities taken *collectively*? University of Tampa Professor Herman J. Saatkamp, Jr., has demonstrated that this question, far from being merely a technical one, bears directly on the morality of affirmative-action programs and how they are implemented.[11]

Saatkamp points out that the question of the conflict between individual and collective merit typifies the debate between government agencies and business over employment policies. On the one hand, business is ordinarily concerned with the individual merit and deserts of its employees. On the other hand, government agencies primarily focus on the relative status of groups within the population at large. To put the conflict in perspective, employment policies based solely on individual merit would try to ensure that only those individuals who could prove they deserved compensation would benefit and only those proved to be the source of discrimination would suffer. Of course, such a focus places an almost unbearable burden on the resources of an individual to provide sufficient, precise data to document employment discrimination, which is commonly acknowledged to exist at times in subtle, perhaps even imperceptible, forms at various organizational levels. Indeed, social policies recognize this difficulty by focusing on discrimination on an aggregate level. Individuals, then, need not prove they themselves were discriminated against, only that they are members of groups that have traditionally suffered because of discrimination.

Taking the collective approach to remedying job discrimination is not without its own disadvantages.

10. Albert W. Flores, "Reverse Discrimination: Towards a Just Society," *in* Business & Professional Ethics, *a quarterly newsletter/report (Troy, N.Y.: Center for the Study of the Human Dimensions of Science & Technology, Rensselaer Polytechnic Institute, Jan. 1978), p. 4.*

11. *Ibid., pp. 5–6.*

1. Policies based on collective merit tend to pit one social group against another. White males face off against all nonwhite males; women find themselves jockeying with other disadvantaged groups for priority employment status; black females can end up competing with Hispanic males for preferred treatment. This factionalizing aspect of policies based on collective merit can prove detrimental to society.

2. Policies based on collective merit victimize some individuals. The individual white male who loses out on a job because of preferential treatment given a woman or a minority-group member is penalized.

3. In some cases the women and minority members selected under preferential treatment are, in fact, less deserving of compensation than those women and minorities who are not selected. In short, those most in need may not benefit at all when preference by group membership is divorced from individual need.

4. Some members of majority groups may be just as deserving or more deserving of compensation than some women or members of minority groups. Many white males, for example, are more seriously limited in seeking employment than some women and minority-group members are.

5. Policies based on collective merit can be prohibitively expensive for business. In order to enforce such programs, businesses must hire people to collect data, process forms, deal with government agencies, and handle legal procedures. From business's viewpoint, this additional time, energy, and expense could have been channeled into more commercially productive directions.

In sum, those who argue that affirmative-action programs will provide adequate compensation for the victims of discrimination must grapple with the problems of determining the focus of the compensation: on the individual or on the group. While both focuses have merit, neither is without disadvantages. Furthermore, it seems neither approach can be implemented without first resolving a complex chain of moral concerns.

But even if we assume that affirmative-action programs will provide adequate compensation, it is still difficult to demonstrate the validity of the second assumption of those who endorse affirmative action by appealing to principles of compensatory justice: that such programs will provide compensation more fairly than any other alternative. By nature, affirmative-action programs provide compensation at the expense of the white males' right to fair and equal employment treatment. In other words, affirmative-action programs in the form of preferential treatment or quota systems undermine the fundamental principle of just employment practice: that a person should be hired or promoted only on job-related grounds. Apparently, then, it is an awesome undertaking to defend the proposition that affirmative action will provide compensation more fairly than any other alternative when such a proposition makes a non-job-related factor (membership in a group) a relevant employment criterion.

Although it would appear that reverse discrimination may not be justified on grounds of compensation, we should not conclude that it cannot be justified. In fact, some people contend that a more careful examination of the principles of justice suggests an alternative defense. As we have mentioned, those who argue against affirmative-action programs do so because such programs allegedly involve unequal treatment and are therefore unjust. The clear assumption here is that whatever involves unequal treatment is in and of itself unjust. But, as Professor Albert W. Flores points out, while justice would demand that equals receive equal treatment, it is likewise true that unequals should receive treatment appropriate to their differences. Hence, he concludes that "unfair or differential treatment may be required by the principles of justice."[12] In other words, unequal treatment is unfair in the absence of any characteristic difference between applicants which, from the viewpoint of justice, would constitute relevant differences. Following this line of reasoning, we must wonder whether being a female or a minority member would constitute a "relevant difference" that would justify unequal treatment.

To illustrate, let's ask how one could justify giving preferential consideration to a female job applicant over an equally qualified white male. Flores contends that while sex may be irrelevant to the job, it may be a relevant consideration as to who should be selected. In effect, he distinguishes between criteria relevant to a job and those relevant to candidate selection. He clearly bases this distinction on a concept of business's social responsibilities. As has been amply demonstrated elsewhere, business does not exist in a commercial vacuum. It is part of a social system and, as such, has obligations that relate to the welfare and integrity of society at large. Thus Flores argues that when a firm must decide between two equally qualified applicants, say a white male and a female, it is altogether justified in introducing as a selection criterion some concept of social justice, which in this case takes cognizance of a fair distribution of society's resources and scarcities among competing groups. From the viewpoint of justice, business may be correct in hiring the qualified female or minority member. Notice, however, that this contention is based primarily not on principles of compensatory justice but on a careful examination of the nature of justice.

The moral issues that affirmative-action programs raise in regard to justice are profound and complex. In this brief overview, we have been able to raise only a few, but these demonstrate that the morality of preferential treatment through affirmative action cuts to our basic assumptions about the nature of human beings and the principles of justice. Any moral resolution of the problem of reverse discrimination in the workplace will not only reflect these assumptions but must justify them.

Arguments against Reverse Discrimination

1. *Reverse discrimination is unequal treatment.*

POINT: "By definition, reverse discrimination means that one sex or race will receive preferential treatment over the other solely for biological reasons. This is inherently unfair because it means unequal treatment. Equality can exist only

12. *Ibid., p. 4.*

where all individuals are treated the same, where they are rewarded or punished to the same degree for the same behavior, regardless of their sex or race. But reverse discrimination precludes this. That's why it's wrong."

COUNTERPOINT: "If your argument was directed at sexism and racism, I'd totally agree with you. Both practices are morally repugnant. But reverse discrimination is different in purpose. First, unlike sexism or racism, reverse discrimination is designed to provide equal opportunity for all, not to ensure unequal opportunity. Second, reverse discrimination is a case not so much of preferring people because of sex or race, but of trying to compensate certain classes of people for the wrongs they've suffered."

2. *Reverse discrimination injures white males.*

POINT: "Surely two of the basic aspects of one's self-concept are the sexual and the racial. In individuals who have what psychologists call a "healthy self-concept," you will inevitably find a healthy sense of sexual and racial self-identity. Conversely, where self-image is damaged, you will likely find serious identity problems. When people have poor self-concepts, they experience anxiety and frustration and cannot attain happiness; indeed, they can hardly pursue happiness. By making individuals feel inferior, inadequate, or incomplete because of their sex or race, we do them incalculable harm by violating their right to a positive self-image. This, I think, is one of the most potent arguments against sexism and racism. But it also applies to reverse discrimination. After all, doesn't the white male have a right to a positive self-image, which reverse discrimination can only undermine?"

COUNTERPOINT: "Why do you focus exclusively on the white male? Considered from the viewpoint of women and minorities, reverse discrimination could have a quite positive effect on self-image. It could help restore to those people the dignity and sense of self-worth that years of sexism and racism have repressed. I doubt very seriously that the occasional white male who may lose an opportunity because of reverse discrimination will be irreparably damaged. After all, he is a member of a class that for centuries has held a preferred position in this society and, consequently, he has considerable resources to draw on when 'wronged.'"

3. *Reverse discrimination wastes the best human resources.*

POINT: "A most insidious part of reverse discrimination is that it wastes human resources. Just think of all the qualified individuals who will not be admitted to medical, dental, or law schools, or given entry into other areas where our nation and the world could use all the human power they can muster. In business, the picture is even bleaker. Under pressure to satisfy government standards, employers sometimes must overlook the one best qualified for a job—who just happens to be a white male. This is fair to neither the employer, the white male, nor society in general."

COUNTERPOINT: "There is no necessary connection between reverse discrimination and the waste of human resources. If anything, reverse discrimination, by enlarging the selection pool, should maximize our chances of securing the most competent people in all human endeavors. I don't doubt that there have been abuses in the administration of affirmative-action programs. But I think it's important to distinguish between the unqualified and the minimally qualified. I agree that nothing would justify employing an unqualified person, no matter the sex or color. But if a person is minimally qualified to do a job, then I don't see any reason other factors can't be introduced. Indeed, they already are: Institutions often consider regional 'qualifications'; businesses and schools have been known to consider 'who you know.' The point is that in the scramble for opportunities, the spoils don't always go to the person who on paper is 'best qualified.' So why not introduce sex and race as two considerations among many in evaluating a candidate?"

Arguments for Reverse Discrimination

1. *Compensatory justice demands reverse discrimination.*

POINT: "As groups, women and minorities traditionally have been discriminated against, often viciously. As individuals and as a nation, we can't ignore the sins of our fathers and mothers. In fact, we have an obligation to do something to help repair the wrongs of the past. Giving women and minorities preferential treatment in things like employment is one sound way to do this."

COUNTERPOINT: "If the living were made to pay for the sins of the dead, we'd be spending all our time making restitution. What's more, we wouldn't even be compensating those who rightly deserved it. So to the people who say, 'You must pay for the past,' I say, 'Why?' I didn't do the wrong; why should I be held accountable for it? And why should I be held accountable to someone who wasn't even the party wronged? What you're proposing will result in the ludicrous situation of an innocent individual being made to compensate someone who wasn't even wronged!"

2. *Reverse discrimination defuses the bomb of social unrest.*

POINT: "Conditions in our society today are volatile. Blacks are pitted against whites, females against males. At the root of class tensions is the fact that women and minorities don't share in the economic bounty of this land to the same degree as white males. Furthermore, women and minorities perceive white males and the establishment they man—no pun intended—as bent on preserving the white male's preferred social and economic position. Whether or not this perception is accurate is irrelevant. One thing's for sure: Women and minorities do, in fact, see it that way. Moreover, the economic gap between white males and others is widening, which can only deepen this perception and increase the chances of serious social unrest, even class warfare. The way to defuse this social bomb is through reverse discrimination. At least in that way, the white male establishment will have gone on record as recognizing and being sympathetic to the plight of the disenfranchised. Also, of course, by introducing women and minorities into the economic mainstream, reverse discrimination will thereby give them a vested interest in the system. This, in turn, will have the effect of getting women and minorities to work constructively within the system and not destructively outside it."

COUNTERPOINT: "I'm not sure I accept the ominous picture you draw of the relations between the sexes and races, but I'll concede it. Still, I doubt that reverse discrimination is going to bring us all together. Indeed, have you contemplated the impact reverse discrimination will have on white males who perceive it as reverse sexism and racism? Already several white males have gone to court crying 'Foul!' And more probably will. How can this be good for society? How can it draw us closer together? If anything, I think it's forcing people to take sides. And no wonder: Can any program that attempts to fight injustice with injustice possibly succeed?"

3. *Reverse discrimination is the only way to eradicate sexism and racism.*

POINT. "If there were any other way to root out sexism and racism in our society, I'd favor it over reverse discrimination. But there isn't. While neither sexism nor racism may be as flagrant as it used to be, each is still virulent in our society. In fact, some would say they are more pernicious today because they're more subtle. Sure, I'd like to count on the good graces of the white male power elite to rid us of these inequities. But there's nothing to suggest that the white male will, in fact, do that. Quite the opposite. Until the passage of various civil rights acts and the Equal Employment Opportunity Act, very little had been done. The lesson of history is clear: Until people are forced to change, they won't; until people are forced to play fair, they will not relinquish their preferred positions."

COUNTERPOINT: "It's funny you mention the Civil Rights Act and the Equal Employment Opportunity Act. Out of these grew the Equal Employment Opportunity Commission and affirmative-action programs, which I believe represent a viable alternative to reverse discrimination. The fact is that already numerous cases of sexism and racism have been argued successfully before the EEOC. Already millions of dollars have been awarded in reparations. All of which leads me to believe that reverse discrimination isn't the way to eradicate sexism and racism. Strict, vigorous, uncompromising enforcement of the law is. If change isn't happening fast enough for some people, then the problem lies with how we're implementing the law, and we should do something about that."

The Justification of Reverse Discrimination

Tom L. Beauchamp

In this essay, philosophy professor Tom L. Beauchamp argues that reverse discrimination can be morally justified. But Beauchamp does not defend reverse discrimination on grounds of compensation owed for past wrongs. On the contrary, he holds that reverse discrimination is

From Social Justice and Preferential Treatment, *edited by William T. Blackstone and Robert D. Heslep.* © 1977 by The University of Georgia Press. Reprinted with permission of The University of Georgia Press and the author.

justified in order to eliminate present discriminatory practices. Clearly, then, Beauchamp must demonstrate that discrimination exists and that it can be eradicated only through methods of reverse discrimination.

Beauchamp approaches his task first by showing that reverse discrimination is compatible with principles of justice and utility. He then turns away from moral considerations to strictly factual ones. The principal factual matter is whether seriously discriminatory conditions exist in our society. To establish this, Beauchamp offers an array of statistical and linguistic evidence. Not only does discrimination exist, Beauchamp claims, it is intractable. Moreover, reverse discrimination is the only way it can be rooted out.

In recent years government policies intended to ensure fairer employment and educational opportunities for women and minority groups have engendered alarm. Although I shall in this paper argue in support of enlightened versions of these policies, I nonetheless think there is much to be said for the opposition arguments. In general I would argue that the world of business is now overregulated by the federal government, and I therefore hesitate to support an extension of the regulative arm of government into the arena of hiring and firing. Moreover, policies that would eventuate in reverse discrimination in present North American society have a heavy presumption against them, for both justice-regarding and utilitarian reasons: The introduction of such preferential treatment on a large scale could well produce a series of injustices, economic advantages to some who do not deserve them, protracted court battles, jockeying for favored position by other minorities, congressional lobbying by power groups, a lowering of admission and work standards in vital institutions, reduced social and economic efficiency, increased racial hostility, and continued suspicion that well-placed women and minority-group members received their positions purely on the basis of quotas. Conjointly these reasons constitute a powerful case against the enactment of policies productive of reverse discrimination in hiring.

I find these reasons against allowing reverse discrimination to occur both thoughtful and tempting, and I want to concede from the outset that policies of reverse discrimination can create serious and perhaps even tragic injustices. One must be careful, however, not to draw an overzealous conclusion from this admission. Those who argue that reverse discrimination creates injustices often say that, because of the injustice, such policies are *unjust*. I think by this use of "unjust" they generally mean "not justified" (rather than "not sanctioned by jus-

tice") But a policy can create and even perpetuate injustices, as violations of the principle of formal equality, and yet be justified by other reasons. It would be an injustice in this sense to fire either one of two assistant professors with exactly similar professional credentials, while retaining the other of the two; yet the financial condition of the university or compensation owed the person retained might provide compelling reasons which justify the action. The first reason supporting the dismissal is utilitarian in character, and the other derives from the principle of compensatory justice. This shows both that there can be conflicts between different justice-regarding reasons and also that violations of the principle of formal equality are not in themselves sufficient to render an action unjustifiable.

A proper conclusion, then—and one which I accept—is that all discrimination, including reverse discrimination, is prima facie immoral, because a basic principle of justice creates a prima facie duty to abstain from such treatment of persons. But no absolute duty is created come what may, for we might have conflicting duties of sufficient weight to justify such injustices. The latter is the larger thesis I wish to defend: Considerations of compensatory justice and utility are conjointly of sufficient weight in contemporary society to neutralize and overcome the quite proper presumption of immorality in the case of some policies productive of reverse discrimination.

I

It is difficult to avoid accepting two important claims: (a) that the law ought never to sanction any discriminatory practices (whether plain old unadorned discrimination or reverse discrimination), and (b) that such practices can be eradicated by bringing the full weight of the law down on those who engage in discriminatory practices. The first claim is a moral one, the second a factual one. I contend in this section that it is unrealistic to believe, as *b* suggests, that in contemporary society discriminatory practices *can* be eradicated by legal measures which do not permit reverse discrimination. And because they cannot be eradicated, I think we ought to relax our otherwise unimpeachably sound reservations (as recorded in *a* and discussed in the first section) against allowing any discriminatory practices whatever.

My argument is motivated by the belief that racial, sexual, and no doubt other forms of discrimination are not antique relics but are living patterns which continue to warp selection and ranking procedures. In my view the difference between the present and the past is that discriminatory treatment is today less widespread and considerably less blatant. But its reduction has produced apathy; its subtleness has made it less visible and considerably more difficult to detect. Largely because of the reduced visibility of racism and sexism, I suggest, reverse discrimination now strikes us as all too harsh and unfair. After all, quotas and preferential treatment have no appeal if one assumes a just, primarily non-discriminatory society. Since the presence or absence of seriously discriminatory conditions in our society is a factual matter, empirical evidence must be adduced to show that the set of discriminatory attitudes and selection procedures I have alleged to exist do in fact exist. The data I shall mention derive primarily from historical, linguistic, sociological, and legal sources.

Statistical Evidence

Statistical imbalances in employment and admission are often discounted because so many variables can be hypothesized to explain why, for non-discriminatory reasons, an imbalance exists. We can all think of plausible non-discriminatory reasons why 22% of Harvard's graduate students in 1969 were women but its tenured Arts and Sciences Faculty in the Graduate School consisted of 411 males and 0 females.[1] But sometimes we are able to discover evidence which supports the claim that skewed statistics are the result of discrimination. Quantities of such discriminatory findings, in turn, raise serious questions about the real reasons for suspicious statistics in those cases where we have *not* been able to determine these reasons—perhaps because they are so subtle and unnoticed.

I shall discuss each factor in turn: (a) statistics which constitute prima facie but indecisive evidence of discrimination; (b) findings concerning discriminatory reasons for some of these statistics; and (c) cases where the discrimination is probably undetectable because of its subtleness, and yet the statistical evidence is overwhelming.

a. A massive body of statistics constituting prima facie evidence of discrimination has been assembled in recent years. Here is a tiny but diverse fragment of some of these statistical findings.[2] (1) Women college teachers with identical credentials in terms of publications and experience are promoted at almost exactly one-half the rate of their male counterparts. (2) In the United States women graduates of medical schools in 1965 stood at 7%, as compared with 36% in Germany. The gap in the number of women physicians was similar. (3) Of 3,000 leading law firms surveyed in 1957 only 32 reported a woman partner, and even these women were paid much less (increasingly so for every year of employment) than their male counterparts. (4) 40% of the white-collar positions in the United States are presently held by women, but only 10% of the management positions are held by women, and their pay again is significantly less (70% of clerical workers are women). (5) 8,000 workers were employed in May 1967 in the construction of BART (Bay Area Rapid Transit), but not a single electrician, ironworker, or plumber was black. (6) In the population as a whole in the United States, 3 out of 7 employees hold white-collar positions, but only 1 out of 7 blacks holds such a position, and these latter jobs are clustered in professions which have the fewest jobs to offer in top-paying positions. (7) In the well-known A. T. & T. case, this massive conglomerate signed a settlement giving tens of millions of dollars to women and minority employees. A. T. & T. capitulated to this settlement based on impressive statistics indicating discriminatory treatment.

b. I concede that such statistics are far from decisive indicators of discrimination. But when further evidence concerning the reasons for the statistics is uncovered, they are put in a perspective affording them greater power—clinching power in my view. Consider (3)—the statistics on the lack of women lawyers. A survey of Harvard Law School alumnae in 1970 provided evidence about male lawyers' attitudes.[3] It showed that businesses and legal firms do not generally expect the women they hire to become lawyers, that they believe women cannot become good litigators, and that they believe only limited numbers of women should be hired since clients generally prefer male lawyers. Surveys of women applicants for legal positions indicate they are frequently either told that a woman will not be hired, or are warned that "senior partners" will likely object, or are told that women will be hired to do only probate, trust, and estate work. (Other statistics confirm that these are the sorts of tasks dominantly given to women.) Consider also (5)—a particular but typical case of hiring in non-white-collar positions. Innumerable studies have shown that most of these positions are filled by word-of-mouth recruitment policies conducted by all-white interviewers (usually all-male as well). In a number of decisions of the Equal Employment Opportunity Commission, it has been shown that the interviewers have racially biased attitudes and that the applications of blacks and women are systematically handled in unusual ways, such as never even being filed. So serious and consistent have such violations been that the EEOC has publicly stated its belief that word-of-mouth recruitment policies without demonstrable supplementary and simultaneous recruitment in minority group communities is in itself a "prima facie violation of Title VII."[4] Gertrude Ezorsky has argued, convincingly I believe, that this pattern of "special ties" is no less present in professional white-collar hiring, which is neither less discriminatory nor more sensitive to hiring strictly on the basis of merit.[5]

c. Consider, finally, (1)—statistics pertaining to the treatment of women college teachers. The Carnegie Commission and others have assembled statistical evidence to show that in even the most favorable construal of relevant variables, women teachers have been discriminated against in hiring, tenuring, and ranking. But instead of summarizing this mountain of material, I wish here to take a particular case in order to illustrate the difficulty in determining, on the basis of statistics and similar empirical data, whether discrimination is occurring even where courts have been forced to find satisfactory evidence of discrimination. In December 1974 a decision was reached by the Commission against Discrimination of the Executive Department of the State of Massachusetts regarding a case at Smith College where the two complainants were women

who were denied tenure and dismissed by the English Department.[6] The women claimed sex discrimination and based their case on the following: (1) Women at the full professor level in the college declined from 54% in 1958 to 21% in 1972, and in the English department from 57% in 1960 to 11% in 1972. These statistics compare unfavorably at all levels with Mt. Holyoke's, a comparable institution (since both have an all-female student body and are located in western Massachusetts). (2) Thirteen of the department's fifteen associate and full professorships at Smith belonged to men. (3) The two tenured women had obtained tenure under "distinctly peculiar experiences," including a stipulation that one be only part-time and that the other not be promoted when given tenure. (4) The department's faculty members conceded that tenure standards were applied subjectively, were vague, and lacked the kind of precision which would avoid discriminatory application. (5) The women denied tenure were at no time given advance warning that their work was deficient. Rather, they were given favorable evaluations of their teaching and were encouraged to believe they would receive tenure. (6) Some stated reasons for the dismissals were later demonstrated to be rationalizations, and one letter from a senior member to the tenure and promotion committee contradicted his own appraisal of teaching ability filed with the department. (7) The court accepted expert testimony that any deficiencies in the women candidates were also found in male candidates promoted and given tenure during this same period, and that the women's positive credentials were at least as good as the men's.

The commissioner's opinion found that "the Complainants properly used statistics to demonstrate that the Respondents' practices operate with a discriminatory effect." Citing *Parham* v. *Southwestern Bell Telephone Co.*,[7] the commissioner argued that "in such cases extreme statistics may establish discrimination as a matter of law, without additional supportive evidence." But in this case the commissioner found abundant additional evidence in the form of "the historical absence of women," "word-of-mouth recruitment policies" which operate discriminatorily, and a number of "subtle and not so subtle, societal patterns" existing at Smith.[8] On December 30, 1974, the commissioner ordered the two women reinstated with tenure and ordered the department to submit an affirmative action program within 60 days.

This case is interesting because there is little in the way of clinching proof that the members of the English Department actually held discriminatory attitudes. Yet so consistent a pattern of *apparently* discriminatory treatment must be regarded, according to this decision, as *de facto* discrimination. The commissioner's ruling and other laws are quite explicit that "intent or lack thereof is of no consequence." If a procedure constitutes discriminatory treatment, then the parties discriminated against must be recompensed. Here we have a case where irresistible statistics and other sociological evidence of "social exclusion" and "subtle societal patterns" provide convincing evidence that strong, court backed measures must be taken because nothing short of such measures is sufficiently strong to overcome the discriminatory pattern, as the Respondents' testimony in the case verifies.[9]

Some understanding of the attitudes underlying the statistical evidence thus far surveyed can be gained by consideration of some linguistic evidence now to be mentioned. It further supports the charge of widespread discrimination in the case of women and of the difficulty in changing discriminatory attitudes.

Linguistic Evidence

Robert Baker has assembled some impressive linguistic evidence which indicates that our language is male-slanted, perhaps male chauvinistic, and that language about women relates something of fundamental importance concerning the males' most fundamental conceptions of women.[10] Baker argues that as the term "boy" once expressed a paternalistic and dominating attitude toward blacks (and was replaced in our conceptual structure because of this denigrating association), so are there other English terms which serve similar functions in regard to women (but are not replaced because not considered by men as in need of replacement). Baker assembles evidence both from the language itself and from surveys of users of the language to show the following.

The term "woman" is broadly substitutable for and frequently interchanged in English sentences such as "Who is that _____ over there?" by terms such as those in the following divisions:

A. *Neutral Categories*	B. *Animal Categories*	C. *Plaything Categories*
lady	chick	babe
gal	bird	doll
girl	fox	cuddly thing
broad	vixen	
(sister)	filly	
	bitch	

D. *Gender Categories*	E. *Sexual Categories*
skirt	snatch
hem	cunt
	ass
	twat
	piece
	lay
	pussy

Baker notes that (1) while there are differences in the frequency of usage, all of these terms are standard enough to be recognizable at least by most male users of the language; (2) women do not typically identify themselves in sexual categories; and (3) typically only males use the nonneutral categories (B-E). He takes this to be evidence—and I agree—that the male conception of women differs significantly from the female conception and that the categories used by the male in classifying women are "prima facie denigrating." He then argues that it is clearly and not merely prima facie denigrating when categories such as C and E are used, as they are either derived from playboy male images or are outright vulgarities. Baker argues that it is most likely that B and D are similarly used in denigrating ways. His arguments center on the metaphorical associations of these terms, but the evidence cannot be further pursued here.

Although Baker does not remark that women do not have a similar language for men, it seems to me important to notice this fact. Generally, any negative categories used by women to refer to men are as frequently or more frequently used by men to apply to women. This asymmetrical relation does not hold, of course, for the language used by whites and blacks for denigrating reference. This fact perhaps says something about how blacks have caught on to the impact of the language as a tool of denigrating identification in a way women have yet to do, at least in equal numbers. It may also say something about the image of submissiveness which many women still bear about themselves—an image blacks are no longer willing to accept.

Baker concludes from his linguistic studies that "sexual discrimination permeates our conceptual structure. Such discrimination is clearly inimical to any movement toward sexual egalitarianism and virtually defeats its purpose at the outset."[11] His conclusion may somewhat overreach his premises, but when combined with the corroborating statistical evidence previously adduced, it seems apt. Linguistic dispositions lead us to categorize persons and events in discriminatory ways which are sometimes glaringly obvious to the categorized but accepted as "objective" by the categorizer. My contention, derived from Baker's and to be supported as we proceed, is that cautious, good faith movements toward egalitarianism such as affirmative action guidelines *cannot* succeed short of fundamental conceptual and ethical revisions. And since the probability of such revisions approximates zero (because discriminatory attitudes are covertly embedded in language and cultural habit), radical expedients are required to bring about the desired egalitarian results, expedients which may result in reverse discrimination.

Conclusions

Irving Thalberg has argued, correctly I believe, that the gravest contemporary problems with racism stem from its "protectively camouflaged" status, which he calls "visceral." Thalberg skillfully points to a number of attitudes held by those whites normally classified as unprejudiced which indicate that racism still colors their conception of social facts.[12] My alliance with such a position ought to be obvious by now. But my overall intentions and conclusions are somewhat different. I hold that because of the peculiarly concealed nature of the protective camouflage under which sexism and racism have so long thrived, it is not a reasonable expectation that the lightweight programs now administered under the heading of affirmative action will succeed in overturning discriminatory treatment. I turn now directly to this topic.

II

The rawest nerve of the social and political controversy concerning reverse discrimination is exposed by the following question: What government policies are permissible and required in order to bring about a society where equal treatment of persons is the rule rather than the exception? Fair-minded opponents of any government policy which might produce reverse discrimination—Carl Cohen and William Blackstone, for example—seem to me to oppose them largely because and perhaps only because of their *factual belief* that present government policies not causing reverse discrimination will, if seriously and sincerely pursued, prove sufficient to achieve the goal of equal consideration of persons.

Once again a significant factual disagreement has emerged: What means are not only fair but also sufficient? I must again support my contentions by adducing factual data to show that my pessimism is sustained by the weight of the evidence. The evidence cited here comes from government data concerning affirmative action programs. I shall discuss the affirmative action program in order to show that on the basis of present government guidelines (which, to my knowledge, are the best either in law or proposed as law by those who oppose reverse discrimination), discriminatory business as usual will surely prevail.

Affirmative Action

I begin with a sample of the affirmative action guidelines, as understood by those who administer them. I use the example of HEW guidelines for educational institutions receiving federal financial aid. These guidelines are not radically different from those directed at hiring practices throughout the world of business. Specifically, these guidelines cover three areas: admission, treatment of students, and employment. A sample of the sorts of requirements universities are under includes: (1) They may not advertise vacant positions as open only to or preferentially to a particular race or sex, except where sex is a legitimate occupational requirement. (2) The university sets standards and criteria for employment, but if these effectively work to exclude women or minorities as a class, the university must justify the job requirements. (3) An institution may not set different standards for admission for one sex, race, etc. (4) There must be active recruitment where there is an underrepresentation of women and minorities, as gauged by the availability of qualified members of these classes.

However, the relevant government officials have from time to time made it clear that (1) quotas are unacceptable, either for admission or employment, though target goals and timetables intended to correct deficiencies are acceptable and to be encouraged. (2) A university is never under any obligation to dilute legitimate standards, and hence there is no conflict with merit hiring. (3) Reserving positions for members of a minority group (and presumably for the female sex) is "an outrageous and illegal form of reverse bias" (as one former director of the program wrote).[13] By affirmative action requirements I mean this latter interpretation and nothing stronger (though I have given only a sample set of qualifications, of course).

The question I am currently asking is whether these guidelines, assuming they will be vigorously pursued, can reasonably be expected to bring about their goal, which is the social circumstance of nondiscriminatory treatment of persons. If they *are* strong enough, then Cohen, Blackstone, and others are right: Reverse discrimination is not under such circumstances justified. Unfortunately the statistical and linguistic evidence previously adduced indicates otherwise. The *Smith College* case is paradigmatic of the concealed yet serious discrimination which occurs through the network of subtle distortions, old-boy procedures, and prejudices we have accumulated. Only when the statistics become egregiously out of proportion is action taken or a finding of mistreatment possible. And that is one reason why it seems unlikely that substantial progress can be made, in any realistic sense of "can," by current government measures not productive of reverse discrimination. According to Peter Holmes, once the Director of HEW's Office for Civil Rights and in charge of interpreting affirmative action guidelines: "It has been our policy that it is the institutions' responsibility to determine nondiscriminatory qualifications in the first instance, and that such qualifications, in conjunction with other affirmative action steps, should yield results."[14] This is the received HEW view, but the last sentence contains an ambiguous use of the word "should." If the "should" in this statement is a moral "should," none will disagree. But if it is an empirical, predictive "should," as I take Mr. Holmes to intend, we are back to the core of the difficulty. I now turn to a consideration of how deficient such affirmative action steps have proven to be.

Government Data

The January 1975 Report of the United States Commission on Civil Rights contains a section on "compliance reviews" of various universities. These are government assessments of university compliance with Executive Orders pertaining to affirmative action plans. The report contains a stern indictment of the Higher Education Division (HED) of HEW—the division in charge of overseeing all HEW civil rights enforcement activities in the area of higher education. It concludes that "HED has, in large part, failed to follow the procedures required of compliance agencies under the Executive order regulations."[15] But more interesting than this mere failure to enforce the law is the report's discussion of how very difficult it is to obtain compliance even when there is a routine attempt to enforce the law. The Commission reviewed four major campuses in the United States (Harvard, University of Michigan, University of Washington, Berkeley). They concluded that there is a pattern of inadequate compliance reviews, inordinate delays, and inexcusable failures to take enforcement action where there were clear violations of the Executive order regulations.[16]

Consider the example of the "case history of compliance contacts" at the University of California at Berkeley. According to HED's own staff a "conciliation agreement" with this university "is now being used as a model for compliance activities with other campuses." When the Office for Civil Rights of HEW determined to investigate Berkeley (April 1971), after several complaints, including a class action sex discrimination complaint, the university refused to permit access to its personnel files and refused to permit the interviewing of faculty members without an administrator present. Both refusals are, as the report points out, "direct violations of the Executive order's equal opportunity clause," under which Berkeley held contracts. Despite this clear violation of the law, no enforcement action was taken. A year and one-half later, after negotiations and more complaints, the university was instructed to develop a written affirmative action plan to correct "documented deficiencies" of "pervasive discrimination." The plan was to include target goals and timetables wherever job underutilization had been identified.[17]

In January 1973 the university, in a letter from Chancellor Albert H. Bowker, submitted a draft affirmative action plan which was judged "totally unacceptable." Throughout 1973 Berkeley received "extensive technical assistance" from the government to aid it in developing a better plan. No such plan emerged, and OCR at the end of the year began to question "the university's commitment to comply with the executive order." The university submitted other unacceptable plans, and finally in March 1974 "a conciliation agreement was reached." However, "the document suffered from such extreme vagueness that, as of August 1974, the university and OCR were in substantial disagreement on the meaning of a number of its provisions," and "the agreement specifically violated OFCC regulations in a number of ways." These violations are extensive and serious, and the report characterizes one part as "outrageous." Four years after this "model" compliance case began, it was unresolved and no enforcement proceedings had been taken against the university. The report concludes: "In its Title VI reviews of colleges and universities, HEW routinely finds noncompliance, but it almost never imposes sanctions; instead HEW responds by making vague recommendations. Moreover, HEW does not routinely require the submission of progress reports or conduct sufficient followup to determine if its recommendations have been followed."

III

No one could be happy about the conclusions I have reached or about the depressing and disturbing facts on which they are based. But I do take it to be a *factual* and not an *evaluative* conclusion both (1) that the camouflaged attitudes I have discussed exist and affect the social position of minority groups and women and (2) that they will in all likelihood continue to have this influence. It is, of course, an evaluative conclusion that we are morally permitted and even required to remedy this situation by the imposition of quotas, target goals, and timetables. But anyone who accepts my *interpretation* of the facts bears a heavy burden of moral argument to show that we ought not to use such means to that end upon which I take it we all agree, viz., the equal consideration of persons irrespective of race, sex, religion, or nationality.

By way of conclusion, it is important to set my arguments in the framework of a distinction between real reverse discrimination and merely apparent reverse discrimination. My evidence demonstrates present, ongoing barriers to the removal of discriminatory practices. My contentions set the stage for showing that *because* of the existence of what Thalberg calls "visceral racism," and because of visceral sexism as well, there will be many occasions on which we can only avoid inevitable discrimination by policies productive of reverse discrimination. Sometimes, however, persons will be hired or admitted—on a quota basis, for example—who appear to be displacing better applicants, but the appearance is the result of visceral discriminatory perceptions of the person's qualifications. In this case there will certainly appear to the visceral racist or sexist to be reverse discrimination, and this impression will be reinforced by knowledge that quotas were used; yet the allegation of reverse discrimination will be a mistaken one. On other occasions there will be genuine reverse discrimination, and on many occasions it will be impossible to determine whether or not this consequence is occurring. The evidence I have adduced is, of course, intended to support the contention that real and not merely apparent reverse discrimination is justified. But it is justified only as a means to the end of ensuring genuinely nondiscriminatory treatment of all persons.

Notes

1. From "Statement of Dr. Bernice Sandler," *Discrimination Against Women: Congressional Hearings on Equal Rights in Education and Employment*, ed. Catharine R. Stimpson (New York: R. R. Bowker Company, 1973), pp. 61, 415. Hereafter *Discrimination Against Women*.

2. All of the statistics and quotations cited are taken from the compilations of data in the following sources: (1) Kenneth M. Davidson, Ruth B. Ginsburg, and Herma H. Kay, eds., *Sex-Based Discrimination: Text, Cases, and Materials* (Minneapolis: West Publishing Company, 1974), esp. Ch. 3. Hereafter *Sex-Based Discrimination*. (2) *Discrimination Against Women*, esp. pp. 397–441 and 449–502. (3) Alfred W. Blumrosen, *Black Employment and the Law* (New Brunswick, N.J.: Rutgers University Press, 1971), esp. pp. 107, 122f. (4) *The Federal Civil Rights Enforcement Effort—1971*, A Report of the United States Commission on Civil Rights.

3. *Discrimination Against Women*, pp. 505f.

4. *Sex-Based Discrimination*, p. 516.

5. "The Fight Over University Women," *The New York Review of Books*, May 16, 1974, pp. 32–39.

6. *Maurianne Adams and Mary Schroeder* v. *Smith College*, Massachusetts Commission Against Discrimination, Nos. 72-S-53, 72-S-54 (December 30, 1974). Hereafter *The Smith College Case.*

7. 433 F.2d 421, 426 (8 Cir. 1970).

8. *The Smith College Case,* pp. 23, 26.

9. *Ibid.,* pp. 26f.

10. Robert Baker, "'Pricks' and 'Chicks': A Plea for Persons," in Richard Wasserstrom, ed., *Today's Moral Problems* (New York: Macmillan Publishing Company, 1975), pp. 152–170.

11. *Ibid.,* p. 170.

12. "Visceral Racism," *The Monist,* 56 (1972), 43–63, and reprinted in Wasserstrom.

13. J. Stanley Pottinger, "Race, Sex, and Jobs: The Drive Towards Equality," *Change Magazine,* 4 (Oct. 1972), 24–29.

14. Peter E. Holmes, "HEW Guidelines and 'Affirmative Action,'" *The Washington Post,* Feb. 15, 1975.

15. *The Federal Civil Rights Enforcement Effort—1974,* 3:276.

16. *Ibid.,* p. 281.

17. *Ibid.,* all subsequent references are from pp. 281–286.

Questions for Analysis

1. What obligations, if any, does Beauchamp draw from claims of compensatory justice?

2. Why does Beauchamp construe reverse discrimination as primarily a factual matter?

3. When Beauchamp says reverse discrimination is compatible with principles of justice, does he mean that no injustice results from reverse discrimination or that these injustices can be justified? Explain the difference, and why the latter claim is a utilitarian one.

4. What are the two minimal principles of justice Beauchamp uses to support the claim that reverse discrimination is compatible with justice? Compare and contrast these principles with Rawls's equality and difference principles.

5. Beauchamp says: ". . . all discrimination, including reverse discrimination, is prima facie immoral." Explain why this admission is not inconsistent with his claim that reverse discrimination can be morally justified.

6. What statistical and linguistic evidence does Beauchamp provide to prove that discrimination still exists?

7. Do you think Beauchamp has established that reverse discrimination is the only way to eradicate intractable discrimination?

A Defense of Programs of Preferential Treatment

Richard Wasserstrom

In this essay, philosophy professor Richard Wasserstrom provides a limited defense of quota hiring by attacking two of the opposition's major arguments. First, opponents of preferential treatment often charge proponents with "intellectual inconsistency." They argue that those now supporting

From Richard Wasserstrom, "A Defense of Programs of Preferential Treatment," Phi Kappa Phi Journal, *LVIII (Winter 1978); originally Part II of "Racism, Sexism, and Preferential Treatment: An Approach to the Topics," 24 U.C.L.A. Law Review, 581 (1977). Reprinted by permission of the author.*

preferential treatment opposed it in the past. But Wasserstrom feels that social realities in respect to the distribution of resources and opportunities make present preferential-treatment programs enormously different from quotas of the past.

The second argument commonly raised against preferential-treatment programs is that such programs, by introducing sex and race, compromise what really should matter: individual qualifications. Wasserstrom counters this charge on both an operational and a theoretical level. He feels that to be decisive, this argument must appeal, not to efficiency, but to desert: Those who are most qualified deserve to receive the benefits. But Wasserstrom sees no necessary connection between qualifications and desert.

Many justifications of programs of preferential treatment depend upon the claim that in one respect or another such programs have good consequences or that they are effective means by which to bring about some desirable end, e.g., an integrated, equalitarian society. I mean by "programs of preferential treatment" to refer to programs such as those at issue in the *Bakke* case—programs which set aside a certain number of places (for example, in a law school) as to which members of minority groups (for example, persons who are non-white or female) who possess certain minimum qualifications (in terms of grades and test scores) may be preferred for admission to those places over some members of the majority group who possess higher qualifications (in terms of grades and test scores).

Many criticisms of programs of preferential treatment claim that such programs, even if effective, are unjustifiable because they are in some important sense unfair or unjust. In this paper I present a limited defense of such programs by showing that two of the chief arguments offered for the unfairness or injustice of these programs do not work in the way or to the degree supposed by critics of these programs.

The first argument is this. Opponents of preferential treatment programs sometimes assert that proponents of these programs are guilty of intellectual inconsistency, if not racism or sexism. For, as is now readily acknowledged, at times past employers, universities, and many other social institutions did have racial or sexual quotas (when they did not practice overt racial or sexual exclusion), and many of those who were most concerned to bring about the eradication of those racial quotas are now untroubled by the new programs which reinstitute them. And this, it is claimed, is inconsistent. If it was wrong to take race or sex into account when blacks and women were the objects of racial and sexual policies and practices of exclusion, then it is wrong to take race or sex into account

when the objects of the policies have their race or sex reversed. Simple considerations of intellectual consistency—of what it means to give racism or sexism as a reason for condemning these social policies and practices—require that what was a good reason then is still a good reason now.

The problem with this argument is that despite appearances, there is no inconsistency involved in holding both views. Even if contemporary preferential treatment programs which contain quotas are wrong, they are not wrong for the reasons that made quotas against blacks and women pernicious. The reason why is that the social realities do make an enormous difference. The fundamental evil of programs that discriminated against blacks or women was that these programs were a part of a larger social universe which systematically maintained a network of institutions which unjustifiably concentrated power, authority, and goods in the hands of white male individuals, and which systematically consigned blacks and women to subordinate positions in the society.

Whatever may be wrong with today's affirmative action programs and quota systems, it should be clear that the evil, if any, is just not the same. Racial and sexual minorities do not constitute the dominant social group. Nor is the conception of who is a fully developed member of the moral and social community one of an individual who is either female or black. Quotas which prefer women or blacks do not add to an already relatively overabundant supply of resources and opportunities at the disposal of members of these groups in the way in which the quotas of the past did maintain and augment the overabundant supply of resources and opportunities already available to white males.

The same point can be made in a somewhat different way. Sometimes people say that what was wrong, for example, with the system of racial discrimination in the South was that it took an irrelevant characteristic, namely race, and used it systematically to allocate social benefits and burdens of various sorts. The defect was the irrelevance of the characteristic used—race—for that meant that individuals ended up being treated in a manner that was arbitrary and capricious.

I do not think that was the central flaw at all. Take, for instance, the most hideous of the practices, human slavery. The primary thing that was wrong with the institution was not that the particular individuals who were assigned the place of slaves were assigned there arbitrarily because the assignment was made in virtue of an irrelevant characteristic, their race. Rather, it seems to me that the primary thing that was and is wrong with slavery is the practice itself—the fact of some individuals being able to own other individuals and all that goes with that practice. It would not matter by what criterion individuals were assigned; human slavery would still be wrong. And the same can be said for most if not all of the other discrete practices and institutions which comprised the system of racial discrimination even after human slavery was abolished. The practices were unjustifiable—they were oppressive—and they would have been so no matter how the assignment of victims had been made. What made it worse, still, was that the institutions and the supporting ideology all interlocked to create a system of human oppression whose effects on those living under it were as devastating as they were unjustifiable.

Again, if there is anything wrong with the programs of preferential treatment that have begun to flourish within the past ten years, it should be evident that the social realities in respect to the distribution of resources and opportunities make the difference. Apart from everything else, there is simply no way in which all of these programs taken together could plausibly be viewed as capable of relegating white males to the kind of genuinely oppressive status characteristically bestowed upon women and blacks by the dominant social institutions and ideology.

The second objection is that preferential treatment programs are wrong because they take race or sex into account rather than the only thing that does matter—that is, an individual's qualification. What all such programs have in common and what makes them all objectionable, so this argument goes, is that they ignore the persons who are more qualified by bestowing a preference on those who are less qualified in virtue of their being black or female.

There are, I think, a number of things wrong with this objection based on qualifications, and not the least of them is that we do not live in a society in which there is even the serious pretense of a qualification requirement for many jobs of substantial power and authority. Would anyone claim, for example, that the persons who comprise the judiciary are there because they are the most qualified lawyers or the most qualified persons to be judges? Would anyone claim that Henry Ford II is the head of the Ford Motor Company because he is the most qualified person for the job? Part of what is wrong with even talking about qualifications and merit is that the argument derives some of its force from the erroneous notion that we would have a meritocracy were it not for programs of preferential treatment. In fact, the higher one goes in terms of prestige, power and the like, the less qualifications seem ever to be decisive. It is only for certain jobs and certain places that qualifications are used to do more than establish the possession of certain minimum competencies.

But difficulties such as these to one side, there are theoretical difficulties as well which cut much more deeply into the argument about qualifications. To begin with, it is important to see that there is a serious inconsistency present if the person who favors "pure qualifications" does so on the ground that the most qualified ought to be selected because this promotes maximum efficiency. Let us suppose that the argument is that if we have the most qualified performing the relevant tasks we will get those tasks done in the most economical and efficient manner. There is nothing wrong in principle with arguments based upon the good consequences that will flow from maintaining a social practice in a certain way. But it is inconsistent for the opponent of preferential treatment to attach much weight to qualifications on this ground, because it was an analogous appeal to the good consequences that the opponent of preferential treatment thought was wrong in the first place. That is to say, if the chief thing to be said in favor of strict qualifications and preferring the most qualified is that it is the most efficient way of getting things done, then we are right back to an assessment of the different consequences that will flow from different programs, and we are far removed from the considerations of justice or fairness that were thought to weigh so heavily against these programs.

It is important to note, too, that qualifications—at least in the educational context—are often not connected at all closely with any plausible conception of social effectiveness. To admit the most qualified students to law school, for example—given the way qualifications are now determined—is primarily to admit those who have the greatest chance of scoring the highest grades at law school. This says little about efficiency except perhaps that these students are the easiest for the faculty to teach. However, since we know so little about what constitutes being a good, or even successful lawyer, and even less about the correlation between being a very good law student and being a very good lawyer, we can hardly claim very confidently that the legal system will operate more efficiently if we admit only the most qualified students to law school.

To be at all decisive, the argument for qualifications must be that those who are the most qualified deserve to receive the benefits (the job, the place in law school, etc.) because they are the most qualified. The introduction of the concept of desert now makes it an objection as to justice or fairness of the sort promised by the original criticism of the programs. But now the problem is that there is no reason to think that there is any strong sense of "desert" in which it is correct that the most qualified deserve anything.

Let us consider more closely one case, that of preferential treatment in respect to admission to college or graduate school. There is a logical gap in the inference from the claim that a person is most qualified to perform a task, e.g., to be a good student, to the conclusion that he or she deserves to be admitted as a student. Of course, those who deserve to be admitted should be admitted. But why do the most qualified deserve anything? There is simply no necessary connection between academic merit (in the sense of being most qualified) and deserving to be a member of a student body. Suppose, for instance, that there is only one tennis court in the community. Is it clear that the two best tennis players ought to be the ones permitted to use it? Why not those who were there first? Or those who will enjoy playing the most? Or those who are the worst and, therefore, need the greatest opportunity to practice? Or those who have the chance to play least frequently?

We might, of course, have a rule that says that the best tennis players get to use the court before the others. Under such a rule the best players would deserve the court more than the poorer ones. But

that is just to push the inquiry back one stage. Is there any reason to think that we ought to have a rule giving good tennis players such a preference? Indeed, the arguments that might be given for or against such a rule are many and varied. And few if any of the arguments that might support the rule would depend upon a connection between ability and desert.

Someone might reply, however, that the most able students deserve to be admitted to the university because all of their earlier schooling was a kind of competition, with university admission being the prize awarded to the winners. They deserve to be admitted because that is what the rule of the competition provides. In addition, it might be argued, it would be unfair now to exclude them in favor of others, given the reasonable expectations they developed about the way in which their industry and performance would be rewarded. Minority-admission programs, which inevitably prefer some who are less qualified over some who are more qualified, all possess this flaw.

There are several problems with this argument. The most substantial of them is that it is an empirically implausible picture of our social world. Most of what are regarded as the decisive characteristics for higher education have a great deal to do with things over which the individual has neither control nor responsibility: such things as home environment, socioeconomic class of parents, and, of course, the quality of the primary and secondary schools attended. Since individuals do not deserve having had any of these things vis-à-vis other individuals, they do not, for the most part, deserve their qualifications. And since they do not deserve their abilities they do not in any strong sense deserve to be admitted because of their abilities.

To be sure, if there has been a rule which connects, say, performance at high school with admission to college, then there is a weak sense in which those who do well at high school deserve, for that reason alone, to be admitted to college. In addition, if persons have built up or relied upon their reasonable expectations concerning performance and admission, they have a claim to be admitted on this ground as well. But it is certainly not obvious that these claims of desert are any stronger or more compelling than the competing claims based upon the needs of or advantages to women or blacks from programs of preferential treatment. And as I have indicated, all rule-based claims of desert are very weak unless and until the rule which creates the claim is itself shown to be a justified one. Unless one has a strong preference for the status quo, and unless one can defend that preference, the practice within a system of allocating places in a certain way does not go very far at all in showing that this is the right or the just way to allocate those places in the future.

A proponent of programs of preferential treatment is not at all committed to the view that qualifications ought to be wholly irrelevant. He or she can agree that, given the existing structure of any institution, there is probably some minimal set of qualifications without which one cannot participate meaningfully within the institution. In addition, it can be granted that the qualifications of those involved will affect the way the institution works and the way it affects others in the society. And the consequences will vary depending upon the particular institution. But all of this only establishes that qualifications, in this sense, are relevant, not that they are decisive. This is wholly consistent with the claim that race or sex should today also be relevant when it comes to matters such as admission to college or law school. And that is all that any preferential treatment program—even one with the kind of quota used in the *Bakke* case—has ever tried to do.

I have not attempted to establish that programs of preferential treatment are right and desirable. There are empirical issues concerning the consequences of these programs that I have not discussed, and certainly not settled. Nor, for that matter, have I considered the argument that justice may permit, if not require, these programs as a way to provide compensation or reparation for injuries suffered in the recent as well as distant past, or as a way to remove benefits that are undeservedly enjoyed by those of the dominant group. What I have tried to do is show that it is wrong to think that programs of preferential treatment are objectionable in the centrally important sense in which many past and present discriminatory features of our society have been and are racist and sexist. The social realities as to power and opportunity do make a fundamental difference. It is also wrong to think that programs of preferential treatment could, therefore, plausibly rest both on the view that such programs are not unfair to white males (except in the weak, rule-dependent sense described above) and on the view that it is unfair to continue the present set of unjust—often racist and sexist—institutions that comprise the social reality. And the case for these programs could rest as well on the proposition that, given the distribution of power and influence in the United States today, such programs may reasonably be viewed as potentially valuable, effective means by which to achieve admirable and significant social ideals of equality and integration.

Questions for Analysis

1. *What does it mean to claim that proponents of preferential treatment are guilty of "intellectual inconsistency"? Do you think that Wasserstrom convincingly refutes this charge?*

2. *What moral principle (or principles) underlies Wasserstrom's objection to slavery?*

3. *How does Wasserstrom respond to the charge that preferential-treatment programs comprise the only thing that really matters: individual qualifications?*

4. *Describe the inconsistency present for the person who favors "pure qualifications" on grounds of maximum efficiency.*

5. *Do you agree that there is no necessary connection between qualifications and desert?*

6. *Do you think Wasserstrom's tennis analogy is a sound one?*

7. *Would it be accurate to say that Wasserstrom unequivocally supports preferential-treatment programs? Explain.*

Reverse Discrimination and Compensatory Justice

William T. Blackstone

In this essay, philosophy professor William T. Blackstone is concerned with a single question: Is reverse discrimination ever justified on grounds of repairing past wrongs done to women and minorities? Blackstone thinks not. In his view, reverse discrimination cannot be so justified either morally or legally.

Blackstone builds his case primarily on a utilitarian foundation. He believes that more harm than good would result from a systematic policy of reverse discrimination. (Curiously, as he points out, reverse discrimination often is justified on an appeal to utility.) Since reverse discrimination is not justified on utilitarian or justice-regarding grounds, Blackstone concludes that compensation through reverse discrimination is not justifiable. Indeed, he argues that affirmative-action programs, despite how they have sometimes been implemented, not only oppose reverse discrimination but forbid it.

Is reverse discrimination justified as a policy of compensation or of preferential treatment for women and racial minorities? That is, given the fact that women and racial minorities have been invidiously discriminated against in the past on the basis of the irrelevant characteristics of race and sex—are we now justified in discriminating in their favor on the basis of the same characteristics? This is a central ethical and legal question today, and it is one which is quite unresolved. Philosophers, jurists, legal scholars, and the man-in-the-street line up on both sides of this issue. These differences are plainly reflected (in the Supreme Court's majority opinion and Justice Douglas's dissent) in *DeFunis v. Odegaard*.[1] . . .

I will argue that reverse discrimination is improper on both moral and constitutional grounds, though I focus more on moral grounds. However, I do this with considerable ambivalence, even "existential guilt." Several reasons lie behind that ambivalence. First, there are moral and constitutional arguments on both sides. The ethical waters are very muddy and I simply argue that the balance of the arguments are against a policy of reverse discrimination.[2] My ambivalence is further due not only to the fact that traditional racism is still a much larger problem than that of reverse discrimination but also because I am sympathetic to the *goals* of those who strongly believe that reverse discrimination as a policy is the means to overcome the debilitating effects of past injustice. Compensation and remedy are most definitely required both by the facts and by our value commitments. But I do not think that reverse discrimination is the proper means of remedy or compensation. . . .

I

Let us now turn to the possibility of a utilitarian justification of reverse discrimination and to the possible conflict of justice-regarding reasons and those of social utility on this issue. The category of morally relevant reasons is broader, in my opinion, than reasons related to the norm of justice. It is broader than those related to the norm of utility. Also it seems to me that the norms of justice and

From Social Theory and Practice, *vol. 3. no. 3 (Spring 1975). Reprinted with permission of the publisher and Mrs. Jean T. Blackstone.*

utility are not reducible one to the other. We cannot argue these points of ethical theory here. But, if these assumptions are correct, then it is at least possible to morally justify injustice or invidious discrimination in some contexts. A case would have to be made that such injustice, though regrettable, will produce the best consequences for society and that this fact is an overriding or weightier moral reason than the temporary injustice. Some arguments for reverse discrimination have taken this line. Professor Thomas Nagel argues that such discrimination is justifiable as long as it is "clearly contributing to the eradication of great social evils."[3] . . .

Another example of what I would call a utilitarian argument for reverse discrimination was recently set forth by Congressman Andrew Young of Georgia. Speaking specifically of reverse discrimination in the context of education, he stated: "While that may give minorities a little edge in some instances, and you may run into the danger of what we now commonly call reverse discrimination, I think the educational system needs this. Society needs this as much as the people we are trying to help . . . a society working toward affirmative action and inclusiveness is going to be a stronger and more relevant society than one that accepts the limited concepts of objectivity. . . . I would admit that it is perhaps an individual injustice. But it might be necessary in order to overcome an historic group injustice or series of group injustices."[4] Congressman Young's basic justifying grounds for reverse discrimination, which he recognizes as individual injustice, are the results which he thinks it will produce: a stronger and more relevant education system and society, and one which is more just overall. His argument may involve pitting some justice-regarding reasons (the right of women and racial minorities to be compensated for past injustices) against others (the right of the majority to the uniform application of the same standards of merit to all). But a major thrust of his argument also seems to be utilitarian.

Just as there are justice-regarding arguments on both sides of the issue of reverse discrimination, so also there are utilitarian arguments on both sides. In a nutshell, the utilitarian argument in favor runs like this: Our society contains large groups of persons who suffer from past institutionalized injustice. As a result, the possibilities of social discord

and disorder are high indeed. If short-term reverse discrimination were to be effective in overcoming the effects of past institutionalized injustice and if this policy could alleviate the causes of disorder and bring a higher quality of life to millions of persons, then society as a whole would benefit.

There are moments in which I am nearly convinced by this argument, but the conclusion that such a policy would have negative utility on the whole wins out. For although reverse discrimination might appear to have the effect of getting more persons who have been disadvantaged by past inequities into the mainstream quicker, that is, into jobs, schools, and practices from which they have been excluded, the cost would be invidious discrimination against majority group members of society. I do not think that majority members of society would find this acceptable, i.e., the disadvantaging of themselves for past inequities which they did not control and for which they are not responsible. If such policies were put into effect by government, I would predict wholesale rejection or noncooperation, the result of which would be negative not only for those who have suffered past inequities but also for the justice-regarding institutions of society. Claims and counter-claims would obviously be raised by other ethnic or racial minorities—by Chinese, Chicanos, American Indians, Puerto Ricans—and by orphans, illegitimate children, ghetto residents, and so on. Literally thousands of types or groups could, on similar grounds as blacks or women, claim that reverse discrimination is justified on their behalf. What would happen if government attempted policies of reverse discrimination for all such groups? It would mean the arbitrary exclusion or discrimination against all others relative to a given purpose and a given group. Such a policy would itself create an injustice for which those newly excluded persons could then, themselves, properly claim the need for reverse discrimination to offset the injustice to them. The circle is plainly a vicious one. Such policies are simply self-destructive. In place of the ideal of equality and distributive justice based on relevant criteria, we would be left with the special pleading of self-interested power groups, groups who gear criteria for the distribution of goods, services, and opportunities to their special needs and situations, primarily. Such policies would be those of special privilege, not the appeal to objective criteria which apply to all.[5] They would lead to social chaos, not social justice.

Furthermore, in cases in which reverse discrimination results in a lowering of quality, the consequences for society, indeed for minority victims of injustice for which reverse discrimination is designed to help, may be quite bad. It is no easy matter to calculate this, but the recent report sponsored by the Carnegie Commission on Higher Education points to such deleterious consequences.[6] If the quality of instruction in higher education, for example, is lowered through a policy of primary attention to race or sex as opposed to ability and training, everyone—including victims of past injustice—suffers. Even if such policies are clearly seen as temporary with quite definite deadlines for termination, I am skeptical about their utilitarian value. . . .

II

The inappropriateness of reverse discrimination, both on utilitarian and justice-regarding grounds, in no way means that compensation for past injustices is inappropriate. It does not mean that those who have suffered past injustices and who have been disadvantaged by them are not entitled to compensation or that they have no moral right to remedy. It may be difficult in different contexts to translate that moral right to remedy into practice or into legislation. When has a disadvantaged person or group been compensated enough? What sort of allocation of resources will compensate without creating additional inequities or deleterious consequences? There is no easy answer to these questions. Decisions must be made in particular contexts. Furthermore, it may be the case that the effects of past injustices are so severe (poverty, malnutrition, and the denial of educational opportunities) that genuine compensation—the balancing of the scales—is impossible. The effects of malnutrition or the lack of education are often nonreversible (and would be so even under a policy of reverse discrimination). This is one of the tragedies of injustice. But if reverse discrimination is inappropriate as a means of compensation and if (as I have argued) it is unjust to make persons who are not responsible for the suffering and disadvantaging of others to suffer for those past injuries, then

other means must be employed unless overriding moral considerations of another type (utilitarian) can be clearly demonstrated. That compensation must take a form which is consistent with our constitutional principles and with reasonable principles of justice. Now it seems to me that the Federal Government's Equal Opportunity and Affirmative Action programs are consistent with these principles, that they are not only not committed to reverse discrimination but rather absolutely forbid it.[7] However, it also seems to me that some officials authorized or required to implement these compensatory efforts have resorted to reverse discrimination and hence have violated the basic principles of justice embodied in these programs. I now want to argue both of these points: first, that these federal programs reject reverse discrimination in their basic principles; secondly, that some implementers of these programs have violated their own principles.

Obviously our country has not always been committed constitutionally to equality. We need no review of our social and political heritage to document this. But with the Fourteenth Amendment, equality as a principle was given constitutional status. Subsequently, social, political, and legal practices changed radically and they will continue to do so. The Fourteenth Amendment declares that states are forbidden to deny any person life, liberty, or property without due process of law or to deny to any person the equal protection of the laws. In my opinion the principles of the Equal Opportunity and Affirmative Action Programs reflect faithfully this constitutional commitment. I am more familiar with those programs as reflected in universities. In this context they require that employers "recruit, hire, train, and promote persons in all job classifications without regard to race, color, religion, sex or national origin, except where sex is a bona fide occupational qualification."[8] They state explicitly that "goals may not be rigid and inflexible quotas which must be met, but must be targets reasonably attainable by means of good faith effort."[9] They require the active recruitment of women and racial minorities where they are "underutilized," this being defined as a context in which there are "fewer minorities or women in a particular job classification than would reasonably be expected by their availability."[10] This is sometimes difficult to determine; but some relevant facts do exist and hence the meaning of a "good faith" effort is not entirely fluid. In any event the Affirmative Action Program in universities requires that "goals, timetables and affirmative action commitment, must be designed to correct any identifiable deficiencies," with separate goals and timetables for minorities and women.[11] It recognizes that there has been blatant discrimination against women and racial minorities in universities and elsewhere, and it assumes that there are "identifiable deficiencies." But it does not require that blacks be employed because they are black or women employed because they are women; that is, it does not require reverse discrimination with rigid quotas to correct the past. It requires a good faith effort in the present based on data on the availability of qualified women and racial minorities in various disciplines and other relevant facts. (Similar requirements hold, of course, for non-academic employment at colleges and universities.) It does not mandate the hiring of the unqualified or a lowering of standards; it mandates only equality of opportunity for all which, given the history of discrimination against women and racial minorities, requires affirmative action in recruitment.

Now if this affirmative action in recruitment, which is not only consistent with but required by our commitment to equality and social justice, is translated into rigid quotas and reverse discrimination by those who implement equal opportunity and affirmative action programs in the effort to get results immediately—and there is no doubt in my mind that this has occurred—then such action violates the principles of these programs.

This violation—this inconsistency of principle and practice—occurs, it seems to me, when employers hire with *priority emphasis* on race, sex, or minority-group status. This move effectively eliminates others from the competition. It is like pretending that everyone is in the game from the beginning while all the while certain persons are systematically excluded. This is exactly what happened recently when a judge declared that a certain quota or number of women were to be employed by a given agency regardless of their qualifications for the job,[12] when some public school officials fired a white coach in order to hire a black one,[13] when a DeFunis is excluded from law school on racial grounds, and when colleges or universities announce that normal academic openings will give preference to female candidates or those from racial minorities.

If reverse discrimination is prohibited by our constitutional and ethical commitments, what means of remedy and compensation are available? Obviously, those means which are consistent with those commitments. Our commitments assure the right to remedy to those who have been treated unjustly, but our government has not done enough to bring this right to meaningful fruition in practice. Sound progress has been made in recent years, especially since the Equal Employment Opportunity Act of 1972 and the establishment of the Equal Employment Opportunities Commission. This Act and other laws have extended anti-discrimination protection to over 60% of the population.[14] The Commission is now authorized to enforce anti-discrimination orders in court and, according to one report, it has negotiated out-of-court settlements which brought 44,000 minority workers over 46 million dollars in back pay.[15] Undoubtedly this merely scratches the surface. But now the framework exists for translating the right to remedy into practice, not just for sloughing off race and sex as irrelevant criteria of differential treatment but other irrelevant criteria as well—age, religion, the size of hips (I am thinking of airline stewardesses), the length of nose, and so on.

Adequate remedy to overcome the sins of the past, not to speak of the present, would require the expenditure of vast sums for compensatory programs for those disadvantaged by past injustice in order to assure equal access. Such programs should be racially and sexually neutral, benefiting the disadvantaged of *whatever sex or race*. Such neutral compensatory programs would have a high proportion of blacks and other minorities as recipients, for they as members of these groups suffer more from the injustices of the past. But the basis of the compensation would be that fact, not sex or race. Neutral compensatory policies have definite theoretical and practical advantages in contrast to policies of reverse discrimination: Theoretical advantages, in that they are consistent with our basic constitutional and ethical commitments whereas reverse discrimination is not; practical advantages, in that their consistency, indeed their requirement by our constitutional and ethical commitments, means that they can marshal united support in overcoming inequalities whereas reverse discrimination, in my opinion, can not.

Notes

1. 94 S. Ct. 1704 (1974).

2. I hasten to add a qualification—more ambivalence!—resulting from discussion with Tom Beauchamp of Georgetown University. In cases of extreme recalcitrance to equal employment by certain institutions or businesses some quota requirements (reverse discrimination) may be justified. I regard this as distinct from a general policy of reverse discrimination.

3. "Equal Treatment and Compensatory Discrimination," *Philosophy and Public Affairs*, 2 (Summer 1974).

4. *Atlanta Journal and Constitution*, Sept. 22, 1974, p. 20-A.

5. For similar arguments see Lisa Newton, "Reverse Discrimination as Unjustified," *Ethics*, 83 (1973).

6. Richard A. Lester, *Antibias Regulation of Universities* (New York, 1974); discussed in *Newsweek*, July 15, 1974, p. 78.

7. See The Civil Rights Act of 1964, especially Title VII (which created the Equal Employment Opportunity Commission), amended by The Equal Employment Opportunity Act of 1972, found in *ABC's of The Equal Employment Opportunity Act*, prepared by the Editorial Staff of The Bureau of National Affairs, Inc., 1972. Affirmative Action Programs came into existence with Executive Order 11246. Requirements for affirmative action are found in the rules and regulations 41-CFR Part 60-2, Order #4 (Affirmative Action Programs) generally known as Executive Order #4 and Revised Order #4 41-CFT 60-2 B. For discussion see Paul Brownstein, "Affirmative Action Programs," in *Equal Employment Opportunities Compliance*, Practising Law Institute, New York City (1972), pp. 73–111.

8. See Brownstein, "Affirmative Action Programs" and, for example, *The University of Georgia Affirmative Action Plan*, Athens, Ga., 1973–74, viii, pp. 133, 67.

9. Brownstein and *The University of Georgia Affirmative Action Plan*, Athens, Ga., 1973–74, p. 71.

10. *Ibid.*, p. 69.

11. *Ibid.*, p. 71.

12. See the *Atlanta Journal and Constitution*, June 9, 1974, p. 26-D.

13. See *Atlanta Constitution*, June 7, 1974, p. 13-B.

14. *Newsweek*, June 17, 1974, p. 75.

15. *Ibid.*, p. 75.

Questions for Analysis

1. Why does Blackstone argue his case with a certain amount of "existential guilt"?

2. State the utilitarian argument for reverse discrimination.

3. Would it be accurate to say that Blackstone rejects utility as a legitimate standard for determining the morality of reverse discrimination?

4. Consider this proposition: "Blackstone is opposed to compensating those who have suffered past injustices." Is this statement true or false? Explain.

5. What are some of the problems that compensation raises?

6. Some people would claim that it is wrong to hold people today responsible for the wrongs of their ancestors and that it is equally as wrong to compensate people today for the wrongs their ancestors may have experienced. Do you agree? Explain your answers by appeal to some concept of justice.

7. What reasons does Blackstone offer for saying that affirmative-action programs actually forbid reverse discrimination? Do you think his argument is persuasive? What objections to his interpretations might you raise?

8. *Granted that reverse discrimination is prohibited by our constitution and ethical commitments, what means of redress are available? Do you agree that a vigorous and unflinching implementation of these means will satisfy the obligation to eradicate discrimination?*

Reverse Discrimination as Unjustified

Lisa Newton

Professor of philosophy Lisa Newton delivered a version of the following essay at a meeting of the Society for Women in Philosophy in 1972. She argues that reverse discrimination cannot be justified by an appeal to the ideal of equality. Indeed, according to Newton, reverse discrimination does not advance but actually undermines equality because it violates the concept of equal justice under law for all citizens.

Specifically, Newton attacks the defense for reverse discrimination on grounds of equality. She contends that no violation of justice can be justified by an appeal to the ideal of equality, for the idea of equality is logically dependent on the notion of justice.

In addition to this theoretical objection to reverse discrimination, Newton opposes it because she believe it raises insoluble problems. Among them are: determining what groups have been sufficiently discriminated against in the past to deserve preferred treatment in the present, and determining the degree of reverse discrimination that will be compensatory. Newton concludes that reverse discrimination destroys justice, law, equality, and citizenship itself.

I have heard it argued that "simple justice" requires that we favor women and blacks in employment and educational opportunities, since women and blacks were "unjustly" excluded from such opportunities for so many years in the not so distant past. It is a strange argument, an example of a possible implication of a true proposition advanced to dispute the proposition itself, like an octopus absentmindedly slicing off his head with a stray tentacle. A fatal confusion underlies this argument, a confusion fundamentally relevant to our understanding of the notion of the rule of law.

Two senses of justice and equality are involved in this confusion. The root notion of justice, progenitor of the other, is the one that Aristotle (*Nicomachean Ethics* 5. 6; *Politics* 1.2; 3.1) assumes to be the foundation and proper virtue of the political association. It is the conclusion which free men establish among themselves when they "share a common life in order that their association bring them self-sufficiency"—the regulation of their relationship by law, and the establishment, by law, of equality before the law. Rule of law is the name and pattern of this justice; its equality stands against the inequalities—of wealth, talent, etc.—otherwise obtaining among its participants, who by virtue of that equality are called "citizens." It is an achievement—complete, or, more frequently, partial—of certain people in certain concrete situations. It is fragile and easily disrupted by powerful individuals who discover that the blind equality of rule of law is inconvenient for their interests. Despite its obvious instability, Aristotle assumed that the establishment of justice in this sense, the creation of citizenship, was a permanent possibility for men and that the resultant association of citizens was

From Lisa H. Newton, "Reverse Discrimination as Unjustified," Ethics 83 (1973): 308–12. Copyright © 1973 by The University of Chicago Press. Reprinted by permission of the publisher and the author.

the natural home of the species. At levels below the political association, this rule-governed equality is easily found; it is exemplified by any group of children agreeing together to play a game. At the level of the political association, the attainment of this justice is more difficult, simply because the stakes are so much higher for each participant. The equality of citizenship is not something that happens of its own accord, and without the expenditure of a fair amount of effort it will collapse into the rule of a powerful few over an apathetic many. But at least it has been achieved, at some times in some places; it is always worth trying to achieve, and eminently worth trying to maintain, wherever and to whatever degree it has been brought into being.

Aristotle's parochialism is notorious; he really did not imagine that persons other than Greeks could associate freely in justice, and the only form of association he had in mind was the Greek *polis*. With the decline of the *polis* and the shift in the center of political thought, his notion of justice underwent a sea change. To be exact, it ceased to represent a political type and became a moral ideal: the ideal of equality as we know it. This ideal demands that all men be included in citizenship— that one Law govern all equally, that all men regard all other men as fellow citizens, with the same guarantees, rights, and protections. Briefly, it demands that the circle of citizenship achieved by any group be extended to include the entire human race. Properly understood, its effect on our associations can be excellent: It congratulates us on our achievement of rule of law as a process of government but refuses to let us remain complacent until we have expanded the associations to include others within the ambit of the rules, as often and as far as possible. While one man is a slave, none of us may feel truly free. We are constantly prodded by this ideal to look for possible unjustifiable discrimination, for inequalities not absolutely required for the functioning of the society and advantageous to all. And after twenty centuries of pressure, not at all constant, from this ideal, it might be said that some progress has been made. To take the cases in point for this problem, we are now prepared to assert, as Aristotle would never have been, the equality of sexes and of persons of different colors. The ambit of American citizenship, once restricted to white males of property, has been extended to

include all adult free men, then all adult males including ex-slaves, then all women. The process of acquisition of full citizenship was for these groups a sporadic trail of half-measures, even now not complete; the steps on the road to full equality are marked by legislation and judicial decisions which are only recently concluded and still often not enforced. But the fact that we can now discuss the possibility of favoring such groups in hiring shows that over the area that concerns us, at least, full equality is presupposed as a basis for discussion. To that extent, they are full citizens, fully protected by the law of the land.

It is important for my argument that the moral ideal of equality be recognized as logically distinct from the condition (or virtue) of justice in the political sense. Justice in this sense exists *among* a citizenry, irrespective of the number of the populace included in that citizenry. Further, the moral ideal is parasitic upon the political virtue, for "equality" is unspecified—it means nothing until we are told in what respect that equality is to be realized. In a political context, "equality" is specified as "equal rights"—equal access to the public realm, public goods and offices, equal treatment under the law— in brief, the equality of citizenship. If citizenship is not a possibility, political equality is unintelligible. The ideal emerges as a generalization of the real condition and refers back to that condition for its content.

Now, if justice (Aristotle's justice in the political sense) is equal treatment under law for all citizens, what is injustice? Clearly, injustice is the violation of that equality, discrimination for or against a group of citizens, favoring them with special immunities and privileges or depriving them of those guaranteed to the others. When the southern employer refuses to hire blacks in white-collar jobs, when Wall Street will only hire women as secretaries with new titles, when Mississippi high schools routinely flunk all the black boys above ninth grade, we have examples of injustice, and we work to restore the equality of the public realm by ensuring that equal opportunity will be provided in such cases in the future. But of course, when the employers and the schools *favor* women and blacks, the same injustice is done. Just as the previous discrimination did, this reverse discrimination violates the public equality which defines citizenship and destroys the rule of law for the areas in which these favors are granted. To the extent that we adopt a program of discrimination, reverse or otherwise, justice in the political sense is destroyed, and none of us, specifically affected or not, is a citizen, a bearer of rights—we are all petitioners for favors. And to the same extent, the ideal of equality is undermined, for it has content only where justice obtains, and by destroying justice we render the ideal meaningless. It is, then, an ironic paradox, if not a contradiction in terms, to assert that the ideal of equality justifies the violation of justice; it is as if one should argue, with William Buckley, that an ideal of humanity can justify the destruction of the human race.

Logically, the conclusion is simple enough: All discrimination is wrong prima facie because it violates justice, and that goes for reverse discrimination too. No violation of justice among the citizens may be justified (may overcome the prima facie objection) by appeal to the ideal of equality, for that ideal is logically dependent upon the notion of justice. Reverse discrimination, then, which attempts no other justification than an appeal to equality, is wrong. But let us try to make the conclusion more plausible by suggesting some of the implications of the suggested practice of reverse discrimination in employment and education. My argument will be that the problems raised there are insoluble, not only in practice but in principle.

We may argue, if we like, about what "discrimination" consists of. Do I discriminate against blacks if I admit none to my school when none of the black applicants are qualified by the tests I always give? How far must I go to root out cultural bias from my application forms and tests before I can say that I have not discriminated against those of different cultures? Can I assume that women are not strong enough to be roughnecks on my oil rigs, or must I test them individually? But this controversy, the most popular and well-argued aspect of the issue, is not as fatal as two others which cannot be avoided: If we are regarding the blacks as a "minority" victimized by discrimination, what is a "minority"? And for any group—blacks, women, whatever—that has been discriminated against, what amount of reverse discrimination wipes out the initial discrimination? Let us grant as true that women and blacks were discriminated against, even where laws forbade such discrimination, and grant for the sake of argument that a history of discrimination must

be wiped out by reverse discrimination. What follows?

First, are there other groups which have been discriminated against? For they should have the same right of restitution. What about American Indians, Chicanos, Appalachian Mountain whites, Puerto Ricans, Jews, Cajuns, and Orientals? And if these are to be included, the principle according to which we specify a "minority" is simply the criterion of "ethnic (sub) group," and we're stuck with every hyphenated American in the lower middle class clamoring for special privileges for *his* group—and with equal justification. For be it noted, when we run down the Harvard roster, we find not only a scarcity of blacks (in comparison with the proportion in the population) but an even more striking scarcity of those second-, third-, and fourth-generation ethnics who make up the loudest voice of Middle America. Shouldn't they demand *their* share? And eventually, the WASPs will have to form their own lobby; for they too are a minority. The point is simply this: There is no "majority" in America who will not mind giving up just a bit of their rights to make room for a favored minority. There are only other minorities, each of which is discriminated against by the favoring. The initial injustice is then repeated dozens of times, and if each minority is granted the same right of restitution as the others, an entire area of rule governance is dissolved into a pushing and shoving match between self-interested groups. Each works to catch the public eye and political popularity by whatever means of advertising and power politics lend themselves to the effort, to capitalize as much as possible on temporary popularity until the restless mob picks another group to feel sorry for. Hardly an edifying spectacle, and in the long run no one can benefit: The pie is no larger—it's just that instead of setting up and enforcing rules for getting a piece, we've turned the contest into a free-for-all, requiring much more effort for no larger a reward. It would be in the interests of all the participants to reestablish an objective rule to govern the process, carefully enforced and the same for all.

Second, supposing that we do manage to agree in general that women and blacks (and all the others) have some right of restitution, some right to a privileged place in the structure of opportunities for a while, how will we know when that while is up? How much privilege is enough? When will the guilt be gone, the price paid, the balance restored? What recompense is right for centuries of exclusion? What criterion tells us when we are done? Our experience with the Civil Rights movement shows us that agreement on these terms cannot be presupposed: A process that appears to some to be going at a mad gallop into a black takeover appears to the rest of us to be at a standstill. Should a practice of reverse discrimination be adopted, we may safely predict that just as some of us begin to see "a satisfactory start toward righting the balance," others of us will see that we "have already gone too far in the other direction" and will suggest that the discrimination ought to be reversed again. And such disagreement is inevitable, for the point is that we could not *possibly* have any criteria for evaluating the kind of recompense we have in mind. The context presumed by any discussion of restitution is the context of the rule of law: Law sets the rights of men and simultaneously sets the method for remedying the violation of those rights. You may exact suffering from others and/or damage payments for yourself if and only if the others have violated your rights; the suffering you have endured is not sufficient reason for them to suffer. And remedial rights exist only where there is law: Primary human rights are useful guides to legislation but cannot stand as reasons for awarding remedies for injuries sus-tained. But then, the context presupposed by any discussion of restitution is the context of preexistent full citizenship. No remedial rights could exist for the excluded; neither in law nor in logic does there exist a right to *sue* for a standing to sue.

From these two considerations, then, the difficulties with reverse discrimination become evident. Restitution for a disadvantaged group whose rights under the law have been violated is possible by legal means, but restitution for a disadvantaged group whose grievance is that there was no law to protect them simply is not. First, outside of the area of justice defined by the law, no sense can be made of "the group's rights," for no law recognizes that group or the individuals in it, qua members, as bearers of rights (hence *any* group can constitute itself as a disadvantaged minority in some sense and demand similar restitution). Second, outside of the area of protection of law, no sense can be made of the violation of rights (hence the amount of the recompense cannot be decided by any objective criterion). For both reasons, the practice of reverse discrimination undermines the foundation of the very ideal in whose name it is advocated; it destroys justice, law, equality, and citizenship itself, and replaces them with power struggles and popularity contests.

Questions for Analysis

1. *What is the "fatal confusion" underlying the argument that "simple justice" requires preferential treatment?*

2. *Can you describe how justice under Aristotle moved from a "political type" to a "moral ideal"?*

3. *Why is it important for Newton's argument that she distinguish the moral ideal of equality from the condition of justice in the political sense?*

4. *Central to Newton's argument is her definition of justice and her assumptions about the relationship between justice and equality. Do you agree with her?*

5. *Do you think Rawls would agree with Newton's analysis? Explain.*

6. *Would you agree that in part Newton objects to reverse discrimination on utilitarian grounds? Explain.*

7. *Do you agree that the problems Newton says surround reverse discrimination really are "insoluble"?*

CASE PRESENTATION
Brian Weber

From its beginning in 1958, the Kaiser Aluminum plant in Grammercy, Louisiana, had very few black workers. By 1965, Kaiser had hired only 4.7 percent blacks, although 39 percent of the local work force were black. As of 1970, none of Kaiser's fifty professional employees was black; of 132 supervisors, one was black; of 146 skilled craft workers, none was black. In the fifteen years between 1958 and 1973, Kaiser had allowed several whites with no prior craft experience to transfer into skilled craft positions, whereas blacks were required to have at least five years' prior craft experience before being permitted to transfer. But getting this experience was difficult, since blacks were largely excluded from craft unions. As a result, only 2 percent of Grammercy's skilled craft workers were black.

A federal review in 1975 found things at Grammercy basically unchanged. 2.2 percent of its 290 craft workers and 7 percent of its professional employees were black. No blacks were among its eleven draftsmen. Although the percentage of blacks in Grammercy's overall work force had increased to 13.3, the local labor force remained constant at 39 percent black. Only the lowest-paying category of workers, so-called unskilled workers, included a large proportion of blacks, 35.5 percent, a proportion brought about by Kaiser's implementing a 1968 policy of hiring one black unskilled worker for every white unskilled worker.

As an upshot of these racial disparities in the allocation of jobs, federal agencies started pressuring Kaiser to employ more blacks in its better-paying skilled craft position. At the same time, the United Steelworkers Union was pressing Kaiser to institute programs for training its own workers in the crafts, instead of hiring all craft workers from outside the company. In response to both pressures, Kaiser set up a training program intended to qualify its own white and black workers for agreed-to craft positions. Under the program, Kaiser would pay for the training of its own workers who would be selected for the program on the basis of seniority. One-half of the training slots would be set aside for blacks until the percentage of black skilled craft workers at Grammercy approximated the percentage of blacks in the local labor force. Openings in the programs would be filled by alternating between the most senior qualified white employee and the most senior qualified black employee.

Thirteen workers—seven blacks and six whites—were selected during the first year of the program. Brian Weber, a young, white, semiskilled worker at Grammercy, was not among those selected, although he'd applied. Upon investigation, Weber discovered that he, in fact, had several months' more seniority than two of the blacks who had been admitted into the training program. Indeed, forty-three other white workers who had applied for the program and had been rejected had even more seniority than Weber. The conclusion was unmistakable:

Junior black employees were receiving training in preference to more senior white employees. Weber didn't think this was fair, especially since none of the blacks admitted to the program had themselves been discriminated against by Kaiser during their prior employment.

Weber decided to sue Kaiser. The case was eventually heard by the U.S. Supreme Court, which ruled that Kaiser's affirmative-action program didn't violate the Civil Rights Act of 1964.

Questions for Analysis

1. *Do you think Kaiser's preferential treatment program was fair? Explain in terms of ethical principles and concepts of justice.*

2. *Do you think Weber was treated unfairly, as he claimed? Defend your response on the basis of the moral principles you think are involved.*

3. *Companies frequently use seniority as the sole or primary basis of promotions or, as in Kaiser's case, for admission into training programs. Do you think this is fair? (Seniority generally refers to longevity on a job or with a company.)*

CASE PRESENTATION
First Hired, First Fired?

Marvin Alcott knew it was foolish. But as a personnel director faced with a sticky decision, he couldn't help wishing that Frank Stimson were anything but a white male.

Things had been going so well with the firm's pilot program for training the hard-core unemployed for positions as assistant machinists. Just a month before, Alcott had placed sixteen workers in the program, one of whom—indeed the first—was Frank Stimson. Having been out of work for the better part of a year and having no specific skills, Stimson had easily met the program's minimal qualifications for training.

A number of things about Stimson had impressed Alcott. It seemed that since returning from his two-year stint in Vietnam, Stimson had found nothing but tough employment sledding. In fact, as Stimson told it, if it hadn't been for the meager income his wife earned waitressing, he would have had to apply for welfare, something he strongly objected to on principle. As Stimson had said in the interview, "I was brought up to believe that you should carry your own weight. Anything less was being a leech, if you know what I mean." Then Stimson had explained how he didn't think it was right to expect society to bear the burden of what he termed a "misspent youth." Stimson had put it quite graphically:

"Why should I expect others to pay for my screw-ups?" Predictably enough, when Alcott informed Stimson that he was the first trainee to be selected, Stimson was elated and expressed every desire to seize this opportunity to make something of himself.

Alcott chuckled on the first day of training when Stimson showed up for work a half-hour before the prescribed time. He appreciated Stimson's enthusiasm, especially since it contrasted sharply with the apparent indifference of some of the other trainees.

After the first week of training, several instructors went out of their way to compliment Alcott on his selection of Stimson, while at the same time indicating that they'd had to admonish several other employees for being tardy, nonchalant, and generally uninterested in the opportunity the program was providing them.

It's little wonder, then, that Marvin Alcott considered Frank Stimson his top job trainee. This is precisely what made the decision he faced so painful.

It seems that when the firm launched the program, it did so with the government's implicit promise to fund sixteen positions. When the grant was actually issued, it covered only fifteen trainees. Alcott was faced with having to drop one.

Being a thoughtful, sensitive, and fair man, Alcott was trying to determine the most equitable way to manage the cut. One possibility was a lottery. He'd simply put the names of the candidates into a hat and draw one to be dropped. He had also considered making the drop on the basis of apparent job potential. But whatever method he contemplated, Alcott was haunted by the fact that Stimson was a white male. The other fifteen trainees were women and members of minority groups, and Alcott was keenly aware of affirmative-action guidelines that prescribed benefits for members of traditionally disadvantaged groups. In short, there was a real question in his mind whether he'd endanger the entire program should he decide to drop one of the fifteen disadvantaged members.

Above all else, Alcott wanted to be fair. There was no doubt in his mind that from what he and other company officials had observed, Stimson was the most promising trainee in the program. At the same time, he felt the press of fairness to members of groups traditionally discriminated against, which left him questioning the fairness of perhaps the most obvious solution: Drop the last selected.

Questions for Analysis

1. *What should Alcott do?*

2. *What moral directions do the principles of chapter 1 provide?*

3. *In the event that Alcott decides to drop Stimson, does he have an obligation to make a case to the firm for underwriting Stimson's training? Do you think the firm has a moral obligation to do this, or at least compensate Stimson in some way?*

Selections for Further Reading

Bittker, Boris. *The Case for Black Reparations*. New York: Random House, 1973.

Blackstone, William, and Robert Heslep. *Social Justice and Preferential Treatment*. Athens: University of Georgia Press, 1977.

Braggin, Mary; Frederick Elliston; and Jane English, eds. *Feminism and Philosophy*, Section 4. Totowa, N.J.: Littlefield, Adams, 1977.

Cohen, Marshall; Thomas Nagel; and Thomas Scanlon, eds. *Equality and Preferential Treatment*.Princeton, N.J.: Princeton University Press, 1976.

DeCrow, Karen. *Sexist Justice*. New York: Vintage, 1975.

Farley, J. *Affirmative Action and the Woman Worker*. New York: AMACOM, 1979.

Glazer, N. *Affirmative Discrimination: Ethnic Inequality and Public Policy*. New York: Basic Books, 1976.

Gross, Barry R., ed. *Reverse Discrimination*. Buffalo, N.Y.: Prometheus Press, 1977.

Livingston, John. *Fair Game*. San Francisco: W. H. Freeman, 1979.

Mill, John Stuart. *Essays on Sex Equality*, A. C. Rossi, ed. Chicago: University of Chicago Press, 1970.

Remick, H. *Comparable Worth and Wage Discrimination*. Philadelphia: Temple University Press, 1985.

9
WORLD HUNGER AND ECONOMIC JUSTICE

There is no question that much of the world population literally is starving to death. Recent figures estimate that at least 10,000 people die of starvation every day, that as many as 2 billion more are malnourished, that annually 14,000 children in India alone go blind because of insufficient protein. In short, two-thirds of the world's population is caught in a seemingly irreversible cycle of hunger-sickness-death.

We in the other one-third, in the West, are lucky. Rarely, if ever, do any of us directly experience the harsh fate of the world's starving masses. Fortunate to have been born in a land of plenty, we seldom realize that we feed our house pets each day enough protein to meet the daily nutritional needs of hundreds of thousands of people, that we throw away in one week more food than countless people will see in a year. Even for many who are aware of massive world starvation, the problem remains remote, even abstract. But to those facing starvation, the problem is not only real, immediate, and paramount, it also appears to have no resolution, except in death.

Given the disparity between those who have and those who have not, a moral question of considerable importance emerges: Do the affluent nations of the world have any moral obligation to help the world's starving masses? If we answer yes, then precisely how should these nations go about sharing their wealth? Stated in more global terms: How should the world's goods be distributed? This last question makes explicit the issue of economic justice, which is implied in the issue of moral obligation and world hunger.

In this chapter, then, we confront two questions of considerable moral importance. The first is whether the affluent nations have an obligation to help the starving nations; the second concerns the fairest distribution of the world's wealth. While these questions are distinct, they are not easily separated. Indeed, as we will see, many of the arguments for an obligation to help are rooted in a concept of economic justice. For this reason, we will consider first the issue of economic justice, then relate it to the problem of moral obligation and world hunger.

Initial Considerations

A number of moral problems cluster around the issues of world hunger and economic justice. Two in particular deserve careful study: the rights to property and liberty, and the causes of world hunger. Additional issues relate to the nature and form of proposed aid, including who will receive it and who should provide it.

Liberty and Property Rights

The belief in a body of rights that belong to all human beings is commonplace in our society and elsewhere. These "human" or "natural" rights are to be distinguished from rights derived from special agreements or restricted to particular groups of people. Whether we ascribe the universal character of these natural rights to God or human nature, or to the logical extension of our beliefs about human beings, there is no question that we talk of some rights as basic and universal.

The British philosopher John Locke (1632–1704) is generally credited with developing the idea that human beings have a natural right to liberty and a natural right to private property. Locke never used his theory of natural rights to argue for free markets (an economic system in which privately owned firms make their own decisions about what they will produce and how they will produce it, and exchange their goods with other firms and consumers at the most advantageous prices they can get), but a number of twentieth-century authors have. In general, they claim that given their natural rights to liberty and property, individuals must be left free to exchange their labor and property as they voluntarily choose. The free-market theorists argue further that only an economy of free private enterprise exchange allows for such voluntary transfers. In short, the existence of Lockean rights to liberty and property presumably implies that societies should include private-property institutions and free markets.

In a pure free-market system, no constraints would exist on the property you or I could own, on what we could choose to do with it, or on the voluntary exchanges we could make. But of course there are no pure free-market systems. Some things may not be owned—for example, slaves. Some things may not be done with property, such as polluting the environment. And some exchanges are not permitted, such as having young children do labor. But apart from such specific constraints, we are free to dispose of our own property as we choose and make exchanges voluntarily, and we typically view and defend these rights as a logical extension of the natural rights to liberty and private property.

In practice, then, the so-called natural rights to liberty and property serve as a basis for claiming that we can do with our holdings whatever we want that is not proscribed by law. If I choose to squander my wealth while others need it to survive, presumably I am free to do that. But am I, or better: Should I be? Is the property right so extensive? Many think not. They argue that my right to my holdings is limited by the satisfaction of the basic needs of other people. Yes, they say, I may do with my wealth whatever I choose, but only after the basic needs of others have been satisfied. But what "others" are intended? Relatives, friends, neighbors, fellow citizens, distant peoples, future generations? There's no easy answer to this question.

Related to our property rights is how we obtained our holdings. Many argue that if property rights exist, they apply only to what an owner has acquired legally and morally. Suppose an honest man inherits a fortune that was amassed in the distant past through others' dishonesty and ruthless exploitation. Does the original taint of the fortune's acquisition cast doubt in his claims to it? The same question may be asked about a nation's wealth acquired through years of dubious moral conduct. Does the nation, therefore, have no claim to its wealth, or no right to determine how it shall spend its riches? Indeed, how can we separate "clean" from "dirty" money in the first place?

Clearly the issue of how far property rights extend bears on the question of world hunger. For if I have an absolute right to dispose of my property however I choose—no matter the genesis of the holding—then seemingly I have no obligation to help the starving masses. But if that right is subordinate to the claims of those seeking to maintain themselves, then I could have an obligation to help. At issue here is the whole notion of Lockean rights—whether in fact such rights exist, and if so, what priority they warrant relative to other rights.

Criticisms of the Lockean natural rights to liberty and property, and by implication of the free-market defense based on it, have focused on several salient weaknesses, two of which concern us here. The first one relates to the assumption that individuals do, in fact, have natural rights. Do they? Critics claim that this assumption is unproven. Locke himself merely asserted that reason teaches all humankind who will consult it that the natural rights he recognizes do exist. Presumably they are self-evident; rational human beings supposedly can intuit that the rights to liberty and property exist. The problem is that plenty of rational humans have tried to intuit the existence of these rights and have failed.

The second criticism of Lockean natural rights concerns the conflict between these and other rights. Let's suppose for argument's sake that humans do have natural rights to liberty and property. Even so, it doesn't follow that these rights override all other rights.

The rights to liberty and property are *negative* rights, which means they are solely defined in terms of the duties others have not to interfere in the activities of the person who holds these rights. But negative rights can conflict with *positive* rights, which impose on some party (it's not always clear whom) *positive duties* to provide the holder of the right with whatever he or she needs to freely pursue his or her interests. Thus the negative rights to liberty and property can easily conflict with someone else's positive right to food, medical care, housing, education, clean air, and so forth. Why must we believe that the negative rights of liberty and property override such positive rights? Some say we in fact shouldn't make such a glib assumption, and others go so far as to assert that positive rights like the aforementioned take precedence. In any event, it should be clear that a crucial question in discussions about feeding and caring for the world's needy is the nature and extent of liberty and property rights.

Causes of World Hunger

As indicated, the chief question that concerns us in this chapter is: Given the wide disparity between the living standards of the developed industrial countries and those of the underdeveloped agricultural or single-resource countries, should rich countries sacrifice some of their wealth for the benefit of the poorer ones? In answering this question, one crucial ethical variable is *responsibility*. Who is responsible for the famine and malnutrition in underdeveloped countries?

Some argue that since overpopulation is the cause of scarcity and people living in poor countries have failed to keep their populations under control, they themselves are primarily responsible for their plight. The key assumption here, and the one which many question, is that overpopulation is the sole cause of the scarcity leading to starvation.

Onora O'Neill, for one, has argued that the international business activities of many corporations have contributed at least partially to the grim conditions of some peoples. She points particularly to foreign-investment activities and commodity-pricing policies.

Regarding foreign investments, O'Neill hypothesizes a case in which a group of investors form a company that invests abroad, perhaps in a plantation or a mine. The investors so manage their affairs that a high level of profits goes back to their homeland, while laborers' wages are so minimal that the laborers' survival rate is reduced—in other words, their life expectancy is lower than it might have been had the company not invested there. It's true that in such a case the investors and company management don't act alone, are not the immediate causes of deaths, don't know in advance who will die, and don't intend the deaths. But they surely can't claim to be "uninvolved" the way a company with no investments there can. Indeed, they are helping set policies that determine the living standards, which in turn determine the survival rate. When people die because of the lowered standard of living established by a firm that dominates a local economy (either by limiting workers to employment on their terms or by reducing the prospects for employment through damaging traditional economic structures), and when these firms could either pay workers more or stay out of the area altogether, they seem to be directly responsible for the suffering and deaths that result.

Furthermore, even when a company investing in an underdeveloped country sets high wages and benefits, and raises the life expectancy of its workers, it often succeeds in combining these payments with high profitability only by achieving a tax-exempt status. This means the company is being subsidized by the general tax revenue of the underdeveloped economy. The company makes no contribution to the country's infrastructure—that is, to the roads, harbors, and airports that benefit it. "In this way," O'Neill writes, "many underdeveloped economies have come to include developed enclaves whose development is achieved in part at the expense of the poorer majority. In such cases, government and company policy combine to produce a high-wage sector at the expense of a low-wage sector; in consequence, some of the persons in the low-wage sector, who would not otherwise have died, may die. Those persons, whoever they may be, are killed and not merely allowed to die."[1] O'Neill concedes that such killings may be justifiable, perhaps if they are outnumbered by lives saved through having a developed society. Nonetheless, they are killings.

Then there are commodity-pricing cases. It's no secret that underdeveloped countries often depend largely on the price level of a few commodities. As a result, a precipitous drop in the world price of, say, coffee or sugar or cocoa could lower survival rates in these countries. Such drops sometimes result from factors beyond human control. But often they result from the action of investors, brokers, or government agencies. In such cases, these people or agencies are choosing policies that will kill some people, albeit not single-handedly, instantaneously, with forethought or intention.

Given the economic interdependence of countries, deaths can also result from dramatic *rises* in the prices of various commodities. Sharp increases in the international prices of essential foodstuffs such as wheat and other grains will be reflected in higher death rates among the world's poorest groups. Living on subsistence level diets to begin with, they simply lack the income to pay proportionately more for food. Where these price increases result directly from human agency, the people involved are responsible for the resulting starvation and deaths—deaths which, again, seem more properly termed killings. As before, some of these may be justifiable killings—for example, if the lives saved as a result of the pricing outnumbered those lost. Even so, they are killings.

The preceding analysis bears directly on the question of whether the rich nations have a moral obligation to help the poor ones. If, for example, one holds that those living in underdeveloped countries are themselves primarily responsible for their plight because they have failed to keep their populations under control, one has a basis, though it's not sufficient, for concluding: (1) those living in industrial countries are under no obligation to provide food, and possibly (2) it would be wrong to do so, inasmuch as such aid might encourage further overpopulation, which would put the world's resources at risk. (I have termed the bases insufficient because the assumption about overpopulation and who is responsible for it does not necessarily commit one to either of the two conclusions; one could still argue that no matter who's responsible, one is morally obliged to prevent or ease pain and suffering where one can with minor or insignificant sacrifice.)

But if variables other than overpopulation cause malnutrition and starvation, then a basis emerges for an obligation to help. Thus if through their international activities corporations are at least partially responsible for the dire conditions in certain underdeveloped countries, and since the economic chains linking U.S. multinational firms and the foreign policy of the U.S. government extend to U.S.

---

1.   *Onora O'Neill, "Lifeboat Earth," in* Ethical Theory and Business, *eds. Tom L. Beauchamp and Norman E. Bowie (Englewood Cliffs, N.J.: Prentice-Hall, 1979), p. 110.*

2.   *O'Neill, "Lifeboat Earth," p. 111.*

citizens, almost all of us are responsible for the deaths of famine victims. From which we might conclude: Our duty is to redirect the policy of the U.S. government and the multinational corporations.

Aid-Related Issues

What will happen if the affluent nations continue to feed the destitute nations? Many claim that the long-term results will spell catastrophe. These Neo-Malthusians,[3] as they are sometimes called, predict food relief will only swell the populations of nations already bursting with more people than they can support. By this account, food relief will increase the net suffering and deprivation not only of recipients but of donors as well. Not everyone agrees, however. Many claim that such dire forecasts are exaggerated. More important, as we've noted, they say such a horrifying outcome could result only if food relief is not coupled with developmental assistance aimed at improving productivity through modernizing agriculture.

All this raises a second issue concerning aid: If the rich nations have an obligation to help the poor ones, just what sort of help are they obliged to provide? It is possible to identify at least three kinds of aid that affluent nations such as the United States give to poor nations: (1) developmental assistance, to help underdeveloped countries educationally and technologically to accumulate capital and raise their standards of living; (2) emergency famine or disaster relief, given in the wake of natural disasters such as drought, flood, and earthquake; (3) relief for countries suffering chronic famine because their birth rate far exceeds their actual or potential productivity. If rich nations are obliged to help, just which, if any, kinds of aid are they obliged to provide?

Some would argue that affluent nations should give only emergency aid; others that they should give only emergency and developmental aid; still others that they should give all three. One common position among Neo-Malthusians is that rich nations should not provide any aid in the third category.

The issue of which kind of aid is to be given is clearly inseparable from the question of who should receive the aid. Perhaps we should dole out aid by *triage* (French for "sorting"), a method of allocating resources used first during World War I. Wounded soldiers were separated into three categories and allocated scarce medical resources on that basis. Those with superficial injuries were given immediate emergency attention; those with serious wounds who could be helped to survive were given the lion's share of intensive care; those beyond hope were allowed to die. Applied to the starving nations of the world, the method of triage might roughly classify the nations as: (1) those with slight food problems who will survive even without aid; (2) those with serious food problems who can benefit from help because they are ready to take steps to control their populations and increase their productivity; (3) those whose problems cannot be solved because they are not prepared to take any measures to help themselves. Given these

---

3. *Named after the English economist John Malthus (1766–1834), who argued that population tends to increase faster than the means of subsistence, unless checked by such factors as war and famine.*

classifications, some would say, "Yes, affluent nations have an obligation to provide help, but only to those nations falling into categories 1 and 2." Indeed, they might and sometimes do argue that rich nations have an obligation *not* to help nations in category 3. Opposed to these positions are those who say the worst-off nations should receive immediate and massive aid. Such appears to be the United States' position. Of course, the question of who, if anyone, ought to receive help grows ever murkier as resources dwindle.

Finally, if there is an obligation to help, whose obligation is it? Is it the obligation of an individual, you and me personally? A nation, such as the United States? A group of nations, perhaps through an international organization such as the United Nations? Our discussion here of world hunger and economic justice focuses on possible obligations that richer nations have to poorer ones. But it is also perfectly reasonable to ask: Can a nation have obligations? Is it sensible to attribute rights, duties, and obligations to some disembodied entity called a nation? And if it is, to whom do nations have responsibilities and against whom do they have claims—other nations, individuals, a combination?

These are only some of the questions that make world hunger and economic justice extraordinarily complex issues. They are questions that can be investigated thoroughly only in a study of social philosophy. Given the narrow scope of our present study, we can merely draw these issues to the reader's attention and encourage a deeper investigation of them elsewhere.

International Economic Justice

Economic justice refers to what people deserve economically. The question of moral obligation regarding world hunger is inseparable from the issue of economic justice. To see why, consider this simple example.

Suppose you're walking down a big-city street with a friend. You're approached by a beggar who asks, "You got some change for a meal, pal?" You fish into your pocket for a couple of quarters and hand them to the man. He thanks you and moves on.

Your friend is outraged. "Why did you do that?" she asks you, in a most disapproving tone.

"Because the guy needed to eat," you reply.

"But the guy was a bum!" she points out. "Let him get a job, not a handout!"

Presumably you feel you have an obligation to help the beggar, but your friend does not. In fact, she seems to think she has an obligation *not* to help him. But notice the reasons behind these judgments, reasons that imply full-blown views on what people deserve economically. You feel the beggar deserves something simply because he *needs* it. Your friend believes you should not give the beggar anything because of the kind of person he is (a "bum") and because he has done nothing to help himself. For her, *need* is not as much a determinant of economic desert as are *merit* and *effort*. For both of you, economic justice is associated with some view of distributive justice.

Distributive Justice

The subject of economic desert touches numerous areas, from jobs to income to taxes to world resources. Thus questions of economic justice would include: How ought jobs be awarded? How should income and taxes be determined? What is the fairest way to allocate the wealth of the world? Any answer to these questions inevitably implies a working principle of *distributive justice: an assumption about what is the proper way of passing out the wealth of a society.* For example, people commonly say: "Jobs should be awarded on the basis of merit"; "Income should be determined on the basis of contribution to society or on the degree of preparation for a job"; "Taxes should be assessed on the basis of ability to pay." Each statement implies some standard that should be considered in the distribution of society's wealth: merit, contribution and effort, capacity. Whether these or other principles should be taken into account is a basic concern of economic justice.

Such a question is also basic to the issue of worldwide hunger. To illustrate: Some argue that the affluent nations have a moral obligation to help feed the hungry nations simply because the latter need help. Others argue that the affluent nations do not have an obligation to share what they have because they have a proprietary right to what they have earned and may dispose of it however they choose. Still others argue that only starving nations that attempt to help themselves (as, for example, by controlling their populations) should receive help. Again, underlying each of these positions is a principle of distributive justice. Thus, in the matter of world hunger, some believe *need* ought to determine the distribution of aid; others feel that *merit* should; and still others that *effort* should.

Whether the entity under consideration is a business, a society, or the world, serious questions of distributive and economic justice arise as soon as we begin to speculate about how—on what basis—the wealth of the entity ought to be parceled out. Well, just what are the options? What are the vying principles on the basis of which we can mete out economic justice? There appear to be five likely candidates, which bear on world hunger: (1) equality, (2) need, (3) merit or achievement, (4) contribution, and (5) effort. The first two can be viewed as egalitarian principles, the last three as desert principles.

EQUALITY. The principle of equality would give each individual an equal share in the distribution, for, it is claimed, as human beings they deserve to be treated equally. By this account, every individual in a society would be entitled to the same portion of a society's goods as every other individual in the society.

Notice that the principle of equality ignores individual merit, contribution, and effort. Most important, claim its critics, it overlooks need. Is a pattern of distribution that ignores individual differences fair? Is any distribution that results from it equitable?

To see the thrust of this criticism, consider that I may need more food than you; and you may need more money than I; and both of us may need less medical attention than somebody else. Under strict equality of distribution, each of us would receive identical shares of the goods and services available. Clearly, there would be no guarantee that any one of us would receive all that we need.

Applied to world hunger, the equality principle would lead to equal shares of the world's food for all the peoples of the world, presumably on a person-by-person basis. Conceivably, as a result of such equal distribution, some individuals who need more food than others might be left malnourished. Or possibly, those starving to death might, as a result of a greater share of food, not only live but add to their nation's population problems, which in turn would reduce the individual share. Operational problems such as these have caused some people who want some sort of egalitarian principle to turn to a different consideration.

NEED.   The principle of need would give to each individual according to his or her needs. Notice that this principle is, like the preceding, an egalitarian principle, in that it treats everyone equally. By the principle of need, each of us should get exactly what we require. Clearly, this principle, unlike the first, squarely faces the problem of differences among individuals. However, it too has several operational challenges.

In a world of limited resources, priorities must be set. Needs must be ranked. But what needs are to receive top priority? After we answer that question, how do we establish whose needs shall be met among those with similar needs when there is not enough to satisfy the needs of all? For example, suppose we give top priority to the need for enough food to maintain life. Taking a global view, let's suppose that a very needy nation will survive if given enough food because it is prepared to take population-control measures. In contrast, another even needier nation probably will not survive even with massive food aid, because it is not prepared to take any population-control measures. Now, let's say that if we fully satisfy the needs of the more desperate nation, we won't be able to satisfy the food needs of the less desperate one. Should we, nevertheless, give the lion's share of the available food to the nation that appears doomed?

As indicated, both the principle of equality and the principle of need rest on considerations of equality, on treating people the same way. The first claims that everyone should receive an equal share; the second holds that everyone should get the share he or she needs. In contrast, the next three principles emphasize desert, not equal treatment.

MERIT OR ACHIEVEMENT.   The principle of merit or achievement would give to each individual according to the kind of person he or she is or the characteristics he or she has. But just what types of characteristic should we consider? Skill, some say. But what kind of skills? If we introduce native skills (inherited aptitude) as a basis of desert, then we seem to reward and punish individuals for their genetic makeup. But since none of us has an opportunity to choose our genes, is it fair that we should be judged on them? Perhaps we should consider acquired or learned skills. While perhaps a fairer consideration than the genetic calculus, acquired skills to a large degree depend on native skills. True, the degree to which we develop our skills is greatly influenced by individual effort: practice, drill, perseverance. But to introduce *effort* as a principle of justice is to depart from the principle of merit or achievement. After all, effort refers to labor; merit to productivity.

Others who advocate merit or achievement want to evaluate merit in terms of virtue: Those individuals who show character qualities such as kindness, courage, diligence, reliability, and the like should receive a greater share of the economic pie than those who are cruel, cowardly, careless, and irresponsible. But by what standard are these traits to be isolated and measured? And even if we can locate and calculate them, are such qualities the sort of things that we want to make economic allotments for? Critics argue that by definition, acts of virtue must result from motives other than pecuniary ones, that tying virtue to material rewards undermines the nature of virtue itself.

Others who espouse principles based on desert focus their nonegalitarian theories not on what one is, but on what one has done. The final two principles typify these views.

CONTRIBUTION.   The principle of contribution would give each individual exactly that portion of a society's wealth he or she has produced. But in as complex a society and economy as ours, this is extraordinarily difficult to determine, if possible at all. It requires not only a precise measurement of the contribution, but an evaluation of its significance toward creating a society's wealth. In the production, say, of a car, what is the comparable worth of the contribution of the designer, the engineer, the assembler, the retailer, the stockholder, and the numerous others involved in the production and sale of the automobile? How is an artist's contribution to society to be measured? What about the people who collect our garbage, wash our laundry, cut our hair?

It might be easier to evaluate the contribution of nations to the world's wealth. Just look at their gross national products. Maybe the world resources should be distributed on that basis: Nations will get back exactly the proportion of the world's food supply that they themselves have created. But is this fair? Surely there is a measure of fortune, of chance, in the development of nations. Like individuals, some nations appear to have begun with a head start; they have had more to work with, to develop and exploit. Also, there is always a line of social factors stretching far back into a nation's history that help account for its present economic status. In short, individuals have no say over the society or nations they are born into. To expect them to reverse in their lifetimes the historical interplay of natural and social forces, or to penalize them by neglect for the decisions and actions of those long since dead, hardly seems fair.

EFFORT.   The principle of effort would give to each according to the degree of his or her labor. Like the principle of contribution, effort focuses on what people have done, not on what they are. But unlike contribution, the principle of effort is not concerned with what individuals have produced, but on the effort they make. By this account, the nature of one's job is irrelevant to justice. Equal effort requires equal remuneration. But how is effort to be measured? Effort appears to be relative to the individual who is doing the work. The effort you expend in writing an essay might be far greater than someone else's because that person happens to be a more "gifted" writer. Also, the degree to which we extend ourselves is largely determined by genetic and early environmental factors.

As with compensation, we might apply the effort principle more easily to nations than to individuals. For example, we might distribute food according to the effort a nation has made to become self-sufficient, as, for example, by controlling its population, utilizing its natural resources, and modernizing its agriculture. Having identified nations who have made the greatest effort, we might evaluate individuals within those nations by the same criteria. It is difficult, however, in instances such as these to separate effort from results. In some cases, the results are appalling; but that does not necessarily mean that the effort was lacking. After all, birth-control programs often must struggle to take hold in the soil of superstition, social taboos, and invincible ignorance. True, a country may fail to control its population, but perhaps not for the lack of effort. The effort simply may be no match for the gargantuan obstacles to be overcome.

These, then, are some common candidates for principles of economic justice. Some people base their views of proper distribution on a single principle. Others appeal to a combination. Whatever one's approach, it will underlie one's position on the issue of moral obligation and world hunger.

But any discussion of international economic justice that focuses exclusively on distributive justice without considering the productive side of economic arrangements seems incomplete. After all, what good does it do to redistribute scarce resources if there simply aren't enough resources to go around? Increasing the supply so that no one suffers certainly is preferable to spreading misery about more equitably. But increasing the supply raises questions not about how goods should be distributed, but about what goods should be produced.

Productive Justice

Howard Richards, for one, believes that by recognizing the importance of the principle of productive justice, concerned individuals might make a more effective response to problems of hunger and malnutrition. In making his case, he provides five considerations he thinks will convince rational men and women of the need to supplement principles of distributive justice with principles of productive justice.[4]

(1) The practices responsible for keeping world food production at dismayingly low levels are unjust because they cause harm that minor, morally insignificant sacrifice could avert. (2) Unproductive practices kill people. They're unjust **because they're analogous to homicide in the morally relevant respects. (3) The** hungry of the earth have a right to a reasonably high level of agricultural production because, as inhabitants of the earth, they, as well as all other people, have a right to a planet that is as productive as people can reasonably be expected to make it. (4) Distributive justice cannot be achieved without production; hence justice requires production. In other words, if distributive justice, for whatever reasons, requires a minimum standard below which no one should fall, distributive justice cannot be achieved without production. Production, then, becomes a requirement of justice. (5) It is misleading to say the practices that sacrifice distributive justice in order to increase production are just without also saying production is required of justice.

4. *Howard Richards, "Productive Justice," in* World Hunger and Moral Obligation, *ed. William Aiken and Hugh LaFollette (Englewood Cliffs, N.J.: Prentice-Hall, 1977), pp. 165–179.*

It's not necessary here to lay out the arguments which underlie these principles as much as to identify the implications of introducing the notion of productive justice into discussions of world hunger. It is a common observation that even if the population explosion could be checked and the rich nations were to share their surpluses with the poor, world hunger wouldn't be solved because world need exceeds surpluses. Then it is concluded that apathy and inaction are justified because nothing can be done. Those arguing this way, however, overlook productive justice. For the point is not what would happen if we'd share what we *have*, but if we'd share what we can *produce*. Even if need exceeds surpluses, it's potential production, not current supplies, that sets the moral standard. Looking at the issue from the view of producing more of those foods that more efficiently satisfy human nutritional requirements, and assuming the population explosion can be brought under control, the world hunger problem seems soluble and the grounds for apathy and inaction shaky.

Considerations of productive justice also seem to properly focus moral sentiments and righteous indignation on the causes and not, as is more often the case, on the effects of world hunger. "It is not the starving child and the extravagant banquet that should awaken our moral sentiments," Richards writes, "but the underutilized land, the unemployed work force, and the factories that are closed waiting for passenger car sales to pick up when they could be making tractors."[5]

Of course, identifying what needs to be produced to meet survival needs of the world's hungry is one thing and designing the economic system to do it is another. The inclusion of productive justice, therefore, ultimately invites a full-scale study of our economic system, with special attention to how well that system fulfills its obligation to produce.

Arguments for an Obligation to Help

1. *All human beings have equal rights to the necessities of life.*

POINT: "Where people are treated differently, the different treatment should be based on their freely chosen actions and not on accidents of birth. But look around you and what do you see? Millions of people who are starving, not because of some action of their own but because they were unlucky enough to be born in a hostile environment. To ignore their plight is the height of moral callousness. We have an obligation to help the starving for one reason and one reason only: They are human beings, and as human beings they have the same rights we all do to the necessities of life."

COUNTERPOINT: "What you say sounds fine until one realizes that it flies in the face of fact. Don't you see that if we equally shared what we have with the starving people of the world, *all* of us would end up suffering? There simply isn't enough food to go around. So if we did what you propose, everybody would end up malnourished."

5. *Ibid.*, p. 178.

2. *People are required to help prevent suffering.*

POINT: "I agree that it's irrational to ask people to help others when such help is going to create great hardship for the 'good samaritans' themselves. But it's altogether reasonable to expect people to help if by so doing they don't seriously injure themselves. This is precisely the situation with world hunger. Two-thirds of the world's people—the so-called Third World—are malnourished. The remaining one-third—the West—are consuming two-thirds of the world's resources. Now, surely that affluent one-third could share their resources and help feed the starving masses, without imperiling themselves. They could and they are obliged to—at least up to the point where any more help would cause them as much suffering as it would prevent. We in the West are far from having reached that point. Just where that point is, it's impossible to say. But surely, since we're dealing with millions of human lives, we are obligated to extend ourselves, even if it means great personal sacrifice and a radical change in our life-styles. After all, by no measure of decency can it be seriously and respectably argued that we are justified in feeding our cats and dogs each day enough protein to meet the daily requirements of thousands of people, who, for lack of protein, are contracting horrible diseases and even dying. We must give, and give until it hurts, to the degree commensurate with the suffering of those starving."

COUNTERPOINT: "I know I must sound like an arch-villain to criticize an argument in behalf of the starving masses, but criticize I must. Let's assume for argument's sake that the affluent Western nations share their food until every Westerner is just well-nourished, no more. At that point the surplus of food is distributed equally to the remaining two-thirds of the world's population. Even then the Third World peoples would still be malnourished. My point is that there simply isn't enough food currently available to feed everyone on an equal basis. And if you're suggesting that the affluent nations should share to the point of leaving themselves malnourished, what's the logic behind that? Is the world better off having four-fifths, five-sixths, maybe even 100 percent of its population malnourished rather than two-thirds? All this aside, why do you focus exclusively on the 'rights' of the starving? What about the rights of the affluent? They're human beings too, you know. On what grounds is it justifiable to expect them to 'give until it hurts, to a degree commensurate with the suffering of the starving'?"

3. *Human beings have a right to be saved from starvation.*

POINT: "Those who claim that the affluent nations have no obligation to help the starving forget what we're dealing with: individual, flesh-and-blood human beings. Human beings who have the same needs, fears, and pains as you or I. When they ask for help, they're not merely begging for charity or pleading for us to be benevolent. To insist that they are is to reduce the urgency of their plight to the level of a street-corner beggar's. But don't kid yourself—the need of these people is neither trivial nor manufactured. Their need is real and dire, and desperate need creates obligations and rights. The starving person has a moral right to get help from those in a position to provide it. This right derives from a more general right to be saved from preventable death due to deprivation, and this general right is based on human need. The bottom line is that anyone starving to death has a right to the goods and services that will prevent his or her death by deprivation. And if you or I happen to have the necessary goods and services, then we have an obligation to prevent the person's death. So it's quite clear that the affluent nations are obliged to help the world's starving masses. Should they not try to meet this obligation, they would be guilty of an act as morally reprehensible as if they had taken a direct action to kill these people."

COUNTERPOINT: "Although I can sympathize with the sincerity, even urgency, of your appeal, I can't get a handle on what you mean by a 'right based on need.' I can understand moral rights resulting from promises, or from special roles and relationships. But when you talk of a right based on need, you lose me. I'll grant that there could be such a category of 'need rights.' Even so, the whole concept is terribly vague. For example, I have a tough time distinguishing 'needs' from 'wants' or 'wishes.' Then there's the matter of how intense a need must be to be considered a right. Some people undoubtedly have a profound 'need' to be loved, and if this need is not met, they seem to languish. Does that mean they have a right to be loved, and that someone has an obligation to provide that love? Another thing: Assuming that a need can be the basis of a right, against whom, if anyone, is this right correctly claimed? Suppose, for example, we consider a person's need for medical care a right. Precisely who is responsible for providing it? If I didn't put the person in the condition of need, why should I be obligated? Then there's the matter of conflicting rights. It's generally acknowledged that individuals and nations have a right to control their resources and property. Does a right based on need automatically take precedence over such ownership rights? If so, why? It could very well be that your central argument is cogent. But until you clear up this concept of 'need right,' I'll remain unconvinced."

Arguments for an Obligation Not to Help

1. *Helping will actually damage some recipient nations.*

POINT: "There's no question that a number of Third World countries have exceeded their 'carrying capacity.' In simple English, that means their populations exceed their productivity. They neither are nor can be self-sufficient. So if we give aid to countries whose reproduction has outstripped their productivity, all we do is increase their population without increasing their rate of productivity. The ironic result is that we increase the number of starving people and produce a net increase in human misery. Now, don't misunderstand. I'm not objecting to our helping countries in biological balance, countries whose populations haven't so outpaced their production that they can never be self-sufficient. On the contrary, I think we ought to help such countries, and also of course those in need of emergency famine or disaster relief. But I don't think we have an obligation to help if by helping we actually increase the net suffering of a recipient country.

And this is precisely what we will do in the case of many countries. In fact, it would be immoral to help, since by 'helping' we would create more pain.''

COUNTERPOINT: "First of all, how does one determine precisely the point at which a country has exceeded its 'carrying capacity'? What criteria do you use to determine that a country can never be self-sufficient? Your whole argument assumes we can clearly identify population trends that indicate major worldwide population growth. And it also assumes that these trends are irreversible. But why couldn't immediate food assistance together with developmental assistance aimed at improved food production contain and even wipe out widespread hunger? India is a case in point. Far from being hopelessly overpopulated, India actually reduced its population-growth rate in many areas as a result of a well-planned birth-control effort. Specifically, during India's third 'Five Year Plan' (1961–1966), the birth rate in Bombay actually declined to only 27 per 1,000 population, which is only slightly higher than the U.S. rate, 23 per 1,000.[6] True, this was the most impressive result in the country, but there were other promising signs. For example, in one rural district of West Bengal the birth rate dropped from 43 to 36 per 1,000. Such results suggest that the hopeless picture you paint grossly distorts the plights of these countries.''

2.   *Helping would ultimately threaten the human species.*

POINT: "Consider a couple of sobering facts. The population of the two-thirds of the world that we call the 'Third World' is increasing more than twice as fast as the population of the one-third we call 'affluent.' What's more, if you compare most Third World countries with just the United States, you'll find that their populations are doubling *three* or *four* times as fast as the U.S. population! Now, suppose we decide to share what we have with these starving nations. What do you think things would be like by the end of this century? Each one of us in the United States would be sharing our resources with about a dozen people. Even if there were still enough to go around, contemplate the miserable conditions we'd all be living under. Of course, ultimately it wouldn't be a question of quality of life; there simply wouldn't be any life left! That's right, the human species would die out. So not only do the affluent nations have *no* obligation to help the starving peoples of the world, they *must not* share their food or even provide developmental assistance. Their moral obligation is to the species, to future generations. Above everything else, we, the affluent, must ensure our own survival by retaining a safety factor of surplus and by preserving the environment for posterity.''

COUNTERPOINT: "Again, you assume not only that population trends are identifiable but that they're not reversible. I remind you of India's experiences, and caution you about such distortive population projections as the ones you make. It wasn't too long ago, you know, that China faced widespread starvation. Many people termed China's plight 'hopeless.' But today China's huge population is adequately fed. What happened? To put it in the vernacular, China got its

6.   *B. L. Raina, "India," in* Family Planning and Populations Programs: A Review of World Developments, *ed. Bernard Berelson (Chicago: University of Chicago Press, 1966), pp. 111–22.*

agricultural act together. So your doomsday forecasts are very misleading. Even worse, they do a dreadful, and potentially fatal, disservice to the world's poor by making their plight appear hopeless, and thus futile to address. I'll give you an example of what I mean. Remember the starvation problem that Bangladesh faced a few years ago? Well, recall how the media represented it. The only pictures that ever appeared in our newspapers and on our television screens were of children and adults with bellies swollen with hunger. No wonder a lot of people in this country got the impression that Bangladesh was beyond hope. But the fact of the matter is that the majority of Bangladeshi have enough to get by and that Bangladesh potentially has some of the world's richest croplands. 'Potentially'—it all depends on whether a well-formulated aid program is forthcoming. But judging from the reporting on Bangladesh, we understandably considered their plight hopeless. In the last analysis, short-term relief programs coupled with long-range population-control programs and assistance to improve local agriculture could minimize if not eradicate starvation."

Argument for Helping as Morally Permissible but Not Obligatory

1. *Helping is an act of charity.*

POINT: "Helping the starving people of the world isn't something we must or must not do. It's something we can do, if we choose. In other words, we should look on such help as charity or benevolence. As with any act of charity, we are not obligated to perform it. Sure, it might be nice if we did, even desirable, noble. But it's not required of us. After all, we have a right to our property and can dispose of it pretty much however we choose. If we choose to share what we have, fine; but we have no duty to do so. Helping to feed the world's needy is an option that the well-fed have. In the last analysis, it's an act of charity or benevolence, but not a duty."

COUNTERPOINT: "Your argument ignores important aspects of the other two positions: (1) that we have a duty to help, (2) that we have a duty not to help. I think those people supporting the first position can legitimately ask: Why do you relegate something as important as preventing massive starvation to 'charity'? If we don't have a duty to help prevent human misery and death, just what duties do we have? To leave such a momentous issue to the benevolent impulses of individuals and nations is wholly unrealistic. Furthermore, you imply that personal property rights are extensive, if not unlimited. Maybe they are, but I find it hard to argue that I have a right to something that is not necessary, such as a second car or a swimming pool, when others will die unless they have the food that could be purchased with the money used to buy these things. If an affluent nation could save millions of people from starvation by diverting a fraction of its GNP into developmental assistance or hunger relief, would that country be morally justified in retaining that wealth? Besides, you don't for a minute consider how the affluent obtained their wealth, which may be morally suspect. Do we have moral rights to what we've acquired nefariously? Similarly, I think those supporting the second position are justified in pointing out that whether the help springs from charity or duty, the result is the same. And, according to the Neo-Malthusians, the result isn't good; in fact, it's calculated to cause overpopulation and increase human misery for recipients and donors alike. Are these dire futuristic projections mistaken, or irrelevant? You're going to have to deal with this question before you can convince any Neo-Malthusian of the merit of your argument."

Lifeboat Ethics: The Case against Helping the Poor

Garrett Hardin

In this essay, biologist Garrett Hardin rejects the claim, and the ethic entailing it, that affluent nations have an obligation to help the world's starving masses. Indeed, Hardin argues that the duty of the affluent nations is to not help. And he implies that this duty includes not providing even developmental assistance.

After criticizing the environmentalists' metaphor of the earth as a spaceship, Hardin sets up an extended metaphor of his own. He asks us to regard each rich nation as a lifeboat with limited capacity and full of relatively rich people. Outside the lifeboat, the sea is full of the poor and needy, who want to get in the boat. Hardin claims that unless the lifeboat's occupants maintain a safety factor—that is, keep people out—the boat will swamp.

But "swamping" is precisely what the "spaceship" or sharing ethic will lead to, Hardin believes. A good example, he feels, can be seen in the international food bank, which he considers nothing more than a device for moving the wealth of the rich, productive nations over to the poor, unproductive ones. Eventually, Hardin predicts, there will be nothing left to withdraw. In the end, the sharing ethic will undo us all.

Thus Hardin concludes that we must reject the sharing ethic. We owe it to future generations, to the species, not to help the starving masses.

Environmentalists use the metaphor of the earth as a "spaceship" in trying to persuade countries, industries and people to stop wasting and polluting our natural resources. Since we all share life on this planet, they argue, no single person or institution has the right to destroy, waste or use more than a fair share of its resources.

But does everyone on earth have an equal right to an equal share of its resources? The spaceship metaphor can be dangerous when used by misguided idealists to justify suicidal policies for sharing our resources through uncontrolled immigration and foreign aid. In their enthusiastic but unrealistic generosity, they confuse the ethics of a spaceship with those of a lifeboat.

A true spaceship would have to be under the control of a captain, since no ship could possibly survive if its course were determined by committee. Spaceship Earth certainly has no captain; the United Nations is merely a toothless tiger, with little power to enforce any policy upon its bickering members.

If we divide the world crudely into rich nations and poor nations, two thirds of them are desperately poor, and only one third comparatively rich, with the United States the wealthiest of all. Metaphorically each rich nation can be seen as a lifeboat full of comparatively rich people. In the ocean outside each lifeboat swim the poor of the world, who would like to get in, or at least to share some of the wealth. What should the lifeboat passengers do?

First, we must recognize the limited capacity of any lifeboat. For example, a nation's land has a limited capacity to support a population and as the current energy crisis has shown us, in some ways we have already exceeded the carrying capacity of our land.

Adrift in a Moral Sea

So here we sit, say fifty people in our lifeboat. To be generous, let us assume it has room for ten more, making a total capacity of sixty. Suppose the fifty of us in the lifeboat see 100 others swimming in the water outside, begging for admission to our boat or for handouts. We have several options: We may be tempted to try to live by the Christian ideal of being "our brother's keeper," or by the Marxist ideal of "to each according to his needs." Since the needs of all in the water are the same, and since they can all be seen as "our brothers," we could take them all into our boat, making a total of 150 in a boat designed for sixty. The boat swamps, everyone drowns. Complete justice, complete catastrophe.

Since the boat has an unused excess capacity of ten more passengers, we could admit just ten more to it. But which ten do we let in? How do we choose? Do we pick the best ten, the neediest ten, "first come, first served"? And what do we say to the ninety we exclude? If we do let an extra ten into our lifeboat, we will have lost our "safety factor," an engineering principle of critical importance. For example, if we don't leave room for excess capacity as a safety factor in our country's agriculture, a new plant disease or a bad change in the weather could have disastrous consequences.

Suppose we decide to preserve our small safety factor and admit no more to the lifeboat. Our survival is then possible, although we shall have to be constantly on guard against boarding parties.

While this last solution clearly offers the only means of our survival, it is morally abhorrent to many people. Some say they feel guilty about their good luck. My reply is simple: "Get out and yield your place to others." This may solve the problem of the guilt-ridden person's conscience, but it does not change the ethics of the lifeboat. The needy person to whom the guilt-ridden person yields his place will not himself feel guilty about his good luck. If he did, he would not climb aboard. The net result of conscience-stricken people giving up their unjustly held seats is the elimination of that sort of conscience from the lifeboat.

This is the basic metaphor within which we must work out our solutions. Let us now enrich the image, step by step, with substantive additions from the real world, a world that must solve real and pressing problems of overpopulation and hunger.

The harsh ethics of the lifeboat become even harsher when we consider the reproductive differences between the rich nations and the poor nations. The people inside the lifeboats are doubling in numbers every eighty-seven years; those swimming around outside are doubling, on the average, every thirty-five years, more than twice as fast as the rich. And since the world's resources are dwindling, the difference in prosperity between the rich and the poor can only increase.

As of 1973, the U.S. had a population of 210 million people, who were increasing by 0.8 percent per year. Outside our lifeboat, let us imagine another 210 million people (say the combined populations of Colombia, Ecuador, Venezuela, Morocco, Pakistan, Thailand and the Philippines), who are increasing at a rate of 3.3 percent per year. Put differently, the doubling time for this aggregate population is twenty-one years, compared to eighty-seven years for the U.S.

Multiplying the Rich and the Poor

Now suppose the U.S. agreed to pool its resources with those seven countries, with everyone receiving an equal share. Initially the ratio of Americans to non-Americans in this model would be one-to-one. But consider what the ratio would be after eighty-seven years, by which time the Americans would have doubled to a population of 420 million. By then, doubling every twenty-one years, the other group would have swollen to 354 billion. Each American would have to share the available resources with more than eight people.

But, one could argue, this discussion assumes that current population trends will continue, and they may not. Quite so. Most likely the rate of population increase will decline much faster in the U.S. than it will in the other countries, and there does not seem to be much we can do about it. In sharing with "each according to his needs," we must recognize that needs are determined by population size, which is determined by the rate of reproduction, which at present is regarded as a sovereign right of every nation, poor or not. This being so, the philanthropic load created by the sharing ethic of the spaceship can only increase.

The Tragedy of the Commons

The fundamental error of spaceship ethics, and the sharing it requires, is that it leads to what I call "the tragedy of the commons." Under a system of private property, the men who own property recognize their responsibility to care for it, for if they don't they will eventually suffer. A farmer, for instance, will allow no more cattle in a pasture than its carrying capacity justifies. If he overloads it, erosion sets in, weeds take over, and he loses the use of the pasture.

If a pasture becomes a commons open to all, the right of each to use it may not be matched by a corresponding responsibility to protect it. Asking everyone to use it with discretion will hardly do, for the considerate herdsman who refrains from overloading the commons suffers more than a selfish one who says his needs are greater. If everyone would restrain himself, all would be well; but it takes only one less than everyone to ruin a system of voluntary restraint. In a crowded world of less than perfect human beings, mutual ruin is inevitable if there are no controls. This is the tragedy of the commons.

One of the major tasks of education today should be the creation of such an acute awareness of the dangers of the commons that people will recognize its many varieties. For example, the air and water have become polluted because they are treated as commons. Further growth in the population or per-capita conversion of natural resources into pollutants will only make the problem worse. The same holds true for the fish of the oceans. Fishing fleets have nearly disappeared in many parts of the world, technological improvements in the art of fishing are hastening the day of complete ruin. Only the replacement of the system of the commons with a responsible system of control will save the land, air, water and oceanic fisheries.

The World Food Bank

In recent years there has been a push to create a new commons called a World Food Bank, an international depository of food reserves to which nations would contribute according to their abilities and from which they would draw according to their needs. This humanitarian proposal has received support from many liberal international groups, and from such prominent citizens as Margaret Mead, U.N. Secretary General Kurt Waldheim, and Senators Edward Kennedy and George McGovern.

A world food bank appeals powerfully to our humanitarian impulses. But before we rush ahead with such a plan, let us recognize where the greatest political push comes from, lest we be disillusioned later. Our experience with the "Food for Peace program," or Public Law 480, gives us the answer. This program moved billions of dollars' worth of U.S. surplus grain to food-short, population-long countries during the past two decades. But when P.L. 480 first became law, a headline in the business magazine *Forbes* revealed the real power behind it: "Feeding the World's Hungry Millions: How It Will Mean Billions for U.S. Business."

And indeed it did. In the years 1960 to 1970, U.S. taxpayers spent a total of $7.9 billion on the Food for Peace program. Between 1948 and 1970, they also paid an additional $50 billion for other economic-aid programs, some of which went for food and food-producing machinery and technology. Though all U.S. taxpayers were forced to contribute to the cost of P.L. 480, certain special interest groups gained handsomely under the program. Farmers did not have to contribute the grain; the Government, or rather the taxpayers, bought it from them at full market prices. The increased demand raised prices of farm products generally. The manufacturers of farm machinery, fertilizers and pesticides benefited by the farmers' extra efforts to grow more food. Grain elevators profited from storing the surplus until it could be shipped. Railroads made money hauling it to ports, and shipping lines profited from carrying it overseas. The implementation of P.L. 480 required the creation of a vast Government bureaucracy, which then acquired its own vested interest in continuing the program regardless of its merits.

Extracting Dollars

Those who proposed and defended the Food for Peace program in public rarely mentioned its importance to any of these special interests. The public emphasis was always on its humanitarian effects. The combination of silent selfish interests and highly vocal humanitarian apologists made a powerful and successful lobby for extracting money from taxpayers. We can expect the same lobby to push now for the creation of a World Food Bank.

However great the potential benefit to selfish interests, it should not be a decisive argument against a truly humanitarian program. We must ask if such a program would actually do more good than harm, not only momentarily but also in the long run. Those who propose the food bank usually refer to a current "emergency" or "crisis" in terms of world food supply. But what is an emergency? Although they may be infrequent and sudden, everyone knows that emergencies will occur from time to time. A well-run family, company, organization or country prepares for the likelihood of accidents and emergencies. It expects them, it budgets for them, it saves for them.

Learning the Hard Way

What happens if some organizations or countries budget for accidents and others do not? If each country is solely responsible for its own well-being, poorly managed ones will suffer. But they can learn from experience. They may mend their ways, and learn to budget for infrequent but certain emergencies. For example, the weather varies from year to year, and periodic crop failures are certain. A wise and competent government saves out of the production of the good years in anticipation of bad years to come. Joseph taught this policy to Pharaoh in Egypt more than 2,000 years ago. Yet the great majority of the governments in the world today do not follow such a policy. They lack either the wisdom or the competence, or both. Should those nations that do manage to put something aside be forced to come to the rescue each time an emergency occurs among the poor nations?

"But it isn't their fault!" some kindhearted liberals argue. "How can we blame the poor people who are caught in an emergency? Why must they suffer for the sins of their governments?" The concept of blame is simply not relevant here. The real question is, what are the operational consequences of establishing a world food bank? If it is open to every country every time a need develops, slovenly rulers will not be motivated to take Joseph's advice. Someone will always come to their aid. Some countries will deposit food in the world food bank, and others will withdraw it. There will be almost no overlap. As a result of such solutions to food shortage emergencies, the poor countries will not learn to mend their ways, and will suffer progressively greater emergencies as their populations grow.

Population Control the Crude Way

On the average, poor countries undergo a 2.5 percent increase in population each year; rich countries, about 0.8 percent. Only rich countries have anything in the way of food reserves set aside, and even they do not have as much as they should. Poor countries have none. If poor countries received no food from the outside, the rate of their population growth would be periodically checked by crop failures and famines. But if they can always draw on a world food bank in time of need, their population can continue to grow unchecked, and so will their "need" for aid. In the short run, a world food bank may diminish that need, but in the long run it actually increases the need without limit.

Without some system of worldwide food sharing, the proportion of people in the rich and poor nations might eventually stabilize. The overpopulated poor countries would decrease in numbers, while the rich countries that had room for more people would increase. But with a well-meaning system of sharing, such as a world food bank, the growth differential between the rich and the poor countries will not only persist, it will increase. Because of the higher rate of population growth in the poor countries of the world, 88 percent of today's children are born poor, and only 12 percent rich. Year by year the ratio becomes worse, as the fast-reproducing poor outnumber the slow-reproducing rich.

A world food bank is thus a commons in disguise. People will have more motivation to draw from it than to add to any common store. The less provident and less able will multiply at the expense of the abler and more provident, bringing eventual ruin upon all who share in the commons. Besides, any system of "sharing" that amounts to foreign aid from the rich nations to the poor nations will carry the taint of charity, which will contribute little to the world peace so devoutly desired by those who support the idea of a world food bank.

As past U.S. foreign-aid programs have amply and depressingly demonstrated, international charity frequently inspires mistrust and antagonism rather than gratitude on the part of the recipient nation.

Chinese Fish and Miracle Rice

The modern approach to foreign aid stresses the export of technology and advice, rather than money and food. As an ancient Chinese proverb goes: "Give a man a fish and he will eat for a day; teach him how to fish and he will eat for the rest of his days." Acting on this advice, the Rockefeller and Ford Foundations have financed a number of programs for improving agriculture in the hungry nations. Known as the "Green Revolution," these programs have led to the development of "miracle rice" and "miracle wheat," new strains that offer bigger harvests and greater resistance to crop damage. Norman Borlaug, the Nobel Prize winning agronomist who, supported by the Rockefeller Foundation, developed "miracle wheat," is one of the most prominent advocates of a world food bank.

Whether or not the Green Revolution can increase food production as much as its champions claim is a debatable but possibly irrelevant point. Those who support this well-intended humanitarian effort should first consider some of the fundamentals of human ecology. Ironically, one man who did was the late Alan Gregg, a vice president of the Rockefeller Foundation. Two decades ago he expressed strong doubts about the wisdom of such attempts to increase food production. He likened the growth and spread of humanity over the surface of the earth to the spread of cancer in the human body, remarking that "cancerous growths demand food; but, as far as I know, they have never been cured by getting it."

Overloading the Environment

Every human born constitutes a draft on all aspects of the environment: food, air, water, forests, beaches, wildlife, scenery and solitude. Food can, perhaps, be significantly increased to meet a growing demand. But what about clean beaches, unspoiled forests, and solitude? If we satisfy a growing population's need for food, we necessarily decrease its per-capita supply of the other resources needed by men.

India, for example, now has a population of 600 million, which increases by 15 million each year. This population already puts a huge load on a relatively impoverished environment. The country's forests are now only a small fraction of what they were three centuries ago, and floods and erosion continually destroy the insufficient farmland that remains. Every one of the 15 million new lives added to India's population puts an additional burden on the environment, and increases the economic and social costs of crowding. However humanitarian our intent, every Indian life saved through medical or nutritional assistance from abroad diminishes the quality of life for those who remain, and for subsequent generations. If rich countries make it possible, through foreign aid, for 600 million Indians to swell to 1.2 billion in a mere twenty-eight years, as their current growth rate threatens, will future generations of Indians thank us for hastening the destruction of their environment? Will our good intentions be sufficient excuse for the consequences of our actions?

My final example of a commons in action is one for which the public has the least desire for rational discussion—immigration. Anyone who publicly questions the wisdom of current U.S. immigration policy is promptly charged with bigotry, prejudice, ethnocentrism, chauvinism, isolationism or selfishness. Rather than encounter such accusations, one would rather talk about other matters, leaving immigration policy to wallow in the crosscurrents of special interests that take no account of the good of the whole, or the interest of posterity.

Perhaps we still feel guilty about things we said in the past. Two generations ago the popular press frequently referred to Dagos, Wops, Polacks, Chinks and Krauts, in articles about how America was being "overrun" by foreigners of supposedly inferior genetic stock. But because the implied inferiority of foreigners was used then as justification for keeping them out, people now assume that restrictive policies could only be based on such misguided notions. There are other grounds.

A Nation of Immigrants

Just consider the numbers involved. Our Government acknowledges a net inflow of 400,000 immigrants a year. While we have no hard data on the extent of illegal entries, educated guesses put the figure at about 600,000 a year. Since the natural increase (excess of births over deaths) of the resident population now runs about 1.7 million per year, the yearly gain from immigration amounts to at least 19 percent of the total annual increase, and may be as much as 37 percent if we include the estimate for illegal immigrants. Considering the growing use of birth-control devices, the potential effect of educational campaigns by such organizations as Planned Parenthood Federation of America and Zero Population Growth, and the influence of inflation and the housing shortage, the fertility rate of American women may decline so much that immigration could account for all the yearly increase in population. Should we not at least ask if that is what we want?

For the sake of those who worry about whether the "quality" of the average immigrant compares favorably with the quality of the average resident, let us assume that immigrants and nativeborn citizens are of exactly equal quality, however one defines that term. We will focus here only on quantity; and since our conclusions will depend on nothing else, all charges of bigotry and chauvinism become irrelevant.

Immigration vs. Food Supply

World food banks *move food to the people*, hastening the exhaustion of the environment of the poor countries. Unrestricted immigration, on the other hand, *moves people to the food*, thus speeding up the destruction of the environment of the rich countries. We can easily understand why poor people should want to make this latter transfer, but why should rich hosts encourage it?

As in the case of foreign-aid programs, immigration receives support from selfish interests and humanitarian impulses. The primary selfish interest in unimpeded immigration is the desire of employers for cheap labor, particularly in industries and trades that offer degrading work. In the past, one wave of foreigners after another was brought into the U.S. to work at wretched jobs for wretched wages. In recent years the Cubans, Puerto Ricans and Mexicans have had this dubious honor. The interests of the employers of cheap labor mesh well with the guilty silence of the country's liberal intelligentsia. White Anglo-Saxon Protestants are particularly reluctant to call for a closing of the doors to immigration for fear of being called bigots.

But not all countries have such reluctant leadership. Most educated Hawaiians, for example, are keenly aware of the limits of their environment, particularly in terms of population growth. There is only so much room on the islands, and the islanders know it. To Hawaiians, immigrants from the other forty-nine states present as great a threat as those from other nations. At a recent meeting of Hawaiian government officials in Honolulu, I had the ironic delight of hearing a speaker, who like most of his audience was of Japanese ancestry, ask how the country might practically and constitutionally close its doors to further immigration. One member of the audience countered: "How can we shut the doors now? We have many friends and relatives in Japan that we'd like to bring here some day so that they can enjoy Hawaii too." The Japanese-American speaker smiled sympathetically and answered: "Yes, but we have children now, and someday we'll have grandchildren too. We can bring more people here from Japan only by giving away some of the land that we hope to pass on to our grandchildren some day. What right do we have to do that?"

At this point, I can hear U.S. liberals asking: "How can you justify slamming the door once you're inside? You say that immigrants should be kept out. But aren't we all immigrants, or the descendants of immigrants? If we insist on staying, must we not admit all others?" Our craving for intellectual order leads us to seek and prefer symmetrical rules and morals: a single rule for me and everybody else; the same rule yesterday, today, and tomorrow. Justice, we feel, should not change with time and place.

We Americans of non-Indian ancestry can look upon ourselves as the descendants of thieves who are guilty morally, if not legally, of stealing this land from its Indian owners. Should we then give back the land to the now living American descendants of those Indians? However morally or logically sound this proposal may be, I, for one, am unwilling to live by it and I know no one else who is. Besides, the logical consequence would be absurd. Suppose that, intoxicated with a sense of pure justice, we should decide to turn our land over to the Indians. Since all our wealth has also been derived from the land, wouldn't we be morally obliged to give that back to the Indians too?

Pure Justice vs. Reality

Clearly, the concept of pure justice produces an infinite regression to absurdity. Centuries ago, wise men invented statutes of limitations to justify the rejection of such pure justice, in the interest of preventing continual disorder. The law zealously defends property rights, but only relatively recent property rights. Drawing a line after an arbitrary time has elapsed may be unjust, but the alternatives are worse.

We are all descendants of thieves, and the world's resources are inequitably distributed. But we must begin the journey to tomorrow from the point where we are today. We cannot remake the past. We cannot safely divide the wealth equitably among all peoples so long as people reproduce at different rates. To do so would guarantee that our grandchildren, and everyone else's grandchildren, would have only a ruined world to inhabit.

To be generous with one's own possessions is quite different from being generous with those of posterity. We should call this point to the attention of those who, from a commendable love of justice and equality, would institute a system of the commons, either in the form of a world food bank, or of unrestricted immigration. We must convince them if we wish to save at least some parts of the world from environmental ruin.

Without a true world government to control reproduction and the use of available resources, the sharing ethic of the spaceship is impossible. For the foreseeable future, our survival demands that we govern our actions by the ethics of a lifeboat, harsh though they may be. Posterity will be satisfied with nothing less.

Questions for Analysis

1. *Why does Hardin object to the environmentalists' metaphor of the earth as a spaceship?*

2. *Hardin seems opposed even to developmental assistance. Why?*

3. *In Hardin's view, "pure justice" is not compatible with survival. What does he mean? Do you agree?*

4. *Do you agree that future generations have a claim against us? If they do, what is the nature of this claim?*

5. *Explain why Hardin's argument can be called utilitarian.*

Famine, Affluence, and Morality

Peter Singer

Unlike Garrett Hardin, professor of philosophy Peter Singer believes that the affluent nations of the world have an obligation to help the poor nations. Singer opens his argument with what he considers are two uncontroversial principles. The first is that suffering and death from lack of food, shelter, and medical care are bad. The second is that if we can prevent something bad from

Peter Singer, "Famine, Affluence, and Morality," *Philosophy & Public Affairs,* Vol. 1, No. 3 (Spring 1972). Copyright © 1972 by Princeton University Press. Reprinted by permission of Princeton University Press.

happening "without thereby sacrificing anything of comparable moral importance," then we should do it. (While Singer believes that this principle is correct, he does offer a "weaker" version of it as well: We ought to prevent something bad from happening unless we have to sacrifice something morally significant.)

Basing his argument on these principles, Singer concludes that help or relief for the starving masses is a duty, not charity. Affluent nations are morally obliged to help; to refrain from helping is not merely uncharitable, it is immoral.

In addition to drawing a philosophical distinction between charity and duty, Singer raises a number of practical concerns. One is whether help to poor nations should be a government responsibility and not a personal one. Another is whether relief to countries lacking effective population-control measures merely postpones starvation.

Still another concern is just how much individually and collectively we ought to be giving away.

In the postscript to his essay, written several years afterward, Singer concedes that there is a serious case to be made for denying aid to countries that refuse to take any population-control measures. He also admits definitional problems with the phrase "moral significance," which, of course, is crucial in his second principle.

As I write this, in November 1971, people are dying in East Bengal from lack of food, shelter, and medical care. The suffering and death that are occurring there now are not inevitable, not unavoidable in any fatalistic sense of the term. Constant poverty, a cyclone, and a civil war have turned at least nine million people into destitute refugees; nevertheless, it is not beyond the capacity of the richer nations to give enough assistance to reduce any further suffering to very small proportions. The decisions and actions of human beings can prevent this kind of suffering. Unfortunately, human beings have not made the necessary decisions. At the individual level, people have, with very few exceptions, not responded to the situation in any significant way. Generally speaking, people have not given large sums to relief funds; they have not written to their parliamentary representatives demanding increased government assistance; they have not demonstrated in the streets, held symbolic fasts, or done anything else directed toward providing the refugees with the means to satisfy their essential needs. At the government level, no government has given the sort of massive aid that would enable the refugees to survive for more than a few days. Britain, for instance, has given rather more than most countries. It has, to date, given £14,750,000. For comparative purposes, Britain's share of the nonrecoverable development costs of the Anglo-French Concorde project is already in excess of £275,000,000, and on present estimates will reach £440,000,000. The implication is that the British government values a supersonic transport more than thirty times as

highly as it values the lives of the nine million refugees. Australia is another country which, on a per capita basis, is well up in the "aid to Bengal" table. Australia's aid, however, amounts to less than one-twelfth of the cost of Sydney's new opera house. The total amount given, from all sources, now stands at about £65,000,000. The estimated cost of keeping the refugees alive for one year is £464,000,000. Most of the refugees have now been in the camps for more than six months. The World Bank has said that India needs a minimum of £300,000,000 in assistance from other countries before the end of the year. It seems obvious that assistance on this scale will not be forthcoming. India will be forced to choose between letting the refugees starve or diverting funds from her own development program, which will mean that more of her own people will starve in the future.[1]

These are the essential facts about the present situation in Bengal. So far as it concerns us here, there is nothing unique about this situation except its magnitude. The Bengal emergency is just the latest and most acute of a series of major emergencies in various parts of the world, arising both from natural and from man-made causes. There are also many parts of the world in which people die from malnutrition and lack of food independent of any special emergency. I take Bengal as my example only because it is the present concern, and because the size of the problem has ensured that it has been given adequate publicity. Neither individuals nor governments can claim to be unaware of what is happening there.

What are the moral implications of a situation like this? In what follows, I shall argue that the way people in relatively affluent countries react to a situation like that in Bengal cannot be justified; indeed, the whole way we look at moral issues—our moral conceptual scheme—needs to be altered, and with it, the way of life that has come to be taken for granted in our society.

In arguing for this conclusion I will not, of course, claim to be morally neutral. I shall, however, try to argue for the moral position that I take, so that anyone who accepts certain assumptions, to be made explicit, will, I hope, accept my conclusion.

I begin with the assumption that suffering and death from lack of food, shelter, and medical care are bad. I think most people will agree about this, although one may reach the same view by different routes. I shall not argue for this view. People can hold all sorts of eccentric positions, and perhaps from some of them it would not follow that death by starvation is in itself bad. It is difficult, perhaps impossible, to refute such positions, and so for brevity I will henceforth take this assumption as accepted. Those who disagree need read no further.

My next point is this: If it is in our power to prevent something bad from happening, without thereby sacrificing anything of comparable moral importance, we ought, morally, to do it. By "without sacrificing anything of comparable moral importance" I mean without causing anything else comparably bad to happen, or doing something that is wrong in itself, or failing to promote some moral good, comparable in significance to the bad thing that we can prevent. This principle seems almost as uncontroversial as the last one. It requires us only to prevent what is bad, and not to promote what is good, and it requires this of us only when we can do it without sacrificing anything that is, from the moral point of view, comparably important. I could even, as far as the application of my argument to the Bengal emergency is concerned, qualify the point so as to make it: If it is in our power to prevent something very bad from happening, without thereby sacrificing anything morally significant, we ought, morally, to do it. An application of this principle would be as follows: If I am walking past a shallow pond and see a child drowning in it, I ought to wade in and pull the child out. This will mean getting my clothes muddy, but this is insignificant, while the death of the child would presumably be a very bad thing.

The uncontroversial appearance of the principle just stated is deceptive. If it were acted upon, even in its qualified form, our lives, our society, and our world would be fundamentally changed. For the principle takes, firstly, no account of proximity or distance. It makes no moral difference whether the person I can help is a neighbor's child ten yards from me or a Bengali whose name I shall never know, ten thousand miles away. Secondly, the principle makes no distinction between cases in which I am the only person who could possibly do anything and cases in which I am just one among millions in the same position.

I do not think I need to say much in defense of the refusal to take proximity and distance into account. The fact that a person is physically near to us, so that we have personal contact with him, may make it more likely that we *shall* assist him, but this does not show that we *ought* to help him rather than another who happens to be further away. If we accept any principle of impartiality, universalizability, equality, or whatever, we cannot discriminate against someone merely because he is far away from us (or we are far away from him). Admittedly, it is possible that we are in a better position to judge what needs to be done to help a person near to us than one far away, and perhaps also to provide the assistance we judge to be necessary. If this were the case, it would be a reason for helping those near to us first. This may once have been a justification for being more concerned with the poor in one's town than with famine victims in India. Unfortunately for those who like to keep their moral responsibilities limited, instant communication and swift transportation have changed the situation. From the moral point of view, the development of the world into a "global village" has made an important, though still unrecognized, difference to our moral situation. Expert observers and supervisors, sent out by famine relief organizations or permanently stationed in famine-prone areas, can direct our aid to a refugee in Bengal almost as effectively as we could get it to someone in our own block. There would seem, therefore, to be no possible justification for discriminating on geographical grounds.

There may be a greater need to defend the second implication of my principle—that the fact that there are millions of other people in the same position, in respect to the Bengali refugees, as I am, does not make the situation significantly different from a situation in which I am the only person who can prevent something very bad from occurring. Again, of course, I admit that there is a psychological difference between the cases; one feels less guilty about doing nothing if one can point to others, similarly placed, who have also done nothing. Yet this can make no real difference to our moral obligations.[2] Should I consider that I am less obliged to pull the drowning child out of the pond if on looking around I see other people, no further away than I am, who have also noticed the child but are doing nothing? One has only to ask this question to see the absurdity of the view that numbers lessen obligation. It is a view that is an ideal excuse for inactivity; unfortunately most of the major evils—poverty, overpopulation, pollution—are problems in which everyone is almost equally involved.

The view that numbers do make a difference can be made plausible if stated in this way: If everyone in circumstances like mine gave £5 to the Bengal Relief Fund, there would be enough to provide food, shelter, and medical care for the refugees; there is no reason why I should give more than anyone else in the same circumstances as I am; therefore I have no obligation to give more than £5. Each premise in this argument is true, and the argument looks sound. It may convince us, unless we notice that it is based on a hypothetical premise, although the conclusion is not stated hypothetically. The argument would be sound if the conclusion were: if everyone in circumstances like mine were to give £5, I would have no obligation to give more than £5. If the conclusion were so stated, however, it would be obvious that the argument has no bearing on a situation in which it is not the case that everyone else gives £5. This, of course, is the actual situation. It is more or less certain that not everyone in circumstances like mine will give £5. So there will not be enough to provide the needed food, shelter, and medical care. Therefore by giving more than £5 I will prevent more suffering than I would if I gave just £5.

It might be thought that this argument has an absurd consequence. Since the situation appears to be that very few people are likely to give substantial amounts, it follows that I and everyone else in similar circumstances ought to give as much as possible, that is, at least up to the point at which by giving more one would begin to cause serious suffering for oneself and one's dependents—perhaps even beyond this point to the point of marginal utility, at which by giving more one would cause oneself and one's dependents as much suffering as one would prevent in Bengal. If everyone does this, however, there will be more than can be used for the benefit of the refugees, and some of the sacrifice will have been unnecessary. Thus, if everyone does what he ought to do, the result will not be as good as it would be if everyone did a little less than he ought to do, or if only some do all that they ought to do.

The paradox here arises only if we assume that the actions in question—sending money to the relief funds—are performed more or less simultaneously, and are also unexpected. For if it is to be expected that everyone is going to contribute something, then clearly each is not obliged to give as much as he would have been obliged to had others not been giving too. And if everyone is not acting more or less simultaneously, then those giving later will know how much more is needed, and will have no obligation to give more than is necessary to reach this amount. To say this is not to deny the principle that people in the same circumstances have the same obligations, but to point out that the fact that others have given, or may be expected to give, is a relevant circumstance: Those giving after it has become known that many others are giving and those giving before are not in the same circumstances. So the seemingly absurd consequence of the principle I have put forward can occur only if people are in error about the actual circumstances—that is, if they think they are giving when others are not, but in fact they are giving when others are. The result of everyone doing what he really ought to do cannot be worse than the result of everyone doing less than he ought to do, although the result of everyone doing what he reasonably believes he ought to do could be.

If my argument so far has been sound, neither our distance from a preventable evil nor the number of other people who, in respect to that evil, are in the same situation as we are, lessens our obligation to mitigate or prevent that evil. I shall therefore take as established the principle I asserted earlier. As I have already said, I need to assert it only in its qualified form: If it is in our power to prevent something very bad from happening, without thereby sacrificing anything else morally significant, we ought, morally, to do it.

The outcome of this argument is that our traditional moral categories are upset. The traditional distinction between duty and charity cannot be drawn, or at least, not in the place we normally draw it. Giving money to the Bengal Relief Fund is regarded as an act of charity in our society. The bodies which collect money are known as "charities." These organizations see themselves in this way—if you send them a check, you will be thanked for your "generosity." Because giving money is regarded as an act of charity, it is not thought that there is anything wrong with not giving. The charitable man may be praised, but the man who is not charitable is not condemned. People do not feel in any way ashamed or guilty about spending money on new clothes or a new car instead of giving it to a famine relief. (Indeed, the alternative does not occur to them.) This way of looking at the matter cannot be justified. When we buy new clothes not to keep ourselves warm but to look "well-dressed" we are not providing for any important need. We would not be sacrificing anything significant if we were to continue to wear our old clothes, and give the money to famine relief. By doing so, we would be preventing another person from starving. It follows from what I have said earlier that we ought to give money away, rather than spend it on clothes which we do not need to keep us warm. To do so is not charitable, or generous. Nor is it the kind of act which philosophers and theologians have called "supererogatory"—an act which it would be good to do, but not wrong not to do. On the contrary, we ought to give the money away, and it is wrong not to do so.

I am not maintaining that there are no acts which are charitable, or that there are no acts which it would be good to do but not wrong not to do. It may be possible to redraw the distinction between duty and charity in some other place. All I am arguing here is that the present way of drawing the distinction, which makes it an act of charity for a man living at the level of affluence which most people in the "developed nations" enjoy to give money to save someone else from starvation, cannot be supported. It is beyond the scope of my argument to consider whether the distinction should be redrawn or abolished altogether. There would be many other possible ways of drawing the distinction—for instance, one might decide that it is good to make other people as happy as possible, but not wrong not to do so.

Despite the limited nature of the revision in our moral conceptual scheme which I am proposing, the revision would, given the extent of both affluence and famine in the world today, have radical implications. These implications may lead to further objections, distinct from those I have already considered. I shall discuss two of these.

One objection to the position I have taken might be simply that it is too drastic a revision of our moral scheme. People do not ordinarily judge in the way I have suggested they should. Most people reserve their moral condemnation for those who violate some moral norm, such as the norm against taking another person's property. They do not condemn those who indulge in luxury instead of giving to famine relief. But given that I did not set out to present a morally neutral description of the way people make moral judgments, the way people do in fact judge has nothing to do with the validity of my conclusion. My conclusion follows from the principle which I advanced earlier, and unless that principle is rejected, or the arguments shown to be unsound, I think the conclusion must stand, however strange it appears.

It might, nevertheless, be interesting to consider why our society, and most other societies, do judge differently from the way I have suggested they should. In a well-known article, J. O. Urmson suggests that the imperatives of duty, which tell us what we must do, as distinct from what it would be good to do but not wrong not to do, function so as to prohibit behavior that is intolerable if men are to live together in society.[3] This may explain the origin and continued existence of the present division between acts of duty and acts of charity. Moral attitudes are shaped by the needs of society, and no doubt society needs people who will observe the rules that make social existence tolerable. From the point of view of a particular society, it is essential to prevent violations of norms against killing, stealing, and so on. It is quite inessential, however, to help people outside one's own society.

If this is an explanation of our common distinction between duty and supererogation, however, it is not a justification of it. The moral point of view requires us to look beyond the interests of our own society. Previously, as I have already mentioned, this may hardly have been feasible, but it is quite feasible now. From the moral point of view, the prevention of the starvation of millions of people outside our society must be considered at least as pressing as the upholding of property norms within our society.

It has been argued by some writers, among them Sidgwick and Urmson, that we need to have a basic moral code which is not too far beyond the capacities of ordinary man, for otherwise there will be a general breakdown of compliance with the moral code. Crudely stated, this argument suggests that if we tell people that they ought to refrain from murder and give everything they do not really need to famine relief, they will do neither, whereas if we tell them that they ought to refrain from murder and that it is good to give to famine relief but not wrong not to do so, they will at least refrain from murder. The issue here is: Where should we draw the line between conduct that is required and conduct that is good although not required, so as to get the best possible result? This would seem to be an empirical question, although a very difficult one. One objection to the Sidgwick-Urmson line of argument is that it takes insufficient account of the effect that moral standards can have on the decisions we make. Given a society in which a wealthy man who gives 5 percent of his income to famine relief is regarded as most generous, it is not surprising that a proposal that we all ought to give away half our incomes will be thought to be absurdly unrealistic. In a society which held that no man should have more than enough while others have less than they need, such a proposal might seem narrow-minded. What it is possible for a man to do and what he is likely to do are both, I think, very greatly influenced by what people around him are doing and expecting him to do. In any case, the possibility that by spreading the idea that we ought to be doing very much more than we are to relieve famine we shall bring about a general breakdown of moral behavior seems remote. If the stakes are an end to widespread starvation, it is worth the risk. Finally, it should be emphasized that these considerations are relevant only to the issue of what we should require from others, and not to what we ourselves ought to do.

The second objection to my attack on the present distinction between duty and charity is one which has from time to time been made against utilitarianism. It follows from some forms of utilitarian theory that we all ought, morally, to be working full time to increase the balance of happiness over misery. The position I have taken here would not lead to this conclusion in all circumstances, for if there were no bad occurrences that we could prevent without sacrificing something of comparable moral importance, my argument would have no application. Given the present conditions in many parts of the world, however, it does follow from my argument that we ought, morally, to be working full time to relieve great suffering of the sort that occurs as a result of famine or other disasters. Of course, mitigating circumstances can be adduced—for instance, that if we wear ourselves out through overwork, we shall be less effective than we would otherwise have been. Nevertheless, when all considerations of this sort have been taken into account, the conclusion remains: We ought to be preventing as much suffering as we can without sacrificing something else of comparable moral importance. This conclusion is one which we may be reluctant to face. I cannot see, though, why it should be regarded as a criticism of the position for which I have argued, rather than a criticism of our ordinary standards of behavior. Since most people are self-interested to some degree, very few of us are likely to do everything that we ought to do. It would, however, hardly be honest to take this as evidence that it is not the case that we ought to do it.

It may still be thought that my conclusions are so wildly out of line with what everyone else thinks and has always thought that there must be something wrong with the argument somewhere. In order to show that my conclusions, while certainly contrary to contemporary Western moral standards, would not have seemed so extraordinary at other times and in other places, I would like to quote a passage from a writer not normally thought of as a way-out radical, Thomas Aquinas.

> Now, according to the natural order instituted by divine providence, material goods are provided for the satisfaction of human needs. Therefore the division and appropriation of property, which proceeds from human law, must not hinder the satisfaction of man's necessity from such goods. Equally, whatever

a man has in superabundance is owed, of
natural right, to the poor for their sustenance.
So Ambrosius says, and it is also to be found
in the *Decretum Gratiani:* "The bread which
you withhold belongs to the hungry; the
clothing you shut away, to the naked; and the
money you bury in the earth is the redemp-
tion and freedom of the penniless."[4]

I now want to consider a number of points,
more practical than philosophical, which are relevant to the application of the moral conclusion we
have reached. These points challenge not the idea
that we ought to be doing all we can to prevent
starvation, but the idea that giving away a great
deal of money is the best means to this end.

It is sometimes said that overseas aid should
be a government responsibility, and that therefore
one ought not to give to privately run charities.
Giving privately, it is said, allows the government
and the noncontributing members of society to
escape their responsibilities.

This argument seems to assume that the more
people there are who give to privately organized
famine relief funds, the less likely it is that the government will take over full responsibility for such
aid. This assumption is unsupported, and does not
strike me as at all plausible. The opposite view—
that if no one gives voluntarily, a government will
assume that its citizens are uninterested in famine
relief and would not wish to be forced into giving
aid—seems more plausible. In any case, unless there
were a definite probability that by refusing to give
one would be helping to bring about massive government assistance, people who do refuse to make
voluntary contributions are refusing to prevent a
certain amount of suffering without being able to
point to any tangible beneficial consequence of their
refusal. So the onus of showing how their refusal
will bring about government action is on those who
refuse to give.

I do not, of course, want to dispute the contention that governments of affluent nations should
be giving many times the amount of genuine, no-
strings-attached aid that they are giving now. I agree,
too, that giving privately is not enough, and that
we ought to be campaigning actively for entirely
new standards for both public and private contributions to famine relief. Indeed, I would sympa-

thize with someone who thought that campaigning
was more important than giving oneself, although
I doubt whether preaching what one does not practice would be very effective. Unfortunately, for many
people the idea that "it's the government's responsibility" is a reason for not giving which does not
appear to entail any political action either.

Another, more serious reason for not giving to
famine relief funds is that until there is effective
population control, relieving famine merely postpones starvation. If we save the Bengal refugees
now, others, perhaps the children of these refugees, will face starvation in a few years' time. In
support of this, one may cite the now well-known
facts about the population explosion and the relatively limited scope for expanded production.

This point, like the previous one, is an argument against relieving suffering that is happening
now, because of a belief about what might happen
in the future; it is unlike the previous point in that
very good evidence can be adduced in support of
this belief about the future. I will not go into the
evidence here. I accept that the earth cannot support indefinitely a population rising at the present
rate. This certainly poses a problem for anyone who
thinks it important to prevent famine. Again, however, one could accept the argument without drawing the conclusion that it absolves one from any
obligation to do anything to prevent famine. The
conclusion that should be drawn is that the best
means of preventing famine, in the long run, is
population control. It would then follow from the
position reached earlier that one ought to be doing
all one can to promote population control (unless
one held that all forms of population control were
wrong in themselves, or would have significantly
bad consequences). Since there are organizations
working specifically for population control, one
would then support them rather than more orthodox methods of preventing famine.

A third point raised by the conclusion reached
earlier relates to the question of just how much we
all ought to be giving away. One possibility, which
has already been mentioned, is that we ought to
give until we reach the level of marginal utility—
that is, the level at which, by giving more, I would
cause as much suffering to myself or my dependents as I would relieve by my gift. This would
mean, of course, that one would reduce oneself to

very near the material circumstances of a Bengali refugee. It will be recalled that earlier I put forward both a strong and a moderate version of the principle of preventing bad occurrences. The strong version, which required us to prevent bad things from happening unless in doing so we would be sacrificing something of comparable moral significance, does seem to require reducing ourselves to the level of marginal utility. I should also say that the strong version seems to me to be the correct one. I proposed the more moderate version—that we should prevent bad occurrences unless, to do so, we had to sacrifice something morally significant—only in order to show that even on this surely undeniable principle a great change in our way of life is required. On the more moderate principle, it may not follow that we ought to reduce ourselves to the level of marginal utility, for one might hold that to reduce oneself and one's family to this level is to cause something significantly bad to happen. Whether this is so I shall not discuss, since, as I have said, I can see no good reason for holding the moderate version of the principle rather than the strong version. Even if we accepted the principle only in its moderate form, however, it should be clear that we would have to give away enough to ensure that the consumer society, dependent as it is on people spending on trivia rather than giving to famine relief, would slow down and perhaps disappear entirely. There are several reasons why this would be desirable in itself. The value and necessity of economic growth are now being questioned not only by conservationists, but by economists as well.[5] There is no doubt, too, that the consumer society has had a distorting effect on the goals and purposes of its members. Yet looking at the matter purely from the point of view of overseas aid, there must be a limit to the extent to which we should deliberately slow down our economy; for it might be the case that if we gave away, say, 40 percent of our Gross National Product, we would slow down the economy so much that in absolute terms we would be giving less than if we gave 25 percent of the much larger GNP that we would have if we limited our contribution to this smaller percentage.

I mention this only as an indication of the sort of factor that one would have to take into account in working out an ideal. Since Western societies generally consider one percent of the GNP an acceptable level for overseas aid, the matter is entirely academic. Nor does it affect the question of how much an individual should give in a society in which very few are giving substantial amounts.

It is sometimes said, though less often now than it used to be, that philosophers have no special role to play in public affairs, since most public issues depend primarily on an assessment of facts. On questions of fact, it is said, philosophers as such have no special expertise, and so it has been possible to engage in philosophy without committing oneself to any position on major public issues. No doubt there are some issues of social policy and foreign policy about which it can truly be said that a really expert assessment of the facts is required before taking sides or acting, but the issue of famine is surely not one of these. The facts about the existence of suffering are beyond dispute. Nor, I think, is it disputed that we can do something about it, either through orthodox methods of famine relief or through population control or both. This is therefore an issue on which philosophers are competent to take a position. The issue is one which faces everyone who has more money than he needs to support himself and his dependents, or who is in a position to take some sort of political action. These categories must include practically every teacher and student of philosophy in the universities of the Western world. If philosophy is to deal with matters that are relevant to both teachers and students, this is an issue that philosophers should discuss.

Discussion, though, is not enough. What is the point of relating philosophy to public (and personal) affairs if we do not take our conclusions seriously? In this instance, taking our conclusion seriously means acting upon it. The philosopher will not find it any easier than anyone else to alter his attitudes and way of life to the extent that, if I am right, is involved in doing everything that we ought to be doing. At the very least, though, one can make a start. The philosopher who does so will have to sacrifice some of the benefits of the consumer society, but he can find compensation in the satisfaction of a way of life in which theory and practice, if not yet in harmony, are at least coming together.

Postscript

The crisis in Bangladesh that spurred me to write the above article is now of historical interest only, but the world food crisis is, if anything, still more serious. The huge grain reserves that were then held by the United States have vanished. Increased oil prices have made both fertilizer and energy more expensive in developing countries, and have made it difficult for them to produce more food. At the same time, their population has continued to grow. Fortunately, as I write now, there is no major famine anywhere in the world; but poor people are still starving in several countries, and malnutrition remains very widespread. The need for assistance is, therefore, just as great as when I first wrote, and we can be sure that without it there will, again, be major famines.

The contrast between poverty and affluence that I wrote about is also as great as it was then. True, the affluent nations have experienced a recession, and are perhaps not as prosperous as they were in 1971. But the poorer nations have suffered at least as much from the recession, in reduced government aid (because if governments decide to reduce expenditure, they regard foreign aid as one of the expendable items, ahead of, for instance, defense or public construction projects) and in increased prices for goods and materials they need to buy. In any case, compared to the difference between the affluent nations and the poor nations, the whole recession was trifling; the poorest in the affluent nations remained incomparably better off than the poorest in the poor nations.

So the case for aid, on both a personal and a governmental level, remains as great now as it was in 1971, and I would not wish to change the basic argument that I put forward then.

There are, however, some matters of emphasis that I might put differently if I were to rewrite the article, and the most important of these concerns the population problem. I still think that, as I wrote then, the view that famine relief merely postpones starvation unless something is done to check population growth is not an argument against aid, it is only an argument against the *type* of aid that should be given. Those who hold this view have the same obligation to give to prevent starvation as those who do not; the difference is that they regard assisting population control schemes as a more effective way of preventing starvation in the long run. I would now, however, have given greater space to the discussion of the population problem; for I now think that there is a serious case for saying that if a country refuses to take any steps to slow the rate of its population growth, we should not give it aid. This is, of course, a very drastic step to take, and the choice it represents is a horrible choice to have to make, but if, after a dispassionate analysis of all the available information, we come to the conclusion that without population control we will not, in the long run, be able to prevent famine or other catastrophes, then it may be more humane in the long run to aid those countries that are prepared to take strong measures to reduce population growth, and to use our aid policy as a means of pressuring other countries to take similar steps.

It may be objected that such a policy involves an attempt to coerce a sovereign nation. But since we are not under an obligation to give aid unless that aid is likely to be effective in reducing starvation or malnutrition, we are not under an obligation to give aid to countries that make no effort to reduce a rate of population growth that will lead to catastrophe. Since we do not force any nation to accept our aid, simply making it clear that we will not give aid where it is not going to be effective cannot properly be regarded as a form of coercion.

I should also make it clear that the kind of aid that will slow population growth is not just assistance with the setting up of facilities for dispensing contraceptives and performing sterilizations. It is also necessary to create the conditions under which people do not wish to have so many children. This will involve, among other things, providing greater economic security for people, particularly in their old age, so that they do not need the security of a large family to provide for them. Thus, the requirements of aid designed to reduce population growth and aid designed to eliminate starvation are by no means separate; they overlap, and the latter will often be a means to the former. The obligation of the affluent is, I believe, to do both. Fortunately, there are now so many people in the foreign aid field, including those in the private agencies, who are aware of this.

One other matter that I should now put forward slightly differently is that my argument does, of course, apply to assistance with development, particularly agricultural development, as well as to direct famine relief. Indeed, I think the former is usually the better long-term investment. Although this was my view when I wrote the article, the fact that I started from a famine situation, where the need was for immediate food, has led some readers to suppose that the argument is only about giving food and not about other types of aid. This is quite mistaken, and my view is that the aid should be of whatever type is most effective.

On a more philosophical level, there has been some discussion of the original article which has been helpful in clarifying the issues and pointing to the areas in which more work on the argument is needed. In particular, as John Arthur has shown in "Rights and the Duty to Bring Aid" . . . something more needs to be said about the notion of "moral significance." The problem is that to give an account of this notion involves nothing less than a full-fledged ethical theory; and while I am myself inclined toward a utilitarian view, it was my aim in writing "Famine, Affluence, and Morality" to produce an argument which would appeal not only to utilitarians, but also to anyone who accepted the initial premises of the argument, which seemed to me likely to have a very wide acceptance. So I tried to get around the need to produce a complete ethical theory by allowing my readers to fill in their own version—within limits—of what is morally significant, and then see what the moral consequences are. This tactic works reasonably well with those who are prepared to agree that such matters as being fashionably dressed are not really of moral significance; but Arthur is right to say that people could take the opposite view without being obviously irrational. Hence, I do not accept Arthur's claim that the weak principle implies little or no duty of benevolence, for it will imply a significant duty of benevolence for those who admit, as I think most nonphilosophers and even off-guard philosophers will admit, that they spend considerable sums on items that by their own standards are of no moral significance. But I do agree that the weak principle is nonetheless too weak, because it makes it too easy for the duty of benevolence to be avoided.

On the other hand, I think the strong principle will stand, whether the notion of moral significance is developed along utilitarian lines, or once again left to the individual reader's own sincere judgment. In either case, I would argue against Arthur's view that we are morally entitled to give greater weight to our own interests and purposes simply because they are our own. This view seems to me contrary to the idea, now widely shared by moral philosophers, that some element of impartiality or universalizability is inherent in the very notion of a moral judgment. (For a discussion of the different formulations of this idea, and an indication of the extent to which they are in agreement, see R. M. Hare, "Rules of War and Moral Reasoning," *Philosophy and Public Affairs* I, no. 2 [1972].) Granted, in normal circumstances, it may be better for everyone if we recognize that each of us will be primarily responsible for running our own lives and only secondarily responsible for others. This, however, is not a moral ultimate, but a secondary principle that derives from consideration of how a society may best order its affairs, given the limits of altruism in human beings. Such secondary principles are, I think, swept aside by the extreme evil of people starving to death.

Notes

1. There was also a third possibility: that India would go to war to enable the refugees to return to their lands. Since I wrote this paper, India has taken this way out. The situation is no longer that described above, but this does not affect my argument, as the next paragraph indicates.

2. In view of the special sense philosophers often give to the term, I should say that I use "obligation" simply as the abstract noun derived from "ought," so that "I have an obligation to" means no more, and no less, than "I ought to." This usage is in accordance with the definition of "ought" given by the *Shorter Oxford English Dictionary*: "the general verb to express duty or obligation." I do not think any issue of substance hangs on the way the term is used; sentences in which I use "obligation" could be all rewritten, although somewhat clumsily, as sentences in which a clause containing "ought" replaces the term "obligation."

3. J. O. Urmson, "Saints and Heroes," in *Essays in Moral Philosophy*, ed. Abraham I. Melden (Seattle: University of Washington Press, 1958), p. 214. For a related but significantly different view see also Henry Sidgwick, *The Methods of Ethics*, 7th edn. (London: Dover Press, 1907), pp. 220–21, 492–93.

4. *Summa Theologica*, II-II, Question 66, Article 7, in *Aquinas, Selected Political Writings*, ed. A. P. d'Entreves, trans. J. G. Dawson (Oxford: Basil Blackwell, 1948), p. 171.

5. See, for instance, John Kenneth Galbraith, *The New Industrial State* (Boston: Houghton Mifflin, 1967); and E. J. Mishan, *The Costs of Economic Growth* (New York: Praeger, 1967).

Questions for Analysis

1. *What is the difference between the strong and weak versions of the principle of preventing bad occurrences?*

2. *What does Singer mean by "without sacrificing anything of comparable importance"?*

3. *Why does Singer say the world would be fundamentally different if we followed his two principles?*

4. *Suppose someone said to Singer: "But I'm not responsible for the starvation that people experience. So why do I have a duty to prevent it?" How might Singer reply?*

5. *Why does Singer not regard helping as charity?*

6. *Suppose one accepts the argument that relief to countries without population-control measures merely postpones starvation. Does this absolve one of the obligation to do anything to prevent starvation?*

7. *Is it accurate to say that while Singer is inclined to the utilitarian view, his principles are essentially nonutilitarian or at least could appeal to nonutilitarians? Explain.*

8. *Does Singer's postscript undercut his original argument?*

Reason and Morality in a World of Limited Food

Richard A. Watson

The principle of equity is central to philosophy professor Richard A. Watson's thesis in this essay. The principle of equity refers to equal sharing. Watson's thesis is that, with respect to world hunger, there should be an equal sharing of food.

Watson is aware of the most trenchant objection to his position: Sharing food may turn out to be futile. Indeed, what if, as a result of sharing, the human species perishes? So be it, Watson answers. No matter how horrendous the consequences, the moral action is to share and share equally. As Watson says, "No principle of morality absolves one of behaving immorally simply to save one's life or nation."

Watson grants that such a suicidal course may be irrational. Nevertheless, he argues that the claims of morality supersede those of conflicting reason. In other words, the moral action may not necessarily be the reasonable or practical action. Where in fact the moral action is unreasonable, **one nevertheless has an obligation to behave morally.**

From Richard A. Watson, "Reason and Morality in a World of Limited Food," in World Hunger and Moral Obligation, *William Aiken and Hugh LaFollette, eds. (Englewood Cliffs, N.J.: Prentice-Hall, 1977). Reprinted by permission of the author.*

Watson believes his conclusion that we must equally share what we have follows inexorably from the assumption that every human life is equal in value. Accepting this assumption, presumably we must conclude that everyone deserves an equal share—no matter what the consequences, even if they be extinction.

Obviously Watson subordinates the principle of survival to the principle of equity. He feels that this is justified because "in the milieu of morality, it is immaterial whether or not the human species survives as a result of individual moral behavior."

Like Singer, Watson is arguing for an obligation to share. But while Singer's basis is utilitarian, Watson rejects any consequential considerations as a basis for morality.

A few years ago, President Johnson said:

> There are 200 million of us and 3 billion of them and they want what we've got, but we're not going to give it to them.

In this essay I examine the conflict between reasonable and moral behavior in a world of limited food. It appears to be unreasonable—and conceivably immoral—to share all food equally when this would result in everyone's being malnourished. Arguments for the morality of unequal distribution are presented from the standpoint of the individual, the nation, and the human species. These arguments fail because, although it is unreasonable to share limited food when sharing threatens survival, the moral principle of equity ranks sharing above survival. I accept the principle of equity, and conclude by challenging the ideological basis that makes sharing unreasonable.

The contrast of the moral with the reasonable depends on distinguishing people from things. Moral considerations pertain to behavior of individuals that affects other people by acting on them directly or by acting on things in which they have an interest. The moral context is broad, for people have interests in almost everything, and almost any behavior may affect someone.

If reasonable and moral behavior were coextensive, then there would be no morality. Thus, there is no contrast at the extremes that bound the moral milieu, reason and morality being the same at one pole, and morality not existing at the other. These extremes meet in evolutionary naturalism: If it is moral to treat people as animals surviving, then reason augmenting instinct is the best criterion for behavior, and a separate discipline of morality is extraneous. Only between the extremes can reason and morality conflict.

Between the extremes, some moralists use "rational" to indicate conclusions that tend toward

moral behavior, and "practical" for conclusions that excusably do not. The use of these terms often constitutes special pleading, either to gain sympathy for a position that is not strictly reasonable but is "rational" (because it is "right"), or that is not strictly moral but is "practical" (because it "should" be done). These hedges hide the sharp distinction between people and things in the context of reason and morality. The rational and the practical are obviously reasonable in a way that they are not obviously either moral or immoral. Reasonable behavior is either moral, immoral, or amoral. When reason and morality conflict, there can be confusion, but no compromise.

Attacks on morality by reason disguised in practical dress are so common as to go almost without notice. The practical ousts morality as a determinant of behavior, particularly in industrialized nations. Many argue that the practical imperatives of survival preclude moral behavior even by those who want to be moral. If only it were practical to be moral, then all would gladly be so.

It is difficult to be moral in a world of limited food because the supreme moral principle is that of equity. The principle of equity is based on the belief that all human beings are moral equals with equal rights to the necessities of life. Differential treatment of human beings thus should be based only on their freely chosen actions and not on accidents of their birth and environment. Specific to this discussion, everyone has a right to an equal share of available food.

However, we find ourselves in a world about which many food and population experts assert the following:

1. One-third of the world's people (the West) consume two-thirds of the world's resources.

2. Two-thirds of the world's people (the Third World) are malnourished.

3. Equal distribution of the world's resources would result in everyone's being malnourished.

There is ample evidence that these statements are true, but for this discussion it is enough that many people in the West—particularly those who occupy positions of responsibility and power—understand and accept them.

These moral and factual beliefs drive one to this practical conclusion: Although morally we should share all food equally, and we in the West eat more than we need, equal sharing would be futile (unreasonable), for then no one would be well nourished. Thus, any food sharing is necessarily symbolic, for no practical action would alleviate the plight of the malnourished.

For example, practical action—moral as far as it goes—might be to reduce food consumption until every Westerner is just well nourished. But if the surplus were distributed equally to the other two-thirds of the world's people, they would still be malnourished. Thus, an easy excuse for not sharing at all is that it would neither solve the nourishment problem nor change the moral situation. Two-thirds would still be malnourished, and one-third would still be consuming more than equal shares of the world's food, to which everyone has equal rights.

Another argument for unequal distribution is as follows: All people are moral equals. Because everyone has a right to be well nourished, it would be immoral to take so much food from someone who has enough as to leave him without enough. Anyone who takes the food would be acting immorally, even if the taker is starving. This argument can go two ways. One could simply say that it would be immoral to deprive oneself of what one has. But if one wanted to discredit morality itself, one could claim that morality in this instance is self-contradictory. For if I behave morally by distributing food equally, I behave immorally by depriving someone (myself) of enough food to remain well nourished. And noticing that if all food were shared equally, everyone would be malnourished instead of just some, one might argue that it cannot be moral to deprive one person of his right to enough food so that two people have less than enough. Proper moral action must be to maintain the inequity, so at least one person can enjoy his rights.

Nevertheless, according to the highest principles of traditional Western morality, available food should be distributed equally even if everyone then will be malnourished. This is belabored by everyone who compares the earth to a lifeboat, a desert island, or a spaceship. In these situations, the strong are expected to take even a smaller share than the weak. There is no need for us to go overboard, however. We shall soon be as weak as anyone else if we just do our moral duty and distribute the food equally.

Given this, the well-nourished minority might try to buttress its position morally by attempting to solve the nourishment problem for everyone, either by producing enough food for everyone, or by humanely reducing the world's population to a size at which equal distribution of food would nourish everyone adequately. The difficulty with this is that national survival for the food-favored industrial nations requires maintenance of political and economic systems that depend on unequal distribution of limited goods.[1] In the present world context, it would be unreasonable (disastrous) for an industrialized nation to attempt to provide food for everybody. Who would pay for it? And after all, well-nourished citizens are obviously important to the survival of the nation. As for humanely reducing the world's population, there are no practical means for doing it. Thus, the practical expediencies of national survival preclude actions that might justify temporary unequal distribution with the claim that it is essential for solving the nourishment problem. Equal distribution is impossible without total (impractical) economic and political revolution.

These arguments are morally spurious. That food sufficient for well-nourished survival is the equal right of every human individual or nation is a specification of the higher principle that everyone has equal right to the necessities of life. The moral stress of the principle of equity is primarily on equal sharing, and only secondarily on what is being shared. The higher moral principle is of human *equity per se.* Consequently, the moral action is to distribute all food equally, *whatever the consequences.* This is the hard line apparently drawn by such moralists as Immanuel Kant and Noam Chomsky—but then, morality is hard. The conclusion may be unreasonable (impractical and irrational in conventional terms), but it is obviously moral. Nor should anyone purport surprise; it has always been understood that the claims of morality—if taken seriously—supersede those of conflicting reason.

One may even have to sacrifice one's life or one's nation to be moral in situations where practical behavior would preserve it. For example, if a prisoner of war undergoing torture is to be a (perhaps dead) patriot even when reason tells him that collaboration will hurt no one, he remains silent. Similarly, if one is to be moral, one distributes available food in equal shares (even if everyone then dies). That an action is necessary to save one's life is no excuse for behaving unpatriotically or immorally if one wishes to be a patriot or moral. No principle of morality absolves one of behaving immorally simply to save one's life or nation. There is a strict analogy here between adhering to moral principles for the sake of being moral, and adhering to Christian principles for the sake of being Christian. The moral world contains pits and lions, but one looks always to the highest light. The ultimate test always harks to the highest principle—recant or die—and it is pathetic to profess morality if one quits when the going gets rough.

I have put aside many questions of detail—such as the mechanical problems of distributing food—because detail does not alter the stark conclusion. If every human life is equal in value, then the equal distribution of the necessities of life is an extremely high, if not the highest, moral duty. It is at least high enough to override the excuse that by doing it one would lose one's own life. But many people cannot accept the view that one must distribute equally even if the nation collapses or all people die.

If everyone dies, then there will be no realm of morality. Practically speaking, sheer survival comes first. One can adhere to the principle of equity only if one exists. So it is rational to suppose that the principle of survival is morally higher than the principle of equity. And though one might not be able to argue for unequal distribution of food to save a nation—for nations can come and go—one might well argue that unequal distribution is necessary for the survival of the human species. That is, some large group—say one-third of the present world population—should be a least well-nourished for human survival.

However, from an individual standpoint, the human species—like the nation—is of no moral relevance. From a naturalistic standpoint, survival does come first; from a moralistic standpoint—as indicated above—survival may have to be sacrificed. In the milieu of morality, it is immaterial whether or not the human species survives as a result of individual moral behavior.

A possible way to resolve this conflict between reason and morality is to challenge the view that morality pertains only to the behavior of individual human beings. One way to do this is to break down the distinction between people and things. It would have to be established that such abstract things as "the people," "the nation," and "the human species" in themselves have moral status. Then they would have a right to survival just as human beings have a right to life: We should be concerned about the survival of these things not merely because human beings have an interest in them, but because it would be immoral *per se* to destroy them.

In the West, corporation law provides the theoretical basis for treating things as people.[2] Corporate entities such as the State, the Church, and trading companies have long enjoyed special status in Western society. The rights of corporate entities are precisely defined by a legal fiction, the concept of the corporate person. Christopher D. Stone says that corporate persons enjoy as many legal rights as, and sometimes more than, do individual human persons.[3] Thus, while most of us are not tempted to confuse ordinary things like stones and houses with people, almost everyone concurs with a legal system that treats corporate entities as people. The great familiarity and usefulness of this system supports the delusion that corporate entities have rights in common with, and are the moral equals of, individual human beings.

On these grounds, some argue that because of size, importance, and power of corporate entities, institutional rights have priority over the rights of individuals. Of course, to the extent that society is defined by the economy or the State, people are dependent on and subordinate to these institutions. Practically speaking, institutional needs come first; people's needs are satisfied perhaps coextensively with, but secondarily to, satisfying institutional needs. It is argued that to put individual human needs first would be both illogical and impractical, for people and their needs are defined only in the social context. Institutions come first because they are prerequisite to the very existence of people.

A difficulty with the above argument as a support for any given institution is that it provides merely for the priority of *some* institutions over human individuals, not, say, for the priority of the United States or the West. But it does appear to provide an argument for the priority of the human species.

Given that the human species has rights as a fictional person on the analogy of corporate rights, it would seem to be rational to place the right of survival of the species above that of individuals. Unless the species survives, no individual will survive, and thus an individual's right to life is subordinate to the species' right to survival. If species survival depends on the unequal distribution of food to maintain a healthy breeding stock, then it is morally right for some people to have plenty while others starve. Only if there is enough food to nourish everyone well does it follow that food should be shared equally.

This might be true if corporate entities actually do have moral status and moral rights. But obviously, the legal status of corporate entities as fictional persons does not make them moral equals or superiors of actual human persons. Legislators might profess astonishment that anyone would think that a corporate person is a *person* as people are, let alone a moral person. However, because the legal rights of corporate entities are based on individual rights, and because corporate entities are treated so much like persons, the transition is often made.

Few theorists today would argue that the state or the human species is a personal agent.[4] But all this means is that idealism is dead in theory. Unfortunately, its influence lives, so it is worth giving an argument to show that corporate entities are not real persons.

Corporate entities are not persons as you and I are in the explicit sense that we are self-conscious agents and they are not. Corporate entities are not *agents* at all, let alone moral agents. This is a good reason for not treating corporate entities even as fictional persons. The distinction between people and other things, to generalize, is that people are self-conscious agents, whereas things are not.

The possession of rights essentially depends on an entity's being self-conscious, i.e., on its actually being a person. If it is self-conscious, then it has a right to life. Self-consciousness is a necessary, but

not sufficient, condition for an entity's also being a responsible moral agent as most human beings are. A moral agent must have the capacity to be responsible, i.e., the capacity to choose and to act freely with respect to consequences that the agent does or can recognize and accept as its own choice and doing. Only a being who knows himself as a person, and who can effect choices and accept consequences, is a responsible moral agent.

On these grounds, moral equality rests on the actuality of moral agency based on reciprocal rights and responsibilities. One is responsible to something only if it can be responsible in return. Thus, we have responsibilities to other people, and they have reciprocal rights. We have no responsibilities to things as such, and they have no rights. If we care for things, it is because people have interests in them, not because things in themselves impose responsibilities on us.

That is, as stated early in this essay, morality essentially has to do with relations among people, among persons. It is nonsense to talk of things that cannot be moral agents as having responsibilities; consequently, it is nonsense to talk of whatever is not actually a person as having rights. It is deceptive even to talk of legal rights of a corporate entity. Those rights (and reciprocal responsibilities) actually pertain to individual human beings who have an interest in the corporate entity. The State or the human species have no rights at all, let alone rights superior to those of individuals.

The basic reason given for preserving a nation or the human species is that otherwise the milieu of morality would not exist. This is false so far as specific nations are concerned, but it is true that the existence of individuals depends on the existence of the species. However, although moral behavior is required of each individual, no principle requires that the realm of morality itself be preserved. Thus, we are reduced to the position that people's interest in preserving the human species is based primarily on the interest of each in individual survival. Having shown above that the principle of equity is morally superior to the principle of survival, we can conclude again that food should be shared equally even if this means the extinction of the human race.

Is there no way to produce enough food to nourish everyone well? Besides cutting down to the minimum, people in the West might quit feeding such nonhuman animals as cats and dogs. However, some people (e.g., Peter Singer) argue that mere sentience—the capacity to suffer pain—means that an animal is the moral equal of human beings.[5] I argue that because nonhuman animals are not moral agents, they do not share the rights of self-conscious responsible persons. And considering the profligacy of nature, it is rational to argue that if nonhuman animals have any rights at all, they include not the right to life, but merely the right to fight for life. In fact, if people in the West did not feed grain to cattle, sheep, and hogs, a considerable amount of food would be freed for human consumption. Even then, there might not be enough to nourish everyone well.

Let me remark that Stone and Singer attempt to break down the distinction between people on the one hand, and certain things (corporate entities) and nonhuman animals on the other, out of moral concern. However, there is another, profoundly antihumanitarian movement also attempting to break down the distinction. All over the world, heirs of Gobineau, Goebbels, and Hitler practice genocide and otherwise treat people as nonhuman animals and things in the name of the State. I am afraid that the consequences of treating entities such as corporations and nonhuman animals—that are not moral agents—as persons with rights will not be that we will treat national parks and chickens the way we treat people, but that we will have provided support for those who treat people the way we now treat nonhuman animals and things.

The benefits of modern society depend in no small part on the institution of corporation law. Even if the majority of these benefits are to the good—of which I am by no means sure—the legal fiction of corporate personhood still elevates corporate needs above the needs of people. In the present context, reverence for corporate entities leads to the spurious argument that the present world imbalance of food and resources is morally justified in the name of the higher rights of sovereign nations, or even of the human species, the survival of which is said to be more important than the right of any individual to life.

This conclusion is morally absurd. This is not, however, the fault of morality. We *should* share all food equally, at least until everyone is well-nour-

ished. Besides food, *all* the necessities of life should be shared, at least until everyone is adequately supplied with a humane minimum. The hard conclusion remains that we should share all food equally even if this means that everyone starves and the human species becomes extinct. But, of course, the human race would survive even equal sharing, for after enough people died, the remainder could be well-nourished on the food that remained. But this grisly prospect does not show that anything is wrong with the principle of equity. Instead, it shows that something is profoundly wrong with the social institutions in which sharing the necessities of life equally is "impractical" and "irrational."

In another ideological frame, moral behavior might also be practical and rational. As remarked above, equal sharing can be accomplished only through total economic and political revolution. Obviously, this is what is needed.

Notes

1. See Richard Watson, "The Limits of World Order," *Alternatives: A Journal of World Policy*, I (1975), 487–513.

2. See Christopher D. Stone, *Should Trees Have Standing? Toward Legal Rights for Natural Objects* (Los Altos, Calif.: William Kaufman, 1974). Stone proposes that to protect such things as national parks, we should give them legal personhood as we do corporations.

3. Ibid., p. 47: "It is more and more the individual human being, with his consciousness, that is the legal fiction." Also: "The legal system does the best it can to maintain the illusion of the reality of the individual human being." (footnote 125) Many public figures have discovered that they have a higher legal status if they incorporate themselves than they do as individual persons.

4. Stone (ibid., p. 47) does say that "institutions . . . have wills, minds, purposes, and inertias that are in very important ways their own, i.e., that can transcend and survive changes in the consciousness of the individual humans who supposedly comprise them, and whom they supposedly serve," but I do not think Stone actually believes that corporate entities are persons like you and me.

5. See Peter Singer, *Animal Liberation* (New York: The New York Review of Books/Random House, 1975).

Questions for Analysis

1. *Describe the conflict between the "reasonable" and the "moral."*

2. *Why does Watson feel that arguments for the morality of unequal distribution fail?*

3. *Why does Watson say: "It is difficult to be moral in a world of limited food because the supreme moral principle is that of equity"? Do you accept the supremacy of equity as a moral principle?*

4. *From what higher principle does Watson say people have a right to food sufficient for well-nourished survival?*

5. *Do you agree with Watson that morality in some cases may be irrational? Is it necessary first to clarify Watson's use of the term* irrational?

6. *If morality may be unreasonable, does this create any special problems for the moralist?*

7. *Do any of the principles of Chapter 1 support the claim that "if one is to be moral, one distributes available food in equal shares (even if everyone then dies)"?*

Equality, Entitlements, and the Distribution of Income

John Arthur

As indicated in the chapter, an alternative to the positions that argue for an obligation to share or not to share food is the position that views sharing as morally permissible but not obligatory. In this essay, professor of philosophy John Arthur argues that sharing ultimately is an act of benevolence. At the same time, he claims that there may be occasions when we have a duty to be so benevolent.

Arthur begins by observing an ambivalence in our moral code. Sometimes we feel obliged to help the needy; other times we feel justified in keeping what we have, even though our sacrifice might cause greater evil to be avoided. How can we resolve the tension?

Singer in his essay suggested a principle of greater moral evil: Any time we can prevent something bad without sacrificing anything of comparable moral significance, we ought to do it. Arthur rejects this response, arguing that it ignores the essential role of entitlements in our moral code. Arthur then goes on to discuss entitlements in terms of rights and desert and demonstrates how they are embedded in our moral outlook. Indeed, by dissecting the nature of morality, with

---

Thanks to Aleta Arthur, Clement Dore, and William Shaw for helpful comments on an earlier version of this paper, and especially to Richard B. Brandt, whose influence is apparent throughout.

special attention to the kind of morality we want to endorse, Arthur champions entitlements as a necessary part of an ideal moral code.

Be careful not to misconstrue Arthur. He is not making entitlements absolute; he is not saying that individuals never have an obligation to help the needy. Quite the opposite: He acknowledges that we likely have obligations to help where there is no substantial cost to ourselves. By the same token, in Arthur's view it is at least sometimes moral to invoke rights and duties as justification for not giving aid.

Introduction

My guess is that everyone who reads these words is wealthy by comparison with the poorest millions of people on our planet. Not only do we have plenty of money for food, clothing, housing, and other necessities, but a fair amount is left over for far less important purchases like phonograph records, fancy clothes, trips, intoxicants, movies, and so on. And what's more, we don't usually give thought to whether or not we ought to spend our money on such luxuries rather than to give it to those who need it more; we just assume it's ours to do with as we please.

Peter Singer, "Famine, Affluence, and Morality," and Richard Watson, "Reason and Morality in a World of Limited Food" [both reprinted in this volume] argue that our assumption is wrong, that we should not buy luxuries when others are in severe need. But are they correct? In the first two sections of this paper my aim is to get into focus just what their arguments are, and to evaluate them. Both Singer and Watson, it seems to me, ignore an important feature of our moral code, namely that it allows people who deserve or have rights to their earnings to keep them.

But the fact that our code encourages a form of behavior is not a complete defense, for it is possible that our current moral attitudes are mistaken. Sections 3 and 4 consider this possibility from two angles: universalizability and the notion of an ideal moral code. Neither of these approaches, I argue, requires that desert and rights be sacrificed in the name of redistribution.

1. Equality and the Duty to Aid

What does our moral code have to say about helping people in need? Watson emphasizes what he calls the "principle of equity." Since "all human life is of equal value," and difference in treatment should be "based on freely chosen actions and not accidents of birth or environment," he thinks that we have "equal rights to the necessities of life." To distribute food unequally assumes that some lives are worth more than others, an assumption which, he says, we do not accept. Watson believes, in fact, that we put such importance on the "equity principle" that it should not be violated even if unequal distribution is the only way for anybody to survive. (Leaving aside for the moment whether or not he is correct about our code, it seems to me that if it really did require us to commit mass suicide rather than allow inequality in wealth, then we would want to abandon it for a more suitable set of rules. But more on that later.)

Is Watson correct in assuming that all life is of equal value? Did Adolph Hitler and Martin Luther King, for example, lead two such lives? Clearly one did far more good and less harm than the other. Nor are moral virtues like courage, kindness, and trustworthiness equally distributed among people. So there are at least two senses in which people are not morally equal.

Yet the phrase "All men are equal" has an almost platitudinous ring, and many of us would not hesitate to say that equality is a cornerstone of our morality. But what does it mean? It seems to me that we might have in mind one of two things. First is an idea that Thomas Jefferson expressed in the *Declaration of Independence.* "All men are created equal" meant, for him, that no man is the moral inferior of another, that, in other words, there are certain rights which all men share equally, including life and liberty. We are entitled to pursue our own lives with a minimum of interference from others, and no person is the natural slave of another. But, as Jefferson also knew, equality in that sense does not require equal distribution of the necessities of life, only that we not interfere with one another, allowing instead every person the liberty to pursue his own affairs, so long as he does not violate the rights of his fellows.

Others, however, have something different in mind when they speak of human equality. I want to develop this second idea by recounting briefly the details of Singer's argument in "Famine, Affluence, and Morality." He first argues that two general moral principles are widely accepted, and then that those principles imply an obligation to eliminate starvation.

The first principle is simply that "suffering and death from lack of food, shelter and medical care are bad." Some may be inclined to think that the mere existence of such an evil in itself places an obligation on others, but that is, of course, the problem which Singer addresses. I take it that he is not begging the question in this obvious way and will argue from the existence of evil to the obligation of others to eliminate it. But how, exactly, does he establish this? The second principle, he thinks, shows the connection, but it is here that controversy arises.

This principle, which I will call the greater moral evil rule, is as follows:

> If it is in our power to prevent something bad from happening, without thereby sacrificing anything of comparable moral importance, we ought, morally, to do it.[1]

In other words, people are entitled to keep their earnings only if there is no way for them to prevent a greater evil by giving them away. Providing others with food, clothing, and housing would generally be of more importance than buying luxuries, so the greater moral evil rule now requires substantial redistribution of wealth.

Certainly there are few, if any, of us who live by that rule, although that hardly shows we are *justified* in our way of life; we often fail to live up to our own standards. Why does Singer think our shared morality requires that we follow the greater moral evil rule? What arguments does he give for it?

He begins with an analogy. Suppose you came across a child drowning in a shallow pond. Certainly we feel it would be wrong not to help. Even if saving the child meant we must dirty our clothes, we would emphasize that those clothes are not of comparable significance to the child's life. The greater moral evil rule thus seems a natural way of capturing why we think it would be wrong not to help.

But the argument for the greater moral evil rule is not limited to Singer's claim that it explains our feelings about the drowning child or that it appears "uncontroversial." Moral equality also enters the picture. Besides the Jeffersonian idea that we share certain rights equally, most of us are also attracted to another type of equality, namely that like amounts of suffering (or happiness) are of equal significance, no matter who is experiencing them. I cannot reasonably say that, while my pain is no more severe than yours, I am somehow special and it's more important that mine be alleviated. Objectivity requires us to admit the opposite, that no one has a unique status which warrants such special pleading. So equality demands equal consideration of interests as well as respect for certain rights.

But if we fail to give to famine relief and instead purchase a new car when the old one will do, or buy fancy clothes for a friend when his or her old ones are perfectly good, are we not assuming that the relatively minor enjoyment we or our friends **may get is as important as another person's life**? And that is a form of prejudice; we are acting as if people were not equal in the sense that their interests deserve equal consideration. We are giving special consideration to ourselves or to our group, rather like a racist does. Equal consideration of interests thus leads naturally to the greater moral evil rule.

2. Rights and Desert

Equality, in the sense of giving equal consideration to equally serious needs, is part of our moral code. And so we are led, quite rightly I think, to the conclusion that we should prevent harm to others if in doing so we do not sacrifice anything of comparable moral importance. But there is also another side to the coin, one which Singer and Watson ignore. This can be expressed rather awkwardly by the notion of entitlements. These fall into two broad categories, rights and desert. A few examples will show what I mean.

All of us could help others by giving away or allowing others to use our bodies. While your life may be shortened by the loss of a kidney or less enjoyable if lived with only one eye, those costs are probably not comparable to the loss experienced by a person who will die without any kidney or who is totally blind. We can even imagine persons who will actually be harmed in some way by your not granting sexual favors to them. Perhaps the absence of a sexual partner would cause psychological harm or even rape. Now suppose that you can prevent this evil without sacrificing anything of comparable importance. Obviously such relations may not be pleasant, but according to the greater moral evil rule, that is not enough; to be justified in refusing, you must show that the unpleasantness you would experience is of equal importance to the harm you are preventing. Otherwise, the rule says you must consent.

If anything is clear, however, it is that our code does not *require* such heroism; you are entitled to keep your second eye and kidney and not bestow sexual favors on anyone who may be harmed without them. The reason for this is often expressed in terms of rights; it's your body, you have a right to it, and that weighs against whatever duty you have to help. To sacrifice a kidney for a stranger is to do more than is required, it's heroic.

Moral rights are normally divided into two categories. Negative rights are rights of noninterference. The right to life, for example, is a right not to be killed. Property rights, the right to privacy, and the right to exercise religious freedom are also negative, requiring only that people leave others alone and not interfere.

Positive rights, however, are rights of recipience. By not putting their children up for adoption, parents give them various positive rights, including the rights to be fed, clothed, and housed. If I agree to share in a business venture, my promise creates a right of recipience, so that when I back out of the deal, I've violated your right.

Negative rights also differ from positive in that the former are natural; the ones you have depend on what you are. If lower animals lack rights to life or liberty it is because there is a relevant difference between them and us. But the positive rights you may have are not natural; they arise because others have promised, agreed, or contracted to give you something.

Normally, then, a duty to help a stranger in need is not the result of a right he has. Such a right would be positive, and since no contract or promise was made, no such right exists. An exception to this would be a lifeguard who contracts to watch out for someone's children. The parent whose child drowns would in this case be doubly wronged. First, the lifeguard should not have cruelly or thoughtlessly ignored the child's interests, and second, he ought not to have violated the rights of the parents that he help. Here, unlike Singer's case, we can say there are rights at stake. Other bystanders also act wrongly by cruelly ignoring the child, but unlike the lifeguard they do not violate anybody's rights. Moral rights are one factor to be weighed, but we also have other obligations; I am not claiming that rights are all we need to consider. That view, like the greater moral evil rule, trades simplicity for accuracy. In fact, our code expects us to help people in need as well as to respect negative and positive rights. But we are also entitled to invoke our own rights as justification for not giving to distant strangers or when the cost to us is substantial, as when we give up an eye or a kidney.

Rights come in a variety of shapes and sizes, and people often disagree about both their shape and size. Can a woman kill an unborn child because of her right to control her body? Does mere inheritance transfer rights to property? Do dolphins have a right to live? While some rights are widely accepted, others are controversial.

One more comment about rights, then we'll look at desert. Watson's position, which I criticized for other reasons earlier, is also mistaken because he ignores important rights. He claims that we must pay no attention to "accidents of birth and environment" and base our treatment of people on "what they freely choose." But think about how you will (or did) select a spouse or lover. Are you not entitled to consider such "accidents of birth and environment" as attractiveness, personality, and intelligence? It is, after all, your future, and it is certainly a part of our shared moral code that you have a right to use those (or whatever) criteria you wish in selecting a mate. It is at best an exaggeration to say we must always "ignore accidents of birth and environment" in our treatment of people.

Desert is a second form of entitlement. Suppose, for example, an industrious farmer manages through hard work to produce a surplus of food for the winter while a lazy neighbor spends his summer fishing. Must our industrious farmer ignore his hard work and give the surplus away because his neighbor or his family will suffer? What again seems clear is that we have more than one factor to weigh. Not only should we compare the consequences of his keeping it with his giving it away; we also should weigh the fact that one farmer deserves the food, he earned it through his hard work. Perhaps his deserving the product of his labor is outweighed by the greater need of his lazy neighbor, or perhaps it isn't, but being outweighed is in any case not the same as weighing nothing!

Desert can be negative, too. The fact that the Nazi war criminal did what he did means he deserves punishment, that we have a reason to send him to jail. Other considerations, for example the fact that nobody will be deterred by his suffering, or that he is old and harmless, may weigh against punishment and so we may let him go; but again that does not mean he doesn't still deserve to be punished.

Our moral code gives weight to both the greater moral evil principle and entitlements. The former emphasizes equality, claiming that from an objective point of view all comparable suffering, whoever its victim, is equally significant. It encourages us to take an impartial look at all the various effects of our actions; it is thus forward-looking. When we consider matters of entitlement, however, our attention is directed to the past. Whether we have rights to money, property, eyes, or whatever, depends on how we came to possess them. If they were acquired by theft rather than from birth or through gift exchange, then the right is suspect. Desert, like rights, is also backward-looking, emphasizing past effort or past transgressions which now warrant reward or punishment.

Our commonly shared morality thus requires that we ignore neither consequences nor entitlements, neither the future results of our action nor relevant events in the past. It encourages people to help others in need, especially when it's a friend or someone we are close to geographically, and when the cost is not significant. But it also gives weight to rights and desert, so that we are not usually obligated to give to strangers.

One path is still open as a defense of the greater moral evil rule, and it deserves comment. I have assumed throughout that Singer wants to emphasize the great disparity in the amount of enjoyment someone may get from, say, a new car, as compared with the misery that could be prevented by using the money to save another's life. The fact that the two are not comparable means that the money should not be spent on the car. It is possible to interpret the rule differently, however. By admitting that having rights and deserving things are also of moral significance, Singer could accept what I have said so that the greater moral evil rule would survive intact.

The problem with this response, however, is that the greater moral evil rule has now become an almost empty platitude, urging nothing more than that we should prevent something bad unless we have adequate moral reason not to do so. Since rights and desert often provide such reasons, the rule would say nothing useful about our obligation to help others, and it certainly would not require us to "reduce ourselves to the level of marginal utility" so that the "consumer society" would "slow down and perhaps disappear" as Singer claims. I will therefore assume he would not accept such an interpretation of his view, that entitlements are not among the sacrifices which could balance off the suffering caused by failing to help people in need.

But unless we are moral relativists, the mere fact that entitlements are an important part of our moral code does not in itself justify such a role. Singer and Watson can perhaps best be seen as moral reformers, advocating the rejection of rules which provide for distribution according to rights and desert. Certainly the fact that in the past our moral code condemned suicide and racial mixing while condoning slavery should not convince us that a more enlightened moral code, one which we would want to support, would take such positions. Rules which define acceptable behavior are continually changing, and we must allow for the replacement of inferior ones.

Why should we not view entitlements as examples of inferior rules we are better off without? What could justify our practice of evaluating actions by looking backward to rights and desert instead of just to their consequences? One answer is that more fundamental values than rights and desert are at stake, namely fairness, justice, and respect. Failure to reward those who earn good grades or promotions is wrong because it's *unfair*; ignoring past guilt shows a lack of regard for *justice*; and failure to respect rights to life, privacy, or religious choice suggests a lack of *respect for other persons*.

Some people may be persuaded by those remarks, feeling that entitlements are now on an acceptably firm foundation. But an advocate of equality may well want to question why fairness, justice, and respect for persons should matter. But since it is no more obvious that preventing suffering matters than that fairness, respect, and justice do, we again seem to have reached an impasse.

3. Universalizability

It is sometimes thought that we can choose between competing moral rules by noting which ones are compatible with some more fundamental rule. One such fundamental standard is attributed to Kant, though it is also rooted in traditional Christian thought. "Do unto others as you would have them do unto you" and the Kantian categorical imperative, "Act only on maxims that you can will would become universal laws," express an idea some think is basic to *all* moral rules. The suggestion is that if you think what you're doing is right, then you have got to be willing to universalize your judgment, that is, to acknowledge that anyone in similar circumstances would be correct if he were to follow the same rule.

Such familiar reasoning can be taken in two very different ways. The first requires only that a person not make himself an exception, that he live up to his own standard. This type of universalizability, however, cannot help choose between the two rules. An advocate of rights and desert would surely agree that whether he were the deserving or undeserving one, whether he had the specific right or did not have it, entitlements still should not be ignored. Nothing about the position of those supporting rights and desert suggests that they must make exceptions for themselves; such rules are in that sense universalizable. But the advocate of the greater moral evil rule can also be counted on to claim that he too should not be made an exception, and that *ignoring* entitlements in favor of the greater moral evil rule is the proper course whether or not he would benefit from the policy. Both views, then, could be universalized in the first sense.

But if we understand universalizability in another sense, neither of the rules passes the test. If being "willing to universalize the judgment" means that a supporter of a particular moral rule would be equally happy with the result were the roles reversed, then there is doubt whether either is universalizable. The rights advocate cannot

promise always to like the outcome; he probably would *prefer*, were the tables turned and his life depended on somebody not keeping his rightfully owned income, that entitlements be ignored in that instance. But his opponent cannot pass the test either, since he would likely prefer that rights and desert *not* be ignored were he in a position to benefit from them. But in any case it is not at all clear why we should expect people who make moral judgments to be neutral as to which position they occupy. Must a judge who thinks justice requires that a murderer go to jail agree that he would prefer jail if he were the murderer? It seems that all he must do to universalize his judgment is agree that it would be *right* that he go to jail if the tables were turned, that, in other words, he is not exempt from the rules. But that is a test, as I said, which supporters of entitlements can pass.

So the test of universalizability does not provide grounds for rejecting entitlement rules, and we are once again at an impasse. A second possibility is to view the egalitarian as a moral reformer. Then, perhaps, the criticism of entitlements can be defended as part of a more reasonable and effective moral system. In the final section I look in detail at the idea that rights and desert would not be part of a such ideal moral code, one which we would support if we were fully rational.

4. Entitlements and the Ideal Moral Code

The idea I want now to consider is that part of our code should be dropped, so that people could no longer invoke rights and desert as justification for not making large sacrifices for strangers. In place of entitlements would be a rule requiring that any time we can prevent something bad without sacrificing anything of comparable moral significance we ought to do it. Our current code, however, allows people to say that while they would do more good with their earnings, still they have rights to the earnings, the earnings are deserved, and so need not be given away. The crucial question is whether we want to have such entitlement rules in our code, or whether we should reject them in favor of the greater moral evil rule.

Universalizability, I argued, gives no clear answer to this. Each position also finds a certain amount of support within our code, either from the idea of equal consideration of interests or from our concerns about fairness, justice, and respect for other persons. The problem to be resolved, then, is whether there are other reasons to drop entitlement rules in favor of the greater moral evil rule.

I believe that our best procedure is not to think about this or that specific rule, drawing analogies, refining it, and giving counterexamples, but to focus instead on the nature of morality as a whole. What is a moral code? What do we want it to do? What type of code do we want to support? These questions will give us a fresh perspective from which to consider the merits of rules which allow people to appeal to rights and desert and to weigh the issue of whether our present code should be reformed.

We can begin with the obvious: A moral code is a system of rules designed to guide people's conduct. As such, it has characteristics in common with other systems of rules. Virtually every organization has rules which govern the conduct of members; clubs, baseball leagues, corporations, bureaucracies, profession associations, even *The* Organization all have rules. Another obvious point is this: What the rules are depends on why the organization exists. Rules function to enable people to accomplish goals which lead them to organize in the first place. Some rules, for example, "Don't snitch on fellow mafioso," "Pay dues to the fraternity," and "Don't give away trade secrets to competing companies," serve in obvious ways. Other times the real purposes of rules are controversial, as when doctors do not allow advertising by fellow members of the AMA.

Frequently rules reach beyond members of a specific organization, obligating everyone who is capable of following them to do so. These include costs of civil and criminal law, etiquette, custom, and morality. But before discussing the specific purposes of moral rules, it will be helpful to look briefly at some of the similarities and differences between these more universal codes.

First, the sanctions imposed on rule violators vary among different types of codes. While in our legal code, transgressions are punished by fines, jail, or repayment of damages, informal sanctions of praise, blame, or guilt encourage conformity to the rules of morality and etiquette. Another difference is that while violation of a moral rule is always a serious affair, this need not be so for legal rules of etiquette and custom. Many of us think it unimportant whether a fork is on the left side of a plate or whether an outmoded and widely ignored Sunday closing law is violated, but violation of a moral rule is not ignored. Indeed, that a moral rule has lost its importance is often shown by its demotion to status of mere custom.

A third difference is that legal rules, unlike rules of morality, custom, and etiquette, provide for a specific person or procedure that is empowered to alter the rules. If Congress acts to change the tax laws, then as of the date stated in the statute the rules are changed. Similarly for the governing rules of social clubs, government bureaucracies, and the AMA. Rules of custom, morals, and etiquette also change, of course, but they do so in a less precise and much more gradual fashion, with no person or group specifically empowered to make changes.

This fact, that moral rules are *in a sense* beyond the power of individuals to change, does not show that rules of morality, any more than those of etiquette, are objective in the same sense that scientific laws are. All that needs to happen for etiquette or morality to change is for people to change certain practices, namely the character traits they praise and blame, or the actions they approve and disapprove. Scientific laws, however, are discovered, not invented by society, and so are beyond human control. The law that the boiling point of water increases as its pressure increases cannot be changed by humans, either individually or collectively. Such laws are a part of the fabric of nature.

But the fact that moral rules, like legal ones, are not objective in the same sense as scientific ones does not mean that there is no objective standard of right or wrong, that one code is as good as another, or even that the "right thing to do" is just what the moral code currently followed in our society teaches is right. Like the rules of a fraternity or corporation, legal and moral rules can serve their purposes either well or poorly, and whether they do is a matter of objective fact. Further, if a moral code doesn't serve its purpose, we have good reason to criticize all or part of it, to ignore it, and to think of a way to change it, just as its serving us well provides a good reason to obey. In important respects morality is not at all subjective.

Take, for example, a rule which prohibits homosexual behavior. Suppose it serves no useful purpose, but only increases the burdens of guilt, shame, and social rejection borne by 10% of our population. If this is so, we have good reason to ignore the rule. On the other hand, if rules against killing and lying help us to accomplish what we want from a moral code, we have good reason to support those rules. Morality is created, and as with other systems of rules which we devise, a particular rule may or may not further the shared human goals and interests which motivated its creation. There is thus a connection between what we ought to do and how well a code serves its purposes. If a rule serves well the general purposes of a moral code, then we have reason to support it, and if we have reason to support it, we also have reason to obey it. But if, on the other hand, a rule is useless, or if it frustrates the purposes of morality, we have reason neither to support nor to follow it. All of this suggests the following conception of a right action: Any action is right which is approved by an ideal moral code, one which it is rational for us to support. Which code we would want to support would depend, of course, on which one is able to accomplish the purposes of morality.

If we are to judge actions in this way, by reference to what an ideal moral code would require, we must first have a clear notion of just what purposes morality is meant to serve. And here again the comparison between legal and moral rules is instructive. Both systems discourage certain types of behavior—killing, robbing, and beating—while encouraging others—repaying debts, keeping important agreements, and providing for one's children. The purpose which both have in discouraging various behaviors is obvious. Such negative rules help keep people from causing harm. Think, for example, of how we are first taught it is wrong to hit a baby brother or sister. Parents explain the rule by emphasizing that it hurts the infant when we hit him. Promoting the welfare of ourselves, our friends and family, and to a lesser degree all who have the capacity to be harmed is the primary purpose of negative moral rules. It's how we learn them as children and why we support them as adults.

The same can be said of positive rules, rules which encourage various types of behavior. Our own welfare, as well as that of friends, family, and others, depends on general acceptance of rules which encourage keeping promises, fulfilling con-tracts, and meeting the needs of our children. Just try to imagine a society in which promises or agreements mean nothing, or where family members took no concern for one another. A life without positive or negative rights would be as Thomas Hobbes long ago observed: nasty, brutish, and short.

Moral rules thus serve two purposes. They promote our own welfare by discouraging acts of violence and promoting social conventions like promising and paying debts, and second, they perform the same service for our family, friends, and others. We have reason to support a moral code because we care about our own welfare, and because we care about the well-being of others. For most of us the ideal moral code, the one we would support because it best fulfills these purposes, is the code which is most effective in promoting general welfare.

But can everyone be counted on to share these concerns? Think, for example, of an egoist, who only desires that *he* be happy. Such a person, if he existed, would obviously like a code which maximizes his own welfare. How can we hope to get agreement about which code it is rational to support, if different people expect different things from moral rules?[2]

Before considering these questions, I want to mention two preliminary points. First, the problem with egoism is that it tends to make morality relative. If we are going to decide moral disputes by considering what would be required by the code which it is rational for people to support, then we must reach agreement about what that code is. Otherwise the right action for an altruist, the one which is required by the code which it's rational for him to support, may be the wrong act for the egoist. Yet how can the very same act done in identical circumstances be wrong for one person yet right for another? Maybe morality is relative in that way, but if so the prospects for peaceful resolution of important disputes is lessened, a result not to be hoped for.

My second point is that while we certainly do not want to assume people are perfect altruists, we also do not want to give people less credit than they deserve. There is some evidence, for example, that concern for others in our species is part of our biological heritage. Some geneticists think that many animals, particularly higher ones, take an innate interest in the welfare of other members of their species.[3] Other researchers argue that feelings of benevolence originate naturally, through classical conditioning; we develop negative associations with our own pain behavior (since we are then in pain) and this attitude becomes generalized to the pain behavior of others.[4] If either of these is true, egoism might be far more unusual than is commonly supposed, perhaps rare enough that it can be safely ignored.

There is also a line of reasoning which suggests that disagreement about which moral code to support need not be as deep as is often thought. What sort of code in fact *would* a rational egoist support? He would first think of proposing one which allows him to do anything whatsoever that he desires, while requiring that others ignore their own happiness and do what is in his interests. But here enters a family of considerations which will bring us back to the merits of entitlements versus the greater moral evil rule. Our egoist is contemplating what code to *support*, which means going before the public and trying to win general acceptance of his proposed rules. Caring for nobody else, he might secretly prefer the code I mentioned, yet it would hardly make sense for him to work for its public adoption since others are unlikely to put his welfare above the happiness of themselves and their families. So it looks as if the code an egoist would actually support might not be all that different from the ideal (welfare maximizing) code; he would be wasting his time to advocate rules that serve only his own interests because they have no chance of public acceptance.

The lesson to be learned here is a general one: The moral code it is rational for us to support must be practical; it must actually work. This means, among other things, that it must be able to gain the support of almost everyone.

But the code must be practical in other respects as well. I have emphasized that it is wrong to ignore the possibilities of altruism, but it is also important that a code not assume people are more unselfish than they are. Rules that would work only for angels are not the ones it is rational to support for humans. Second, an ideal code cannot assume we are more objective than we are; we often tend to rationalize when our own interests are at stake, and a rational person will also keep that in mind when choosing a moral code. Finally, it is not rational to support a code which assumes we have perfect knowledge.

We are often mistaken about the consequences of what we do, and a workable code must take that into account as well.

I want now to bring these various considerations together in order to decide whether or not to reject entitlements in favor of the greater moral evil rule. I will assume that the egoist is not a serious obstacle to acceptance of a welfare maximizing code, either because egoists are, like angels, merely imaginary, or because a practical egoist would only support a code which can be expected to gain wide support. We still have to ask whether entitlements would be included in a welfare maximizing code. The initial temptation is to substitute the greater moral evil rule for entitlements, requiring people to prevent something bad whenever the cost to them is less significant than the benefit to another. Surely, we might think, total welfare would be increased by a code requiring people to give up their savings if a greater evil can be prevented.

I think, however, that this is wrong, that an ideal code would provide for rights and would encourage rewarding according to desert. My reasons for thinking this stem from the importance of insuring that a moral code really does, in fact, work. Each of the three practical considerations mentioned above now enters the picture. First, it will be quite difficult to get people to accept a code which requires that they give away their savings, extra organs, or anything else merely because they can avoid a greater evil for a stranger. Many people simply wouldn't do it: they aren't that altruistic. If the code attempts to require it anyway, two results would likely follow. First, because many would not live up to the rules, there would be a tendency to create feelings of guilt in those who keep their savings in spite of having been taught it is wrong, as well as conflict between those who meet their obligations and those who do not. And, second, a more realistic code, one which doesn't expect more than can be accomplished, may actually result in more giving. It's a bit like trying to influence how children spend their money. Often they will buy less candy if rules allow them to do so occasionally but they are praised for spending on other things than if its purchase is prohibited. We cannot assume that making a charitable act a requirement will always encourage such behavior. Impractical rules not only create guilt and social conflict, they often tend to encourage the opposite of the desired result. By giving people the right to use their savings for themselves, yet praising those who do not exercise the right but help others instead, we have struck a good balance; the rules are at once practical yet reasonably effective.

Similar practical considerations would also influence our decision to support rules that allow people to keep what they deserve. For most people, working is not their favorite activity. If we are to prosper, however, goods and services must be produced. Incentives are therefore an important motivation, and one such incentive for work is income. Our code encourages work by allowing people to keep a large part of what they earn, indeed that's much the point of entitlements. "I worked hard for it, so I can keep it" is an oft-heard expression. If we eliminate this rule from our code and ask people to follow the greater moral evil rule instead, the result would likely be less work done and so less total production. Given a choice between not working and continuing to work knowing the efforts should go to benefit others, many would choose not to work.

Moral rules should be practical in a third sense, too. They cannot assume people are either more unbiased or more knowledgeable than they are. This fact has many implications for the sorts of rules we would want to include in a welfare maximizing code. For example, we may be tempted to avoid slavish conformity to counterproductive rules by allowing people to break promises whenever they think doing so would increase total welfare. But again we must not ignore human nature, in this case our tendency to give special weight to our own welfare and our inability to be always objective in tracing the effects of our actions. While we would not want to teach that promises must never be broken no matter what the consequences, we also would not want to encourage breaking promises any time a person can convince himself the results of doing so would be better than if he kept his word.

Similar considerations apply to the greater moral evil rule. Imagine a situation where someone feels he can prevent an evil befalling himself by taking what he needs from a large store. The idea that he's preventing something bad from happening (to himself) without sacrificing anything of compara-

ble moral significance (the store won't miss the goods) would justify robbery. Although sometimes a particular act of theft really is welfare maximizing, it does not follow that we should support a *rule* which allows theft whenever the robber is preventing a greater evil. Such a rule, to work, would require more objectivity and more knowledge of long-term consequences than we have. Here again, including rights in our moral code serves a useful role, discouraging the tendency to rationalize our behavior by underestimating the harm we may cause to others or exaggerating the benefits that may accrue to ourselves.

The first sections of this paper attempted to show that our moral code is a bit schizophrenic. It seems to pull us in opposite directions, sometimes toward helping people who are in need, other times toward the view that rights and desert justify keeping things we have even if greater evil could be avoided were we to give away our extra eye or our savings account. This apparent inconsistency led us to a further question: Is the emphasis on entitlements really defensible, or should we try to resolve the tension in our own code by adopting the greater moral evil rule and ignoring entitlements? In this section I considered the idea that we might choose between entitlements and the greater moral evil rule by paying attention to the general nature of a moral code; and in particular to the sort of code we might want to support. I argued that all of us, including egoists, have reason to support a code which promotes the welfare of everyone who lives under it. That idea, of an ideal moral code which it is rational for everyone to support, provides a criterion for deciding which rules are sound and which ones we should support.

My conclusion is a conservative one: Concern that our moral code encourages production and not fail because it unrealistically assumes people are more altruistic or objective than they are means that our rules giving people rights to their possessions and encouraging distribution according to desert should be part of an ideal moral code. And since this is so, it is not always wrong to invoke rights or claim that money is deserved as justification for not giving aid, even when something worse could be prevented by offering help. The welfare maximizing moral code would not require us to maximize welfare in each individual case.

I have not yet discussed just how much weight should be given to entitlements, only that they are important and should not be ignored as Singer and Watson suggest. Certainly an ideal moral code would not allow people to overlook those in desperate need by making entitlements absolute, any more than it would ignore entitlements. But where would it draw the line?

It's hard to know, of course, but the following seems to me to be a sensible stab at an answer. Concerns about discouraging production and the general adherence to the code argue strongly against expecting too much; yet on the other hand, to allow extreme wealth in the face of grinding poverty would seem to put too much weight on entitlements. It seems to me, then, that a reasonable code would require people to help when there is no substantial cost to themselves, that is, when what they are sacrificing would not mean *significant* reduction in their own or their families' level of happiness. Since most people's savings accounts and nearly everybody's second kidney are not insignificant, entitlements would in those cases outweigh another's need. But if what is at stake is trivial, as dirtying one's clothes would normally be, then an ideal moral code would not allow rights to override the greater evil that can be prevented. Despite our code's unclear and sometimes schizophrenic posture, it seems to me that these judgments are not that different from our current moral attitudes. We tend to blame people who waste money on trivia when they could help others in need, yet not to expect people to make large sacrifices to distant strangers. An ideal moral code thus might not be a great deal different from our own.

Notes

1. Singer also offers a "weak" version of this principle which, it seems to me, is *too* weak. It requires giving aid only if the gift is of *no* moral significance to the giver. But since even minor embarrassment or small amounts of happiness are not completely without moral importance, this weak principle implies little or no obligation to aid, even to the drowning child.

2. This difficulty leads many to think the choice of a code should be made behind a "veil of ignorance" about one's particular station in life, talents, class, and religious or other moral values. The major proponent of this view is John Rawls, *A Theory of Justice* (Cambridge: Harvard University Press, 1971).

3. Stephen Jay Gould, "So Cleverly Kind an Animal" in *Ever Since Darwin* (New York: W. W. Norton Co., 1977).

4. Richard B. Brandt, *Theory of Right and Good* (New York: Oxford University Press, 1979).

Questions for Analysis

1. What is the "greater moral evil principle"?

2. What does Arthur mean by "entitlements"?

3. What is the difference between negative and positive rights?

4. Arthur claims that the greater moral evil principle is forward-looking, while matters of entitlement are directed to the past. What does he mean?

5. In what sense can both the greater moral evil rule and the rights-and-desert rule be universalized? In what sense can they not?

6. Explain how a consideration of the nature of morality demonstrates the need for entitlements.

7. According to Arthur, what two purposes do moral rules serve?

8. Are there features of Arthur's presentation that remind you of Rawls's ethics? Explain.

CASE PRESENTATION
To Aid or Not to Aid

The conference on world hunger had promised to be uneventful. Such conferences had convened periodically over the past forty years. Invariably they did little more than tell those assembled what they already knew: World hunger is still with us.

The first hint that this conference would be different came when the secretary of the U.S. Commission on World Hunger injected a political note. He suggested that the declining trend in U.S. foreign assistance had to be reversed if American leadership in the world was to continue.

"Intelligently administering foreign aid," the secretary pointed out, "is in America's self-interest and in the interest of world security." Then, as if to reinforce his point, he added, "Make no mistake about it. The purpose of our international aid program is self-serving. It's an approach that makes sense not only in international relations, but also in managing our families, businesses, and other aspects of our lives. That approach recognizes that it's safer and cheaper to anticipate a problem than to wait for it to become a crisis."

Thus the secretary concluded that it was in our national interest to do all we could to combat the conditions that would otherwise likely drive people to desperation. By slashing international programs, he said finally, we're not saving money but merely postponing, even raising, the costs that we'll one day have to pay.

Not everyone agreed, however. In fact, one panel member strongly objected to the secretary's remarks. She suggested that our international aid might actually be hurting the very people we want to help.

"Our aid fails to help," she argued, "because it assumes that aid can reach the powerless, even though it's funneled through the powerful. Well, it can't." She went on to insist that our aid to those countries where economic control is concentrated in the hands of a few merely underwrites the local, national, and international elites whose control over the land and other productive resources is generating the poverty and hunger we are trying to eradicate.

The secretary listened attentively to her remarks. When she finished, he said, "What would you propose we do?"

"Cut aid to all countries where a genuine redistribution of control over productive resources isn't under way," she shot back.

"Do you know how many countries that would involve?" the secretary asked her.

"Dozens," she said. "Perhaps scores."

The secretary agreed. "And do you know how many people would starve?"

"Millions," she said without hesitation. Then she asked the secretary, "Do you know how many people we're sentencing to a life of suffering and to a death by starvation through our well-intentioned but tragically misguided aid?"

Questions for Analysis

1. *How would Kant evaluate aid given primarily out of self-interest?*

2. *Do you think it would be moral to allow people to starve so long as their nation was not taking measures to redistribute control of its productive resources?*

3. *Would it be accurate to describe both the secretary's and the panel member's positions as utilitarian?*

4. *If the secretary agreed that the panel member is correct in her assessment of the impact of U.S. aid, could he continue to argue that it is still in our best interest to provide aid?*

5. *Do you think a rich nation such as the United States is morally justified in using its aid program as a weapon for molding the social and economic infrastructures of recipient nations?*

CASE PRESENTATION
The Way Out

"You know the worst of it?" Lila Robbins asked her companion Walter Moore, who was decrying the grayish-brown poison that passed for air in the Los Angeles basin.

"Sure," said Walt. "It's killing us." With that he honked the car's horn. Not that it would do any good. As usual during rush hour, the freeway traffic had backed up. Walt knew that at best they'd crawl at a snail's pace for the next thirty minutes or so. But it always made him feel better to honk the horn, as if he still had some control over things.

"No," Lila said. "The worst thing is that there is absolutely nothing anyone of us can do to stop its spread."

"How depressing!"

"Depressing but true. An individual act of renunciation would be meaningless."

"Unless everyone else did the same thing," Walt said.

Lila wagged her head from side to side and said, "It'll never happen."

The young couple took on the gloom of the day. Unconsciously they checked to see if their windows were sealed.

"So what's the solution?" Walt asked with a sigh.

"Control the behavior that's causing the problem," Lila answered firmly.

"You mean get people off the roads?"

"I'm not just talking about smog," Lila said. "The smog's just a symptom of a far more serious problem."

"Which is?"

"The pursuit of private gratification. That's what's responsible for pollution, world hunger, dwindling resources—what environmentalists call 'ecological scarcity.' "

She went on to explain that ecological scarcity is upon us. We live on a finite planet containing limited resources, and we appear to be approaching those limits at breakneck speed. In short, "We're about to overtax the carrying capacity of our planet."

Walt disagreed. "What you fail to take note of," he told Lila, "is that technology is simultaneously expanding the limits."

Lila shook her head. "Look," she said. "We're like fish in a pond where all life is rapidly being suffocated by a water lily that doubles in size every day and will cover the whole pond in a month."

"I don't deny that the lily—to use your metaphor—is growing really fast. But the pond can be made to grow even faster. We'll never run out of resources because economics and technology will always keep finding ways for us to meet our needs."

"You miss the point."

"What point?"

"That either way we lose." Walt didn't catch her drift. "If," Lila said, "I'm right, then sooner or later—probably sooner—we'll reach the physical limits and all hell will break loose. It'll be every person for himself, dog-eat-dog, sheer anarchy. The only way to restore order will be through dictatorship."

"And if I'm right?" Walt asked her.

"If you're right, the result will be much the same. Think about it. If we can save ourselves technologically, we'll still have to vigilantly guard our resources, and that means we must control human behavior—through strong-arm tactics, if necessary. In the end, the measures we'll have to adopt to survive won't be much different from the future that I'm predicting when we reach our physical limits."

The traffic inched forward and then stopped. Walt craned his head out his window, but he couldn't see much. Up ahead the smog hung thicker. He rolled his window up again and dabbed his stinging eyes. "So what's the way out?"

"We have to abandon our political corruption. We must stop using liberty as a license for self-indulgence. We must recognize that we can lead a very good life, even an affluent one, without wasteful use of our resources. When we recognize that the pursuit of happiness doesn't mean an insane, lustful quest for material gain, then we'll start dealing with the crisis of ecological scarcity. Then we'll seriously start dealing with problems like world poverty, sickness, and starvation."

Walt mulled over what Lila had said. After several minutes he spoke. "You make it sound like our real shortage is in moral resources."

"Exactly!" Lila was quick to agree. "There's no real scarcity in nature. It's just that our wants have outstripped nature's bounty. If we're to avoid a grim future, we must assume full moral responsibilities."

"Thank God!" Walt blurted as the traffic bolted forward. He turned on the headlights and started to think about something to eat. "I'm famished!" he said.

But Lila wasn't listening. She was recalling a quotation from the Chinese sage Lao-tzu:

> Nature sustains itself through three precious principles, which one does well to embrace and follow. These are gentleness, frugality, and humility.

Questions for Analysis

1. *Do you agree with Lila?*

2. *What do you think Lila means by "assuming full moral responsibilities"?*

3. *What connection, if any, do you see between ecological scarcity and our alleged failure to assume moral responsibilities?*

4. *How is ecological scarcity related to world hunger?*

5. *An essay entitled "The Scarcity Society" inspired this case presentation. In it the author, William Ophuls, writes: "If this inexorable process is not controlled by prudent and, above all, timely political restraints on the behavior that causes it, then we must resign ourselves to ecological self-destruction."[7] What political restraints do you think are necessary?*

Selections for Further Reading

Aiken, William, and Hugh LaFollette. *World Hunger and Moral Obligation.* Englewood Cliffs, N.J.: Prentice-Hall, 1977.

Bauer, P. T. *Equality, the Third World and Economic Delusion.* Cambridge, Mass.: Harvard University Press, 1981.

Bayles, Michael D. *Morality and Population Policy.* Birmingham: University of Alabama Press, 1980.

Brown, Peter R., and Erik P. Eckholm. *By Bread Alone.* New York: Praeger, 1974.

Brown, Peter, and Henry Shue. *Boundaries.* Totowa, N.J.: Rowman and Littlefield, 1981.

Ehrlich, Paul. *The Population Bomb.* New York: Ballantine, 1971.

Hardin, Garrett. *Promethean Ethics.* Seattle: University of Washington Press, 1980.

Kahn, Herman; William Brown; and Leon Martel. *The Next 200 Years.* New York: William Morrow, 1976.

Lucan, George R., Jr., and Thomas W. Ogletree. *Lifeboat Ethics.* New York: Harper and Row, 1976.

Partridge, Ernest. *Responsibilities to Future Generations.* Buffalo, N.Y.: Prometheus, 1981.

---

7. *William Ophuls, "The Scarcity Society," Harper's, April 1974, pp. 29–37.*

Sikora, R. I., and Brian Barry. *Obligations to Future Generations*. Philadelphia: Temple University Press, 1978.

Simon, Arthur, and Paul Simon. *The Politics of World Hunger*. New York: Harper's Magazine Press, 1973.

Wortman, Sterling, and Ralph Cummings, Jr. *To Feed This World*. Baltimore: Johns Hopkins University Press, 1978.

10
ANIMAL RIGHTS

In 1975, Australian philosopher Peter Singer published his landmark book, *Animal Liberation*. The title of the first chapter, like the title of the book itself, clearly announced the author's basic moral message: "All Animals Are Equal." Succeeding chapters documented another message: All animals are not treated equally.

The dividing line is drawn between human and nonhuman animals. While our shared morality protects *human* animals from innumerable kinds of treatment we find intolerable, it is far less protective of *nonhuman* animals. Here are some of the things that readers of Singer's book learned:

1. Psychologist Martin Seligman performed a series of experiments involving dogs and a contraption known as the shuttle box. A shuttle box is a box with two compartments. One has electrified floors, allowing the experimenter to administer shocks to its occupant. The other, separated from the first by a barrier, does not. The experiments concerned two groups of dogs. The "naive" group (dogs with no prior training) reacted to the electric shocks by howling, running about, and defecating and urinating until they managed to escape to the other compartment. The trained group (dogs who had been given inescapable electric shocks before being put in the box) reacted differently. After some initial running, howling, and so forth, they simply gave up. That is, they lay in the box and passively accepted the shocks. Moreover, repeated trials brought out another difference. The naive group learned to escape more quickly. The trained group learned not to make any attempt to escape.

2. The U.S. Food and Drug Administration tests new cosmetics by dripping concentrated solutions of the products into the eyes of rabbits and then measuring the amount of damage, which may include total loss of vision. To keep the squealing rabbits from clawing at and shutting their eyes and thereby removing the drops, researchers often immobilize the rabbits and clamp their eyes open.

3. Chickens raised for food on "factory" farms are packed so tightly into long windowless sheds that by the end of their short lives each chicken has as little as a half square foot of space. The crowding is so stressful to them that they take to pecking one another's feathers and even eating one another. Farmers often solve the problem by painfully removing the chickens' beaks.

4. Veal calves are raised in stalls so narrow that they cannot even turn around. The purpose of confining the calves is to keep them from grazing (grass makes the color of veal meat less appealing to veal eaters) and developing muscles (which make the meat tough). The purpose of confining them in stalls so narrow is to prevent them from licking their own urine to satisfy their natural craving for iron. (Because the meat of anemic calves has a more appealing color to veal eaters, their diet is kept low in iron.)

It is difficult to read detailed accounts of these and other experiments and farm procedures without feeling great sympathy for the animals involved. To be sure, scientists and farmers have what they take to be good reasons for doing such things. Seligman's experiments provided a new understanding of human depression and led to new therapies for treating it. FDA tests help to ensure that new products are safe for human consumers. Factory farm practices allow for efficient food production. Standard treatment of veal calves results in the kind of meat humans desire.

But are these reasons good enough? Can they morally justify such cruel treatment of nonhuman animals? Aren't the human interests served by such treatment (a new line of make-up or an "appealing" color of meat) downright trivial compared to the nonhuman interests denied by it? Aren't those of us who support such treatment by eating veal and buying cosmetics guilty of *speciesism*— the view that all human animals have greater moral worth than nonhuman animals? And isn't that just as bad as racism or sexism?

What Do We Owe Nonhuman Animals?

Singer's point is simple. Nonhuman animals, like human animals, can experience both pleasure and pain. And that is a morally important fact. If it is wrong to cause human suffering to achieve a good that does not outweigh that suffering, Singer argues, it is wrong to cause nonhuman suffering to achieve such a good. Given the variety of nutritious and tasty vegetarian recipes available to us, the suffering caused by factory farms is not justified by human desire for meat. Given the availability of canvas shoes and leather substitutes for belts and such, human demand for leather is not worth the suffering it brings to nonhuman animals.

Historically, the weight of Western opinion has not been on Singer's side. Both our religious and philosophical traditions have been inhospitable to the notion that we have moral obligations to other animals. Let's take a brief look at both.

The Judeo-Christian Tradition

Beginning with the creation story of Genesis, Judeo-Christian thought has told us that other animals were put here for our purposes. According to that story, we are to "fill the earth and subdue it; and have dominion over the fish of the sea and over the birds of the air and over every living thing that moves upon the earth." And later in Genesis, after the flood, we are told, "Every moving thing that lives shall be food for you; and as I gave you the green plants, I give you everything."

These biblical injunctions have been supported by centuries of Christian theology. Humans are created in the image of God; other animals are not. Humans have immortal souls; other animals do not. Humans belong to both the spiritual and the material worlds; other animals belong only to the material. Given these differences, plus the influence of Christian thought on Western culture, no one should be surprised by our treatment of nonhuman animals.

The Philosophical Tradition

Secular philosophers have, in the main, given nonhuman animals no greater consideration. Writing at a time when such scientists as Galileo were ushering in the era of modern science, the great French philosopher René Descartes (1596–1650) argued that nonhuman animals are no better than biological robots, incapable of feeling any sensations, even pain. The nonphysical mind is the seat of sensation, he argued, and only creatures capable of reason have nonphysical minds. Since nonhuman animals cannot reason, they are simply physical creatures. Therefore, they cannot feel pain.

Immanuel Kant had other reasons for excluding nonhuman animals from moral consideration. As we saw in Part I, Kant put respect for *persons* at the center of morality—we are not to treat other *persons* merely as a means to our own ends. Although Kant did not deny that animals can suffer, he did deny that they are persons. To be a person, he said, is to be an autonomous being, one that has the capacity to act for reasons and to reason about its reasons. And that capacity does not belong to nonhuman animals. They are, then, beyond the pale of morality. (Kant did recommend that we be nice to animals, though—not out of moral obligation, of course, but for another reason. If we treat animals cruelly, he felt, we run the risk of developing insensitive characters.)

Another strain in moral philosophy—*social contract theory*—is equally exclusive of nonhuman animals. According to this way of looking at morality, morality is the product of an informal agreement among the members of society. Each of us agrees to follow certain rules on the condition that others do the same. The purpose of the agreement is to ensure that all of us act in dependable ways, providing the mutual trust necessary for social cooperation. An important aspect of social contract theory is that this informal agreement is the source of all moral obligation. We have moral obligations to others who have entered into the agreement with us. We have no such obligations to those who are not part of the agreement. Nonhuman animals, who are incapable of entering into contracts, are not part of the agreement. Therefore, we have no moral obligations to them.

In traditional Western views, then, we owe nonhuman animals nothing. We have no moral obligations to them. We may have moral obligations *concerning* them, but those obligations are *to* other people. We ought not, for example, poison somebody else's pet, for the same reason that we ought not destroy somebody else's sofa. The pet and the sofa are another person's property, and our obligations to that person forbid us to destroy his property. The pet itself is due no more moral consideration than the sofa—none.

To be sure, current practices are not quite as harsh as the above might lead you to think. Since we no longer believe that animals cannot suffer, our natural feelings of sympathy have led us to condemn cruel treatment of at least some of them—household pets, in particular, but some work animals like horses, as well. But as Singer's book clearly shows, most of the animal kingdom does not benefit from our sympathy, and even the small part that does is hardly granted full moral consideration. A cat's suffering simply does not count for most of us as much as a person's suffering.

Animal Rights

The basis of Singer's moral appeal is the principle of utility: Since we morally ought to maximize happiness and minimize suffering, and since nonhuman animals are just as capable of happiness and suffering as human animals, our calculations ought to include them as well. Against our own pleasure in eating veal, we ought to balance the suffering of veal calves. Against the benefits of research on animals, we ought to balance the suffering of laboratory animals. Their pain should matter just as much as ours.

Other animal advocates make a different moral appeal. As they see it, the principle of utility does not guarantee fit treatment of nonhuman animals. Suppose, for example, that the elimination of factory farms would create such havoc in our economy that utility is maximized by keeping them. Would that justify keeping them? If our answer is yes, we should ask ourselves an analogous question: Suppose we could maximize utility by reintroducing slavery. Would that justify doing so? Presumably, our answer to that question is no. Humans have certain rights that we morally cannot violate, regardless of utility. If we do not feel the same about at least some animals, aren't we guilty of speciesism?

Thus, philosophers like Tom Regan focus their attention on animal rights. He argues that just as respect for persons requires that we not treat other humans in certain ways, regardless of utility, so should respect for at least some nonhuman animals require that we not treat them in certain ways, regardless of utility.

Which animals? At the very least, those that, like us, are experiencing subjects of their own lives. By that phrase, Regan means the following: conscious creatures that are aware of their environment, that have desires, feelings, emotions, memories, beliefs, preferences, goals, and a sense of their own identity and future. Although we cannot be sure precisely where we can draw the line between animals that meet these criteria and animals that do not, we can be sure of one thing, he says. Adult mammals do. And because they do, their lives, like ours, have inherent value—value independent of any use they may be to us. In that case, we ought not use them merely as a means to our own ends.

What's Wrong with Speciesism?

Most of us are, undeniably, speciesists. But what, you may be wondering, is wrong with that? Most of us agree that pointless cruelty to animals should not be tolerated, but that is a far cry from agreeing that animals are our moral equals. Why should they be? Shouldn't human beings matter more than other animals?

The Conventional View Defended

Certainly, speciesism doesn't *seem* to be as bad as racism or sexism. To deny full moral equality to other people on the basis of skin color is totally arbitrary, since skin color is of no moral importance whatever. We are all capable of the same aspirations, we desire to be treated with dignity and respect, we participate in social arrangements believing that we deserve from others what they believe they deserve from us, we can develop the same virtues and talents—we can, in short, belong to the same moral community regardless of race. To exclude someone from that community because of race is unjustifiable.

The same remarks hold for sex, of course. But for species? Can pigs and cows make the same moral claims on us as other people? Can we really say that the differences between rabbits and humans are as trivial, morally speaking, as the differences between blacks and whites, women and men? The commonsense answer to these questions is, of course, no. The conventional view is that morality is our own—humankind's—institution, developed and maintained and improved for our own purposes, for our own individual and social good. To the extent that the good of other animals contributes to our own good, it should be of concern to us. Because our pets play unique and rewarding roles in our lives, we should treat them as more than mere things. Because sympathy, compassion, and kindness contribute in crucial ways to the human good, we should not accept needless cruelty to nonhuman animals. But we have no obligation to promote the good of nonhuman animals at humankind's own expense. To do that would be to undercut the whole purpose of morality.

In other words, the conventional view says this: The difference between human and nonhuman animals is not merely a matter of species, while the difference between black and white is merely a matter of race, and the difference between women and men is merely a matter of sex. If there were another species that was not unlike us in morally relevant ways—the highly evolved apes of the *Planet of the Apes* film series, for example, or people from Mars—then we would welcome them into our moral community. That is, we don't discriminate against rabbits on the basis of species. We exclude them from our moral community because of crucial moral distinctions. So it is unfair to call us "speciesists," since the term implies otherwise. Like "racism" and "sexism," it implies that our distinctions cannot be morally justified.

This conventional view reflects, of course, the influence of Kant and the social contract view of morality. Like Kant, it draws the line at persons, although not necessarily human persons. And like the social contract view, it emphasizes a moral community of fully participating members, again not necessarily human. Moreover, as conventional views always do, it strikes us as eminently reasonable, even if we have never heard of Kant or social contract theory.

The Conventional View Criticized

However reasonable the conventional view may seem, animal rights advocates attack it on two fronts. First, they claim, we do not apply the conventional view consistently. Humans who are not fully persons are protected by our morality; humans who cannot fully participate in our moral community are granted moral rights. We do not test new cosmetics on the severely retarded. We do not run cruel psychological experiments on infants. We do not conduct medical experiments on irreversibly comatose humans. Why not? Because they are human. Why do we test cosmetics on rabbits, experiment on dogs, raise veal calves for food? Because they are not human. And that, animal rights activists say, *is* discrimination purely on the basis of species.

Second, even if the conventional view were applied consistently, they claim, it would still be inadequate. Granted, difference of species is not the only difference between normal adult humans and farm animals, but the differences stressed by the conventional view are not morally crucial ones. What is so morally important about the fact that steers cannot enter into our social contract? Why should it matter so much that pigs can't have all the aspirations that humans have, that sheep can't develop the same virtues and talents? What the conventional view boils down to, they say, is this: Only moral *agents* can have rights.

What are moral agents? Creatures that have two closely related abilities. The first is the ability to take on moral duties toward others, to understand that they have obligations toward others that they ought to fulfill. The second is the ability to make moral claims against others, to understand that they have moral rights that others can violate. But why, critics of the conventional view ask, should those abilities be crucial?

For Singer, we saw earlier, the really crucial thing is the ability to feel pleasure and pain. Calves, chickens, and rabbits can suffer, they have a real interest in avoiding suffering, and that interest matters. The fact that they are not human or persons does not make that interest any less real, nor should it make that interest matter any less.

For Regan, the crucial thing is inherent value. Whatever has inherent value deserves respect, and whatever deserves respect should not be used as a mere thing. Any creature that is a subject of its own life passes that crucial test, regardless of its inability to be a moral agent. Such a creature is still a moral *patient*. It may not have any duties toward us, but we have duties toward it. It may not be able to respect our rights, but we ought to respect its rights.

The Conventional View Reconsidered

The above criticisms show that the acceptability of our treatment of other animals turns on two points. The first is consistency. Do we apply the conventional view consistently? And if not, can we justify our inconsistency? The second strikes at the heart of the conventional view. Does it draw a morally defensible line between human and nonhuman animals? And if so, is there an even better place to draw the line between creatures with rights (or, as Singer would put it, creatures whose interests matter as much as our own) and creatures without rights (or creatures whose interests do not matter as much as our own)?

Regarding the first point, defenders of current treatment of other animals can say this: If we do apply the conventional view inconsistently, we do so in a *principled* way. Moral agents—persons—stand at the center of our morality. They are the primary holders of moral rights. We grant rights to human infants because they will *become* moral agents and so deserve our respect. We grant rights to humans in comas because they *were* moral agents and so also deserve our respect. We grant rights to severely retarded humans because they are so much like some other holders of rights that it seems almost incoherent not to. In other words, we welcome these noncentral humans into our moral community because of the important similarities they bear to the rest of us. Not only that. They are also our parents, our children, our brothers and sisters. Their good is deeply connected to our good.

As for the second point, defenders of current practices can do little more than repeat the reasons for drawing the line where we now do and then throw the question back to their critics: Why is Singer's dividing line or Regan's any better than the one we now draw? The fact that nonhuman animals can suffer should certainly have some moral weight, but why should it lead us to put them on an equal footing with full members of our moral community? The fact that some of them are experiencing subjects of their own lives should also have some moral weight, but why should it have as much weight as other facts about ourselves?

Whether these answers are acceptable depends on two further questions. First, are at least some nonhuman animals so much like some humans that it seems almost incoherent to deny them rights? Second, assuming that morality did arise to advance the human good, should we now say that the time has come to recognize that other goods are of equal value? Critics of our treatment of other animals answer yes to both questions. Defenders answer no.

Arguments for Equal Treatment of Animals

1. *Human beings hold no special place in nature.*

POINT: "What's so special about humans, anyway? From Mother Nature's point of view, *all* animals are equal. We all evolved from the same beginnings, we're all made of the same stuff, and we all belong to the same biosphere. The world wasn't made for any one species. It's here for all of us. And it's nothing but pure arrogance for humans to think that *we're* the pinnacle of creation, that we have the right to treat the rest of the animal kingdom any way we want. It's time we recognize that we're part of nature, not lords over it, and we ought to act accordingly."

COUNTERPOINT: "Of course, we're part of nature. But what does that prove? Tigers, eagles, and other predators are also part of nature. What can be more natural than eating other animals? Besides, why stop at animals? Plants are part of nature, too. So are rocks, rivers, and dirt. From Mother Nature's point of view, they must matter just as much as animals. Should we treat them equally, too? Finally, why should we even care about Mother Nature's point of view (whatever *that* might be)? We have our own point of view—the human point of view—and if that point of view is no better than any other, it's no worse, either. It's ours, and we're entitled to live our lives according to it."

2.   *All pain is equally bad.*

POINT: "We all know that pain is bad. We begin to think morally when we recognize that somebody else's pain is just as bad as our own pain and that we shouldn't cause unnecessary pain to others. Well, an animal's pain is just as bad as a human being's pain—it hurts every bit as much as ours, and animals try just as hard to avoid it as we do. So the moral thing is to recognize that. We have to admit that all pain is equally bad, and we have to stop causing unnecessary pain to animals. We don't need to do cruel research on animals, so we should stop it. We don't need to eat meat, so we should become vegetarians. We should treat all animals, human and nonhuman, equally."

COUNTERPOINT: "Sure, pain is bad. And I'm willing to admit that animal pain is bad, too. I'm even willing to admit that we shouldn't cause unnecessary pain to animals. But a lot of pain that you call unnecessary isn't. What makes something necessary, after all, is that we need it to serve our interests. We have an interest in medical and other kinds of scientific research, and even if we don't always have to experiment on live subjects to serve that interest, sometimes we do. And even if we don't absolutely have to eat meat, most of us certainly like to, and that makes meat eating a real human interest. What you're missing is this: Even if all pain is bad, that doesn't mean that nonhuman interests count as much as human interests."

3.   *Trivial human interests don't count as much as important animal interests.*

POINT: "Now *you're* missing the point. Maybe some animal pain really is necessary to serve important human interests. But how important are the interests you mentioned? Take eating meat. That's downright trivial. It's not needed for health, and vegetarian meals can taste every bit as good. And what about eye make-up? You can't call that an important interest. I'll concede that some research isn't trivial, but you have to concede that a whole lot of it is. And even when we're dealing with important research interests, there are a lot of ways of finding out what we want to know without torturing animals. The only reason we go on as we do is because we're too lazy or thoughtless to change."

COUNTERPOINT: "Whether an interest is trivial or not depends on how much it matters to us, and what you call trivial matters a whole lot to a whole lot of people. Look at what a big deal most of us make about going out for a steak dinner. We get all dressed up and spend a fortune. To some people, it's more than just nontrivial—it's the highlight of their week. Besides, what does it matter even if we say that such interests *are* trivial? If humans matter more to us than nonhumans, why shouldn't even trivial human interests matter more to us than any animal interest?"

4.   *The interests of at least some animals count as much as ours.*

POINT: "Let's talk about what makes an interest important. What makes one of *your* interests important to *you* is that it matters to you. And that makes it important to *me*, too. Since I want you to respect the interests that matter to me, simple golden-rule reasoning tells me to do likewise. Well, there are at least some animals who care about their own interests as much as we care about ours. The animals I have in mind are the ones that are aware of themselves and their futures, and have memories and beliefs and preferences, just like us. Their interests matter to them and that makes their interests important to them. And that should make their interests important to us, too."

COUNTERPOINT: "What you're saying is that the golden rule applies to monkeys and pigs. But an important part of the golden rule is reciprocity. If we're going to count on others to treat us in certain ways, then we ought to treat them the same. And that makes no sense when those others are monkeys and pigs. They can't reciprocate. All we can expect of them is that they'll act like monkeys and pigs. We certainly can't expect them to apply the golden rule to us. If you want to apply it to them, if it makes you feel better to do it, fine. But you can't tell me we have a moral *obligation* to do it."

Arguments Against Equal Treatment of Animals

1.   *Equal treatment would have disastrous consequences.*

POINT: "Have you thought of the consequences of your position? Suppose we did treat other animals as equals. What would that do to ranchers, farmers, workers at meat packaging plants, butchers, fishermen, and all the other people whose livelihoods would disappear? And think what that would mean for the economy as a whole. What you're talking about is the closing of vast markets and the dislocation of millions of people. You're also talking about giving up important research and who knows what else. Whatever good would come to nonhuman animals, the consequences for humans would be disastrous. And that can't be right."

COUNTERPOINT: "Slave-holders could have used—and did use—the same arguments against abolitionists before the Civil War. Don't forget, the economies of many states depended on slavery then even more than the economies of many states depend on meat today. And the answer to the arguments is the same now as it was then. If something's wrong, it's wrong, and we have no right to base our economies on enslavement or slaughter. Besides, the dislocations will be temporary. The South did rise again, and so will we."

2. *You can't compare other species to minorities and women.*

POINT: "All this talk of animal liberation, animal rights, and speciesism is an insult to women and minorities. How can you equate sheep and women, cows and blacks? How can you compare raising animals for food to denying our fellow human beings the attainment of their most fundamental aspirations? Farm animals can't feel humiliated. They can't feel robbed of their dignity. They can't feel the outrage that humans feel when denied recognition of their worth. They can't know what it's like to be treated like a thing instead of a person. They have no idea what it means to be a person, to have rights, to be treated fairly."

COUNTERPOINT: "My point isn't to compare animals *just* to women and minorities, but to *all* humans—and that includes white men. It's not to insult anybody, either. Nobody wants to demean humans. I just want to give nonhumans the respect they deserve. And all that stuff about a sense of dignity and the rest is irrelevant. All it shows is that some things that matter to us don't matter to them. But other things do. Avoiding pain, for instance. And freedom. And to many of them, their lives. Animals want to roam free, have enough space to do what comes natural to them, and lead pain-free lives. Their aspirations may not be precisely the same as ours, but they're equally real."

3. *Giving animals rights would lead to absurd interference with nature.*

POINT: "Humans aren't the only animals that eat other animals, you know. What about wolves, eagles, tigers, and other predators? If we grant rights to their prey, then we'll have to protect animals from each other, not just from ourselves. After all, if we don't have the right to violate another animal's rights, neither does a wolf. But if we do protect the prey, what happens to the predator? What, for that matter, happens to all of nature? If you follow your position to its logical conclusion, the results are absurd."

COUNTERPOINT: "The kind of interference that worries you is *not* a logical consequence of my position. What you're forgetting is that tigers and wolves aren't moral *agents*. They don't have any obligations to other animals, so there's nothing immoral about their preying on other animals. Humans *are* moral agents, though, so there *is* something immoral about our preying on other animals."

4. *Putting our own species first is the natural thing to do.*

POINT: "It's only natural that we care more about other humans than we care about nonhumans. After all, being members of the same species is an important relationship, like being members of the same family. We care more about our parents than we do about strangers, so why shouldn't we care more about our fellow humans than we do about sheep? And just take a look at the rest of the animal kingdom. A lot of animals cooperate with members of their own species but not with other animals, and in some cases, animals will even lay down their lives for other members of their species. As the old saying goes, birds of a feather flock together. Why should humans be any different?"

COUNTERPOINT: "Humans *are* different. We can rise above our natural inclinations. That's what civilization and culture are all about. It's why we have laws and morality. And, since you're so fond of old sayings, it's why a tiger can't change its stripes but a human can. We know the difference between right and wrong, and the point of teaching that difference is to get people to put a check on some of their natural inclinations. Selfishness is just as natural as altruism, you know—maybe even more natural—but I don't hear you saying that we shouldn't try to curb our selfishness. So even if speciesism is natural, if it's wrong we should stamp it out."

All Animals Are Equal . . . or why supporters of liberation for Blacks and Women should support Animal Liberation too

Peter Singer

In this selection from the first chapter of Animal Liberation, *Peter Singer compares speciesism to sexism and racism, and he argues that the same considerations that make sexism and racism morally unjustifiable make speciesism morally unjustifiable. He bases his argument on the principle of equal consideration, according to which the pain that nonhuman animals feel is of equal moral importance to the pain that humans feel.*

While supporting the principle of equal consideration, Singer stresses that it does not always require equal treatment of all animals, since the same treatment can cause unequal amounts of suffering to different animals. He also points out that the principle does not require us to say that all lives are equal. Often, a human life is morally more important than the life of a nonhuman animal. Sometimes, though, it is not. When forced to choose between a human and nonhuman animal's life, we should base our decision on the mental capacities of the individuals involved, not on species.

"Animal Liberation" may sound more like a parody of other liberation movements than a serious objective. The idea of "The Rights of Animals" actually was once used to parody the case for women's rights. When Mary Wollstonecraft, a forerunner of today's feminists, published her *Vindication of the Rights of Women* in 1792, her views were widely regarded as absurd, and before long an anonymous publication appeared entitled *A Vindication of the Rights of Brutes.* The author of this satirical work (now known to have been Thomas Taylor, a distinguished Cambridge philosopher) tried to refute Mary Wollstonecraft's arguments by showing that they could be

carried one stage further. If the argument for equality was sound when applied to women, why should it not be applied to dogs, cats, and horses? The reasoning seemed to hold for these "brutes" too; yet to hold that brutes had rights was manifestly absurd; therefore the reasoning by which this conclusion had been reached must be unsound, and if unsound when applied to brutes, it must also be unsound when applied to women, since the very same arguments had been used in each case.

In order to explain the basis of the case for the equality of animals, it will be helpful to start with an examination of the case for the equality of women.

From Peter Singer, Animal Liberation *(New York: New York Review, 1975), pp. 1–23. Reprinted with permission of the author.*

Let us assume that we wish to defend the case for women's rights against the attack by Thomas Taylor. How should we reply?

One way in which we might reply is by saying that the case for equality between men and women cannot validly be extended to nonhuman animals. Women have a right to vote, for instance, because they are just as capable of making rational decisions about the future as men are; dogs, on the other hand, are incapable of understanding the significance of voting, so they cannot have the right to vote. There are many other obvious ways in which men and women resemble each other closely, while humans and animals differ greatly. So, it might be said, men and women are similar beings and should have similar rights, while humans and nonhumans are different and should not have equal rights.

The reasoning behind this reply to Taylor's analogy is correct up to a point, but it does not go far enough. There *are* important differences between humans and other animals, and these differences must give rise to *some* differences in the rights that each have. Recognizing this obvious fact, however, is no barrier to the case for extending the basic principle of equality to nonhuman animals. The differences that exist between men and women are equally undeniable, and the supporters of Women's Liberation are aware that these differences may give rise to different rights. Many feminists hold that women have the right to an abortion on request. It does not follow that since these same feminists are campaigning for equality between men and women they must support the right of men to have abortions too. Since a man cannot have an abortion, it is meaningless to talk of his right to have one. Since a dog can't vote, it is meaningless to talk of its right to vote. There is no reason why either Women's Liberation or Animal Liberation should get involved in such nonsense. The extension of the basic principle of equality from one group to another does not imply that we must treat both groups in exactly the same way, or grant exactly the same rights to both groups. Whether we should do so will depend on the nature of the members of the two groups. The basic principle of equality does not require equal or identical *treatment*; it requires equal *consideration*. Equal consideration for different beings may lead to different treatment and different rights.

So there is a different way of replying to Taylor's attempt to parody the case for women's rights, a way that does not deny the obvious differences between humans and nonhumans but goes more deeply into the question of equality and concludes by finding nothing absurd in the idea that the basic principle of equality applies to so-called "brutes." At this point such a conclusion may appear odd; but if we examine more deeply the basis on which our opposition to discrimination on grounds of race or sex ultimately rests, we will see that we would be on shaky ground if we were to demand equality for blacks, women, and other groups of oppressed humans while denying equal consideration to nonhumans. To make this clear we need to see, first, exactly why racism and sexism are wrong.

When we say that all human beings, whatever their race, creed, or sex, are equal, what is it that we are asserting? Those who wish to defend hierarchical, inegalitarian societies have often pointed out that by whatever test we choose it simply is not true that all humans are equal. Like it or not we must face the fact that humans come in different shapes and sizes; they come with different moral capacities, different intellectual abilities, different amounts of benevolent feeling and sensitivity to the needs of others, different abilities to communicate effectively, and different capacities to experience pleasure and pain. In short, if the demand for equality were based on the actual equality of all human beings, we would have to stop demanding equality.

Still, one might cling to the view that the demand for equality among human beings is based on the actual equality of the different races and sexes. Although, it may be said, humans differ as individuals there are no differences between the races and sexes *as such*. From the mere fact that a person is black or a woman we cannot infer anything about that person's intellectual or moral capacities. This, it may be said, is why racism and sexism are wrong. The white racist claims that whites are superior to blacks, but this is false—although there are differences among individuals, some blacks are superior to some whites in all of the capacities and abilities that could conceivably be relevant. The opponent of sexism would say the same: a person's sex is no guide to his or her abilities, and this is why it is unjustifiable to discriminate on the basis of sex.

The existence of individual variations that cut across the lines of race or sex, however, provides us with no defense at all against a more sophisticated opponent of equality, one who proposes that, say, the interests of all those with IQ scores below 100 be given less consideration than the interests of those with ratings over 100. Perhaps those scoring below the mark would, in this society, be made the slaves of those scoring higher. Would a hierarchical society of this sort really be so much better than one based on race or sex? I think not. But if we tie the moral principle of equality to the factual equality of the different races or sexes, taken as a whole, our opposition to racism and sexism does not provide us with any basis for objecting to this kind of inegalitarianism.

There is a second important reason why we ought not to base our opposition to racism and sexism on any kind of actual equality, even the limited kind that asserts that variations in capacities and abilities are spread evenly between the different races and sexes: we can have no absolute guarantee that these capacities and abilities really are distributed evenly, without regard to race or sex, among human beings. So far as actual abilities are concerned there do seem to be certain measurable differences between both races and sexes. These differences do not, of course, appear in each case, but only when averages are taken. More important still, we do not yet know how much of these differences is really due to the different genetic endowments of the different races and sexes, and how much is due to poor schools, poor housing, and other factors that are the result of past and continuing discrimination. Perhaps all of the important differences will eventually prove to be environmental rather than genetic. Anyone opposed to racism and sexism will certainly hope that this will be so, for it will make the task of ending discrimination a lot easier; nevertheless it would be dangerous to rest the case against racism and sexism on the belief that all significant differences are environmental in origin. The opponent of, say, racism who takes this line will be unable to avoid conceding that *if* differences in ability do after all prove to have some genetic connection with race, racism would in some way be defensible.

Fortunately there is no need to pin the case for equality to one particular outcome of a scientific investigation. The appropriate response to those who claim to have found evidence of genetically based differences in ability between the races or sexes is not to stick to the belief that the genetic explanation must be wrong, whatever evidence to the contrary may turn up: instead we should make it quite clear that the claim to equality does not depend on intelligence, moral capacity, physical strength, or similar matters of fact. Equality is a moral idea, not an assertion of fact. There is no logically compelling reason for assuming that a factual difference in ability between two people justifies any difference in the amount of consideration we give to their needs and interests. *The principle of the equality of human beings is not a description of an alleged actual equality among humans: it is a prescription of how we should treat humans.*

Jeremy Bentham, the founder of the reforming utilitarian school of moral philosophy, incorporated the essential basis of moral equality into his system of ethics by means of the formula: "Each to count for one and none for more than one." In other words, the interests of every being affected by an action are to be taken into account and given the same weight as the like interests of any other being. A later utilitarian, Henry Sidgwick, put the point in this way: "The good of any one individual is of no more importance, from the point of view (if I may say so) of the Universe, than the good of any other." More recently the leading figures in contemporary moral philosophy have shown a great deal of agreement in specifying as a fundamental presupposition of their moral theories some similar requirement which operates so as to give everyone's interests equal consideration—although these writers generally cannot agree on how this requirement is best formulated.[1]

It is an implication of this principle of equality that our concern for others and our readiness to consider their interests ought not to depend on what they are like or on what abilities they may possess. Precisely what this concern or consideration requires us to do may vary according to the characteristics of those affected by what we do: concern for the well-being of a child growing up in America would require that we teach him to read; concern for the well-being of a pig may require no more than that we leave him alone with other pigs in a place where there is adequate food and room to run freely. But the basic element—the taking into account of the interests of the being, whatever those interests may be—must, according to the principle of equality, be extended to all beings, black or white, masculine or feminine, human or nonhuman.

Thomas Jefferson, who was responsible for writing the principle of the equality of men into the American Declaration of Independence, saw this point. It led him to oppose slavery even though he was unable to free himself fully from his slave-holding background. He wrote in a letter to the author of a book that emphasized the notable intellectual achievements of Negroes in order to refute the then common view that they had limited intellectual capacities:

> Be assured that no person living wishes more sincerely than I do, to see a complete refutation of the doubts I have myself entertained and expressed on the grade of understanding allotted to them by nature, and to find that they are on a par with ourselves . . . but whatever be their degree of talent it is no measure of their rights. Because Sir Isaac Newton was superior to others in understanding, he was not therefore lord of the property or person of others.[2]

Similarly when in the 1850s the call for women's rights was raised in the United States a remarkable black feminist named Sojourner Truth made the same point in more robust terms at a feminist convention:

> . . . they talk about this thing in the head; what do they call it? ["Intellect," whispered someone near by.] That's it. What's that got to do with women's rights or Negroes' rights? If my cup won't hold but a pint and yours holds a quart, wouldn't you be mean not to let me have my little half-measure full?[3]

It is on this basis that the case against racism and the case against sexism must both ultimately rest; and it is in accordance with this principle that the attitude that we may call "speciesism," by analogy with racism, must also be condemned. Speciesism—the word is not an attractive one, but I can think of no better term—is a prejudice or attitude of bias toward the interests of members of one's own species and against those of members of other species. It should be obvious that the fundamental objections to racism and sexism made by Thomas Jefferson and Sojourner Truth apply equally to speciesism. If possessing a higher degree of intelligence does not entitle one human to use another for his own ends, how can it entitle humans to exploit nonhumans for the same purpose?[4]

Many philosophers and other writers have proposed the principle of equal consideration of interests, in some form or other, as a basic moral principle; but not many of them have recognized that this principle applies to members of other species as well as to our own. Jeremy Bentham was one of the few who did realize this. In a forward-looking passage written at a time when black slaves had been freed by the French but in the British dominions were still being treated in the way we now treat animals, Bentham wrote:

> The day *may* come when the rest of the animal creation may acquire those rights which never could have been withholden from them but by the hand of tyranny. The French have already discovered that the blackness of the skin is no reason why a human being should be abandoned without redress to the caprice of a tormentor. It may one day come to be recognized that the number of the legs, the villosity of the skin, or the termination of the *os sacrum* are reasons equally insufficient for abandoning a sensitive being to the same fate. What else is it that should trace the insuperable line? Is it the faculty of reason, or perhaps the faculty of discourse? But a full-grown horse or dog is beyond comparison a more rational, as well as a more conversable animal, than an infant of a day or a week or even a month, old. But suppose they were otherwise, what would it avail? The question is not, Can they *reason?* nor Can they *talk?* but, *Can they suffer?*[5]

In this passage Bentham points to the capacity for suffering as the vital characteristic that gives a being the right to equal consideration. The capacity for suffering—or more strictly, for suffering and/or enjoyment or happiness—is not just another characteristic like the capacity for language or higher mathematics. Bentham is not saying that those who try to mark "the insuperable line" that determines whether the interests of a being should be considered happen to have chosen the wrong characteristic. By saying that we must consider the interests of all beings with the capacity for suffering or enjoyment Bentham does not arbitrarily exclude from consideration any interests at all—as those who draw the line with reference to the possession of reason or language do. The capacity for suffering and enjoyment is *a prerequisite for having interests at all*, a condition that must be satisfied before we can speak of interests in a meaningful way. It would be nonsense to say that it was not in the interests of a stone to be kicked along the road by a schoolboy. A stone does not have interests because it cannot suffer. Nothing that we can do to it could possibly make any difference to its welfare. A mouse, on the other hand, does have an interest in not being kicked along the road, because it will suffer if it is.

If a being suffers there can be no moral justification for refusing to take that suffering into consideration. No matter what the nature of the being, the principle of equality requires that its suffering be counted equally with the like suffering—insofar as rough comparisons can be made—of any other being. If a being is not capable of suffering, or of experiencing enjoyment or happiness, there is nothing to be taken into account. So the limit of sentience (using the term as a convenient if not strictly accurate shorthand for the capacity to suffer and/or experience enjoyment) is the only defensible boundary of concern for the interests of others. To mark this boundary by some other characteristic like intelligence or rationality would be to mark it in an arbitrary manner. Why not choose some other characteristic, like skin color?

The racist violates the principle of equality by giving greater weight to the interests of members of his own race when there is a clash between their interests and the interests of those of another race. The sexist violates the principle of equality by favoring the interests of his own sex. Similarly the speciesist allows the interests of his own species to override the greater interests of members of other species. The pattern is identical in each case.

Most human beings are speciesists. The following chapters show that ordinary human beings—not a few exceptionally cruel or heartless humans, but the overwhelming majority of humans—take an active part in, acquiesce in, and allow their taxes to pay for practices that require the sacrifice of the most important interests of members of other species in order to promote the most trivial interests of our own species.

There is, however, one general defense of the practices to be described in the next two chapters that needs to be disposed of before we discuss the practices themselves. It is a defense which, if true, would allow us to do anything at all to nonhumans for the slightest reason, or for no reason at all, without incurring any justifiable reproach. This defense claims that we are never guilty of neglecting the interests of other animals for one breathtakingly simple reason: they have no interests. Nonhuman animals have no interests, according to this view, because they are not capable of suffering. By this is not meant merely that they are not capable of suffering in all the ways that humans are—for instance, that a calf is not capable of suffering from the knowledge that it will be killed in six months time. That modest claim is, no doubt, true; but it does not clear humans of the charge of speciesism, since it allows that animals may suffer in other ways—for instance, by being given electric shocks, or being kept in small, cramped cages. The defense I am about to discuss is the much more sweeping, although correspondingly less plausible, claim that animals are incapable of suffering in any way at all; that they are, in fact, unconscious automata, possessing neither thoughts nor feelings nor a mental life of any kind.

Although, as we shall see in a later chapter, the view that animals are automata was proposed by the seventeenth-century French philosopher René Descartes, to most people, then and now, it is obvious that if, for example, we stick a sharp knife into the stomach of an unanesthetized dog, the dog will feel pain. That this is so is assumed by the laws in most civilized countries which prohibit wanton cruelty to animals. Readers whose common sense tells them that animals do suffer may prefer to skip the remainder of this section, moving straight on to page [395], since the pages in between do nothing but refute a position which they do not hold. Implausible as it is, though, for the sake of completeness this skeptical position must be discussed.

Do animals other than humans feel pain? How do we know? Well, how do we know if anyone, human or nonhuman, feels pain? We know that we ourselves can feel pain. We know this from the direct experiences of pain that we have when, for instance, somebody presses a lighted cigarette against the back of our hand. But how do we know that anyone else feels pain? We cannot directly experience anyone else's pain, whether that "anyone" is our best friend or a stray dog. Pain is a state of consciousness, a "mental event," and as such it can never be observed. Behavior like writhing, screaming, or drawing one's hand away from the lighted cigarette is not pain itself; nor are the recordings a neurologist might make of activity within the brain observations of pain itself. Pain is something that we feel, and we can only infer that others are feeling it from various external indications.

In theory, we *could* always be mistaken when we assume that other human beings feel pain. It is conceivable that our best friend is really a very cleverly constructed robot, controlled by a brilliant scientist so as to give all the signs of feeling pain, but really no more sensitive than any other machine. We can never know, with absolute certainty, that this is not the case. But while this might present a puzzle for philosophers, none of us has the slightest real doubt that our best friends feel pain just as we do. This is an inference, but a perfectly reasonable one, based on observations of their behavior in situations in which we would feel pain, and on the fact that we have every reason to assume that our friends are beings like us, with nervous systems like ours that can be assumed to function as ours do, and to produce similar feelings in similar circumstances.

If it is justifiable to assume that other humans feel pain as we do, is there any reason why a similar inference should be unjustifiable in the case of other animals?

Nearly all the external signs which lead us to infer pain in other humans can be seen in other species, especially the species most closely related to us—other species of mammals, and birds. Behavioral signs—writhing, facial contortions, moaning, yelping or other forms of calling, attempts to avoid the source of pain, appearance of fear at the prospect of its repetition, and so on—are present. In addition, we know that these animals have nervous systems very like ours, which respond physiologically as ours do when the animal is in circumstances in which we would feel pain: an initial rise of blood pressure, dilated pupils, perspiration, an increased pulse rate, and, if the stimulus continues, a fall in blood pressure. Although humans have a more developed cerebral cortex than other animals, this part of the brain is concerned with thinking functions rather than with basic impulses, emotions, and feelings. These impulses, emotions, and feelings are located in the dience-

phalon, which is well developed in many other species of animals, especially mammals and birds.[6]

We also know that the nervous systems of other animals were not artificially constructed to mimic the pain behavior of humans, as a robot might be artificially constructed. The nervous systems of animals evolved as our own did, and in fact the evolutionary history of humans and other animals, especially mammals, did not diverge until the central features of our nervous systems were already in existence. A capacity to feel pain obviously enhances a species' prospects of survival, since it causes members of the species to avoid sources of injury. It is surely unreasonable to suppose that nervous systems which are virtually identical physiologically, have a common origin and a common evolutionary function, and result in similar forms of behavior in similar circumstances should actually operate in an entirely different manner on the level of subjective feelings.

It has long been accepted as sound policy in science to search for the simplest possible explanation of whatever it is we are trying to explain. Occasionally it has been claimed that it is for this reason "unscientific" to explain the behavior of animals by theories that refer to the animal's conscious feelings, desires, and so on—the idea being that if the behavior in question can be explained without invoking consciousness or feelings, that will be the simpler theory. Yet we can now see that such explanations, when placed in the overall context of the behavior of both human and nonhuman animals, are actually far more complex than their rivals. For we know from our own experience that explanations of our own behavior that did not refer to consciousness and the feeling of pain would be incomplete; and it is simpler to assume that the similar behavior of animals with similar nervous systems is to be explained in the same way than to try to invent some other explanation for the behavior of nonhuman animals as well as an explanation for the divergence between humans and nonhumans in this respect.

The overwhelming majority of scientists who have addressed themselves to this question agree. Lord Brain, one of the most eminent neurologists of our time, has said:

> I personally can see no reason for conceding mind to my fellow men and denying it to animals. . . . I at least cannot doubt that the

interests and activities of animals are corre-lated with awareness and feeling in the same way as my own, and which may be, for aught I know, just as vivid.[7]

While the author of a recent book on pain writes:

Every particle of factual evidence supports the contention that the higher mammalian vertebrates experience pain sensations at least as acute as our own. To say that they feel less because they are lower animals is an absurd-ity; it can easily be shown that many of their senses are far more acute than ours—visual acuity in certain birds, hearing in most wild animals, and touch in others; these animals depend more than we do today on the sharp-est possible awareness of a hostile environ-ment. Apart from the complexity of the cere-bral cortex (which does not directly perceive pain) their nervous systems are almost identi-cal to ours and their reactions to pain remark-ably similar, though lacking (so far as we know) the philosophical and moral over-tones. The emotional element is all too evi-dent, mainly in the form of fear and anger.[8]

In Britain, three separate expert government committees on matters relating to animals have accepted the conclusion that animals feel pain. After noting the obvious behavioral evidence for this view, the Committee on Cruelty to Wild Animals said:

. . . we believe that the physiological, and more particularly the anatomical, evidence fully justifies and reinforces the common-sense belief that animals feel pain.

And after discussing the evolutionary value of pain they concluded that pain is "of clear-cut biological usefulness" and this is "a third type of evidence that animals feel pain." They then went on to con-sider forms of suffering other than mere physical pain, and added that they were "satisfied that ani-mals do suffer from acute fear and terror." In 1965, reports by British government committees on experiments on animals, and on the welfare of ani-mals under intensive farming methods, agreed with this view, concluding that animals are capable of suffering both from straightforward physical inju-ries and from fear, anxiety, stress, and so on.[9]

That might well be thought enough to settle the matter; but there is one more objection that needs to be considered. There is, after all, one behavioral sign that humans have when in pain which nonhumans do not have. This is a devel-oped language. Other animals may communicate with each other, but not, it seems, in the compli-cated way we do. Some philosophers, including Descartes, have thought it important that while humans can tell each other about their experience of pain in great detail, other animals cannot. (Inter-estingly, this once neat dividing line between humans and other species has now been threat-ened by the discovery that chimpanzees can be taught a language.)[10] But as Bentham pointed out long ago, the ability to use language is not relevant to the question of how a being ought to be treated—unless that ability can be linked to the capacity to suffer, so that the absence of a language casts doubt on the existence of this capacity.

This link may be attempted in two ways. First, there is a hazy line of philosophical thought, stem-ming perhaps from some doctrines associated with the influential philosopher Ludwig Wittgenstein, which maintains that we cannot meaningfully attribute states of consciousness to beings without language. This position seems to me very implau-sible. Language may be necessary for abstract thought, at some level anyway; but states like pain are more primitive, and have nothing to do with language.

The second and more easily understood way of linking language and the existence of pain is to say that the best evidence that we can have that another creature is in pain is when he tells us that he is. This is a distinct line of argument, for it is not being denied that a non-language-user con-ceivably *could* suffer, but only that we could ever have sufficient reason to *believe* that he is suffering. Still, this line of argument fails too. As Jane Goodall has pointed out in her study of chimpanzees, *In the Shadow of Man,* when it comes to the expressions of feelings and emotions language is less important than in other areas. We tend to fall back on nonlin-guistic modes of communication such as a cheering pat on the back, an exuberant embrace, a clasp of the hands, and so on. The basic signals we use to convey pain, fear, anger, love, joy, surprise, sexual arousal, and many other emotional states are not specific to our own species.[11]

Charles Darwin made an extensive study of this subject, and the book he wrote about it, *The Expression of the Emotions in Man and Animals,* notes countless nonlinguistic modes of expression. The statement "I am in pain" may be one piece of evidence for the conclusion that the speaker is in pain, but it is not the only possible evidence, and since people sometimes tell lies, not even the best possible evidence.

Even if there were stronger grounds for refusing to attribute pain to those who do not have a language, the consequences of this refusal might lead us to reject the conclusion. Human infants and young children are unable to use language. Are we to deny that a year-old child can suffer? If not, language cannot be crucial. Of course, most parents understand the responses of their children better than they understand the responses of other animals; but this is just a fact about the relatively greater knowledge that we have of our own species, and the greater contact we have with infants, as compared to animals. Those who have studied the behavior of other animals, and those who have pet animals, soon learn to understand their responses as well as we understand those of an infant, and sometimes better. Jane Goodall's account of the chimpanzees she watched is one instance of this, but the same can be said of those who have observed species less closely related to our own. Two among many possible examples are Konrad Lorenz's observations of geese and jackdaws, and N. Tinberger's extensive studies of herring gulls.[12] Just as we can understand infant human behavior in the light of adult human behavior, so we can understand the behavior of other species in the light of our own behavior—and sometimes we can understand our own behavior better in the light of the behavior of other species.

So to conclude: there are no good reasons, scientific or philosophical, for denying that animals feel pain. If we do not doubt that other humans feel pain we should not doubt that other animals do so too.

Animals can feel pain. As we saw earlier, there can be no moral justification for regarding the pain (or pleasure) that animals feel as less important than the same amount of pain (or pleasure) felt by humans. But what exactly does this mean, in practical terms? To prevent misunderstanding I shall spell out what I mean a little more fully.

If I give a horse a hard slap across its rump with my open hand, the horse may start, but it presumably feels little pain. Its skin is thick enough to protect it against a mere slap. If I slap a baby in the same way, however, the baby will cry and pre-

sumably does feel pain, for its skin is more sensitive. So it is worse to slap a baby than a horse, if both slaps are administered with equal force. But there must be some kind of blow—I don't know exactly what it would be, but perhaps a blow with a heavy stick—that would cause the horse as much pain as we cause a baby by slapping it with our hand. That is what I mean by "the same amount of pain" and if we consider it wrong to inflict that much pain on a baby for no good reason then we must, unless we are speciesists, consider it equally wrong to inflict the same amount of pain on a horse for no good reason.

There are other differences between humans and animals that cause other complications. Normal adult human beings have mental capacities which will, in certain circumstances, lead them to suffer more than animals would in the same circumstances. If, for instance, we decided to perform extremely painful or lethal scientific experiments on normal adult humans, kidnaped at random from public parks for this purpose, every adult who entered a park would become fearful that he would be kidnaped. The resultant terror would be a form of suffering additional to the pain of the experiment. The same experiments performed on nonhuman animals would cause less suffering since the animals would not have the anticipatory dread of being kidnaped and experimented upon. This does not mean, of course, that it would be right to perform the experiment on animals, but only that there is a reason, which is *not* speciesist, for preferring to use animals rather than normal adult humans, if the experiment is to be done at all. It should be noted, however, that this same argument gives us a reason for preferring to use human infants—orphans perhaps—or retarded humans for experiments, rather than adults, since infants and retarded humans would also have no idea of what was going to happen to them. So far as this argument is concerned nonhuman animals and infants and retarded humans are in the same category; and if we use this argument to justify experiments on nonhuman animals we have to ask ourselves whether we are also prepared to allow experiments on human infants and retarded adults; and if we make a distinction between animals and these humans, on what basis can we do it, other than a barefaced—and morally indefensible—preference for members of our own species?

There are many areas in which the superior mental powers of normal adult humans make a difference: anticipation, more detailed memory, greater knowledge of what is happening, and so on. Yet these differences do not all point to greater suffering on the part of the normal human being. Sometimes an animal may suffer more because of his more limited understanding. If, for instance, we are taking prisoners in wartime we can explain to them that while they must submit to capture, search, and confinement they will not otherwise be harmed and will be set free at the conclusion of hostilities. If we capture a wild animal, however, we cannot explain that we are not threatening its life. A wild animal cannot distinguish an attempt to overpower and confine from an attempt to kill; the one causes as much terror as the other.

It may be objected that comparisons of the sufferings of different species are impossible to make, and that for this reason when the interests of animals and humans clash the principle of equality gives no guidance. It is probably true that comparisons of suffering between members of different species cannot be made precisely, but precision is not essential. Even if we were to prevent the infliction of suffering on animals only when it is quite certain that the interests of humans will not be affected to anything like the extent that animals are affected, we would be forced to make radical changes in our treatment of animals that would involve our diet, the farming methods we use, experimental procedures in many fields of science, our approach to wildlife and to hunting, trapping and the wearing of furs, and areas of entertainment like circuses, rodeos, and zoos. As a result, a vast amount of suffering would be avoided.

So far I have said a lot about the infliction of suffering on animals, but nothing about killing them. This omission has been deliberate. The application of the principle of equality to the infliction of suffering is, in theory at least, fairly straightforward. Pain and suffering are bad and should be prevented or minimized, irrespective of the race, sex, or species of the being that suffers. How bad a pain is depends on how intense it is and how long it lasts, but pains of the same intensity and duration are equally bad, whether felt by humans or animals.

The wrongness of killing a being is more complicated. I have kept, and shall continue to keep, the question of killing in the background because in the present state of human tyranny over other species the more simple, straightforward principle of equal consideration of pain or pleasure is a sufficient basis for identifying and protesting against all the major abuses of animals that humans practice. Nevertheless, it is necessary to say something about killing.

Just as most humans are speciesists in their readiness to cause pain to animals when they would not cause a similar pain to humans for the same reason, so most humans are speciesists in their readiness to kill other animals when they would not kill humans. We need to proceed more cautiously here, however, because people hold widely differing views about when it is legitimate to kill humans, as the continuing debates over abortion and euthanasia attest. Nor have moral philosophers been able to agree on exactly what it is that makes it wrong to kill humans, and under what circumstances killing a human being may be justifiable.

Let us consider first the view that it is always wrong to take an innocent human life. We may call this the "sanctity of life" view. People who take this view oppose abortion and euthanasia. They do not usually, however, oppose the killing of nonhumans—so perhaps it would be more accurate to describe this view as the "sanctity of *human* life" view.

The belief that human life, and only human life, is sacrosanct is a form of speciesism. To see this, consider the following example.

Assume that, as sometimes happens, an infant has been born with massive and irreparable brain damage. The damage is so severe that the infant can never be any more than a "human vegetable," unable to talk, recognize other people, act independently of others, or develop a sense of self-awareness. The parents of the infant, realizing that they cannot hope for any improvement in their child's condition and being in any case unwilling to spend, or ask the state to spend, the thousands of dollars that would be needed annually for proper care of the infant, ask the doctor to kill the infant painlessly.

Should the doctor do what the parents ask? Legally, he should not, and in this respect the law reflects the sanctity of life view. The life of every human being is sacred. Yet people who would say this about the infant do not object to the killing of nonhuman animals. How can they justify their different judgments? Adult chimpanzees, dogs, pigs, and many other species far surpass the brain-damaged infant in their ability to relate to others, act independently, be self-aware, and any other capacity that could reasonably be said to give value to life. With the most intensive care possible, there are retarded infants who can never achieve the intelligence level of a dog. Nor can we appeal to the concern of the infant's parents, since they themselves, in this imaginary example (and in some actual cases), do not want the infant kept alive.

The only thing that distinguishes the infant from the animal, in the eyes of those who claim it has a "right to life," is that it is, biologically, a member of the species Homo sapiens, whereas chimpanzees, dogs, and pigs are not. But to use *this* difference as the basis for granting a right to life to the infant and not to the other animals is, of course, pure speciesism.* It is exactly the kind of arbitrary difference that the most crude and overt kind of racist uses in attempting to justify racial discrimination.

This does not mean that to avoid speciesism we must hold that it is as wrong to kill a dog as it is to kill a normal human being. The only position that is irredeemably speciesist is the one that tries to make the boundary of the right to life run exactly parallel to the boundary of our own species. Those who hold the sanctity of life view do this because while distinguishing sharply between humans and other animals they allow no distinctions to be made within our own species, objecting to the killing of the severely retarded and the hopelessly senile as strongly as they object to the killing of normal adults.

To avoid speciesism we must allow that beings which are similar in all relevant respects have a

*I am here putting aside religious views, for example the doctrine that all and only humans have immortal souls, or are made in the image of God. Historically these views have been very important, and no doubt are partly responsible for the idea that human life has a special sanctity. Logically, however, these religious views are unsatisfactory, since a reasoned explanation of why it should be that all humans and no nonhumans have immortal souls is not offered. This belief too, therefore, comes under suspicion as a form of speciesism. In any case, defenders of the "sanctity of life" view are generally reluctant to base their position on purely religious doctrines, since these doctrines are no longer as widely accepted as they once were.

similar right to life—and mere membership in our own biological species cannot be a morally relevant criterion for this right. Within these limits we could still hold that, for instance, it is worse to kill a normal adult human, with a capacity for self-awareness, and the ability to plan for the future and have meaningful relations with others, than it is to kill a mouse, which presumably does not share all of these characteristics; or we might appeal to the close family and other personal ties which humans have but mice do not have to the same degree; or we might think that it is the consequences for other humans, who will be put in fear of their own lives, that makes the crucial difference; or we might think it is some combination of these factors, or other factors altogether.

Whatever criteria we choose, however, we will have to admit that they do not follow precisely the boundary of our own species. We may legitimately hold that there are some features of certain beings which make their lives more valuable than those of other beings; but there will surely be some nonhuman animals whose lives, by any standards, are more valuable than the lives of some humans. A chimpanzee, dog, or pig, for instance, will have a higher degree of self-awareness and a greater capacity for meaningful relations with others than a severely retarded infant or someone in a state of advanced senility. So if we base the right to life on these characteristics we must grant these animals a right to life as good as, or better than, such retarded or senile humans.

Now this argument cuts both ways. It could be taken as showing that chimpanzees, dogs, and pigs, along with some other species, have a right to life and we commit a grave moral offense whenever we kill them, even when they are old and suffering and our intention is to put them out of their misery. Alternatively one could take the argument as showing that the severely retarded and hopelessly senile have no right to life and may be killed for quite trivial reasons, as we now kill animals.

Since the focus of this book is on ethical questions concerning animals and not on the morality of euthanasia I shall not attempt to settle this issue finally. I think it is reasonably clear, though, that while both of the positions just described avoid speciesism, neither is entirely satisfactory. What we need is some middle position which would avoid speciesism but would not make the lives of the retarded and senile as cheap as the lives of pigs and dogs now are, nor make the lives of pigs and dogs so sacrosanct that we think it wrong to put them out of hopeless misery. What we must do is bring nonhuman animals within our sphere of moral concern and cease to treat their lives as expendable for whatever trivial purposes we may have. At the same time, once we realize that the fact that a being is a member of our own species is not in itself enough to make it always wrong to kill that being, we may come to reconsider our policy of preserving human lives at all costs, even when there is no prospect of a meaningful life or of existence without terrible pain.

I conclude, then, that a rejection of speciesism does not imply that all lives are of equal worth. While self-awareness, intelligence, the capacity for meaningful relations with others, and so on are not relevant to the question of inflicting pain—since pain is pain, whatever other capacities, beyond the capacity to feel pain, the being may have—these capacities may be relevant to the question of taking life. It is not arbitrary to hold that the life of a self-aware being, capable of abstract thought, of planning for the future, of complex acts of communication, and so on, is more valuable than the life of a being without these capacities. To see the difference between the issues of inflicting pain and taking life, consider how we would choose within our own species. If we had to choose to save the life of a normal human or a mentally defective human, we would probably choose to save the life of the normal human; but if we had to choose between preventing pain in the normal human or the mental defective—imagine that both have received painful but superficial injuries, and we only have enough painkiller for one of them—it is not nearly so clear how we ought to choose. The same is true when we consider other species. The evil of pain is, in itself, unaffected by the other characteristics of the being that feels the pain; the value of life is affected by these other characteristics.

Normally this will mean that if we have to choose between the life of a human being and the life of another animal we should choose to save the life of the human; but there may be special cases in which the reverse holds true, because the human being in question does not have the capacities of a normal human being. So this view is not speciesist, although it may appear to be at first glance. The preference, in normal cases, for saving a human life over the life of an animal when a choice *has* to be made is a preference based on the characteristics that normal humans have, and not on the mere fact that they are members of our own species. This is why when we consider members of our own species who lack the characteristics of normal humans we can no longer say that their lives are always to be preferred to those of other animals. This issue comes up in a practical way in the following chapter. In general, though, the question of when it is wrong to kill (painlessly) an animal is one to which we need give no precise answer. As long as we remember that we should give the same respect to the lives of animals as we give to the lives of those humans at a similar mental level, we shall not go far wrong.

In any case, the conclusions that are argued for in this book flow from the principle of minimizing suffering alone. The idea that it is also wrong to kill animals painlessly gives some of these conclusions additional support which is welcome, but strictly unnecessary. Interestingly enough, this is true even of the conclusion that we ought to become vegetarians, a conclusion which in the popular mind is generally based on some kind of absolute prohibition on killing.

Notes

1. For Bentham's moral philosophy, see his *Introduction to the Principles of Morals and Legislation*, and for Sidgwick's see *The Methods of Ethics* (the passage quoted is from the seventh edition, p. 382). As examples of leading contemporary moral philosophers who incorporate a requirement of equal consideration of interests, see R. M. Hare, *Freedom and Reason* (New York: Oxford University Press, 1963) and John Rawls, *A Theory of Justice* (Cambridge: Harvard University Press, Belknap Press, 1972). For a brief account of the essential agreement on this issue between these and other positions, see R. M. Hare, "Rules of War and Moral Reasoning," *Philosophy and Public Affairs*, vol. 1, no. 2 (1972).

2. Letter to Henri Gregoire, February 25, 1809.

3. Reminiscences by Francis D. Gage, from Susan B. Anthony, *The History of Woman Suffrage*, vol. 1; the passage is to be found in the extract in Leslie Tanner, ed., *Voices from Women's Liberation* (New York: Signet, 1970).

4. I owe the term "speciesism" to Richard Ryder.

5. *Introduction to the Principles of Morals and Legislation*, chapter 17.

6. Lord Brain, "Presidential Address" in C. A. Keele and R. Smith, eds., *The Assessment of Pain in Men and Animals* (London: Universities Federation for Animal Welfare, 1962).

7. Ibid., p. 11.

8. Richard Serjeant, *The Spectrum of Pain* (London: Hart-Davis, 1969), p. 72.

9. See the reports of the Committee on Cruelty to Wild Animals (Command Paper 8266, 1951), paragraphs 36-42; the Departmental Committee on Experiments on Animals (Command Paper 2641, 1965), paragraphs 179-182; and the Technical Committee to Enquire into the Welfare of Animals Kept under Intensive Livestock Husbandry Systems (Command Paper 2836, 1965), paragraphs 26-28 (London: Her Majesty's Stationery Office).

10. One chimpanzee, Washoe, has been taught the sign language used by deaf people, and acquired a vocabulary of 350 signs. Another, Lana, communicates in structured sentences by pushing buttons on a special machine. For a brief account of Washoe's abilities, see Jane van Lawick-Goodall, *In the Shadow of Man* (Boston: Houghton Mifflin, 1971), pp. 252–254; and for Lana, see *Newsweek*, 7 January 1974, and *New York Times*, 4 December 1974.

11. *In the Shadow of Man*, p. 225; Michael Peters makes a similar point in "Nature and Culture," in Stanley and Roslind Godlovitch and John Harris, eds., *Animals, Men and Morals* (New York: Taplinger Publishing Co., 1972).

12. Konrad Lorenz, *King Solomon's Ring* (New York: T. Y. Crowell, 1952); N. Tinbergen, *The Herring Gull's World*, rev. ed. (New York: Basic Books, 1974).

Questions for Analysis

1. *What does Singer mean by his claim that the principle of human equality is not a description of actual equality, but a prescription of how we should treat humans?*

2. *On what grounds does Singer equate speciesism with sexism and racism?*

3. *What reasons have been advanced in favor of the view that animals cannot suffer? How does Singer rebut them?*

4. *Singer notes certain differences between human and nonhuman capacities and the complications that follow from them. What are these differences, and what kinds of complications follow from them?*

5. *To reject speciesism, Singer says, is not to say that all lives are of equal worth. Why not?*

6. *Normally, Singer says, we should choose a human over a nonhuman life if forced to choose between them. Why? Under what circumstances should we choose the nonhuman one?*

7. *In what way is Singer's principle of equal consideration related to the principle of utility?*

The Case for Animal Rights

Tom Regan

In this essay, Tom Regan offers an alternative approach to Peter Singer's. Like Singer, he opposes speciesism. Unlike Singer, he does not offer a utilitarian moral theory. He argues that the focus of our moral concern should not be to minimize suffering and maximize pleasure but to avoid treating individual animals (human and nonhuman alike) in certain ways regardless of the consequences.

All animals that are the experiencing subjects of their own lives, he says, have inherent value. They, like humans, deserve what we called in Part I Kantian respect. They are not to be treated as mere things, even if we can maximize happiness by doing so. What makes eating meat or experimenting on animals wrong, then, is not that the human benefit does not outweigh the animal suffering, but that such practices deny the inherent value of the animals involved.

In defending his position, Regan criticizes contractarian views of morality, which deny that nonhuman animals can have rights. He also disagrees with Singer's view that some lives of creatures with the right to life are more valuable than others. All lives that have inherent value, he says, are equal.

I regard myself as an advocate of animal rights—as a part of the animal rights movement. That movement, as I conceive it, is committed to a number of goals, including:

> the total abolition of the use of animals in science;
>
> the total dissolution of commercial animal agriculture;
>
> the total elimination of commercial and sport hunting and trapping.

There are, I know, people who profess to believe in animal rights but do not avow these goals. Factory farming, they say, is wrong—it violates animals' rights—but traditional animal agriculture is all right. Toxicity tests of cosmetics on animals violates their rights, but important medical research—cancer research, for example—does not. The clubbing of baby seals is abhorrent, but not the harvesting of adult seals. I used to think I understood this reasoning. Not any more. You don't change unjust institutions by tidying them up.

What's wrong—fundamentally wrong—with the way animals are treated isn't the details that vary from case to case. It's the whole system. The forlornness of the veal calf is pathetic, heart wrenching; the pulsing pain of the chimp with electrodes planted deep in her brain is repulsive; the slow, tortuous death of the raccoon caught in the leg-hold trap is agonizing. But what is wrong isn't the pain, isn't the suffering, isn't the deprivation. These compound what's wrong. Sometimes—often—they make it much, much worse. But they are not the fundamental wrong.

The fundamental wrong is the system that allows us to view animals as *our resources*, here for *us*—to be eaten, or surgically manipulated, or exploited for sport or money. Once we accept this view of animals—as our resources—the rest is as predictable as it is regrettable. Why worry about their loneliness, their pain, their death? Since animals exist for us, to benefit us in one way or another, what harms them really doesn't matter—or matters only if it starts to bother us, makes us feel a trifle uneasy when we eat our veal escalope, for example. So, yes, let us get veal calves out of solitary confinement, give them more space, a little straw, a few companions. But let us keep our veal escalope.

From "The Case for Animal Rights," in In Defense of Animals *edited by Peter Singer (1985), pp. 13–26. Reprinted by permission of Peter Singer and Tom Regan.*

But a little straw, more space and a few companions won't eliminate—won't even touch—the basic wrong that attaches to our viewing and treating these animals as our resources. A veal calf killed to be eaten after living in close confinement is viewed and treated in this way: but so, too, is another who is raised (as they say) 'more humanely.' To right the wrong of our treatment of farm animals requires more than making rearing methods 'more humane'; it requires the total dissolution of commercial animal agriculture.

How we do this, whether we do it or, as in the case of animals in science, whether and how we abolish their use—these are to a large extent political questions. People must change their beliefs before they change their habits. Enough people, especially those elected to public office, must believe in change—must want it—before we will have laws that protect the rights of animals. This process of change is very complicated, very demanding, very exhausting, calling for the efforts of many hands in education, publicity, political organization and activity, down to the licking of envelopes and stamps. As a trained and practising philosopher, the sort of contribution I can make is limited but, I like to think, important. The currency of philosophy is ideas—their meaning and rational foundation—not the nuts and bolts of the legislative process, say, or the mechanics of community organization. That's what I have been exploring over the past ten years or so in my essays and talks and, most recently, in my book, *The Case for Animal Rights*. I believe the major conclusions I reach in the book are true because they are supported by the weight of the best arguments. I believe the idea of animal rights has reason, not just emotion, on its side.

In the space I have at my disposal here I can only sketch, in the barest outline, some of the main features of the book. Its main themes—and we should not be surprised by this—involve asking and answering deep, foundational moral questions about what morality is, how it should be understood and what is the best moral theory, all considered. I hope I can convey something of the shape I think this theory takes. The attempt to do this will be (to use a word a friendly critic once used to describe my work) cerebral, perhaps too cerebral. But this is misleading. My feelings about how animals are sometimes treated run just as deep and just as strong as those of my more volatile compatriots. Philosophers do—to use the jargon of the day—have a right side to their brains. If it's the left side we contribute (or mainly should), that's because what talents we have reside there.

How to proceed? We begin by asking how the moral status of animals has been understood by thinkers who deny that animals have rights. Then we test the mettle of their ideas by seeing how well they stand up under the heat of fair criticism. If we start our thinking in this way, we soon find that some people believe that we have no duties directly to animals, that we owe nothing to them, that we can do nothing that wrongs them. Rather, we can do wrong acts that involve animals, and so we have duties regarding them, though none to them. Such views may be called indirect duty views. By way of illustration: suppose your neighbour kicks your dog. Then your neighbour has done something wrong. But not to your dog. The wrong that has been done is a wrong to you. After all, it is wrong to upset people, and your neighbour's kicking your dog upsets you. So you are the one who is wronged, not your dog. Or again: by kicking your dog your neighbour damages your property. And since it is wrong to damage another person's property, your neighbour has done something wrong—to you, of course, not to your dog. Your neighbour no more wrongs your dog than your car would be wronged if the windshield were smashed. Your neighbour's duties involving your dog are indirect duties to you. More generally, all of our duties regarding animals are indirect duties to one another—to humanity.

How could someone try to justify such a view? Someone might say that your dog doesn't feel anything and so isn't hurt by your neighbour's kick, doesn't care about the pain since none is felt, is as unaware of anything as is your windshield. Someone might say this, but no rational person will, since, among other considerations, such a view will commit anyone who holds it to the position that no human being feels pain either—that human beings also don't care about what happens to them. A second possibility is that though both humans and your dog are hurt when kicked, it is only human pain that matters. But, again, no rational person can believe this. Pain is pain wherever it occurs. If your neighbour's causing you pain is wrong because of the pain that is caused, we cannot rationally ignore or dismiss the moral relevance of the pain that your dog feels.

Philosophers who hold indirect duty views—and many still do—have come to understand that they must avoid the two defects just noted: that is, both the view that animals don't feel anything as well as the idea that only human pain can be morally relevant. Among such thinkers the sort of view now favoured is one or other form of what is called *contractarianism*.

Here, very crudely, is the root idea: morality consists of a set of rules that individuals voluntarily agree to abide by, as we do when we sign a contract (hence the name contractarianism). Those who understand and accept the terms of the contract are covered directly; they have rights created and recognized by, and protected in, the contract. And these contractors can also have protection spelled out for others who, though they lack the ability to understand morality and so cannot sign the contract themselves, are loved or cherished by those who can. Thus young children, for example, are unable to sign contracts and lack rights. But they are protected by the contract none the less because of the sentimental interests of others, most notably their parents. So we have, then, duties involving these children, duties regarding them, but no duties to them. Our duties in their case are indirect duties to other human beings, usually their parents.

As for animals, since they cannot understand contracts, they obviously cannot sign; and since they cannot sign, they have no rights. Like children, however, some animals are the objects of the sentimental interest of others. You, for example, love your dog or cat. So those animals that enough people care about (companion animals, whales, baby seals, the American bald eagle), though they lack rights themselves, will be protected because of the sentimental interests of people. I have, then, according to contractarianism, no duty directly to your dog or any other animal, not even the duty not to cause them pain or suffering; my duty not to hurt them is a duty I have to those people who care about what happens to them. As for other animals, where no or little sentimental interest is present—in the case of farm animals, for example, or laboratory rats—what duties we have grow weaker and weaker, perhaps to vanishing point. The pain and death they endure, though real, are not wrong if no one cares about them.

When it comes to the moral status of animals, contractarianism could be a hard view to refute if it were an adequate theoretical approach to the moral status of human beings. It is not adequate in this latter respect, however, which makes the question of its adequacy in the former case, regarding animals, utterly moot. For consider: morality, according to the (crude) contractarian position before us, consists of rules that people agree to abide by. What people? Well, enough to make a difference—enough, that is, *collectively* to have the power to enforce the rules that are drawn up in the contract. That is very well and good for the signatories but not so good for anyone who is not asked to sign. And there is nothing in contractarianism of the sort we are discussing that guarantees or requires that everyone will have a chance to participate equally in framing the rules of morality. The result is that this approach to ethics could sanction the most blatant forms of social, economic, moral and political injustice, ranging from a repressive caste system to systematic racial or sexual discrimination. Might, according to this theory, does make right. Let those who are the victims of injustice suffer as they will. It matters not so long as no one else—no contractor, or too few of them—cares about it. Such a theory takes one's moral breath away . . . as if, for example, there would be nothing wrong with apartheid in South Africa if few white South Africans were upset by it. A theory with so little to recommend it at the level of the ethics of our treatment of our fellow humans cannot have anything more to recommend it when it comes to the ethics of how we treat our fellow animals.

The version of contractarianism just examined is, as I have noted, a crude variety, and in fairness to those of a contractarian persuasion it must be noted that much more refined, subtle and ingenious varieties are possible. For example, John Rawls, in his *A Theory of Justice*, sets forth a version of contractarianism that forces contractors to ignore the accidental features of being a human being—for example, whether one is white or black, male or female, a genius or of modest intellect. Only by ignoring such features, Rawls believes, can we ensure that the principles of justice that contractors would agree upon are not based on bias or prejudice. Despite the improvement a view such as Rawls's represents over the cruder forms of contractarianism, it remains deficient: it systematically denies that we have direct duties to those human beings who do not have a sense of justice—young children, for instance, and many mentally retarded humans. And yet it seems reasonably certain that, were we to torture a young child or a retarded elder, we would be doing something that wronged him or her, not something that would be wrong if (and only if) other humans with a sense of justice were upset. And since this is true in the case of these humans, we cannot rationally deny the same in the case of animals.

Indirect duty views, then, including the best among them, fail to command our rational assent. Whatever ethical theory we should accept rationally, therefore, it must at least recognize that we have some duties directly to animals, just as we have some duties directly to each other. The next two theories I'll sketch attempt to meet this requirement.

The first I call the cruelty-kindness view. Simply stated, this says that we have a direct duty to be kind to animals and a direct duty not to be cruel to them. Despite the familiar, reassuring ring of these ideas, I do not believe that this view offers an adequate theory. To make this clearer, consider kindness. A kind person acts from a certain kind of motive—compassion or concern, for example. And that is a virtue. But there is no guarantee that a kind act is a right act. If I am a generous racist, for example, I will be inclined to act kindly towards members of my own race, favouring their interests above those of others. My kindness would be real and, so far as it goes, good. But I trust it is too obvious to require argument that my kind acts may not be above moral reproach—may, in fact, be positively wrong because rooted in injustice. So kindness, notwithstanding its status as a virtue to be encouraged, simply will not carry the weight of a theory of right action.

Cruelty fares no better. People or their acts are cruel if they display either a lack of sympathy for or, worse, the presence of enjoyment in another's suffering. Cruelty in all its guises is a bad thing, a tragic human failing. But just as a person's being motivated by kindness does not guarantee that he or she does what is right, so the absence of cruelty does not ensure that he or she avoids doing what is wrong. Many people who perform abortions, for example, are not cruel, sadistic people. But that fact alone does not settle the terribly difficult question of the morality of abortion. The case is no different when we examine the ethics of our treatment of animals. So, yes, let us be for kindness and against cruelty. But let us not suppose that being for the one and against the other answers questions about moral right and wrong.

Some people think that the theory we are looking for is utilitarianism. A utilitarian accepts two moral principles. The first is that of equality: everyone's interests count, and similar interests must be counted as having similar weight or importance. White or black, American or Iranian, human or animal—everyone's pain or frustration matters, and matters just as much as the equivalent pain or frustration of anyone else. The second principle a utilitarian accepts is that of utility: do the act that will bring about the best balance between satisfaction and frustration for everyone affected by the outcome.

As a utilitarian, then, here is how I am to approach the task of deciding what I morally ought to do: I must ask who will be affected if I choose to do one thing rather than another, how much each individual will be affected, and where the best results are most likely to lie—which option, in other words, is most likely to bring about the best results, the best balance between satisfaction and frustration. That option, whatever it may be, is the one I ought to choose. That is where my moral duty lies.

The great appeal of utilitarianism rests with its uncompromising *egalitarianism:* everyone's interests count and count as much as the like interests of everyone else. The kind of odious discrimination that some forms of contractarianism can justify—discrimination based on race or sex, for example—seems disallowed in principle by utilitarianism, as is speciesism, systematic discrimination based on species membership.

The equality we find in utilitarianism, however, is not the sort an advocate of animal or human rights should have in mind. Utilitarianism has no room for the equal moral rights of different individuals because it has no room for their equal inherent value or worth. What has value for the utilitarian is the satisfaction of an individual's interests, not the individual whose interests they are. A universe in which you satisfy your desire for water, food and warmth is, other things being equal, better than a universe in which these desires are frustrated. And the same is true in the case of an animal with similar desires. But neither you nor the animal has any value in your own right. Only your feelings do.

Here is an analogy to help make the philosophical point clearer: a cup contains different liquids, sometimes sweet, sometimes bitter, sometimes a mix of the two. What has value are the liquids: the sweeter the better, the bitterer the worse. The cup, the container, has no value. It is what goes into it, not what they go into, that has value. For the utilitarian you and I are like the cup; we have no value as individuals and thus no equal value. What has value is what goes into us, what we serve as receptacles for; our feelings of satisfaction have positive value, our feelings of frustration negative value.

Serious problems arise for utilitarianism when we remind ourselves that it enjoins us to bring about the best consequences. What does this mean? It doesn't mean the best consequences for me alone, or for my family or friends, or any other person taken individually. No, what we must do is, roughly, as follows: we must add up (somehow!) the separate satisfactions and frustrations of everyone likely to be affected by our choice, the satisfactions in one column, the frustrations in the other. We must total each column for each of the options before us. That is what it means to say the theory is aggregative. And then we must choose that option which is most likely to bring about the best balance of totaled satisfactions over totaled frustrations. Whatever act would lead to this outcome is the one we ought morally to perform—it is where our moral duty lies. And that act quite clearly might not be the same one that would bring about the best results for me personally, or for my family or friends, or for a lab animal. The best aggregated consequences for everyone concerned are not necessarily the best for each individual.

That utilitarianism is an aggregative theory—different individuals' satisfactions or frustrations are added, or summed, or totaled—is the key objection to this theory. My Aunt Bea is old, inactive, a cranky, sour person, though not physically ill. She prefers to go on living. She is also rather rich. I could make a fortune if I could get my hands

on her money, money she intends to give me in any event, after she dies, but which she refuses to give me now. In order to avoid a huge tax bite, I plan to donate a handsome sum of my profits to a local children's hospital. Many, many children will benefit from my generosity, and much joy will be brought to their parents, relatives and friends. If I don't get the money rather soon, all these ambitions will come to naught. The once-in-a-lifetime opportunity to make a real killing will be gone. Why, then, not kill my Aunt Bea? Of course I *might* get caught. But I'm no fool and, besides, her doctor can be counted on to cooperate (he has an eye for the same investment and I happen to know a good deal about his shady past). The deed can be done . . . professionally, shall we say. There is *very* little chance of getting caught. And as for my conscience being guilt-ridden, I am a resourceful sort of fellow and will take more than sufficient comfort—as I lie on the beach at Acapulco—in contemplating the joy and health I have brought to so many others.

Suppose Aunt Bea is killed and the rest of the story comes out as told. Would I have done anything wrong? Anything immoral? One would have thought that I had. Not according to utilitarianism. Since what I have done has brought about the best balance between totaled satisfaction and frustration for all those affected by the outcome, my action is not wrong. Indeed, in killing Aunt Bea the physician and I did what duty required.

This same kind of argument can be repeated in all sorts of cases, illustrating, time after time, how the utilitarian's position leads to results that impartial people find morally callous. It *is* wrong to kill my Aunt Bea in the name of bringing about the best results for others. A good end does not justify an evil means. Any adequate moral theory will have to explain why this is so. Utilitarianism fails in this respect and so cannot be the theory we seek.

What to do? Where to begin anew? The place to begin, I think, is with the utilitarian's view of the value of the individual—or, rather, lack of value. In its place, suppose we consider that you and I, for example, do have value as individuals—what we'll call *inherent value*. To say we have such value is to say that we are something more than, something different from, mere receptacles. Moreover, to ensure that we do not pave the way for such injustices as slavery or sexual discrimination, we must believe that all who have inherent value have it equally, regardless of their sex, race, religion, birthplace and so on. Similarly to be discarded as irrelevant are one's talents or skills, intelligence and wealth, personality or pathology, whether one is loved and admired or despised and loathed. The genius and the retarded child, the prince and the pauper, the brain surgeon and the fruit vendor, Mother Teresa and the most unscrupulous used-car salesman—all have inherent value, all possess it equally, and all have an equal right to be treated with respect, to be treated in ways that do not reduce them to the status of things, as if they existed as resources for others. My value as an individual is independent of my usefulness to you. Yours is not dependent on your usefulness to me. For either of us to treat the other in ways that fail to show respect for the other's independent value is to act immorally, to violate the individual's rights.

Some of the rational virtues of this view—what I call the rights view—should be evident. Unlike (crude) contractarianism, for example, the rights view in *principle* denies the moral tolerability of any and all forms of racial, sexual or social discrimination; and unlike utilitarianism, this view *in principle* denies that we can justify good results by using evil means that violate an individual's rights—denies, for example, that it could be moral to kill my Aunt Bea to harvest beneficial consequences for others. That would be to sanction the disrespectful treatment of the individual in the name of the social good, something the rights view will not—categorically will not—ever allow.

The rights view, I believe, is rationally the most satisfactory moral theory. It surpasses all other theories in the degree to which it illuminates and explains the foundation of our duties to one another—the domain of human morality. On this score it has the best reasons, the best arguments, on its side. Of course, if it were possible to show that only human beings are included within its scope, then a person like myself, who believes in animal rights, would be obliged to look elsewhere.

But attempts to limit its scope to humans only can be shown to be rationally defective. Animals, it is true, lack many of the abilities humans possess. They can't read, do higher mathematics, build a bookcase or make *baba ghanoush*. Neither can many

human beings, however, and yet we don't (and shouldn't) say that they (these humans) therefore have less inherent value, less of a right to be treated with respect, than do others. It is the *similarities* between those human beings who most clearly, most non-controversially have such value (the people reading this, for example), not our differences, that matter most. And the really crucial, the basic similarity is simply this: we are each of us the experiencing subject of a life, a conscious creature having an individual welfare that has importance to us whatever our usefulness to others. We want and prefer things, believe and feel things, recall and expect things. And all these dimensions of our life, including our pleasure and pain, our enjoyment and suffering, our satisfaction and frustration, our continued existence or our untimely death—all make a difference to the quality of our life as lived, as experienced, by us as individuals. As the same is true of those animals that concern us (the ones that are eaten and trapped, for example), they too must be viewed as the experiencing subjects of a life, with inherent value of their own.

Some there are who resist the idea that animals have inherent value. "Only humans have such value," they profess. How might this narrow view be defended? Shall we say that only humans have the requisite intelligence, or autonomy, or reason? But there are many, many humans who fail to meet these standards and yet are reasonably viewed as having value above and beyond their usefulness to others. Shall we claim that only humans belong to the right species, the species *Homo sapiens*? But this is blatant speciesism. Will it be said, then, that all—and only—humans have immortal souls? Then our opponents have their work cut out for them. I am myself not ill-disposed to the proposition that there are immortal souls. Personally, I profoundly hope I have one. But I would not want to rest my position on a controversial ethical issue on the even more controversial question about who or what has an immortal soul. That is to dig one's hole deeper, not to climb out. Rationally, it is better to resolve moral issues without making more controversial assumptions than are needed. The question of who has inherent value is such a question, one that is resolved more rationally without the introduction of the idea of immortal souls than by its use.

Well, perhaps some will say that animals have

some inherent value, only less than we have. Once again, however, attempts to defend this view can be shown to lack rational justification. What could be the basis of our having more inherent value than animals? Their lack of reason, or autonomy, or intellect? Only if we are willing to make the same judgment in the case of humans who are similarly deficient. But it is not true that such humans—the retarded child, for example, or the mentally deranged—have less inherent value than you or I. Neither, then, can we rationally sustain the view that animals like them in being the experiencing subjects of a life have less inherent value. *All* who have inherent value have it *equally*, whether they be human animals or not.

Inherent value, then, belongs equally to those who are the experiencing subjects of a life. Whether it belongs to others—to rocks and rivers, trees and glaciers, for example—we do not know and may never know. But neither do we need to know, if we are to make the case for animal rights. We do not need to know, for example, how many people are eligible to vote in the next presidential election before we can know whether I am. Similarly, we do not need to know how many individuals have inherent value before we can know that some do. When it comes to the case for animal rights, then, what we need to know is whether the animals that, in our culture, are routinely eaten, hunted and used in our laboratories, for example, are like us in being subjects of a life. And we do know this. We do know that many—literally, billions and billions—of these animals are the subjects of a life in the sense explained and so have inherent value if we do. And since, in order to arrive at the best theory of our duties to one another, we must recognize our equal inherent value as individuals, reason—not sentiment, not emotion—reason compels us to recognize the equal inherent value of these animals and, with this, their equal right to be treated with respect.

That, *very* roughly, is the shape and feel of the case for animal rights. Most of the details of the supporting argument are missing. They are to be found in the book to which I alluded earlier. Here, the details go begging, and I must, in closing, limit myself to four final points.

The first is how the theory that underlies the case for animal rights shows that the animal rights movement is a part of, not antagonistic to, the human rights movement. The theory that rationally grounds the rights of animals also grounds the rights of humans. Thus those involved in the animal rights movement are partners in the struggle to secure respect for human rights—the rights of women, for example, or minorities, or workers. The animal rights movement is cut from the same moral cloth as these.

Second, having set out the broad outlines of the rights view, I can now say why its implications for farming and science, among other fields, are both clear and uncompromising. In the case of the use of animals in science, the rights view is categorically abolitionist. Lab animals are not our tasters; we are not their kings. Because these animals are treated routinely, systematically as if their value were reducible to their usefulness to others, they are routinely, systematically treated with a lack of respect, and thus are their rights routinely, systematically violated. This is just as true when they are used in trivial, duplicative, unnecessary or unwise research as it is when they are used in studies that hold out real promise of human benefits. We can't justify harming or killing a human being (my Aunt Bea, for example) just for these sorts of reason. Neither can we do so even in the case of so lowly a creature as a laboratory rat. It is not just refinement or reduction that is called for, not just larger, cleaner cages, not just more generous use of anaesthetic or the elimination of multiple surgery, not just tidying up the system. It is complete replacement. The best we can do when it comes to using animals in science is—not to use them. That is where our duty lies, according to the rights view.

As for commercial animal agriculture, the rights view takes a similar abolitionist position. The fundamental moral wrong here is not that animals are kept in stressful close confinement or in isolation, or that their pain and suffering, their needs and preferences are ignored or discounted. All these *are* wrong, of course, but they are not the fundamental wrong. They are symptoms and effects of the deeper, systematic wrong that allows these animals to be viewed and treated as lacking independent value, as resources for us—as, indeed, a renewable resource. Giving farm animals more space, more natural environments, more companions does not right the fundamental wrong, any more than giving lab animals more anaesthesia or bigger, cleaner cages would right the fundamental wrong in their case. Nothing less than the total dissolution of commercial animal agriculture will do this, just as, for similar reasons I won't develop at length here, morality requires nothing less than the total elimination of hunting and trapping for commercial and sporting ends. The rights view's implications, then, as I have said, are clear and uncompromising.

My last two points are about philosophy, my profession. It is, most obviously, no substitute for political action. The words I have written here and in other places by themselves don't change a thing. It is what we do with the thoughts that the words express—our acts, our deeds—that changes things. All that philosophy can do, and all I have attempted, is to offer a vision of what our deeds should aim at. And the why. But not the how.

Finally, I am reminded of my thoughtful critic, the one I mentioned earlier, who chastised me for being too cerebral. Well, cerebral I have been: indirect duty views, utilitarianism, contractarianism—hardly the stuff deep passions are made of. I am also reminded, however, of the image another friend once set before me—the image of the ballerina as expressive of disciplined passion. Long hours of sweat and toil, of loneliness and practice, of doubt and fatigue: those are the discipline of her craft. But the passion is there too, the fierce drive to excel, to speak through her body, to do it right, to pierce our minds. That is the image of philosophy I would leave with you, not "too cerebral" but *disciplined passion*. Of the discipline enough has been seen. As for the passion: there are times, and these not infrequent, when tears come to my eyes when I see, or read, or hear of the wretched plight of animals in the hands of humans. Their pain, their suffering, their loneliness, their innocence, their death. Anger. Rage. Pity. Sorrow. Disgust. The whole creation groans under the weight of the evil we humans visit upon these mute, powerless creatures. It *is* our hearts, not just our heads, that call for an end to it all, that demand of us that we overcome, for them, the habits and forces behind their systematic oppression. All great movements, it is written, go through three stages: ridicule, discussion, adoption. It is the realization of this third stage, adoption, that requires both our passion and our discipline, our hearts and our heads. The fate of animals is in our hands. God grant we are equal to the task.

Questions for Analysis

1. *What is the difference between direct and indirect duties? Why does Regan reject the view that we can have only indirect duties to nonhuman animals?*

2. *On what grounds does Regan reject contractarian views of moral obligations?*

3. *What is the cruelty-kindness view of morality? Why does Regan find it inadequate?*

4. *What does Regan find appealing about utilitarian thinking? What does he find objectionable about it?*

5. *What does Regan mean by inherent value? What traits must a creature possess to have it?*

6. *What objections to the view that some animals have inherent value does Regan consider? How does he rebut them?*

7. *What practical differences can you see between Regan's view and Singer's?*

Immoral and Moral Uses of Animals

Christina Hoff

The following essay by Christina Hoff deals with a particular issue of the animal rights movement—experimentation on animals. The view she defends is sympathetic to the animal rights movement, but her position is more moderate than both Regan's and Singer's.

She begins by rejecting traditional arguments against animal rights, but she does not draw the conclusion that nonhuman animals deserve consideration equal to that of humans. Although nonhuman animals are equally capable of suffering pain, she says, morally critical differences remain between humans and other animals. Her conclusion, then, is that dangerous and painful animal experimentation may be morally permissible, but only if they yield "vital benefits for humans or other animals."

One can do something wrong to a tree, but it makes no sense to speak of wronging it. Can one wrong an animal? Many philosophers think not, and many research scientists adopt the attitude that the use of laboratory animals raises no serious moral questions. It is understandable that they should do so. Moral neutrality toward the objects of one's research is conducive to scientific practice. Scientists naturally wish to concentrate on their research and thus tend not to confront the problems that may arise in the choice of techniques. In support of this attitude of indifference, they could cite philosophers who point to features peculiar to human life, by virtue of which painful experimentation on unwilling human beings is rightly to be judged morally reprehensible and that on animals not. What are these features?

Rationality and the ability to communicate meaningfully with others are the most commonly mentioned differentiating characteristics. Philosophers as diverse as Aristotle, Aquinas, Descartes, and Kant point to man's deliberative capacities as the source of his moral preeminence. Animals, because they are irrational, have been denied standing. The trouble is that not all human beings are rational. Mentally retarded or severely brain-damaged human beings are sometimes much less intelligent than lower primates that have been successfully taught to employ primitive languages and make simple, logical inferences beyond the capac-ity of the normal three-year-old child. The view that rationality is the qualifying condition for moral status has the awkward consequence of leaving unexplained our perceived obligations to nonrational humanity.

Some philosophers have therefore argued that man's privileged moral status is owed to his capacity for suffering. To be plausible, this way of explaining man's position as the only being who can be wronged must discount the apparent suffering of mammals and other highly organized creatures. It is sometimes assumed that the subjective experience of pain is quite different for animals and human beings. Descartes, for example, maintains that animals are machines: he speaks of tropisms of avoidance and desire rather than pleasure and pain.[1] Although it is true that human beings can suffer in ways that animals cannot, the idea that animals and human beings experience physical pain differently is physiologically incoherent. We know that animals feel pain because of their behavioral reactions (including writhing, screaming, facial contortions, and desperate efforts to escape the source of pain), the evidence of their nervous systems, and the evolutionary value of pain. (By "animals" I mean mammals, birds, and other organisms of comparable evolutionary complexity.)

There are other sources of human suffering besides pain, but they too are not peculiarly human.

From The New England Journal of Medicine, *Vol. 302, No. 2, pp. 115–118, January 10, 1980. Reprinted with permission of the publisher.*

One has only to consult the reports of naturalists or go to the zoo or own a pet to learn that the higher animals, at least, can suffer from loneliness, jealousy, boredom, frustration, rage, and terror. If, indeed, the capacity to suffer is the morally relevant characteristic, then the facts determine that animals, along with all human beings, are the proper subjects of moral consideration.

There is, however, another common way of defending human privilege. It is sometimes asserted that "just being human" is a sufficient basis for a protected moral status, that sheer membership in the species confers exclusive moral rights. Each human life, no matter how impoverished, has a depth and meaning that transcends that of even the most gifted dolphin or chimpanzee. One may speak of this as the humanistic principle. Cicero was one of its earliest exponents: "Honor every human being because he is a human being."[2] Kant called it the Principle of Personality and placed it at the foundation of his moral theory.[3] The principle appears evident to us because it is embodied in the attitudes and institutions of most civilized communities. Although this accounts for its intuitive appeal, it is hardly an adequate reason to accept it. Without further argument the humanistic principle is arbitrary. What must be adduced is an acceptable criterion for awarding special rights. But when we proffer a criterion based, say, on the capacity to reason or to suffer, it is clearly inadequate either because it is satisfied by some but not all members of the species *Homo sapiens*, or because it is satisfied by them all—and many other animals as well.

Another type of argument for denying equal consideration to animals goes back at least to Aristotle. I refer to the view that man's tyranny over animals is natural because his superiority as an animal determines for him the dominant position in the natural scale of things. To suggest that man give up his dominance over animals is to suggest that he deny his nature. The argument assumes that "denial of nature" is ethically incoherent. But conformity with nature is not an adequate condition for ethical standards. Being moral does not appear to be a question of abiding by the so-called laws of nature; just as often it seems to require us to disregard what is "natural" in favor of what is compassionate. We avoid slavery and child labor, not because we have discovered that they are unnatural, but because we have discovered that slaves and children have their own desires and interests and they engage our sympathy. Social Darwinism was an ethical theory that sought to deduce moral rules from the "facts" of nature. Wealthy 19th-century industrialists welcomed a theory that seemed to justify inhumane labor practices by reference to the "natural order of things." It has become clear that these so-called "laws" of nature cannot provide an adequate basis for a moral theory, if only because they may be cited to support almost any conceivable theory.

It is fair to say that no one has yet given good reasons to accept a moral perspective that grants a privileged moral status to all and only human beings. A crucial moral judgment is made when one decides that a given course of action with respect to a certain class of beings does not fall within the range of moral consideration. Historically, mistakes at this level have proved dangerous: they leave the agent free to perpetrate heinous acts that are not regarded as either moral or immoral and are therefore unchecked by normal inhibition. The exclusion of animals from the moral domain may well be a similar and equally benighted error. It is, in any case, arbitrary and unfounded in good moral argument.

Whatever belongs to the moral domain can be wronged. But if one rejects the doctrine that membership in the moral domain necessarily coincides with membership in the human species, then one must state a satisfactory condition for moral recognition. Bentham offers an intuitively acceptable starting point. "The question is not, Can they *reason*?, nor, Can they *talk*? but Can they *suffer*?"[4] The capacity to suffer confers a minimal prima facie moral status on any creature, for it seems reasonable that one who is wantonly cruel to a sentient creature wrongs that creature. Animals too can be wronged; the practical consequences of such a moral position are, however, not as clear as they may seem. We must consider what we may and may not do to them.

I begin with a word about the comparative worthiness of human and animal life. Although animals are entitled to moral consideration, it does not follow that animals and human beings are always equal before the moral law. Distinctions must still be made. One may acknowledge that animals have rights without committing oneself to a radical egalitarianism that awards to animals complete parity with human beings. If hunting animals for sport is wrong, hunting human beings for the same purpose is worse, and such a distinction is not inconsistent with recognizing that animals have moral status. Although some proponents of animal rights would deny it, there are morally critical differences between animals and human beings. Animals share with human beings a common interest in avoiding pain, but the complexities of normal human life clearly provide a relevant basis for assigning to human beings a far more serious right to life itself. When we kill a human being, we take away his physical existence (eating, sleeping, and feeling pleasure and pain), but we deprive him of other things as well. His projects, his friendships, and his sense of himself as a human being are also terminated. To kill a human being is not only to take away his life, but to impugn the special meaning of his life. In contrast, an animal's needs and desires are restricted to his place in time and space. He lives "the life of the moment." Human lives develop and unfold; they have a direction. Animal lives do not. Accordingly, I suggest the following differential principle of life worthiness: Human lives are generally worthier than animal lives, and the right to life of a human being generally supersedes the right to life of an animal.

This differential principle rejects the Cartesian thesis, which totally dismisses animals from moral consideration, and it is consistent with two other principles that I have been tacitly defending: animals are moral subjects with claims to considerations that should not be ignored; and an animal's experience of pain is similar to a human being's experience of pain.

In the light of these principles I shall try to determine what general policies we ought to adopt in regulating the use of animals in experimental science. I am limiting myself to the moral questions arising in the specific area of painful or fatal animal experimentation, but some of the discussion will apply to other areas of human interaction with animals. Space does not allow discussion of killing animals for educational purposes.

Scientists who perform experiments on animals rarely see the need to justify them, but when they do they almost always stress the seriousness of the research. Although it may be regrettable that animals are harmed, their suffering is seen as an unavoidable casualty of scientific progress. The

moral philosopher must still ask: is the price in animal misery worth it?

That the ends do not always justify the means is a truism, and when the means involve the painful treatment of unwilling innocents, serious questions arise. Although it is notoriously difficult to formulate the conditions that justify the consequences, it is plausible that desired ends are not likely to justify onerous means in the following situations: when those who suffer the means are not identical with those who are expected to enjoy the ends; when there is grave doubt that the justifying ends will be brought about by the onerous means; and when the ends can be achieved by less onerous means.

When a competent surgeon causes pain he does not run afoul of these conditions. On the other hand, social policies that entail mass misery on the basis of tenuous sociopolitical assumptions of great future benefits do run afoul of the last two conditions and often of the first as well. The use of laboratory animals often fails to satisfy these conditions of consequential justification; the first is ignored most frequently (I shall argue that this can often be justified), but scientists often violate the others as well when they carry out painful or fatal experiments with animals that are poorly designed or could have been just as well executed without intact living animals.

We can be somewhat more specific in formulating guidelines for animal experimentation if we consider the equality of animals and human beings with respect to pain. Because there are no sound biologic reasons for the idea that human pain is intrinsically more intense than animal pain, animals and men may be said to be equals with respect to pain. Equality in this case is a measure of their shared interest in avoiding harm and discomfort. The evil of pain, unlike the value of life, is unaffected by the identity of the individual sufferer.

Animals and human beings, however, do differ in their experience of the aftereffects of pain. When an injury leaves the subject cosmetically disfigured, for example, a human being may suffer from a continuing sense of shame and bitterness, but for the animal the trauma is confined to the momentary pain. Even the permanent impairment of faculties has more serious and lasting aftereffects on human beings than on animals. It can be argued that a person who is stricken by blindness suffers his loss more keenly than an animal similarly stricken.

More important than the subjective experience of privation is the objective diminishment of a valuable being whose scope of activity and future experience have been severely curtailed. In terms of physical privation animals and human beings do not differ, but the measure of loss must be counted far greater in human beings. To sum up: human beings and animals have a parity with respect to the trauma of a painful episode but not with respect to the consequences of the trauma. Yet when an experiment involves permanent impairment or death for the subject and thus considerations of differential life worthiness make it wrong to use most human beings, the pain imposed on the animals should still be counted as intrinsically bad, as if human beings had been made to suffer it, regardless of the aftereffects.

Although I believe that the general inferiority of animal lives to human life is relevant to the formation of public policy, I cannot accept the view that their relative inferiority licenses harming animals except for very serious purposes in rather special circumstances. However, the special circumstances are not necessarily extraordinary. Many experiments, although not as many as is generally supposed, are medically important and needed. The researcher who is working to control cancer and other fatal and crippling diseases may be able to satisfy the conditions that justify the use of laboratory animals. Because I believe that normal human lives are of far greater worth than animal lives, I accept a policy in which those who suffer the means are not those who may enjoy the ends, which violates the first of the conditions of consequential justification mentioned above, by permitting the infliction of pain on animals to save human lives or to contribute substantially to their welfare. However, when researchers intend to harm an animal, they need more than a quick appeal to the worthiness of human life. They ought to be able to show that the resulting benefits are outstandingly compensatory; if the scientist cannot make a good case for the experiment, it should be proscribed. (On the other hand, if suffering is the main consideration in judging the admissibility of experiments with animals, then nonpainful experiments, even fatal ones, may be under fewer constraints than painful, nonfatal experiments. Although this idea may seem paradoxical, it is in accord with the common moral intuition that condones those who put a kitten "to sleep" while condemning those who torment one.) The implementation of this policy raises questions that cannot be dealt with here. Yet one might expect that research proposals involving painful animal experimentation should be reviewed by a panel of experts, perhaps composed of two scientists in the field of the experiment and a scientifically knowledgeable philosopher versed in medical ethics.

In closing, I wish to indicate how I would deal with a possible objection. It may appear that my criteria of life worthiness place human idiots on a par with animals. On what grounds could I prohibit the painful or fatal experimental use of human subjects whose capacity does not differ from that of many animals? I would be prepared to rethink or even abandon a position that could not distinguish between animal and human experimentation. Fortunately, this distinction can be made.

I oppose painful or fatal experimentation on defective, nonconsenting human beings not because I believe that any person, just because he is human, has a privileged moral status, but because I do not believe that we can safely permit anyone to decide which human beings fall short of worthiness. Judgments of this kind and the creation of institutions for making them are fraught with danger and open to grave abuse. It is never necessary to show that an animal's life is not as valuable as that of a normal human being, but just such an initial judgment of exclusion would have to be made for idiots. Because there is no way to circumvent this problem, experiments on human beings are precluded and practically wrong. There are other arguments against experimenting on mentally feeble human beings, but this one seems to me to be the strongest and to be sufficient to support the view that whereas animal experimentation is justifiable, no dangerous or harmful experiments involving unwilling human subjects could be.

Accordingly, I have reached the following conclusions concerning the painful exploitation of animals for human rewards. Animals should not be used in painful experiments when substantial benefits are not expected to result. Even when the objective is important, there is a presumption against the use of animals in painful and dangerous experiments that are expected to yield tenuous results of doubtful value. Animals but not human beings may be used in painful and dangerous experiments that are to yield vital benefits for human beings (or other animals).

Vast numbers of animals are currently being used in all kinds of scientific experiments, many of which entail animal misery. Some of these studies, unfortunately, do not contribute to medical science, and some do not even require the use of intact animals. Even the most conservative corrective measures in the implementation of a reasonable and morally responsible policy would have dramatic practical consequences.

Notes

1. Descartes, R. Letter to the Marquess of Newcastle. In: Kenny A., ed. *Philosophical letters*. Oxford: Oxford University Press, 1970.

2. Cicero. *De Finibus*.

3. Kant, I. In: Paton H. J., ed. *Groundwork for a metaphysic of morals*.

4. Bentham, J. *The principles of morals and legislation*. New York: Hafner Publishing, 1948:311n.

Questions for Analysis

1. On what does Hoff base her conclusion that "no one has yet given good reasons to accept a moral perspective that grants a privileged moral status to all and only human beings"?

2. What important moral differences does Hoff find between human and nonhuman animals?

3. What does Hoff mean by her claim that although all animals are equal with respect to pain, they are not equal with respect to the consequences of pain?

4. How does Hoff justify different treatment of animals and human idiots on a par with animals? How would Singer and Regan respond?

5. How would you apply Hoff's reasoning to other animal rights issues, such as meat eating?

Speciesism and the Idea of Equality

Bonnie Steinbock

This essay by Bonnie Steinbock is a defense of our common practice of putting human interests ahead of the interests of other animals. Although Singer is right in claiming that nonhuman pain deserves some moral consideration, she says, he is wrong in claiming that there are no morally important differences between humans and other animals. Among the important differences are the human capacities to be held morally responsible for their actions, to reciprocate in ways that nonhuman animals can't, and to desire self-respect.

Against Singer's charge that we treat humans who don't have these capacities better than nonhuman animals, she argues as follows: To extend special care to others out of sympathy is not morally wrong, even if we don't extend it to all. It is not, for example, wrong to go beyond our

From Philosophy, *Vol. 53, No. 204 (April 1978), pp. 247–256.* © 1978 Cambridge University Press. Reprinted by permission of the publisher.

obligations to members of our own race, as long as we do not fail in our obligations to members of other races. Similarly, it is not wrong to give special care to severely retarded humans out of sympathy for them, even though we don't do the same for nonhuman animals.

Most of us believe that we are entitled to treat members of other species in ways which would be considered wrong if inflicted on members of our own species. We kill them for food, keep them confined, use them in painful experiments. The moral philosopher has to ask what relevant difference justifies this difference in treatment. A look at this question will lead us to re-examine the distinctions which we have assumed make a moral difference.

It has been suggested by Peter Singer[1] that our current attitudes are "speciesist," a word intended to make one think of "racist" or "sexist." The idea is that membership in a species is in itself not relevant to moral treatment, and that much of our behaviour and attitudes towards nonhuman animals is based simply on this irrelevant fact.

There is, however, an important difference between racism or sexism and "speciesism." We do not subject animals to different moral treatment simply because they have fur and feathers, but because they are in fact different from human beings in ways that could be morally relevant. It is false that women are incapable of being benefited by education, and therefore that claim cannot serve to justify preventing them from attending school. But this is not false of cows and dogs, even chimpanzees. Intelligence is thought to be a morally relevant capacity because of its relation to the capacity for moral responsibility.

What is Singer's response? He agrees that nonhuman animals lack certain capacities that human animals possess, and that this may justify different *treatment*. But it does not justify giving less consideration to their needs and interests. According to Singer, the moral mistake which the racist or sexist makes is not essentially the factual error of thinking that blacks or women are inferior to white men. For even if there were no factual error, even if it were true that blacks and women are less intelligent and responsible than whites and men, this would not justify giving less consideration to their needs and interests. It is important to note that the term "speciesism" is in one way like, and in another way unlike, the terms "racism" and "sexism." What the term "speciesism" has in common with these terms is the reference to focusing on a characteristic which

is, in itself, irrelevant to moral treatment. And it is worth reminding us of this. But Singer's real aim is to bring us to a new understanding of the idea of equality. The question is, on what do claims to equality rest? The demand for *human* equality is a demand that the interests of all human beings be considered equally, unless there is a moral justification for not doing so. But why should the interests of all human beings be considered equally? In order to answer this question, we have to give some sense to the phrase, "All men (human beings) are created equal." Human beings are manifestly *not* equal, differing greatly in intelligence, virtue and capacities. In virtue of what can the claim to equality be made?

It is Singer's contention that claims to equality do not rest on factual equality. Not only do human beings differ in their capacities, but it might even turn out that intelligence, the capacity for virtue, etc., are not distributed evenly among the races and sexes:

> The appropriate response to those who claim to have found evidence of genetically based differences in ability between the races or sexes is not to stick to the belief that the genetic explanation must be wrong, whatever evidence to the contrary may turn up; instead we should make it quite clear that the claim to equality does not depend on intelligence, moral capacity, physical strength, or similar matters of fact. Equality is a moral ideal, not a simple assertion of fact. There is no logically compelling reason for assuming that a factual difference in ability between two people justifies any difference in the amount of consideration we give to satisfying their needs and interests. The principle of equality of human beings is not a description of an alleged actual equality among humans: it is a prescription of how we should treat humans.[2]

Insofar as the subject is human equality, Singer's view is supported by other philosophers. Bernard Williams, for example, is concerned to show that demands for equality cannot rest on factual equality among people, for no such equality exists.[3] The only respect in which all men are equal, according to Williams, is that they are all equally men. This seems to be a platitude, but Williams denies that it is trivial. Membership in the species *homo sapiens* in itself has no special moral significance, but rather the fact that all men are human serves as a *reminder* that being human involves the possession of characteristics that are morally relevant. But on what characteristics does Williams focus? Aside from the desire for self-respect (which I will discuss later), Williams is not concerned with uniquely human capacities. Rather, he focuses on the capacity to feel pain and the capacity to feel affection. It is in virtue of these capacities, it seems, that the idea of equality is to be justified.

Apparently Richard Wasserstrom has the same idea as he sets out the racist's "logical and moral mistakes" in "Rights, Human Rights and Racial Discrimination."[4] The racist fails to acknowledge that the black person is as capable of suffering as the white person. According to Wasserstrom, the reason why a person is said to have a right not to be made to suffer acute physical pain is that we all do in fact value freedom from such pain. Therefore, if anyone has a right to be free from suffering acute physical pain, *everyone* has this right, for there is no possible basis of discrimination. Wasserstrom says, "For, if all persons do have equal capacities of these sorts and if the existence of these capacities is the reason for ascribing these rights to anyone, then all persons ought to have the right to claim equality of treatment in respect to the possession and exercise of these rights."[5] The basis of equality, for Wasserstrom as for Williams, lies not in some uniquely human capacity, but rather in the fact that all human beings are alike in their capacity to suffer. Writers on equality have focused on this capacity, I think, because it functions as some sort of lowest common denominator, so that whatever the other capacities of a human being, he is entitled to equal consideration because, like everyone else, he is capable of suffering.

If the capacity to suffer is the reason for ascribing a right to freedom from acute pain, or a right to well being, then it certainly looks as though these rights must be extended to animals as well. This is the conclusion Singer arrives at. The demand for human equality rests on the equal capacity of all human beings to suffer and to enjoy well being. But if this is the basis of the demand for equality, then this demand must include all beings which have an equal capacity to suffer and enjoy well being. That is why Singer places at the basis of the demand for equality, not intelligence or reason, but sentience. And equality will mean, not equality of treatment, but "equal consideration of interests." The equal consideration of interests will often mean quite different treatment, depending on the nature of the entity being considered. (It would be as absurd to talk of a dog's right to vote, Singer says, as to talk of a man's right to have an abortion.)

It might be thought that the issue of equality depends on a discussion of rights. According to this line of thought, animals do not merit equal consideration of interests because, unlike human beings, they do not, or cannot, have rights. But I am not going to discuss rights, important as the issue is. The fact that an entity does not have rights does not necessarily imply that its interests are going to count for less than the interests of entities which are right-bearers. According to the view of rights held by H. L. A. Hart and S. I. Benn, infants do not have rights, nor do the mentally defective, nor do the insane, in so far as they all lack certain minimal conceptual capabilities for having rights.[6] Yet it certainly does not seem that either Hart or Benn would agree that *therefore* their interests are to be counted for less, or that it is morally permissible to treat them in ways in which it would not be permissible to treat right-bearers. It seems to mean only that we must give different sorts of reasons for our obligations to take into consideration the interests of those who do not have rights.

We have reasons concerning the treatment of other people which are clearly independent of the notion of rights. We would say that it is wrong to punch someone because doing that infringes his rights. But we could also say that it is wrong because doing that hurts him, and that is, ordinarily, enough of a reason not to do it. Now this particular reason extends not only to human beings, but to all sentient creatures. One has a *prima facie* reason not to pull the cat's tail (whether or not the cat has rights) because it hurts the cat. And this is the only thing, normally, which is relevant in this case. The fact that the cat is not a "rational being," that it is not capable of moral responsibility, that it cannot make free choices or shape its life—all of these differences from us have nothing to do with the justifiability of pulling its tail. Does this show that rationality and the rest of it are irrelevant to moral treatment?

I hope to show that this is not the case. But first I want to point out that the issue is not one of cruelty to animals. We all agree that cruelty is wrong, whether perpetrated on a moral or nonmoral, rational or nonrational agent. Cruelty is defined as the infliction of unnecessary pain or suffering. What is to count as necessary or unnecessary is determined, in part, by the nature of the end pursued. Torturing an animal is cruel, because although the pain is logically necessary for the action to be torture, the end (deriving enjoyment from seeing the animal suffer) is monstrous. Allowing animals to suffer from neglect or for the sake of large profits may also be thought to be unnecessary and therefore cruel. But there may be some ends, which are very good (such as the advancement of medical knowledge), which can be accomplished by subjecting animals to pain in experiments. Although most people would agree that the pain inflicted on animals used in medical research ought to be kept to a minimum, they would consider pain that cannot be eliminated "necessary" and therefore not cruel. It would probably not be so regarded if the subjects were nonvoluntary human beings. Necessity, then, is defined in terms of human benefit, but this is just what is being called into question. The topic of cruelty to animals, while important from a practical viewpoint, because much of our present treatment of animals involves the infliction of suffering for no good reason, is not very interesting philosophically. What is philosophically interesting is whether we are justified in having different standards of necessity for human suffering and for animal suffering.

Singer says, quite rightly I think, "If a being suffers, there can be no moral justification for refusing to take that suffering into consideration."[7] But he thinks that the principle of equality requires that, no matter what the nature of the being, its suffering be counted equally with the like suffering of any other being. In other words sentience does not simply provide us with reasons for acting; it is the *only* relevant consideration for equal consideration of interests. It is this view that I wish to challenge.

I want to challenge it partly because it has such counter-intuitive results. It means, for example, that feeding starving children before feeding starving dogs is just like a Catholic charity's feeding hungry Catholics before feeding hungry non-Catholics. It is simply a matter of taking care of one's own, something which is usually morally permissible. But whereas we would admire the Catholic agency which did not discriminate, but fed all children, first come, first served, we would feel quite differently about someone who had this policy for dogs and children. Nor is this, it seems to me, simply a matter of sentimental preference for our own species. I might feel much more love for my dog than for a strange child—and yet I might feel morally obliged to feed the child before I fed my dog. If I gave in to the feelings of love and fed my dog and let the child go hungry, I would probably feel guilty. This is not to say that we can simply rely on such feelings. Huck Finn felt guilty at helping Jim escape, which he viewed as stealing from a woman who had never done him any harm. But while the existence of such feelings does not settle the morality of an issue, it is not clear to me that they can be explained away. In any event, their existence can serve as a motivation for trying to find a rational justification for considering human interests above non-human ones.

However, it does seem to me that this *requires* a justification. Until now, common sense (and academic philosophy) have seen no such need. Benn says, "No one claims equal consideration for all mammals—human beings count, mice do not, though it would not be easy to say *why* not. . . . Although we hesitate to inflict unnecessary pain on sentient creatures, such as mice or dogs, we are quite sure that we do not need to show good reasons for putting human interests before theirs."[8]

I think we do have to justify counting our interests more heavily than those of animals. But how? Singer is right, I think, to point out that it will not do to refer vaguely to the greater value of human life, to human worth and dignity:

> Faced with a situation in which they see a need for some basis for the moral gulf that is commonly thought to separate humans and animals, but can find no concrete difference that will do this without undermining the equality of humans, philosophers tend to waffle. They resort to high-sounding phrases like 'the intrinsic dignity of the human individual.' They talk of 'the intrinsic worth of all men' as if men had some worth that other beings do not have or they say that human beings, and only human beings, are 'ends in themselves,' while 'everything other than a

person can only have value for a person'. . . . Why should we not attribute 'intrinsic dignity' or 'intrinsic worth' to ourselves? Why should we not say that we are the only things in the universe that have intrinsic value? Our fellow human beings are unlikely to reject the accolades we so generously bestow upon them, and those to whom we deny the honour are unable to object.[9]

Singer is right to be skeptical of terms like "intrinsic dignity" and "intrinsic worth." These phrases are no substitute for a moral argument. But they may point to one. In trying to understand what is meant by these phrases, we may find a difference or differences between human beings and non-human animals that will justify different treatment while not undermining claims for human equality. While we are not compelled to discriminate among people because of different capacities, if we can find a significant difference in capacities between human and non-human animals, this could serve to justify regarding human interests as primary. It is not arbitrary or smug, I think, to maintain that human beings have a different moral status from members of other species because of certain capacities which are characteristic of being human. We may not all be equal in these capacities, but all human beings possess them to some measure, and nonhuman animals do not. For example, human beings are normally held to be responsible for what they do. In recognizing that someone is responsible for his or her actions, you accord that person a respect which is reserved for those possessed of moral autonomy, or capable of achieving such autonomy. Secondly, human beings can be expected to reciprocate in a way that non-human animals cannot. Non-human animals cannot be motivated by altruistic or moral reasons; they cannot treat you fairly or unfairly. This does not rule out the possibility of an animal being motivated by sympathy or pity. It does rule out altruistic motivation in the sense of motivation due to the recognition that the needs and interests of others provide one with certain reasons for acting.[10] Human beings are capable of altruistic motivation in this sense. We are sometimes motivated simply by the recognition that someone else is in pain, and that pain is a bad thing, no matter who suffers it. It is this sort of reason that I claim cannot motivate an animal or any entity not possessed of fairly abstract concepts. (If some non-human animals do possess the req-

uisite concepts—perhaps chimpanzees who have learned a language—they might well be capable of altruistic motivation.) This means that our moral dealings with animals are necessarily much more limited than our dealings with other human beings. If rats invade our houses, carrying disease and biting our children, we cannot reason with them, hoping to persuade them of the injustice they do us. We can only attempt to get rid of them. And it is this that makes it reasonable for us to accord them a separate and not equal moral status, even though their capacity to suffer provides us with some reason to kill them painlessly, if this can be done without too much sacrifice of human interests. Thirdly, as Williams points out, there is the "desire for self-respect": "a certain human desire to be identified with what one is doing, to be able to realize purposes of one's own, and not to be the instrument of another's will unless one has willingly accepted such a role."[11] Some animals may have some form of this desire, and to the extent that they do, we ought to consider their interest in freedom and self-determination. (Such considerations might affect our attitudes toward zoos and circuses.) But the desire for self-respect *per se* requires the intellectual capacities of human beings, and this desire provides us with special reasons not to treat human beings in certain ways. It is an affront to the dignity of a human being to be a slave (even if a well-treated one); this cannot be true for a horse or a cow. To point this out is of course only to say that the justification for the treatment of an entity will depend on the sort of entity in question. In our treatment of other entities, we must consider the desire for autonomy, dignity and respect, but only where such a desire exists. Recognition of different desires and interests will often require different treatment, a point Singer himself makes.

But is the issue simply one of different desires and interests justifying and requiring different treatment? I would like to make a stronger claim, namely, that certain capacities, which seem to be unique to human beings, entitle their possessors to a privileged position in the moral community. Both rats and human beings dislike pain, and so we have a *prima facie* reason not to inflict pain on either. But if we can free human beings from crippling diseases, pain and death through experimentation which involves making animals suffer, and if this is the only way to achieve such results, then

I think that such experimentation is justified because human lives are more valuable than animal lives. And this is because of certain capacities and abilities that normal human beings have which animals apparently do not, and which human beings cannot exercise if they are devastated by pain or disease.

My point is not that the lack of the sorts of capacities I have been discussing gives us a justification for treating animals just as we like, but rather that it is these differences between human beings and nonhuman animals which provide a rational basis for different moral treatment and consideration. Singer focuses on sentience alone as the basis of equality, but we can justify the belief that human beings have a moral worth that nonhuman animals do not, in virtue of specific capacities, and without resorting to "high-sounding phrases."

Singer thinks that intelligence, the capacity for moral responsibility, for virtue, etc., are irrelevant to equality, because we would not accept a hierarchy based on intelligence any more than one based on race. We do not think that those with greater capacities ought to have their interests weighed more heavily than those with lesser capacities, and this, he thinks, shows that differences in such capacities are irrelevant to equality. But it does not show this at all. Kevin Donaghy argues (rightly, I think) that what entitles us human beings to a privileged position in the moral community is a certain minimal level of intelligence, which is a prerequisite for morally relevant capacities.[12] The fact that we would reject a hierarchical society based on degree of intelligence does not show that a minimal level of intelligence cannot be used as a cut-off point, justifying giving greater consideration to the interests of those entities which meet this standard.

Interestingly enough, Singer concedes the rationality of valuing the lives of normal human beings over the lives of nonhuman animals.[13] We are not required to value equally the life of a normal human being and the life of an animal, he thinks, but only their suffering. But I doubt that the value of an entity's life can be separated from the value of its suffering in this way. If we value the lives of human beings more than the lives of animals, this is because we value certain capacities that human beings have and animals do not. But freedom from suffering is, in general, a minimal condition for exercising these capacities, for living a fully human life. So, valuing human life more involves regard-ing human interests as counting for more. That is why we regard human suffering as more deplorable than comparable animal suffering.

But there is one point of Singer's which I have not yet met. Some human beings (if only a very few) are less intelligent than some nonhuman animals. Some have less capacity for moral choice and responsibility. What status in the moral community are these members of our species to occupy? Are their interests to be considered equally with ours? Is experimenting on them permissible where such experiments are painful or injurious, but somehow necessary for human well being? If it is certain of our capacities which entitle us to a privileged position, it looks as if those lacking those capacities are not entitled to a privileged position. To think it is justifiable to experiment on an adult chimpanzee but not on a severely mentally incapacitated human being seems to be focusing on membership in a species where that has no moral relevance. (It is being "speciesist" in a perfectly reasonable use of the word.) How are we to meet this challenge?

Donaghy is untroubled by this objection. He says that it is fully in accord with his intuitions, that he regards the killing of a normally intelligent human being as far more serious than the killing of a person so severely limited that he lacked the intellectual capacities of an adult pig. But this parry really misses the point. The question is whether Donaghy thinks that the killing of a human being so severely limited that he lacked the intellectual capacities of an adult pig would be less serious than the killing of that pig. If superior intelligence is what justifies privileged status in the moral community, then the pig who is smarter than a human being ought to have superior moral status. And I doubt that this is fully in accord with Donaghy's intuitions.

I doubt that anyone will be able to come up with a concrete and morally relevant difference that would justify, say, using a chimpanzee in an experiment rather than a human being with less capacity for reasoning, moral responsibility, etc. Should we then experiment on the severely retarded? Utilitarian considerations aside (the difficulty of comparing intelligence between species, for example), we feel a special obligation to care for the handicapped members of our own species, who cannot survive in this world without such care. Non-human animals manage very well, despite their "lower intelligence" and lesser capacities; most of them do not require special care from us. This does not, of course, justify experimenting on them. However, to subject to experimentation those people who depend on us seems even worse than subjecting members of other species to it. In addition, when we consider the severely retarded, we think, "That could be me." It makes sense to think that one might have been born retarded, but not to think that one might have been born a monkey. And so, although one can imagine oneself in the monkey's place, one feels a closer identification with the severely retarded human being. Here we are getting away from such things as "morally relevant differences" and are talking about something much more difficult to articulate, namely, the role of feeling and sentiment in moral thinking. We would be horrified by the use of the retarded in medical research. But what are we to make of this horror? Has it moral significance or is it "mere" sentiment, of no more import than the sentiment of whites against blacks? It is terribly difficult to know how to evaluate such feelings.[14] I am not going to say more about this, because I think that the treatment of severely incapacitated human beings does not pose an insurmountable objection to the privileged status principle. I am willing to admit that my horror at the thought of experiments being performed on severely mentally incapacitated human beings in cases in which I would find it justifiable and preferable to perform the same experiments on non-human animals (capable of similar suffering) may not be a moral emotion. But it is certainly not wrong of us to extend special care to members of our own species, motivated by feelings of sympathy, protectiveness, etc. If this is speciesism, it is stripped of its tone of moral condemnation. It is not racist to provide special care to members of your own race; it is racist to fall below your moral obligation to a person because of his or her race. I have been arguing that we are morally obliged to consider the interests of all sentient creatures, but not to consider those interests equally with human interests. Nevertheless, even this recognition will mean some radical changes in our attitude toward and treatment of other species.[15]

Notes

1. Peter Singer, *Animal Liberation* (A New York Review Book, 1975).

2. Singer, 5.

3. Bernard Williams, "The Idea of Equality," *Philosophy, Politics and Society* (Second Series), Laslett and Runciman (eds.) (Blackwell, 1962), 110–131, reprinted in *Moral Concepts*, Feinberg (ed.) (Oxford, 1970), 153–171.

4. Richard Wasserstrom, "Rights, Human Rights, and Racial Discrimination," *Journal of Philosophy* 61, No. 20 (1964), reprinted in *Human Rights*, A. I. Melden (ed.) (Wadsworth, 1970), 96–110.

5. Ibid., 106.

6. H. L. A. Hart, "Are There Any Natural Rights?," *Philosophical Review* 64 (1955), and S. I. Benn, "Abortion, Infanticide, and Respect for Persons," *The Problem of Abortion*, Feinberg (ed.) (Wadsworth, 1973), 92–104.

7. Singer, 9.

8. Benn, "Equality, Moral and Social," *The Encyclopedia of Philosophy* 3, 40.

9. Singer, 266–267.

10. This conception of altruistic motivation comes from Thomas Nagel's *The Possibility of Altruism* (Oxford, 1970).

11. Williams, op. cit., 157.

12. Kevin Donaghy, "Singer on Speciesism," *Philosophic Exchange* (Summer 1974).

13. Singer, 22.

14. We run into the same problem when discussing abortion. Of what significance are our feelings toward the unborn when discussing its status? Is it relevant or irrelevant that it looks like a human being?

15. I would like to acknowledge the help of, and offer thanks to, Professor Richard Arneson of the University of California, San Diego; Professor Sidney Gendin of Eastern Michigan University; and Professor Peter Singer of Monash University, all of whom read and commented on earlier drafts of this paper.

Questions for Analysis

1. *In the beginning of the essay, Steinbock writes, "We do not subject animals to different moral treatment simply because they have fur and feathers, but because*

they are in fact different from human beings in ways that could be morally relevant." What ways does she mean? Are they morally relevant?

2. *On what points does Steinbock agree with Singer?*

3. *Steinbock says that the issue between her and Singer is not cruelty to animals. Why not?*

4. *According to Steinbock, the view that the capacity to feel pain is the only relevant consideration for equal consideration leads to counterintuitive results. What results does she mean? Do they run counter to your intuitions?*

5. *How does Steinbock answer Singer's charge that unequal treatment of animals and severely retarded humans is speciesist? How would Singer respond?*

6. *Does Steinbock provide a compelling refutation of Singer? Do her arguments have any force against Regan?*

CASE PRESENTATION
"Putting Her to Sleep"

In their first home, the cat had always used the litterbox. Now, after a couple of days in their new home, they noticed the smell of cat urine on the landing of the stairs. They scrubbed the carpet and sprayed it with disinfectant, but soon afterward the urine smell returned.

They tried covering the spot that the cat had chosen as its new urinating site, but she picked another place, two steps down. They bought child barriers for the top and bottom of the stairs, but she had little trouble negotiating them. They tried yelling at her, rubbing her nose in the spot, and even whacking her with rolled-up newspaper as they would a dog, but nothing worked.

They'd have to give the cat away.

It was a painful realization. They'd had her for six years, ever since she turned up at their door as a forlorn kitten who, from the looks of her, had lost at least one fight. And though they'd often joked about how silly it was that two intelligent adults could grow so fond of a creature as dumb as a cat, they were indeed fond of her and knew that they would miss her. What they did not yet know, however, was that none of their acquaintances would take her.

That left them with two options—keep the cat and live with the urine smell, which was beginning to penetrate into the wood beneath the carpet, or take her to the SPCA, which would keep her in a cage for a week or so and then, they didn't doubt, destroy her. She was a beautiful animal, but people looking to "adopt" a pet are not looking for a six-year-old cat, however beautiful. Although they considered the first option intolerable, they put off taking the second for one week, then another, hoping that the cat would return to using her litterbox.

Finally, tears streaming down his face, he took her to the SPCA. The woman who accepted the cat from him told him what she must have told countless children. "She's so beautiful, maybe I'll take her home myself."

He was feeling childlike enough to pretend to believe her, but the tears did not stop.

Questions for Analysis

1. Some animal rights activists think that owning house pets is a form of slavery. Does anything about this incident suggest that they might have a point?

2. Pet owners love their pets, but they often declaw them, spay them, or neuter them. What would Singer say about such ordinary practices? Regan?

3. Dogs and cats, like other animals, like to roam free. If a cat is always kept indoors, or a dog is confined to a small apartment and allowed outside only at the end of a leash, is it being treated immorally?

4. Did the couple miss any options? Should they have taken their cat into the country and set it free, for example?

5. Did the cat's interest in staying alive outweigh the couple's interest in protecting their floor or getting rid of the urine smell? What would Singer say?

6. Did the couple, despite loving the cat, treat her as a mere thing? What would Regan say?

CASE PRESENTATION
Animal Liberators

On May 24, 1984, five members of the Animal Liberation Front (ALF) raided the University of Pennsylvania's Experimental Head Injury Lab, located in the sub-basement of the Anatomy-Chemistry Building. Although the purpose of most ALF raids is to liberate laboratory animals, this raid was different. This time the goal was to "liberate" videotapes of the experiments being conducted in the lab, experiments that included using a hydraulic jack to compress the heads of monkeys. They found what they came for, and along the way they ransacked the lab—destroying equipment and removing files.

What the videotapes showed was gruesome. There were images of pistons piercing the heads of baboons and of unanesthetized primates crawling in pain from operating tables. There were also images that showed clear violations of standard research procedures, such as operations performed without surgical masks while workers were smoking cigarettes.

A great controversy followed the release of the tapes. Dr. Thomas Gennarelli, head of the lab, defended his research and decried the raid. All animals were anesthetized and felt no pain, he insisted, and the raid had seriously set back important medical research. The university also defended Dr. Gennarelli's research, as did the National Institute of Health (NIH), which, despite protests from People for the Ethical Treatment of Animals, gave the lab a new grant of $500,000.

The raiders, in an interview that appeared in the November, 1986 issue of *Omni* ("Inhuman Bondage," by Robert Weil), likened the research to the cruel medical experiments that Nazi Dr. Josef Mengele conducted on humans. (Indeed, one of the raiders was himself a survivor of a Nazi concentration camp.)

As the controversy continued, protesters demonstrated at the Penn campus, and animal rights activists staged a sit-in at the NIH until Secretary of Health and Human Services Margaret Heckler ordered a halt to all federal funding of the Head Injury Lab. That was July 18, 1985. Four months later, Penn agreed to pay a $4,000 fine for violating the Animal Welfare Act. The university also agreed to improve its use of pain-relieving drugs, its care of injured animals, and its training of research workers who handle laboratory animals.

And the raiders? Despite a grand jury investigation, no indictments were handed down. ALF members, invoking their Fifth Amendment rights, refused to testify against themselves.

Questions for Analysis

1. *Is the comparison between Drs. Gennarelli and Mengele justified?*

2. *Dr. Gennarelli and the NIH obviously believed that his research would bring significant medical benefit. If his research workers had not violated standard research procedures, would that benefit have justified it?*

3. *Suppose that ALF and Tom Regan are right about such experiments violating animals' rights. Does that justify ALF's tactics?*

4. *Which is the more important moral issue—the research itself or the violations of the Animal Welfare Act? Why?*

5. *If similar research was done on mice, would your reaction to it be any different?*

Selections for Further Reading

Callicott, J. Baird, ed. *Companion to a Sand County Almanac.* Madison, Wis.: University of Wisconsin Press, 1987.

Frey, R. G. Interests and Rights: *The Case Against Animals.* Oxford: The Clarendon Press, 1980.

Leopold, Aldo. *A Sand County Almanac.* New York: Oxford University Press, 1966.

Passmore, John. *Man's Responsibility for Nature.* New York: Scribner's, 1974.

Rollin, Bernard E. *Animal Rights and Human Morality.* Buffalo, N.Y.: Prometheus, 1981.

Regan, Tom. *And All That Dwell Therein: Essays on Animal Rights and Environmental Ethics.* Berkeley and Los Angeles: University of California Press, 1982.

———. *The Case for Animal Rights.* Berkeley and Los Angeles: University of California Press, 1983.

———— , and Peter Singer, eds. *Animal Rights and Human Obligations.* Englewood Cliffs, N.J.: Prentice-Hall, 1976.

Stone, Christopher. *Should Trees Have Standing?* Los Altos, Calif.: Kaufman, 1974.

Taylor, Paul W. *Respect for Nature: A Theory of Environmental Ethics.* Princeton, N.J.: Princeton University Press, 1986.

11
CORPORATE RESPONSIBILITY

It comes as no surprise to you to hear that the United States is a capitalist society. Nor should it come as a surprise to you to hear what that means. Primarily, it means that the means of production—factories, mines, farms, and such—are for the most part in private hands. It also means that our economy is for the most part a market economy. That is, economic choices are by and large made by private individuals—business people, workers, and consumers—in response to conditions of a competitive marketplace, and those choices then bring about new market conditions, which in turn lead to new economic decisions, followed by new market conditions and further economic decisions in a continuous flow of economic activity. It is through this activity that prices and wages rise or fall, production of various products increases or decreases, and workers and manufacturers enter, leave, or relocate themselves in the market.

To be sure, the market is not entirely autonomous. It is not affected only by private decisions and such economic forces as supply and demand. That was the point of the qualifying phrase, "by and large." The government is an economic player too, and its decisions also affect the market and private economic decisions, often deliberately. The Federal Reserve Board, for example, manipulates interest rates and the money supply in order to increase or decrease economic activity. Congress sets tax rates and spending programs toward the same end. Regulatory agencies, such as the Environmental Protection Agency (EPA) and the Occupational Safety and Health Administration (OSHA), issue regulations to force economic players to make decisions they would not otherwise make to protect the environment and individuals. Plus, we have minimum-wage laws, antitrust laws, and a host of other laws to help ensure fairness and competition in the market.

Still, we remain largely a market economy, and among the chief players in the economy are business corporations, which are the primary concern of this chapter.

Corporations

Many of the issues we've looked at so far have turned on the legal and moral concepts of a person. Is a fetus a person in the legal or moral sense of the word? Is a newborn infant? Is an adult chimpanzee? These questions have been important because their answers help determine our legal and moral responsibilities to a fetus, a newborn infant, or an animal, and how we may treat it. Since the U.S. Supreme Court has ruled that a fetus is not a legal person, a fetus does not have the legal rights that the rest of us do. In the early months of pregnancy, then, women have the legal right to an abortion. On the other hand, many people feel that the fetus is a moral person, that it has (or ought to have) such moral rights as the right to life, in which case women do not have a moral right to an abortion.

It may surprise many of you to learn that, unlike a fetus, General Motors *is* a legal person. It has legal rights and obligations. It can sue and be sued in civil court, and it can be tried in criminal court. It can own property and enter into contracts. Indeed, the same is true for any corporation. All are persons according to the law.

A corporation is an organization owned by its stockholders—individuals or other organizations who contribute capital to the corporation in return for shares (partial ownership) in the corporation. In most cases, purchasers of stock in business corporations are primarily interested in its short- or long-term investment value. That is, they are looking to sell their stocks at a profit or to keep their stocks in hope that their value will increase over a long period of time. Few are interested in controlling the corporation's operations.

Although stockholders are the corporation's owners, their control over it is indirect. They vote for the corporate directors (the number of votes for each shareholder being a function of the number of shares held), who appoint the corporation's officers, who, along with other managers, are in charge of the corporation's day-to-day operations. Although shareholders have an opportunity to vote on other matters from time to time, most assign their proxy votes to the directors. Still, the directors, the officers, and other managers of the corporation remain responsible to the shareholders.

Responsibility to Shareholders

An obvious consequence of the above observations is that business corporations have an obligation to protect their shareholders' investments, which means concerning themselves with profits, market share, reinvestment, corporate assets, and the like, all of which can affect a stock's market value. The stakes involved, we should point out, can be very high.

Although the value of outstanding stocks varies from transaction to transaction on the stock exchanges, this figure should give some idea of the amount of money at stake: Between August 25 and October 26, 1987, the value of all stocks traded on the New York Stock Exchange dropped over a *trillion* dollars—most of the drop occurring on one day, October 19. That's over a trillion dollars lost by private investors, pension funds, charitable foundations, university endowments, and other stockholders.

Of course, these losses were spread out among the stockholders of all corporations listed on the exchange, and a crash like that cannot be blamed on the directors and officers of any one corporation, but the amount of money involved does show that a corporation's responsibility to its investors is not to be taken lightly.

Responsibility to Obey the Law

As legal persons, corporations also have legal obligations. They must obey federal, state, and local laws, they must adhere to the regulations of various regulatory agencies (like the EPA and OSHA), they must follow court orders, and they must avoid fraud, breach of contract, and various other legal wrongs.

On these matters, there is no controversy. There might be a good deal of controversy over the wisdom of any particular law or regulation, but corporations, as legal persons, enjoy the full protection of the law. Like the rest of us, then, they ought to obey it. Similarly, no controversy surrounds the claim that corporations have a responsibility to protect their shareholders' investments. Another matter, though, is highly controversial. That is the issue of a corporation's social responsibility.

Corporate Social Responsibility

Adult human beings are not just legal persons. We are also moral persons. We have moral as well as legal obligations. Other things being equal, we ought to avoid harming others, even if the harm is not forbidden by law, and in certain cases we ought to help others in need, even if that help is not required by law. We have general moral obligations to treat others decently, and we have specific moral obligations to particular people—our parents, for example, and our friends, neighbors, and other associates.

What about business corporations? Do their obligations to their investors and the law exhaust their responsibilities, or do they, their directors, officers, and other managers have additional responsibilities? And if they do, what are they?

To ask such questions is to raise the issue of corporate social responsibility. It is to ask whether corporations and corporate officials have moral obligations to the communities in which they operate, to their employees, to the environment, to their customers, to the nation as a whole, responsibilities that go beyond what the law requires of them. It is to ask whether they ought to make safer products than the law requires, spew fewer pollutants into the air and water than the law requires, voluntarily limit layoffs and plant closings, provide retraining programs and day-care centers, make extended parental leaves available to their employees, pull out of a country like South Africa, with its racist system of apartheid, and consider the social ramifications of a wide range of economic decisions.

As the above list shows, critics of corporate activities have come up with many proposals for what they take to be due exercise of corporate responsibility. And many have argued that if corporations are not willing to assume these responsibilities themselves, Congress and the appropriate regulatory agencies ought to force them to assume them. Since airbags are more effective than safety-belts, for example, shouldn't car manufacturers be required to make them standard on all models if they will not do so voluntarily?

Our immediate concern, though, is not the issue of airbags. Nor is it whether any particular law or regulation should be put in place. Rather, it is whether corporations should be viewed as morally responsible members of the larger community.

A Narrow View

The traditional view of corporate responsibility is a narrow one, according to which corporations have only two obligations—to obey the law and to make money for their stockholders.

One of the basic reasons for this view concerns the peculiar status of corporations. Although corporations are legal persons, the argument goes, they cannot be considered persons in the moral sense. Corporations are nothing more than artificial creations of the legal system, and that makes their status as legal persons a mere legal fiction. Unlike a real person, a corporation cannot be a moral agent, someone who can assume moral responsibility for its actions and be held morally accountable for them. It cannot, rightly speaking, act at all. Individuals in the corporation can act, and they can certainly be held morally responsible for what they do, but how can a corporation, which is nothing but an organization composed of individual agents, be itself an agent that acts morally or immorally?

We can speak of a corporation as having *legal* responsibilities, because it is, according to law, created for specific purposes and forbidden to engage in certain kinds of activities. But as long as it is not a real person—as long as it is not a person in the moral sense of the word—we cannot speak of it as having *moral* obligations.

What about a corporation's directors, officers, and other managers, then? Don't they have moral responsibilities beyond their legal ones? Of course, but we must be careful to separate their moral responsibilities as private individuals from their moral responsibilities as corporate officials. As private individuals away from the office, they have the same moral obligations as the rest of us. At the office, however, they are agents of the corporation's stockholders, with the primary obligation to protect their investments. If they want to give to the Sierra Club out of their own pockets, fine, but they do not have the right to take it upon themselves to jeopardize shareholders' money by engaging in costly measures to protect the environment at the expense of corporate profits, unless those measures are required by law.

That is one line of defense for the narrow view: the special obligation of directors and officers to shareholders. Another line has its antecedents in the work of the great classical economist, Adam Smith (1723–1790). According to Smith and his contemporary followers, if all participants in the market act in their own economic interests, the result will be in the best interest of everyone alike. It is, according to his famous metaphor, as if an invisible hand guided the economy, coordinating the self-interested economic decisions of independent individuals in a way that brings about the most efficient allocation of resources and the greatest economic benefit to the economy as a whole.

If demand for a particular product falls, for example, producers may choose to cut back production and lay off workers. The workers, in turn, will find employment in another industry, one that needs more workers to keep up with consumer demand. In the end, society is the winner. Workers go where they are needed, overextended industries regain their health, and consumers get what they want and need. Should economic decisions be made on the basis of a misbegotten notion of corporate social responsibility, however, the entire economy—not just shareholders—will suffer. Inefficient and overextended industries will sap needed resources, shortages of needed goods will appear, and prices and wages will not reflect market conditions, leading to further unwelcome consequences.

This line of defense relies not only on Adam Smith's economics, but also on John Stuart Mill's principle of utility. Its point is to secure the greatest happiness for the greatest number of people. Another line also reflects utilitarian reasoning. Our society, as we saw in chapter 1, is a pluralistic one. Within certain limits, each institution is free to pursue its own ends in its own way without government interference. If corporations take it upon themselves to assume responsibility in broad areas of social concern and allow that responsibility to take precedence over market forces in economic decisions, the argument goes, they are in effect pursuing government ends instead of corporate ones. And that is unwise for two reasons. First, nobody elected corporate officials to set social policy. Second, corporate power is so great that the assumption of responsibility presents equally great dangers.

How great is their power? Consider these figures: In 1987, the five hundred largest U.S. industrial corporations (the *Fortune* 500) combined for sales of close to $1.9 trillion. For the same year, their combined profits amounted to $90.6 billion, and their combined assets totaled over $1.7 trillion. Thus, these corporations control great amounts of wealth, and with that wealth goes corresponding power. Although corporate critics assume that this power will be used for the public good, it can just as easily be used in support of causes and programs that have the opposite effect.

Moreover, the *Fortune* 500 employed 13.1 million people in 1987. That's over 13 million people whose lives are directly affected by corporate decisions. And, given their numbers, whatever affects them must also affect local and regional economies. Thus, the best that corporations can do for them and the nation is to maintain the best state of financial health. Or, as Charles Wilson, Secretary of Defense under Dwight Eisenhower, famously put it, what's good for General Motors is good for America.

A Broader View

Defenders of the narrow view of corporate responsibility base their case on certain assumptions about the nature and purpose of business corporations and on a particular economic theory. Defenders of a broader view, one that assigns social responsibility to business corporations, begin elsewhere. Their starting point is the array of social problems we now face.

In the summer of 1988, for example, much of the United States suffered a prolonged period of dry, hot weather that led to dangerously low water supplies in many areas and ravaged the country's farm belt. Although nobody blamed this particular drought on atmospheric pollution, a consensus among scientists quickly emerged. The long awaited greenhouse effect was now upon us. World-wide average temperatures are rising due to pollutants in the air that allow solar energy to reach the earth but trap the heat radiated by the earth, just as the glass walls and roof of a greenhouse (or the windows of a car parked in direct sunlight) trap heat inside. The greenhouse effect, of course, is just one serious environmental problem. Additional ones include dead fish washed up onto New Jersey beaches and toxic waste dumps that threaten the health of people who live nearby.

Changing patterns in the work force provoke other concerns. Increasingly, we see married couples in which both spouses work. Must one spouse risk losing his or her job to stay home with a newborn child? This question is particularly pressing for those couples that depend on both incomes to maintain a decent standard of living. Equally pressing for such couples is the cost of day care for their children. That problem, of course, can be even more pressing for the growing number of single mothers who must either work or receive welfare payments to care for their children.

Consider also the changes in our economy as we shift from manufacturing to service industries. Plants close or relocate and workers are laid off. Some find lower paying jobs, some find none, others are forced to move to another region. Meanwhile, local economies are devastated, unemployment compensation, welfare payments, and shelter for the homeless strain government budgets, and jobs go begging for lack of people with the requisite skills.

That these and other social problems exist not even defenders of the narrow view can deny. But they do deny that business corporations should, at cost to their investors, assume responsibility for them. Defenders of the wider view, of course, think otherwise.

For one thing, they argue that corporations must accept responsibility for problems they themselves have caused—most obviously, environmental problems. It was morally wrong to harm our air and water as much as they did before the era of environmental legislation, and it remains morally wrong not to alleviate the damage if present environmental controls are not strict enough.

As for the claim that alleviating the damage would violate the corporation's obligation to its stockholders, defenders of the broader view argue this way: No obligation is absolute. Whenever we obligate ourselves to another person, it should be understood by all concerned that there are moral limits to the obligation. If fulfilling it requires immoral behavior on our part, we ought not fulfill it. In the case of a corporation's obligations to its shareholders, that means that the corporation has moral limits on what it can do to maximize their profits, and those limits include not destroying the environment.

Of course, even defenders of the broader view of corporate responsibility recognize that many social problems cannot be blamed on past corporate acts. Why should corporations assume responsibility for solving these problems? Why, for example, should they provide retraining for laid-off workers, or extended parental leave to employees, or make airbags standard on all automobile models if consumers do not demand them, or give advanced word to workers and communities before closing a plant? After all, business corporations are chartered to do business, not solve social problems, and their purpose is to make money for their shareholders, not to tend to all of society's needs.

Defenders of the broader view respond that the conception of business corporations as just money-making enterprises is based on outmoded assumptions. Corporations are chartered for the public good, they say, and the reason we have not required them to act in socially responsible ways is the assumption that Adam Smith's invisible hand will achieve the best utilitarian results if they act only as money-making enterprises. But that assumption, they argue, is no longer valid. Smith's invisible hand works only in an economy marked by perfect competition, not one dominated by giant corporations. It requires markets that new manufacturers can easily enter, not markets with prohibitively high entry costs. Moreover, in today's economy, laid-off assembly-line workers cannot find similar work at similar wages. Those jobs aren't there. And they rarely have the special skills required for the new jobs that are there. A healthy economy requires that these workers be retrained, and business corporations are in the best position to do the retraining. Similarly, the economies of many communities depend on particular corporations. If a plant suddenly shuts down, so does the community's economy.

Besides, they argue, it is a mistake to think of business corporations as merely private enterprises. Not only are they chartered by state governments, they also receive a wide variety of benefits from our local, state, and federal governments. They are given tax breaks to locate in certain areas, special leasing provisions, and other incentives and exemptions. Roads may be built for them. The power of eminent domain may be exercised for them. All of this (and more) amounts to public contributions to business corporations for the public good. Corporations, defenders of the broader view conclude, owe the public something in return. All of us, not just stockholders, are investors in corporations.

Arguments for Corporate Social Responsibility

1. *Responsibility goes hand in hand with power.*

POINT: "The issue's simple. We face a lot of serious social problems in today's world, and it's going to take a lot of our resources to solve them. And that means that all of us have to chip in. The more resources each of us has, the more power each of us has to do something about the problems we face, and the more each of us must chip in. And nobody has more resources and power than business corporations. After all, each of our largest corporations takes in more money than the governments of most countries have to spend. Surely they can spare some of it to help society. It's just a matter of ordinary fairness—with power comes responsibility. Since the corporations have the power, they also have the responsibility."

COUNTERPOINT: "You're forgetting two important points. First, corporations already contribute in accordance with their resources and power. They do pay taxes, you know, and the more money they make the more taxes they pay. In fact, corporations are subject to double taxation. Not only does each corporation pay taxes on its earnings, but its stockholders have to pay taxes on their earnings—their dividend checks. Also, the bigger they are, the more people they employ and the more wealth they pump into the economy. Second, corporate officials don't even have the right to contribute more than the law demands of them, let alone the responsibility. It's not their money they're sacrificing—it's the shareholders'."

2. *Corporations owe something back to society.*

POINT: "Corporations don't exist in a vacuum. They exist in society, and they receive a lot of benefits from society. And I don't just mean things like an educated work force and police and fire protection. I mean special benefits. When Chrysler was going under, who bailed it out? The federal government. When manufacturers complain about foreign competition, who does something about it? The federal government. And when corporations go shopping around for the best places to put their plants, who comes up with the special favors to attract them? State and local governments. Don't they owe us something in return for that?"

COUNTERPOINT: "You make it sound as though we do all that for the corporations' sake. But we don't. We do it for ours. A ruined Chrysler would have meant thousands of people out of work, and unfair foreign competition hurts all of us, not just the corporations. And why do you think states and municipalities vie for factories the way they do? Obviously, because they want the new jobs and the boost to their economies that come with them. And that's the real bottom line—corporations do good by doing good business."

3. *Not all corporate activity brings benefits.*

POINT: "Now you're the one who's forgetting an important point. Corporations also do harm by doing what you call 'good business.' They lay off workers as well as hire them. They close plants as well as open them. They also make unsafe products and pollute our air and water. And they lure people into buying things they don't need through their advertising, while many things that people do need—like decent and affordable housing for the poor—are in pitifully short supply. And don't forget the huge sums of money corporations give politicians through their political action committees and 'honoraria' to get them to vote their way, instead of in the public interest. The question isn't whether or not corporations will affect today's social realities, but whether they will affect them positively or negatively."

COUNTERPOINT: "I agree that corporations sometimes cause harm, but let's take a closer look at the list you just gave. Sure, they close plants and lay off workers, but whatever harm that causes workers and the communities they live in is more than offset by the long-term benefits to society as a whole. In the long run, society is best served by letting corporations respond to market forces. I'm not saying that laid-off workers should be forgotten. They shouldn't. They should get adequate unemployment compensation, food stamps if they need them, and help in finding other work. But those kinds of responsibility belong to governments, not corporations. As for environmental damage and unsafe products, of course some corporations have behaved irresponsibly. If they've dumped pollutants into the atmosphere in violation of EPA regulations, they should be punished. If, either through negligence or deliberate intent, they've put defective products on the market or products that carry risks that consumers had absolutely no reason to suspect, then people who've been harmed should sue them for whatever they can get. Nobody denies that corporations have legal responsibilities in these matters. But you're asking more than that. You're asking car makers to drive up the cost of their cars with safety features that buyers don't want, and you're asking manufacturers to spend millions of their shareholders' dollars to reduce pollution beyond the point that the public's representatives demand. And as for political contributions and advertising, come on. It is a free country, isn't it? Don't you think people should have the right to get involved in the political process, or the right to advertise their products?"

4. *Social responsibility is in corporations' own interests.*

POINT: "You talk as though corporations and their shareholders don't have common interests with the rest of us. But they do. They have to exist in the same environment as the rest of us. They have to worry as much as we do about the crime and other social costs associated with poverty. And their stake in a well-educated and trained public is every bit as high as ours. After all, it's their own work force we're talking about here. And don't forget this—what corporations aren't willing to do themselves, the public will eventually force them to do, and that means a whole lot more regulations and red tape. All I'm really saying is that corporations ought to show a little enlightened self-interest, rather than the narrow and unenlightened kind they're following now."

COUNTERPOINT: "That corporations should pursue an enlightened self-interest is not something I'm going to deny. But don't be so sure that everything you're suggesting they do really is in their own interest, or even society's interest. The more burdens we place on our corporations, the higher the prices we have to pay for their products and the less money they have for investment. Higher prices and less investment mean declining economic growth, which hurts the rest of us as much as it hurts stockholders. And it's certainly not in a corporation's interest to impose on itself restrictions it doesn't want the government to impose on it—even if that would keep the government from imposing them, which it probably wouldn't anyway. Most workplaces are safe, but we still have OSHA, don't we? And even though most corporations do give adequate notice of plant closings, that didn't stop Congress from enacting the requirement that they do it into law."

Arguments Against Corporate Social Responsibility

1. *Corporate social responsibility is unfair to shareholders.*

POINT: "Why do you think people buy stock, anyway? Not to solve social problems, but to invest their money the best way they see fit. And don't forget who most of the investors are—ordinary working people who buy stocks themselves to build up a nest egg or belong to pension plans that invest their funds in the stock market. To say that corporate officials should eat into these people's profits in the name of social responsibility just isn't fair to them—especially when you consider that they pay taxes on their earnings and privately contribute to the causes that matter to them most. What you're really demanding is that corporations shirk their most important responsibility—to their shareholders."

COUNTERPOINT: "Nobody's demanding that they shirk their responsibility to their shareholders, only that they recognize other responsibilities as well. Besides, what makes you think that most shareholders disagree with that? Do you really think they want to make the biggest profits they can without any concern for the environment, or public health and safety, or the economic well-being of depressed regions of the country, or the welfare of laid-off workers? When's the last time you heard about a stockholders' revolt against a corporation that showed some social responsibility? Did the price of Chrysler stock plummet in the summer of 1988 when Lee Iacocca announced that he'd start making cars with airbags?"

2.   *Corporate social responsibility is economic irresponsibility.*

POINT: "What you're suggesting is just bad economics. The job of corporations is to pursue, within the limits of the law, their own economic interests. If they do that, everybody benefits. That's what a free-market economy is all about, and it's the way we get the most efficient allocation of resources. Let's not forget Adam Smith's invisible hand."

COUNTERPOINT: "Let's also not forget that Smith wrote *The Wealth of Nations* over two hundred years ago, before we had giant corporations that exercise such powerful control over the economy. He was writing about an economy with perfect competition, easy entrance into the market, and a variety of conditions that no longer exist. Since then, we've had other books, like Michael Harrington's *The Other America*, which shows how whole regions of the country can remain impoverished while the rest of the economy booms. We've also learned how public goods like clean air and water can be sacrificed in the chase after private profits. Public goods may not show up on any corporation's balance sheets, but they sure make a difference to society's balance sheets. I'm not saying we should give up on the market economy altogether, but I am saying we should recognize its defects and do something about them."

3.   *Demanding social responsibility of corporations is changing the rules of the game.*

POINT: "Corporations and society have something like a social contract with each other. We charter them to mine, manufacture, and sell products like oil and cars for profit, and they promise to obey the laws of the land. You're saying that society should unilaterally change that contract; that we should hold corporations responsible for things that weren't part of the original deal. That's changing the rules of the game on them, and it's not fair."

COUNTERPOINT: "Well, you're right about one thing—we are asking for a change in what you call the social contract. But there's nothing unfair about it, as long as we don't ask more of corporations than we're justified in asking. You may think we're asking more than that, but we're not. We're asking only that they conduct themselves as morally responsible members of society, which includes taking their fair part in helping to advance the public good. If we didn't ask that before, it's only because we were mistaken about the best role of corporations in society. You certainly can't believe that we chartered corporations for any other ultimate purpose than to serve the public good."

4. *There's no way of knowing how a socially responsible corporation should act.*

POINT: "You make it sound as though it's perfectly obvious what a socially responsible corporation should do. But the truth of the matter is that it's one thing to identify social problems and quite another to figure out the right way to deal with them. Then again, we don't all agree on what counts as a social problem to begin with. Everybody wants clean air and water, for example, but there's hardly any agreement about how clean is clean enough, or about what costs we ought to pay to make them cleaner. Who's right? The Sierra Club or farmers and manufacturing workers? Everybody wants safe products, too, but how safe is safe enough, and when does it become too expensive to make them safer? Right now we deal with these kinds of questions two ways. First, we leave them to market forces. We let consumers decide what they're willing to pay for. And if the public is unhappy about the way that works out, we go to the second way. We get our democratically elected government to do something. What you're proposing is that corporations settle these questions for us, and that's not only undemocratic, it's dangerous. What are you going to do if you don't like their solutions?"

COUNTERPOINT: "Again, you're right about one thing. People do disagree about a lot of things, so corporations should be careful in exercising social responsibility. But careful isn't the same thing as derelict. Being careful here is a matter of discussing social problems with community leaders, labor leaders, elected officials, and civic groups and acting on these problems when there's a consensus over what should be done about them. It's a matter of cooperation and good faith. And there's nothing dangerous or undemocratic about it."

The Social Responsibility of Business Is to Increase Its Profits

Milton Friedman

In the following essay, Nobel Prize-winning economist Milton Friedman defends the narrow view of corporate responsibility. If corporate executives exercise social responsibility at the expense of shareholder profit, he argues, they neglect their obligations to shareholders and assume a government role they have no right to assume. He also argues that defenders of a broader view of corporate responsibility are advocating socialism and that their view is incompatible with a free society. If executives believe that it is in the corporation's economic interest to attack certain social problems, they should do so, but they should not justify their actions by claiming to be socially responsible. That, he argues, is to invite undue interference with the legitimate economic role of corporations.

When I hear businessmen speak eloquently about the "social responsibilities of business in a free-enterprise system," I am reminded of the wonderful line about the Frenchman who discovered at the age of 70 that he had been speaking prose all his life. The businessmen believe that they are defending free enterprise when they declaim that business is not concerned "merely" with profit but also with promoting desirable "social" ends; that business has a "social conscience" and takes seriously its responsibilities for providing employment, eliminating discrimination, avoiding pollution and whatever else may be the catchwords of the contemporary crop of reformers. In fact they are—or would be if they or anyone else took them seriously—preaching pure and unadulterated socialism. Businessmen who talk this way are unwitting puppets of the intellectual forces that have been undermining the basis of a free society these past decades.

The discussion of the "social responsibilities of business" are notable for their analytical looseness and lack of rigor. What does it mean to say that "business" has responsibilities? Only people can have responsibilities. A corporation is an artificial person and in this sense may have artificial responsibilities, but "business" as a whole cannot be said to have responsibilities, even in this vague sense. The first step toward clarity to examining the doctrine of the social responsibility of business is to ask precisely what it implies for whom.

Presumably, the individuals who are to be responsible are businessmen, which means individual proprietors or corporate executives. Most of the discussion of social responsibility is directed at corporations, so in what follows I shall mostly neglect the individual proprietors and speak of corporate executives.

In a free-enterprise, private-property system, a corporate executive is an employee of the owners of the business. He has direct responsibility to his employers. That responsibility is to conduct the business in accordance with their desires, which generally will be to make as much money as possible while conforming to the basic rules of the society, both those embodied in law and those embodied in ethical custom. Of course, in some cases his employers may have a different objective. A group of persons might establish a corporation for an eleemosynary purpose—for example, a hospital or a school. The manager of such a corporation will not have money profit as his objectives but the rendering of certain services.

In either case, the key point is that, in his capacity as a corporate executive, the manager is the agent of the individuals who own the corporation or establish the eleemosynary institution, and his primary responsibility is to them.

Needless to say, this does not mean that it is easy to judge how well he is performing his task. But at least the criterion of performance is straightforward, and the persons among whom a voluntary contractual arrangement exists are clearly defined.

Of course, the corporate executive is also a person in his own right. As a person, he may have many other responsibilities that he recognizes or assumes voluntarily—to his family, his conscience, his feelings of charity, his church, his clubs, his city, his country. He may feel impelled by these responsibilities to devote part of his income to causes he regards as worthy, to refuse to work for particular corporations, even to leave his job, for example, to join his country's armed forces. If we wish, we may refer to some of these responsibilities as "social responsibilities." But in these respects he is acting as a principal, not an agent; he is spending his own money or time or energy, not the money of his employers or the time or energy he has contracted to devote to their purposes. If these are "social responsibilities," they are the social responsibilities of individuals, not of business.

What does it mean to say that the corporate executive has a "social responsibility" in his capacity as businessman? If this statement is not pure rhetoric, it must mean that he is to act in some way that is not in the interest of his employers. For example, that he is to refrain from increasing the price of the product in order to contribute to the social objective of preventing inflation, even though a price increase would be in the best interests of the corporation. Or that he is to make expenditures on reducing pollution beyond the amount that is in the best interests of the corporation or that is required by law in order to contribute to the social objective of improving the environment. Or that, at the expense of corporate profits, he is to hire "hardcore" unemployed instead of better qualified available workmen to contribute to the social objective of reducing poverty.

In each of these cases, the corporate executive would be spending someone else's money for a general social interest. Insofar as his actions in accord with his "social responsibility" reduce returns to stockholders, he is spending their money. Insofar as his actions raise the price to customers, he is spending the customers' money. Insofar as his actions lower the wages of some employees, he is spending their money.

The stockholders or the customers or the employees could separately spend their own money on the particular action if they wished to do so. The executive is exercising a distinct "social responsibility," rather than serving as an agent of the stockholders or the customers or the employees, only if he spends the money in a different way than they would have spent it.

But if he does this, he is in effect imposing taxes, on the one hand, and deciding how the tax proceeds shall be spent, on the other.

This process raises political questions on two levels: principle and consequences. On the level of political principle, the imposition of taxes and the expenditure of tax proceeds are governmental functions. We have established elaborate constitutional, parliamentary and judicial provisions to control these functions, to assure that taxes are imposed so far as possible in accordance with the preferences and desires of the public—after all, "taxation without representation" was one of the battle cries of the American Revolution. We have a system of checks and balances to separate the legislative function of imposing taxes and enacting expenditures from the executive function of col-lecting taxes and administering expenditure programs and from the judicial function of mediating disputes and interpreting the law.

Here the businessman—self-selected or appointed directly or indirectly by stockholders—is to be simultaneously legislator, executive and jurist. He is to decide whom to tax by how much and for what purpose, and he is to spend the proceeds—all this guided only by general exhortations from on high to restrain inflation, improve the environment, fight poverty and so on and on.

The whole justification for permitting the corporate executive to be selected by the stockholders is that the executive is an agent serving the interests of his principal. This justification disappears when the corporate executive imposes taxes and spends the proceeds for "social" purposes. He becomes in effect a public employee, a civil servant, even though he remains in name an employee of a private enterprise. On grounds of political principle, it is intolerable that such civil servants—insofar as their actions in the name of social responsibility are real and not just window-dressing—should be selected as they are now. If they are to be civil servants, then they must be elected through a political process. If they are to impose taxes and make expenditures to foster "social" objectives, then political machinery must be set up to make the assessment of taxes and to determine through a political process the objectives to be served.

This is the basic reason why the doctrine of "social responsibility" involves the acceptance of the socialist view that political mechanisms, not market mechanisms, are the appropriate way to determine the allocation of scarce resources to alternative uses.

On the grounds of consequences, can the corporate executive in fact discharge his alleged "social responsibilities"? On the one hand, suppose he could get away with spending the stockholders' or customers' or employees' money. How is he to know how to spend it? He is told that he must contribute to fighting inflation. How is he to know what action of his will contribute to that end? He is presumably an expert in running his company—in producing a product or selling it or financing it. But nothing about his selection makes him an expert on inflation. Will his holding down the price of his product reduce inflationary pressure? Or, by leaving more spending power in the hands of his customers, simply divert it elsewhere? Or, by forcing him to produce less because of the lower price, will it simply contribute to shortages? Even if he could answer these questions, how much cost is he justified in imposing on his stockholders, customers, and employees for this social purpose? What is his appropriate share and what is the appropriate share of others?

And, whether he wants to or not, can be get away with spending his stockholders', customers' or employees' money? Will not the stockholders fire him? (Either the present ones or those who take over when his actions in the name of social responsibility have reduced the corporation's profits and the price of its stock.) His customers and his employees can desert him for other producers and employers less scrupulous in exercising their social responsibilities.

This facet of "social responsibility" doctrine is brought into sharp relief when the doctrine is used to justify wage restraint by trade unions. The conflict of interest is naked and clear when union officials are asked to subordinate the interest of their members to some more general purpose. If the union officials try to enforce wage restraint, the consequence is likely to be wildcat strikes, rank-and-file revolts and the emergence of strong competitors for their jobs. We thus have the ironic phenomenon that union leaders—at least in the U.S.—have objected to Government interference with the market far more consistently and courageously than have business leaders.

The difficulty of exercising "social responsibility" illustrates, of course, the great virtue of private competitive enterprise—it forces people to be responsible for their own actions and makes it difficult for them to "exploit" other people for either selfish or unselfish purposes. They can do good—but only at their own expense.

Many a reader who has followed the argument this far may be tempted to remonstrate that it is all well and good to speak of Government's having the responsibility to impose taxes and determine expenditures for such "social" purposes as controlling pollution or training the hard-core unemployed, but that the problems are too urgent to wait on the slow course of political processes, that the exercise of social responsibility by businessmen is a quicker and surer way to solve pressing current problems.

Aside from the question of fact—I share Adam Smith's skepticism about the benefits that can be expected from "those who affected to trade for the public good"—this argument must be rejected on grounds of principle. What it amounts to is an assertion that those who favor the taxes and expenditures in question have failed to persuade a majority of their fellow citizens to be of like mind and that they are seeking to attain by undemocratic procedures what they cannot attain by democratic procedures. In a free society, it is hard for "evil" people to do "evil," especially since one man's good is another's evil.

I have, for simplicity, concentrated on the special case of the corporate executive, except only for the brief digression on trade unions. But precisely the same argument applies to the newer phenomenon of calling upon stockholders to require corporations to exercise social responsibility (the recent G.M. crusade for example). In most of these cases, what is in effect involved is some stockholders trying to get other stockholders (or customers or employees) to contribute against their will to "social" causes favored by the activists. Insofar as they succeed, they are again imposing taxes and spending the proceeds.

The situation of the individual proprietor is somewhat different. If he acts to reduce the returns of his enterprise in order to exercise his "social responsibility," he is spending his own money, not someone else's. If he wishes to spend his money on such purposes, that is his right, and I cannot see that there is any objection to his doing so. In the process, he, too, may impose costs on employees and customers. However, because he is far less likely than a large corporation or union to have monopolistic power, any such side effects will tend to be minor.

Of course, in practice the doctrine of social responsibility is frequently a cloak for actions that are justified on other grounds rather than a reason for those actions.

To illustrate, it may well be in the long-run interest of a corporation that is a major employer in a small community to devote resources to providing amenities to that community or to improving its government. That may make it easier to attract desirable employees, it may reduce the wage bill or lessen losses from pilferage and sabotage or have other worthwhile effects. Or it may be that, given the laws about the deductibility of corporate charitable contributions, the stockholders can contribute more to charities they favor by having the corporation make the gift than by doing it themselves, since they can in that way contribute an amount that would otherwise have been paid as corporate taxes.

In each of these—and many similar—cases, there is a strong temptation to rationalize these actions as an exercise of "social responsibility." In the present climate of opinion, with its widespread aversion to "capitalism," "profits," and "soulless corporation" and so on, this is one way for a corporation to generate goodwill as a by-product of expenditures that are entirely justified in its own self-interest.

It would be inconsistent of me to call on corporate executives to refrain from this hypocritical window-dressing because it harms the foundations of a free society. That would be to call on them to exercise a "social responsibility"! If our institutions, and the attitudes of the public make it in their self-interest to cloak their actions in this way, I cannot summon much indignation to denounce them. At the same time, I can express admiration for those individual proprietors or owners of closely held corporations or stockholders of more broadly held corporations who disdain such tactics as approaching fraud.

Whether blameworthy or not, the use of the cloak of social responsibility, and the nonsense spoken in its name by influential and prestigious businessmen, does clearly harm the foundations of a free society. I have been impressed time and again by the schizophrenic character of many businessmen. They are capable of being extremely farsighted and clear-headed in matters that are internal to their businesses. They are incredibly short-sighted and muddle-headed in matters that are outside their businesses but affect the possible survival of business in general. This short-sightedness is strikingly exemplified in the calls from many businessmen for wage and price guidelines or controls or income policies. There is nothing that could do more in a brief period to destroy a market system and replace it by a centrally controlled system

than effective governmental control of prices and wages.

The short-sightedness is also exemplified in speeches by businessmen on social responsibility. This may gain them kudos in the short run. But it helps to strengthen the already too prevalent view that the pursuit of profits is wicked and immoral and must be curbed and controlled by external forces. Once this view is adopted, the external forces that curb the market will not be the social consciences, however highly developed, of the pontificating executives; it will be the iron fist of Government bureaucrats. Here, as with price and wage controls, businessmen seem to me to reveal a suicidal impulse.

The political principle that underlies the market mechanism is unanimity. In an ideal free market resting on private property, no individual can coerce any other, all cooperation is voluntary, all parties to such cooperation benefit or they need not participate. There are no values, no "social" responsibilities in any sense other than the shared values and responsibilities of individuals. Society is a collection of individuals and of the various groups they voluntarily form.

The political principle that underlies the political mechanism is conformity. The individual must serve a more general social interest—whether that be determined by a church or a dictator or a majority. The individual may have a vote and say in what is to be done, but if he is overruled, he must conform. It is appropriate for some to require others to contribute to a general social purpose whether they wish to or not.

Unfortunately, unanimity is not always feasible. There are some respects in which conformity appears unavoidable, so I do not see how one can avoid the use of the political mechanism altogether.

But the doctrine of "social responsibility" taken seriously would extend the scope of the political mechanism to every human activity. It does not differ in philosophy from the most explicitly collectivist doctrine. It differs only by professing to believe that collectivist ends can be attained without collectivist means. That is why, in my book *Capitalism and Freedom,* I have called it a "fundamentally subversive doctrine" in a free society, and have said that in such a society, "there is one and only one social responsibility of business—to use its resources and engage in activities designed to increase its profits so long as it stays within the rules of the game, which is to say, engages in open and free competition without deception or fraud."

Questions for Analysis

1. Can a corporation have moral responsibilities, or can only individuals have them?

2. Friedman makes a distinction between an individual's responsibilities as a principal and as an agent. What does he mean by that distinction? How does he use it to support his case?

3. According to Friedman, the exercise of social responsibility by corporate executives amounts to "taxation without representation." Why?

4. On what grounds does Friedman claim that calls for corporate social responsibility are socialistic and undemocratic? Do you agree?

5. To what extent are Friedman's arguments based on principles of social justice? On the principle of utility? On respect for persons?

The Corporate Social Responsibility Debate

Christopher D. Stone

In the following excerpts from his book The Social Control of Corporate Behavior, *law professor Christopher D. Stone defends the broad view of corporate responsibility. His argument proceeds in three steps. First, he rejects four arguments against the broader view: that corporate executives who exercise social responsibility violate a promise to shareholders, that they violate their duty as the shareholders' agents, that exercising social responsibility violates their proper social role, and that it is in the best interest of society that they do not exercise social responsibility. Second, he argues that we cannot rely totally on market forces to influence corporations to act in socially desirable ways. Third, he argues that legal mechanisms are not sufficient to ensure that corporations act in socially desirable ways. Therefore, he concludes, something more—the exercise of social responsibility by corporations—is required.*

Why Shouldn't Corporations Be Socially Responsible?

[T]he opposition to corporate social responsibility comprises at least four related though separable positions. . . . Each assumes in its own degree that the managers of the corporation are to be steered almost wholly by profit, rather than by what they think proper for society on the whole. Why should this be so? So far as ordinary morals are concerned, we often expect human beings to act in a fashion that is calculated to benefit others, rather than themselves, and commend them for it. Why should the matter be different with corporations?

The Promissory Argument

The most widespread but least persuasive arguments advanced by the "antiresponsibility" forces take the form of a moral claim based upon the corporation's supposed obligations to its shareholders. In its baldest and least tenable form, it is presented as though management's obligation rested upon the keeping of a promise—that the management of the corporation "promised" the shareholders that it would maximize the shareholders' profits. But this simply isn't so.

Consider for contrast the case where a widow left a large fortune goes to a broker, asking him to invest and manage her money so as to maximize her return. The broker, let us suppose, accepts the money and the conditions. In such a case, there would be no disagreement that the broker had made a promise to the widow, and if he invested her money in some venture that struck his fancy for any reason other than that it would increase her fortune, we would be inclined to advance a moral (as well, perhaps, as a legal) claim against him. Generally, at least, we believe in the keeping of promises; the broker, we should say, had violated a promissory obligation to the widow.

But that simple model is hardly the one that obtains between the management of major corporations and their shareholders. Few if any American shareholders ever put their money into a corporation upon the express promise of management that the company would be operated so as to maximize their returns. Indeed, few American shareholders ever put their money directly *into* a corporation at all. Most of the shares outstanding today were issued years ago and found their way to their current shareholders only circuitously. In almost all cases, the current shareholder gave his money to some prior shareholder, who, in turn, had gotten in from B, who, in turn, had gotten it from A, and so on back to the purchaser of the original issue, who, many years before, had bought the shares through an underwriting syndicate. In the course of these transactions, one of the basic elements that exists in the broker case is missing: The manager of the corporation, unlike the broker, was never even offered a chance to refuse the shareholder's "terms" (if they were that) to maximize the shareholder's profits.

There are two other observations to be made about the moral argument based on a supposed promise running from the management to the shareholders. First, even if we do infer from all the circumstances a "promise" running from the management to the shareholders, but not one, or not one of comparable weight running elsewhere (to the company's employees, customers, neighbors, etc.), we ought to keep in mind that as a moral matter (which is what we are discussing here) sometimes it is deemed morally justified to break promises (even to break the law) in the furtherance of other social interests of higher concern. Promises can advance moral arguments, by way of creating presumptions, but few of us believe that promises, per se, can end them. My promise to appear in class on time would not ordinarily justify me from refusing to give aid to a drowning man. In other words, even if management *had* made an express promise to its shareholders to "maximize your profits," (a) I am not persuaded that the ordinary person would interpret it to mean "maximize *in every way you can possibly get away with*, even if that means polluting the environment, ignoring or breaking the law"; and (b) I am not persuaded that, even if it were interpreted as so blanket a promise, most people would not suppose it ought—morally—to be broken in some cases.

Finally, even if, in the face of all these considerations, one still believes that there is an overriding, unbreakable, promise of some sort running from management to the shareholders, I do not think that it can be construed to be any stronger than one running to *existent* shareholders, arising from *their* expectations as measured by the price *they* paid. That is to say, there is nothing in the argument from promises that would wed us to a regime in which management was bound to maximize the income of shareholders. The argument might go so far as to support compensation for existent shareholders if the society chose to announce that henceforth management would have other specified obligations, thereby driving the price of shares to a lower adjustment level. All future shareholders would take with "warning" of, and a price that discounted for, the new "risks" of shareholding (i.e., the "risks" that management might put corporate resources to *pro bonum* ends).

The Agency Argument

Related to the promissory argument but requiring less stretching of the facts is an argument from agency principles. Rather than trying to infer a promise by management to the shareholders, this argument is based on the idea that the shareholders designated the management their agents. This is the position advanced by Milton Friedman in his

New York Times article. "The key point," he says, "is that . . . the manager is the agent of the individuals who own the corporation. . . ."[1]

Friedman, unfortunately, is wrong both as to the state of the law (the directors are *not* mere agents of the shareholders)[2] and on his assumption as to the facts of corporate life (surely it is closer to the truth that in major corporations the shareholders are *not*, in any meaningful sense, selecting the directors; management is more often using its control over the proxy machinery to designate who the directors shall be, rather than the other way around).

What Friedman's argument comes down to is that for some reason the directors ought morally to consider themselves more the agents for the shareholders than for the customers, creditors, the state, or the corporation's immediate neighbors. But why? And to what extent? Throwing in terms like "principal" and "agent" begs the fundamental questions.

What is more, the "agency" argument is not only morally inconclusive, it is embarrassingly at odds with the way in which supposed "agents" actually behave. If the managers truly considered themselves the agents of the shareholders, as agents they would be expected to show an interest in determining how their principals wanted them to act—and to act accordingly. In the controversy over Dow's production of napalm, for example, one would expect, on this model, that Dow's management would have been glad to have the napalm question put to the shareholders at a shareholders' meeting. In fact, like most major companies faced with shareholder requests to include "social action" measures on proxy statements, it fought the proposal tooth and claw.[3] It is a peculiar agency where the "agents" will go to such lengths (even spending tens of thousands of dollars of their "principals'" money in legal fees) to resist the determination of what their "principals" want.

The Role Argument

An argument so closely related to the argument from promises and agency that it does not demand extensive additional remarks is a contention based upon supposed considerations of *role*. Sometimes in moral discourse, as well as in law, we assign obligations to people on the basis of their having assumed some role or status, independent of any specific verbal promise they made. Such obligations are assumed to run from a captain to a sea-

man (and vice versa), from a doctor to a patient, or from a parent to a child. The antiresponsibility forces are on somewhat stronger grounds resting their position on this basis, because the model more nearly accords with the facts—that is, management never actually promised the shareholders that they would maximize the shareholders' investment, nor did the shareholders designate the directors their agents for this express purpose. The directors and top management are, as lawyers would say, fiduciaries. But what does this leave us? So far as the directors are fiduciaries of the shareholders in a legal sense, of course they are subject to the legal limits on fiduciaries—that is to say, they cannot engage in self-dealing, "waste" of corporate assets, and the like. But I do not understand any proresponsibility advocate to be demanding such corporate largesse as would expose the officers to legal liability; what we are talking about are expenditures on, for example, pollution control, above the amount the company is required to pay by law, but less than an amount so extravagant as to constitute a violation of these legal fiduciary duties. (Surely no court in America today would enjoin a corporation from spending more to reduce pollution than the law requires.) What is there about assuming the role of corporate officer that makes it immoral for a manager to involve a corporation in these expenditures? A father, one would think, would have stronger obligations to his children by virtue of his status than a corporate manager to the corporation's shareholders. Yet few would regard it as a compelling moral argument if a father were to distort facts about his child on a scholarship application form on the grounds that he had obligations to advance his child's career; nor would we consider it a strong moral argument if a father were to leave unsightly refuse piled on his lawn, spilling over into the street, on the plea that he had obligations to give every moment of his attention to his children, and was thus too busy to cart his refuse away.

Like the other supposed moral arguments, the one from role suffers from the problem that the strongest moral obligations one can discover have at most only prima facie force, and it is not apparent why those obligations should predominate over some contrary social obligations that could be advanced.

Then, too, when one begins comparing and

weighing the various moral obligations, those running back to the shareholder seem fairly weak by comparison to the claims of others. For one thing, there is the consideration of alternatives. If the shareholder is dissatisfied with the direction the corporation is taking, he can sell out, and if he does so quickly enough, his losses may be slight. On the other hand, as Ted Jacobs observes, "those most vitally affected by corporate decisions—people who work in the plants, buy the products, and consume the effluents—cannot remove themselves from the structure with a phone call."[4]

The "Polestar" Argument

It seems to me that the strongest moral argument corporate executives can advance for looking solely to profit is not one that is based on a supposed express, or even implied promise to the shareholder. Rather, it is one that says, if the managers act in such fashion as to maximize profits—if they act *as though* they had promised the shareholders they would do so—then it will be best for all of us. This argument might be called the polestar argument, for its appeal to the interests of the shareholders is not justified on supposed obligations to the shareholders per se, but as a means of charting a straight course toward what is best for the society as a whole.

Underlying the polestar argument are a number of assumptions—some express and some implied. There is, I suspect, an implicit positivism among its supporters—a feeling (whether its proponents own up to it or not) that moral judgments are peculiar, arbitrary, or vague—perhaps even "meaningless" in the philosophic sense of not being amenable to rational discussion. To those who take this position, profits (or sales, or price-earnings ratios) at least provide some solid, tangible standard by which participants in the organization can measure their successes and failures, with some efficiency, in the narrow sense, resulting for the entire group. Sometimes the polestar position is based upon a related view—not that the moral issues that underlie social choices are meaningless, but that resolving them calls for special expertise. "I don't know any investment adviser whom I would care to act in my behalf in any matter except turning a profit. . . . The value of these specialists . . . lies in their limitations; they ought not allow themselves to see so much of the world that they become distracted."[5] A slightly modified point emphasizes not that the executives lack moral or social expertise per se, but that they lack the social authority to make policy choices. Thus, Friedman objects that if a corporate director took "social purposes" into account, he would become "in effect a public employee, a civil servant. . . . On grounds of political principle, it is intolerable that such civil servants . . . should be selected as they are now."[6]

I do not want to get too deeply involved in each of these arguments. That the moral judgments underlying policy choices are vague, I do not doubt—although I am tempted to observe that when you get right down to it, a wide range of actions taken by businessmen every day, supposedly based on solid calculations of "profit," are probably as rooted in hunches and intuition as judgments of ethics. I do not disagree either that, ideally, we prefer those who have control over our lives to be politically accountable; although here, too, if we were to pursue the matter in detail we would want to inspect both the premise of this argument, that corporate managers are not *presently* custodians of discretionary power over us anyway, and also its logical implications: Friedman's point that "if they are to be civil servants, then they must be selected through a political process"[7] is not, as Friedman regards it, a *reductio ad absurdum*—not, at any rate, to Ralph Nader and others who want publicly elected directors.

The reason for not pursuing these counterarguments at length is that, whatever reservations one might have, we can agree that there is a germ of validity to what the "antis" are saying. But their essential failure is in not pursuing the alternatives. Certainly, *to the extent* that the forces of the market and the law can keep the corporation within desirable bounds, it may be better to trust them than to have corporate managers implementing their own vague and various notions of what is best for the rest of us. But are the "antis" blind to the fact that there are circumstances in which the law—and the forces of the market—are simply not competent to keep the corporation under control? The shortcomings of these traditional restraints on corporate conduct are critical to understand, not merely for the defects they point up in the "antis' " position. More important, identifying where the traditional forces are inadequate is the first step in the design of new and alternative measures of corporate control.

Why the Market Can't Do It

In my view, much of the literature today reflects too little appreciation that, whatever its limits, the "invisible" hand of the market is the most effective force we have to keep corporations operating within socially desirable bounds, especially when the various costs of our legal mechanisms are considered. Nonetheless, the case for the market (as well as the case against it) is easily and often overstated.

For one thing, even at its ideal best, the market is not a remedy for all the problems a society may have with its commercial actors, but plays a general allocative role, encouraging capital, labor, and other factors of production to flow to those industries and firms that can put them to the most beneficial social use. One's willingness to trust to the market to fulfill the resource allocation function, such as by leaving firms autonomous in their pricing policies, rises or falls depending upon how he responds to a series of questions. To what extent is one willing to accept dollar values as the measure of most beneficial social use? To what extent are giant modern corporations freeing themselves of the forces that restrained small producers historically, allowing them to administer prices and manipulate their own consumer demand? These questions have been discussed too fully and too well elsewhere to reiterate the matter anew. It is safe to say, however, that, although economists may differ as to the advisability of various *forms* of intervention with market dictates, or as to the various *sectors* at which intervention best takes place (banking, farming), few if any are satisfied that the market of itself can allocate resources adequately to fill social needs.

What is more, when one turns from the market as resource allocator to inspect its capacity to fulfill other societal desiderata, the case of the free-market man is even harder to support. One ought to be clear that those who have faith that profit orientation is an adequate guarantee of corporations realizing socially desirable consumer goals are implicitly assuming: (1) that the persons who are going to withdraw patronage know *the fact* that they are being "injured" (where injury refers to a whole range of possible grievances, from getting a worse deal than he might get elsewhere, to purchasing a product that is defective or below warranted standards, to getting something that produces actual physical injury); (2) that they know *where* to apply pressure of some sort; (3) that they are in a *posi-*

tion to apply pressure of some sort; and (4) that their pressure will be *translated* into warranted changes in the institution's behavior. None of these assumptions is particularly well-founded.

As for the first, over a range of important cases the person who, under this model, should be shifting his patronage, does not even know that he is being "injured" (in the broad sense referred to above). For example, from our vantage point in the present, we can look back on history and appreciate some of the dangers of smoking on a cigarette consumer's health, or of coal dust on a worker's lungs. But the basis for these doubts was not adequately appreciated by the earlier consumer, who might have wanted to shift his patronage from, say, nonfilter to filter cigarettes, or to the worker who might have shifted his career from coal mining to something else. It hardly strains the imagination to believe that we today, as consumers, employees, investors, and so forth, are being subjected by corporations to all sorts of injuries that we will learn about only in time. But we are not able to translate these general misgivings into market preferences because we simply do not know enough about where dangers lie.

Second, that the individual knows *where* to apply pressure, is, in many instances also, too facile an assumption. Consider the case of the consumer disaffected by a certain product. If the free-market mechanism is working perfectly, he would be expected to withdraw his patronage from the management that produced that product, thereby "penalizing" those responsible for it and encouraging their rivals. But to do so, what exactly is he supposed to "boycott"? Consumers identify products by brand name, not usually by the producing company, of whose identity they are often ignorant. A dissatisfied Tide user who shifted from Tide to Dash, or to Duz—or to Bold, Oxydol, Cascade, Cheer, or Ivory Soap—would still, whether he knows it or not, be patronizing Proctor & Gamble. Or suppose another sort of problem: Theoretically, people concerned over ITT's involvement with the federal government might withdraw patronage from ITT products and services. But to judge the effectiveness of this "remedy" the reader has only to ask himself if he can identify the stereo set, color TV, hotel, bread, plumbing fixture, book, or windshield wiper behind which ITT, at varying degrees of distance, stands. The consumer could, at a cost, undertake to find out what other products were produced by the company that had produced brand Z, or was engaged in the undesirable activity, but even this search could be unsatisfactory. The company he finds at the end of his chase may itself be part of a larger shell of corporations so complex that even the Congress sometimes has trouble determining what are the "real" interests behind a corporate name.

Even where the first two criteria are met—that is, the person being injured knows the fact that he is being injured and can discover against whom to apply pressure—he may still not be in a position in which he can apply pressure. This could come about for at least two major reasons.

First, the model presupposes the existence of some negotiating interface between the corporation and the person disaffected with it. Such a relationship is available for a worker who is a member of a union recognized by the corporation, and for a person who is directly a consumer of the corporation's products or services. But consider, for example, a person whose grievance is with an aluminum company that is showering his land with pollutants, or that is, in his estimate, exercising objectionable influences in Latin America. If, as is likely, he is not a direct purchaser of aluminum, what recourse does he have: to do a study of all the products he is contemplating buying that contain aluminum so as to determine the "parentage" of their aluminum components and know which of them to boycott? The problem is hardly an isolated one. We are living in a society in which a number of major companies—for example North American Aviation and General Dynamics—produce too few consumer products, even indirectly, such as submit them to classic market pressures. Furthermore, the problems of our society are increasingly of a sort in which those affected are third parties to the negotiation; even when a company sits down with its union to discuss pulling up roots from some small towns, the town itself may have almost no say.

Second, even if such a negotiating interface exists, the person dealing with the company may have no viable alternative source of supply or employment. The most obvious example is when the company with whose actions someone is concerned is a monopoly or near-monopoly. . . . And even where one is not confronted with a monopoly

in the strict sense (such as a regulated utility), often as a practical matter the availability of desired products is in the hands of but one or two corporations. . . .

Finally, one ought to be chary, too, of the assumptions that even if economic pressure can be brought to bear on the "offending" corporation, the pressure will be smoothly translated into changes in the institution's behavior. . . . A company whose customers are being "turned off" for one reason or another may . . . turn their patronage elsewhere. But this does not assure that the management will know why it lost sales, or, discovering the reason, that it will remedy the problem in the most desirable way possible. There is a vivid example of this in a recent episode involving "snack packs," little cans of pudding with metal, tear-away lids, that had become a popular lunch box item for school children. Unfortunately, not only were children cutting their fingers on the sharp, serrated edges, but they were regularly licking the custard from the snapped-off metal top, which Consumers Union found sharp enough to cut a chicken leg.[8] Reports began to filter in of cuts. The surest remedy for this would presumably have been to replace the metal snap-off top with a plastic or screw-on variant. "It is easier to change the design of the can," one third-grade teacher wrote Consumers Union, "than it is to change the natural tendencies of a child." Well— that's what the third-grade teacher thought. What she overlooked is that for the company to change its top called for it to change its way of doing things— its own "natural tendencies." Instead of changing its tops, the company undertook an advertising campaign, distributing posters that told kiddies, in essence, to be careful. It took who knows how many complaints before the company finally gave in and promised to start using a safety lid or withdraw the product. The episode is not atypical. What those who put all their faith in the market fail to account for is one of the most fundamental principles of organizational theory: All large organizations seek to seal off or "buffer" their technical core from disruptive environmental influences (like the market—or the law).[9] So far as possible their tendency is to fight rather than to switch.

Why the Law Can't Do It

Wherever the market is inadequate as a control, one can, of course, act to shore it up by law. . . .

[This is] accounted for in the position that a corporation's social responsibilities are discharged if it follows the dictates of the market within the constraints of the law. Its fundamental idea is that laws, as the expression of popular sentiment, should be the source of guidance for corporate direction, not the personal preferences of each corporation's management. If the majority of the people believe the market and present laws inadequate to keep corporations within socially desirable bounds, the society can, through its democratic processes, make tougher laws. But unless and until such laws are made, this argument goes, it is best for all of us if the corporation managers guide themselves by profit.

. . . [E]ven if one regards this position persuasive generally, it does not really prove that corporate social responsibility is unnecessary; it merely invites the "pros" to identify more clearly just exactly where and in what ways reliance on the law is an inadequate method of keeping corporations within socially desirable bounds.

. . . [T]hose who trust to the law to bind corporations have failed to take into account a whole host of reasons why the threat of legal sanction is apt to lack the desired effects when corporate behavior is its target—for example, limited liability, the lack of congruence between the incentives of top executives and the incentives of "the corporation," the organization's proclivity to buffer itself against external, especially legal, threats, and so on. But . . . even if the corporation followed the law anyway, it would not be enough. The first set of reasons involves what I shall call the "time-lag problem"; the second concerns limitations connected with the making of law; the third concerns limitations connected with the mechanisms for implementing the law.

The Time-lag Problem

Even if we put aside the defects in the impact of the sanctions, there still remains the problem that the law is primarily a reactive institution. Lawmakers have to appreciate and respond to problems that corporate engineers, chemists, and financiers were anticipating (or could have anticipated) long before—that the drugs their corporations are about to produce can alter consciousness or damage the gene pool of the human race, that they are on the verge of multinational expansion that will

endow them with the power to trigger worldwide financial crises in generally unforeseen ways, and so on. Even if laws could be passed to deal effectively with these dangers, until they are passed a great deal of damage—some perhaps irreversible—can be done. Thus, there is something grotesque—and socially dangerous—in encouraging corporate managers to believe that, until the law tells them otherwise, they have no responsibilities beyond the law and their impulses (whether their impulses spring from the id or from the balance sheet). We do not encourage human beings to suppose so. And the dangers to society seem all the more acute where corporations are concerned.

Limitations Connected with the Making of Law

To claim society's desires will be realized so long as the corporations "follow the edict of the populus" fails to take into account *the role of corporations in making the very law that we trust to bind them.* This is, incidentally, not an especially modern development or one peculiar to laws regulating corporations. The whole history of commercial law is one in which, by and large, the "legislation" has been little more than an acknowledgment of rules established by the commercial sector, unless there are the strongest and most evident reasons to the contrary. Thus, in many areas such as food, drug, and cosmetic regulation, and, more recently, with respect to the promulgation of safety rules by the Department of Transportation, the government effectively adopts the standards worked out with the industry. Such processes do not always bespeak, as is sometimes intimated, sinister sales of power. The real roots are more cumbersome, more bureaucratic, more "necessary," and therefore more difficult to remedy: The regulating body is considerably outstaffed and relatively uninformed; it knows that it has to "live with" the industry it is regulating; it does not want to set standards that it always will be having to fight to enforce.

A related problem arises when an overseeing agency is in fact staffed with industry personnel—a problem that reaches its extreme form when the law that establishes the agency expressly provides for industry representatives to sit on the board. By its very constitution, California's Dickie Act, for example, effectually seats representatives of polluters on the Water Pollution Control Board.[10] The milk laws put the producers on the board that determines the distribution and price levels of milk.[11] Now, I am not here arguing the concept of having industry representatives on some regulatory boards. There are good reasons (whether or not they should ultimately prevail) for doing so in some cases. What I am saying is just that insofar as the corporations are engaged in making the regulations to which they are supposedly subject, it is absurdly circular to argue that their social responsibilities are discharged so long as they are living within the constraints of the law. . . .

The "anti" position implicitly assumes also that the lawmaking body is as informed on the relevant facts as is the regulatee. Often this is more or less true. When a lawmaking body considers, for example, what the speed limit ought to be, it can obtain as well as the companies such relevant data as injuries at various speeds.

But when we attempt to legislate in more complex areas, we find an information gap. Even the specialized regulatory agencies, much less the Congress, cannot in their rule-making capacities keep technically abreast of the industry. Are employees who work around asbestos being subjected to high risks of cancer? What psychological and physical dangers lurk in various forms of manufacturing processes? What are the dangers to field workers, consumers, and the environment of various forms of pesticides? Congress and the various regulatory bodies can barely begin to answer these questions. The companies most closely associated with the problems may not know the answers either; but they certainly have the more ready access to the most probative information. It is their doctors who treat the employees' injuries; it is their chemists who live with and test the new compounds; it is their health records that gather absentee data. . . .

Limitations Connected with Implementing the Law

. . . [A] combination of factors, including the increased expectations of today's citizens and the increasingly technical nature of the society, have left our traditional legal mechanisms unsatisfactory to cope with the problems that currently concern people. Consider, for example, the law of torts, the ordinary rules for recovering damages against someone who has injured you. A model tort case is one in which Smith, who is walking across the

street, is accidentally but negligently driven into by Jones. Smith falls, suffering internal injuries, and sues for damages. Now, I call this "a model" case because certain of its features make it so well suited to traditional legal recovery. Note that (a) Smith knows *the fact* that he has been injured; (b) Smith knows *who* has caused the injury; (c) one can assess, fairly well, the *nature and extent* of his injuries; and (d) the *technical inquiry* involved in analyzing causality is not too extensive—that is, simple laws of physics are involved, not beyond commonsense experience.

But contrast that model case—a case in which the tort laws may be fairly adequate to make restitution—with the sort of case that is increasingly of concern in the society today. The food we will eat tonight (grown, handled, packaged, distributed by various corporations) may contain chemicals that are killing us, or at least reducing our life expectancy considerably. But (a) we cannot know with certainty the fact that we are being injured by any particular product; (b) it is difficult determining who might be injuring us—that is, even if we know that our bodies are suffering from a build-up of mercury, we are faced with an awesome task of pinning responsibility on any particular source of mercury; (c) we would have a difficult time proving the extent of our injuries (the more so proving the extent attributable to any particular source); and (d) the nature of the evidence that would have to be evaluated by the court is far more complex and technical than that in the "model" case above—perhaps too technical realistically to trust to courts or even agencies to handle. Thus, it seems inevitable that a certain percentage of harmful, even seriously harmful activity is not going to be contained by trusting to traditional legal mechanisms. . . .

The question of how well regulatory agencies can repair the various weaknesses of traditional legal mechanisms is a significant one, too vast to be reviewed here thoroughly. But several points have to be mentioned. First, one ought to recognize that the mere establishment of regulatory agencies does not get around the most significant weaknesses of traditional legal strategies when they are applied to corporate problems. In the last analysis, agencies, too, have to fall back on court enforcement and thus on fines and civil penalties with all the infirmities I have emphasized. . . .

. . . [Second, the] agencies do not as a whole seem capable of developing consistent policies; they are often ineffective, and, if rarely corrupt, more than occasionally subject to influence peddling. Some agencies, from whatever the cause, do go through phases of getting tough on their regulatees. But even these episodes do not guarantee that the public interest will be served. . . .

. . . [Third, the] vague generality of the agencies' ground rules produces, understandably, all sorts of difficulties. The FCC, trying to work out some tangible criteria as guidelines for the granting of licenses, has produced some that seem almost inconsistent—as in seeking to maximize both broadcast experience and diversification of ownership—with no evident overriding principles to arbitrate the conflicts. Often the looseness of the agencies' mandate results in their turning over to their staffs equally foggy assignments, such as when the Civil Aeronautics Board directed one hearing examiner (with a total staff of one secretary) to "review the local air service pattern in the area covered by [seven] states and develop a sound pattern of service to meet the needs of the entire area."[12] If such generalities were products of carelessness or lack of attention, they could be remedied. But a good deal of the vagueness is more deep-seated and even inherent in the nature of the relationship between Congress and the agencies. The very situations that gave rise to agencies are those where Congress could not lay down hard-and-fast rules; if it could have, it would have. What is more, some measure of congressional vagueness may be born of political necessity: To muster enough votes for passage, proposed bills may have to become more and more watered down and ambiguous, leaving it to the agency to figure out what Congress "meant." (Consider, for example, the National Labor Relation Act's provision that the NLRB should get both sides to "bargain in good faith," a proviso that could be read by the Senate's labor supporters as a victory for them, and yet at the same time appear toothless enough to garner the votes that were promanagement.) With the agencies' basic ground rules cast in terms as open-ended as "the public interest," it is almost inevitable that the regulatees will have a disproportionately strong hand in filling in content. "The public," whatever it is, is distant and disorganized, "its" interests unclear, while the regulatees are present, organized, and vigilant—and they know what they want.

Let me close by observing that in these and many criticisms of the federal agencies, I often find myself in strong agreement with the so-called "antis." But, in my mind, they fail to draw from their skepticism the correct implication for the corporate social-responsibility debate. If the agencies—or the other public control mechanisms—*were* effective, then it would be proper to brush aside the calls for corporate social responsibility by calling on the law to keep corporations in line. But the weaknesses of the agencies are simply a further argument that trust in our traditional legal machinery as a means of keeping corporations in bounds is misplaced—and that therefore something more is needed.

NOTES

1. *New York Times*, September 12, 1962, sect. 6, p. 33, col. 2.
2. See, for example, *Automatic Self-Cleansing Filter Syndicate Co. Ltd.* v. *Cunninghame* (1906) 2 Ch. 34.
3. "Dow Shalt Not Kill," in S. Prakash Sethi, *Up Against the Corporate Wall*, (Englewood Cliffs, N.J.: Prentice-Hall, 1971), pp. 236–266, and the opinion of Judge Tamm in *Medical Committee for Human Rights* v. *S.E.C.*, 432 F.2d 659 (D.C. Cir. 1970), and the dissent of Mr. Justice Douglas in the same case in the U.S. Supreme Court, 404 U.S. 403, 407–411 (1972).
4. Theodore J. Jacobs, "Pollution, Consumerism, Accountability," *Center Magazine* 5, 1, (January-February 1971): 47.
5. Walter Goodman, "Stocks Without Sin," *Harper's*, August 1971, p. 66.
6. *New York Times*, September 12, 1962, sect. 6, p. 122, col. 3.
7. Ibid, p. 122, cols. 3–4.
8. "Little Puddings in Dangerous Cans," *Consumer Reports*, July 1971, p. 406–407.
9. James D. Thompson, *Organizations in Action* (New York: McGraw-Hill, 1967), pp. 20–23.
10. Cal. Water Code § 13201.
11. Cal. Agricultural Code §§ 62115, 62121, 62152.
12. See Louis J. Hector, "Problems of the C.A.B. and the Independent Regulatory Commissions," *Yale Law Journal* 69 (1960): 933–934.

Questions for Analysis

1. *On what grounds does Stone reject the promissory, agency, and role arguments? How might Friedman respond to Stone's rebuttals?*

2. *When he considers the "polestar" argument, Stone admits that there is a "germ of validity" to what his opponents say. What is that germ of validity? Why does he reject the argument anyway?*

3. *Why does Stone think it difficult for consumers to exert market pressures on corporations that behave irresponsibly? Why does he think that consumers may not succeed in changing the behavior as they would like, even if they manage to exert such pressure?*

4. *What is the time-lag problem with legal attempts to change corporate behavior?*

5. *Why, according to Stone, is it difficult to enact adequate legislation controlling corporate behavior? How serious are those difficulties?*

6. *What failures does Stone point out in the implementation of tort law? Why does he think that regulatory agencies face similar and other difficulties?*

7. *Has Stone refuted Friedman?*

Changing the Rules

Norman E. Bowie

This essay by Norman E. Bowie addresses an important question in the debate over corporate responsibility: Why should business corporations agree to exercise social responsibility? Why, that is, should they agree to a new social contract with society? He provides three reasons: self-interest, corporate contribution to social problems, and corporate resources for dealing with social problems. Bowie concludes, however, that business corporations have the right to ask for something in return. First, they have the right to participate in the redrawing of the contract. Second, they have the right to ask other contributors to social problems to participate in their solution in accordance with their own resources.

It is not merely the introductory philosophy students who ask, "Why be moral?" An examination of much of the contemporary literature in business ethics indicates that the "Why be moral" question is very much on the mind of business persons as well.

One possibility for providing an answer to the "why be moral" question is to indicate the contractual basis on which business rests. The operation of a business, particularly when the business is a corporation, is not a matter of right. Rather the individuals enter into a contract with society. In turn for the permission to do business, the society places certain obligations and duties on the business. The corporation is created by society for a specific purpose or purposes. Robert A. Dahl has put the point this way:

> Today it is absurd to regard the corporation simply as an enterprise established for the sole purpose of allowing profit making. We

the citizens give them special rights, powers, and privileges, protection, and benefits on the understanding that their activities will fulfill purposes. Corporations exist only as they continue to benefit us. . . . Every corporation should be thought of as a social enterprise whose existence and decisions can be justified only insofar as they serve public or social purposes.[1]

Actually not only does Dahl's quotation indicate that the relation between business and society is contractual, but Dahl spells out the nature of that contract. The corporation must not only benefit those who create it, it must benefit those who permit it (namely society as a whole).

In many discussions of business ethics no one defines terms like "moral" or "corporate responsibility." This inadequacy can be corrected by adopting the perspective of the contract analysis. The morality of business or corporate responsibility is determined by the terms of the contract with society. The corporation has those obligations which the society imposes on it in its charter of incorporation. In accepting its charter, the corporation accepts those moral constraints. Failure to be moral is a violation of the principle of fairness. The corporation which violates the moral rules contained in or implied by its charter is in the position of agreeing to the rules and then violating them. It is in the position of one who makes a promise and then breaks it. Such unfairness is often considered a paradigm case of injustice and immorality. The corporation which finds itself in the position of breaking the agreements it has made is in a particularly vulnerable position, since the corporate enterprise depends for its survival on the integrity of contractual relations. Understanding business as a contractual relation between the corporation and the society as a whole provides a preliminary answer to our "why be moral" question. The corporation should be moral because it has agreed to be. However, what a corporation's moral obligations are is contained in the contract itself.

Although this analysis does provide the framework for showing that certain corporate activities are immoral and provides a moral *reason* for indicating why a corporation should not engage in them, many complicated questions remain to be answered.

The first focuses on the content of the contract. Many corporate executives could accept the contract analysis as outlined thus far and argue that current demands on corporations to be more socially responsible are themselves violations of the contract. After all, corporate charters do not contain an open-ended moral requirement that the corporation promote the public interest. Rather, corporations are founded primarily to promote the financial interests of the investors (the stockholders). Society had believed that by furthering the interests of the stockholders, society as a whole benefited. Now society has changed its mind, and frustrated corporation executives rightly argue that it is the corporate responsibility zealots and not the corporate executives who are changing the terms of the contract.

In several respects the corporate response is appropriate. Society is changing the rules of the game and it is appropriate to ask why corporations should acquiesce in these unilateral changes. Before considering these issues, however, I should like to point out one respect in which the corporate officials' charge that the rules are being changed is incorrect. In addition to the obligations spelled out in the contract itself, there are certain moral requirements, moral background conditions, if you will, which are assumed. Certain moral rules are rules that are required if contracts are to be made at all. These moral requirements are as obligatory as the obligations spelled out in the contract itself. After all, when I agree to pay my bills in order to get a Master Charge card, I do not also sign a meta-agreement that I keep my agreements. The whole market exchange mechanism rests on conditions of trust which can be embodied in moral principles. What is shocking about some of the current corporate scandals—bribery, falsification of records, theft, and corporate espionage—is that these acts violate the conditions for making contracts and market exchanges, conditions which are at the very heart of the free enterprise system. Such violations cannot be excused by saying that they do not appear in the contract. Such excuses are almost as absurd as someone defending the murder of a creditor by saying: I only promised to pay him back; I didn't promise not to murder him. Hence we can conclude that a company has moral obligations in the contract it makes with society and it has obligations to those moral rules which make contracts possible. Its agreement in the former is explicit; its agreement in the latter, implicit. Violation of either is a violation of fairness—a failure to keep one's promises.

We can now return to the charge that it is society which is changing the terms of the contract. Fortunately, not all the charges of immorality and irresponsibility leveled at corporations are directed at violations of contractual morality. Corporations are charged with neglecting to solve such social problems as pollution, racism, sexism, and urban blight. They are charged with sins of omission. At this point the corporation can argue that they have no obligation to resolve all of society's problems. Such a broad-based moral obligation is not a part of their contract with society. That corporations do not have such general contractual obligations is conceded by most experts in the field.

We now face a more complicated form of the "why be moral" question. Why should the corporation agree to a rewriting of its contract with society—a rewriting which will impose greatly expanded social responsibilities on it?

One answer is prudential. It is in the interests of the corporation to do so. This idea has been expressed in the form of a law called the Iron Law of Responsibility: In the long run those who do not use power in a manner which society considers socially responsible will tend to lose it.[2] If society demands a rewriting of the contract, society has the *power* to rewrite it unilaterally. However, can we go beyond prudence to offer any moral reasons for business to revise its agreements? I believe there are several.

One might be called the principle of contribution: If one contributes to a social harm, then one has a proportional obligation to contribute to its alleviation. Since business clearly does contribute to social problems, it has at least some obligation to correct them. In saying that business has some responsibility, I do not wish to imply that it has the only responsibility. Government, labor, and all of us as consumers contribute our part to the problems and hence have some responsibility to work toward solutions. It is neither fair nor prudent to expect one segment of society to shoulder the entire burden. Hence only a *contribution* is required.

Another moral reason for business to accept a new contract might be based on the notion of power. Those constituents of society which have the most in the way of resources should contribute the most to resolving social ills. Since business is either the most powerful force or second only to the federal government, its superior resources impose special obligations upon it. There is an analogy here to arguments made on behalf of progressive taxation.

If the moral arguments are sound, there are moral reasons as well as a very strong prudential reason for corporations to revise their contractual relations with society. However, the corporation can reciprocally require certain agreements on the part of society. First, since a contract should be mutually acceptable, the contract cannot be rewritten unilaterally. Representatives from the corporate sector have a right to participate in the redrafting. Second, grounds of consistency require that other contributors to society's problems also contribute to their solution and that the requirements for the more powerful constituencies be stronger. So long as these conditions are met, corporations should agree to a revised contract and our original fairness arguments can be used to show why individual corporations should follow it.

NOTES

1. Robert A. Dahl, "A Prelude to Corporate Reform." In *Corporate Social Policy,* ed. Robert L. Heilbroner and Paul London (Reading, Mass.: Addison-Wesley Publishing Company, 1975), pp. 18–19.

2. Keith Davis and Robert L. Blomstrom, *Business and Society: Environment and Responsibility,* 3rd ed. (New York: McGraw-Hill Book Company, 1975), p. 50.

Questions for Analysis

1. According to Bowie, "The corporation should be moral because it has agreed to be." What does he mean by that?

2. *Bowie claims that corporations are in some respects right to say that society is changing the rules of the game and in one respect wrong. In what ways does he agree with corporations on the point? In what way does he disagree?*

3. *Why does Bowie think that prudence dictates that corporations agree to a new contract? Is he correct?*

4. *At the end of his essay, Bowie tells us what corporations can require of society in return for agreeing to a new contract. Do you agree with him? Do you think corporations can require even more than he allows?*

5. *How would Friedman respond to Bowie's arguments?*

Constructing a Social Contract for Business

Thomas Donaldson

The following essay by Thomas Donaldson, like the essay by Bowie, looks at the issue of corporate responsibility in the context of a social contract. There is, however, an important difference between the two essays. Unlike Bowie, Donaldson does not consider the social contract for business to be an agreement between corporations and society. Rather, he thinks of it as an agreement among individuals who live in a society that does not yet have corporations. The idea is to ask ourselves what we would agree to among ourselves if we were starting from scratch. Why should we have corporations? What should we expect them to do for us? What should we not allow them to do? By answering these questions, Donaldson feels, we can best discover how corporations should conduct themselves in our own society. To justify his approach, he compares it to the approach of political philosophers like John Locke (and John Rawls), who seek to discover the rightful powers and obligations of governments by imagining a social contract drawn up among individuals before the existence of any government.

In a speech to the Harvard Business School in 1969, Henry Ford II stated:

> The terms of the contract between industry and society are changing . . . Now we are being asked to serve a wider range of human values and to accept an obligation to members of the public with whom we have no commercial transactions.

The "contract" to which Henry Ford referred concerns a corporation's *indirect* obligations. It represents not a set of formally specified obligations, but a set of binding, abstract ones. A social contract for business, if one exists, is not a typewritten contract in the real world, but a metaphysical abstraction not unlike the "social contract" between citizens and government that philosophers have traditionally discussed. Such a contract would have concrete significance, for it would help to interpret the nature of a corporation's indirect obligations—ones which are notoriously slippery.

The aim of this essay is to discover a corporation's indirect obligations by attempting to clarify the meaning of business's so-called "social contract." The task is challenging. Although people speak frequently of such a contract, few have attempted to specify its meaning.

A good starting point is the so-called "social contract" that philosophers have spoken of between society and the state. This political contract has usually been viewed as a theoretical means for justifying the existence of the state. Philosophers have asked, "Why should people let a government exist

Thomas Donaldson, Corporations and Morality, *© 1982, pp. 36–57. Reprinted by permission of Prentice Hall, Inc., Englewood Cliffs, New Jersey.*

at all?" in other words, "Why should people prefer to have a government control much of their actions—to impose taxes, raise armies, and punish criminals—instead of having no government at all?" They never doubted for a moment the need for a state, but they believed raising such questions would clarify not only the justification for the state's existence, but also the reciprocal obligations between the state and its citizens. If a government began to abuse its citizenry, to trample on its rights or to diminish social welfare, then according to such philosophers it had broken the tenets of the social contract and could be overthrown. Such a theory in the hands of the seventeenth-century English philosopher John Locke, provided much of the theoretical support for the American Revolution and design of the Declaration of Independence and the U.S. Constitution.

The political social contract provides a clue for understanding the contract for business. If the political contract serves as a justification for the existence of the state, then the business contract by parity of reasoning should serve as the justification for the existence of the corporation.

Thus, crucial questions are: Why should corporations exist at all? What is the fundamental justification of their activities? How can we measure their performance and say when they have achieved their fundamental purpose? Consider a case involving General Motors and the production of automobiles. The automobiles that General Motors produced during the 1950s and 1960s all had non-collapsible steering wheels (called by Ralph Nader "ram-rodding" steering wheels), and evidence indicated that they contributed to hundreds of thousands of highway deaths. But General Motors and other auto manufacturers kept them on the cars anyway, claiming the added expense of collapsible steering wheels would reduce car sales and profits. Their claim may well have been true. However, by refusing to install safer steering wheels, had they failed to achieve a fundamental corporate mission? Had they violated a tenet of an implied social contract between them and society? Or had they just attended to business—although in a way which had unfortunate consequences for society? To answer these questions, we must first know what justifies General Motors' existence.

It is reasonable to look for a fundamental purpose, or set of purposes, that justifies corporate existence. Doing so makes conceptual sense, despite the fact one would never look for what justifies, say, human existence. Corporations, unlike humans, are artifacts, which is to say *we* create them. We *choose* to create corporations and we might choose either not to create them or to create different entities. Corporations thus are like political states in their need for justification.

One might attempt to justify corporate existence by appealing to corporate productivity: to the automobiles, irons, tools, clothing, and medical equipment corporations create. Because society demands such items, it seemingly also requires the corporations that produce them. Adam Smith, the eighteenth-century Scottish philosopher, emphasizes productivity when he justifies a szet of economic practices through their contribution to the wealth of nations. But although productivity is surely a crucial piece in the puzzle of corporate justification, it fails to provide a full solution. To say that an organization produces wealth for society is not sufficient to justify it from a moral perspective, since morality encompasses the entire range of human welfare. To say something produces wealth is to say something morally good about it—assuming that wealth is counted as a human good—but it fails to tell us what else the thing does, or how its process of creation affects society. Consider the example of a nuclear power reactor. To say that a nuclear reactor generates electricity is to say something good about it, but it fails to consider the reactor in the context of the possibility of melt-downs, the storage of nuclear waste, the costs of alternative production, and so forth. (This is true even if we suppose that ultimately nuclear reactors are fully justified.) The logic of the problem of corporate justification is similar. To achieve a complete moral picture of a corporation's existence, we must consider not only its capacity to produce wealth, but the full range of its effects upon society.

Before we attempt to spell out the terms of the social contract, a prior issue must be settled; namely, *who* are the parties to the contract? So far we have spoken of a contract between society and business, but the concepts of "business" and "society" are vague. Let us stipulate that "business" refers to *productive organizations*, i.e., ones where people cooperate to produce at least one specific product or service. Productive organizations would include corporations (of the productive sort), but would also include government owned businesses, large business partnerships, and productive firms in socialist countries.

By attempting to find the moral underpinnings of all productive organizations, we will indirectly be searching for the moral underpinnings of corporations, since virtually all corporations are productive organizations. Once the moral underpinnings of productive organizations are known, it will be possible to answer from a moral perspective the question: Why does Exxon exist? Or, speaking more precisely, it will be possible to answer this question when Exxon is considered *as a member of the class of productive organizations.*

The term "society" is similarly vague. It might refer to the aggregate of individuals who make up society, or to something over and above the sum of those individuals. For clarity, let us stipulate that the contract is between productive organizations and *individual members of society*, not between productive organizations and some supra-individual, social entity.

The simplest way of understanding the social contract is in the form: "We (the members of society) agree to do X, and you (the contracting organizations) agree to do Y." Applying this form to General Motors (or any productive organization) means that the task of a social contract argument is to specify X, where X refers to the obligations of society to productive organizations, and to specify Y, where Y refers to the obligations of productive organizations to society.

It is relatively easy in this context to specify X, because what productive organizations need from society is:

1. Recognition as a single agent, especially in the eyes of the law.

2. The authority: (a) to own or use land and natural resources, and (b) to hire employees.

It may appear presumptuous to assume that productive organizations must be warranted by society. Can one not argue that any organization has a *right* to exist and operate? That they have this right *apart* from the wishes of society? When asking such questions, one must distinguish between claims about rights of mere organizations and claims about rights of organizations with special powers, such as productive organizations. A case can be made for the unbridled right of the Elks Club, whose members unite in fraternal activities, to exist and operate (assuming it does not discriminate against minorities or women); but the same cannot be said for Du Pont Corporation, which not only must draw on existing stores of mineral resources, but must find dumping sites to store toxic chemical by-products. Even granted that people have an inalienable right to form and operate organizations, and even granted that this right exists apart from the discretion of society, the productive organization requires special status under the law and the opportunity to use society's resources: two issues in which every member of society may be said to have a vested interest.

Conditions 1 and 2 are obviously linked to each other. In order for a productive organization to use land and hire employees (conditions of 2) it must have the authority to perform those acts as if it were an individual agent (the condition of 1). The philosophical impact of 1 should not be exaggerated. To say that productive organizations must have the authority to act as individual agents is not necessarily to affirm that they are abstract, invisible persons. Rather it is a means of stating the everyday fact that productive organizations must, for a variety of purposes, be treated as individual entities. For example, a corporation must be able to hire new employees, to sign contracts, and to negotiate purchases without getting the O.K. from *all* its employees and stockholders.

Defining the Y side of the contract is as difficult as defining the X side is easy. It is obvious that productive organizations must be allowed to exist and act. But it is not obvious precisely why societies should allow them to exist, that is, what specific benefits society should hope to gain from the bargain. What specific functions should society expect from productive organizations? What obligations should it impose? Only one assumption can be made readily: that the members of society should demand at a minimum that the benefits from authorizing the existence of productive organizations outweigh the detriments of doing so. This is nothing other than the expectation of all voluntary agreements: that no party should be asked to conclude a contract which places him or her in a position worse than before.

To specify society's terms for the social contract, let us return to a traditional device in social contract theory, the device of imagining society *without* the institution that is being analyzed. In short, let us consider society without productive organizations, in a "state of nature." Instead of the traditional state of nature where people live without government, we shall consider a state where people live without *productive organizations*. To avoid confusing this state with the traditional ones, let us call it the "state of individual production." Thus, the strategy involves:

1. Characterizing conditions in a state of individual production (without productive organizations).

2. Indicating how certain problems are remedied by the introduction of productive organizations.

3. Using the reasons generated in the second step as a basis for specifying a social contract between society and its productive organizations.

The details must be spelled out. How are we to imagine the state of individual production? What people occupy it? Are they selfish? Charitable? How do they labor?

At a minimum the people in the state of individual production should be imagined as having "economic interests," i.e., as being people for whom it is desirable to have some things or services produced by human labor. Under such a definition almost any human would qualify, except perhaps ascetics or persons who prefer death to life. Thus, the people envisioned by the present strategy are ordinary, economically interested persons who have not yet organized themselves, or been organized, into productive organizations.

Should they be imagined as purely egoistic, wanting only to satisfy their own selfish interests, or as purely benevolent, wanting only to satisfy the interests of others? In the real world both characterizations are extreme—ordinary people are neither devils nor saints—and thus is suggested the strategy of assuming the same about people in the state of individual production. Let us adopt this strategy; if the contract has application to ordinary people, it will help to keep ordinary people in mind.[1]

To imagine a state of individual production, i.e., without productive organizations, is to imagine a society in which individuals produce and work alone. It is to imagine society without factories, banks, hospitals, restaurants, or railroads, since all these organizations, as well as many others, count

as productive organizations, that is, they are organizations in which people cooperate to produce at least one specific product or service. (For our purposes, noneconomic factors such as family structure, religious attitudes, and educational interests shall be disregarded.) Now in such a state we may imagine any level of technology we wish. The only crucial fact is that people produce *individually*.

The Terms of the Contract

Two principal classes of people stand to benefit or be harmed by the introduction of productive organizations: (1) people who consume the organizations' products, i.e., consumers; and (2) people who work in such organizations, i.e., employees. The two classes are broadly defined and not mutually exclusive. "Consumer" refers to anyone who is economically interested; hence virtually anyone qualifies as a consumer. "Employee" refers to anyone who contributes labor to the productive process of a productive organization, including managers, laborers, part-time support personnel, and (in corporations) members of the board of directors.

Consumers

From the standpoint of our hypothetical consumers, productive organizations promise to *enhance the satisfaction of economic interests*. That is to say, people could hope for the introduction of productive organizations to better satisfy their interests for shelter, food, entertainment, transportation, health care, and clothing. The prima facie benefits for consumers include:

1. *Improving efficiency* through:
   a. Maximizing advantages of specialization.
   b. Improving decision-making resources.
   c. Increasing the capacity to use or acquire expensive technology and resources.

2. *Stabilizing levels of output and channels of distribution.*

3. *Increasing liability resources.*

Each benefit needs explanation.

The first benefit, improving efficiency, is the special excellence of productive organizations. Productive organizations tend to generate products that are equal or better in quality and price, with lower expenditures of human labor, than is possible in the state of individual production. Let us examine a few of the reasons for this remarkable capacity.

1A. Maximizing the advantages of specialization. Adam Smith's well-known thought-experiment in the *Wealth of Nations* provides ready evidence for the truth that two can often be more efficient than one. He showed that in the production of pins, one person working alone could account for a mere handful of pins, whereas in a system of first-order specialization—where one cuts the wire, another points the wire, and so on—the proportionate share of pins per worker increases dramatically. The same is true today. To produce clocks, erasers, and antibiotics efficiently, an enormous degree of cooperative specialization is required: the mere existence of products like the Space Shuttle owes itself to such specialization. Economists agree that many products are further subject to *economies of scale;* that is, their efficient production is dependent not only upon cooperative specialization, but on a certain level of it. Because of this factor, a company like American Motors may be too small to compete successfully with General Motors in the production of automobiles.

1B. Improving decision-making resources. Productive organizations share with individual persons the tendency to err in decision-making. Despite this, such organizations have decision-making advantages. First, they can utilize the ongoing talents of people with different backgrounds. Thus, a decision by Westinghouse, Inc., to manufacture a new appliance may call on the knowledge of chemists, accountants, engineers, and marketing specialists. One person could never possess such knowledge.

Second, they can increase information storage. In the same way a person can collect and remember information on a small scale, organizations do so on a large scale. Productive organizations can have superhuman memories: some corporations have libraries larger than those in universities.

1C. Increasing the capacity to use and acquire expensive technology and resources. This advantage is nearly self-evident. All other things being equal, two or more people will have greater financial resources than one; hence productive organizations can make capital expenditures on a larger scale than single individuals. Often the use of large, expensive equipment is important not only for increasing production, but for generating higher quality production, since expensive equipment is frequently necessary to improve productive efficiency.

2. Stabilizing levels of output and channels of distribution. The imaginary inhabitants of our state of individual production stand to benefit by the merging of individual craftsmen into organizations which are relatively stable, and whose level of output and pattern of distribution are relatively constant. Individual craftsmen are subject to illness, psychological problems, and the need for rest. For example, to rely on an individual mail carrier for the delivery of one's mail is riskier than depending on a large postal organization. Individuals must sleep, eat, and rest, but a large postal organization never sleeps, never eats—it even grows larger at Christmas.

3. Increasing liability resources. Under this heading are grouped the benefits that consumers reap because organizations, in contrast to individuals, have "deep pockets." In short, they are better able to compensate injured consumers. In the late 1970's Ford Motor Company was forced by the courts to compensate victims of the Ford Pinto's exploding gas tank. Because of design defects, the Pinto's tank was prone to ignite when hit from behind. The money paid by Ford to victims (and relatives of victims) was astounding; it ran into the millions of dollars. Although few productive organizations are as large as Ford, it remains true that organizations are better able to back their products with financial resources than individuals.

Employees

These, then, are the prima facie benefits from introducing productive organizations for consumers. But productive organizations should also be viewed from the standpoint of their effects on people as workers, that is, from the standpoint of their effects upon individual laborers and craftsmen in the state of individual production who opt to work for productive organizations.

It is not difficult to discover certain prima facie benefits, such as the following:

1. Increasing income potential (and the capacity for social contributions).

2. Diffusing personal liability.

3. Adjusting personal income allocation.

1. Increasing income potential and capacity for social contributions. This benefit follows immediately from the earlier fact that second-order-cooperative specialization increases productive efficiency. The person, like Smith's hypothetical pin maker, who joins others in the production of pins is able to make many times more pins than he would alone. This increase also represents an increase in his chance to receive a higher income.

2. Diffusing personal liability. A second prima facie benefit from the standpoint of workers lies in the capacity of an organization to diffuse liability, or in short, to insure the individual against the risk of massive compensation demands. A worker in the state of individual production who sells faulty, dangerous products is morally liable for the damages her product causes. But the extent of this liability can exceed her capacity to pay. Therefore she stands to gain by working with others in a productive organization, for it then becomes the productive organization, not she, who assumes ultimate liability.

3. Adjusting personal income allocation. The increased resources of the productive organization allow the worker to participate in an income-allocation scheme which is detached from the vicissitudes of his capacity to produce, and which is more closely tied to his actual needs. The vicissitudes of the worker's capacity include occasional illness, disabling accidents, and a tendency to lose speed and strength as he ages. Yet his needs persist and sometimes even increase in the face of these vicissitudes. The employee can work harder when he is healthy: but he needs as much money, and sometimes more, when he is ill. The worker may not be able to produce more when he is 50 than when he was 20, but if he marries and has a family his need for income may be greater at 50. When the worker joins a productive organization, the organization can allocate personal income according to a scheme more equitable for him and everyone else.

These prima facie benefits to the worker may be added to the prima facie consumer benefits discussed earlier. Together they constitute a set of reasons which rational people living in a state of individual production might use to justify the introduction of productive organizations. Indeed, if some such set of prima facie benefits did *not* exist,

then people would be foolish to introduce such organizations; there would be nothing to gain.

It now becomes possible in light of this analysis to begin the task of specifying the general character of a hypothetical social contract. From the standpoint of society, the goal of a productive organization may be said to be *to enhance the welfare of society through a satisfaction of consumer and worker interests.* In turn, each of the prima facie benefits that we have discussed can be construed as specific terms of the social contract.

Minimizing Drawbacks:

An obvious question arises. If people in the state of individual production must agree upon the terms of the social contract, and if these terms directly relate to the task of enhancing society's welfare, then why stop with maximizing prima facie benefits? Why not also minimize prima facie drawbacks? John Locke employed a similar strategy in structuring his political social contract; he not only specified the positive goals of government, but, recognizing government's tendency to abuse privilege, also saw fit to specify certain pitfalls that government must avoid. Are there prima facie drawbacks from introducing productive organizations as well?

Our imaginary consumer stands to benefit because productive organizations, along with the technology they encourage, improve productivity and put more shoes, clothing, electricity, and automobiles on the market. But there is an unwanted consequence of which twentieth-century consumers are painfully aware: increased production tends to deplete natural resources while increasing pollution. More shoes, clothing, electricity, and automobiles require more leather, cotton, coal, and iron. The world has a finite supply. Moreover, the amazing machines so well adapted to productive organizations—the gas engines, the coal furnaces, and the nuclear reactors—all generate by-products which render the environment less fit for human life.

The problem of the increased pollution and depletion of natural resources is more obvious than a second problem, namely the diffusion of individual moral responsibility which sometimes occurs in productive organizations. In the state of individual production, consumers buy their goods from the individual craftsman who stands behind his product, or at least if he does not, the consumers know where to find him. When the cobbler sells a pair of shoes to John Doe and the shoes fall apart, he must confront Doe face to face. Contrast this situation with that of productive organizations, in which workers never see the consumer. To the employee, the consumer is faceless, and the employee's level of psychic accountability tends to lower along with a rise in consumer anonymity. The employee is responsible for his behavior, but to his superior, not to the customer; and his superior sometimes is more apathetic than he. In extreme instances the employee may participate in a form of rebellion unknown to the independent craftsman: "industrial sabotage," where workers retaliate against management by intentionally damaging products.

While speaking of potential drawbacks of productive organizations, one must also acknowledge that the political power of productive organizations is sometimes used to enhance individual interests. Such power sometimes is used to secure favors from government which damage both consumer interests and the interests of the general public. Organizations can receive favors which bolster monopoly power and aggravate inefficiency, as when the railroads in the United States in the late nineteenth century used government grants and privileges to develop a stranglehold on public transportation. Organizations can also use power to divert government expenditures from consumer items to items that actually harm the consumers' interests. In Germany prior to World Wars I and II, for example, large munitions manufacturers used their political influence to increase taxation, and thus decrease consumers' buying power, for massive purchases of cannons, tanks, fighter planes, and warships. Undeniably, from the overall standpoint of the German public, these purchases were disastrous.

From the perspective of consumers these problems represent potential drawbacks often associated with the introduction of productive organizations. But drawbacks also exist for employees.

Workers in the state of individual production possess a few obvious advantages. For one, they are close to the product and able to take pride in

their own creations and the fact that their hands were responsible for the lamp, the soap, or the shirt being sold. But workers in productive organizations are typically removed from the product. They can be, in the words of Marx, "alienated" in a way that blocks their very capacity for self-realization. During World War II the U.S. aircraft manufacturers discovered that alienation was hampering production. Production was shown to increase when the draftsmen, riveters, and sheetmetal workers were taken to *see* the finished product they had worked on—the airplane itself.

In addition to possible alienation and loss of pride, the worker may also suffer from losing control over the design of the product and of his or her work structure. Whereas the individual craftsman can structure her hours and conditions to suit herself, the organizational worker must suit the needs of the overall organization. A man or woman working on an assembly line is powerless to improve the design of the product, and equally powerless to change the design of the work process. The look of the product, the speed of the conveyer belt, and even the number of steps to perform the task all have been determined by others, who are frequently strangers to the worker. Seldom even does the worker have control over safety arrangements or levels of in-plant pollutants.

The increased capacity of productive organizations (over individuals) to use large, expensive technology and massive resources reveals on the other side a decreased capacity of the workers to control their lives. They must adapt to the machines. If a machine operates most efficiently at a certain pace, then the worker must, like the spool boys of the nineteenth-century cotton industry, hurry to meet that pace. In such cases it is as if the machine were controlling the person instead of the person controlling the machine. Similarly, the increased efficiency which results from specialization reveals, on its reverse, the monotony of the simple task repeated thousands of times. The man who knocked the struts into place on the wheels of Henry Ford's Model T was far more efficient than the old craftsman who built a carriage from the bottom up. But the Ford worker knocked struts in place on wheels every minute of every working day.

These prima facie *drawbacks* may be seen as reasons for *not* introducing productive organizations. Unless the prima facie benefits discussed earlier outweigh these prima facie drawbacks, no contract will be concluded because rational people will not choose a lesser over a greater good. And if the benefits outweigh the drawbacks, it follows that in order maximally to enhance welfare, productive organizations should both pursue positive goals and minimize negative ones. Thus, using our discussion as a basis for this list of negative goals, we have:

From the standpoint of *consumers*, productive organizations should minimize:

1. Pollution and the depletion of natural resources.

2. The destruction of personal accountability.

3. The misuse of political power.

From the standpoint of *workers* productive organizations should minimize:

1. Worker alienation.

2. Lack of worker control over work conditions.

3. Monotony and dehumanization of the worker.

The social contract sketched out requires, then, that productive organizations maximize goods and minimize evils relative to consumer and worker welfare. But how, from a moral point of view, should the inevitable trade-offs be made between maximizing and minimizing, and between consumer interests and worker interests? For example, a corporate decision may impair worker interests while at the same time enhancing consumer interests. Consider the age-old trade-off between higher salaries and lower consumer prices. If coffee workers are paid higher salaries, then coffee drinkers pay higher prices. Conversely, if doctors are paid lower salaries, then the patients pay lower prices. These trade-offs are common not only in the area of salaries, but in many others as well.

How would the rational inhabitants of our state of individual production answer this question? Because the contract specifies that the function of productive organizations is to enhance the welfare of society, our inhabitants might choose a utilitarian standard for making trade-offs, that is, a standard that would specify that organizational policies or action should aim for *the greatest good for the greatest number*. On the other hand, they might prefer a nonutilitarian, or deontological standard, which would specify that *organizational action should accord with general policies or rules which could be universalized for all productive organizations* (i.e., which society would want all productive organizations to adopt).

Whatever the standard—and it must be acknowledged that determining the standard is difficult—two things seem certain. First, society does acknowledge that trade-offs often must be made. Society could not reasonably expect productive organizations to maximize worker interests come what may, say by adopting the policy of paying workers the absolute maximum possible at a given time, for to do so would grossly neglect consumers. If General Motors expended every bit of its resources on employees, the result for society would be catastrophic. Similarly, the consumer must not receive all the attention. Such a policy would result in poor working conditions, low salaries, and frustrated workers (no matter how satisfied employees might be in their life as consumers).

Because trade-offs must be made, it remains logically possible that people in the state of individual production would choose to introduce productive organizations and to establish the social contract, even when they expected either worker interests or consumer interests to be less satisfied than in the state of nature—so long as *overall* welfare were enhanced. In other words, the inhabitants might believe that, on balance, people as workers stand to lose from the introduction of productive organizations, and that potential alienation, loss of control, and other drawbacks make the overall condition of the worker worse than before. But if the benefits to people as consumers fully *overshadowed* these drawbacks, we should still expect the contract to be enacted.

There is a caveat which has application to the overall contract. People would make a trade-off of the kind just discussed only on the condition that it did not violate certain minimum standards of justice, however these are specified. For example, they would refuse to enact the contract if they knew that the existence of productive organizations would systematically reduce a given class of people to an inhuman existence, subsistence poverty, or enslavement. Although the contract might allow productive organizations to undertake actions requiring welfare trade-offs, it would prohibit organizational acts of injustice. It might allow productive organizations to institute layoffs under certain conditions, say, to block skyrocketing production costs; here, worker welfare would be diminished while consumer welfare would be enhanced. But it is another matter when companies commit gross injustices in the process—for example, if they lie to workers, telling them that no layoffs are planned merely to keep them on the job until the last minute. Similarly, it is another matter when organizations follow discriminatory hiring policies, refusing to hire blacks or women, in the name of "consumer advantage." These are clear injustices of the kind that society would want to prohibit as a condition of the social contract. We may infer, then, that a tenet of the social contract will be that productive organizations are to remain within the bounds of the general canons of justice.

Determining what justice requires is a notoriously difficult task. The writings of Plato, Aristotle, and more recently, John Rawls, have shed considerable light on this subject, but unfortunately we must forgo a general discussion of justice here. At a minimum, however, the application of the concept of justice to productive organizations implies *that productive organizations avoid deception or fraud, that they show respect for their workers as human beings, and that they avoid any practice that systematically worsens the situation of a given group in society.* Despite the loud controversy over what justice means, most theorists would agree that justice means at least this much for productive organizations.

Our sketch of a hypothetical social contract is now complete. By utilizing the concept of rational people existing in a state of individual production, we have indicated the terms of a contract which they would require for the introduction of productive organizations. The questions asked in the beginning were: Why should corporations exist at all? What is the fundamental justification for their activities? How can we measure their performance, to say when they have performed poorly or well? A social contract helps to answer these questions. Corporations considered as productive organizations exist to enhance the welfare of society through the satisfaction of consumer and worker interests, in a way which relies on exploiting corporations' special advantages and minimizing disadvantages. This is the *moral foundation* of the corporation when considered as a productive organization.

It is well to notice that the social contract does not specify additional obligations or rights which *corporations* have in contrast to *productive organizations* in general. The social contract justifies corporations as *productive organizations*, not as *corporations*. Presumably, then, further reasons remain to be discovered for society's establishing a certain type of productive organization, such as the corporation—with limited liability, stockholder ownership, and its other characteristics. The important task of discovering those reasons, however, must wait for another occasion. Our development of the social contract has fallen short of a full moral comprehension of corporations, but it has secured a solid footing in an equally important area: comprehending the moral underpinnings of productive organizations.

We have seen that the productive organization cannot be viewed as an isolated moral entity unconstrained by the demands of society, for its very reason for existing lies with its capacity to satisfy certain social interests. Productive organizations, whether U.S. corporations or not, are subject to moral evaluations which transcend the boundaries of the political systems that contain them. When an organization, in the United States or elsewhere, manufactures a product that is inherently dangerous, or when it pushes its employees beyond reasonable limits, it deserves moral condemnation: the organization has failed to live up to a hypothetical contract—a contract between itself and society.

When Henry Ford II referred to the social contract, he left the term "social contract" undefined. This essay has attempted to sharpen the focus of what such a contract might mean, and thereby clarify the content of a corporation's societal obligations. The social contract expresses the underlying conviction that corporations exist to serve more than themselves. This conviction emerges in the speeches of businesspeople as well as in the writings of philosophers. It is the conviction expressed by the inventor of the Model T, the grandfather of Henry Ford II, when he said: "For a long time people believed that the only purpose of industry is to make a profit. They were wrong. Its purpose is to serve the general welfare."[2]

NOTES

1. Some social contract theorists, e.g., Thomas Hobbes and John Rawls, have adopted a different approach, preferring to emphasize people's self-interested tendencies in the state of nature. This view has some definite advantages, since one can say "Even self-interested people will agree to such and such a principle," and, in turn, one's argument gains a persuasive edge. Rawls does not literally assume that people are egoists, but he does assume that they wish to maximize their possession of primary goods. But in the present instance, no compelling reasons exist for representing people to be worse than they are, and one good reason does exist for representing them to be as they are: the presence of even ordinary (i.e., non-self-interested) motives can help clarify the conditions of the social contract.

2. Quoted in David Ewing, *Freedom Inside the Organization*, (New York: McGraw-Hill, 1977), p. 65.

Questions for Analysis

1. *Donaldson considers and rejects the view that corporations have a right to exist apart from the wishes of society. What does he find wrong with the view? Is he right? What would Friedman say?*

2. *Why does Donaldson conceive of the social contract for business as a contract among individuals, rather than one between corporations and society? Do you think that his approach is better than Bowie's?*

3. *Donaldson defines his project as a search for "the moral underpinnings of corporations." What does he mean by "moral underpinnings"? Why does he think the search worthwhile?*

4. *What benefits does Donaldson believe consumers have a right to expect from corporations? Do you agree with them all? Has he left any out?*

5. *What benefits does he believe employees have a right to expect? Do you agree with all of them? Has he left any out?*

6. *Donaldson takes his approach to the social contract from John Locke. But Locke, we saw in Chapter 1, believed that individuals have the natural right to property, which puts moral limits on what can be agreed to in a social contract. Does Donaldson's contract violate those limits?*

CASE PRESENTATION
Educating Tomorrow's Workers

One of the most serious social problems we face is the quality of education in our public schools, especially in our major cities and most especially among minority students. Most disturbing, perhaps, is the drop-out rate. According to an article in the July 4, 1988 issue of *Fortune*, 35 percent of U.S. black students and 45 percent of U.S. Hispanic students drop out before high school graduation, and 40 percent of the U.S. minority population is barely literate.

What were these figures doing in a business magazine? The following figures from the same article answer that question: The majority of new jobs over the next fifteen years will require some education past high school, while the number of young people entering the work force over the same period will decline by 10 percent. Moreover, the majority of public school students in the U.S.'s forty-five largest cities are minority students. In New York City, for example, 70 percent are black or Hispanic.

The minority dropout problem, then, is business's problem. So is the problem of educational quality. In the past, the article noted, Motorola hired eight of ten applicants for entry-level jobs. Today it must screen as many as fifteen applicants to fill one such job—even though the company requires only seventh-grade English skills and ninth-grade math skills. The article was about the attempts by U.S. business corporations to help solve these problems.

Here are two approaches that brought quick and demonstrable results:

1. In New York City's Spanish Harlem, General Electric spends $50,000 a year providing mentors and special classes for its "GE scholars" at the Manhattan Center for Science and Mathematics, a new school located in the building of a school that closed in 1982. The goal of the program is to help the best students in the school get into the country's best universities, but it has produced another benefit as well. The old school graduated only thirty students out of a class of a thousand its last year. In two years, the new one graduated 95 percent of its seniors.

2. In South Carolina, Governor Richard Riley called on the state's business leaders to help write a new education bill. Thirty business leaders joined with educators to produce the 1984 Education Improvement Act, which called for such improvements as higher salaries for teachers and remedial education programs. Real estate developer Robert Selman was selected as chief lobbyist for the bill, and the directors of Keenan Co., the business he ran, gave him 40 percent released time to lobby state legislators. The bill was passed, and since 1984 the average SAT scores for the state rose 34 percent—the highest gain in the nation.

Elsewhere, other approaches are being tried. In Pittsburgh, for example, Westinghouse Electric, the Dravo Corporation, and others support the Allegheny Conference Education Fund, which awards grants to teachers and principals to develop imaginative teaching methods. And in Philadelphia, executives from forty companies meet with teachers to plan courses to help students meet employer needs, while the Philadelphia High School Academies Program offers low-income students a combination of job experience and education.

The results of these programs are difficult to measure. One other program, unfortunately, provided a sad example of the difficulties that those who would try to help face. In 1985, American Express started a work-study program for students at Prospects High School in Brooklyn. Designed to prevent the students from dropping out, the program offered them part-time jobs and the promise of permanent work for students who graduate. In 1988, however, American Express cancelled the program without notice. For many of the students, it seemed, the help was too little too late. American Express was not prepared to deal with such problems as drugs, alcohol, and parental abuse. As Dee Topol, vice president of the American Express Foundation, put it, the $97,000 per year program was "not cost effective."

Questions for Analysis

1. Are the programs discussed in the *Fortune* article examples of corporations exercising social responsibility, pursuing the financial interests of their shareholders, or both?

2. Do these programs strike you as examples of corporations doing their fair share, more than their fair share, or less than their fair share? What do you think Friedman would say? Stone?

3. Should the American Express Foundation have canceled its program because of its lack of cost effectiveness, or should it have tried to improve it to make it cost effective?

4. How do you think corporations measure the cost effectiveness of such programs? How should they measure it?

CASE PRESENTATION
Rose Cipollone and the Tobacco Companies

In 1984, at the age of 58 years, Rose Cipollone died of cancer. For most of her life she'd been a cigarette smoker. Until 1955 she'd smoked Chesterfields. Then, out of concern for her health, she decided to switch to L&M, a brand of filtered cigarettes that were, the ads assured her, "just what the doctor ordered."

In 1981, doctors removed part of her right lung, which was cancerous. Despite family pleas, she did not quit smoking. She was unable to quit, she said. A year later, the rest of the lung was removed. Eventually, she did manage to give up her habit, and before she died she and her husband Tony brought suit against the Liggett Group, makers of both Chesterfield and L&M. The suit charged that Liggett had conspired with other tobacco companies to conceal the dangers of cigarette smoking, and that it had presented its products as safe even though it knew that medical research linked cigarette smoking to lung cancer. By the time that Rose Cipollone knew that she should stop, it was too late, the suit claimed. She was addicted.

As evidence, Tony Cipollone's attorney introduced memos and reports by tobacco industry executives, including Liggett Group executives, showing that cigarette makers knew of the cigarette-cancer link as early as the early forties. Still, they represented their products as safe with such advertising slogans as "Play safe—smoke Chesterfield," "Smoke a Lucky to feel your level best," and "More doctors smoke Camels than any other cigarettes." And as popular media like *Reader's Digest* began to publish information about the cancer risk of smoking, the tobacco industry disputed the evidence.

The Liggett Group spent $75 million on its defense, which included three dozen lawyers. Although the company won on the conspiracy charge, the Newark, New Jersey jury found that it had falsely given Rose Cipollone an "express warranty" that its products were safe. So in June, 1988, four years after her death, her husband was awarded $400,000.

That was the first of over three hundred cases brought by smokers since 1954 that the tobacco industry lost. Yet the Liggett Group claimed victory just the same. Given the high cost of the Cipollone suit and the relatively small award, few victims of cigarette smoking or their attorneys would be encouraged to bring similar suits, its representatives reasoned.

Questions for Analysis

1. *If a corporation has reason to believe that its product presents a health risk, is it morally obligated to inform consumers of the possible risk, even if the evidence is not conclusive?*

2. *Researchers have turned up evidence that passive smoking—inhaling air filled with smoke from the cigarettes of others—presents a health risk to nonsmokers. The tobacco industry is disputing that evidence, just as it earlier disputed the evidence that cigarette smoking causes cancer. Is it acting irresponsibly in doing so?*

3. *Cigarette advertisements, like advertisements for other products, sell an image as well as a product. The makers of Marlboro, for example, present their product as the cigarette of the rugged cowboy, and the makers of Virginia Slims present their product as the cigarette of the independent woman. Critics complain that such advertising is immoral, particularly when the product is known to present health risks. Are they right?*

4. *All cigarette advertising in the United States must carry a surgeon general's warning. Does that absolve cigarette makers of moral obligation to their customers?*

5. *Suppose the jury had decided against Cipollone. Would the Liggett Group have a moral obligation to pay damages anyway?*

Selections for Further Reading

Barry, Vincent. *Moral Issues in Business.* Belmont, Calif.: Wadsworth, 1979.

Beauchamp, Tom L. *Case Studies in Business, Society, and Ethics.* Englewood Cliffs, N.J.: Prentice-Hall, 1983.

———— and Norman E. Bowie, eds. *Ethical Theory and Business.* 3rd ed. Englewood Cliffs, N.J.: Prentice-Hall, 1988.

Donaldson, Thomas, and Patricia H. Werhane, eds. *Ethical Issues in Business: A Philosophical Approach.* 3rd ed. Englewood Cliffs, N.J.: Prentice-Hall, 1988.

Friedman, Milton. *Capitalism and Freedom.* Chicago: University of Chicago Press, 1981.

Galbraith, John K. *The New Industrial State.* 4th ed. Boston: Houghton Mifflin, 1985.

Harrington, Michael. *The Other America*. New York: Penguin, 1971.

Hoffman, W. and Jennifer Mills Moore, eds. *Business Ethics*. New York: McGraw-Hill, 1984.

Regan, Tom, ed. *Just Business: New Introductory Essays in Business Ethics*. Philadelphia: Temple University Press, 1983.

Smith, Adam. *An Inquiry into the Nature and Causes of the Wealth of Nations*, R. H. Campbell, ed. New York: Oxford University Press, 1976.

Snoeyenbos, Milton; Robert Almeder; and James Humber, eds. *Business Ethics*. Buffalo, N.Y.: Prometheus Books, 1983.

INDEX